THE
LOYAL NORTH LANCASHIRE
REGIMENT

THE
LOYAL NORTH LANCASHIRE
REGIMENT

By

COLONEL H. C. WYLLY, C.B.

1914—1919

The Naval & Military Press Ltd

Reproduced by kind permission of the Central Library,
Royal Military Academy, Sandhurst

Published by

The Naval & Military Press Ltd

Unit 10, Ridgewood Industrial Park,

Uckfield, East Sussex,

TN22 5QE England

Tel: +44 (0) 1825 749494

Fax: +44 (0) 1825 765701

www.naval-military-press.com

www.military-genealogy.com

© The Naval & Military Press Ltd 2007

The Naval & Military Press ...

...offer specialist books for the serious student of conflict. The range of titles stocked covers the whole spectrum of military history with titles on uniforms, battles, official histories, specialist works containing Medal Rolls and Casualties Lists, and numismatic titles for medal collectors and researchers.

The innovative approach they have to military bookselling and their commitment to publishing have made them Britain's leading independent military bookseller.

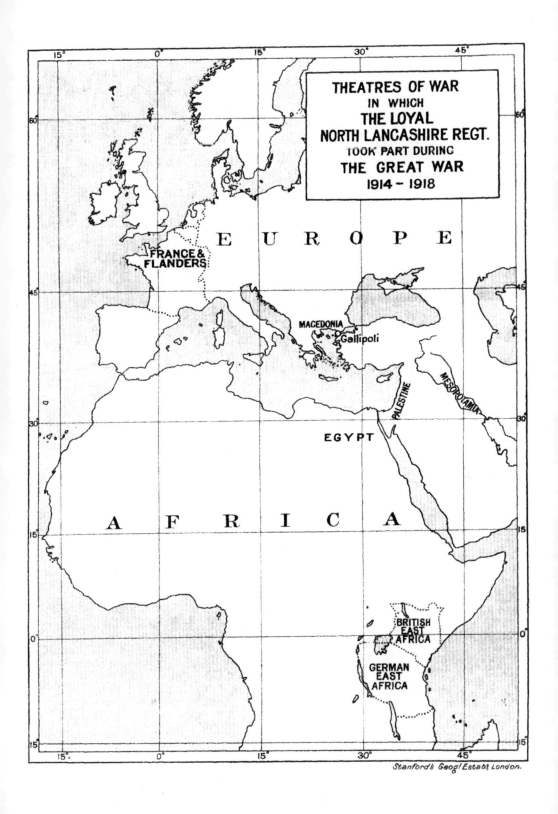

THEATRES OF WAR
IN WHICH
THE LOYAL
NORTH LANCASHIRE REGT.
TOOK PART DURING
THE GREAT WAR
1914 – 1918

EUROPE

FRANCE &
FLANDERS

MACEDONIA
Gallipoli

PALESTINE

MESOPOTAMIA

EGYPT

AFRICA

BRITISH
EAST
AFRICA

GERMAN
EAST
AFRICA

Stanford's Geogl Establ London.

THEATRES OF WAR,
1914–1918

CONTENTS

THE LOYAL NORTH LANCASHIRE REGIMENT

THE 1ST BATTALION

CONTENTS

APPENDICES

By K. R. Wilson

ILLUSTRATIONS

xvii

MAPS

THE
BATTLE HONOURS

THE GREAT WAR

(21 Battalions)

" Mons "
" Retreat from Mons "
" Marne, 1914, '18 "
" Aisne, 1914, '18 "
" Ypres, 1914, '17, '18 "
" Langemarck, 1914 "
" Gheluvelt "
" Nonne Bosschen "
" Givenchy, 1914 "
" Aubers "
" Festubert, 1915 "
" Loos "
" Somme, 1916, '18 "
" Albert, 1916 "
" Bazentin "
" Pozières "
" Guillemont "
" Ginchy "
" Flers-Courcelette "
" Morval "
" Ancre Heights "
" Ancre, 1916 "
" Arras, 1917, '18 "

" Scarpe, 1917 "
" Arleux "
" Messines, 1917 "
" Pilckem "
" Menin Road "
" Polygon Wood "
" Poelcappelle "
" Passchendaele "
" Cambrai, 1917, '18 "
" St. Quentin "
" Bapaume, 1918 "
" Lys "
" Estaires "
" Bailleul "
" Kemmel "
" Béthune "
" Scherpenberg "
" Soissonnais-Ourcq "
" Drocourt-Quéant "
" Hindenburg Line "
" Epéhy "
" Canal du Nord "
" St. Quentin Canal "

" Courtrai "
" Selle "
" Sambre "
" France and Flanders, 1914–1918 "
" Doiran, 1917 "
" Macedonia, 1917 "
" Suvla "
" Sari Bair "
" Gallipoli, 1915 "
" Egypt, 1916 "
" Gaza "
" Nebi Samwil "
" Jerusalem "
" Jaffa "
" Tell 'Asur "
" Palestine, 1917–18 "
" Tigris, 1916 "
" Kut-al-Amara, 1917 "
" Baghdad "
" Mesopotamia, 1916–18 "
" Kilimanjaro "
" E. Africa, 1914–16 "

THE
LOYAL NORTH LANCASHIRE
REGIMENT

CHAPTER XXIX

THE 1st BATTALION
THE LOYAL NORTH LANCASHIRE REGIMENT

1914

THE GREAT WAR. FRANCE AND FLANDERS.
MONS, THE BATTLE OF THE AISNE, THE FIRST BATTLE OF YPRES

IN August, 1914, the 2nd Infantry Brigade was differently commanded and constituted to what it had been at the date when the 1st Battalion The Loyal North Lancashire Regiment first joined it. In the previous year the command of the Brigade had been assumed by Brigadier-General E. S. Bulfin, while it was now composed of the 2nd Bn. The Royal Sussex Regiment, the 1st Bn. The Loyal North Lancashire Regiment, the 1st Bn. The Northamptonshire Regiment and the 2nd Bn. The King's Royal Rifle Corps.

The 5th August was the first day of mobilization, and from then on to the day of entrainment for the port of embarkation all were very busy, engaged in route marching and in drilling and exercising in musketry the reservists who joined from the Depot in two batches, each about three hundred strong. On the 12th the Battalion, 1,007 all ranks, left Tournay Barracks in two parties for Farnborough Station, the first party, composed of " A " and " B " Companies, under the command of Lieut.-Colonel G. C. Knight, at 1.15 p.m., and the second party, under Major W. R. Lloyd, an hour later. The following are the names of the officers who accompanied the Battalion : Lieut.-Colonel G. C. Knight ; Majors W. R. Lloyd and A. Burrows ; Captains G. T. Body, R. H. Watson, H. L. Helme, A. W. Colley, L. T. Allason and B. J. Wakley ; Lieutenants E. J. W. Spread, G. H. Goldie, H. R. Loomes, J. G. Halsted, E. F. Cunningham, E.

Robinson, R. C. Mason and J. G. W. Hyndson ; 2nd Lieutenants S. H. Batty-Smith, H. L. L. Knowles, N. Collins, W. R. L. Calrow, C. E. Wallis and G. C. Kingsley ; Captain and Adjutant R. Howard-Vyse, Lieutenant and Quartermaster E. Wilkinson and Captain W. C. Nimmo, R.A.M.C., in medical charge.

The following were attached to the staff : Captain E. R. Fitzpatrick, Assistant Provost-Marshal, Captain J. F. Allen, Billeting Officer, and 2nd Lieutenant W. C. Rowell with 1st Division Cyclist Platoon.

Southampton was reached late in the afternoon, when the Battalion embarked in the S.S. " Agapenor " and sailed at midnight for " an unknown destination " ; this turned out to be Havre, which was reached soon after midday on the 13th and disembarkation was at once proceeded with, and at six o'clock the same evening the Battalion marched off to a camp about six miles from the town, where the other regiments of the 2nd Brigade were found to be already established. The camp was left again at 6.45 p.m. on the 14th, the Battalion marching down to the railway station and there entraining for Le Nouvion, which was reached by way of Rouen, Paris, Amiens, Arras and Cambrai. After spending twenty-four hours here, the Brigade marched on again, the Battalion halting at and being accommodated in billets at Esquehéries.

" On the 14th and following days," so the *Official History of the War* states,* the troops began to move up by train to the areas of concentration, which were arranged so that the Army was assembled in a pear-shaped area between Maubeuge and Le Cateau, about twenty-five miles long from north-east to south-west, and averaging ten miles wide. The cavalry was at the north-eastern end, ready to join hands with the Fifth French Army.

" In detail the areas were :—

1st Corps : East of Bohain ; Headquarters, Wassigny.

1st Division : Boué, Esquehéries, Leschelles.

2nd Division : Grougis, Mennevret, Hannappes."

The Battalion now spent nearly a week in Esquehéries, and during this time as many officers and men as possible were inoculated against enteric fever ; and it was probably while quartered here that the message of His Majesty The King was read out to the troops, and that copies of Field-Marshal Lord Kitchener's letter were distributed to the non-commissioned officers and men. The King's message was as follows :—

" You are leaving home to fight for the safety and honour of My Empire.

" Belgium, whose country we are pledged to defend, has been attacked, and France is about to be invaded by the same powerful foe.

* 1914, Vol. I, pp. 47, 48.

" I have implicit confidence in you, My soldiers. Duty is your watchword, and I know your duty will be nobly done.

" I shall follow your every movement with deepest interest and mark with eager satisfaction your daily progress ; indeed your welfare will never be absent from My thoughts.

" I pray God to bless and guard you, and bring you back victorious."

The letter from Lord Kitchener was as under :—

" You are ordered abroad as a soldier of the King to help our French comrades against the invasion of a common enemy. You have to perform a task which will need your courage, your energy, your patience. Remember that the honour of the British Army depends on your individual conduct.

" It will be your duty not only to set an example of discipline and perfect steadiness under fire, but also to maintain the most friendly relations with those whom you are helping in this struggle. The operations in which you are engaged will, for the most part, take place in a friendly country, and you can do your own country no better service than in showing yourself in France and Belgium in the true character of a British soldier.

" Be invariably courteous, considerate and kind. Never do anything likely to injure or destroy property, and always look upon looting as a disgraceful act. You are sure to meet with a welcome and to be trusted ; your conduct must justify that welcome and that trust.

" Your duty cannot be done unless your health is sound, so keep constantly on your guard against any excesses. In this new experience you may find temptations both in wine and women. You must entirely resist both temptations, and, while treating all women with perfect courtesy, you should avoid any intimacy.

" Do your duty bravely. Fear God. Honour The King."

The Division began to move forward again on the 20th August in readiness for the general advance which was now commencing ; and on the following day the Battalion marched from Esquehéries by way of Le Nouvion, Fontanelle, Floyon to billets in a village to the south-west of Avesnes. The general effect of these moves now being carried out " would be that on August 23rd, the Army would be aligned on a front, roughly facing north-east, from Estinne-au-Mont, near Binche, on the south-east, to Lens, eight miles north of Mons, on the north-west, with the Cavalry Division on the left ; while the 5th Cavalry Brigade, having covered the right flank during the movement, would find itself finally in advance of the right front. The daily moves were to be as follows. . . .

" On the 21st the I. Corps to the line Avesnes–Landrécies ; on the

22nd north-east to the line Hautmont–Hargnies ; on the 23rd the I. Corps was to incline north-east and come up on the left of the II., on a line from Estinne-au-Mont west to Harmignies, immediately south-east of Spiennes." *

The march was continued on the 22nd, the Battalion being that night billeted in the village of Villers-Sire-Nicole, receiving en route the news from an airman that forty thousand Germans had been seen marching towards Mons. "Next morning," 23rd, writes a diarist of the Battalion, "we are hurried out at daybreak and rushed into Belgium. We cross the frontier about 7.30 a.m. and shortly afterwards turn into a field and stay there for several hours. We see the enemy for the first time in the shape of a Taube, who hovers over us for about five minutes. Towards evening we move forward and go into billets at Givry. Guns have been distinctly heard since leaving La Fontaine and we know that soon we shall be in battle."

"The ground on which the British Army had taken up its position is a narrow belt of coalfield which extends roughly for rather more than twenty miles west from Maurage (six miles east of Mons) along the Mons Canal, and has an average breadth, from the Canal south, of two miles. South of this belt the country gradually rises to a great tract of rolling chalk downs, cut into by many streams and with numerous outlying spurs. . . . In describing the general disposition of the troops, it must be remembered that, as the Army had halted whilst in the course of wheeling or forming to face towards Nivelles, the front of the I. Corps was already turned north-east, whereas the II. Corps, upon the wheeling flank, still mainly faced to the north. The general front, therefore, formed an obtuse angle, the I. Corps being on the right half of the south-eastern arm, and the II. Corps round the apex and along the western arm. The south-eastern arm from Peissant to Mons was about ten miles long, and the arm along the canal from Mons to Condé seventeen miles. The I. Corps was extended, roughly speaking, from the Sambre to the Aisne ; the 1st Division being on the right, with the 3rd Infantry Brigade in front between Peissant and Haulchin (about four miles) ; the 1st (Guards) Brigade in rear of its right at Grand Reng and Vieux Reng ; and the 2nd Infantry Brigade in rear of its left at Villers Sire Nicole and Rouveroy." †

Up to about 2 p.m. on the 23rd August all remained quiet in front of the I. Corps, the advanced line of which was held by the 3rd Brigade of the 1st Division and by the 6th Brigade of the 2nd.

It was not until 6 p.m. that the 2nd Brigade received orders to be ready

* *Official History,* 1914, Vol. I, pp. 49, 50.
† *Official History,* 1914, Vol. I, pp. 52–64.

to move at a moment's notice, and two hours later the Battalion marched about two and a half miles down the road, then receiving fresh orders that the men were to fall out and sleep by the roadside, pending the receipt of fresh instructions as to further movements. While the men were trying to get what sleep they could, the draught animals of two ammunition wagons stampeded, these running over some men of the Battalion, three being severely and two slightly injured.

The night of the 23rd–24th August passed without any serious annoyance from the enemy, and by dawn on the 24th the British Army was occupying a line roughly facing north-east, seventeen miles long, with the centre some three miles south of Mons, the 1st Division being on the line Grand Reng, Rouveroy, Givry. The troops had by this time been subjected to great fatigue, and even "the 1st Division, though scarcely engaged, had been hurried into its place by a forced march during the night of the 22nd–23rd, and had been under arms for eighteen hours before it could billet, or bivouac."

Already late on the night of the 23rd Sir John French had decided to make a general retreat southwards of about eight miles to the line La Longueville–Bavai–La Boiserette, the I. Corps covering the retirement of the II. ; and the 1st and 2nd Divisions received orders during the course of the night to retire by two roads on Feignies and Bavai.

At 4 a.m. on the 24th the Battalion marched off by Villers Sire Nicole and Battignies and thence northwards, about 8.30 entrenching in a position south and north of the road leading to Qugny-le-Grand. "Here a brisk engagement was going on between the 2nd Division and the Germans on our left," so writes a Battalion diarist, "and we could see the German guns in action on our front from just south of Mons." Here the Battalion remained during the rest of the 24th and was not called upon to act, marching on late in the evening to Feignies, where the night was passed.

On the 25th another officer writes : "We are up at dawn and move back in the direction of Maubeuge, which we pass on the outskirts, leaving the city and its forts on the left. I think the men began to see that something was wrong, as just about this time they began to grouse a good deal. Before we got to Maubeuge our billeting party had to repulse a small party of German cavalry who had got in behind us, and as we passed the fortress its great guns had already begun to fire. We march on well into the night and take up billets at Marbaix, very tired "—a march of some fifteen miles ending at 9 p.m.

On the 26th the Battalion moved by Le Grand Fayt and Favril to Oisy where it bivouacked at 9.30 p.m. in a field in pouring rain ; on the 27th —again in heavy rain—by Wassigny, Venerolles, Hannappée, Vadencourt and Noyale to Hauteville, which was reached at eight o'clock at night and where a position was taken up on the hill, to the east of the town, from the right bank of the River Oise to the vicinity of the Flavigny–Mont d'Origny road. During this day's march German aeroplanes were flying over the column and the Northamptonshire Regiment had a brush with German cavalry. The 2nd Brigade being on rearguard to the Division and the Battalion to the Brigade, the 1st Loyal North Lancashire did not leave Hauteville until midday on the 28th, joining up with the rest of the 2nd Brigade at Lucy, and then, moving on for two hours without a halt, Fressancourt was reached at 1 a.m. on the 29th, everybody dead-beat. Fortunately it was possible to halt here for twenty-four hours and give the weary troops a day's rest.

On the 30th there followed a very hot and dusty march of about twenty miles to Anizy-le-Chateau ; and so the great retreat was continued through Soissons and Villers-Cotterets ; and on the 2nd September, so one of the Battalion records, " we crossed a river—the Marne, and scarcely had we done so when the Engineers blew up the bridge ; we were the last regiment to cross. We only go a few miles, then wheel into a field and snatch an hour or two's sleep ; we are roused before daybreak and march off once more." On the 5th the Battalion was at Aulnoy and on the 6th at Bernay, where the welcome news came to hand that the Retreat from Mons had at long last come to an end, and that the British Army was now to turn upon the pursuing enemy.

" The retreat of the British Expeditionary Force had continued, with only one halt, for thirteen days over a distance as the crow flies of 136 miles, and as the men marched, at least 200 miles, and that after two days' strenuous marching in advance to the Mons Canal. The mere statement of the distance gives no measure of the demands made upon the physical and moral endurance of the men, and of but little idea of the stoutness with which they had responded to these demands. . . . The troops suffered under every disadvantage. The number of reservists in the ranks was on an average over one half of the full strength, and the units were, owing to force of circumstances, hurried away to the area of concentration before all ranks could resume acquaintance with their officers and comrades, and re-learn their duty as soldiers. Arrived there, they were hastened forward by forced marches to the battle, confronted with greatly superior numbers of the most renowned army in Europe, and condemned at the very outset to undergo the severest ordeal which can be imposed upon an army. They were short of food and sleep when they began their re-treat ; they continued it, always short of food and sleep, for thirteen days, as has been told ; and at the end they were still an army, and a formidable

army. They were never demoralized, for they rightly judged that they
had never been beaten." *

The British Army was now to move forward again and operate over a
very open, highly-cultivated country, containing many woods and villages,
crossed from east to west by the deep valleys of the Grand and Petit Morin,
the Marne, the Ourcq, the Vesle, the Aisne and the Ailette—none of these
passable except at the bridges. The I. Corps Operation Orders of the 5th
September laid down that the Corps front extended from La Chapelle
Iger to Lumigny, that the advance would be made on the 6th in the general
direction of Montmirail, and that by 9 a.m. on this day the front of the
1st Division would be from Courpalay to Rozoy, with one brigade in reserve
in rear of the right flank.

The 2nd Brigade was at the outset in reserve, and the Battalion moved
out no further than a mile or two and bivouacked for the night in a field,
and this was also the experience of the 8th and 9th. On the last-named
date Lieutenant J. H. Miller joined with a draft of eighty men.

The orders issued on the night of the 8th had directed the continuation
of the northward advance of the Army, and it had been anticipated that
the Germans would stubbornly resist the passage of the Marne ; later
reports made it clear, however, that the enemy was moving rapidly to
the north—so rapidly indeed that only at three places had the bridges
been destroyed. By an early hour on the 9th our cavalry had seized the
bridges at Nogent, Charly and Azy, and it was at the first of these that the
Battalion passed the Marne and pushed on through the hilly country beyond. Near Priez the 2nd Brigade was checked, and the Royal Sussex
and Northamptonshire suffered considerable loss ; but the advance was
continued on the 11th and 12th. On the 10th the casualties in the
Battalion were three killed ; three officers and twenty-four men wounded ;
one of the officers was Lieut.-Colonel G. C. Knight, commanding the 1st
Loyal North Lancashire, who was hit by a shrapnel bullet and died on
the following day, the other two were Lieutenant J. G. Halsted and 2nd
Lieutenant W. C. Rowell.

The orders for the 12th September were that the march of the Army
was to be continued to the Aisne, that all crossing places should be seized,
and the high ground on the north bank secured, the I. Corps marching
by Rocourt, Fère-en-Tardenois, Loupeigne, Bazoches, Longueval and Bourg
on the eastern road, and by Latilly, Ouchy-le-Chateau, Arcy Ste. Restitue,
Jouaignes, Courcelles and Pont Arcy on the western.

The Battalion passed the night of the 11th–12th in billets in Coincy,
and that of the 12th–13th in a village a few miles further on. On the

* *Official History*, 1914, Vol. I, pp. 260, 261.

night of the 12th two of the three Army Corps composing the British Force were halted two miles from the Aisne, the seizure of the line of which presented many difficulties, since the nature of the country made delaying tactics easy for the enemy; while the river was here wide and unfordable, there was but scanty cover for infantry advancing from the south and few positions for artillery support. The advance was, however, ordered to be resumed on the 13th, the I. Corps again moving by two roads, the one by Longueval, Bourg, Chamouille and Bruyères to Athies, the other through Braine, Presles, Chavonne and Lierval to Laon ; and the I. Corps orders directed that patrols were to push forward to the river crossings, of which there were at least seven between Bourg and Venizel, the divisions remaining close at hand, ready to act on such information as should come in. If the enemy stood, he was to be attacked ; if he continued to fall back, the 1st and 2nd Divisions were to occupy ground beyond the Aisne, holding the crossing places and pushing out reconnaissances towards the enemy.

"The ground facing the British I. Corps presented a series of high spurs projecting generally south from the Chemin-des-Dames ridge towards the Aisne. First, commencing from the east, are the Paissy–Pargnan and Bourg spurs, both extending nearly to the river, with the village of Moulins at the top of the valley between them. Next is the short Troyon spur, with Vendresse in the valley east of it, and Beaulne and Chivy west of it. Westwards of those again are the three spurs at the foot of which lie Moussy and Soupir and Chavonne respectively ; only the last of these comes close down to the river." *

The account of the events of the next few days is largely taken from the diary of an officer of the Battalion :

"On the 13th we moved forward to a village and halted for several hours. Heavy guns are just on our left and have already opened on the enemy's position across the Aisne. The passage is forced by the 1st Brigade and we move down and cross at Bourg, where were strong barricades and concealed trenches, which, if held, would certainly have cost us casualties. Towards dusk the Regiment moved into billets at Moulins, except ' A ' Company which is left out on the hill. Pass a good night, but called out hurriedly before daybreak and told to move. We move down the road to Vendresse and lie down under cover of the hedge, where things are beginning to liven up and bullets are falling all round us. Captain Body, who has taken over the company, calls all company officers together and explains the situation, and we are shortly moved up to Troyon to support the attack on the factory."

* *Official History*, 1914, Vol. I, p. 331.

This was at 10.30 a.m. on the 14th, and two and a half companies of the Battalion were sent up to the right of the 2nd King's Royal Rifles, one company was ordered to support the Royal Sussex, the remaining half-company being held in reserve at Vendresse.

The position was reached, the factory carried and held ; but the enemy was in great strength and counter-attacked heavily, while the Battalion ammunition supply had begun to run out, and the 2nd Brigade was ordered to fall back to the ridge previously occupied, arriving there about 3 p.m. and " digging in."

The losses incurred on this day by the Battalion, in this its first general action of the war, amounted to fourteen officers and over 500 non-commissioned officers and men killed, wounded and missing, and in " B " Company alone three officers out of five and 175 out of 220 other ranks were casualties.

The names of the fourteen officers were as follows : killed or died of wounds, Major W. R. Lloyd ; Captains G. T. Body, R. H. Watson, H. L. Helme and R. Howard-Vyse, adjutant ; Lieutenants G. H. Goldie, H. R. Loomes, R. C. Mason and E. Robinson ; wounded, Major A. Burrows, Lieutenants E. J. W. Spread, E. F. Cunningham, C. E. Wallis and 2nd Lieutenant N. Collins.

Matters were tolerably quiet during the 15th September, passed by the Battalion in shallow trenches just below the crest of the hill, subjected only to some intermittent shelling. On the next day the trenches were deepened, a fortunate thing since in the afternoon the enemy attacked, but were repulsed with the bayonet ; and when the firing ceased and darkness fell stragglers and slightly wounded men began to find their way back from the ground fought over on the 14th. It may be considered that on this day, the 16th, the conditions of trench warfare, which was so long to endure, actually commenced.

Here the 2nd Brigade, and the Battalion with it, remained until the 19th, enduring very considerable discomfort, the weather being very wet and the trenches over the men's ankles in mud and water, but on the whole, and considering all the circumstances, the health of the men was wonderfully good. On the early morning of the 19th an officer of the 1st Battalion East Yorkshire Regiment arrived upon the scene, and stated that his battalion was to relieve the 1st Loyal North Lancashire, and that the 18th Brigade, then just out from England, was to take the place on the ridge of the 2nd Infantry Brigade.

At 2 p.m. the relieving battalion came up and took over, and half an hour later the Battalion marched back by way of Vendresse to the village of Pargnan, where half the companies were accommodated in some wretched billets, the remainder finding shelter in some caves half a mile further to the east.   A reinforcement of one hundred men under Lieutenant S. T. Lucey now joined.   Here the Battalion remained until the 25th when the 2nd Brigade moved back again to Troyon in relief of the 18th.   While at Pargnan, however, the Battalion was twice called out in support of other portions of the line, and on the 23rd Lieutenant J. H. Miller and thirteen men were wounded by shrapnel fire.

This tour of the trenches did not terminate until the 16th October, when the Battalion, having been relieved by French troops, withdrew by way of Vendresse, Bourg and Longueville to Vauxcère, where it went for one night only into billets ; but the events of those days up in the front line are generally described as follows by an officer of the Regiment :

" It was one continual round of trench warfare.   The trenches of the West Yorkshire Regiment were still full of their dead, and it was almost impossible to dig in some places without coming upon dead bodies.   We were subjected to several attacks, and in no case did the enemy set foot in our trench.   The bombardment was the worst and we suffered several casualties.   One day " (this appears to have been the 7th October) " Major Burrows, Allason, Allen, Calrow, Reid—who had only joined that day—and I were all sitting in the mess talking when a shell burst just at the door. Allason and Calrow were killed, Reid was wounded and also Major Burrows, but Allen and I were not touched.   One of the mess carts was completely blown up.   On another occasion a minenwerfer came into a trench and burst, where five officers and a few men were standing, and only wounded three of them slightly."

The Battalion was now to move to another part of the " far-flung battle line," and the circumstances leading up to this are described as follows in the *Official History of the War* :

" Towards the close of September Sir John French had suggested to General Joffre the transfer of the British Army to its former place on the left of the line   Other British troops were about to be landed in the north of France, and it was obviously desirable that all the forces of the Nation should act in one body.   The line of communication also of the British Expeditionary Force would be greatly shortened by its being near the coast.   The British were specially concerned in preventing the fall of Antwerp, and were interested, above all nations, in barring the way to the Channel ports, from which the Germans could threaten the transport of troops from England to France and block the vital avenues of water-borne traffic converging on London.   If the British were restored to their old place on the left of the line, they could be reinforced with swiftness and secrecy impossible elsewhere. . . .

" General Joffre agreed to Sir John French's proposal; and on the night of October 1st–2nd was begun the withdrawal of the British troops from the Aisne. Their movements were carefully concealed; all marches were made by night and the men confined to their billets by day, so that no sign of their departure from the Aisne should be visible to enemy aircraft."

The I. Corps was the last to move, but the evacuation of the trenches then held by its components was not completed until the 15th, while it was the 19th before the Corps detrained and concentrated at Hazebrouck, moving thence to Ypres.

The 1st Battalion The Loyal North Lancashire, moving the last of its brigade, did not leave the Troyon position until 2.30 a.m. on the 15th, and on the night of the following day entrained at Fismes, and, moving by St. Denis, Amiens and Abbeville, finally detrained on the night of the 18th–19th at Cassel, near which town the Battalion went into billets. The 19th was more or less a day of rest, but early on the 20th the Brigade marched by Steenevoorde and Poperinghe to Boesinghe, which it reached on the evening of the 21st ready to play its part in the great struggle known as the First Battle of Ypres.

Prior to the arrival of the I. Corps in the neighbourhood of Ypres, there had been very heavy fighting about Zonnebeke, the enemy making persistent attempts to break through to Ypres ; these attempts the timely arrival of the I. Corps had greatly helped to frustrate. The I. Corps now took over the line from Bixschoote to Zonnebeke, and on the 22nd two brigades of the 2nd Division assisted in the repulse of a renewed German attack. The 1st Brigade on the left of the Corps about Pilckem was now attacked in great force, the main onset of the enemy being directed against an inn held by the Cameron Highlanders, situated about a mile and a half north of Pilckem on the Bixschoote–Langemarck road ; after repulsing more than one attack the Highlanders were forced back to another position further south on the afternoon of the 22nd. Part of the position was recovered, but the line itself was too strongly held and further help was called for.

At 5 p.m. on the 22nd the Battalion was ordered to move up from Boesinghe to St. Jean which was reached at 8 p.m. ; but very shortly afterwards fresh orders came to hand for a further advance—this time to Pilckem, which was reached just after dawn on the 23rd. Here, while the men lay down and took what rest they could, Major-General Bulfin assembled commanding officers and issued orders as follows : the Northamptonshire, the 2nd King's Royal Rifles and the Cameron Highlanders were to remain in occupation of the trenches they were then holding ; the 1st Queen's, lent from the 3rd Brigade, was to attack over the open ground to the right of the Pilckem road, while the 1st Loyal North Lancashire was to work through the more enclosed country to the left of the road and attack the trenches to the west of the line, these two battalions then pushing home the assault on the line simultaneously.

As soon as it was sufficiently light the Battalion moved forward to the attack, " C " Company on the right and " A " on the left advancing by sections under command of Major Burrows, " B " and " D " being in support under Major A. J. Carter. " In this order they advanced to within 300 yards of the trenches where they began to come under a very heavy shell fire. Major Carter decided to charge at once with the bayonet, and he sent a message to this effect to the K.R.R. on his left, asking them to advance with him. This, however, they were unable to do, and Major Carter accordingly decided to attack alone. Captain Henderson, with the Machine Gun Section, pushed forward to a very advanced position on the left, from which he was able to get a clear field of fire for his guns, and the Battalion formed up for the attack. Captain Crane's and Captain Prince's companies were in the first line ; the other two were in support. The order to fix bayonets was given ; a bugle sounded the charge, and with loud cheers the Battalion dashed forward, and in less than ten minutes had carried the trenches and cleared them of the enemy. Six hundred prisoners were taken, a number which might have been increased but that further pursuit was checked by our own artillery." *

The fire of our guns obliged the Battalion to evacuate the captured trenches for a time, but they were re-occupied and held all that night, and in the morning they were linked up with those of the Highlanders on the right and of the Rifles on the left.

Parties were pushed forward in the morning and some twenty wounded were brought in. Later the enemy shelled the position and at 6 p.m. a violent attack opened all along the line, but this ceased at the end of half an hour. At 9.30 p.m. the Battalion was relieved by a French Territorial Regiment—the 80th—and withdrew by Pilckem to Ypres, where it arrived in the early morning of the 25th.

In this action the Battalion had two officers killed—Captain Miller and Lieutenant Kingsley ; four wounded—Majors Burrows and Powell, Lieutenants Griffith and Hickling (both Gloucestershire Regiment, attached), while 178 non-commissioned officers and men were killed, wounded or missing.

On the 28th October Major-General Bulfin, commanding 2nd Brigade, caused the following Brigade Order to be published :—

" In spite of the stubborn resistance offered by the German troops,

* Lord Ernest Hamilton, *The First Seven Divisions*, pp. 228, 229.

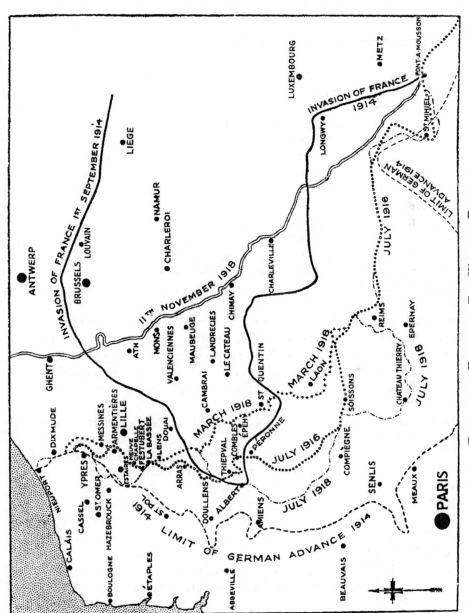

FRANCE AND FLANDERS—THE WESTERN FRONT.

1914–1918.

the object of the engagement was accomplished, but not without many casualties in the Brigade. By nightfall the trenches captured by the Germans had been re-occupied, about 600 prisoners captured and fully 1,500 German dead were lying out in front of our trenches.

"The Brigadier-General congratulates the 1st Loyal North Lancashire Regiment, the 1st Northamptonshire Regiment, and the 2nd King's Royal Rifle Corps : but desires specially to commend the fine soldier-like spirit of the 1st Loyal North Lancashire Regiment, which, advancing steadily under heavy shell and rifle fire, and aided by its machine-guns, was enabled to form up within a comparatively short distance of the enemy trenches. Fixing bayonets, the Battalion then charged, carried the trenches, and then occupied them, and to them must be allotted the majority of the prisoners captured.

"The Brigadier-General congratulates himself on having in his Brigade a battalion which, after marching the whole of the previous night without food or rest, was able to maintain its splendid record in the past by the determination and self-sacrifice displayed in this action."

Indirectly the German Official History pays a no less striking tribute to the successes of the Battalion in that day's fighting :—

"With the failure of the 46th Reserve Division to gain a decisive victory between Bixschoote and Langemarck on the 22nd and 23rd October, the fate of the XXVI. and XXVII. Reserve Corps (which attacked the 2nd and 7th British Divisions respectively) was also settled ; for the time being any further thought of a break-through was out of the question."

While resting near Ypres 2nd Lieutenant A. M. Ker joined and also Captain H. F. B. Ryley.

On the morning of the 26th the 2nd Brigade moved about 1,000 yards nearer to the front, but remained that day in Corps Reserve, while the remaining two brigades of the 1st Division and other units were heavily engaged in the front. Sir John French has described the days from the 27th to the 31st October as more momentous and fateful than any others during the time that he was commanding in the field, adding that "October 31st and November 1st will remain for ever memorable in the history of our Country, for, during those two days, no more than one thin and straggling line of tired-out British soldiers stood between the Empire and its practical ruin as an independent first-class Power."

At 7 a.m. on the 27th October the Battalion left its field bivouac and marched through Hooge to a large wood east of that village, and on this night the 1st Division was disposed as follows : it held a line of front from the Menin Road to a point immediately west of Reutel village, the 1st

Brigade only being in the front line, while the 2nd Brigade was concentrated in bivouac near Veldhoek, and the 3rd near Hooge.

Towards 11.30 a.m. on the 29th reports came in that the Germans were massing opposite the centre of the 1st Brigade, and the 1st Battalion Loyal North Lancashire and 2nd King's Royal Rifles were ordered forward by General Bulfin in support of a counter-attack about to be made by the 3rd Brigade. The King's Royal Rifles moved off first, the Battalion following in echelon on their left, " A " Company (Lieutenant Lucey) on the right and " D " (Captain Colley) on the left, with " B " and " C " Companies in support under Captains Ryley and Prince. It was 4 p.m. before any attack actually developed, the two battalions then advancing to the north of the village of Gheluvelt and the whole digging in on either side of the village.

" As a result of the hasty reinforcing of the line during the day, units were now much mixed up, and sorting and reorganization went on for long after dark. And there was other work to be done. A new line of trenches, roughly north and south through the 8th kilometre-stone, opposite the cross-roads captured by the enemy, and half a mile from them, had to be dug during the night, and the line re-allotted ; entrenching tools were scarce and time was lost in trying to find more." *

During the night of the 30th–31st the four companies of the Battalion were strung out along a line of trenches, most of the time under a heavy bombardment ; and on the early morning of the 31st the Battalion was ordered to retire through the wood to Hooge, where it formed up. On the receipt of fresh orders it went forward again at 9 a.m. and, in company with the Gordon Highlanders, made a successful attack, ending with a bayonet charge on the enemy, inflicting considerable loss upon him. Advancing again, the Battalion occupied a position facing the village of Gheluvelt.

By this time the losses in the Battalion were very serious, some eight officers and four hundred other ranks being missing, while their fate, whether killed or wounded, was wholly uncertain, but so far as can be traced the following were the officer-casualties in the Battalion during the Ypres fighting : killed or died of wounds, Major A. J. Carter, D.S.O., Captains H. F. B. Ryley, J. F. Allen, A. L. Prince, C. G. M. Slade and E. C. Miller ; Lieutenant G. C. Kingsley, Lieutenant and Quartermaster E. Wilkinson ; wounded, Majors Burrows and Powell, Lieutenants S. T. Lucey, Hickling and W. Jackson, 2nd Lieutenants S. H. Batty-Smith and H. L. L. Knowles ; taken prisoner, Captain A. W. Colley, Lieutenants T. C. Griffith and D. H. Garden.

* *Official History*, 1914, Vol. II, p. 273.

The results of the week's fighting may be epitomized from the diary of one of the few officers who came through. "On the 31st, which was the worst day of all, the bombardment began at dawn. At 9 we were sent for to attempt a counter-attack and try to move through the village of Gheluvelt, but in crossing a lane we are enfiladed by a machine-gun, and Major Carter sent Captain Ryley off to try and locate the gun. That was the last heard or seen of him. We reach the main road of Gheluvelt and then come to a standstill, for it is quite impossible to advance any further on account of the terrific shelling. I confer with Captain Prince and we decide that it is impossible to advance through what is in front of us with the few men we have got, so we withdraw again to our trenches. This movement has lasted only half an hour and has cost us dear—two officers and half the two companies have been placed *hors de combat*.

"After being here till about 1 p.m. we are ordered to withdraw, the Germans having rushed our front line to the extent of a couple of miles. We are not strong enough to counter-attack, so retire under very heavy shell fire, units terribly mixed up and we only manage to keep together five officers and about forty men. Pursued by shells the whole way, we retire on Hooge and find that a general retirement has been ordered, but this is almost immediately countermanded and we advance, the whole Brigade numbering about two hundred. We press forward and attack, driving the enemy out of a wood on the side of the Menin Road ; we bayonet and shoot hundreds and are weary with fighting. We did not advance beyond the wood.

"On the 3rd November things were very critical for we have no reserves in case the Germans break through. Spend a fairly quiet day the next day, except for shelling, the enemy attempt no infantry attack ; we are relieved at night and go into reserve for a couple of days."

It was on the 4th November that Sir John French published the following Order of the Day :

"The Field-Marshal Commanding in Chief has watched with the deepest admiration and solicitude the splendid stand made by the soldiers of His Majesty The King in their successful effort to maintain the forward position which they have won by their gallantry and steadfastness. He believes that no other army in the world would show such tenacity, especially under the tremendous artillery directed against it. Its courage and endurance are beyond all praise. It is an honour to belong to such an army.

"The Field-Marshal has now to make one more call upon the troops. It is certainly only a question of a few days, and it may be only a few hours, before, if they only stand firm, strong support will come, the enemy will be driven back, and in his retirement will suffer at their hands losses even greater than those which have befallen him under the terrific blows by which, especially during the last few days, he has been repulsed. The Commander-in-Chief feels sure that he does not make the call in vain."

To continue the diary extracts. "We take over trenches to the west of the Menin Road, south of Gheluvelt. Subjected to two days' terrific shelling, the C.O.—Major Carter, and Captain Allen killed—the latter was wounded so badly that he died shortly after. Our guns are unable to reply to this shelling, for they are only allowed a certain amount of ammunition and that has already been exceeded. At night we were relieved and proceeded to Hooge, but before leaving we buried Major Carter and several men—Major Carter is a great loss. Slade is now in command and I am acting adjutant, we have only two very weak companies—one commanded by Prince and the other by Ker. Total strength, including draft brought up by Slade on the 3rd, does not exceed two hundred and thirty rifles. Sergeants Greaves and Bailey are invaluable.

"We are allowed a day's rest and told that we will be relieved the next day, instead of which, on the 7th November, we are again sent up to the front line east of the Menin Road on the Ypres side of Veldhoek, and have one company in the trenches and one in reserve, relieving the Berkshire who informed us it was a quiet part of the line.

"At dawn on the 8th the Germans commenced shelling and plastered the front trenches of the French and our Company, followed by a heavy attack, when the French position was captured. This forced our Company in the front trench to give ground, and then the Germans succeeded in forcing the line and penetrating as far as the Chateau. We immediately found it necessary to attack with the reserve company and, led by Slade, Prince, Ker and me, we succeeded in not only stemming the attack, but in recapturing the whole of the lost trenches. All was done under a very heavy shell and rifle fire and we lost about one hundred men, while Slade was killed and Ker wounded, and Prince assumed command of the Battalion.

"We were very soon counter-attacked again and forced out of the newly gained trenches, and for a time it looked as if the Germans would conquer; but strong attacks by the rest of the Regiment, ably aided by the West Riding Regiment and the French, checked the Germans at the Chateau. They were in very superior numbers but were killed with rifle and bayonet, and some prisoners were taken. All these attacks were made on the initiative of the West Riding and Loyal North Lancashire alone, no orders being received from the Brigade. The numbers of the Regiment were very considerably reduced and Prince and I were the only officers left, and a hundred rifles only could be relied upon in case of need ; Sergeants Greaves and Bailey still rendered yeoman service. Darkness now stopped the German infantry attacks, though they were not yet played out.

"They were still in very large numbers and in possession of our front trenches, but their massed attacks in the morning had cost them dear.

"Captain Fortune, 42nd, was sent over to us to arrange a night attack and brought a company to assist, but a council-of-war decided against any immediate attack and it was determined to reconnoitre the ground thoroughly. With this object, Prince and I with thirty men crept towards the front trench, and, finding the Germans had made the mistake of holding it very lightly, we made a sudden onslaught and regained the whole of the main trench without loss to ourselves. Touch was established with the Guards on our left, while our right was thrown back. This news was communicated to the Headquarters 1st Brigade, and reinforcements were sent to help us hold our ground, which we did in spite of counter-attacks.

"Prince thought we ought to join up our smaller trench, and sent me to ask the O.C. French troops on our right to cease fire until we had attained this object. I went on my errand and made them stop firing, but on getting back to the company I found Prince had already attempted to take the trench and had been killed with half his men. He tried to do this with twelve men and found the enemy too much on the alert. Thus perished a very able and gallant officer. The command then reverted to me, and I at once sent back to the Brigade, reporting the occurrence, and stating that I did not think it advisable to renew the attempt unless with fresh troops. Steps were taken to block up the end of the trench which was only five yards from the nearest German trench. They were noticed to be very busy consolidating and another attack was expected.

" During the night two attempts to attack us were defeated

" Day broke on the 9th and with it came renewed activity on the part of the enemy. The rest of that day was a terribly anxious one, the Germans more than once attempting to attack ; but that night we were relieved and went into reserve trenches in a wood near Hooge. By morning on the 10th the men were still very exhausted, but we were to have no rest, for about 1 p.m. I got a sudden order to proceed with all speed and make a counter-attack upon the enemy about Nonne Bosschen, the attack by the Prussian Guard having come off and a gap having been made here on a front of about a mile. We went off at full speed, heavily shelled at Hell Fire Corner, advanced in two lines and were then stopped by rifle fire. We managed, however, to form some kind of a line and dug in, when other troops came up and the gap was made good.　At dusk we were ordered back again into reserve.　By this time we only numbered eighty rifles.

"The attack took place next day, the 11th, but failed."

And so matters went on, attacks, withdrawals and counter-attacks, in rain and snow, with ever-decreasing numbers, until at last on the night of the 14th what remained of a hard-fighting battalion marched to Vlamertinghe, where two officers and 150 men joined from England, the two officers being Major Powell and Captain Lucey, both wounded at Ypres, who now took over the duties of C.O. and adjutant.

The 1st Division was now withdrawn from the front for a complete and very much-needed rest, the divisional headquarters being established at the village of Merris, while the Battalion occupied billets at Hazebrouck, remaining here until the 21st December, when it was suddenly recalled to the front.

"The German retaliation for the Allied offensive in Flanders came on the 20th December, and, as usual, against a weak spot in the line.　At daylight on this day the whole front of the Indian Corps was severely bombarded by heavy artillery and trench mortars. . . . It soon became evident that the attack was a serious one," and in the first instance the 1st Brigade of the 1st Division was ordered up to assist the Indian Corps. This was almost immediately followed by the 3rd Brigade, and finally the 2nd Brigade, dispatched later in motor-buses, reached Le Touret, two and a half miles west of Richebourg L'Avoué, at 3 p.m. on the 21st.　It was at once ordered to retake the left sector of the Indian front near the Orchard, about one mile north-east of Festubert, which had been lost that morning.

The attack by the Battalion began at 7.20 p.m. and in little more than an hour later the lost trenches had been recaptured, the line occupied by the Indian Divisions was taken over by the I. Corps, and the Indian Corps went into reserve.

In this action, known as "Givenchy," the Battalion had six officers and 408 non-commissioned officers and men killed, wounded and missing ; the officers were : killed, Captains Smart and Graham ; wounded, Captain Hay, while missing were Captain de Carteret, Lieutenant Batty-Smith and 2nd Lieutenant Gilliland.　The Battalion was brought out of action by 2nd Lieutenant J. G. W. Hyndson.

The Battalion spent Christmas Day in billets at Essars, cheered by the receipt of presents from members of the Royal Family, many gifts from friends at home, and by a message from the G.O.C.

In a letter home, an officer of the Battalion wrote as follows : "To-day, Christmas Day, has been celebrated in the time-honoured way, carols have been sung and there is not a man who has been forgotten by those he has left behind. Relatives and friends and charitable organizations have combined to make our Christmas as festive and happy as it possibly could be ; plum puddings have been received, tobacco and cigarettes have been literally showered upon us in almost staggering quantities ; whilst warm clothing, gloves, mufflers and many other personal comforts have been distributed with a lavish hand. The gratitude of the men who have received these gifts is profound, far more so than words can tell. The Christmas card which Their Majesties the King and Queen graciously sent to each man made a cheery opening for the day and the Royal message ' May God protect you and bring you safely home ' roused lusty cheers which were repeated again and again."

The following was the message from the G.O.C. :—

"In offering to the Army in France my earnest and most heartfelt good wishes for Christmas and the New Year, I am anxious once more to express the admiration I feel for the valour and endurance they have displayed throughout the campaign, and to assure them that to have commanded such magnificent troops in the field will be the proudest remembrance of my life."

The last day of the first year of the war found the Battalion in occupation of billets at Cambrin, being then reserve battalion to the Brigade.

The officers on this day present with the Battalion were distributed as follows : Headquarter Company : Major Powell, Captain Lucey, adjutant ; Captain Nimmo, R.A.M.C., 2nd Lieutenants Hyndson and Callard and Lieutenant and Quartermaster Fenton.

"A" Company : Captain Hay, 2nd Lieutenants Williams and Burdekin.
"B"   „   Captain Dare and 2nd Lieutenant Nailer.
"C"   „   Lieutenant Kearns and 2nd Lieutenant Thomas.
"D"   „   Lieutenant Wilberforce, 2nd Lieutenants Metcalfe and Rowell.

A column to the memory of those who made the supreme sacrifice was subsequently erected at Troyon, on the Aisne, where the 1st Battalion went into action in September, 1914. This memorial was unveiled on 22nd September, 1923, by General Sir James Willcocks, Colonel, The Loyal Regiment (North Lancashire), at which ceremony a representative detachment of the Regiment was present.

CHAPTER XXX

1915

THE BATTLES OF AUBERS RIDGE AND LOOS

ON the 25th December, 1914, the British Expeditionary Force, which then consisted of five cavalry and eleven infantry divisions, organized in four Army Corps, was reorganized for fighting purposes into two Armies.

The new order of battle was as follows :—

The First Army under General Sir D. Haig :

      I. Corps—Lieut.-General Sir C. C. Monro.
      IV. Corps—Lieut.-General Sir H. S. Rawlinson.
      Indian Corps—Lieut.-General Sir J. Willcocks.

The Second Army under General Sir H. L. Smith-Dorrien :

      II. Corps—Lieut.-General Sir C. Fergusson.
      III. Corps—Lieut.-General Sir W. P. Pulteney.
      27th Division—Major-General T. D' O. Snow.
      Cavalry Corps—Lieut.-General Sir E. H. H. Allenby.
      Indian Cavalry Corps—Major-General M. Rimington.

Major-General Haking was now in command of the 1st Division *vice* Major-General Lomax, who had been mortally wounded at the Battle of Ypres.

" The five hundred miles of the allied line were held as to one-tenth by the British, and for the rest by the Belgians and French. It ran from Nieuport generally east of the Yser, along the Ypres Canal, in a salient in front of Ypres, behind Messines to just east of Armentières ; then west of Neuve Chapelle to Givenchy, across the La Bassée Canal, east of Vermelles, west of Lens, to just east of Arras. From Arras it lay by Albert and Noyons to Soissons, east along the Aisne to just north of Rheims by Viennes to Varennes, then, making a wide curve round Verdun, to the west bank of the Meuse opposite St. Mihiel, and so on to Pont-à-Mousson on the Moselle. Thence it passed east of Luneville to just east of St. Dié, ten miles inside the frontier. It reached the crest of the Vosges about the Col de Bonhomme, and then ran in German territory to Belfort and the Swiss border. . . . The winter's record was a chronicle of small things —a sandhill won east of Nieuport, a trench or two at Ypres, a corner of a brickfield at La Bassée, a few hundred yards near Arras, a farm on the Oise, a mile in northern Champagne, a coppice in the Argonne, a hillock on the Meuse, part of a wood on the Moselle, some of the high glens in the Vosges and a village or two in Alsace." *

The opening days of the year 1915 were passed by the troops in extreme discomfort, rain, frost and storms succeeding each other, the ground became too sodden for any forward movement, and the trenches were full of mud and water, in some places up to the men's knees and in others to their hips.

On the 5th January the Battalion—its strength was now no more than fourteen officers and 385 other ranks—was occupying billets in rear of the Cambrin area at Beuvry, when it was ordered up to the trenches about Cuinchy, relieving there the 2nd King's Royal Rifles about 8.30 p.m. Here the enemy trenches were only 200 yards distant and the occupants kept up a continual sniping by day and night. In this position the Battalion remained tolerably quiescent until the 13th, when, on relief by the Royal Sussex, it withdrew to billets at Annequin, about a mile in rear of the front line, finding on arrival that a draft had reached that village, consisting of 360 men and three officers under Lieutenant Halsted, the other two officers being 2nd Lieutenants F. H. Maynard and W. L. Wasbrough. On the 15th four more subaltern officers joined—2nd Lieutenants C. E. Dawes, R. A. Barker, T. M. Garrod and W. H. Roy, this bringing the total strength up to twenty-two officers and 740 non-commissioned officers and men. On the 16th when the Battalion returned to the line, 2nd Lieutenant H. Caffyn joined the service companies, but at this time the dearth of senior and experienced officers and non-commissioned officers was much felt. During this tour of the trenches the weather improved and the ground was drier, while an issue of gum-boots was made for wear in the trenches.

On the 21st January the 1st Brigade relieved the 2nd, which went back to the comparative civilization of Bethune, where the men of the Battalion found comfortable billets in the tobacco factory, and here it remained until the 25th. On the early morning of this day, heavy gun-fire was heard from the direction of Givenchy and a few shells fell in Bethune itself : the Brigade was at once warned to stand by, and within half an hour it had moved forward to Beuvry, whence the Battalion was detached to Le Préol, coming there under the orders of the O.C. 3rd Brigade.

* Buchan, *A History of the Great War*, Vol. I, p. 458.

Early on this morning a German deserter had brought in notice of an intended enemy attack on a larger scale than usual against Cuinchy and Givenchy held by the 1st and 3rd Brigades respectively ; and units from two German Corps (the VII. and XIV.) had in fact attacked on both sides of the Canal ; but at the time of the arrival of the Battalion at 3rd Brigade Headquarters, the G.O.C. was uncertain whether his front-line troops about Givenchy were or were not holding out, or to what extent the German attack had been successful.

At 12.30 p.m. the Battalion advanced along the Canal bank in support of the Highland Light Infantry, which had been directed to counter-attack any enemy body which might have broken through. On arriving near the Pont Fixe road, it was found that the line originally held by the 3rd Brigade had been re-taken by local counter-attacks and was now secure ; the Battalion was then withdrawn by way of Le Préol to Beuvry, where the night was passed, being held ready to move again at short notice if required.

Here at 9.30 a.m. on the 26th, orderly room was being held in a paved yard surrounded by buildings, and an unusually large number of officers and other ranks were unfortunately present, when a high-explosive shell fell almost perpendicularly in the middle of the yard, exploding with great violence and causing many casualties. 2nd Lieutenant G. E. Burdekin, five non-commissioned officers and seven other ranks were killed on the spot, while Lieutenant J. G. Halsted, 2nd Lieutenant M. E. Callard, Sergeant-Major Hodgson and eighteen men were more or less severely injured, one dying of his wounds the same day.

At 4.30 p.m. the Battalion moved to Cambrin and became the reserve battalion to the others of the Brigade holding the front line ; but on the afternoon of the 27th the relief of the Royal Sussex was effected, and in the course of the night that followed the Battalion was ordered to carry out two offensive operations as follows :—

On the left a party of thirty men, under 2nd Lieutenant Dawes, attacked the north side of the railway embankment with a view to capturing a German post situated about one hundred yards east of the culvert. The attack was started at 2 a.m., ten men advancing with hand grenades and slung rifles, while another ten men followed with fixed bayonets, the rest of the party moving in rear carrying tools and sandbags. 2nd Lieutenant Dawes was almost at once mortally wounded, being shot through the chest, and this initial attack failed. A second attempt, led by 2nd Lieutenant Barker, was made two hours later and this party succeeded in entering the enemy trench ; a very hot fire was then opened by the Germans occupying a trench running at right angles to the railway embankment, and 2nd Lieutenant Barker being also wounded, his men fell back, this, the second, attack having thus also failed.

At 2.30 p.m. some only moderately successful bombing operations were carried out by " A " Company, and the operations ended in our casualties being two killed and five wounded. There were a few more men hit on the following day by enemy snipers, whose posts were very close—indeed, at one point British and Germans were actually occupying the same trench ! At the end of the 28th the Battalion was relieved and went back into reserve trenches near the Pont Fixe road. On the 29th January, however, a very violent enemy attack developed on the front line then held by the Sussex and Northamptonshire, and two companies of the Battalion were ordered up in support, while the billets occupied by the remaining companies were heavily shelled.

The Battalion was now to leave the Cuinchy area, the 2nd Brigade being relieved on the 30th—the 2nd Division taking the place of the 1st—and after spending a few days in Bethune, the Battalion moved to Allouagne, where it remained until the end of the third week of February, reorganizing and training. During the short time passed at Bethune Lieut.-Colonel R. R. Bowlby joined and took over command of the Battalion.

While at Allouagne several officers and nearly a hundred men joined the Battalion in drafts—many of the officers from other regiments or battalions ; the names of these officers were : Captains St. J. Adcock and C. R. Etches, 2nd Lieutenants W. Scott, S. Waterworth, W. Fisher, R. Potter, C. N. Andrews and C. G. Treatt.

On the afternoon of the 21st February the Battalion moved to new billets at Lozinghem, and the 5th Battalion Royal Sussex Regiment joined the 2nd Brigade, while the Battalion was greatly occupied with company training and musketry ; here 2nd Lieutenant D. R. Curwen and some machine-gunners joined. When on the last day of February the Battalion marched out to new, very indifferent and very scattered billets at Hinges, the fighting strength stood at nineteen officers and 580 non-commissioned officers and men.

Early in March a move was made to Les Choquaux, and here a serious misfortune overtook the Battalion, Company Quartermaster-Sergeant Bearder and Sergeant Forester dying from suffocation caused by the fumes of a coke-fire in a closed room, while Company Sergeant-Major Wheatley and two men were also very seriously affected, but happily recovered.

On the 10th March the 2nd Brigade moved to Locon, where it was in the First Army Reserve for the Battle of Neuve Chapelle which had opened on the morning of this day, and the object of which, as stated in the Field-Marshal's despatch of the 5th April of this year, was " the capture of the village of Neuve Chapelle and the enemy's position at that point, and the establishment of our line as far forward as possible to the east of that place." For this purpose it was proposed to employ the units of the First Army, supported by troops of the Second Army and the General Reserve. " The 1st Division, the left division of the I. Corps, occupied an exceptionally water-logged sector of the front over which an attack was not considered practicable. It therefore assisted the attacks both of the 2nd Division on its right and the Indian Corps on its left by a bombardment of the enemy's defences, and by periodic bursts of rifle fire so as to hold the enemy " * ; consequently the 1st Division, and the units composing it, were debarred from taking any really prominent part in this battle.

The troops were, however, a good deal moved about during the next three or four days, the Battalion going first into divisional reserve at Le Touret, thence to billets at Les Facons, back again to Le Touret, and finally on the 13th back to Les Choquaux. On the following day there was a further move—to Essars, where the Battalion remained in peace and quietness for four days, the weather having now greatly improved and " the roads," so the Battalion War Diary gleefully states, " are actually dusty " !

On March 18th the 2nd Brigade relieved the 3rd in the Festubert sector, the portion of the front here held running just east of Festubert and being divided into two sections, each occupied by one battalion with two companies in the front line and two in support. When out of the line the Battalion occupied billets at Gorre. Here a draft of ninety-nine non-commissioned officers and men came out direct from the 3rd Battalion, this reinforcement bringing up the Battalion's strength to twenty-two officers and 781 other ranks. On the 23rd the 2nd Brigade took over a very extended line at the Rue de l'Epinette, one which had hitherto been held by the 1st Brigade plus two Indian infantry battalions, and the stretch of trench-line taken over by the Battalion was 900 yards in length. Matters here were on the whole tolerably quiet, but some casualties were incurred, and on the 24th 2nd Lieutenant C. N. Andrews was killed in one of the advanced posts.

While here Captains F. W. Greenhill and W. D. Hill and 2nd Lieutenant C. R. P. Diver joined. The first of the Service Battalions were now beginning to make their appearance at the front, and on the 26th March officers of the 9th (Service) Battalion Liverpool Regiment were sent up to the trenches for a tour of instruction. At the end of the month the Brigade went back to billets about Les Choquaux as Corps Reserve.

During the greater part of April the Battalion was in and out of the

* *Official History*, 1915, Vol. I, p. 115.

northern part of the line, engaged in no major operations, but occupied in building up its strength for work of a more decisive character ; and it may not be without interest to show what was the actual composition of a typical English Battalion at this comparatively early stage of the war.

On the 27th April, then, the strength stood at twenty-three officers and 826 other ranks, these last being made up as under :

Regular Soldiers	209
Rejoined from the Army Reserve	109
Re-enlisted men who had originally been Regulars . .	166
Re-enlisted from the Militia	71
Re-enlisted men who were originally Volunteers, or Territorials	24
Men of the Special Reserve	209
Men who had enlisted in " Kitchener's Army " for the "Duration"	37
Re-enlisted from the Royal Navy	1
Total . . .	826

During the earlier operations of the Second Battle of Ypres, which endured from the 22nd April to the 24th May, the 2nd Brigade in general and the 1st Battalion, Loyal North Lancashire Regiment, in particular had no share ; but in the early part of May the Battalion was called up to play its part in some serious and costly fighting. In his despatch of the 15th June, 1915, Sir John French wrote that "in pursuance of a promise which I made to the French Commander-in-Chief to support an attack which his troops were making on May 9th between the right of my line and Arras, I directed Sir Douglas Haig to carry out on that date an attack on the German trenches in the neighbourhood of Rouges Bancs (north-west of Fromelles) by the IV. Corps, and between Neuve Chapelle and Givenchy by the I. and Indian Corps."

On the 7th May it was announced in 1st Division orders that the First Army was attacking next day with the object of breaking through the enemy's line and gaining the La Bassée–Lille road between La Bassée and Fournes, and then advancing to the line Bauvin–Don. The Indian Corps was to attack on the left of the 1st Division, which was to assault the enemy's line from a Map point Q. 2. on the right to a point opposite the south-west corner of the Orchard on the left. The attack was to be carried out by the 2nd and 3rd Brigades with the 1st in reserve ; the 2nd Brigade to be on the right of the divisional front of attack from Chocolat Ménier Corner to the Cinder Track exclusive, each brigade attacking with two battalions in the front line, one in the second and one in reserve. The objective of the 2nd Brigade was from the point P.8. to the road junction

Q.12., both inclusive ; this line reached, it was to be entrenched and strong points established. This was to be followed by a rapid advance to gain a foothold on Aubers Ridge.

The attack was subsequently postponed till the morning of the 9th May.

May 7th was for the Battalion a long day of preparation, and every man was issued with 220 rounds of ammunition, a gas mask and two sand-bags—" the men," so we read in the War Diary, " are in splendid spirits and everything promises well." At 8 p.m. on the 8th, the Battalion moved off to the position of readiness behind the Rue du Bois, arriving here about midnight ; just before the Battalion marched off two young officers joined —2nd Lieutenants F. Holmes and G. Hawksley of the 4th Battalion, Royal Inniskilling Fusiliers.

The fighting strength this day was nineteen officers and 806 other ranks.

The following is Lieut.-Colonel Sanderson's account of the part played in the action of the 9th May by the Battalion under his command :—

" 8th May. The Battalion left Les Choquaux at 8 p.m. and moved into battle position in the third line of breastworks behind the Rue du Bois, and was in position there by midnight.

" 9th May. The deliberate bombardment of the enemy's trenches commenced at 5 a.m. and at 5.30, when the intense bombardment had started, the Battalion moved forward to the second and first lines of breast-works. ' A ' and ' B ' Companies in front, supported by ' C ' and ' D ' respectively, filed through the Rue du Bois and advanced, partly in the open and partly through the communication trenches, with little difficulty and only a few casualties. A machine-gun accompanied each of the front companies, and two guns were kept in reserve with ' C ' Company. About 6.5 a.m. a report was received from the O.C. ' A ' Company on the left near the Cinder Track, that the assaulting battalions were held up by machine-gun fire from the direction of Ferme du Bois. About this time Battalion H.Q. arrived in the front breastworks, which were then very crowded with men of the 2nd and 5th Royal Sussex Regiment and our own Battalion.

" The assaulting troops could be clearly seen lying in the open in front of the enemy's wire entanglements, and a message was sent to 2nd Brigade H.Q. by signal, that the assault was held up by machine-gun fire from the left of D.2., and that further artillery support was necessary to continue the advance. At 6.45 orders were received to reinforce the front line and assault the trench on completion of the bombardment at 6.45. A quarter of an hour elapsed before the contents of this message could be made known to the companies, and shortly after 7, ' A ' and ' B ' and ' D ' Companies climbed over the parapet and moved forward at the double.

"They were met with a very hot fire from the front and left flank, which ultimately checked the line about a hundred yards in front of our breastworks. Every officer in front was hit, and the casualties in other ranks were very heavy. Our machine-guns then opened fire from the breastworks, and, later, in accordance with instructions from 2nd Brigade H.Q., received about 7.50 a.m., as many men as possible were withdrawn behind the front parapet. Previous to this a message had been sent to the 2nd Brigade that the enemy's wire to our front had not been successfully cut.

"Between 9 and 10 a.m., after the relief by the 1st Brigade, the Battalion withdrew to the breastworks in rear of the Rue du Bois and re-organized. The machine-guns remained in position in the front line. There were now only seven officers available for duty.

"At 1 p.m., according to verbal orders received, the Battalion again took over the front line of breastworks, and prepared for the second assault, with 'C' and 'D' Companies in the front line, supported by 'A' and 'B.' Shortly after 2 p.m. the orders for the assault were cancelled, and the Battalion was to hold the front-line trenches from Tin Cross to the Cinder Track, while the 1st Brigade assaulted at 4 p.m. Companies were then distributed along the whole line and all hand-bombs in our possession were handed over to the Black Watch. At 4.15 a verbal order through the telephone was received to support the Black Watch, who had then assaulted the enemy's lines. This was cancelled a few minutes later. From 3 to 5 p.m. the enemy bombarded our front line of breastworks very heavily, causing considerable damage to the parapet, especially in the right sector.

"At about 6 p.m. all other troops left the breastworks and the Battalion held the front line until relieved at about 3 a.m. on the 10th by the Highland Light Infantry. During the night a large number of wounded were recovered from in front of the breastworks and the parapet was repaired as far as possible. After relief the Battalion assembled at Chocolat Ménier Corner and withdrew to billets at Long Cornet. The behaviour of all ranks throughout the action was excellent."

The losses as stated in the War Diary are, killed or died of wounds, seven officers—Captains G. W. Hay and St. J. Adcock, Lieutenant T. M. Garrod, 2nd Lieutenants R. Potter, T. W. Williams, F. Holmes, W. Fisher and nineteen other ranks ; wounded, Lieut.-Colonel R. R. Bowlby, Captain W. D. Hill, 2nd Lieutenants W. H. Roy, W. Scott, S. Waterworth and G. C. Morris and 190 non-commissioned officers and men, with twenty-one men missing.

The casualties in the 1st Division totalled 160 officers and 3,808 other ranks, and amounted to over 11,600 in the eight divisions this day engaged ; and it was in view of these losses, the small amount of rifle ammunition now available, and the defective character of some of the big-gun ammunition that General Haig decided to cancel his orders for an attack arranged for the same afternoon. " The failure at Aubers Ridge was in fact due to three causes," so the *Official History* states : " first, the strength of the German defences and the clever concealment of machine-guns in them ; secondly, the lack on the British side of sufficient shells of large calibre to deal with such defences ; and thirdly, the inferior quality of much of the ammunition supplied and the difficulties of ranging, so that the British gunners were unable to hit their targets, and the German counter-batteries and machine-guns were not silenced. . . . The brief 40-minutes' bombardment did no appreciable damage, and merely gave the enemy warning to stand-to to meet an assault which he had been expecting."

The week following the battle of the 9th May was passed by the Battalion in billets at Beuvry, the 1st and 47th Divisions being temporarily formed into a separate force under Major-General Barter, which was responsible for the defence of the line from Festubert southwards across the canal to the Vermelles–Loos road, and at the outset the 2nd Brigade was held in reserve to this force. On the 20th, however, the 2nd Brigade relieved the 1st in the trenches on the south of the La Bassée–Bethune road, the Battalion being in billets at Annequin. Here the Battalion was in brigade reserve—fortunately, perhaps, since, according to the War Diary of the 20th May, only six officers were available for duty !

Now followed some two months of comparative quiet during which drafts of officers and men arrived from home, and brought the Battalion up to something like its original strength. During the latter part of May a draft of ninety-four other ranks joined under 2nd Lieutenants A. Livings and J. H. Gardner, while six more officers arrived at different times— Captain R. B. Flint, who only two days later was seriously wounded in the head by a sniper during his second day's tour in the trenches, Lieutenants R. A. Barker, P. A. Burridge, T. R. Parry, H. C. Maule, L. A. G. Flint and L. L. Penno, all these last five from the Special Reserve of other corps. In June thirteen officers were posted to the Battalion and two large drafts arrived, the one 156 strong, the other 184 non-commissioned officers and men, the officers being Major E. Monteagle-Browne, Captain R. S. J. Faulknor, 2nd Lieutenants V. W. Newman, J. A. B. Gemmell, G. F. Bunbury, O. M. Sutton, R. J. P. Hewetson, W. M. Porritt, P. Healey, F. Gowan-Taylor, S. Blythen, P. F. Goldie and R. Goldie. In July there arrived for duty Captain N. C. Phillips and 2nd Lieutenant S. Clements and 84 other ranks in four small drafts ; and in August two drafts totalling thirty-five men joined, as did the following officers—Captain F. H. E. Torbett, Lieutenants N. Collins and H. G. Wood, 2nd Lieutenants F. H. Wharton and W. L. Wasbrough.

It was consequently a strong battalion at the beginning of September, a month in which hostilities of an active character were to recommence, for during the preceding weeks the casualties at the hands of the enemy had been few, though an officer and several men had been injured—one indeed killed—while practising with the bombs issued to the troops.

The operations which commenced in the latter half of September, and which are known as the Battle of Loos, were undertaken in consequence of a decision for joint action come to between the British and French commanders ; and so far as the British share in this was concerned, it consisted of a main attack and several subsidiary or holding attacks. The main assault upon the German positions was delivered by the I. and IV. Corps between the La Bassée Canal on the north, and a point of the enemy's line opposite the village of Grenay on the south. Secondary attacks, designed with the object of distracting the enemy's attention and holding his troops to their ground, were made by the III., V. and Indian Corps. The IV. Corps, in which the 1st Division was now included, was to attack on the right, the I. Corps on the left. In Sir John French's despatch of the 15th October, 1915, he states that "opposite the front of the main line of attack, the distance between the enemy's trenches and our own, varied from about 100–500 yards ; the country is open and overgrown with long grass and self-sown crops. From the Vermelles–Hulluch road southwards the advantage of height is on the enemy's side, as far as the Bethune–Lens road."

The 1st Division was to attack with the 15th Division on its right and the 7th on its left ; and the objectives for the 1st Division were, first, a line about the south-west edge of Hulluch village, and, secondly, a support line of trenches running from east of Bois Hugo to the south-east of Hulluch. The 1st Brigade was to attack on the left, the 2nd on the right, the 3rd Brigade being in support. In the 2nd Brigade the 1st Loyal North Lancashire and 2nd King's Royal Rifles were to be in the front line, the Royal Sussex in support and the 1st Northamptonshire in reserve.

From the 21st to the 25th September—the day appointed for the attack —the enemy position was subjected to a very heavy bombardment, to which, however, the German guns made little response ; and at 9.45 p.m. on the 24th the Battalion moved forward from Marles-les-Mines, where the last few days had been spent, into battle positions. The advance was to have been heralded by a gas attack, but the hour for this was more than once altered, and when at 6.34 a.m. on the 25th gas was at last released

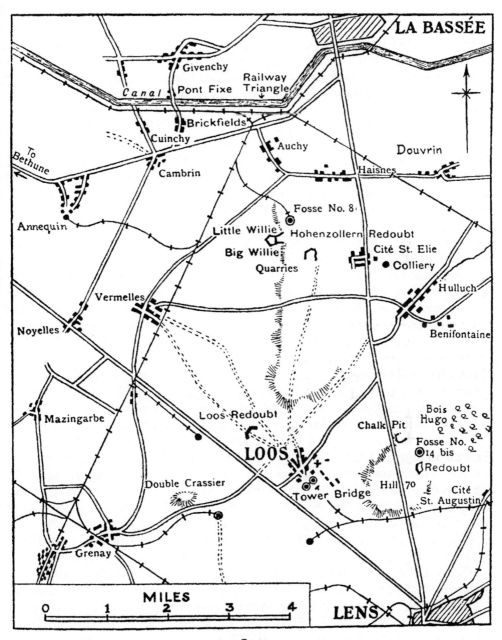

LOOS.

———

1915.

31

from the British trenches, the wind changed and blew it back on the attackers, the front and support lines suffering considerably, while the presence of the gas had the effect of causing the advancing lines to become somewhat intermingled. The attack moved forward right up to the German wire, but this was found to be uncut and the Battalion fell back again to its starting-point.

Lieut.-Colonel Sanderson led out once more as many men as could be collected, but the attempt was fruitless, Colonel Sanderson and the adjutant, Captain Diver, being both wounded almost at once, while 2nd Lieutenant R. Goldie was killed, and the bodies of Captain Faulknor, 2nd Lieutenants Livesey, Wharton and Healey were afterwards found right up by the German wire.

2nd Lieutenant Wasbrough, the Machine-Gun Officer, took his two guns practically up to the enemy wire, where he too was killed ; 2nd Lieutenant Gardner, the other Machine-Gun Officer, went out on the left flank with the two guns in his charge, but nearly all his detachment were at once gassed, and he carried on practically single-handed with one gun until he also was gassed, but none the less went back for more ammunition.

Many isolated attempts were made to advance, but these all failed, and what was left of the Battalion—three officers and 159 other ranks—then remained in the trenches until the afternoon, when these moved with the rest of the Brigade into the Chalk Pit, where 2nd Lieutenant Gardner joined, though still suffering much from the effects of the gas.

A position was now taken up for the night along the Lens–La Bassée road, the right on Puits 14 and the left on the Chalk Pit, the rain coming down all night. Captain Phillips, who that day had also been badly gassed, came up and took over command, and early on the morning of the 26th, on relief by troops of the 11th Division, the Battalion went back to the trenches in rear, finally, on the 28th, retiring to the shelter of some cellars at Mazingarbe, Temporary Major Edwards being now in command.

The losses of the Battalion on the 25th were very heavy, comprising sixteen officers and 489 other ranks, killed, wounded and missing. The officers killed were Captains R. S. J. Faulknor, V. W. Newman and E. J. Nangle, R.A.M.C., Lieutenant H. G. Wood, 2nd Lieutenants P. Goldie, P. Healey, A. G. H. Livesey, F. H. Wharton and W. L. Wasbrough ; wounded were Lieut.-Colonel W. D. Sanderson, Captain C. R. P. Diver, 2nd Lieutenants R. J. P. Hewetson, F. H. Maynard and S. Clements ; missing were 2nd Lieutenants R. Helme (wounded) and W. M. Porritt. Captain Nangle, the Medical Officer, " was killed while attending a wounded man, a great loss to the Battalion."

During the early days of October the Battalion was at Nœux Les Mines and here nearly two hundred men joined in drafts and also the following officers : Captain J. R. Acton, Lieutenant R. M. Sterndale, 2nd Lieutenants T. A. Bold, M. H. C. Firmin, H. G. Gilliland, W. R. Keeble, S. W. Shippard, J. Lindsell, K. H. Leake, R. W. M. Hyndson, D. O. Tripp, H. D. F. Haggar and M. D. G. Scott.

The Battalion now again took its place in the trenches in front of Mazingarbe, where the shelling was usually heavy and casualties were incurred ; on the 9th Captain Meers, the Medical Officer, was mortally wounded while attending to wounded in the trenches.

It had been arranged that on the 13th October the First Army was to make an attack upon the Quarries, Hohenzollern Redoubt and Fosse 8, the 1st Division being detailed for the capture of a new German trench along the Lens road from the junction of the Loos–Hulluch and Lens–La Bassée roads northwards to opposite Hulluch, a distance of 1,400 yards, there consolidating and connecting up with a trench leading south to the Chalk Pit.   The 1st Brigade was to attack, with the 2nd in support in the old German trenches, the 3rd remaining to hold the line through Chalk Pit Wood to the Loos–Puits 14 Bis track.   The wire having been insufficiently cut the attack failed, and the 2nd Brigade was then ordered up on the night of the 13th–14th to make a further attack, but these orders were later cancelled, the day's fighting having cost the 1st Division 1,200 casualties.   The Battalion, however, got off with but small loss.

The *Official History* sums up the result of the fighting on the 13th–14th October, stating that it " had not improved the general situation in any way and had brought nothing but useless slaughter of infantry ; what the British won was lost again for lack of a sufficient supply of effective hand grenades. . . .   The British IV. Corps, in touch with the French left, had gained no ground and continued to hold the line of trenches west of the Lens road by Chalk Pit Wood to the Vermelles–Hulluch Road."

In the Battle of Loos the losses in the 1st Division amounted to 246 officers and 5,784 non-commissioned officers and men killed, wounded and missing.

During the remaining months of the year 1915 the Battalion was engaged in holding the trenches in the neighbourhood of Loos, varied by periods of rest, recuperation and training about Lillers.   During this time Major B. J. Wakley arrived and took over command of the Battalion, but at the end of November he, and Captain Acton, were wounded when up in the trenches.   Among other officers who now joined were 2nd Lieutenants M. Wilson, H. T. Emerson, B. O. Ware, N. Kelley and A. A. McIlwaine.

The close of the year found the Battalion in support trenches in front of Philosophe, where all ranks were greatly cheered by the receipt of a very gracious and kindly message, showing that His Majesty The King did not forget his soldiers fighting on so many different fronts :—

" Another Christmas," so the message ran, " finds all the resources of the Empire still engaged in war, and I desire to convey on My own behalf, and on behalf of the Queen, a heartfelt Christmas greeting and Our good wishes for the New Year to all who, on Sea and Land, are upholding the honour of the British name. In the Officers and Men of My Navy, on whom the security of the Empire depends, I repose, in common with all My subjects, a trust that is absolute. On the Officers and Men of My Armies, whether now in France, in the East or in other fields, I rely with an equal faith, confident that their devotion, their valour and their self-sacrifice will, under God's guidance, lead to Victory and an honourable Peace. There are many of their comrades now, alas, in hospital, and to these brave fellows, also, I desire, with the Queen, to express Our deep gratitude and Our earnest prayers for their recovery.

" Officers and Men of the Navy and Army, another year is drawing to a close, as it began, in toil, bloodshed and suffering ; but I rejoice to know that the goal to which you are striving draws nearer into sight.

" May God bless you and all your undertakings.

(sd.) " GEORGE R.I."

Just a week before Christmas a change had been effected in the command of the British Expeditionary Force, which on the 19th December Field-Marshal Sir John French resigned into the able hands of General Sir Douglas Haig, then proceeding to England to take over the command of the Home Forces.

The difficulty of reinforcement, and the insistent call from Mesopotamia for more Indian troops, had caused the withdrawal from France of the Indian Corps, and on the 26th December the last of the units composing it had sailed from Marseilles, leaving behind, however, certain Special Reserve and Territorial Battalions which, latterly, had been attached to it, as well as three brigades of its artillery.

The 1st Division was now, as has been mentioned, in the IV. Corps, commanded by Lieut.-General Sir H. S. Rawlinson, Bt., the Division being under Major-General A. E. A. Holland and the 2nd Brigade under Brig.-General J. H. W. Pollard. In addition to its original Regular Battalions, the 1/9th Battalion The King's Regiment was also included in the 2nd Brigade.

CHAPTER XXXI

1916

THE BATTLES OF THE SOMME

AFTER the conclusion of the Battle of Loos many months were to elapse before the Battalion was again to be engaged in any major operations, and it remained during the whole of this period of comparative inaction in the same quarter of the front as at the end of 1915.

Trench warfare was carried on during this time and under better conditions than had prevailed when the initial advance was stopped, and the long line from the Alps to the sea was first taken over. The trenches were now better drained and protected, " Trench feet " had been more or less successfully combated, reliefs were more regular and the time spent at rest in rear was profitably and even pleasantly occupied.

The inevitable casualties went on—hardly a day passing without some officer or man being hit when up in the front line ; thus between the 26th and 28th February Lieutenant M. H. C. Firmin was killed, Captain D. O. Tripp was wounded while holding Hart's Crater single-handed against an enemy bombing attack, and some sixteen other casualties occurred. On the 4th March 2nd Lieutenant A. A. McIlwaine was killed by a shell, on the 18th Captain P. A. Edwards was shot dead by a German sniper in the trench known as the north arm of the Double Crassier, and on the 23rd, 2nd Lieutenant A. A. Smith was wounded by shell in the village of Maroc. Finally on the last day of June, when a local attack on the German front line was carried out by parties from the Battalion, the Royal Sussex and the King's Royal Rifles : in the 1st North Lancashire ten men were killed, two officers—2nd Lieutenants Ward and Shippard—and thirty-five other ranks were wounded.

The *London Gazette* of the 30th March, 1916, announced the award of the Victoria Cross to Pte. H. Kenny, 1st Battalion, " for most conspicuous bravery."

During the first six months of this year small reinforcing drafts were constantly arriving, and officers joined in ones and twos and threes—among these were Captain Walworth, 2nd Lieutenants Gifford, Cragg, Pearson, Molyneux, Carmichael, Stone, Nichol and Harrison.

35

With the opening of the month of July the Battalion was now again to be called to the scene of important and far-reaching operations, and to be engaged for many weeks in real hard fighting.

During the past winter and spring considerable reinforcements had reached the British Army in France, and the provision of these had been greatly simplified and eased by the recent introduction in Great Britain of compulsory service.

The four British Armies now in the field were distributed as follows : the Second was about Ypres, the First opposite Neuve Chapelle, the Third covered the new French sector down to Arras, while the Fourth held the line from Albert to the Somme, where it joined on to the French left.   In the spring of the year the enemy had made a very determined attack upon the Ypres Salient, and by the middle of March the pressure upon the French about Verdun had become so severe, that the British troops had taken over an additional twelve miles of front from their allies.   In March and April there had been heavy fighting about St. Eloi and Loos, attacks being made here by the enemy in the hope of holding us to our ground while he continued his offensive at Verdun ; possibly also he hoped to provoke a premature attack on our front, since he had good reason for believing that an allied offensive on a really large scale was then under consideration.

In Sir Douglas Haig's despatch of the 23rd December, 1916, we read :—

" The principle of an offensive campaign during the summer of 1916 had already been decided upon by the Allies. . . .   Preparations for our offensive had made considerable progress ; but as the date on which the attack should begin was dependent on many doubtful factors, a final decision on that point was delayed until the general situation should become clearer."

General Haig was anxious to delay the attack as long as possible, for although the strength of his army and his ammunition supplies were daily increasing, his reinforcements were not fully trained, while his store of supplies was still hardly sufficient for a really great battle.   Against any delay the fact had to be considered that the French were being seriously pressed at Verdun, while in the Italian theatre of war the Austrians appeared to be gaining ground.   Having carefully considered all the points the Allied Commanders agreed that an offensive ought not to be postponed much later than the end of June, and that it should be directed from the junction point of the British and French lines—any attack must in fact be a combined one since neither of the Allies was at this time sufficiently strong to undertake any really great offensive single-handed.   This attack, then, was to be conducted by the Fourth British Army, which then held the front from Gommecourt across the Ancre valley to Maricourt ; and by the Sixth French Army, which lay from Maricourt, astride the Somme, to opposite the village of Fay.

" The enemy's position to be attacked was of a very formidable character, situated on a high undulating tract of ground, which rises to more than 500 feet above sea-level, and forms the watershed between the Somme on the one side, and the rivers of south-west Belgium on the other. On the southern face of this watershed, the general trend of which is from east-south-east to west-north-west, the ground rises in a series of long irregular spurs and deep depressions to the valley of the Somme. Well down the forward slopes of this face, the enemy's first system of defence, starting from the Somme near Curlu, ran at first north for 3,000 yards, then west for 7,000 yards to near Fricourt, where it turned nearly due south, forming a great salient angle in the enemy's line.

" Some 7,000 yards north of Fricourt the trenches crossed the River Ancre, a subsidiary of the Somme, and, still running north, passed over the summit of the watershed, about Hébuterne and Gommecourt, and then down its northern spurs to Arras. On the 20,000 yards' front between the Somme and the Ancre, the enemy had a strong second line of defence, sited generally on or near the southern crest of the highest part of the watershed, at an average distance of from 3,000 to 5,000 yards behind his first system of trenches. . . . The first and second systems each consisted of several lines of deep trenches, well provided with bomb-proof shelters and with numerous communicating trenches connecting them. The front of the trenches in each system was protected by wire entanglements, many of them in belts forty yards broad, built of iron stakes interlaced with barbed wire, often almost as thick as a man's finger." *

The long-enduring Battle of the Somme may be divided into three stages : the first commencing on the 1st July and ending on the 17th ; the second continuing from this latter date and going on until the end of the first week in September ; while the third and last stage, commencing on the 9th September, did not end until the 19th November. The objects of the Somme battle, as stated in the official despatches, were three in number : to lighten the pressure on the French at Verdun ; to prevent the transfer of German troops from the Western to the Russian front ; and to wear down the strength of the opposing forces.

During the early days of July the 1st Division was relieved by the 40th, and on the 5th the 1st Battalion, The North Lancashire Regiment, moved back to Divion, and from here on the afternoon of the following day it marched to Lillers and proceeded by train to Flesselles, where the 1st Division now found itself attached to the III. Corps of the Fourth

* Despatch of 23rd December, 1916.

Army. The III. Corps was covering the front Ovillers–la-Boisselle–Bécourt, and had the XIV. Corps on its right and the X. on its left. From Flesselles the 2nd Brigade moved on by Frechencourt and Albert to Bresle, where it was in support to the 1st Brigade holding Contalmaison village, which had been recaptured that afternoon, the 3rd Brigade being in reserve in Albert ; all were in position by the night of the 10th, in preparation for heavy fighting on the 14th and 15th.

By 7 a.m. on the 14th the Battalion was occupying a position in trenches between the point O.B.I. and Bécourt Wood, and at 11.30 orders were received for " A " and " B " Companies to move up at once and take part in an attack which was to be made by the 1st Brigade on the German second-line system immediately north-west of Bazentin-le-Petit Wood. This attack opened at 2.30 p.m. at which time " C " Company was sent forward to form a guard for 1st Brigade headquarters. The 21st Division had been directed to take the offensive on the right of the 1st Division, but these orders were cancelled, with the result that the right of the 1st Division became rather exposed : none the less the 2nd Brigade succeeded in capturing and consolidating 500 yards of the support line and 300 yards of the front line from the west edge of Bazentin-le-Petit Wood to points X.12.A.82 and X.12.C.86, taking prisoners one German officer and ninety-nine men.

About 6 p.m. " C " Company came up in support, and at nine o'clock it moved forward with Battalion headquarters to Mametz Wood.

In this day's fighting Lieutenant A. Livings and 2nd Lieutenant J. Wardle were wounded, and there were fifty casualties among the other ranks.

The night passed quietly, but at 7.15 on the morning of the 15th the Battalion received orders to attack again at 9 a.m. and bomb up 1,200 yards of trench to a point just east of Pozières on the line X.5.B.10–42. Owing to the short notice given, but small preparation could be made for this attack, which was, however, tolerably successful during the early stages, 150 yards of support trench and 400 of the front line being quickly captured, but further advance was checked by machine-gun fire from the enemy trench itself and from the flanks where the trenches had been levelled by the British bombardment. " D " Company was then thrown in to reinforce, but by 11.30 it was evident that no further advance could be made for the present, in view of the open nature of the ground and the weight of the German machine-gun fire ; and consolidation was then put in hand, one and a half companies of the 2nd Battalion Welsh Regiment coming up to assist.

At noon a strong German counter-attack was launched against the Battalion position in the support line, and it was at first forced to fall back for a hundred and fifty yards, but almost immediately recovered the ground lost. Unfortunately, however, British shells now began to fall on the Battalion, and it was obliged to evacuate a large portion of the re-captured trench ; our shells also caused several casualties in the companies.

Towards 4 p.m. the G.O.C. 3rd Brigade arrived upon the scene and ordered a further attack to be attempted by the 2nd Welsh following upon half-an-hour's concentrated bombardment ; this attack also failed of success, and about 8.30 p.m. the Welsh Regiment took over the line, the Battalion moving back first to Mametz Wood and thence to Bécourt Wood, which was reached in the very early hours of the 16th.

On the 15th 2nd Lieutenant H. W. Gifford was killed, while Lieutenant L. G. Holt was wounded : there were also seventy-five casualties among the non-commissioned officers and men this day engaged.

Things were fairly quiet from the 16th to the 21st July, the Battalion being occupied in improving the existing trenches and in digging a new advanced assembly trench, to be known as Lancashire Trench ; but orders were now issued for an attack by the 2nd Brigade on the 22nd upon what was known as the " German Switch Line," and this attack was to be carried out by the 2nd Royal Sussex and 2nd King's Royal Rifles, with the 1st Northamptonshire in support and the North Lancashire in brigade reserve, the Battalion supplying five officers and 250 men to carry up consolidation material to the advanced troops. 2nd Lieutenant E. Molyneux was here very badly gassed.

This attack, which was carried out in conjunction with the 1st Brigade on the right and the Australian Division on the left, failed by reason of the very heavy artillery and machine-gun fire brought to bear by the Germans. Orders for a fresh attack by the 2nd Brigade on Munster Trench were then issued and almost immediately cancelled, revised instructions being given out about 5 p.m., and in these it was directed that the Battalion, with the Australians on its left, was to capture and consolidate Munster Alley, also seizing and fortifying the junction of Munster Alley and the German support line. This scheme was in turn abandoned, and at 9.30 p.m. a new one was announced, and now the Battalion was, single-handed, to attack Munster Alley, the Australians being responsible for the " strong points " in its vicinity. Later again it was discovered that the Australians were not available, and the capture of Munster Alley was thus left to the Battalion alone.

Preparations were made during the night of the 23rd–24th July, and by 3.30 a.m. on the 24th all were in position, " C " Company being detailed to make the attack, while " D " was to dig a trench which it was considered would facilitate the capture of Munster Alley. The enemy was, however, fully on the alert and his fire was too heavy and too well-directed to allow any chance of the assault being successful, and it was therefore not persisted in. On relief by the 2nd Welsh, the Battalion was moved back to trenches in Bécourt Wood.

On the 26th the 23rd Division relieved the 1st and the 69th Brigade the 2nd, and the Battalion then went back to rest at Franvillers.

This period of rest lasted but little more than a week, for on the 4th August the Battalion relieved the 10th Battalion Royal Fusiliers of the 111th Brigade, 23rd Division, as reserve battalion of the 2nd Brigade in trenches about High Wood. Here the 2nd Brigade was in the front line with the 1st Brigade on its left, and the 33rd Division on its right. For a time matters were generally quiet, except for some spells of heavy shelling, which caused eleven casualties in the Battalion, and on the 17th Lieutenant H. D. F. Huggan—attached No. 2. Trench Mortar Battery—was killed.

At this time the trench-strength of the Battalion was sixteen officers and 522 non-commissioned officers and men.

The following is Major Phillips' account of some operations in which the Battalion took part on the 18th August : " In conjunction with attacks by the French and ourselves from Thiepval to the Somme, the Battalion attacked the German line from the right of the 1st Northamptonshire to the north-west corner of High Wood, and also a trench running along its western edge. At zero time—2.45 p.m.—the right platoon, which was detailed to attack the trench and to form a strong point at the north-west corner of High Wood, left its trenches and was seen to advance into our own bombardment, which was not timed to lift until later. The remainder appear to have followed too quickly and suffered a similar fate, though up to the present "—this account is dated 28th August—" no survivors have been found able to give any reliable account.

" The left platoon delayed its assault until about 3.2 p.m. and, advancing close under our barrage, entered the German trench without difficulty, assisted by the Northamptonshire attack on our left. By the time the third line got in only one officer had not become a casualty ; he, realizing that on the right the trench was unoccupied, extended his men down the trench to within 200 yards of High Wood and commenced to consolidate the position. A further advance was made later, and our right now rests within 120 yards of the north-west corner of High Wood.

" At 4 p.m. two platoons of the 2nd King's Royal Rifles were placed at my disposal to hold the old front line between Sutherland Avenue and Leith Walk ; and later in the day two companies of the same regiment were sent up, one of which relieved the company in support, which had been working hard all day carrying up stores to the occupied position, the

other remaining in reserve near Battalion headquarters and carried up
water, ammunition, rations, bombs, etc., to our forward line.

" During the night patrols were pushed out to the north-west corner
of High Wood and also to our front without being able to establish touch
with the enemy : our advance on the right was stopped by an artillery
barrage set up in answer to signal lights the moment our patrols attempted
to approach High Wood."

The casualties this day were again very heavy, Captains M. A. Cross,
D. O. Tripp, D.S.O., and thirty other ranks were killed ; Lieutenant
E. F. Nichol, 2nd Lieutenants B. O. Ware, F. Stephenson, G. H. Harrison,
J. P. Heaton, A. E. Bulling and 110 non-commissioned officers and men
were wounded, while fifty were missing.

These losses reduced the strength of the Battalion to no more than seven
officers and 310 other ranks, and consequently on the 27th of the month
" A " Company was amalgamated with " B " under the command of
Captain Leake, and " C " with " D " under that of Captain Saunders.

On the next day the following reported themselves for duty : 2nd
Lieutenants J. A. B. Gemmel, J. S. H. Palmer, J. G. Sandie, R. A. Alldred
and J. H. Mort.

On the 2nd September, while the Battalion was in Mametz Wood, six
officers reported themselves for duty, all coming from the 3rd Battalion
The Sherwood Foresters—Lieutenants G. D. M. Abbotts, J. E. Richards,
S. Boyd, S. S. Horwitz, H. A. Robb and L. R. Allen ; these were accompanied by a small draft of twenty-nine other ranks, and two or three days
later 347 non-commissioned officers and men joined the Battalion, the
number being made up by 194 from the Durham Light Infantry, 73 from
the Depot and 80 from the Cheshire Regiment.

On the 9th an attack was carried out by the 2nd Brigade upon the
German line in High Wood and the trench running thence to the south-
east, and in these operations, though the Battalion was nominally in brigade
reserve, three of its companies were placed at the disposal of other battalions
of the Brigade—" A " and " B " working with the 2nd Royal Sussex and
" C " with the 2nd King's Royal Rifles. The attack was only partially
successful and these companies were chiefly employed in digging and
improving the communication trenches.

On the 11th the 47th Division relieved the 1st and the 23rd Battalion
London Regiment took the place of the 2nd North Lancashire, which then
moved back to billets in Albert, having been reinforced by a small draft
with three officers—Captain W. A. Campbell, 2nd Lieutenants R. M. Leake
and N. J. Sanderson. A few days were then spent in Bresle, fitting and
reorganizing, but on the 25th the 2nd Brigade was back again in the front

line in the Mametz Wood area. Here orders were issued that on the night of the 26th at 11 p.m. the Battalion, in conjunction with the 2nd Royal Sussex and with the 50th Division on its left, was to attack the German trench running from Flers Line to the Crescent in front of Eaucourt L'Abbaye. Owing to the extreme darkness of the night direction was unfortunately lost and this attack failed. At 2 p.m. on the 28th a patrol started out from the British trenches with orders to ascertain if the trench previously attacked was still occupied by the enemy, but the patrol had only advanced a few yards when it was stopped by rifle and machine-gun fire from Flers Line. At 6.30 p.m. the Battalion was ordered to attack this trench.

" B " Company then " went over the top " in two lines followed by two platoons of " A," and on drawing near to the trench at Flers Line, the men holding it fired a couple of rounds and then fell back, the attackers at once occupying it and making a block 200 yards from Flers Line. At 1.30 on the morning of the 29th September the Battalion was relieved by one from the 49th Division and marched back to a camp at Millencourt. The casualties during the four days in the line, from the 25th to the 28th, had again been very heavy, amounting to eleven officers and 201 other ranks killed, wounded and missing. The following detailed list of the officers who became casualties, shows from how many different regiments and battalions officers were drawn at this stage of the war :—

Killed : Temp. Captain L. G. Holt, 3rd Bn. Loyal North Lancashire.
      ,,   ,,   ,, C. P. G. Saunders, 3rd Bn. Loyal North Lancashire.
Wounded : Temp. Major W. A. Campbell, 1st Bn. Loyal North Lancashire.
Wounded : Lieut. G. D. M. Abbotts, 3rd Bn. The Sherwood Foresters.
    ,,   ,,   J. E. Edwards   ,, ,, ,,   ,,   ,,
    ,,   ,,   S. Boyd   ,, ,, ,,   ,,   ,,
    ,,   ,,   S. S. Horwitz   ,, ,, ,,   ,,   ,,
    ,, 2nd Lieut. R. A. Alldred, 3rd Bn. Loyal North Lancashire.
    ,,   ,,   J. S. H. Palmer, 1st ,, ,,   ,,   ,,
    ,,   ,,   J. A. B. Gemmel, ,, ,, ,,   ,,   ,,
    ,,   ,,   N. J. Sanderson, 3rd ,, ,,   ,,   ,,
Lieutenant Boyd died later of his wounds.

The 1st Division spent the whole of the month of October at rest in the Millencourt area, being now in the X. Corps of the Fourth Army, and during this time no fewer than twenty officers joined for duty : from the West India Regiment, Major A. E. Norton and Lieutenant E. A. M. Bear ; from the 3rd Battalion, Lieutenant A. B. Bratton and 2nd Lieutenant E. Gladding ; from the East Kent Regiment, 2nd Lieutenants B. L. James and R. H. D'Elboux; from the Middlesex Regiment, 2nd Lieutenants H. W. Smith, L. Edwards, W. H. Ward, G. B. Boulton, W. C. Goulden, G. A. Miller, J. A. Turner, H. P. Burton, F. E. Towers, D. H. Towers, E. M. Davies, R. A. Smith, J. H. Jeffreys and S. A. Bond.

On the 21st October Lieutenant Horwitz and Private Turner were accidentally killed by a premature bomb explosion.

At the end of October the 1st Division was moved back to the Somme area, being the reserve division to the III. Corps; rather more than a fortnight the Battalion spent in billets in Albert, and on the 19th the Division was moved to a new front near Bazentin-le-Grand, and during the relief of the trenches 2nd Lieutenant H. W. Smith was wounded.

In these parts, or in the old area about Mametz Wood, the Battalion passed the remaining weeks of the year 1916, taking its share of trench duty, and spending the " rest-period " in rear in organizing and assimilating the new drafts which continued to arrive in small and larger parties. Of the general results of the fighting of the latter part of this year, Sir Douglas Haig writes as follows in his despatch of the 23rd December, written when the Somme Battle had at long last come to an end with the capture of Beaumont Hamel:—

" The three main objects with which we had commenced our offensive in July had already been achieved at the date when this account closes; in spite of the fact that the heavy autumn rains had prevented full advantage being taken of the favourable situation created by our advance, at a time when we had good grounds for hoping to achieve yet more important successes.

" Verdun had been relieved; the main German force had been held on the Western Front; and the enemy's strength had been very considerably worn down.

" Any one of these three results is in itself sufficient to justify the Somme Battle. The attainment of all three of them affords ample compensation for the splendid efforts of our troops and for the sacrifices made by ourselves and our Allies. They have brought us a long step forward towards the final victory of the Allied cause."

Between the 1st July and the 18th November the British Army in France had captured over thirty-eight thousand prisoners and taken from the Germans over one hundred guns, nearly one hundred and fifty trench-mortars and more than five hundred machine-guns; and these results were largely due to troops of which the vast majority had been raised and trained during the war—many of these indeed counted their service only by months and gained in the Somme battle their first experience of war. " That these troops should have accomplished so much under such conditions, and against an army and a nation whose chief concern for so many years has been preparation for war, constitutes a feat of which the history of our nation records no equal."

Christmas Day, 1916, was spent by the Battalion in Camp No. 5 at the north end of Mametz Wood ; "No fatigues to-day," we read in the War Diary, " but owing to some block on the railway, no parcels arrived, so that all entertainments were somewhat curtailed."

All ranks were, however, cheered and sustained by the following message of goodwill and remembrance from His Majesty The King :—

> "I send you, My Sailors and Soldiers, hearty good wishes for Christmas and the New Year. My grateful thoughts are ever with you for victories gained, for hardships endured, and for your unfailing cheerfulness. Another Christmas has come round and we are still at war, but the Empire, confident in you, remains determined to win.
> "May God bless and protect you."

The year had been one of extreme anxiety for those in authority, both at home and overseas. The output of munitions had been vastly increased ; the success of voluntary enlistment and of the " Derby Scheme " although great had not been great enough, and the Country had accepted, without a murmur, the measure for compulsory service. Thus fortified from home, Sir Douglas Haig found himself able at the beginning of July to advance, in conjunction with the French, and to win those long-continued battles on the Rivers Somme and Ancre, which, together with the magnificent defeat, by the French Army, of the Crown Prince's desperate attacks upon Verdun, mark the history of the year 1916.

CHAPTER XXXII

1917

NIEUPORT. THE THIRD BATTLE OF YPRES

IN Sir Douglas Haig's despatch of the 31st May, 1917, we find the
following :—

" Our operations prior to the 18th November, 1916, had forced
the enemy into a very pronounced salient in the area between the Ancre
and the Scarpe valleys, and had obtained for us greatly improved opportunities for observation over this salient. A comparatively short further
advance would give us complete possession of the few points south of the
Ancre to which the enemy still clung, and would enable us to gain entire
command of the spur above Beaumont Hamel."

By the middle of November, 1916, the Allied Commanders had made
their plans for the coming year, deciding that a strong pressure was to be
maintained upon the enemy during the winter, and that all was to be
ready for an offensive early in the spring—the British attacking on the
1st February between Bapaume and Vimy Ridge, while the French
advanced between the Oise and the Somme. By the 16th December,
however, a change had been made in the command of the French armies,
General Nivelle replacing General Joffre, and the plans were changed, the
arrangement now being that the chief part in the proposed operations was
to fall upon our allies, who, employing a very large number of divisions,
were to try and break through the German line on the Aisne. To make
sure of having a preponderance of force available, as many French divisions
as possible were to be replaced by British units, and Sir Douglas Haig
was asked to extend his line south of the Somme as far as a point opposite
the town of Roye.

This request was complied with and the proposed extension of the
British line was completed by the 26th February, 1917. As stated in
the despatch already above quoted, " this alteration entailed the maintenance by British forces of an exceptionally active front of one hundred
and ten miles, including the whole of the Somme battle-front, and, combined with the continued activity maintained throughout the winter, inter-
fered to no small extent with any arrangement for reliefs. The training

of the troops had consequently to be restricted to such limited opportunities as circumstances from time to time permitted."

While the Battle of the Somme was still in progress the Germans had commenced the preparation of elaborate defensive lines in their rear, upon which their armies might fall back and there make a fresh stand ; by the British these lines were generally and collectively known as " the Hindenburg Line," called after the general of that name who was believed to have had much to do with their creation, and who had now arrived at the western front from the eastern theatre of war.   The flanks of the Hindenburg Line rested on Vimy Ridge in the north, and on the St. Gobain Forest and the Chemin-des-Dames in the south.

When the extension of our line above alluded to had been completed, the British Armies were generally disposed as follows :—the Second Army under General Plumer was about the Ypres Salient ; south of this, in the Armentières area, was the First Army under General Horne ; while General Allenby's Third Army carried the line onwards to the south of Arras.   From the point upon which the British line had hinged during the Somme Battle, General Gough's Fifth Army took over the line, joining on to the Fourth Army, commanded by General Rawlinson, near the old French position.

The new year opened with bitter frost and heavy snow-storms, but when the worst of this weather seemed past and active operations once again became possible, the enemy was attacked and in the first fortnight of January was driven from that part of the Beaumont–Hamel spur of which he was still in possession.   Hard fighting during the early part of February enabled the British to push forward north of the Ancre to the level of Grandcourt, so forcing the Germans to abandon the remaining portion of their second-line system which they were here still holding. A few days later our pressure caused the enemy to vacate Miraumont and Serre.   Between the 25th February and the 2nd March a series of attacks was carried out against " a strong secondary line of defence, which, from a point in the Le Transloy–Loupart line due west of the village of Beaulencourt, crossed in front of Ligny–Tilloy and Le Barque to the southern defences of Loupart Wood."

At the beginning of January, 1917, the 1st Division was relieved by the 50th and moved back into what was known as "the Support Area," and in regard to the disposition of the 2nd Brigade, one battalion was at Millencourt, two battalions—of which the 1st North Lancashire was one— were in Albert, while the fourth was employed in road-mending about Fricourt.   On the 24th the Battalion moved into camp at Bresle where ten days were passed, moving on the 3rd February to Maricourt and neighbourhood, where the troops were practised in the open warfare to which all were now, somewhat prematurely, as it turned out, looking forward. During this month the following officers joined for duty from the 3rd Reserve Battalion : 2nd Lieutenants S. E. Matthews, V. F. Spurgeon, A. C. V. Ferguson and G. O. Parry.

At the end of February reports were persistent that the Germans were falling back, and on the 25th three strong fighting patrols were sent forward to verify the truth of these reports. That under Lieutenant H. W. Smith got through the German wire, and this officer, accompanied by Sergeant Flanagan, entered the enemy trench, but was forced to retire, Lieutenant Smith having his hand blown off and dying a few days later of the wound ; ten men of the patrol were reported missing.

During the month of March the Battalion took part in some raids on the enemy's positions, the objects of these activities being to capture prisoners, machine-guns and trench mortars, to destroy dug-outs and mine shafts and to inflict the utmost damage upon the German trenches. One of these was undertaken on the night of the 6th–7th March against the enemy trenches about Barleux Quarry, and Captain E. F. Nichol was in charge of the Battalion raiding party, which consisted of five officers and 137 non-commissioned officers and men, divided into four columns each of four waves. Some of each of the four parties reached the immediate vicinity of the German trenches, but these were particularly strongly held, which was to be expected, since the Quarry formed a natural raiding point and our recent wire-cutting must have shown that a raid was possible. Severe bomb-fighting resulted and was maintained until the withdrawal signal was given and Captain Nichol's men fell back to their lines. As the German stretcher-bearers were noticed to be very busy collecting wounded the next morning, the raiding party probably inflicted considerable loss upon the enemy ; but the casualties among our own people were many, Captain E. F. Nichol and forty-five other ranks being wounded, while killed or died of wounds were 2nd Lieutenant W. H. Ward and ten men, with six men missing.

In a Divisional Order issued on the 9th March, Major-General Strickland, who in June, 1916, had been appointed to the command of the 1st Division, made the following appreciative remarks on the operations carried out :—

" I much appreciate the fine offensive spirit shown by all ranks of the 1st Loyal North Lancashire and 1st Northamptonshire in the raids they carried out. Their efforts were deserving of better results, and had it not been that the enemy were in a great state of preparedness, I am convinced that the success in both cases would have been great.

" In spite of being met by a barrage, and knowing that the enemy was quite prepared, the way the raiding parties advanced and endeavoured to achieve their object is much to be admired. It shows that the right spirit is there, and I look forward to the day when the opportunity will come of action under more favourable circumstances, the result of which can never be in doubt.

"The arrangements for these raids, in every detail, could not have been better, and every credit is due to those responsible."

On the morning of the 17th March it was noticed that the enemy in front of the 2nd Brigade was commencing the evacuation of his trenches, and twenty hours later he had fallen back several miles east of the Somme River. During the 19th to the 27th the Battalion was employed in assisting the Royal Engineers to bridge the river at Brie and in improving the road from Villers Carbonnel eastward to the river-bank. When all was completed, the III. Corps Commander expressed his entire satisfaction with the work done by the Battalion in enabling the bridge to be so quickly constructed. During the last four days of March all available men were busily engaged on the roads about Estrées.

The month of April was passed first at Assevillers, then at Chuignolles and latterly at Morcourt, all ranks chiefly engaged in carrying out training schemes ; at the middle of the month the strength of the Battalion reached a very high point—39 officers and 986 other ranks, of whom nine officers and sixty-nine men had joined during the month, while six officers and fifty-six other ranks had left.

The officers who joined were—on the 2nd, 2nd Lieutenants Allsup and Brown ; on the 11th, 2nd Lieutenant Hibberd ; on the 14th, Major Huntingdon, D.S.O., Lieutenant A. Livings, M.C., 2nd Lieutenants S. A. W. Ward and L. Balchin ; on the 17th, Lieutenant and Quartermaster J. A. Cover, and on the 26th, Lieutenant F. B. C. Barrett.

May was spent very much in the same area until the 19th, when the 1st Division was moved to Villers–Bretonneux, where it remained while arrangements were being made for its transfer to the north to join the XIV. or Reserve Corps, of the Second Army.

During the past weeks while the 1st Division had remained tolerably inactive, several important actions had taken place on the western front, and some mention of these, and of their effect upon the general situation, must now be given. The German retreat to the Hindenburg Line, which had been carried out during the last fortnight in March and the first week in April, was followed by an event which was to have an immense influence upon the result of the war, for on the 6th April the United States of America declared war upon Germany.

On the 9th April the Battle of Arras opened with the Battles of Vimy

Ridge and of the Scarpe, was continued with the Second Battle of the Aisne, and endured until the 4th May ; while the Battle of Bullecourt, which commenced on the 3rd of that month, went on until the 17th. The results of the spring offensive of this year are summed up as follows in General Haig's despatch of the 31st December, 1917 : "On the British front alone, in less than one month's fighting, we had captured over 19,500 prisoners, including over 400 officers, and had also taken 257 guns, including ninety-eight heavy guns, with 464 machine-guns, 227 trench mortars, and immense quantities of other war material. Our line had been advanced to a greatest depth exceeding five miles on a total front of over twenty miles, representing a gain of some sixty square miles of territory. A great improvement had been effected in the general situation of our troops on the front attacked, and the capture of Vimy Ridge had removed a constant menace to the security of our line."

On the 11th June the Battalion moved with the 2nd Brigade to the small town of Terdeghem, two and a half miles south-west of Cassel, remaining here until the 20th, when the march to the coast, which was now the real destination of the 1st Division, was resumed. Moving by march and train, on the evening of the 23rd the Battalion found itself at Coxyde-les-Bains, a village some five miles to the west of the line in the Nieuport sector. Here the 1st Division formed with the 32nd the XV. Corps of General Rawlinson's Fourth Army, the XV. Corps being then in process of relieving the French Marines, which had been holding this portion of the line since the very early days of the war.

"The appearance of British troops on the coast seems to have alarmed the enemy and caused him to launch a counter-offensive.

"The positions which we had taken from the French in this area, included a narrow strip of polder and dune, some two miles in length and from 600 to 1,200 yards in depth, lying on the right bank of the canalized Yser between the Plasschendaele Canal, south of Lombartzyde, and the coast. Midway between the Plasschendaele Canal and the sea those positions were divided into two parts by the dyke known as the Geleide Creek, which flows into the Yser south-west of Lombartzyde. If the enemy could succeed in driving us back across the canal and river on the whole of this front, he would render the defence of the sector much easier for him." *

Of the two divisions holding this front, the 2nd covered some 1,400 yards of frontage from the sea, near the small town of Nieuport, to Lombartzyde, whence the 32nd Division carried on the line. In the left sector the three brigades of the 1st Division were distributed in depth, the one in front having two battalions holding the line to the east of Nieuport,

* Despatch of the 25th December, 1917.

the two other battalions in support behind the River Yser. The supporting brigade occupied huts between Dunkerque and Coxyde-les-Bains, and the reserve brigade was in billets to the west of Coxyde-les-Bains.

On the night of the 4th July the Battalion became left support battalion, occupying houses and cellars in Nieuport-les-Bains, the 2nd King's Royal Rifles taking its place in the front line, which lay among the sandhills where the soil was too light to allow of the digging of trenches and the only protection afforded was by earthworks, which were, of course, both conspicuous and vulnerable.

Of the tragedy which, on the 10th July, overtook the 2nd Royal Sussex and the 2nd King's Royal Rifles on that day holding the front line, the following account is given in the Battalion War Diary : " About 6 a.m. on the 10th the enemy commenced a heavy bombardment of the front system—the river, Nieuport-les-Bains, and the back areas, Coxyde and Coxyde-les-Bains. This increased during the day and about 7.25 p.m. the enemy successfully attacked, taking our trenches up to the east bank of the river. The two battalions in the front line were practically annihilated. An advance party, totalling four officers and thirty-six other ranks, which went up to the left battalion in the early morning of the 10th, was present during the attack, and of these only two men returned.

" The Battalion occupied the trenches on the west bank of the Yser as the front line, ' A ' and ' B ' Companies being in front and ' C ' and ' D ' in support. After the attack the bombardment slackened slightly, but it was not until five the following morning that it really ceased. About eight o'clock in the evening the enemy's aeroplanes dropped bombs on Rinck Camp, which was occupied by details of the Battalion, and one man was killed and an officer and six other ranks were wounded, the officer and one of the men being attached. Total casualties for the day were four officers and thirty-four other ranks missing, three officers and twenty-eight other ranks wounded and two men killed."

The 11th was spent in reorganizing the defence, and about half-past eight in the evening three men of the King's Royal Rifles swam across from the enemy's side of the river and reported that there were still some twenty men on the further bank. Immediately this was made known No. 23983 Private Higson, one of the battalion scouts, secured a rope and swam with it across the Yser, closely followed by Captain H. A. Pallant, M.C., R.A.M.C., attached to the Battalion ; and these two were largely responsible for bringing over men who were unable to swim or who were in the last stage of exhaustion. By the joint efforts of Captain Pallant and Private Higson the whole party—twenty of the King's Royal Rifles —were safely passed over the stream.

On the 30th July the 1st Division moved to Le Clipon Camp and lived there for many weeks in an atmosphere of mystery. "Some time before the opening of the offensive of the Battle of Ypres of this month, the 1st Division suddenly developed an acute attack of cerebro-spinal meningitis of a highly contagious form, and retired behind barbed-wire fencing in an unfrequented area of sandland dune behind Dunkirk. There the Division strove manfully against the disease by novel methods. . . . It need scarcely be explained that the 'meningitis' was of a purely official, or semi-official character, invented for the benefit of any inquisitive person who might wonder what had become of the 1st Division, and why its sudden disappearance had been made the subject of so much secrecy"! *

The real cause of the withdrawal and concealment of the 1st Division was the decision which had recently been come to for the carrying out of a scheme, originally drafted as early as 1915, whereby the proposed offensive in the Ypres Salient was to be accompanied by a landing upon and seizure of a portion of the Belgian coast, enabling us to mount heavy guns within range of Bruges and Zeebrugge. The 1st Division was detailed to carry out this landing, and this was to have taken place in the first half of August. Postponement succeeded postponement until at the end of October the project was finally abandoned, and the Division then began to move off to the Ypres area to take part in the Passchendaele Battle, the Battalion arriving on the 6th November in Dirty Bucket Camp to the north-west of Vlamertinghe.

As to the need for the Passchendaele offensive Sir Douglas Haig writes as follows in his despatch of the 25th December, 1917 : "At this date the need for the policy of activity outlined above had been still further emphasized by recent developments in Italy. Additional importance was given to it by the increasing probability that a time was approaching when the enemy's power of drawing reinforcements from Russia would increase considerably. In pursuance of this policy, therefore, two short advances were made on the 30th October and the 6th November, by which we gained possession of Passchendaele."

In the early part of the Passchendaele offensive the 1st Division took no part ; and it was not indeed until the 10th that the units composing it were engaged, when, as stated in the same despatch, "in very unfavourable weather, British and Canadian troops attacked northwards from Passchendaele and Goudberg, and captured further ground on the main ridge, after heavy fighting."

The 1st Division, now in the II. Corps, was to come up on the left of the Canadian divisions, and endeavour to co-operate with them in extending

* Dewar, *Sir Douglas Haig's Command*, Vol. I, pp. 361, 362.

the position and clearing the whole of the Passchendaele Ridge, part of which these had captured in the previous fighting. The rain at this time was heavy and continuous and the ground a quagmire.

At ten o'clock on the morning of the 9th November, the Battalion, then in School Camp, a mile and a half to the west of Poperinghe, suddenly received orders to move to Irish Camp, to the north-west of Ypres, there taking over billets from a battalion of the 3rd Brigade which was then about to join in the attack. The 3rd Brigade did not move out until that evening, and the attack then made was a failure, whereupon the Battalion was ordered forward to support the 3rd Brigade, two of the battalions of which—the South Wales Borderers and the Royal Munster Fusiliers—had suffered heavy casualties. The Battalion accordingly advanced to the support area about Kron Prinz Farm, and on the 11th moved up to the front line with three companies, the fourth being in support. The relief was a somewhat complicated one and was not completed till early on the 12th.

On the morning of this day the enemy opened a heavy bombardment from his guns which he had succeeded in moving to a position from which he could reach the ridge held by our troops, while the British artillery, practically immobile in the deep mud, could not make any adequate reply. The Battalion casualties, however, were but slight, though Lieutenant W. Allsup was wounded and on his way back to the dressing-station was blown up by a shell and badly "concussed."

During the night "A" Company managed to push forward and occupied Valour Farm without opposition, while "B" Company's posts were also advanced to conform with the movements of "A."

On the 13th the Germans again bombarded the position very heavily at intervals, and in the afternoon massed opposite the Canadians on the right with the evident intention of attacking; but their formations were broken up by the heavy counter-battery work of our guns. Only on the extreme left of the Battalion position did the enemy succeed in making any advance, and this he did supported by his barrage and machine-gun fire; he was, however, brought to a standstill fifty yards from the line. During these operations Lieutenant H. P. Bruton was wounded and there were some fifteen other casualties in the Battalion.

The Battalion was relieved during the night of the 13th–14th by troops of the 3rd Brigade, and many casualties were incurred during the relief—Captain R. M. Leake, M.C., Lieutenant G. L. Brown, 2nd Lieutenants W. Roberts and L. Edwards being among the wounded. The Battalion now went back to Kron Prinz Farm.

The 15th was again a day of heavy shelling by the enemy, and many disturbing reports of German activity came to hand: but matters were

YPRES.

1917.

The Imperial War Museum—Copyright.

otherwise quiet, and in the evening the Battalion was withdrawn to dug-outs in the canal bank, about three-quarters of a mile to the north of Ypres. "Unfortunately," so the Battalion War Diary tells us, "bad luck still dogged us, and Headquarter Company and 'D' Company were caught by enemy shell-fire on the way out. In the former case only a few minor wounds were caused, but a direct hit on the last platoon of 'D' Company killed four other ranks and severely wounded Lieutenant E. H. Pinches and six men."

The total casualties for this tour of duty were thus seven officers wounded—of whom Lieutenants G. L. Brown and E. H. Pinches succumbed to their wounds on the 15th and 16th respectively—twenty-six other ranks killed, seventy-six wounded and eleven missing.

On the afternoon of the 19th the Battalion moved up to the front again, taking over from the 1st Black Watch a line of posts running just in front of Vocation and Virile Farms, joining up with the 8th Division. And so during the remainder of this year the same monotonous record continues—periods up in the line varied by periods of comparative rest in the more peaceful areas in rear ; casualties, however, showed no perceptible decrease, and by the end of the year two more officers—Captain G. E. Grove and 2nd Lieutenant S. Haworth—had been wounded, while eight men had been killed, forty-four wounded and three men were missing.

For some considerable time past the different commanders of the French Army had urged that the British should take over a larger extent of the allied line in the west. The matter had repeatedly to be shelved by reason of the heavy fighting to which our troops were everywhere committed, but the request had been renewed, and with increased urgency, whenever these attacks in any way died down. " The discussions of negotiations continued into November and December, 1917. We proposed to relieve the French as far as the Basse Forêt–St. Gobain railway, provided additional British troops were not sent to Italy and the French would take over the Nieuport sector ; and Pétain agreed to this on November 27th." *

The 1st Division was one of the units of the British Expeditionary Force told off to relieve a portion of the line held by French troops, and early in December it was moved down towards the Houthulst Forest area. On the 7th, then, the Battalion marched to Chauney Camp in the neighbourhood of Crombeke and took over from the 24th Brigade French Artillery, and here the Battalion was stationed when the year came to an end. " The health of the Battalion," we are told, " was splendid during the month," and its fighting strength on the 31st December stood at twenty-one officers and 676 non-commissioned officers and men.

* Dewar, *Sir Douglas Haig's Command*, Vol. II, pp. 35, 36.

CHAPTER XXXIII

1918

THE BATTLE OF THE LYS ; THE BATTLE OF BETHUNE. THE SECOND BATTLE OF ARRAS ; THE BATTLE OF EPEHY ; THE BATTLE OF THE ST. QUENTIN CANAL ; THE BATTLE OF THE SELLE AND THE BATTLE OF THE SAMBRE ; END OF THE WAR

THE opening of the year 1918—the last year of the Great War —found the Battalion occupying much the same area and experiencing terribly wet weather. The rapid thaw which had now set in, was accompanied by heavy rain, " and the effect of this was to turn the water-logged valleys into raging torrents. The one bridge over the St. Jans Beek had been washed away, while of the three bridges leading from Mondovi Farm, one only was above water, and the main road to Carre de Londres was at least four feet under water for a distance of 250 yards. The conditions of the front area were naturally very bad. No-Man's-Land had become a swamp, through which the patrols had to progress by swimming, but the actual posts in the outpost line were kept sufficiently dry to be tolerable, and none were evacuated though permission to do so, if necessary, had been received."

During January, 2nd Lieutenants P. G. Phillips, G. P. Etches and T. M. McCall joined the Battalion.

On the 5th February the following entry occurs in the Battalion War Diary :—

"After rather over four years' service together, the Battalion was transferred from the 2nd to the 1st Brigade, consequent upon the reorganization of brigades into three battalions instead of four ; the record of four years' continuous service as a brigade—three and a half years of war— was one of which no other brigade could boast, and consequently the parting, although merely changing brigades within the division, was rather a wrench."

For some time past there had been a feeling abroad, and especially among the Allies, that the resistance of Germany was weakening, and more and more was it believed that the war could not last very much longer, and that when it did come to an end victory would rest with the

Western Powers. This feeling was engendered and strengthened by the fact that in almost every other theatre of war, except the western front, the Allied Powers had gained many real and important successes; and though there can be no doubt that the Germans were daily experiencing in ever-increasing degree the cramping effects of British sea-power, there were at the same time certain influences at work which encouraged Germany to hold on and prolong her resistance. Russia had by this time practically given up the fight and Roumania had been compelled to make terms with Germany, and consequently it had been possible to strengthen the enemy line in France and Flanders by transferring thither many German divisions from the Russian and Roumanian fronts.

In consequence of the arrival of these reinforcements for the German main enemy, it had been necessary to recall to France several French and British divisions which had been sent to the assistance of Italy after the defeat at Caporetto, and this despite the fact that large Austrian forces were threatening the Italians on the Piave.

In Great Britain, too, the heavy and continued drains upon the manhood of the nation had become a source of very considerable anxiety, equally to those who had to find the material for our armies and to those who had to train and prepare them for war. This had led to the forming of a decision to effect a very drastic reorganization of the divisions of the British Expeditionary Force. This measure was quickly taken in hand and as rapidly carried into execution, and during the month of February, 1918, the number of battalions in each infantry division was reduced from thirteen to ten, and those in each brigade from four to three.

" This measure, which was the consequence of the failure of the Government to provide the drafts, caused a drastic change in the organization and tactics of our infantry at a critical period when there was no time to accustom commanders and troops to the new conditions. . . . Nor was this all. Owing to the decline of the strength of the French Army the French Government became more and more insistent that we should take over a longer stretch of the front. After prolonged negotiations between the two Governments the French arguments prevailed, and Haig, in order to meet the wishes of the British Government, agreed with Pétain to take over an additional twenty-eight miles of front, and to extend his front south of the Somme as far as the Oise. This extension made the length of our line one hundred and thirty miles, the greatest length of front we had ever held, while the number of rifles to hold it was approximately equal to that in March, 1916, when the length of our front was eighty miles and the Germans still had great armies on the Russian front." *

* Maurice, *The Last Four Months*, pp. 22–4.

Under the reorganization scheme of brigades and divisions which now came into force, the 8th Bn. Royal Berkshire and the 10th Bn. Gloucestershire Regiment had been taken out of the 1st Brigade to make way for the 1st Bn. The Loyal North Lancashire Regiment; and the 1st Brigade of the 1st Division now contained the 1st Bn. The Black Watch, the 1st Bn. The Loyal North Lancashire Regiment, the 1st Bn. The Cameron Highlanders and the 1st Trench Mortar Battery, the commander being Brig.-General W. B. Thornton, D.S.O.

On the 9th February the 1st Division moved and took over the Poelcapelle sector from the 35th Division, when the 2nd Brigade was in the front line, the 1st in support and the 3rd in reserve. The Battalion, now in the 1st Brigade, relieved a battalion of the Durham Light Infantry in what were known as " California Dug-outs," slightly to the north of Wieltje, arriving just as the enemy was shelling the sector, when thirteen casualties were incurred, of which three were fatal. There were occasional bouts of enemy shelling during the remainder of this month, which the War Diary generally describes as " quiet " ; and by the end of February several more officers had joined—2nd Lieutenants G. W. P. Howarth, H. P. Crane, J. Midgeley and Bell, and also a large draft, nearly 200 strong, from the 7th Battalion of the Regiment ; so that by the 28th the fighting strength stood as high as 40 officers and 969 other ranks—fortunate, perhaps, in view of the demands which the next month was to make upon all ranks and units of the British Army in France.

On the 4th March the 1st Brigade was relieved in the front line, which for some days past it had been holding, and the Battalion went back by rail to a camp about half a mile south of Elverdinghe ; but on the very next day a warning order was received directing the Battalion to be ready to move back again to the front to relieve the right battalion of the 35th Division. Later, definite orders for the move came to hand, and on the 9th the Battalion proceeded by train and by march route to Langemarck and the front area. The front of the 1st Division was now from Poelcapelle to the Ypres–Staden railway.

The Battalion was here placed under the orders of the G.O.C. 3rd Brigade, who was in charge of the whole divisional front.

The reason for this recent constant movement of troops is to be gathered from a paragraph in Sir Douglas Haig's despatch of the 20th July, 1918, which runs as follows : " Towards the middle of February, 1918, it became evident that the enemy was preparing for a big offensive on the Western Front. It was known from various sources that he had been steadily increasing his forces in the western theatre since the beginning of November, 1917. In three and a half months twenty-eight infantry divisions had been transferred from the eastern theatre and six infantry divisions from the Italian theatre.   There were reports that further reinforcements were on their way to the west, and it was also known that the enemy had greatly increased his heavy artillery in the western theatre during the same period.   These reinforcements were more than were necessary for defence, and as they were moved at a time when the distribution of food and fuel to the civil population in Germany was rendered extremely difficult through lack of rolling stock, I concluded that the enemy intended to attack at an early date.''

Early on the morning of the 21st March the German attack opened with very great vigour against the Third and Fifth British Armies, which were holding the front from south of Barisis to south of Gavrelle, a total distance of sixty-nine miles, with twenty-nine infantry and three cavalry divisions.   At the outset, however, the 1st Division had no part or lot in these operations, but remained holding the most northerly sector of the Ypres Salient, endeavouring by frequent raids and a show of much activity, to hold the enemy in its immediate front, and identify the German units still there.

Early in April there were indications that the Division was shortly to be relieved by one of those which had been seriously reduced in strength in the recent heavy fighting in the south ; and on the 8th the Battalion proceeded by march route and by train to Lapugny, which was reached at 3 a.m. on the 9th.   Here the 1st Division was in the I. Corps of the First Army.

Lapugny was left again on the 11th, the Battalion moving by way of Houchin to Beuvry by roads which were under shell-fire of the enemy, and some ten casualties were incurred, but all happily of a minor character.   On the 15th the Battalion took over the defences of Le Préol, occupying the sector from the La Bassée Canal northwards and being the right battalion of the brigade line.

It had been anticipated that the enemy would attack the 1st Division on the 18th, and at 4.15 on the morning of this day a bombardment was opened upon the whole length of the divisional front, becoming every moment more intense ; and about eight o'clock the Germans attacked from the north, succeeding in reaching and occupying the main line of resistance before any counter-measures could be taken.   " C " and " D " Companies of the 1st Loyal North Lancashire then vigorously attacked and eventually succeeded in ejecting the enemy from our main line, so that by eleven o'clock he was in possession of no more than a few isolated posts in the divisional outpost line.   On the next day the remainder of the position was cleared by an attack by the 1st Northamptonshire of the

2nd Brigade, and a period of quiet then followed during which all concentrated on improving the defensive system. The Battalion was relieved in the front line on the 23rd–24th, and went back by bus to Houchin.

During these operations the Battalion losses had been heavy, two officers and 46 other ranks being killed, five officers and 105 men were wounded, while five officers and 189 non-commissioned officers and men were missing. The officers were, killed, 2nd Lieutenants J. N. King and W. Pettitt; wounded, Captains A. R. Bare, M.C., and J. H. Jeffreys, 2nd Lieutenants Bell, E. T. Mallett and Allen, and missing were Captain Smith, M.C., Lieutenant E. Gladding, 2nd Lieutenants Smith, C. G. Claridge and W. G. Whitehead.

These casualties in officers were to some extent made good by the following arrivals during the month—Captain Leake, M.C., Lieutenant Sandie, M.C., 2nd Lieutenants Howard, Hardy, Moykopf, Pardoe, Horrocks and Page-Wood.

As a temporary measure, and owing to the weakness in numbers of these companies, " A " and " B " were now amalgamated, and for some time the Battalion remained in the Noeux-les-Mines sector of the front. The month of May passed tolerably quietly, beyond occasional " area straffs," the enemy making little reply to the harassing fire from our guns. During the month six officers joined or rejoined, while reinforcements of 165 non-commissioned officers and men arrived in four drafts ; the officers were Captain G. W. Ainsworth, Lieutenant D. E. Pollard, 2nd Lieutenants J. R. McHugh, A. Gillingham, F. James and J. C. Wright. The casualties had not been heavy—one man killed and eleven wounded.

Matters continued much as above during the weeks that followed, and it was not until the end of August that the 1st Division made any move from this sector. It was now, however, sent for to support the Canadian Corps in the attack which it was about to make on the Drocourt–Quéant switch line, timed to commence on the 2nd September ; and on the afternoon of the 31st August the Battalion marched to the railway station at Anvin, where it entrained for Arras, arriving there at 7 a.m. on the 1st September.

The Division was pushed forward immediately on arrival, moving through an assembly position south-east of Guémappe, ready to reinforce the Canadian Corps ; but the attack had been so successful that the services of the 1st Division were not required, though the Battalion sustained some few casualties during its advance from bombs and machine-gun fire from low-flying enemy aeroplanes. During the week that followed some seventy of the Battalion were killed, wounded, gassed or missing.

A certain number of units were now to be used to strengthen the Fourth Army in its projected advance, and the 1st Division was detailed as one of those to be thus transferred. Consequently, at midday on the 10th September the Battalion entrained at Maroeuil and moved by way of Doullens to Marcelcave, about nine miles south-east of Amiens ; having detrained here it marched on to Morcourt, where the companies found shelter, of a kind, in a high bank on the east side of the village.

The 1st Division now, with the 6th, 32nd and 46th, formed the IX. Corps of the Fourth Army under General Sir H. Rawlinson ; the IX. Corps, which had been comparatively recently constituted, was commanded by Lieut.-General Sir W. Braithwaite, and stood on the extreme right of the British Army.

Of this period of the campaign the Field-Marshal wrote as follows in his despatch of the 21st December, 1918 : " The 1st September marks the close of the second stage in the British offensive. Having in the first stage freed Amiens by our brilliant success east of that town, in the second stage the troops of the Third and Fourth Armies, comprising twenty-three British divisions, by skilful leading, hard fighting and relentless and un-remitting pursuit, in ten days had driven thirty-five German divisions from one side of the old Somme battle-field to the other, thereby turning the line of the River Somme. In so doing they had inflicted upon the enemy the heaviest losses in killed and wounded, and had taken from him over 35,000 prisoners and 270 guns. . . . In the obstinate fighting of the past few days the enemy had been pressed back to the line of the Somme River and the high ground about Rocquigny and Beugny, where he had shown an intention to stand for a time. Thereafter his probable plan was to retire slowly, when forced to do so, from one intermediary position to another, until he could shelter his battered divisions behind the Hinden-burg defences. . . . A sudden and successful blow, of weight sufficient to break through the northern hinge of the defences to which it was his design to fall back, might produce results of great importance. At this date our troops were already in position to deliver such a stroke."

Still advancing, the Battalion on the 13th September was at Estrées, on the 14th at Poeilly and on the 15th at Vermand. It was expected that the Germans would make a stand on the heights commanding St. Quentin to the north and south, but since the enemy was known to be losing moral and to be somewhat disorganized, it was not anticipated that his resistance would be great. On the night of the 17th orders were given out that on the next morning the 34th French Division on the right, the 6th British Division in the centre and the 1st British Division on the left, were to attack and capture the high ground held by the enemy, so as to form a " jumping-off place " for the attack on the Hindenburg Line, which ran just outside St. Quentin to the canal at Bellenglise.

" The IX. Corps front extended from the south-eastern outskirts of Holnon to a point 500 yards north of Vadencourt, some 7,000 yards in all. The 6th and 1st Divisions were in line on the right and left respectively, the former holding 3,000, and the latter 4,000 yards." * Six tanks were detailed to accompany and work with the IX. Corps, and the 1st Division formed up with the 1st and 2nd Brigades on the right and left respectively, and the 3rd in reserve. The attack by the 1st Division, once started, made excellent progress. The 1st Brigade on the right was somewhat delayed by machine-gun fire from the valley north of Fresnoy-le-Petit and from the trenches north-east of that village ; but with the assistance of the 2nd Brigade, which had reached the first objective at 7.30 a.m., the 1st Brigade secured the first objective from Fresnoy-le-Petit northwards to its junction with the Australian Corps. The advance towards the second objective was resumed at 8.30 a.m., but the progress of the right of the 1st Division met with very considerable opposition and the line was only advanced a few hundred yards beyond the Fresnoy-le-Petit–Berthancourt road ; but Berthancourt was captured by 10.30 and the second objective half an hour later. Early in the afternoon the enemy made several determined counter-attacks against the 6th and 1st Divisions, and fighting continued throughout the rest of the day, no further advance being made.

So far the general outline of the operations of the 1st Division, and we may now follow the Battalion's account of this day's operations.

At 4.45 a.m. on the 18th September the Battalion was formed up preparatory to attack—" D " and " C " Companies on the right and left respectively, " A " Company in support and " B " in reserve, and at 5.30 the advance commenced in rain and mist so thick that no landmarks could be recognized. " D " Company reached the first objective at schedule time, but " C " was held up by very heavy machine-gun fire, and " B " Company was then sent forward with orders to establish touch with " D " and advance with it to the second objective, " C " Company falling back into reserve. Villemay Trench, the Battalion's first objective, was secured, but the enemy now counter-attacked, debouching from two woods in the front under cover of the fire of his machine-guns from some high ground, completely enfilading the position held by " B " Company. After a strong resistance, during which the company commander, Captain Leake, was killed, the Company had temporarily to give ground, but being again led forward re-established itself in part of the position, the remainder being still in German hands.

" When darkness set in our line ran along the eastern edge of Holnon village, where a junction was established with the French north of Selency,

* Montgomery, *The Story of the Fourth Army*, p. 124.

through the western outskirts of Fresnoy-le-Petit, with a few posts in the
village, thence due north, keeping just west of Pontruet and Ste Hélène,
near which village the 1st Division was in touch with the Australians. . . .
On the flanks of the Army neither the IX. nor the III. Corps had reached
all their objectives on the 18th September. The attack was, therefore,
continued on the fronts of these two corps on the morning of the 19th
as it was essential that all objectives of the 18th should be secured as early
as possible, with a view to future operations.

   " On the IX. Corps front the 6th and 1st Divisions endeavoured to gain
ground round the Quadrilateral, Fresnoy-le-Petit, and east of Berthancourt. Attempts by the 1st Division, east of Berthancourt, were checked
by heavy machine-gun fire ; on the other hand, a counter-attack, launched
against the 1st Division at Berthancourt at 8 a.m., was completely repulsed."

   During the 19th and 20th the Battalion remained in the positions arrived
at on the previous evening, and on the 21st took the place of the Cameron
Highlanders, as left battalion of the Brigade. On the night of the 22nd
the Battalion was engaged in heavy fighting about Callchet Trench, and
twenty-four hours later the 1st Brigade was relieved in the front line and
the Battalion was withdrawn to a bivouac in Caulaincourt Wood, near
Vermand.

   Major-General Strickland, commanding 1st Division, now issued the
following order : " The Field-Marshal Commanding-in-Chief has to-day
personally directed me to convey to all ranks of the 1st Division his congratulations on their splendid successes in the recent fighting, with which
he is much pleased."

   The 1st Brigade returned to the front on the evening of the 26th, the
Battalion occupying part of the line running north of the village of Pontruet, where two tolerably quiet days were passed, for the Germans were
falling back all along the front, and the main task now remaining to the
Fourth Army was the forcing of the Hindenburg Line. The front of attack
of the Fourth Army extended from Selency to Vendhuile, a distance of
twelve miles, the IX. Corps, on the right, occupying a front of 10,000
yards. The 1st Division, operating between Cricourt and Bellenglise and
keeping west of the canal, was to press forward towards Thorigny and Le
Tranquoy.

   Zero hour for the attack on the Hindenburg Line was fixed for 5.30
a.m. on the 29th September, and in the 1st Division the 1st and 3rd Brigades
were employed in front, in the 1st Brigade the 1st Black Watch being on
the right and the 1st Loyal North Lancashire on the left. " The mission
of the 1st Division was to secure the right flank of the 46th Division in
its advance to the canal, to gain the high ground north of Thorigny, and

join hands with the 32nd Division at the Tunnel defences south of Le Tranquoy. The 1st Loyal North Lancashire and the 1st Black Watch of the 1st Brigade, the former battalion operating in close liaison with the right of the 46th Division, cleared the trenches west of the canal astride of the Bellenglise–Ste Hélène road. The 3rd Brigade on the right sent forward the 1st Gloucestershire towards the high ground around Sycamore Wood. . . . Meanwhile the 1st Black Watch, with the 1st Loyal North Lancashire in support, had swung round its left west of the canal and was clearing the trenches in the area as far east as the main St. Quentin–Cambrai road. The clearing of this maze of trenches was no easy task, and the fighting was severe, but the 1st Black Watch and the 1st South Wales Borderers of the 3rd Brigade were not to be denied, and early in the afternoon the high ground around Road Wood and the trenches between it and the canal were captured.

"During the remainder of the afternoon little progress was made by the troops of the 1st Division beyond the St. Quentin–Cambrai road, on account of heavy enfilade fire from the south, but connection was established with the 6th Division." *

On the night of the 29th orders were issued that the IX. Corps was to secure the whole of the tunnel defences, and it was hoped that when these and other objectives were in our hands, it would be possible to advance our line to within striking distance of the Masnières–Beaurevoir–Fonsomme Line, and thence force this by another organized attack on a wide front. The task of the 1st Division on the 30th September was to secure Thorigny and Talana Hill with its left flank on the canal south of Le Tranquoy, where touch was to be gained with the 32nd Division.

The 1st Infantry Brigade was to fight forward on the low ground between the ridge and the canal in co-operation with the 3rd Brigade, which was to attack along the high ground from Road Wood to Thorigny, capturing the last-named place and also Talana Hill.

On the morning of the 30th these places were taken by the 3rd Brigade with but little opposition, while the 1st Brigade fought its way forward, capturing many prisoners. That night the 3rd Brigade relieved the 1st, south of the canal at Le Tranquoy, while the 1st North Lancashire and 1st Cameron Highlanders took the place of portions of the 32nd Division before Le Tranquoy and Levergies. The French Division on the right had not been as successful and little progress was made by it. During the 1st October the Battalion maintained the position it had taken up the previous day; but on the 2nd when the advance was resumed, only the 1st Brigade of the 1st Division was employed. Its rôle was to keep touch

* *Story of the Fourth Army*, p. 158.

with the left of the 32nd Division on the Le Tranquoy–Sequehart Ridge and also with the flank of the 47th French Division, which, having now fought its way forward, was crossing the canal and attacking in a south-easterly direction.   The advance of the 32nd Division was met by counter-attack, whereby it was driven out of Sequehart which it had occupied, and the two battalions of the 1st Brigade—1st North Lancashire and 1st Cameron Highlanders—though not actually engaged—suffered many casualties from enemy shell-fire.

On the 3rd the operations, cut short on the 2nd, were resumed, and about 7.45 a.m. a body of the enemy about two hundred and fifty strong, accompanied by machine-guns and under cover of heavy gun-fire, suddenly emerged from Cerise Wood and attempted to work round the village of Sequehart, the troops holding which fell back.   " A," " C " and " D " Companies of the Battalion promptly formed a defensive flank on the high ground near at hand, met the enemy and repulsed him at the point of the bayonet, capturing from thirty to forty prisoners.

The following message was received from the commander of the 1st Brigade by the officer-in-command of the Battalion :—

" Will you please express to all ranks my appreciation of their fine work during the recent operations, and my satisfaction on their excellent turn-out this morning after hard and strenuous fighting."

This night the 1st Brigade was relieved and withdrew to the south of the canal, again occupying bivouacs in Caulaincourt Wood near Vermand, but the Battalion, owing to delay in the relief, did not rejoin its brigade until the 5th.   From this date until the evening of the 16th the 1st Division remained in the Bellenglise area, moving up to the front again to take part in the Battle of the Selle.

Lieut.-General Sir W. Braithwaite, commanding IX. Corps, " decided to attack with the 46th Division on the right and the 6th Division on the left, while the 1st Division, which had moved up from Bellenglise during the night of the 16th, was concentrated just north and west of Bohain. This last division was held in readiness to pass through the 6th Division and capture the second and third objectives, including the villages of Wassigny and La Vallée Mulâtre, after the 46th and 6th had secured the first objective.   The attack of the IX. Corps, owing to the lie of the ground, and to the position of Riqerval Wood in the south end of the Bellevue spur in the north, was complicated and required careful preparation, good preliminary staff work, and exceptional leadership from battalion and company commanders." *

The 1st and 2nd Brigades were told off to carry out the attack on the

* *The Story of the Fourth Army*, p. 209.

second and third objectives, capturing the second under a barrage, and having taken it, were then to wait under a protective barrage lasting three hours, during which time artillery and machine-guns were to be brought up to furnish another barrage for the attack on the third objective.

In front of the 1st Brigade on the right of the Division were the southern outskirts of La Vallée Mulâtre and the northern portion of the Andigny Forest.

The account of the fighting that now followed is almost wholly drawn from *The Story of the Fourth Army*, p. 214 *et seq.* : The attacking troops advanced at 5.30 a.m. on the 17th October through a dense mist, in the 1st Brigade the Battalion being ordered to attack on the right, with the Cameron Highlanders on the left and the Black Watch in support. Owing to the mist the march to the starting-point had to be made by the main road on which the enemy guns concentrated a heavy fire ; fire from " machine-gun nests " was also opened on the two leading brigades as they appeared east of Vaux Andigny and while still a considerable distance from their " jumping-off point." During this approach march the Battalion, after helping to capture the Bellevue Spur, whence the machine-gun fire had been very hot, pushed forward into Andigny-les-Fermes to get touch with the 46th Division and it assisted one of its brigades to " mop up " that village.

" The manner in which the four leading battalions of the 1st and 2nd Brigades, moving by compass bearing throughout the advance, maintained their cohesion and reached their starting line on the first objective, practically up to time, constituted a very fine achievement."

The four leading battalions had, however, by now lost touch with the barrage, but none the less they fought their way forward for about 1,000 yards, some little way short of the objective. By midday the divisional line was roughly from Andigny-les-Fermes northwards, through the centre of La Vallée Mulâtre, to the railway north of that village.

Major-General Strickland now decided to pause awhile, and prepare for an organized attack by both brigades in the evening.

The attack re-started at 5.15 p.m. under a somewhat insufficient barrage, but the Battalion and the Cameron Highlanders succeeded in reaching the edge of the wood south-east of La Vallée Mulâtre, although here a very heavy gas-shelling forced the battalions to fall back.

" As the result of the day's operations the IX. Corps had advanced its line to a depth of 4,500 yards ; it had firmly established itself on the crest of the watershed which divided the Selle and the Sambre valleys, and was in an excellent position to continue its advance next day. It had engaged and defeated the 5th Reserve, 29th and 81st Reserve Divisions, and portions of the 3rd Naval, 15th Reserve and 24th Divisions. To accomplish this, it had employed three divisions, but of these one brigade of each was still untouched."

The attack, renewed about 11.30 on the morning of the 18th by the 1st and 3rd Brigades of the 1st Division, was entirely successful, and Wassigny and the line of road from Wassigny cemetery to Ribeauville were captured. On this day, however, the Battalion was in reserve, and, not being required to support either of the other units of the brigade, it remained about Angin Farm, moving back on the 19th to billets in La Vallée Mulâtre. Here it remained until the 24th, when it again moved up to the front and took over a line of 4,000 yards beyond the Oise Canal. The last days of October were spent by the Battalion in billets in Wassigny.

On the 21st October the Brigadier wrote as follows to Lieut.-Colonel Berkeley, 1st Battalion, The Loyal North Lancashire Regiment, who had taken over command early in the month :

" I am very pleased to send the attached on to you. On the 17th and 18th October every unit in the 1st Brigade pulled its full weight and maintained the best traditions of the British Army. I especially congratulate the 1st Bn. The Loyal North Lancashire Regiment and the 1st Bn. The Cameron Highlanders on their fine work on the 17th, and the 1st Bn. The Black Watch on theirs on the 18th."

The " attached " documents referred to are as follows :

From the G.O.C. 46th Division : " In forwarding the attached letter from the O.C. 1st/5th Lincolns, I would like to add in the name of the 46th Division, my appreciation of the 1st Loyal North Lancashire. Without their help my left would have suffered heavily, and the success of the whole operation might have been jeopardized.

" I would deem it a favour if you would convey my thanks to the Commanding Officer."

From the O.C. 138th Brigade, 46th Division : " I should be glad if you would send my thanks to the Brigade concerned, as the 1st Bn. The Loyal North Lancashire Regiment undoubtedly contributed to our success."

From the O.C. 1st/5th Lincolnshire Regiment : " On the 17th inst. when my leading companies were moving forward to their objectives they were held up by heavy flanking fire from Bellevue Ridge and the village of Andigny-les-Fermes. They were in a very insecure position until the 1st Bn. The Loyal North Lancashire Regiment pushed forward and in the face of great opposition charged the ridge and secured the left edge of the village. I understand they had several casualties in so doing, and I should like to express my thanks for the great assistance they rendered my Battalion."

Finally, from Major-General E. P. Strickland, commanding 1st Division, to whom these messages were in the first instance addressed, came the following appreciative letter to the commanding officers of the two battalions specially mentioned :—

" It gives me particular pleasure to forward the attached, and to express my admiration of the fine spirit shown by the 1st Loyal North Lancashire and the 1st Cameron Highlanders on this occasion. Nor is this the only occasion on which they have very materially assisted other divisions, in addition to carrying out their own task ; their action at Sequehart showed a fine soldierly spirit and unselfish and whole-hearted devotion to duty. Any troops may well be glad to be associated with them in action."

During the operations commencing in September and enduring until the end of October, the losses suffered by the Battalion appear to have been heavier than during any other period of the war ; when fighting was practically continuous, and the periods of rest, during which no man was safe from the German long-range guns, were but short, it does not always seem to have been possible for the casualties to be fully recorded in the Battalion War Diary as they occurred, and some may inadvertently have been omitted, while others again may possibly have been recorded more than once. The following may, however, perhaps be accepted as a tolerably accurate statement of the losses suffered by the Battalion during the " Hundred Days " :

Officers : killed, 9 ; wounded, 25 ; missing, 2.

Other Ranks : killed, 113 ; wounded, 511 ; missing, 50 ; or a total casualty list of 710 all ranks !

By the end of October the defeat of Germany seemed assured ; in the series of battles just concluded her armies had been beaten, suffering heavy losses in men and material, while no longer could she count upon her allies to hold the armies of the Western Powers in the other theatres of the World War. Turkey and Bulgaria had surrendered and Austria was quite incapable of taking any further part in the struggle. What the Allied commanders now sought was to inflict such a defeat upon the enemy as should convert his inevitable withdrawal into a positive rout.

On the 29th October Sir Douglas Haig had issued orders for a concerted attack by the Fourth, Third and First Armies in the general direction of Maubeuge and Mons, the First French Army, on General Rawlinson's right, pushing forward in the direction of La Capelle.

On the morning of the 4th November the attack opened on a thirty-mile front between Valenciennes and Oisy on the Sambre, the Fourth Army on the right moving to cross the Sambre south of the Mormal Forest, the Third Army in the centre advancing to clear the forest, while the

First Army was to pass the marshes north of Valenciennes and advance east of the Aunelle River. The IX. Corps was on the right of the British Army and the 1st Division on the right of the Corps.

To force the Sambre and Oise Canal the O.C. IX. Corps employed the 1st and 32nd Divisions, the 46th Division being in reserve with orders to follow immediately in rear of the 1st Division, taking its place on the capture of the first objective. On the eve of the attack the 1st Division was holding a front of 7,000 yards from Oisy to the north of Catillon, and it was arranged that the 1st and 2nd Brigades were to cross the canal south of Catillon under cover of a heavy barrage accompanied by a smoke screen.   Each brigade was allotted a separate crossing-place, the 1st at a point north-west of Bois l'Abbaye, the 2nd about two miles south of Catillon. The crossing effected, a bridge-head was to be established, followed by a pause of an hour and a half to allow of our guns moving forward ; the advance was then to be resumed to the first objective—Petit Cambrésis–Hautrève–Catillon–Petit Versaille–La Folie. The 3rd Brigade was ordered to clear Catillon from the south and establish a bridge-head east of the canal, pending the establishment of touch with the 32nd Division further to the east.

At zero hour—5.45 a.m. on the 4th November—the 1st Brigade advanced, the Battalion and the Cameron Highlanders in front on right and left respectively, the Black Watch following in support. The leading battalions carried bridges up to the canal with them, those used by the battalions of the 1st Brigade being floating bridges carried on German steel floats, of which many had lately been captured in the German engineer parks. On the barrage lifting off the east bank of the canal, four floating bridges were pushed across. The first party of the Battalion to cross was a Lewis Gun section intended to cover the crossing, and this came under short-range enemy machine-gun fire, but was able to silence the guns and capture the teams. The companies then began to double forward and crossed by two of the bridges in the following order—" A," " B " and " C,"—" D " Company remaining behind to help launch more bridges.

The Battalion only took fifteen minutes to pass over the canal, the whole operation being completed by twenty minutes after zero.*

A halt of some forty minutes now took place during which large numbers of the enemy, seeing themselves in danger of being outflanked, showed a general disposition to surrender, few putting up anything of a resistance.

* In *The Story of the Fourth Army* it is stated that the Battalion and the Cameron Highlanders had a bet on which should be first across the Canal, the Highlanders winning by a narrow margin of half a minute !   Actually there was a very dense mist, and it was impossible to say which battalion was across first. When Battalion Headquarters crossed the bridges, great difficulty was experienced, owing to the mist and the large number of German prisoners being sent back.

On the barrage lifting, the advance was resumed, the Battalion moving forward, " A," " B " and " C " Companies in front and " D " in support ; but the mist was very thick and the operations, so far as fighting was concerned, developed into a series of hand-to-hand combats between small opposing parties. Fighting their way forward in this manner, clearing houses and accepting surrenders, the Battalion front line arrived in good time on the Catillon Road in touch with the 3rd Brigade, " D " Company being hard at work consolidating east of the Canal.

The first objective of the Division was now reached and occupied, and the Black Watch came forward to take the place of the Battalion, which had no further part in the action. Late that night the 1st Brigade was relieved by one from the 46th Division and withdrew, the Battalion concentrating at Molain, whence on the 6th it marched into camp at Fresnoy-le-Grand.

During these final operations the Battalion experienced a loss of seven killed, forty-one wounded and four missing.

The operations of the 4th were a brilliant success ; the canal had been forced on a wide front, a bridge-head had been established, and the Forest of Mormal had been penetrated to a great depth, while over four thousand prisoners and close upon eighty guns had been captured.

On the 7th November the Brigadier sent the following letter to Lieut.-Colonel R. E. Berkeley, D.S.O., Commanding the Battalion :—

" I wish to express to you personally and to the 1st Bn. The Loyal North Lancashire Regiment my admiration of the completeness of your arrangements for the operation of crossing the Sambre Canal and subsequent exploitation of the eastern side. Your Battalion and the 1st Bn. The Cameron Highlanders reached the eastern bank simultaneously, and the complete co-operation which existed was entirely responsible for the success of the operation.

" I congratulate all ranks on their staunch devotion to duty and hope that the 4th November, 1918, may be a memorable day in the history of the war, and add one more to the gallant records of your Regiment."

On the night of the 4th November the Germans began to fall back on the whole battle front and by the 9th the enemy was in full retreat. The German generals now admitted that their cause was hopeless, Germany itself was in the throes of revolution, the High Seas Fleet refused to move out of harbour and the Emperor had fled into Holland. On the evening of the 7th November German delegates ventured into the French lines, deputed to make the best terms that were obtainable ; and at 5 a.m. on the 11th they agreed to the terms which Marshal Foch demanded. These were briefly that all allied prisoners were to be at once released, the left bank of the Rhine was to be handed over, 5,000 guns, 3,000 machine-guns and 2,000 aeroplanes were to be at once surrendered, and all submarines and many German warships were to be given up to the Allies.

Such a complete surrender was inevitable, in view of the military situation at the time as visualized in Sir Douglas Haig's despatch on the 21st December, 1918 : " The military situation on the British front on the morning of the 11th November can be stated very shortly. In the fighting since the 1st November our troops had broken the enemy's resistance beyond possibility of recovery, and had forced on him a disorderly retreat along the whole front of the British armies. Thereafter the enemy was capable neither of accepting nor refusing battle. The utter confusion of his troops, the state of his railways congested with abandoned trains, the capture of huge quantities of rolling stock and material, all showed that our attack had been decisive. . . . A continuance of hostilities could only have meant disaster to the German armies and the armed invasion of Germany."

At 11 a.m. on the 11th November, the right of the Fourth Army was east of the Franco-Belgian frontier, and thence northwards our troops had reached the general line Sivry–Erquelines–Boussu–Jurbise–Herghies–Ghislenghien–Lassnies–Grammont ; but the 1st Battalion, The Loyal North Lancashire Regiment, was still in billets at Fresnoy-le-Grand, when on the morning of the 11th the following telegram was issued from the headquarters of the 1st Division :—

> " Following message from G.H.Q. begins. Hostilities will cease 11.00 November 11th. Troops will stand fast on the line reached at that hour. Defensive precautions will be maintained. There will be no intercourse with the enemy until receipt of instructions from G.H.Q. Further instructions follow."

The Great War was over, and His Majesty The King, who throughout had followed with so keen an interest the movements of His troops, now sent the following gracious and congratulatory message to their Commander :—

" I desire to express at once, through you, to all ranks of the British Empire, Home, Dominion, Colonial and Indian troops, My heartfelt pride and gratitude at the brilliant success which has crowned more than four years of effort and endurance.

" Germany, our most formidable enemy, who planned the war to gain the supremacy of the world, full of pride in her armed strength, and of contempt for the small British Army of that day, has now been forced to acknowledge defeat. I rejoice that in this achievement the British forces now grown from small beginnings to the finest army in our history, have borne so gallant and distinguished a part.

" Soldiers of the British Army ! In France and Belgium the prowess of your arms, as great in retreat as in victory, has won the admiration alike of friend and foe, and has now by a happy and historic fate, enabled you to conclude the campaign by capturing Mons, where your predecessors of 1914 shed the first British blood. Between that date and this you have traversed a long and weary road, defeat has more than once stared you in the face, your ranks have been thinned again and again by wounds, sickness and death, but your faith has never faltered, your courage has never failed, your hearts have never known defeat. With your allied comrades you have won the day.

" Others of you have fought in more distant fields, in the mountains and plains of Italy, in the rugged Balkan ranges, under the burning sun of Palestine, Mesopotamia and Africa, amid the snows of Russia and Siberia, and by the shores of the Dardanelles.

" Men of the British race who have shared these successes have felt in their veins the call of the blood and joined eagerly with the Mother Country in the fight against tyranny and wrong. Equally those of the ancient and historic peoples of India and Africa, who have learnt to trust the flag of England, hastened to discharge their debt of loyalty to the Crown.

" I desire to thank every officer, soldier and woman of our Army for service nobly rendered, for sacrifices cheerfully given, and I pray that God, who has been pleased to grant a victorious end to this great crusade for justice and right, will prosper and bless our efforts in the immediate future to secure for generations to come the hard-won blessings of freedom and peace.

" GEORGE R.I."

The final official despatch states : " Despite the enormous development of mechanical invention in every phase of warfare, the place which the infantryman has always held as the main substance and foundation of an army is as secure to-day as in any period of history. The infantryman remains the backbone of defence and the spear-head of the attack. At no time has the reputation of the British infantryman been higher, or his achievement more worthy of his renown. The same infantry divisions have advanced to the attack day after day, and week after week, with an untiring irresistible ardour which refused to be denied ; no praise can be too high for the valour they have shown, no gratitude too deep for the work they have accomplished."

CHAPTER XXXIV

1918–1919

THE BRITISH ARMY OF OCCUPATION IN GERMANY
DEMOBILIZATION AND RETURN TO ENGLAND

THE IX. Corps was now transferred from the Fourth to the Second Army, under General Sir H. Plumer, to whom had been assigned the command of the British Army of Occupation in Germany, and on the 16th November the Battalion marched to billets in Hestrup, ready for the advance to the Rhine. The march began on the 18th, the Division moving by easy stages and with many halts. The Battalion passed through Boussu-lez-Walcourt, Fraire, Flavion—where the inhabitants, now freed from four years of German domination, presented the Battalion with an address of welcome—and Onhaye, this last halting-place being reached on the 25th and the march not being resumed until the 2nd December. Then marching by Celles, Chevetogne, Baillonville, Barvaux, Mormont, Odeigne and Les Sarts, the eastern frontier of Belgium was reached on the evening of the 15th and preparations were made for the entry next day on to German soil.

So soon as the Armistice had been signed, Lieutenant Heath and 2nd Lieutenant Utting had been sent to England to bring out the Colours, and, with these flying and drums beating, the Battalion crossed the German frontier on the 16th December, the Divisional Commander standing on the line of demarcation to watch his troops go by.

At the outset of the march occasional long halts were obliged to be made owing to the difficulty of feeding the leading divisions ; the necessity, in some cases, of supplying rations to the local population ; by the destruction caused by the Germans to the roads and railways and also to the German retirement not being always carried out according to the scheduled programme. Up to the Belgian frontier the roads had been much damaged and many of the bridges blown up, whereby our march was impeded, but once across the German frontier the roads were found to be in splendid condition.

The first billets of the Battalion in Germany were in Krombach, " a poor and dirty hamlet."

Moving on again through Manderfeld, Dahlem, Blankenheim, Minstereifel, Kluckenheim was reached on the 23rd, " the end of our march to

71

the Rhine.   Unfortunately bad weather, and the absence of any kind of a road for two miles in the middle of the march, made it rather a trying day. Our final destination—Bornheim—was reached about 2.30 p.m.   Billets were found to be quite good, and the Battalion settled down to enjoy its well-earned rest.   We had marched for thirteen days, from the 9th to the 23rd, and covered one hundred and thirty-five miles.   During that period only two men fell out and the total sick admissions from all causes were only twenty-six men, in spite of the fact that owing to the adverse weather the troops were frequently soaked through on arrival in billets.''

At Bornheim the Battalion remained during the remainder of the time that it formed part of the Army of Occupation in Germany.

On the 26th demobilization commenced.   For this preparations had been made while yet the war had hardly more than commenced, for it was realized from the outset that, when peace came round again, very much would have to be done to lessen the confusion and dislocation which might be occasioned by the sudden and wholesale disbandment of many thousands of men before labour had sufficiently recovered its poise to provide enough employment for those seeking it.   Already in January, 1915, a scheme was drawn up and submitted to the Cabinet of the day, containing proposals for meeting some at least of the many difficulties which had been envisaged when the wage-earners of our huge army should be ready to return to civil life.   The proposals then put forward were provisionally approved, but as there seemed at the time to be no hurry for their application, they were put aside until the need for their further re-consideration might arise.

As the war went on and its conclusion came daily nearer into sight, committees were appointed to deal with demobilization in more detail— there was a Reconstruction Committee, an Army Demobilization Committee and several others, and eventually it was decided to offer the following to each soldier on leaving the Army :—

1. A furlough with pay and separation allowances for four weeks from the date of demobilization.

2. A railway warrant to his home.

3. A twelve-months' policy of insurance against unemployment.

4. A money gratuity in addition to the ordinary service gratuity.

Various different methods of dispersal were considered, and in the first instance the principle was accepted and followed of granting men release from army service in order of priority, determined by individual qualifications, the idea of an early reconstruction of the army after the declaration of peace being kept in view.   It followed, then, that in considering and endeavouring to solve the demobilization problem, the authorities appear to have been influenced by national interests—that is, that the army was to be dispersed in accordance with the needs of the reconstruction of industry, and by individuals rather than by military units.   This scheme, as initially administered, caused considerable opposition in many quarters, while a system of " special releases," which formed no part of the original plan, was open to the charge of favouritism, for serving soldiers could not easily be made to understand that other men had stronger claims for early discharge than they considered themselves to possess ; hopes were raised which could not be gratified ; and considerable difficulty was experienced in making men retained with the Colours understand that a state of war still existed, and that a considerable army must for some time be maintained in the field.

In consequence of the many representations made, Army Order No. 55 of 1919, finally abolished the principle of demobilization on industrial grounds, substituting that of release by reason of age and length of army service.

At the end of the year the new educational training scheme was inaugurated, under which men were given a training calculated to help them to obtain employment on their return to civil life.

On the 1st January, 1919, the first party of men for demobilization—fifty-six strong—left the Battalion for home, and this appears to have been the only party that left during this month, since on the 31st, the effective strength of the Battalion was as high as thirty-six officers and 824 non-commissioned officers and men.   On the 1st March, however, demobilization re-commenced and proceeded steadily all through the month ; some of the newly-raised Young Soldiers' Battalions were now joining the Army of Occupation, and to the 52nd (Young Soldiers) Battalion The Bedfordshire Regiment all transport and all mobilization equipment, not actually carried on the soldier, were handed over.

In March, 1919, the 1st Battalion being still at Bornheim and the 2nd Battalion at Siegburg, the two battalions, for the first time in their history, found themselves sufficiently close to one another to be able to meet and full advantage was taken of the opportunity.   Amongst other events, a football match, between the two battalions, was played at Bornheim with the appropriate result of a draw—two goals each.   The Colours being with the battalions, the chance of having a combined photograph was too good to be missed ; this photograph, taken on the banks of the Rhine, appears facing page 74 ; reading from left to right the names of the officers are as follows :—

1st Battalion : Captain R. Rowley, D.C.M. ; Lieut.-Colonel R. E. Berkeley, D.S.O. ; Lieutenant J. Lindsell, M.C.
2nd Battalion : Lieutenant H. Wilkinson, M.C. ; Lieut.-Colonel T. Mc. G. Bridges ; Captain W. Halton; M.C.

On the 8th March all officers and other ranks, liable for retention in the Army of Occupation, left the Battalion and proceeded to Bonn, there to join the 12th (Service) Battalion, The Loyal North Lancashire Regiment, and in all twenty-one officers and 313 other ranks were thus sent away. In addition to this party, another large dispersal draft was sent home, and the effect of these measures was to reduce the Battalion to no more than nine officers and 103 men, which was composed of the Battalion cadre, details still awaiting demobilization, re-enlisted men awaiting final approval, and a few others who were earmarked for service with No. 1. Trench Mortar Battery, if and when this unit should be re-formed.

The Battalion was now formed into a single composite company.

During the next few days all were awaiting orders to proceed home and the details still remaining for dispersion were gradually dispatched to their destinations. On the 10th a Regimental Dinner was held and was attended by representatives of five battalions of The Loyal North Lancashire Regiment, viz. the 1st, 2nd, 2/4th, 2/5th and 12th.

The reconstruction of the various divisions composing the Army of Occupation had now for some little time past been in progress, and on the 15th March the 1st Division ceased to exist and was re-named the Western Division, and this, when finally reconstituted, was composed of the following units : the 1/4th, 1/7th and 9th Battalions The Cheshire Regiment, the 51st, 52nd and 53rd Battalions The South Wales Borderers, and the 1/6th, 51st, 52nd and 53rd Battalions The Welsh Regiment.

On the 25th the first of the cadres to which battalions had now been reduced began to leave the 1st Division for embarkation, and at the end of the month the strength of the Battalion stood at six officers and only sixty-eight other ranks. At last on the 3rd April definite information was received that the cadre would entrain for Dunkirk on the 13th, and the few remaining details were sent off to concentration camps.

On the early morning of the 13th April the Battalion cadre was sent by bus from Bornheim to Cologne where it entrained and proceeded to Dunkirk ; it arrived here about two o'clock on the morning of the 14th and, after spending the rest of the night in the train, marched to " A " Camp, where it remained until the morning of the 16th. On this day the cadre marched down to the docks, and at 9.45 sailed for England, finally disembarking at Dover and being at once sent off by train to the Depot at Preston.

The officers who returned home with the cadre were : Lieut.-Colonel R. E. Berkeley, D.S.O., Captains J. Lindsell, M.C. and A. B. Bratton, D.S.O., M.C., Lieutenant A. J. Smith, M.C., and Captain and Quartermaster R. Rowley, D.C.M.

THE COLOURS OF THE 1ST AND 2ND BATTALIONS ON THE RHINE.

March, 1919.

CHAPTER XXXV

THE 2ND BATTALION
THE LOYAL NORTH LANCASHIRE REGIMENT

1914

OPERATIONS IN EAST AFRICA
TANGA

WHEN in August, 1914, the Great War broke out there were fifty-two battalions of British infantry serving in India and Burma, seventeen of these being stationed in Bengal, fourteen in the Punjab, twelve in Bombay, six in Madras, and only three in Burma. On the 17th September Lord Kitchener wrote out to India asking that thirty-nine of those still in India at that date, might be sent to England, stating that their places would be taken by such battalions of the Territorial Force as had volunteered for service in India.

Before the end of September ten British infantry battalions had sailed from India, some of these proceeding direct to France with the Indian Army Corps, while others voyaged to England, joining on arrival those divisions still being organized at home. By the end of the year 1914 fifteen more British battalions had left India for other theatres of the World War, so that by the beginning of 1915 there were scarcely twelve of these remaining in India. Actually, as the war went on the British military establishment in India was reduced as follows :—

Seven cavalry regiments out of nine were sent overseas.

Forty-four infantry battalions out of fifty-two had sailed.

Forty-three out of fifty-six artillery batteries were sent away, while in place of these twenty-nine batteries of Territorial artillery and thirty-five battalions of Territorial infantry arrived from England, but not, however, before the strength of the British garrison of India had been reduced by at least fifteen thousand men.

India's effort is thus summed up in *India's Contribution to the Great War*, pp. 76, 77 : " Thirty-two Regular British Infantry Battalions and the bulk of the Regular Horse, Field and Heavy Batteries were sent to England. By the early spring of 1915 two more Infantry Brigades were dispatched from India, to form, with a brigade already overseas, a new Division, and also another Cavalry Brigade, thus bringing India's initial effort up to :—

Two Indian Army Corps,
Seven Infantry Brigades,
One Mixed Force, including three Infantry Battalions,
Two Cavalry Divisions,
Two Cavalry Brigades,

plus Corps, Divisional, attached troops, administrative services and rein-forcements.''

A request was received by the Government of India very shortly after the opening of the war '' for the preparation of a mixed force including six battalions to deal with German East Africa, and for three additional battalions for the protection of Zanzibar and the Mombasa–Nairobi Railway, the operation of the latter being controlled by the Colonial Office. The dispatch of the former was somewhat delayed by the shortage of shipping and the difficulty of providing naval escort, as the German cruisers ' Emden ' and ' Königsberg ' were at large and the former had even appeared off Madras. But the force eventually arrived off Mombasa on the 31st October and sailed for Tanga next day. One of the three battalions for British East Africa, the 29th Punjabis, sailed on the 19th August, and was in action at Tsavo on the 6th September. With the arrival of the remaining two battalions the two forces were amalgamated under one command. The strength of those two contingents, which contained a large proportion of Imperial Service Troops, amounted approximately to 1,500 British and 10,250 Indian ranks.'' *

When on the outbreak of war troops were sent from India to German East Africa, this was principally as a defensive measure, since the only Regular forces at that time in the British East Africa Protectorate and Uganda were two battalions of the King's African Rifles, '' a garrison barely sufficient for internal police work and for guarding against native uprising and tribal feuds. Consequently for defence against a German attack, still more for an offensive against German East Africa, troops from overseas were required, and in the initial stages of the war they came exclusively from India.'' Several months before war was declared—in January, 1914—an enemy commander of unusual ability, resourcefulness and strength of character, General von Lettow-Vorbeck, had arrived in German East Africa, and in his *Reminiscences* he tells us that '' at the outbreak of war the Protective Force consisted of 216 Europeans (from whom a part must be deducted as on leave) and 2,540 Askari ; there were, further, in the Police Force forty-five Europeans and 2,154 Askari ; these were later increased

* Lucas, *The Empire at War*, Vol. V, p. 180.

by the ship's company of the ' Königsberg,' which had put to sea, 322 men, and of the ' Möwe,' 102 men. The total number enrolled in the Force during the war were about 3,000 Europeans and 11,000 Askari."

It having been decided to attempt to gain a footing in German East Africa, two practically simultaneous attacks were planned to be made upon Moshi, not far from the Anglo-German frontier at Taveta, and also the terminus of the Usambara Railway, connecting it with the capital, Wilhelmstadt, and the coast at the port of Tanga. Moshi was to be attacked from the north-west round the southern slopes of Mount Kilimanjaro by such troops as were already in the country, while " Indian Expeditionary Force B " was to force a landing at Tanga and work up-country along the line of the railway.

" B " Force was composed of two infantry brigades with divisional troops ; only one of the brigades was a regular unit, being the Bangalore Brigade under the command of Brigadier-General R. Wapshare, and containing the 2nd Battalion The Loyal North Lancashire Regiment, the 63rd Palamcottah Light Infantry, the 98th Infantry and the 101st Grenadiers. The other brigade was under the command of Brigadier-General M. J. Tighe, and included in it were the 13th Rajputs, the 2nd Battalion Kashmir Imperial Service Infantry, and a composite battalion of Kashmir and Gwalior Imperial Service Infantry. The divisional troops were the 61st Pioneers, the 28th Indian Mountain Battery, and an Imperial Service Company of Sappers and Miners. The force was commanded by Brigadier-General A. E. Aitken.

The ships which carried the troops of " Expeditionary Force B " were part of a convoy of forty-five vessels, taking troops to places as far apart as Basra, Egypt, Marseilles and East Africa. The 2nd Battalion, The Loyal North Lancashire Regiment, sailed at 5 p.m. on the 16th October in the " Karmala " at a strength of nineteen officers and 830 other ranks. The officers were Lieut.-Colonel C. E. A. Jourdain, D.S.O., Majors W. D. Sanderson, H. A. Robinson, F. J. Braithwaite and T. McG. Bridges ; Captains E. C. Halton and R. E. Berkeley ; Lieutenants R. H. Logan, C. V. M. Bell (adjutant), D. P. J. Collas, C. J. de V. l'Anson, J. F. B. Watson, W. H. Anderson and C. G. Dickson, 2nd Lieutenants S. V. Einem-Hickson, B. H. Withers, R. L. C. Keays and G. G. R. Williams ; Lieutenant and Quartermaster R. Rowley ; attached were Captain C. A. T. Conyngham, R.A.M.C., and Assistant-Surgeon A. R. Emmett.

After a slow passage across the Indian Ocean in perfect weather, the " Karmala " put into Kilindini Harbour on the south side of Mombasa Island on the 31st, the rest of the convoy remaining out of sight.

The General Officer Commanding, with his Staff, went ashore to confer with the Governor of British East Africa, Sir Henry Belfield, and Brigadier-General L. J. M. Stewart, who commanded the smaller Indian Expeditionary Force which had landed the month before.   At this conference the following plan of operations was settled : Indian Expeditionary Force " B " was to land at Tanga, form a base there and work up the Usambara Railway, General Stewart co-operating from Voi and Longido.   A small expedition was to be sent, as soon after landing as possible, from Tanga towards Vanga, to co-operate with a detachment of " C " force at Gazi. Information available pointed to the probability of the enemy's chief concentration being between Moshi and Mombo.   Should it be evident after engagements at Mombo and elsewhere on the railway that the enemy's remaining power of resistance was inconsiderable, it was thought that General Stewart might be able to complete the subjugation of the Moshi section without further assistance.   In this case " B " Force could be withdrawn from the Usambara Railway to Tanga to commence the second phase of the operation against Dar-es-Salaam and the Central Railway at a later date.

This decision having been taken, combined naval and military operation orders for disembarkation at Tanga were issued.   The naval force consisted of H.M.S. " Fox " and three tugs, the " Khalifa," used as a despatch vessel and the " Mombasa " and " Helmuth," fitted as mine sweepers, and these ships, with the transports, were to rendezvous at a point fifteen miles east of Tanga Island at 6 a.m. on 2nd November, where the lighters and tugs for disembarkation were to join the flotilla.   Unfortunately the battleship " Goliath," which should have accompanied the flotilla, was obliged to be left at Mombasa for an engine overhaul.

Before going into the details of the landing, there are one or two incidents of the voyage which are memorable in the Regiment : The force was exceedingly weak in artillery—there was only one mountain battery with it— therefore the naval commander-in-chief at Bombay offered to lend some light guns with shore mountings for use on arrival, and to train gun crews on the voyage.   To this end Lieutenant R. H. Logan, with a corporal and twelve men, were sent on board H.M.S. " Goliath," there to be made into gunners in a fortnight by intensive training on Navy lines.   They practised incessantly with 3-pounders, 6-pounders and 12-pounders, while the ship's artificers fitted up two 3-pounder (Q.F.) guns with shore carriages.

On one occasion, the gun detachment was indulging in a rest, and, taking advantage of the glorious weather, the men were snatching a spell of sleep.   A strange sail was sighted and challenged by H.M.S. " Goliath " and, for some reason best known to herself, was lamentably slow in answering the signals of the warship ; so slow was she, in fact, that she was reckoned a suspicious character and the order came down to "clear for action." The resulting evolution was literally an eye-opener to the gun detachment. As one of them put it : "Everything fell down all round us, the matlows all seemed to be falling over each other, and before we could sit up and ask what was happening, the guns were swinging round on their target right over the top of us. Just as the last armoured door was closing the one remaining passage inside the ship, a voice suggested that we had better come inside and look slippy."

Breathless and bewildered, the detachment scrambled "inside"—just in time. However, by this time the casual tramp had condescended to answer the "Goliath's" signals and so the alarm passed off. When the battleship parted company from the convoy at Mombasa, "Logan's Battery" as it came to be termed, was transferred to the "Barjora" complete with its two 3-pounders and limbers, upon which ship it made the voyage to Tanga.

The situation, as appreciated by General Aitken, led to the expectation that the landing at Tanga would not be opposed, and this view was supported by the fact that the German civil authorities at Dar-es-Salaam and elsewhere had entered into unofficial arrangements with the local British naval forces to avoid the risk of bombardment of the open coast towns. Apparently this arrangement extended to Tanga, which fact, coupled with one other unknown, or unappreciated, factor, made all the difference to the fate of the expedition : this factor was the powerful and resolute character of the German Commander-in-Chief, General von Lettow-Vorbeck. This officer felt it his duty to defend the German colony to the utmost of his ability, but, at the outset, he was none too well supported in his views by the Civil Governor, and the fight at Tanga appears to have been undertaken largely, if not wholly, on his individual responsibility ; but there is small room for doubt that the issue of this first trial of strength confirmed the confidence of the German colonists in themselves and their leader and caused the campaign to run the full length of the Great War in Europe.

At dawn on 2nd November the convoy was at its appointed rendezvous, whence H.M.S. "Fox" went into Tanga Harbour under a flag-of-truce to demand the unconditional surrender of the place. The provincial commissioner came on board and was informed that the truce was at an end, and he was given an hour to haul down his flag ; but at the end of that time (9.30 a.m.) the German flag was still flying and the "Fox" returned to the convoy to bring in the troopships. In the absence of any knowledge as to whether the harbour was mined and to avoid the delay which the sweeping operations would entail, it was decided that the first landing should be made on the seaward side of Ras Kasone, a headland which covers the entrance to Tanga Bay about one and a half miles east of Tanga town ; so for this point the ships were headed. Several hours were lost at the start, for in the unexpected absence of H.M.S. " Goliath " the convoy could not be marshalled at the rendezvous until the " Fox " returned to it, also the shortage of pilots made it necessary for the ships to come in a few at a time and in daylight only ; but by 4.30 p.m. the " Fox " and three of the transports were anchored in the outer roads, opposite the spot selected for disembarkation. This was a small sandy beach beneath a building called " The Red House "—the only break in the long line of dark-leaved mangrove-trees which covered the whole of the low cliffs nearly to low-water mark—from which stretched seaward for some five hundred yards a flat reef. On the edge of this the laden lighters grounded and the troops had to wade ashore. Such was " Landing Place A," from which one or two narrow tracks led upwards to the low, tree-clad plateau above ; the great point in its favour was, however, that it was screened from view of Tanga. Two other landing-places were selected and used next day—Landing Place " B," about fifteen hundred yards from " A," on the extreme northern point of Ras Kasone, beneath the Signal Tower ; and " C," a good, steep beach on the western side of the headland some one thousand yards south of " B,"—but " A " Beach was the vital point, both in the first landing and subsequent re-embarkation.

According to Operation Order No. 1, issued by Major-General A. E. Aitken,* dated Mombasa 1st November, opposition to the landing was not anticipated, but resistance was to be expected further up the railway ; wherefore a covering force was to be landed on the 2nd to cut communications with the interior, picquet the roads, and generally cover the formation of the base. This was modified by a second order, No. 2, changing the landing-place to " A " Beach, detailing the covering force—13th Rajputs and 61st Pioneers and three hundred porters under Brigadier-General Tighe —and ordering the town of Tanga to be seized that night. Although the transports had anchored at 4.30 p.m., the first of the lighters did not reach the shore till nearly 9 p.m. and as they grounded on the reef fire was opened upon them from the cliffs, and from one or two isolated houses in the vicinity. To this H.M.S. " Fox " replied ; after one or two rounds the fire from the shore ceased and the landing proceeded unmolested, the troops having suffered no casualties. Nevertheless disembarkation was slow, and by the time General Tighe landed at midnight only two companies of the 13th Rajputs and the scouts of the Imperial Service Brigade were on shore ; these, however, pushed out patrols towards Tanga, and

* Temporary Major-General 10th October, 1914.

soon afterwards a report came in to the effect that the enemy had an out-post line covering Tanga from the east, and that machine-guns had been located near Tanga Station. At 3.30 a.m. a hostile patrol attempted to rush a picquet of the 13th Rajputs but was repulsed.

By 4.30 a.m. eight companies of the 13th Rajputs and four companies of the 61st Pioneers were landed, and Brigadier-General Tighe sent forward four companies of the Rajputs to seize the railway station and workshops. Firing soon broke out, and within an hour the increasing volume of musketry showed plainly enough that the Rajputs were heavily engaged with the enemy. Communication with them was interrupted, so General Tighe advanced to their support with the remainder of the force, leaving only one company of the 61st Pioneers to cover the landing-place. By 6.30 a.m. touch was gained with the firing-line and a double company of the 13th was sent in to prolong it to the left, after which the advance pro-ceeded and the enemy fell back to what appeared to be a prepared position on the railway line. But now his reinforcements, both of European and Native troops, were beginning to come into action; the firing-lines were in close touch, casualties, particularly among the British officers, were becoming heavy; supports were being absorbed, the remainder of the 13th having been thrown in: then it became evident that these two Battalions were not sufficiently strong to deal with the situation. In the beginning it was simply that the flank guard of the 13th had not gone out far enough, and so failed to deal with a machine-gun which was enfilading the whole firing-line. One more company of the 61st was thrown into the line and the enfilading machine-gun was dislodged; but the same company of the 61st then found itself within fifty yards of the enemy firing-line and was unable to compete with the situation, and the advance on the left came to a standstill about 7.30 a.m. A strong counter-attack then developed against the left of General Tighe's line and the 61st failed to make ground. Half an hour later the crisis came. All the supports had been absorbed and had failed to carry the line forward; now the enemy's threat of a counter-attack on the left flank of the 61st proved successful and General Tighe deemed it advisable to disengage the force.

So much for the left of the line. On the right it was no better, for on moving thither the General found the 13th already falling back, and there was nothing for it but retirement on the landing-place. Fortunately touch was gained with H.M.S. " Fox," whose guns now began to shell the woods east of the town; whereupon the enemy's pressure relaxed and General Tighe's withdrawal was accomplished without further molestation, the regi-ments finding themselves by 10 a.m. safely within an outpost line which was being taken up by the Loyal North Lancashire who had just landed.

The " Karmala " with Headquarters, Indian Expeditionary Force " B " and the 2nd Battalion, Loyal North Lancashire Regiment, on board, had been one of the three transports brought to Ras Kasone on the afternoon of 2nd November, but at first no orders were sent to Lieut.-Colonel Jourdain as to disembarkation.   At 6.30 a.m. on 3rd November the Battalion was ordered to hold two double companies ready for disembarkation at short notice, and at 8 a.m., following an urgent call from General Tighe for reinforcements, No. 1 Company (Major Robinson) and No. 2 Company (Major Bridges) under Major Sanderson, disembarked into lighters and were towed, in pouring rain, to Landing Place " B."   The lighters grounded about fifty yards from the shore, from which point light draught boats from H.M.S. " Fox " were laid to their bows to make some sort of a bridge to the shore ; for the last few yards it was a case of splashing through the water on to the gently-sloping, muddy beach.   Ere the half-battalion was clear of the ship orders had come in for the remainder to be landed, and by 9.30 a.m. Nos. 3 and 4 Companies—Captain Halton and Major Braithwaite—and Battalion Headquarters had followed the right half battalion ashore ; only the Quartermaster, Lieutenant Rowley, and a few details, mostly sick, remaining on board.   That the landing was uncomfortably precipitate can be gathered from a diary, which tells us :—

" The 2nd Battalion received orders to disembark at very short notice ; the enemy's resistance disorganized our plans.   The Battalion landed with rations for only twenty-four hours carried by the men, reserve ammunition and a few entrenching tools ; it was put on shore in two lighters, near the Signal Tower."

Once concentrated on shore, the Battalion was moved towards " A " Beach and ordered to entrench a line covering the Red House (where the 13th and 61st had landed the previous night) and running about nine hundred yards northward in front of Ras Kasone point, to G.H.Q. at " The White House."   This position was occupied for the day to cover the disembarkation of more troops, and as these landed the entrenchments were extended to the right to cover the Signal Tower and " B " Beach. The rest of the day passed quietly.   The only contact with the enemy was on the extreme left where a picquet, under Lieutenant Hickson, lay at a fork road clear of the entrenched line ; here shots were exchanged with a hostile patrol about 7 p.m.   During the night rations for the following day were brought ashore and the Battalion was ordered to be ready to move at 8 a.m. next day.

Before passing on to the larger events of 4th November it will be as well to note briefly what had been passing in the enemy's camp to lead up to the situation which existed when the Battalion landed.   General von Lettow-Vorbeck has put it on record that he always expected a descent by the British on Tanga in the event of hostilities, and that in a capture of mails made early in the war there was found evidence which changed the possibility into a strong probability. Consequently he reconnoitred the whole country thoroughly a month before the landing took place, and made the disposition of his forces in such a way that though his scattered troops were actually watching the frontier, they could, by hard marching and the use of the Usambara Railway, quickly be concentrated at Tanga. It was with no surprise that von Lettow-Vorbeck, then at New Moshi, heard of the appearance off Tanga of the transports conveying Indian Expeditionary Force " B," and he set his concentration going at once. The delay caused by the formal demand for the surrender of Tanga, the time lost in bringing the transports into the outer roads, the slowness of disembarkation, were all pieces of good fortune for him, and the twenty-four hours which elapsed between the appearance of the fleet in Tanga Bay and the launching of the first attack, were of inestimable value. Two companies of Askari, which were in the neighbourhood of Tanga, started south at once by forced marches, though one did not arrive in time for the action of 3rd November ; one and a half companies of Askari actually in New Moshi were sent down by rail on 3rd November, the Police Askari and Railway Protection detachments being swept along with them ; two companies of Europeans followed from Moshi by the railway, down to the coast, in short, the Usambara Railway continued to pour troops into Tanga to the utmost of its capacity from early on 2nd November right up to the close of the action on the 4th. General von Lettow-Vorbeck and his Headquarters did not arrive until the evening of the 3rd, and it is not quite clear who was in supreme command at the first action ; but it seems fairly certain that the forces opposed to General Tighe's first attack consisted of the 17th Askari Company, the Railway Protection and Police Askari, probably about one company strong, a local European Volunteer Company, and one and a half companies of Askari which arrived from Moshi during the action and made the counter-attack on the left flank of the 61st which closed the action. The actual figures are not available, but the total strength may be taken at about four hundred men and six machine-guns. The action itself was the simplest possible, and the German account agrees with that given above from our point of view. The 17th Askari Company held an outpost position covering Tanga from the east, and when attacked in force this company fell back on a prepared position along the railway cutting and eastern edge of the town, where it was reinforced by the local Volunteers, Police Askari, etc. ; the opportune arrival of one and a half companies of Askari from Moshi during the action made an effective counter-attack possible at the crucial moment and completed the discomfiture of the two Indian regiments.

General von Lettow-Vorbeck arrived at a point some four miles west of Tanga about 3 a.m. on 4th November. Here he met some of the senior officers who had taken part in the previous day's action and, after a conference, reconnoitred the position at Tanga for himself during the night. He was quite convinced the attack would be renewed and made his dispositions accordingly, although there was a feeling among some of his subordinates that the British forces in their full strength were too powerful to justify a decisive engagement. His troops had been augmented by the arrival of further companies by rail and road and still more were on their way, and with this fact in mind he posted his men so as to meet the attack on the eastern edge of Tanga, with strong reserves behind his right flank for the purpose of counter-attack. When day broke on 4th November he had available four companies of Askari and two or three companies of Europeans with about twelve machine-guns, while two more companies of Askari each with six machine-guns were on their way from Moshi—in all about thirteen hundred men and twenty machine-guns came into action against General Aitken's force.

While the Loyal North Lancashire were holding the outpost position, the rest of the transports had been brought into the outer roads, and the disembarkation continued during the 3rd and 4th, until, by 10 a.m. on the latter day, the whole of the force was ashore. At 10.15 a.m. the G.O.C. issued an order stating that the enemy was reported in considerable force west of the German Hospital, and that the G.O.C. intended to attack them and occupy Tanga. It directed that the Imperial Service Brigade, under General Tighe (less three companies Gwalior Infantry left to cover the landing-places), should advance on a front of about six hundred yards with its right on Tanga Bay, while the 27th Brigade under General Wapshare should continue the line to the left, with its left flank echeloned to the left rear ; the right of the 27th Brigade was to direct ; the 61st Pioneers were to be in reserve. The advance was to commence at 12 noon, being covered as far as possible by the guns of H.M.S. " Fox " and the 28th Mountain Battery on the " Bharata." The necessary dispositions were made, and by noon the force was deployed on a front of two thousand yards in the following order :—

On the right was the Imperial Service Brigade consisting of the 2nd Battalion Kashmir Rifles and the Composite Battalion (less three companies Gwalior Infantry) in the firing-line, with the 13th Rajputs in support. On the left was the 27th Brigade, whose right-flank battalion—the Loyal North Lancashire—was the directing unit of the operation ; the

63rd Palamcottah L.I. followed next in the line, while the 101st Grenadiers, with their four companies, echeloned to their left rear at one hundred yards' distance and interval, covered the left flank ; the 98th Native Infantry was in support. The 61st Pioneers formed the reserve in rear of the Imperial Service Brigade. The 28th Mountain Battery was not landed, as it was considered that too much time would be lost in waiting for its disembarkation ; it was, however, ordered to have its guns ready for action on the deck of the " Bharata " to support the attack. The " Fox " and the " Bharata " were moved into the inner harbour to co-operate with the movements on land, but the guns of neither ship could be used to much effect, as the tall, dense trees at the top of the cliffs lining Tanga Bay hid most of the town and all the battlefield from view. Observation and control of fire were therefore impossible. " Logan's Battery " remained on the " Barjora " off " A " Beach. Definite orders were given at the commencement of the action not to shell Tanga Town ; these were only countermanded late in the day.

When operation orders were received at about 8 a.m. on the 4th from 27th Brigade Headquarters, the Battalion fell in rapidly and marched off to the rendezvous, a sector a little in advance of the position held by Lieutenant Hickson's picquet the night before. This operation order is interesting, for in two important points it differs from Operation Order No. 3 as issued by the G.O.C.—the objective and the directing unit. For whereas the latter gave a somewhat indefinitive objective—to attack the enemy (west of the German Hospital) and occupy Tanga, the former gave a perfectly definite objective—Tanga Mission Station—which tended to draw the troops of the 27th Brigade across the front of those in the Imperial Service Brigade ; moreover, the G.O.C.'s orders named the right of the 27th Brigade (i.e. The Loyal North Lancashire) as the directing unit, but the 27th Brigade orders bade it " keep touch with the left of the Imperial Service Brigade."

Having arrived at the allotted station Lieut.-Colonel Jourdain deployed the Battalion as follows : in a firing-line with a frontage of about two hundred yards were No. 2 Company (Major Bridges) on the right and No. 4 Company (Major Braithwaite) on the left, each company finding its own supports ; No. 3 Company (Captain Halton) and No. 1 Company (Major Robinson) formed local reserves to Nos. 2 and 4 Companies respectively, while the machine-gun section remained with Battalion Headquarters in the initial stages of the operation. The dispositions were completed and the force received orders to advance between 12 noon and 1 p.m. The day was intensely hot, and in the dense, steamy rubber plantation through which the path of the Battalion lay, touch was hard to keep ; consequently the advance was slow, in fact the whole force broke up into open order, or small columns, as soon as the advance started, thus adding to the difficulty of control. The Battalion moved with each company in column of platoons at fifty yards' distance, the men being in open order at three paces interval.

Incidentally, the communications of the force ran from front to rear in each brigade by telephone cables laid along the two roads leading to Tanga, and so back to the Signal Tower on Ras Kasone Point, whence touch was kept with the ships by visual signalling. Lateral communication was very difficult and had to be maintained entirely by runners ; consequently it was slow and doubtful. The troubles experienced in this direction had not a little to do with the uncertainty and incoherence which eventually settled down on the action.

During the first half-mile of the advance, that is to say, until the forward companies approached the boundary of the dense undergrowth, the advance was without opposition, although by no means without incident. Swarms of wild bees whose hives were in the trees resented the movement of these lines of intruders and showed it in no uncertain fashion.

Just before the Battalion advanced up to the track running across their front, at about 2.30 p.m., there was a halt of about half an hour. During this halt two platoons of No. 3 Company were moved up on the right of No. 2 Company and filled a gap between the right of the Battalion and the Composite Battalion.

When the advance was resumed at about 3 p.m., firing broke out from the Town and from the Railway Workshops (Baumstark's Battalion) and it became evident that the main strength of the enemy was opposed to General Aitken's left Brigade, as the firing in front of the Brigade on the right was comparatively light and the advance proceeded there with little opposition towards the European Town of Tanga.

When the enemy's resistance strengthened on the left, the 63rd Palamcottah Light Infantry did not advance with the other forward battalions of the 27th Brigade, with the result that the 101st Grenadiers realized that there was a big gap on their right flank. They were placed in a very difficult position and with a view to filling the gap they changed direction right, advanced in the direction of the Town, and their left flank became exposed to Baumstark's Battalion which was holding a position in the vicinity of the Railway Workshops.

Meanwhile the Loyal North Lancashire continued their advance under a fire which was very hard to locate in the tall crops.

When nearing the railway cutting, the Battalion was shot at in front by the 6th Askari Company defending Tanga and in flank by the companies near the Workshops ; in addition, enemy snipers were concealed

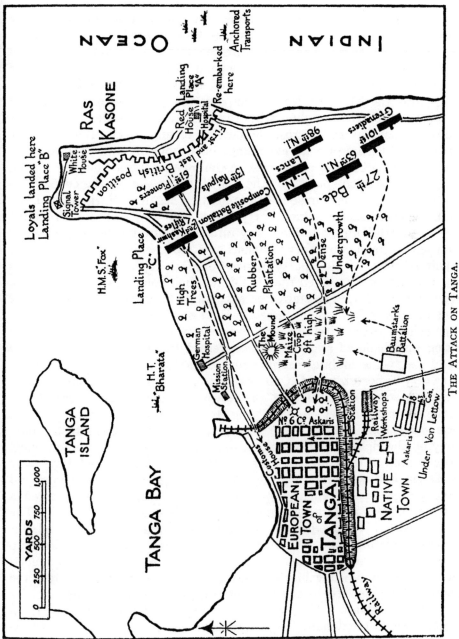

THE ATTACK ON TANGA.

4th November, 1914.
12.0 Noon.

87

in the houses. The Maxim-guns came into action and beat down the fire of such hostile machine-guns as could be located, and under their cover the Loyal North Lancashire pressed forward towards a collection of huts on a higher piece of ground beyond which the sheer sides of the railway cutting, thirty feet deep, stretched across the front of the advance. By this time the whole of No. 3 Company was extended on the right of Nos. 2 and 4, partly mingling with the 3rd Kashmir Rifles, and in this formation a rush was made across the cutting to some open ground, on the far side of which lay a road encircling the European town of Tanga. A number of casualties were sustained as the men emerged from the cutting and crossed the open space, but the line still swept on to the edge of the town, where street and house-to-house fighting began. On the right Lieutenant Anderson and a mixed party of his men and Gurkhas (from the Composite Battalion) made their way into some outlying houses, accounting for one German, a number of Askari and one machine-gun in the course of their search; of this party Lance-Corporal Taylor (killed), Privates Allen and Ridgway received the D.C.M. for their conduct on this occasion. Windows, doors and even staircases were found barricaded and the shower of bullets from rifles and machine-guns did not lessen, hostile fire seemed to come from every direction and from every level, for each corner and crossing was disputed and the houses were defended sometimes by three tiers of fire, while mobile machine-guns darted about the streets and let fly at every opportunity. On the extreme right the 2nd Kashmir Rifles penetrated some distance into the town, capturing the Kaiser Hotel and the German flag which was flying from it. Further inland, platoons of the 3rd Kashmir Rifles made some progress through the streets immediately on the right of the Battalion, some of the 13th Rajputs following.

By 4 p.m. three companies of the Battalion had forced their way into Tanga and were making slow headway against the tenacious and elusive groups of the enemy opposed to them; they had captured a number of houses and had secured a large open space, known as "The Square," with a revetted earth platform, of unknown use, called, for the sake of distinction, "The Barricade." As No. 3 Company drew up to the Barricade Lieutenant Hickson was hit in the arm and pulled under the lee of it while his wound was dressed, but unfortunately the supposed shelter proved to be enfiladed, and the stretcher-bearer who was dressing him (Private Smith) was wounded; then, before either of them could be moved, Lieutenant Hickson was hit again in the chest—this time fatally. Beyond the Square and among the houses, the companies became rather broken up and each platoon or section selected an immediate objective for its attention.

In the meantime, No. 1 Company (Major H. A. Robinson) had come up on the left and made good a position between the cutting and the Town, but owing to the heavy fire from the Workshops and Baumstark's Battalion, was unable to advance further.

When the 6th Askari Company was driven in from the east of the Town and the three companies of the Battalion with the Kashmir Rifles on their right were making good their position there, Captain von Prince (who was killed during the afternoon) reinforced the Askari company with two companies of Europeans, who brought heavy fire to bear down the streets of the Town.

Shortly afterwards (about 4.30 p.m.) General von Lettow-Vorbeck " considered the pressure on his front so strong that he could not delay the decision any longer and that he must make a counter-stroke." This he did with the 13th Company and with Baumstark's Battalion.

This counter-attack was directed against the 101st Grenadiers who had already suffered severely from heavy rifle and machine-gun fire from the Railway Workshops. They were taken in flank, fought gallantly, but were almost annihilated.

In the German accounts of the action, this counter-attack is invariably spoken of as being against the whole British line—this is not so, as the Loyal North Lancashire were in the Town at the time and realized that the counter-attack was being made.

The company commanders in Tanga were now faced with a very difficult situation. The heavy firing of the enemy's counter-attack indicated that the enemy was getting round behind them, so that not only were they heavily engaged but it appeared that they would be cut off. The company commanders discussed the situation and decided that it was expedient to withdraw to the east of the cutting, and orders were issued to this effect. Colonel Jourdain had moved up Battalion Headquarters to a point on the east side of the cutting, but owing to the open ground between the east of the Town and the cutting, communication was very difficult. In the words of the G.O.C.'s report: " The Loyal North Lancashire in the town, being unsupported (there were no troops available for effective support), had to retire across the railway into the fringe of the woods."

In the close fighting to which the Battalion was committed there was a strong probability of heavy losses in an attempt to disengage, and this probability was, unfortunately, fulfilled. It fell back to the edge of the Town, where a stand was made for some little time to collect the scattered parties. It was in re-crossing this open space and the railway cutting beyond that the Battalion suffered many of its casualties, for the enemy followed up at close range and had several machine-guns trained on the retirement. In reply the Battalion could bring but one machine-gun into action, for the other had broken both locks during the day and now lay abandoned in the railway cutting ; but Lieutenant J. F. B. Watson did most excellent work with the remaining gun on the left flank, covering the retirement of the Battalion as he had covered its advance.

There were certain landmarks, like the footbridge over the cutting and the water steps down the face of it, upon which the hostile machine-guns had ranged and it was under a very heavy cross-fire directed upon these and sweeping the whole face of the cutting, that the Battalion regained comparative shelter. During the crossing of the open space to the cutting Major Braithwaite was killed and Captain Halton was wounded. Second-Lieutenant G. G. R. Williams received a wound in the head which rendered him insensible, and he was taken prisoner.

When the companies arrived on the east of the cutting they were directed to the position selected for them by Major W. D. Sanderson ; this position faced in a south-westerly direction with the right near the Mound with three companies in line and one company echeloned behind the left company. Command of Nos. 2 and 4 Companies had now, owing to casualties, been taken over by Captain R. E. Berkeley and Lieutenant C. G. Dickson.

By 5.30 p.m. the new position had been taken up and Colonel Jourdain went over to where General Aitken and his staff were standing by a knoll, and explained the situation briefly. Here the machine-guns of the 61st Pioneers were put in position, together with one from the 13th Rajputs and one belonging to the 63rd Native Infantry (worked by two men of the Battalion). The position of General Aitken's force at 5.30 p.m. was, according to his report, as follows : On the right the Kashmir Rifles held the railway cutting and some houses on the edge of the town nearest the Jetty ; on their left were three companies of Rajputs, a party of the Loyal North Lancashire and a double company of the 61st with the greater part of the officers of that regiment. The line then curved round to the knoll near which were the Maxims of the 13th and 61st, and was continued southward by the Loyal North Lancashire. In continuation of this line there were no troops, as the 101st were practically out of action owing to casualties and the 63rd Palamcottah L.I. and the 98th had retired. The General Reserve (61st Pioneers), as stated above, had a double company and machine-gun section in the line.

About 5.30 p.m. the last reinforcement destined to reach the enemy that day appeared on the field—the 4th Company of Askari from Moshi. General von Lettow-Vorbeck at once sent it in the wake of his previous counter-attack, but instead of following the line intended, it cut in to the left of the 13th Company and passing rather across the front of the new line of resistance, was brought to a standstill by the Battalion in the above position.   During this counter-attack Lieutenant C. G. Dickson was killed. This was the enemy's final effort ; soon afterwards bugles rang out all down his line and all but desultory firing ceased.   By one of the strange accidents of war an impression prevailed on the German side that, on the conclusion of the action, the scattered companies were to return to their camp several miles west of Tanga.   This they did, and it was well into the night before their commander discovered the misunderstanding which had arisen !   At the same time, there is a strong probability that disorganization by casualties and loss of touch, together with the decisive repulse of the last counter-attack, quickened the inclination of the subordinate commanders to obey the supposed order.

Although the new position was firmly established, there was no water in the area held.   The G.O.C. therefore decided to retire to another line in the neighbourhood of the German Hospital, which was the only place between Ras Kasone and the town where water was to be found, with a view to renewing the attack in the morning.   However, later and more disconcerting reports compelled him to abandon the idea, and General Aitken decided to re-embark his force next day and issued orders to General Tighe, who had been left in charge of the line around the German Hospital. to withdraw his command to the Ras Kasone position.

The Battalion heard of the proposed withdrawal from the position in front of Tanga with dismay, and it was not until written orders reached Colonel Jourdain about 6 p.m. that the truth was realized.   In the sudden dusk of a tropical evening the retirement was organized, and Colonel Jourdain issued orders to each company to move away by the road leading towards the German Hospital and the seashore.   The Battalion reached the new line and started to dig in ; but soon after 10 p.m. a further retirement was ordered and the men finally reached the trenches from which they had started that morning at 11.30 p.m., after thirteen hours of hard marching and fighting.   In spite of exhaustion and lack of food, the Battalion at once began to improve the trenches, working till 2.30 a.m.   Two hours of uneasy rest followed, after which all in the line resumed work to strengthen the position.

Early on the 5th the defensive line covered Beaches " A " and " B." The North Lancashire trench ran like the arc of a circle about the former, falling back to the seashore about five hundred yards north and one hundred yards south ;   on the northern (right) flank it joined a trench line which intersected it at an obtuse angle, so placing the holders—the Kashmir Rifles—in a good position either to enfilade an attack on the Battalion front, or to counter-attack with advantage.   The line terminated at the

Signal Tower over Landing Place " B." The re-embarkation was to take place from Beach " A," which was entirely concealed from view of the enemy, and was to be covered by the Loyal North Lancashire, the Kashmir Rifles, except for the Loyal North Lancashire, being the last unit to embark. About 8 a.m. Colonel Jourdain was sent for by the G.O.C., who thanked him for the work of the Battalion and said they had done magnificently, and gave orders for covering the evacuation. After the Battalion had taken over the whole sector allotted, parts of which had been held by Indian infantry during the night, the commanding officer went round and explained the situation to each company in turn. The arrangement was that when all other units had embarked, the withdrawal should be by half companies, the last to retire to be the scouts and the machine-guns, who were to hold on as long as possible to give time to gain the boats. In the whole line there were nine machine-guns, two on the left flank, and seven on the right flank under Lieutenant Watson. At 11.30 a.m. one of the transports signalled a report that the enemy was advancing in force along the shore on the left flank. No. 2 Company was sent out to reconnoitre for half a mile, but found the report to be incorrect. At the same time the flank was reinforced by two companies of the Kashmir Rifles as a precaution.

Thanks to the admirable arrangements made by the Senior Naval Officer, the embarkation proceeded with extraordinary rapidity and smoothness. Six tugs were sent in to the Reef, each having a lighter lashed on either beam and another towing astern. These tugs and their lighters lay just clear of the Coral Reef, while ships' boats worked as far as they could over the shallow intervening lagoon, conveying parties of men to them. As each lighter was filled it was towed to the seaward side of its particular transport so that the re-embarkation of the troops should be screened from view, and possibly from fire. The operation began at dead-low water, 12 noon, and was completed just after 4 p.m. The first to be taken off were some coolies, with the 61st and the 63rd ; then the rest of the coolies, the 98th and the 101st ; then the 13th and Headquarter details ; next the Composite Battalion ; the 2nd Kashmir Rifles and lastly the Loyal North Lancashire. A regrettable feature of the operation was that the muddy, slippery nature of the foreshore made it impossible to carry off any bulky loads ; for this reason orders were issued to abandon considerable quantities of ammunition, stores and heavy kits.

Except for the badly wounded cases left in the German Hospital and at the Red House, the whole of Force " B " was now re-embarked, the transports remaining at their anchorages while a staff officer was sent on shore to negotiate arrangements for removing the wounded. A convention was concluded the same evening, whereby it was agreed that those

TANGA   RE-EMBARKATION   OF   INDIAN TROOPS

5th November, 1914.

who would give parole and were fit to be moved should be taken off on the 6th.   To assist the wounded a party of two hundred of the North Lancashire was sent shoreward, unarmed, about 3 p.m., in the charge of Lieutenant and Quartermaster R. Rowley, who had been informed that permission had been given to search the battlefield for wounded and missing combatants ;   but by some misunderstanding it was not allowed to land. Cooped up in a lighter and cast off by the tug, this party was left to drift about aimlessly all the afternoon in the harbour.   About 5 p.m. warning was received that guns had arrived in Tanga and were being mounted on shore to shell the transports, upon which the ships were ordered to weigh anchor and get out of range.   The lighter of " Lancashire " men seems to have been forgotten ;   and was left behind at the mercy of the wind and tide ;   fortunately these were kind, and bore it towards Mansa Bay, off which the convoy was reassembling ;   and there, in the small hours of the morning, it was picked up and brought back to the " Karmala " to rejoin the rest of the Battalion, after being adrift for fourteen hours, without food or water.

In the course of the three days the Battalion lost four officers killed— Major F. J. Braithwaite, Captain C. A. T. Conyngham (R.A.M.C., attached), Lieutenant C. G. Dickson and 2nd Lieutenant S. V. Einem-Hickson ;   one wounded—Captain E. C. Halton ;   and one wounded and prisoner—2nd Lieutenant G. G. R. Williams.   Among the other ranks 26 were killed, 62 wounded, and 22 missing, 18 of whom were wounded—116 casualties for all ranks being the total.   The total losses of the Expeditionary Force, including the above, were 900 in killed, wounded and missing.

The following extracts from an officer's diary survey the situation during the voyage from Bombay to East Africa and the landing at Tanga.

" Previous to the landing at Tanga the Expeditionary Force was three weeks at sea, crossing the Indian Ocean by convoy, during which time the speed had to be kept down to 8 knots, which was the fastest that the slowest of the hired transports could steam.   There were several reasons which placed the attacking force in a particularly disadvantageous position. The enemy were prepared for, if not actually expecting, the Expeditionary Force to make an attack there, so the required element of surprise was entirely lacking.   The country over which the attacking force had to advance was very enclosed, which made reconnaissance more than usually imperative.   The attack on the 2nd inst. was held up before any information could be obtained, either with regard to the approach on Tanga or the position itself.   If the suggestion to blow up the railway line south of Moshi had been adopted, it would have been impossible for the troops in Tanga to have been reinforced by the additional companies and it was these companies that turned the scale at the critical moment. The task set the Indian units of the Expeditionary Force in the attack was a severe one for native troops, which in certain cases were not recruited from the best fighting races of the Indian Empire."

The following are extracts from a book, recently published, by General von Lettow-Vorbeck, on the East African campaign :—

" The enemy's advance through the sheltered bush was slow, it lasted three hours for the one and a half miles. The left brigade changed direction to the right and exposed its left flank more and more to the German front.

" The 101st behaved pluckily, attacking in places with the bayonet and the brave Lancs. and Kashmir Rifles set an example, in spite of heavy losses.

" Their northern flank in the Town was driven back, Captain von Prince attacked with a handful of whites against superior numbers and when he himself fell his example inspired both whites and natives to dogged determination in the bitter house-fighting.

" The south German flank began to give way—now the decision stood on the edge of a knife—it could only be handled on the moment.

" The German commander had only his last reserve—a single company ; the counter-attack took the 101st straight on their flank and the German machine-guns mowed down their ranks."

In a survey of the dispositions General von Lettow says :—

" On the left flank, where freedom of manœuvre exists, the troops fail. One looks in vain here, where undoubtedly the decision will come, for the best regiment. This, the Loyal North Lancs., one finds in the centre of the front of the Indian Regiments, so that the core of the force (diese Kerntruppe) has no freedom of movement."

The illustration facing page 92 shows the re-embarkation of the Indian troops from Beach " A " ; meanwhile the Loyal North Lancashire and a small party of Kashmir Rifles were holding the final trench, covering the re-embarkation.

After re-concentrating in Mansa Bay the convoy headed up for Mombasa, and about noon on 7th November the " Karmala " came into Kilindini. Later in the day some companies disembarked and then proceeded to unload baggage and stores. After a night spent in the Customs sheds the unloading was completed and early next morning the Battalion, less the machine-gun detachment and a few details, entrained for Nairobi, arriving there on the 9th after an uncomfortable journey, and marched straight into camp on the old parade ground of the King's African Rifles.

CHAPTER XXXVI

1914–1916

OPERATIONS IN EAST AFRICA

FOR a week the Battalion remained concentrated at Nairobi before being scattered over the country—which was its ultimate fate. During this time it was inspected by H.E. The Governor who, addressing the men, complimented the Battalion on its present turn-out and the example it had set ; he added : " I am informed that you conducted yourselves on a recent occasion with consummate bravery and exemplary discipline, under most trying conditions, and that you set an example of steadiness and pluck to some other units of the force who would appear to have been much in need of it. In short, you have most worthily sustained the best traditions of your Regiment and the prestige of the British Army, in the same way as your brothers-in-arms are at this time upholding it upon the Continent of Europe. It is quite apparent to me that you were placed at a disadvantage only on account of conditions which could not be foreseen, and that you only need a further opportunity to add to the credit which you have already earned."

After the inspection came a march through Nairobi, which was the cause of a display of considerable enthusiasm on the part of the inhabitants.

Major-General Aitken also addressed the officers on their return to camp ; in making some very appreciative remarks, he thanked them for what they had done and asked them to pass his thanks on to the men.

Then a few days' rest, to re-fit as far as possible. The lull was quite accidental and was undoubtedly due to the fact that G.H.Q. was uncertain what to do next, and was discussing the problem with " Higher Authority." The outcome of these cable deliberations was a decision that the British forces in East Africa were not strong enough for offensive operations, so that they must remain on the defensive until reinforcements could be sent, and meanwhile, no reinforcements were available ! Then, on 24th November, the War Office assumed control of operations in this theatre of war, but the policy remained unchanged. The crisis in France was too urgent —side-shows, however important, must wait.

On the 16th November, the Left Wing of the Battalion (Nos. 3 and 4

Companies) was detached from Headquarters, under Major Sanderson, and sent to Kajiado, thirty miles south of Nairobi, by train. Hence No. 3 Company (Captain Berkeley) was dispatched by march-route to Longido where it arrived on the 24th. The other officers with these companies were Lieutenants l'Anson, Watson and Anderson and 2nd Lieutenant Withers. Thus began the vigil so long kept there by one detachment or another from the Battalion; and it may be of interest to see how the spot struck one of our diarists, who spent some time there. He says:—

" Longido is about ten miles across the border in German East Africa and the geographical features of the camp are most remarkable. The system of hills called Longido stands up from perfectly level plain country (bush), and the camp itself is in the centre of a complete circle of hills. These hills are highest on the west side, where they are certainly two thousand feet above the camp itself. The perimeter of the circle of hills is from twenty-five to thirty miles. On arrival the country abounded with game; but by degrees, on account of shooting and the movement of troops, it afterwards became scarce and wild. Personally, I saw rhino, koodoo, zebra, kongoni, wildebeeste, giraffe, leopard, innumerable smaller antelope, such as Thompson's and Grant's gazelle, and plenty of tracks of elephant. Several lion were also reported. I shot two very good oryx, two lesser koodoo and some impala."

There had been an action at Longido on 3rd November, when a British force attacked the German detachment, which was holding the post, but without success. Subsequently, between 3rd and 23rd November, the German detachment at Longido was withdrawn to Engari Nairobi, some thirty miles to the eastward, as the communications with Longido were too uncertain.

The approach to the plateau was quite a formidable matter, for the road was so bad that kits had to be off-loaded at the entrance to Longido Nek and carried up to the camp by hand. The machine-gun detachment was also ordered to Longido and joined No. 3 en route. On arrival it transpired that the duty of the North Lancashire Regiment was to find a post of forty rifles on Sandback Kopje, a hill about twelve hundred feet higher than the camp, which formed the key to the whole position; and this post was mounted next day. Until the end of the year the story is simply one of ordinary reliefs of the garrison of Sandback Kopje, interspersed with extraordinary reliefs of sick officers and men, while the defences and living accommodation of the camp were steadily improved. It is believed that No. 3 Company was the only company of British regular infantry occupying German territory on Christmas Day, 1914, in any part of the world. And so the year closed on the 2nd Battalion, Loyal North Lancashire; Headquarters and the Right Wing being still at Nairobi.

During the month of December the following officers joined for duty: Captain Woodruffe, Royal Sussex Regiment, Captain Mintoff and 2nd Lieutenant Bowden, Yorkshire Regiment, and 2nd Lieutenant Almond on promotion from R.S.M.

Meanwhile the theatre of war had been split up into two commands, the North Lancashire being in the " Lake Area " under Brigadier-General Stewart; and General Tighe was advancing from Gazi into the Umba Valley, towards Jassin.

The first day of 1915 saw the introduction of the double-company system in the 2nd Battalion by Indian Army Orders; from the tactical point of view it had been working for some months, but it was now officially installed for all purposes.

On 4th January, No. 2 Company, under Major Bridges, was ordered up from Nairobi to Kisumu, on Lake Victoria, to take part in an attack on the German defended post at Sherati, also on the Lake, ten miles south of the frontier. Leaving Kisumu by steamer, a small force under Brigadier-General Stewart, of which No. 2 Company formed part, landed in the face of slight opposition, shelled the fort and occupied Sherati on the 8th, no casualties being suffered. At Sherati the company remained till 29th January, taking part in some minor expeditions and reconnaissances, and incurring no losses save from sickness; but these latter were considerable, for when the company arrived back at Nairobi on 1st February forty-six fever cases were sent straight to hospital.

In the meantime No. 4 Company was at Lone Hill and No. 3 still at Longido. The last-named had led a somewhat monotonous existence till the 27th of January, when part of it went out to support a reconnaissance made by Wilson's scouts towards Ol Molog, on the slopes of Kilimanjaro. The detachment was out two days and suffered much from thirst in an entirely waterless country; and in the end no contact was made with the enemy.

On the 18th January, No. 1 Company, under Major Robinson, received sudden orders to move from Nairobi to Mombasa, with two days' rations and full battle ammunition; and that evening it entrained —strength eight officers (including two regimental staff) and one hundred and ninety-nine other ranks. Jassin was heavily attacked; but by the time the company detrained at Mombasa the place had fallen.

General Tighe had been pushing down the Umba Valley, the German patrols falling back before him, until the British advanced troops occupied the post of Jassin, south of Vanga, on German soil. To the German commander-in-chief this was a serious menace, for such a force might filter slowly down the coast to Tanga, securing the country by means of block-houses, and cut the Usambara Railway; such a threat needed to be countered at once. The main British force was at Vanga, just on the British side of the border, with Jassin held by one battalion. Quietly von Lettow-Vorbeck concentrated nine companies (nominally 1,800 men) and two guns at a plantation seven miles to the south and on the morning of the 18th he fell upon the isolated battalion, which appears to have been unconscious of its impending danger. Surrounding Jassin with six companies, he interposed the remainder between that place and Vanga, to beat off any attempt at relief—and in this he was perfectly successful. For twenty-four hours a fierce battle raged, in which both sides nearly exhausted their ammunition and the Germans came within an ace of breaking off the engagement; but Jassin village had been lost by the British troops in the first attack and the water supply in the trenches was exhausted. Wherefore, after an abortive sortie on the morning of the 19th, Jassin surrendered. But the victory had been dearly bought, both in casualties and ammunition, and von Lettow-Vorbeck realized at once that further actions on a similar scale would exhaust his resources entirely. Perhaps, therefore, the defence of Jassin was not entirely in vain.

Naturally, the narrow margin by which the enemy had carried off his victory was unknown to General Tighe, who became anxious as to the safety of his main body. To strengthen him, No. 1 Company of the Loyal North Lancashire was sent down to Vanga, where it arrived at Umba Camp on the 21st January; while No. 4 Company, with "Logan's Battery," was afterwards brought down to Kilindini (26th January) in case further reinforcement should be needed. However, the evacuation of Vanga had been ordered in the meantime, so No. 4 was not sent there. No. 1 moved into the entrenched camp at M'goa—a most unhealthy place, reeking with fever, on the 22nd January, where Major Robinson had the command of a reserve force consisting of his own double-company, some of the 101st Grenadiers, and some companies of the Kashmir Rifles and some machine-gun Volunteers. Here it remained till Vanga was evacuated on the 9th of February, chiefly engaged in patrol and reconnaissance work, in the course of which a number of German Askaris were accounted for, and 2nd Lieutenant Grove particularly distinguished himself. Sniping was continuous and some men were wounded, but the serious feature of this phase was the speed at which fever began to appear in the ranks; by the end of a fortnight twenty-five per cent. of the men were sick. Therefore, it was with much relief that No. 1 Company re-embarked for Mombasa on the 8th of the month, finally arriving back at Nairobi on the 12th.

Thirty-five malarial cases went to hospital next day; Vanga had taken its toll.

To revert for a moment to No. 4. This company had been ordered in from Lone Hill on 21st January and left the position at 4 p.m. on that afternoon. At 9 a.m. on the 24th it marched into Kajiado, having covered fifty-five miles in sixty-five hours, a very good performance, considering that the march was not a forced one. The company entrained at once for Nairobi, where it was to re-fit; but next day, in the very midst of the process, was suddenly ordered down to Mombasa, as previously related. There it remained till 3rd February, when it returned to Nairobi, bringing " Logan's Battery."

The beginning of March found the Battalion more or less reunited at Nairobi, except for No. 3 Company, which was still on the Longido line, and half of No. 4, which had been sent to Kiu to disarm some disaffected Somali levies; but this condition was not to last. Sickness of a peculiar nature had broken out at Longido whence, on the 3rd of March, Captain Berkeley reported thirty cases of beriberi in his command. The medical authorities recommended a move, so No. 2 Company and the remainder of No. 4 were ordered out in relief. No. 3 received orders to leave Longido on the evening of 5th March, and marched next morning to Namanga. Here, in spite of the orders for relief, it was kept for a week to find various posts; and here also, on the 13th, No. 2 arrived, the companies spending the day together. On the 14th No. 2 marched out for Longido and on the 15th, at 4 a.m., No. 3 started on its trek to railhead, marching by El Olokenoni and Bissel to Kajiado, where it arrived at 6.30 a.m. on the 19th: Here it was detained for a day on account of a report of a German raid on Longido which had taken place on the morning of the 15th; but on the arrival of General Stewart next morning it was ordered to hand over its tents and ammunition to the Rhodesian Regiment and to go on to Nairobi. There it ultimately arrived late on the 20th. The German raid on Longido took place between the departure of No. 3 Company and the arrival there of No. 2; but no mention of it is made in the war diary, which explicitly states that No. 2 took over at Longido on 16th March.

The Field State of the 2nd Battalion in East Africa is given, on the 8th of March, 1915, at 31 officers and 870 other ranks, of which approximately 150 were in hospital; a return made a week later shows that, in addition to the " admitted " cases, 100 men were attending hospital for quinine daily. The state of health of the Battalion was giving rise to anxiety; in fact, the C.O. was compelled to write to India for mosquito curtains as they seemed to be unobtainable locally.

New moves were shortly to scatter the companies again. On the 9th of March the machine-gun section went to Lone Hill and on the 12th No. 1 Company (strength 4 officers and 101 other ranks), under Lieutenant Atkinson, left Nairobi for Lake Victoria.   Going to Kisumu, it joined " Logan's Battery " aboard H.M.S. " Usoga," and, a company of the 4th King's African Rifles embarking at the same time in the " Winifred," the flotilla set sail for Karungu, arriving there on the night of the 15th.   Next morning the force was ordered to go on to Sherati, some twenty miles further down the coast and ten miles south of the German border ; sailing again at midday it landed at the latter place the same night, to find a small party of Ross's Scouts already in possession.   Although Sherati did not yield much in the way of booty, a most welcome acquisition was that of some German maps of the Colony, which were unearthed by Lieutenant Atkinson ; they ultimately proved most useful.   Guided by Ross's Scouts, the combined column left Sherati at 1 p.m. on the 17th and camped at Ukina the same night.   Next day touch was gained with Colonel Hickson's column, but movement was handicapped by shortage of rations and forage, also by heavy rain.   However, a further advance was made towards the south-east until, on the 20th, the communications of the force were endangered by the rising of the Mori River as a result of the continuous rain. No contact with the enemy having been made, it was decided to return ; Ukina Camp was reached once more on 22nd March and Sherati on the 23rd.   Next day Sherati was evacuated.   Part of the force went to Karungu ; but No. 1 Company took ship again for Kisumu, where it entrained for Nairobi, rejoining Battalion Headquarters on 26th March with the remarkable report of " no sick."

In the meantime there had been two minor events of interest in the life of the Battalion at Nairobi.   On 22nd March 2nd Lieutenant Parker with twenty-nine men and mules left for Kiu to form part of a mounted infantry company which was there being constituted.   This " M.I." Troop of the Battalion ultimately grew until it became a Mounted Infantry Company with a separate existence, but whose history and movements were intimately related to those of the Battalion ; its story will be told in due course.   The other incident was the arrival from India of a draft of forty-three men from the Depot at Bangalore.   Finally, the monsoon burst on the 28th of the month with a force sufficient to get itself " noted " in the war diary.

April was for the most part a quiet month.   Two outlying detachments came in during the early days : part of No. 4 Company from Kiu on the 6th and No. 2 from Longido on the 11th.   On the 12th, Major-General Wapshare inspected the Battalion, then at full strength, except for sick and the M.I. detachment, prior to his departure for the Persian Gulf.

LONGIDO.

1915.

Expressing his pleasure at the appearance of the Battalion and at its good behaviour and soldier-like conduct while under his command, he wished it success and bade all farewell. The command of the up-country district then devolved upon General Tighe, General Malleson taking over the coastal area.

For the first three weeks of April the Battalion remained at Nairobi, improving quarters, making roads in the cantonments and carrying out company training; then, on the 19th, orders for further moves were received.

In accordance with these No. 3 Company (Captain Berkeley) and No. 4 (Captain Woodruffe), total strength eleven officers, 293 other ranks and 19 followers, together with a Volunteer machine-gun detachment and a section of a mountain battery, left Nairobi on the 20th April for the Lake District. Arriving at Kisumu next day, they were embarked in lake steamers for Karungu, where they arrived on the night of the 22nd and disembarked next morning, encamping on the Karungu promontory. The O.C. Lake Area—Colonel Hickson—was stationed there, the 98th Indian Infantry and some King's African Rifles forming the garrison. Two detachments were sent out in the course of the next few days—Captain Watson and thirty-seven men going to reinforce the post of Nyesuku, some twenty miles up-country; while 2nd Lieutenant Bowden and a platoon of No. 3 went to form a post at Kuja Ferry, on the Gori River, fourteen miles to the south.

It was during the stay of these companies at Karungu that the " Sybil " incident took place. One morning early in October, the " Sybil " was proceeding in the neighbourhood of Majita, in the south-east corner of Lake Victoria and well within German territorial waters, and during this particular trip the navigator elected to take her through a channel which was notoriously dangerous, but which provided a short cut. Like many another short cut, this one ultimately proved to be the longest way round, for in the middle the ship hit something so hard and unpleasant that she had to be beached at once to save her from going down into deep waters. The ship's company got away and, on his return to Karungu, the skipper excused himself with the statement that the " Sybil " had been mined by the enemy.

On this account an officer was sent to investigate the circumstances. His report is laconic; he wired " Sybil holed by an unexpected mine laid by the Almighty about 4000 B.C." Subsequently it was reported that the ship could be salved, and there was no doubt but that she was worth the trouble. Early in November the Germans at Muanza sent an expedition to seize the wreck—they were terribly short of steamers—but could not get her off ; failing to do so, they looted everything portable and left her hard and fast ashore.   Nevertheless a repairable hull and a perfectly good set of engines remained ; and when the detachment of the North Lancashire came to Karungu the O.C. Lake Area decided to make an attempt to salve her.

Wherefore, on 11th May, seven officers and one hundred and fifty men of the North Lancashire, one hundred King's African Rifles, a 12-pounder of "Logan's Battery" and a machine-gun under Captain Berkeley, together with a salvage party, set forth from Karungu in three steamers to attempt to recover the remains of the " Sybil."   Arriving off Majita next morning, an unopposed landing was effected some two miles from the scene of the wreck, after which the force moved inland to clear a range of three rocky kopjes.   These were found to be held by a German force whose strength was ultimately ascertained to be three " Whites " and thirty Askaris ; but after a half-hearted resistance the enemy evacuated the kopjes and retired into the interior before any encircling movement could be attempted, leaving behind one dead and one wounded Askari, who was made a prisoner. All was over by noon, at which hour the force took up a position to cover salvage operations ; the three kopjes were held—one by Lieutenant Kerr's platoon, one by Lieutenant Almond's platoon and one by a platoon of the King's African Rifles—while the remainder of the force took up an outpost position to cover the actual salvage operations.   Next day the 12-pounder gun and the machine-gun were landed to strengthen the position.   The salvage was a slow process, and it was not until noon on the 16th that the wreck was floated off and towed in triumph to Irungwa Island, some four miles away, to be made fit to return to Karungu.   The covering force was also withdrawn to the island.   Of this expedition an officer records :—

" We spent three of the worst nights at Majita it has ever been my misfortune to spend.   About midnight it would pour with rain and after an hour of it we would be attacked by thousands of mosquitoes.   Every officer and man was down with fever within sixteen days of their arrival on the Victoria Nyanza.   The rain by night, mosquitoes and the great heat by day, contributed to make things very unpleasant at Majita."

On the night of the 18th the expedition re-embarked for Karungu, the " Sybil " being now thoroughly dry and seaworthy ; but as the convoy was approaching Karungu on the 19th, the O.C. Lake sent urgent word by heliograph for the North Lancashire to land as soon as possible, as he had received word of a large German force near the border, towards Buda, and was moving immediately up to Marotchi ; so they hardly set foot in Karungu again before they were out of it.   The detachment was rushed

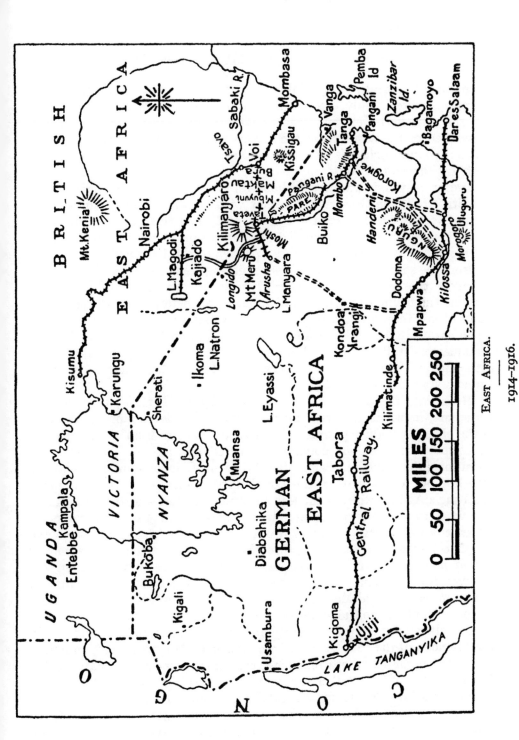

EAST AFRICA.
1914–1916.

103

up-country to Errah, to a point about mid-way between Marotchi and Nyesuku, where it duly arrived in position by the evening of the 21st ; but the expected German attack never developed, as the enemy was forewarned of the strength of the troops awaiting him by the treachery of a native, and held off.   The Battalion returned to Nyesuku, remaining there till the end of May.

Life at Karungu was not without its compensations and lighter side. On 28th April, the Governor, together with Generals Tighe and Stewart, visited Karungu to inspect the camp ; and upon this occasion an officer of the headquarters staff recorded his impression of the place : " Every-one seemed very cheerful in camp ; parties of the Lancashires were fish-ing from the shore, whilst others were shooting geese, hippos and crocodiles. At night the monotony is varied by hippos strolling into the camp. Imagine the feelings of a mule which has never before in its life seen any-thing bigger than an Abottabad bullock, waking up to find an enormous hippo eating its hay ! "   Incidentally, it was upon this occasion that the headquarters staff made a preliminary reconnaissance of Bukoba, a pretty little port and settlement on the west side of the Lake, where the German wireless station was situated.

Meanwhile the M.I. Company, under Captain Berkeley-Cole, was at Katetema, in which direction much activity was developing on the part of the enemy's raiding patrols.   To clear the raiders from the Simba and Katetema area a mobile column was fitted out for one week's special operations, the command being given to Lieut.-Colonel Jourdain, who had with him No. 1 Company of the Loyal North Lancashire, " D " Company 3rd King's African Rifles, some M.I., machine-gunners and the 27th Moun-tain Battery ; in all approximately 20 officers and 560 other ranks, of whom 200 were mounted troops, exclusive of signal, field ambulance and supply columns.   On 10th May, this column concentrated at Simba, moved out at noon and arrived at Katetema at 5 p.m.   Here information was received from headquarters to the effect that other columns were moving out from Maktau and Mazima on the 11th to join in sweeping operations of considerable magnitude ; but the very first day the Simba column was in difficulties with the water supply and the plans had to be changed.   In the forenoon of the 12th the column marched to Muguri River (ten miles), where the mounted troops remained, the infantry moving on later in the day to Hill 419.B.—another seven miles ; on this same day the Maktau column was intended to attack Salaita Hill and the Mazima column to move on Kiulikoni.   After waiting for a day while nothing happened, the Simba column moved to attack the German camp known to be situated on Loosoito Hill.   After a night march—in the course of which the Masai guides got lost—it approached the hill about 5 a.m. on the 14th, only to find that the enemy had evacuated the place. Straightway the Simba column turned about and marched back to camp at Lemeboti Hill, where it arrived about 5 p.m., the infantry having done thirty-six miles in twenty-two and a half hours, while the guns and mounted troops had covered considerably more. Next day the column returned to Katetema, ultimately reaching Nairobi on the 18th. On the 20th, Headquarters issued a complimentary order congratulating the troops on their keenness, good spirit and good marching; at the same time regret was expressed that the information regarding the enemy was "stale."

The May returns show the strength of the Battalion in East Africa at thirty-one officers, 885 other ranks, four machine-guns and two 3-pounder Hotchkiss guns; of the above total, fourteen officers and 327 men were at Nairobi on 3rd May. It is further recorded that on 5th May, two 15-pounder guns were handed over to "Logan's Battery" by the Calcutta Battery in place of the 3-pounder Hotchkiss.

To close the month of May it remains just to trace out the movements of the Marotchi detachment during the last few days. After its return there on the 23rd the men began to develop fever in large numbers, as a result of their exposure in the pestilential swamps around Majita; so that when another move was ordered on the 28th, only ninety men out of two double companies were fit to march. Information had been received that an enemy force was in the neighbourhood of Mobachi and the detachment was sent out to endeavour to round it up. Moving from Nyesuku about midnight on the 27th–28th it reached Mobachi about 4 a.m. on the 28th, whence, when day dawned, enemy movements were noticed on the slopes of Geribi Hill. The party hid all day in the long grass, hoping to have laid the foe an ambush; but hour after hour passed and nothing happened. Ultimately, about 10 a.m. the enemy moved, but the fact was observed too late to give any hope of cutting him off; and all that could be done was to follow up and occupy Geribi, where all ranks spent a most uncomfortable night in the pouring rain. Next day, after a further search of the hill, the detachment returned to Nyesuku. The men had suffered severely from exposure and cold and now seemed so pulled down as to be unable to keep up any sustained period of hard work; particularly did this apply to those who had been at Majita.

From the latter end of 1914 until the summer of 1915 the Germans had exercised continuous pressure on the Uganda Border, and Major-General Tighe decided early in June to relieve the situation by destroying the enemy's base. This was the port of Bukoba, on the western shore of Lake Victoria Nyanza and about twenty-five miles south of the British frontier. Here the Germans had a fort and had accumulated warlike stores of all kinds. General Tighe arranged for a simultaneous advance on two sides—one column starting from the Kagera River, while the main body, under the command of Brigadier-General Stewart, was to move across the lake.

Brigadier-General Stewart's force was made up of the 2nd Loyal North Lancashire, the 29th Punjabis, the 3rd King's African Rifles, detachments of the Royal Fusiliers, a machine-gun company and other details.

From headquarters at Nairobi this force journeyed by rail to Kisumu, 237 miles, and on 20th June embarked there on steamers on a voyage of 240 miles to Bukoba, and the following extracts from the official report give an account of the action which followed : " The bulk of our forces, including our mountain guns, were landed about three miles north of Bukoba at dawn on the 22nd June, a hostile picquet being surprised and driven off. At daybreak the fight was opened by the enemy making an attack on our right centre, closely supported by machine-guns, which gave us considerable trouble in the dense banana plantations, till our guns finally located and silenced theirs. All was ready for a final advance, when a drenching rainstorm held us up till 9.15 a.m.

" About 11 a.m. the enemy attempted to withdraw their guns, but a direct hit from one of our mountain guns forced them to abandon the attempt, and the gun lay at our mercy on the road south of Bukoba, whence we recovered it and brought it aboard our convoy. By 12.30 p.m. our right had made progress and the enemy commenced to retire. The Loyal North Lancashire, who had made a wide detour, entered the town from the west, and the enemy, by now thoroughly demoralized, broke and fled in a disorganized rabble and were not seen again.

" The British casualties were ten men killed, two officers and twenty-five men wounded ; and we destroyed or captured one machine-gun, two field-guns, thirty-two thousand rounds of small-arm ammunition, one motor-launch, three small boats and a quantity of explosives. As it was not our intention to hold Bukoba, re-embarkation commenced at 6 p.m. on 23rd June and was complete by 2 a.m. on the 24th when the Battalion returned to Nairobi."

In these operations the Battalion had one man killed and six wounded.

The following is Colonel Jourdain's account of these operations taken —and to some small extent abridged—from the Battalion War Diary :

" It was 11.50 a.m. on the 22nd June when Lieut.-Colonel Jourdain left the ship. No. 1 Company, under Captain Stokes, had reached the heights above where Colonel Driscoll was at about 10 a.m., and had been

ordered to cover Colonel Driscoll's right flank. When Colonel Jourdain
met Colonel Driscoll and his staff officer on the top of the hill an attack
in small detachments had begun and the two guns had opened fire, while
a report had come in that some Germans were moving round the right flank
of Captain Stokes' company.

"About 1 p.m. the 29th Punjabis began to arrive on the top of the
Kanwazi Hill, while Brigadier-General Stewart had also come up and
assumed command; he now directed Colonel C. E. A. Jourdain to attack the
high ground across the valley, known as Arab Ridge, with the remainder
of his own Battalion—one and a half companies—and be responsible for
the security of the northern flank. General Stewart had already sent two
platoons of No. 2 Company of the Battalion to support the attack of the
25th Bn. Royal Fusiliers. Shortly afterwards—about 2.30 p.m.—Major
Bridges arrived with two more platoons of No. 2 Company, and was sent
off in support of No. 1, leaving a weak platoon of No. 4 and a machine-
gun to watch the northern flank. Captain Stokes had in the meantime
made good progress under a brisk fire from rifles and machine-guns posted
on the heights above him, while he had experienced some difficulty in crossing the boggy stream at the bottom of the valley. On being joined by
Major Bridges, the two continued to move forward, using their machine-
guns with good effect.

"By 4.30 p.m. No. 1 and the half of No. 2 Companies was nearly at
the top of Arab Ridge, where they outflanked the main enemy position;
but as ammunition was now running rather short, Captain Woodruffe was
sent back to bring some up from the ship, while Colonel Jourdain proceeded
to the ground overlooking the landing-place with a view to arranging for
night outposts; on return, he found that General Stewart had ordered
all the troops to move forward to Fusilier Knoll, and that the advance
had been led by two platoons of the Battalion under Lieutenants Keays
and Leeb. By the same time Major Bridges had gained the top of Arab
Ridge and had moved south-east to join Captain Stokes, the enemy finally
evacuating the ridge about 5 p.m.

"This ended the operations for the day, but firing was kept up all
night, so that little sleep could be obtained.

"The occupation of the whole of this ridge was practically entirely due
to the outflanking of the German positions by Nos. 1 and 2 Companies
of the Battalion, and the frontal advance of two platoons of No. 2, while
the mountain guns also did good work in covering the advance of the 25th
Bn. Royal Fusiliers.

"Early in the morning of the 23rd ammunition was taken up to Major
Bridges, under fire from a German Maxim and snipers.

" Colonel Jourdain had been ordered to advance on the Protestant Mission House, which was flying the Red Cross Flag, but where a German gun was in action, and to hold the high ground on the right, while the 25th Royal Fusiliers advanced through the town.   On relief on Arab Ridge by some of the King's African Rifles, orders were given for the advance down the spur running roughly south-west and ending in a stony kopje, and, when the advance commenced, the enemy opened fire with Maxims and rifles.   No. 1 Company was on the right and No. 2 on the left, while one platoon of No. 4 Company was in reserve.   The spur, however, was found to consist of a succession of three steep scarps, of which the first was unclimbable except at the sides.   One of the Battalion Maxims got into position at the edge of the first scarp, but could get no further.   The enemy here seemed to number 30–40 rifles with one or two machine-guns, the latter being especially well handled and opened fire immediately any of our men appeared in sight.

" A very heavy rain-storm now came on, lasting for about an hour, the advance being then continued over difficult ground.

" The scouts reached the foot of Rocky Kopje just as a German machine-gun was seen being removed ; the enemy was evidently preparing to withdraw and a company of the 29th Punjabis arriving as a reinforcement, the whole force now advanced on the Mission House, leaving a small party of Punjabis and a Battalion Maxim on the kopje.   The first ridge was seized and held by the 29th while the North Lancashire pushed on ;   a couple of shells falling near them as they closed on the Mission House.

" The first point to seize was the bridge over the Kanoni River, and this was ordered to be rushed by successive platoons under the command of Captain Woodruffe.   The advance was made through some deserted villages on the far side of which two of the Battalion Maxims came into action, accounting for some of the German white troops who were falling back over the hill to the north of the Mission.   Two platoons were then hurried over the Kanoni Bridge and directed to assault the hills and there establish themselves.   The enemy snipers still maintained an intermittent fire, but about 2 p.m., after a steep climb, several platoons were in position and communication was then established with the Signal Station on Gun Spur, while a German gun fell into the hands of the North Lancashire and was wheeled away to the rear.

" About 7 p.m. orders received to re-embark at 5.30 next morning.

" 24th.   After the last of the 25th Bn. Royal Fusiliers had left, the North Lancashire began to re-embark about 6 a.m., outposts being withdrawn, and all were in boats or aboard the ' Rosinga ' by 7.30."

The stay here was only a brief one, for on the 3rd July the Battalion left by train for Maktau, which was reached on the 5th; on the 8th Headquarters with Nos. 2 and 4 Companies—strength nine officers and 246 non-commissioned officers and men—proceeded by train to Bura, leaving Major H. A. Robinson at Maktau in command of No. 1 and part of No. 3 Companies; from both these stations small posts were established along the railway line to keep German raiders in check. On the 13th a larger affair took place. Major Robinson, with twelve officers and two hundred of the Battalion, being sent out from Maktau as part of a force commanded by Brigadier-General Malleson, which was to make an attack on Mbuyuni, but the enemy was found to be in greater strength than had been reported, and General Malleson's force had to fall back. The Battalion covered the retirement and had a sergeant, a corporal and six men wounded.

On the 14th August a draft of seventy non-commissioned officers and men joined the Battalion from India by the hired transport "Tabora"; and on the last day of this month a further draft joined—this one from England—composed of two officers—Captain J. S. Gaskell and 2nd Lieutenant J. G. W. Hyndson—and one hundred and ten other ranks.

On the 3rd September the Mounted Infantry Company, containing men of the Battalion and commanded by Captain Woodruffe, Royal Sussex Regiment, attached, was engaged with the enemy some five miles distant from Maktau; an account of this affair will be found in Chapter XXXVII.

About 4 p.m. local scouts reported that a strong party of Germans had reached a point about eight or nine miles south of Bura at about 2 p.m. Two platoons of No. 3 Company, under Captain Berkeley, were ordered at 5 p.m. to take up positions on, and to reconnoitre, both banks of the Bura River on the following morning.

29th September. At 5 a.m. Captain Stokes and party left by armoured train for a "point some three miles on the railway towards Maktau, at Mile 26–27. The armoured train returned to Bura and the party took up a position near the railway; they were heavily attacked by a strong force of the enemy about 6.10 a.m., and Captain Stokes was killed. One platoon of No. 3 Company, under Lieutenant O. E. Almond, hearing the firing, moved in that direction, and in the thick bush ran into the retreating enemy. A fierce hand-to-hand encounter took place. Casualties were very heavy on both sides. German casualties were subsequently reported to have been three whites and thirty Askaris killed, whilst our casualties consisted of Captain R. G. Stokes, 2nd Lieutenant O. E. Almond and twelve other ranks killed and five wounded.

Lieutenant Almond's body was found lying across that of a German white, whom he appeared to have bayoneted ; all the casualties occurred in a very small area.

Owing to the very great density of the bush, firing was not heard by the other platoon which was on the far bank of the river. The gallant action of the platoon under 2nd Lieutenant Almond was referred to and commended by G.O.C. Nairobi.

On the 31st October the following remarkable entry appears in the Battalion War Diary, clearly showing the nature of the climate to which the Battalion had for so long been exposed : " Of soldiers of the Battalion since the beginning of the war in East Africa, 836 have been admitted to hospital, and only 278 have not yet been admitted to hospital to date ! "

The headquarters of the Battalion was now to leave Bura, and on the morning of the 13th November it marched out to Mashoti, distance nine miles, the marching-out strength being thirteen officers and 395 other ranks ; and at Mashoti the Battalion Headquarters remained for the remainder of the year.

" Beyond these small local activities no military operations of any importance took place during 1915. The Germans had not sufficient strength to take the offensive in force ; and we had so many preoccupations elsewhere that we could not afford to send troops enough to distant East Africa. Thus the year 1915 came to an end without any appreciable change in the situation in East Africa, except that the German Colony, completely cut off by sea and thrown upon its own resources, had to watch the gradual strengthening of the British position and to see the weak points at which blows might have been struck, secured and made good. In the operations by which this was done, a very large share of the work fell on the Indian troops whom Generals Stewart and Aitken had brought out. . . . Without the assistance of the contingent from India, British East Africa and Uganda would have fared badly." *

With the successful conclusion of General Botha's operations in German South-West Africa, considerable numbers of South African troops became available for service in East Africa ; while, on the withdrawal of the Indian Corps from France, several Indian regiments were dispatched to East Africa in time to take part in the offensive now about to be opened.

" Large contingents were raised in South Africa, some of which at the end of 1915 began to arrive. There were two formed divisions in the country, apart from the forces on the lakes and the Rhodesia and Nyasaland forces—the 1st Division, under General Stewart, at Longido, and the 2nd Division, under General Tighe, on the Voi–Maktau line." † Early

---

* Lucas, *The Empire at War*, Vol. V, p. 321.
†,Buchan, *A History of the Great War*, Vol. IV, p. 110.

in 1916, on the arrival of the South African troops in East Africa, General Smuts took over the command of the East African expeditionary force and in his despatch of the 30th April, 1916, he estimates the strength of the German forces at the outset of the campaign of 1916, at 16,000 men, of whom 2,000 were white, with sixty guns and eighty machine-guns. They were organized in companies, varying from 150 to 200 strong, with ten per cent. of whites and an average of two machine-guns per company.

In General Smuts' despatch of the 30th April, 1916, he gives a general review of the military situation as it existed at the beginning of that year : " The enemy," he writes, " occupied a considerable tract of British territory. At Taveta they had established a large entrenched camp, with an advanced position at Salaita, an entrenched camp at Serengeti and an outpost at Mbuyuni, the latter places thirteen and seventeen miles respectively east of Taveta. At Kasigau they maintained a garrison of 500–600 rifles with the object of delaying our concentration by blowing up the Uganda Railway and the Voi–Maktau Railway. . . . At numerous points throughout the six hundred miles of land frontier the opposing troops were in touch, and the result was that General Tighe had to disseminate widely his small force, and was unable to keep any large reserve in hand to meet a sudden call. . . . He organized such of his infantry as could be spared for active operations into the 1st and 2nd East African Brigades, acting on the Taveta and Longido lines respectively, and proceeded to develop the organization of the whole force into two divisions and line-of-communication troops.

" On the 15th January, 1916, the 1st Division, under Major-General Stewart, was ordered to occupy Longido and to develop the lines-of-communication between that place and Kajiado, on the Magadi Railway. On the 22nd January the 2nd Division, under Brigadier-General Malleson, advanced from Maktau to Mbuyuni, and on the 24th occupied Serengeti camp. This advance had the immediate effect of making the enemy evacuate Kasigau. The railway was advanced from Maktau to Njoro drift, three miles east of Salaita, and arrangements made for the concentration of a large force at and near Mbuyuni.

" Early in February the 2nd South African Infantry Brigade arrived, and on the 12th of that month General Tighe directed the 2nd Division to make a reconnaissance in force on Salaita, and if possible to occupy that position. General Malleson carried out this operation with three battalions 2nd South African Brigade, and three battalions 1st East African Brigade, supported by eighteen guns and howitzers. The enemy was found in force and counter-attacked vigorously. General Malleson was compelled to withdraw to Serengeti, but much useful information had been gained."

The 2nd Battalion Loyal North Lancashire was at Maktau when, on

the 20th January, it was informed that it was to move with the bulk of
the force there stationed to Mbuyuni by way of Bibi, and a start was made
the following afternoon, Mbuyuni being occupied with little opposition on
the morning of the 22nd. Such skirmishing as occurred on this day and
the next fell almost entirely upon the mounted troops with the column,
and 2nd Lieutenant W. Parker, of the Battalion M.I., was severely wounded.
On the 24th, Indian troops occupied the enemy camp at Serengeti which
the Germans evacuated on our approach.

The Brigade with which the Battalion was working had hitherto been
known as the Voi Brigade, but on the 7th February its title was changed
to that of the 1st East African Brigade.

On the 11th February the Battalion moved up to Serengeti, and on
the evening of arrival at this place, orders were received that the following
day an attack would be made upon the enemy occupying Salaita, a strong
natural position on high ground surrounded by bush, some eight miles to
the east of Taveta. The troops to be employed were the 2nd Loyal North
Lancashire, the 2nd Rhodesia Regiment, and the 130th Baluchis.

The Battalion War Diary gives the following account of the action :
" The Battalion—strength twenty-five officers and 552 other ranks—left
Serengeti at 6.25 a.m. on the 12th with the guns of the force, and marched
along a track north of the Taveta road in order to avoid a steep drift ; two
platoons of No. 1 Company and No. 2 Company were escort to the guns,
four of which opened fire at 8.20. The guns having come into action,
the Battalion advanced and the Rhodesians took up a position on the
left of the Battalion. At 9.45 a.m. the O.C. Battalion sent Captain Collas,
the adjutant, to report to the O.C. Brigade, that the German trenches
were at the foot of Salaita Hill with most of their guns south of the hill.

" At about ten o'clock the attack of the 2nd Rhodesia Regiment was
repulsed with loss and the Battalion was now ordered to move forward
for 500 yards. This advance, and another which followed later, brought
the leading platoons nearly up to the edge of the bush in front of the German
trenches. This was about 12.20 p.m. The German gunners kept up an
intermittent shell fire—pompoms and field guns—on any parties of infantry
that could be seen, and also on our guns in rear of the Battalion.

" At 1.20 p.m. Lieut.-Colonel Jourdain was ordered to take command
of the firing line and cover the retirement of the force north of the Taveta
road, with the 130th Baluchis on the right, or northern, flank. The enemy
showed great enterprise, using their machine-guns and stampeding the
mules of the Battalion M.G. Company under Captain Watson, which was
operating near the Baluchis. A small party of the enemy attacked the
rearmost party of the Battalion, but was dispersed. Progress was slow,

as some of the wounded had to be carried and the bearers were quite exhausted.

" At 6.15 p.m. as the company on rear guard was a quarter of a mile from Njoro drift, fire was opened by our Maxims from the east side of the drift in order to cover the retirement ; the mountain battery also fired. The whole force returned to Serengeti."

During this day's operations the Battalion suffered a serious loss in the death in action of Assistant-Surgeon A. R. Emmett, who had been with the Battalion since November, 1914, and had always shown great gallantry and devotion to duty ; he was killed while attending to the wounded in the firing-line.   Second-Lieutenant A. Wale and four men were wounded.

On the 16th February the 3rd Battalion King's African Rifles arrived at Serengeti and joined the 1st East African Brigade.   Another welcome arrival was a consignment of chargers for the mounted officers, but the war diary regretfully records that the " two horses issued to the O.C. Battalion and adjutant had only two eyes between them ! "

On the 29th February the Battalion was sent out with a small mobile column in the direction of Luchoro ; some slight opposition was met with and the Battalion had a sergeant and two men wounded.

General Smuts had assumed the chief command, and he at once commenced operations with the object of clearing the Kilimanjaro area before the rainy season as a preliminary to a sustained offensive later on. The plan of campaign he now outlined was as follows : the 1st Division was to cross the thirty-five miles of waterless bush lying between Longido and the Engare Nanyuki River, occupy the latter, and then advance between Meru and Kilimanjaro to Boma ya Ngombe.   Thereafter this division was to move on Kahe and cut the enemy's line of communication by the Usambara Railway.

The 2nd Division, with the 1st South African Mounted Brigade, was to advance through the gap between Kilimanjaro and the Paré Hills against the enemy's main body, reported as being concentrated near Taveta, with strong detachments at the head of Lake Jipe, in the bush country east of the River Lumi and at Salaita.

The advance of the 1st and 2nd Divisions commenced on the 7th and 8th March respectively, but it was not until the afternoon of the 11th that the Battalion left Serengeti for Taveta, which had been seized by some of our mounted troops on the previous day, the enemy retiring to and taking up a strong position on the Latema–Reata neck.   It was obviously necessary to clear the Germans out of this position before the main force could advance, since any counter-attack on Taveta from the south-west might have seriously hampered our movements.

The work of driving the enemy from the Latema–Reata neck was entrusted to Brigadier-General Malleson, but on his falling sick Major-General Tighe took charge of the operation in person. At his disposal were the following troops : Belfield's Scouts, the Machine-Gun Company of the 2nd Battalion North Lancashire Regiment, the M.I. Company, two field and one howitzer batteries, the 2nd Rhodesia Regiment, 130th Baluchis and 3rd King's African Rifles.

The Battalion was this day not actually engaged, but its Machine-Gun Company moved in support of the 130th Baluchis who were on the right of the attack. The enemy made a very obstinate resistance and was still in position after several hours' fighting, when General Tighe judged it best not further to press the attack on the Latema–Reata position, but to await the effect of a turning movement to be carried out next day by mounted troops. The whole attacking force was then withdrawn, but while the retirement was in progress the defending party evacuated the position, which our troops then occupied. With the end of this action the first phase of the struggle for Kilimanjaro came to a conclusion.

In the Battalion Machine-Gun Company Captain Pigot, 3rd Battalion South Lancashire Regiment, attached, and two men were wounded.

On the 13th March the Battalion advanced to and took over charge of the position on the Latema–Reata ridge, but moved back to Taveta two days later. About this time several changes were made in commands, Brigadier-General S. H. Sheppard, D.S.O., taking over the 1st East African Brigade and Major-General A. R. Hoskins, C.M.G., D.S.O., the 1st Division.

On the 24th the following special Brigade Order was issued :—

" Brig.-General Malleson in handing over command of the 1st East African Brigade desires to thank all ranks for the excellent work done under trying circumstances during many months, and wishes them a victorious issue to the campaign and all good fortune in the future."

The following gives the strength and disposal of the Battalion at this date :—

	Officers.	Other Ranks.
Present with Headquarters.	19	403
Machine-Gun Company	4	77
With Transport	2	12
Hospital and Attending	4	217
Unfit at Maktau	1	19
On Command, etc.	5	108
Total	35	836

The men were now, however, going sick daily in increasing numbers, for the climate at this time was very trying, the sick-rate being largely due to the stay in low mosquito-infected ground. At the end of March the Battalion moved back again to Mbuyuni and encamped on the top of the ridge ; sickness did not, however, diminish and at the beginning of April it was decided to move the Battalion from East Africa for reasons of health. On the 15th the Battalion was warned to be ready to move to the Cape of Good Hope at the end of the week.

The departure of the Battalion was, however, delayed considerably beyond the date first notified, and it was not until the 29th April that it paraded before Brigadier-General Sheppard, who addressed to the officers and other ranks the following farewell remarks :—

" I deeply regret what I trust may be no more than a temporary absence of the Battalion from East Africa. General Officers have to make many speeches—some they mean and some they do not mean, but I mean every word of what I now say to you. The Battalion has had as hard a time of it as any unit in this war. Though we have not had the fighting like in Flanders or in the Dardanelles, the climate and country of this campaign have proved a severe strain on anybody. Such was the trust in the Regiment and in its reliability that when any particular work had to be done, no matter the locality, the North Lancashire were always sent to assist. From Tanga to Lake Victoria, from Sonju to Gazi, from Umba Valley to Voi, the North Lancashire have always been sent to help. That the men are now in bad health, is not a mark of reproach but rather of honour. If you had had no work to do, doubtless you would all be fit enough. I hope your absence is only temporary, and that the men who were at the beginning of the campaign may see the final act.

" It has always been my hope that when I got command of a brigade, the Battalion would form part of it. There is much work still in front of us all in this country. I will say ' au revoir ' and not good-bye, and I wish you all a quick return to health and to the old Voi Brigade."

The Battalion finally left Mbuyuni by train at 1 p.m. on the 7th May, and arrived at Kilindini at four o'clock on the following morning, embarking at once in the S.S. " Professor " at a strength of sixteen officers, five warrant officers and 516 other ranks. All the remaining fit men of the Battalion were left behind in East Africa with the M.I. and Machine-Gun Companies.

Sailing on the afternoon of the 10th the " Professor " put into Zanzibar next day for water, and reached Durban at 11 a.m. on the 18th. Here the Battalion disembarked and was entertained during the afternoon by the Mayor and residents at a tea and concert before leaving again by two trains in the evening, thirty-seven men remaining in hospital at Durban as being too ill to travel further.   Passing through Ladysmith, Bethlehem, Bloemfontein, Worcester and Wynberg, the Battalion arrived on the evening of the 21st at Simonstown, being met at the railway station by the band of H.M.S. " Kent," which played the companies to the barracks, where all now settled down for a greatly needed change and rest.

On the 26th May, H.E. Lord Buxton, the Governor-General of South Africa, inspected the Battalion on parade and spoke to the following effect :—

" Lieut.-Colonel Jourdain, Officers and Men of the 2nd Battalion The Loyal North Lancashire Regiment.

" I am very glad to have the opportunity of meeting you and thanking you on behalf of His Majesty The King, as well as to thank you myself on behalf of this part of the Empire which I represent.   Your Battalion has had for a very long time very arduous and difficult duties to perform, and to fight against a brave and determined enemy in a very unhealthy climate under worse conditions perhaps than on any of the other fronts.   We are therefore all the more grateful for the fine work that you have done under such difficult conditions, and I hope that you will all return to East Africa after your period of rest, much improved in health, and that you have laid the foundation for a further period of activity there.   When victory is ours I hope you will be in at the death.

" We all feel, hope and believe that the occupation of that portion of German territory will have a great moral effect on the general situation— some people may think that it will have very little effect, but I do not agree.   I think that a victorious conclusion there will have a great effect in Germany, in England, and in allied countries, but more especially in neutral countries.

" I desire again to express my very great appreciation of the very excellent service you have already rendered to the Empire in East Africa, and when you return there you will carry with you our very best wishes.   Men have come forward in very large numbers from all parts of this Empire to serve their King and Country in this great war, and we, as well as our allies, are determined to win this war, however long it may continue.

" Again I thank you, Officers and Men, for the excellent service you have rendered to your King and Country."

On the 31st Major H. A. Robinson died suddenly.

On the 9th June the Depot of the Battalion left Bangalore, where for some time it had been stationed, for Bombay to embark for home.

At this time the strength of the Battalion in South Africa was sixteen officers and 553 non-commissioned officers and men, of whom one officer —Captain A. T. T. Storey, South Lancashire Regiment, attached—and 144 other ranks were in hospital. The names of the other fifteen officers are as follows : Lieut.-Colonel C. E. A. Jourdain, Captains J. S. Gaskell, D. P. J. Collas, adjutant, J. F. B. Watson, B. H. Withers and R. L. C. Keays, Lieutenants J. G. W. Hyndson, W. McDonald, F. W. Walker and M. E. Leeb, 2nd Lieutenants P. Chalk, C. S. Chambers, R. Forrest and C. H. A. Grierson, and Lieutenant and Quartermaster R. Rowley.

On the 20th June the Commanding Officer was informed that the Battalion would be moved back to East Africa early in August, and on the 20th of that month fourteen officers and 355 other ranks disembarked from the " Comrie Castle " at Kilindini. More officers and other ranks also arrived from England, and by the 22nd the total strength of the Battalion stood at twenty-one officers, thirty-one warrant officers and sergeants, seventy-one corporals and lance-corporals, four drummers and 404 privates.

On this latter date orders were received directing the Commanding Officer to hold the Battalion in readiness to embark in the S.S. " Rajput " at a moment's notice for Bagamoyo, in view of operations which were to commence there on the 29th August.

While the Battalion had been away in South Africa building up its strength, General Smuts had reorganized his forces and advanced from several directions against the troops of von Lettow-Vorbeck and his subordinate commanders. In his despatch of the 27th October, 1916, General Smuts gives the following appreciation of the general situation in German East Africa in the first week of August : " Van Deventer had occupied the Central Railway from Kilimatinde to Dodoma ; in the Lake area the British and Belgian forces were well south of Lake Victoria and preparing for a combined move towards Tabora. Further west a Belgian force had crossed Lake Tanganyika and occupied Ujiji and Kigoma, the terminus of the Central Railway. In the south-west General Northey's force had occupied Malangali after a brilliant little action, and was prepared to move towards Iringa, seventy miles further north-east. All coast towns as far south as Sadani had been occupied, and a small column was working its way southward to the Wami River and clearing the country between the Nguru mountains and the coast. The time had therefore come for the 1st and 3rd Divisions to resume the advance to the Central Railway."

The coast region was also dealt with, and assisted by the Navy, Tanga, Pangani, Sadani and Bagamoyo were successively occupied between the 17th July and the 15th August.

Arrived at Bagamoyo, the Battalion left again at 2 p.m. on the 31st

August, forming one of the units of a column which was the centre one of three marching upon Dar-es-Salaam ; a small depot with surplus kits was left behind at Bagamoyo in charge of Sergeant Clifford of the Battalion and three unfit men.   At the start the Battalion furnished the advanced guard, the rest of the companies moving at the head of the main body, each company with its own machine-gun section and its first-line transport in rear.

At the end of a very hot and dusty march the column halted and bivouacked at a place known as Singa.

Marching on by Matinga and Magosa, on arrival on the early morning of the 2nd September near Gunja Peak a few Germans were seen and fired on, with what effect was not discernible ; and about midday on the 4th the column reached Dar-es-Salaam, which had surrendered to the Navy on the previous day, for, as General Smuts states in his despatch of the 27th October, " the enemy, aware of the overwhelming force moving against Dar-es-Salaam, was determined to avoid capture and also anxious to avoid siege operations against a town containing a large German non-combatant population, and so had decided not to defend the place."

On arrival the Battalion was at first housed in the Boma Barracks, but later occupied the Sewa-Hadji hospital, remaining tolerably quiescent until the 10th September, on the morning of which day orders were received to prepare for a further move.   Accordingly at 6 a.m. on the 11th the Battalion embarked in H.M.S. " Hyacinth " and disembarked twenty-four hours later at Kilwa, some 150 miles to the south, the Battalion finding quarters there in the Custom House sheds.

During the time that the Battalion remained at or in the immediate vicinity of Kilwa, it was engaged in operations of no more than a very minor character, companies being sent out singly or in pairs to occupy distant posts or to search for small parties of the enemy reported as being in the neighbourhood.   The hospital returns for this period, however, show only too plainly that the Battalion had benefited but little by the change to South Africa, and the rate of admission to hospital grew higher month by month ; in November 241 men were admitted to hospital and in the first fortnight of December eight-five, while the State for December shows only fourteen officers and 333 other ranks fit for duty.   Of the sickness in his force generally the following statement occurs in General Smuts' despatch of the 28th February, 1917 :—

" Disease had played havoc among the troops, of whom large numbers were totally unfit, without medical attention, prolonged rest, change of climate and nourishment, to make any sustained effort.   The wastage due to the above cause was enormous, and the reduction in the number of

effective rifles was alone enough to stop all further movement until reinforcements were available. . . . The strain upon all ranks of all units
and services due to the steadily increasing effect of disease had reached the
limit which was endurable."

The transport question had been beset with every kind of difficulty
and its provision had demanded considerable knowledge and forethought ;
there were few real roads and the conditions were unlike those experienced
in any previous campaign in which forces of such a number had been engaged.   Continuing his despatch General Smuts wrote : " The mechanical
transport was in a seriously damaged condition in consequence of the
strain of continuous work over appalling roads, or trackless country, and
extensive repairs, for which there had been no time, were essential ; the
personnel of this transport suffered, as did every other branch of the forces,
from the same diseases as affected the fighting troops and as men dropped
out increasing strain was thrown on those able to keep going, until the
loss of men threw scores of vehicles out of work.   Animal diseases had
wiped out horses, mules and oxen by thousands, and it was therefore necessary to replace this transport in some way or other before movement was
possible."

The enemy's transport was a simpler matter ; operating in their own
country, each unit possessed a full complement of native porters, who were
able, to a certain extent, to live on the country, with the result that his
mobility was in no way impeded, which in itself gave him an inestimable
advantage over our own troops, especially during the rainy seasons.

General von Lettow-Vorbeck was an accomplished soldier and a determined leader.   In the defence of Tanga and in the subsequent operations he
deserved well of his country and earned the ungrudging admiration of all
those who fought against him.   He clearly foresaw that the ultimate fate
of the German colony would not depend on the result of the campaign in
East Africa but rather on the result of the war as a whole, and shrewdly
made his plans accordingly.   He was of the opinion that he could best
serve his country's interests by compelling the British to keep as large a
force as possible, for an indefinite period, in the field, and that his best
course to pursue was to fight delaying actions only, and to avoid risking
the destruction of his force, against probably superior numbers, in a general
engagement fought to a finish ; how well, or not, he succeeded, history
alone can now only tell.

In recognition of the services of the 2nd Battalion, the battle-honours
" Kilimanjaro " and " East Africa, 1914–16 " were subsequently awarded ;
the former honour now being borne on the Colours.

CHAPTER XXXVII

1914–1917

OPERATIONS IN EAST AFRICA

A SHORT ACCOUNT OF THE DETACHED UNITS FOUND BY THE BATTALION

I. Small 12-pounder Battery, under Captain R. H. Logan, 1914–1916.

II. Mounted Infantry Company, originally under Captain J. S. Woodruffe, Royal Sussex Regiment (attached) and afterwards under Captain G. P. Atkinson. August, 1915–July, 1916.

III. Machine-Gun Company, under Major R. E. Berkeley. May, 1916–December, 1916.

IV. Second Machine-Gun Company, under Major R. E. Berkeley. December, 1916–December, 1917.

CAPTAIN LOGAN'S BATTERY

1914–1916

"LOGAN'S BATTERY" was born on the battleship "Goliath," one of the escort of the East African Expeditionary Force during its journey from Bombay to East Africa. Lieutenant R. H. Logan was ordered from the "Karmala" to the "Goliath" to take over two 3-pounder Q.F. Guns; one sergeant, one corporal and thirteen men went with him. Soldiers in one of H.M. ships are more or less like bulls in china shops and all manner of sacred places were invaded before they learnt what was what. The 3-pounders had of course no land mountings, so these were improvised on board during the voyage,—they eventually proved to be useless; thirteen bluejackets were told off to join the Battery, but these were later withdrawn.

At Tanga the Battery did not land the guns, being merely held in readiness. On returning to Mombasa the Battery was sent to guard the bridges to the mainland, and after a short time there it was sent to Nairobi where serviceable carriages and limbers were provided, each gun being drawn by a team of oxen; these were eventually withdrawn and the Battery ordered to Lake Victoria, where it was stationed for six months in the steamship " Usoga," one of the fleet of the Uganda Marine.   There they took part in the action of Bukoba, shelling the wireless station which was eventually destroyed.   From Victoria Nyanza they were sent to the coast and placed in the British India steamer " Barjora," which proceeded up and down the coast of German East Africa, shelling enemy dhows. Then they were ordered to Maktau, the advance camp in British East Africa, where the 3-pounders were handed into store and two 12-pounder 8-cwt. naval landing guns were taken over.   These guns were excellent in their way, having good carriages with limbers especially made and mounted on pneumatic tyres.

They were drawn at first by Hupmobile cars which were soon replaced by Reo lorries.   The Battery was then properly constituted and appeared in orders as " Logan's Battery " ; five cars were allotted, two to draw the guns, two for ammunition and one for kit.   The Battery took part in the general advance with the South African troops and was engaged in many actions, the most important of which was at Taveta, where it was in action from dawn until darkness made further shooting impossible. The dreadful climate and conditions under which the men worked had gradually taken toll of all ranks, and notwithstanding regular doses of quinine and insistence on mosquito-nets the Battery was greatly reduced in personnel.   After Taveta Captain Logan, as he then was, was sick, as was also Lieutenant Brown, an attached officer who was generally known as " Dynamite Brown," as he had come from an armoured train on which he was regularly blown up on Sunday mornings at 11.30 a.m., the Germans being very methodical.   The men were in a bad way from malaria and dysentery.   The Battery, however, struggled along and eventually the officers and sick men rejoined.   All this time the Reo lorries with drivers from South Africa had done excellent work ; the South African drivers, though certainly not used to discipline, behaved well and soon became interested in their work and the Battery never had a breakdown.   It must be remembered that there were no roads, just virgin bush, and it was necessary for water, for men and animals, to be brought up by a pipe line which was carried in sections and moved along with the force.

A time came, however, when no amount of manhandling of guns, or cars, could get the Battery any further nor could any wheeled transport proceed ; this was near the Rufiji River in German East Africa and so the guns had to be dismounted and with great exertion carried by porters to the Rufiji, and there, after two years of strenuous life, it was disbanded, the men returning to their Regiment, Lieutenant Brown to England to finish his training as a doctor, and Major Logan, as he then was, to work under the G.O.C. Lines-of-Communication.

THE MOUNTED INFANTRY COMPANY

August, 1915–July, 1916

During the campaign the Battalion, in conjunction with the 25th (Service) Battalion Royal Fusiliers, found officers, N.C.O.s and men for a Mounted Infantry Company.

As there were very few mounted troops in the country and as duties in the way of reconnoitring, reporting on movements of the enemy, blowing up railway lines, looking for water, etc., were continuous, work was very arduous.

The Company was originally formed in August, 1915, and was eventually broken up in July, 1916, by which time the Company was very much under strength and no reinforcements were available.

Captain J. S. Woodruffe was in command of the Company until he was wounded, and Captain G. P. Atkinson continued to command it until it was broken up.

In August, 1915, when first formed, the Company Officers were :—

Captain J. S. Woodruffe, Royal Sussex Regiment
Lieutenant A. T. T. Storey, South Lancashire Regiment
} Attached, Loyal North Lancashire Regiment.

Lieutenant W. Dartnell
Lieutenant M. Ryan
} 25th (Service) Bn. Royal Fusiliers.

2nd Lieutenant W. Parker, 2nd Loyal North Lancashire Regiment.

The Loyal North Lancashire Regiment and the 25th (Service) Battalion Royal Fusiliers each found approximately seventy-five men and a proportion of N.C.O.s

Officers were mounted on Somali ponies and N.C.O.s and men on mules, as, on account of the country being infested with tsetse-fly, horses and ponies could only be kept alive for a very short time. Mules were practically immune and with ten grains of arsenic administered every evening were able to carry on with no forage ration and with only grazing to see them through. The Company was formed from officers and men who were accustomed to horses and were for this reason qualified for the work, though none of them had done a mounted infantry course. Two of the officers, however, had received their commissions from the ranks of cavalry regiments.

When the Company was first formed in August, 1915, the Battalion was at Maktau (the garrison in perimeter camp), which was then railhead of the light military railway line which eventually ran from Voi via Maktau and Taveta to Moshi, the terminus of the German Moshi to Tanga line.

The country in this district is comparatively open, consisting of rolling downs of a wooded park-like nature, with water very scarce and visibility from high ground quite good except during the middle of the day, when owing to the sun being overhead there was generally a very bad haze which caused a mirage ; in places there were patches of bush.

Very shortly after its formation, the Company, on 3rd September, had its first engagement with a patrol of the enemy.

A small force of Germans was reported to have laid a mine on the Mombasa–Nairobi line and to be returning to the German border by a route passing a few miles from Maktau.

The Mounted Infantry (strength four officers and sixty-three non-commissioned officers and men) were ordered out to intercept this party.

At 10.15 a.m. the Company was in position facing east, on a slope in bushy country, with mules about a hundred yards in rear, when the picquets were suddenly attacked by a strong force of the enemy at about one hundred yards' range.

The picquets withdrew, as previously ordered, on to the firing-line and desperate fighting took place at very short range.

Fighting continued for about half an hour, during which time Captain Woodruffe was wounded and Lieutenant Dartnell, Royal Fusiliers, was killed. The enemy was numerically in considerably greater force and seeing that they were sending up supports to outflank the position, Captain Woodruffe, who, in spite of a severe wound in the back, continued to command, gave the order to withdraw. This was effected and the total casualties, in addition to the above, consisted of seven killed and seven wounded. The enemy who, it was afterwards ascertained, were one hundred and fifty strong, left five dead Askaris on the field. They adopted their usual method for removing the dead and wounded, which consisted of carrying them away in hammocks, slung on bamboo poles which they carried for use, when required.

Captain Atkinson took over command of the Company from Captain Woodruffe.

A similar affair took place shortly afterwards—on the 13th and 14th September.

Tracks of a strong patrol of Germans, moving south of Maktau to the railway, were discovered by the Company on the 12th instant and at 6 a.m. on the 14th the Company (four officers and sixty-three N.C.O.s and men) with one hundred men of the 130th Baluchis (under Lieutenant Wildman) were in position to hold up the enemy on his return.

The field of fire was only about two hundred yards, owing to scattered bush, but an open strip of country running two miles north and one mile south behind the position, was covered by the support (fifty Baluchis under Lieutenant Wildman) in the event of the enemy crossing this opening.

At 9.20 a.m. five buck ran across in front of the position, indicating the enemy's approach. A few minutes later the enemy, about eighty strong, came into the open at about two hundred yards' range, advancing directly on to the position. Very heavy fire was opened, the enemy suffered heavily and the Baluchis in support were moved up to enfilade the enemy's left flank. Enemy survivors then crawled back into the bush where the force scattered, leaving one white German, twenty-eight Askaris and three porters dead on the field. Our casualties were Lieutenant Wildman and four men killed and eight wounded.

This was the last occasion on which the enemy raided the railway line.

From this time until the capture of Latema and Reata at the foot of Kilimanjaro, on March 11th, 1916, the Company was continually employed in reconnoitring enemy positions at Kampi ya Bibi, Mbuyuni, Serengeti, Salaita, Taveta and took part in the attack on each of them, being generally employed to take up a position to a flank to guard against any turning movement.

In the attack on Latema and Reata the Company, after reconnoitring Reata and reporting the hill to be held in strength, was ordered to watch the left flank of the 1st East African Brigade attacking Reata. The same night the South African Infantry with this Brigade attacked the Reata position and as it was a very dark night and the bush thick, it was very difficult to keep touch and small units penetrated well behind the enemy's position. The position, however, was not captured the same night, but as the enemy were driven from Latema, the Reata position was evacuated by the enemy the following day.

The rainy season had now set in and our forces occupied Kahe, Arusha, Latema and Reata, the bulk of the troops being withdrawn to Mbuyuni, thus facilitating the question of supplies. On the 4th May, Lieutenant C. Crosby joined the Company for duty, and on the 6th all officers, N.C.O.s and men of the Royal Fusiliers still with the Company returned to their Battalion. On the 7th, Captain A. T. T. Storey was invalided with the Battalion to South Africa and Captain A. P. V. Pigot joined the Company.

After this date the only officer doing duty with the Company, not belonging to the Regiment, was 2nd Lieutenant Holmes of the E.A.P. Forces. The position of Mbuyuni was particularly well suited for the reconnoitring of the Paré mountains and the enemy's positions on the Tanga to Moshi railway—on which duties the Company was continually employed.

On the 21st May the main East African force under General Smuts commenced its advance down the Pangani River.

The Mounted Infantry Company formed part of the 1st (East African) Division, which was divided into three columns under Lieut.-Colonel Fitzgerald, Brig.-General Hannyngton and Brig.-General Sheppard, and being divisional troops received their orders from the Division and did duty with the leading column.

At places during this advance the grass was so high that men and animals were completely hidden. On the 7th June the Company crossed the Pangani River at Buiko by Berthon boat bridges—the carts and baggage being taken over by rafts. The river was very swollen owing to the recent rains and great difficulty was experienced.

After attacking Mzinga on the 23rd June, bandas (grass huts) for three German field companies were found, also several dead and dying Askaris and porters, and stores and supplies which the enemy was unable to get away were burning.

In the action at Kwa Di Rema on the 24th June, which will be referred to in the Machine-Gun record, the Mounted Infantry also took part. With the 17th Cavalry and armoured cars they took up a position about three hundred yards from the enemy and moved forward in support of General Hoskins' attack, capturing four whites and a number of Askaris.

By the beginning of July the strength of the Company had dwindled to such small figures, that its disbandment was ordered, Captain Atkinson being sent to the 17th Cavalry to be attached for duty, while Captain Pigot and Lieutenant Crosby were sent to the Machine-Gun Company.

Some of the names of places where the Company carried out reconnaissances and generally had small affairs with the enemy read like a selection of names from Rider Haggard and the following are a few of them : Nkangata, Mzinga, Kwadirewa, Mkomazi, Makayo, Mbugwe, Mkokoni, Nguguini, Sangeni, Pongwe.

THE MACHINE-GUN COMPANY
May, 1916–December, 1916

When the Battalion entrained at Mbuyuni to proceed to South Africa in May, 1916, to recuperate after eighteen months in East Africa from casualties and sickness caused by malaria and dysentery, a Machine-Gun Company composed of all available fit men (about one hundred and forty strong), under Major R. E. Berkeley, was left behind in the country.

The following officers also remained for duty with the Company : Lieutenants G. E. Bowden, H. Wilkinson and W. Halton, and 2nd Lieutenant H. P. Woodgate ; 2nd Lieutenants A. Schofield and W. M. Liesch-ing, Machine-Gun Corps, were attached for duty.

Major T. McG. Bridges also remained for duty with column H.Q.

The equipment and transport with the Company consisted of eight ·303 Maxim guns, one hundred and twenty first-line porters to carry first-line ammunition, water for guns, spare parts, etc., five hundred second-line porters (not with Company on the march) to carry baggage, supplies, additional ammunition, etc., and forty mules to carry guns and first supply ammunition on the march.

At this stage it was obvious that to maintain men and animals in the field great difficulty on account of climate would be encountered, and from now until the end of the campaign ten grains (whenever available) of quinine were issued daily to all ranks and ten grains of arsenic daily to each mule.

During the first two months preparations were made for the great drive under General Smuts, and during these preparations General Van Deventer with South African mounted troops captured and occupied Kondoa Irangi, where he became immobile owing to loss of animals from tsetse-fly and shortness of supplies.

At the same time the main force of the enemy was attacked in strength and forced to retire from Kahe on the Moshi–Tanga railway.

The drive was commenced in June and was supported by the Belgians who operated in the direction of Tabora, on the Dar-es-Salaam to Lake Tanganyika railway, from the west, and by General Northey with a Rhodesian force towards Iringa from the south-west.

The Machine-Gun Company, the Mounted Infantry Company and Logan's Battery were with the 1st East African Division during the con-tinual fighting and rapid advance down the Usambara valley along the Pangani River ; the Division incidentally consisted of British, South African, Indian, East African troops and was shortly afterwards joined by a Nigerian brigade from West Africa. The river was crossed at Palms and on arrival at Mombo, the Division left the river and proceeded in the direction of Handeni along the light trolley line. The enemy left com-panies to hold up the advance and to cover their retirement, but it was generally possible to advance rapidly and marches were occasionally as long as twenty miles in very hot weather, it being necessary at times to cut a way through the bush. Only half and sometimes quarter rations were issued. After leaving Handeni a small force under General Hoskins, who afterwards commanded the Expeditionary Force, carried out a march with Indian troops and the Machine-Gun Company to make a surprise attack against the enemy's camp at Kwa Di Rema. Leaving at about

10 p.m. after a march of over thirty miles, the enemy was surprised at sundown the following evening and after a running fight his camp was captured and a small force of enemy whites and Askaris was taken prisoner.

For this march, owing to the scarcity of supplies, biltong (sun-dried meat), which had been prepared in the country, was issued to the troops. After capturing this camp our force was heavily shelled by the 4-in. and 3·5-in. naval guns from the "Königsberg," but suffered no casualties. From this camp a short advance along the Mgeta River was made and here the column, having outrun its supplies and heavier artillery, remained for six weeks in what became known as Shell Camp. During this time the camp was shelled daily from Tuliani (Kanga mountains), and as the enemy's guns outranged any guns with the column it was not possible to reply to their fire.

Dug-outs for troops and shelters for animals and porters were constructed.

It was here that C.S.M. Nelson was killed by gun-fire, a great loss to the Machine-Gun Company.

During the period that our forces occupied Shell Camp, and the enemy occupied Tuliani, the enemy temporarily held a post at Maomondo, north of Tuliani. This post was attacked and hand-to-hand fighting took place. The post was withdrawn and retired to the main position at Tuliani. The enemy commander, General von Lettow-Vorbeck, realized the necessity of safeguarding his supplies on the Central Railway, and with this in view now withdrew the bulk of the force in front of Kondoa, marched to Dodoma, proceeded by rail to Morogoro and moved up in support of Kraut to Tuliani. In Shell Camp troops suffered more from the climate than when on the march, all supplies, medical comforts, etc., in the early days of the occupation of this camp still having to come from Mombasa by rail via Voi and Moshi to the Tanga railway, and then for two hundred miles by lorries and porters to advanced supply depots. No forage was issued for mules, mails were only received at intervals of several weeks and no clothing was available for issue to the men.

The mules kept their condition in an extraordinary way, which was unquestionably due to the daily issue of arsenic, and eighty per cent. were able to carry their loads after working for over eight months under these conditions.

On the 13th August our force facing Tuliani attacked in two columns —the main column against the enemy's position, the other (the Machine-Gun Company with this column) by the Wami River, and after heavy casualties forced the enemy to retire ; the advance to the Central Railway, being thereby opened, was not seriously opposed. On Morogoro being threatened the enemy retired into the Uluguru mountains, which, being very steep and rocky, offered excellent opportunities for the enemy's smaller force to hold up the advance.

It is a point of great interest to note that General von Lettow-Vorbeck states in his diary that the impression at the British headquarters that he was likely to make a final stand at Morogoro and then surrender was a strange one, as his object being to keep a British force in the field his future action naturally consisted of continuing his retirement.

Dar-es-Salaam had fallen in August, and consequently after the capture of the Central Railway it was possible to use Morogoro as a supply base ; but owing to the bridge across the Ruvu River having been destroyed, it was necessary to run the train in two sections. Thus ended the necessity of transporting all supplies, ammunition, etc., by rail for some hundred of miles and then by lorries for anything up to two hundred miles, a tremendous saving when it is remembered that all the petrol had to be brought into the country at a time when there was a very serious shortage of shipping.

The Germans had collected a large amount of supplies at Kisaki on the south-west of the mountains and a force under Captain Stammermann, with the bulk of the enemy's force, held up our advance whilst these supplies were being withdrawn. After the enemy's advanced troops had been driven back, the first attack on Kisaki was made by South African mounted troops under General Enslin, who had moved round by the west of the mountains and was repulsed with severe loss. On the same night General von Lettow-Vorbeck moved the greater part of his force from Kisaki to reinforce Stammermann's column which had retired on Dutumi and there awaited our main force advancing through the mountains by the eastern road. Great difficulties were encountered in moving along this road as gradients were very steep and in places it was necessary to construct bridges, whilst at other places it was necessary to swim the mules and it was only just possible for the porters to keep loads out of the water when fording the streams.

On the 9th September the two enemy forces had concentrated at Dutumi and a three-day battle ensued. On the first day of the attack, the Kashmir Rifles and the Machine-Gun Company attacked the enemy's right flank, through sugar-cane and long grass and established a position about five hundred yards from the enemy. On the second day half the Company was withdrawn and took up a position on the slopes of the mountains, where they had a bird's-eye view of the enemy's endeavour to turn the flank on the low ground and as the enemy's flank attack was within range of the machine-guns, they were able to assist in repelling this counter-attack.

During the night the enemy commenced their withdrawal, and on the following day they evacuated the position and began their retirement to Beho-Beho, near the Rufiji River.

Beho-Beho was later attacked and there Selous, probably the greatest of all African game hunters, was killed, serving with the 25th Royal Fusiliers.

The Machine-Gun Company, which had received no reinforcements since its formation in March, had now been reduced to a strength of under thirty non-commissioned officers and men and received orders to return to Morogoro with a view to proceeding via Dar-es-Salaam to rejoin the Battalion which had in the meantime returned to East Africa and was now at Kilwa.　Owing to the very great difficulties connected with getting up supplies, ammunition, petrol, etc., no clothing had been obtainable for several months.　When the Company was halted at various supply dumps on its march to Morogoro, many South Africans passed through clothed only in a ragged shirt, a helmet and a pair of boots.

At one of these dumps an order was received for an officer of the Company to be detailed to bury a South African who had died on the road. Like most South Africans he was a member of the Dutch Reformed Church of South Africa.　The only prayer book available was one of the Church of England and incidentally the officer who conducted the service was a Presbyterian!　From a medical point of view the Company had to rely largely on its own resources and was lucky in having one or two men who had been trained in India as medical orderlies ; these men were invaluable and kept officers and men in the field who would otherwise have found it impossible to "stick it."　At this time, amongst other makeshifts, the enemy had had to improvise field dressings made from the bark of trees.

On arrival at Morogoro the Company, after several months, saw for the first time a British Hospital complete with nurses, which brought home to them the fact that they had been through the very unusual experience of not having seen a member of the other sex (black or white) for over seven months !

Here things were comparatively civilized and a new base was being formed.　The cases quoted above have been given with a view to trying to describe the conditions under which the force operated at this period of the campaign.

The Company received orders to march from Morogoro to Dar-es-Salaam and to commandeer local guides along the road to find an old slave route which had practically ceased to be used and had in places practically disappeared since the construction of the railway.　The strength of the Company at this time consisted of five officers and twenty other ranks, with thirty-five mules and about one hundred first-line porters, and eight days' supplies were carried by second-line porters. The length of the march was about one hundred and twenty miles.

The Company arrived at Dar-es-Salaam on the morning of the eighth day. Here it was medically inspected. Three officers (Major R. E. Berkeley, Lieutenant G. E. Bowden and Lieutenant W. Halton) and seventeen rank and file were found fit to continue in the field and they proceeded to rejoin the Battalion at Kilwa with a view to the formation of another Machine-Gun Company.

LOYAL NORTH LANCASHIRE MACHINE-GUN COMPANY

(Afterwards No. 259 Company, Machine-Gun Corps)

December, 1916–December, 1917

On rejoining the Battalion at Kilwa on 15th November, 1916, the situation was as follows :—

The Battalion had received orders to proceed to Egypt, leaving behind all fit men to form a Machine-Gun Company, the small fit remnant of the previous Company forming the nucleus.

The officers with this Company were as follows : Major R. E. Berkeley, Lieutenants G. E. Bowden and W. Halton, 2nd Lieutenants H. J. Prout, J. R. Godfrey, H. C. Tunnadine, N. McDonald, and E. Fellowes.

The medical officers with great difficulty selected the one hundred and twenty fittest men and the company commander was given a free hand to select a warrant officer and non-commissioned officers from the Battalion.

The formation of the Company was proceeded with as rapidly as possible, and after about ten days' training received orders to proceed on December 11th to Kibata, about sixty miles by track in a north-westerly direction. This post was under command of Brigadier-General O'Grady with detachments of King's African Rifles, Baluchis and Mountain Battery. It consisted of a mission station, from which the Germans had been driven, but they had taken up positions on the higher hills which commanded the position and from which they could bring rifle and machine-gun fire to bear.

The force holding Kibata was a small one, and the situation more closely resembled trench warfare than at any time during the campaign.

The Company left Chuma at 6 p.m. on the evening of the 17th December in a torrential downpour of rain, the darkness being typical of the tropical density of the country, and arrived at Kibata at 6 a.m. the following morning. The country through which the march was made was thick bush, and for a newly-formed Company to move with one hundred and twenty porters and forty mules under these conditions was of considerable difficulty, but was carried out without a hitch. One of the positions held by the enemy was within forty yards of one of our posts and was known as " The Lodgement " and had already changed hands twice. It dominated our position and orders were received for the Company to support with two sections of guns the attack to be made the same night by a party of Baluchis and bombers from the King's African Rifles.

The Germans, in place of barbed wire, had fixed sharpened bamboo spikes in front of their position, and the Baluchis crawled under the enemy's fire and removed these before rushing in, and a hand-to-hand fight ensued, the enemy being literally hurled down the slope on the other side. A section of machine-guns assisted in holding the captured position, and during the following morning 2nd Lieutenant N. McDonald, who was in command and attending a wounded man, was hit and died in the improvised hospital at Kibata a week later—on Christmas Day. A 4-in. " Königsberg " gun, two field howitzers and two mountain guns, under Lieutenant-Commander Apel, did considerable execution.

A force under Brigadier-General Hannyngton, composed chiefly of the W.A.A.F.s, had occupied a position north-west of Kibata, locally known as Gold Coast Hill, and this position was strongly attacked and shelled by the Germans, the W.A.A.F.s holding the hill but suffering heavy casualties.

Owing to the advance from the north of our forces which had crossed the Rufiji at Kongolio in boats, the enemy's supply depots were threatened, and General von Lettow-Vorbeck was forced to withdraw in a southwesterly direction.

It was during the early days of the Company's occupation of Kibata that the following incident, which may be of sufficient interest to record, occurred. A small party of German porters was surprised while trying to get out of camp with various loads which they were endeavouring to get away from the Mission Station, two of these loads consisting of elephant tusks. It was obviously undesirable that they should get away with these, and they eventually represented the only memento of the campaign in possession of the Company when it left the country. One tusk was presented to the 2nd Battalion Mess and the other to the Machine-Gun Corps Depot at Shorncliffe.

As the Battalion was at this time in Egypt, and it was impossible for reinforcements to be sent to the Company a wireless message was sent to the War Office asking how casualties were to be made good. A reply was received stating that all officers, N.C.O.s and men had been transferred to the Machine-Gun Corps, and that the Company would be known as No. 259 Company, Machine-Gun Corps, date of transfer being 31st January, 1917.

The Company left Kibata in the middle of January, and until the 14th February took part in operations in the Mtumbei Valley, the enemy slowly withdrawing. The long period of two or three months' very wet weather was now commencing, and during this time operations would, of necessity, have to be at a standstill. The Company received orders to return to Kilwa and found much difficulty on this march owing to casualties amongst the porters. To cope with this difficulty, a herd of several thousand donkeys which had been imported into the country was utilized for carrying rations. Owing to the rain several streams had to be forded on the return to Kilwa and the method of getting across these consisted of swimming the mules and donkeys, and taking guns, ammunition and rations over on rafts improvised from petrol tins and branches of trees. The route followed was by Chini Mjingo—Mitoli and Migerigeri, the Company arriving at Kilwa on the 21st February.

It was now clear that some months must elapse before operations could be resumed, orders were issued for the Company to proceed to Nakuru on the Uganda Railway (midway between Nairobi and the Victoria Nyanza Lake), about 8,000 feet above sea-level, to recuperate.

The Company embarked in H.M.T. "Barjora" on March 8th and, after putting in at Dar-es-Salaam and Zanzibar, disembarked at Kilindini (Mombasa) and trained to Nakuru. Here the Company was under canvas, but owing to the extreme cold at night and heat by day (Nakuru is practically on the Equator) the extremes of temperature increased rather than decreased the prevalence of malaria, although otherwise the better climate and food were conducive to a general improvement in health.

The Company remained here until May 11th and then trained to Kilindini where it embarked on May 19th for Lindi, putting in for three days at Dar-es-Salaam. On arrival the Company went into bivouac on the slopes of the hills overlooking the sea. Up to this time it had only been armed with ·303 Maxim machine-guns, but was now issued with Lewis guns and trench mortars.

The force at Lindi was not sufficiently strong at this time to advance, and whilst the column was being concentrated, the Company was engaged in training and exercising to keep fit. The camp shortly became unhealthy, but sickness was kept to a minimum as porters had constructed bandas (grass huts) and beds, and the whole Company was under cover.

On June 10th a force under Brigadier-General O'Grady moved out at night and H.M.S. "Severn" and "Thistle" and two whalers sailed up the reedy creek at the mouth of the Lukuledi River in support, and fired

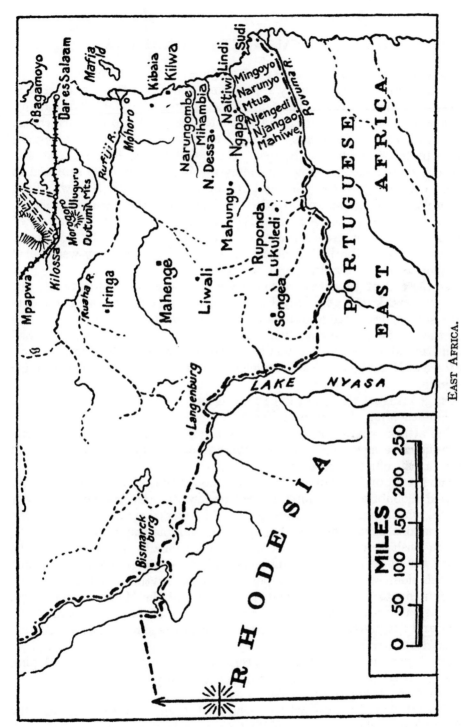

EAST AFRICA.

1917.

on the enemy's positions.   Other naval guns from the Watch Tower at Lindi also fired on the enemy's positions and from there saw H.M.S. " Thistle " struck by one of the enemy's shells, but fortunately little damage was done and she was able to put about and steam back to Lindi Harbour.

A small force under Colonel Wood (two sections of the machine-guns being this force) moved to Ngapa.   The country was found to be still very heavy, and after engaging the enemy at Mingoyo the force returned to Lindi.   On June 30th the 5th Light Infantry advanced to Naitiwi, about three miles from Ngapa, and attacked and captured the enemy's position. The enemy having received immediate reinforcements, counter-attacked with a force under General von Lettow-Vorbeck and inflicted heavy casualties, most of the British officers of the 5th Light Infantry were killed and they lost one hundred and thirty men.

By the end of July preparations were completed for the advance, but units were weak, the 25th Royal Fusiliers, who at one time at Lindi were fairly strong, were reduced to a fighting strength of seventy.   By this time the enemy's communications being threatened from Kilwa, they had fallen back along the trolley line to Narunyo, leaving only a small covering force at Mingoyo which was driven out on the 31st, and we then occupied Mingoyo.

On 3rd August the Lindi force moved out from Mingoyo to attack the Tandamutu–Mihambia positions.

The attack was unsuccessful, and the 30th Punjabis, operating along the trolley line against Mihambia, suffered very heavy casualties, most of their British officers being killed.

The attack on Tandamutu failed to dislodge the enemy from a strongly fortified redoubt and the force retired to Ziwani.   An advanced dressing-station, which had been established for this operation, was raided by the enemy and a large supply of dressings and quinine was taken.

The bush here was so thick that it occasionally happened that the enemy would be heard speaking German, fire would suddenly be opened by both sides, without it being possible to see anything of the enemy.

Lieutenants T. S. Glover and A. H. Daly, of the Machine-Gun Corps, with a small draft, joined the Company on July 13th and Lieutenant C. H. Frost and Lieutenant L. H. D. Castle, both of the same Corps, on August 5th and 12th respectively.

On August 10th the attack was renewed, and in face of an enveloping attack carried out by Colonel Taylor, the enemy under General Wahle fell back on Narunyo and Ruho.

General von Lettow-Vorbeck, who had been operating against the Kilwa force in the Mihambia–Ndessa area, moved his force to Nyengedi and went himself to Narunyo to inform General Wahle of his arrival—where he found the opposing forces facing one another at close quarters—in almost impenetrable country broken by numerous ravines, at the bottom of which lay deep swamps.

On August 18th the Narunyo position was attacked under conditions as described above—perimeter camps were formed at night—the enemy attacked one of these and mistaking its position suffered heavily and little progress could be made. These camps were fired on by the enemy with their " Königsberg " 10·5-centimetre guns when located, and consequently had frequently to be moved. During this period, to prevent the location of camps being disclosed to the enemy, it was necessary to do all cooking at selected places some distance from camp and only by daylight.

Smoke from fires was not so easily seen during the day as in the early hours when in the heavy morning air it hung over the tree-tops.

There was no further advance till September 10th when the enemy withdrew towards Massasi on account of the advance of other British forces advancing from the south and south-west. A small covering force was left at Narunyo—the Kilwa force at this date had arrived at Mahungu and Njangao, capturing supply dumps at these places. After desultory fighting, the enemy retired slowly, concentrating their main force at Mahiwe.

General von Lettow-Vorbeck stated in his diary that on joining General Wahle at Mahiwe he hoped to strike a decisive blow without the Lindi force getting information of this move.

On the evening of the 14th General von Lettow-Vorbeck, with five enemy companies and two guns, arrived at Mancho and left at daybreak on the 15th, joining forces that evening with General Wahle who was then in action against the Lindi force at Mahiwe.

The Lindi force was now concentrated at Njangao with the Kilwa force advancing on Mahiwe from the north, and practically the whole of the German forces still in the field were concentrated at Mahiwe.

At 4 a.m. on October 17th the 3rd/4th King's African Rifles attacked, with the Punjabis, 25th Royal Fusiliers and Machine-Gun Company in reserve.

The attack developed quickly and the Machine-Gun Company sent its Lewis guns forward in close support. In endeavouring to capture a position held by an advanced party of the enemy Lieutenant Frost was killed.

The machine-guns were brought into position on a ridge on the left flank within a hundred yards of the enemy's trenches and heavy fighting continued all day ; and during this Lieutenants Daly, Glover and Prout were wounded, four non-commissioned officers and men were killed and eight wounded : amongst the killed was Sergeant Peduzzi, who had won many a fight in the boxing ring for the Regiment. A heavy fire was kept up all night.

The following day the Lindi force continued to make strong attacks, but the enemy held his ground and fierce fighting at very short range ensued. On account of the strength of these attacks the enemy had to concentrate his force in the centre to hold his ground and the fighting was without any material success on either side. During this day Lieutenant Tunnadine was wounded and Private Wray, who had served continuously with both Machine-Gun Companies, was killed.

On October 18th, Major Kraut at Lukuledi was attacked by the Gold Coast Regiment and retired on Chigugu.

On account of his line of retirement being threatened and of his casualties at Mahiwe—over five hundred killed and wounded—the enemy withdrew on the 19th in the direction of Lukuledi.

This ended the fighting at Mahiwe, and a few days later the Company received orders to move back to Lindi, as all white troops were to be withdrawn from the country.

During one of the halts on the way to the coast Captain G. G. R. Williams, who had been a prisoner in the enemy's hands for three years, was handed over.

On arrival at Lindi the Company embarked for Dar-es-Salaam and sailed for England on 10th December, 1917, putting in at Durban and Cape Town en route.

Summarizing the hardships endured and the enthusiasm displayed by all ranks during the campaign in German East Africa, General J. C. Smuts said :—

" Their work has been done under tropical conditions which not only produce bodily weariness and unfitness, but which create mental languor and depression and, finally, appal the stoutest of hearts. To march day by day, and week by week, through the African jungle or high grass, in which vision is frequently limited to a few yards, in which danger always lurks near but seldom becomes visible, even when experienced, supplies a test to human nature often in the long run beyond the limits of human endurance."

CHAPTER XXXVIII

December, 1916–April, 1918

EGYPT AND PALESTINE

IT was not surprising that a British battalion whch had suffered so much from the climate, as had the 2nd Loyal North Lancashire in East Africa, should now be selected for transfer to another and a less unhealthy theatre of war than was that in which for just over two years it had now been serving ; and at the end of December, 1916, the Battalion embarked for Egypt in the hired transport " Elele " at a strength of ten officers and 442 non-commissioned officers and men. The officers proceeding with the Battalion were Lieut.-Colonel Jourdain, D.S.O., Captains Collas, adjutant, Walsh and Withers, Lieutenants Walker, Chambers, Martin, Hooper, Schofield and Wilkinson, acting quartermaster.

Aden was reached on the 11th January, 1917, and Suez on the 18th, and in the afternoon the Battalion was sent on by rail to Cairo, where it was accommodated in comfortable quarters in Preston Barracks.

Five men had died of the effects of malaria during the voyage.

In Cairo the Battalion found itself in what was known as the Delta District, the troops in which were the 2nd Battalion Loyal North Lancashire, the 1/4th Duke of Cornwall's Light Infantry and five Garrison Battalions, these last composed of men—in part old Regular soldiers— past marching age, and younger men incapacitated by wounds or other disabilities from more active service ; the Delta District was under the command of Brigadier-General H. G. Casson, C.M.G., and was directly under G.H.Q.

On the 5th February the remaining officers and other ranks of the Battalion arrived at Suez from East Africa in the " Desna " and reached Cairo the same evening ; this party numbered ten officers and 365 other ranks, and the officers accompanying it were Major Bridges, Captain Thorne, Lieutenants Schofield, McDonald and Crosby, 2nd Lieutenants Woodgate, Baldwin, Marsh, Hill and Spencer. A return dated the 9th of this month gives the total strength of the united Battalion as twenty officers and 802 other ranks, but of these no fewer than two officers and 293 non-commissioned officers and men were either in or attending hospital.

During the closing months of 1916 General Sir A. Murray, commanding the Egyptian Expeditionary Force, in view of an advance which he proposed making in the ensuing year, had asked to be reinforced by two infantry divisions and any spare mounted troops which might be available. On the 11th January, 1917, he had been informed that the military situation did not at present permit the dispatch of the reinforcements for which General Murray had asked, and that the prosecution of all large-scale operations in Palestine must be deferred until the autumn of this year.

" The general policy during the summer was therefore to prepare for such a campaign, but meanwhile—here was the rub—to be ready to release for service in France one or two divisions. . . . The blow fell sooner than was expected, for on the 17th January the War Office ordered a division to be prepared for dispatch to France. Sir A. Murray selected the 42nd and re-arranged his forces. The 54th Division was moved up from the Canal to Romani, while the 53rd took the place of the 42nd further forward. The 42nd Division began embarkation in Egypt early in February. Once again Sir A. Murray felt it his duty to repeat to the War Office his estimate that he needed five infantry divisions in addition to his mounted troops." *

On the 19th February the Battalion was inspected by General Sir A. Murray, who remarked to the Commanding Officer—" I have nothing but praise for all I have seen."

The Battalion was ordered on the 9th March to prepare to move from Cairo, and it left by train on the morning of the 14th for Kantara, on arrival at which place it marched to the Standing Camp ; but on the 19th the Battalion left again for El Arish, where it took the place of other troops which were marching out to take part in the operations leading up to the First Battle of Gaza.

On the 6th April the Battalion received from home the first draft which had joined since arrival in Egypt ; it was, however, only fourteen strong. Ten days later the Battalion moved to Khan Yunis, where at this time was railhead and consequently was a post of some importance ; while it was also the site of a very fine well, which, when a pumping-station was later there established, supplied an almost unlimited quantity of water for the pipe line, which was being pushed forward as our troops advanced.

From this time on there appear to have been constant changes as to the brigading and disposal of the Battalion. On the 20th April Lieut.-Colonel Jourdain was informed that the Battalion was to be posted to the 232nd Infantry Brigade under Brigadier-General H. J. Huddleston, C.M.G., D.S.O., M.C., with the 1/4th Duke of Cornwall's Light Infantry, the 1/5th

* *Military Operations, Egypt and Palestine*, Vol. I, pp. 272, 273.

Devonshire Regiment and the 2/5th Hampshire Regiment, but this arrangement appears to have been at least postponed, when, on the 24th, the Battalion was sent back to El Arish.   Here on the 11th May the Brigadier-General arrived with the other two units of the Brigade.

On the 1st June the Brigade was informed that it was now part of the 75th Division.

On the 19th June another change took place, the Brigadier informing the Commanding Officer that the Brigade was moving on to Rafa, and that the Battalion was to be attached to the 123rd Indian Infantry Brigade on the lines-of-communication ; this was no doubt occasioned by the continued bad health of the Battalion, of which it had recently been reported that only fifty per cent. were fit for service in the field.   But on the 25th June, Colonel Jourdain was notified that the Battalion was now to form part of the 234th Brigade, commanded by Brigadier-General F. G. Anley, C.B., C.M.G., of the 75th Division—Major-General P. C. Palin, C.B., C.M.G. —the other battalions of the Brigade being the 1/4th Duke of Cornwall's Light Infantry and the 123rd Outram's Rifles, Indian Army.

On the 28th June General Sir E. H. H. Allenby arrived in Egypt and took over command of the Expeditionary Force from General Sir A. Murray.

In the second week in August the Battalion moved from El Arish to the neighbourhood of Alexandria, and on the 12th of this month three Army Corps were formed and to that numbered XXI., to be commanded by Lieut.-General E. S. Bulfin, the 75th Division, with the 52nd and 54th Divisions, was posted.   It was not, however, until the 10th December that the O.C. Battalion was informed that it would shortly move from Alexandria to Gaza, there to rejoin the 75th Division.   Attached to the XXI. Corps this division had assisted in the capture of Gaza on November 7th, and a fortnight later had arrived within five miles of Jerusalem ; while on the very day before the Battalion received notice to rejoin its division, Jerusalem had surrendered to the force under General Allenby's command.

It was not, however, until the 15th December that the Battalion, strength twenty-five officers and 694 other ranks, left Sidi Bishr Station by train and arrived at Gaza early on the morning of the 17th.   Here the Battalion was at once employed in the clearing of the battle-field—a work which went on until Christmas Day, all kinds of warlike stores being retrieved.

On the 1st January, 1918, the Battalion, now at an effective strength of twenty-five officers and 703 other ranks, was finally passed as medically fit for active service ; but it was not until the 22nd February that intimation was received that it would shortly march to Jaffa to join the XXI. Corps.   Jaffa had been captured on the 16th November, and here and to the south and east of it the XXI. Corps had been somewhat heavily engaged about the middle of December.

The Battalion moved off on the 23rd February from Gaza, and, marching along the coastal road by Deir Sineid, El Mejdel, Nahr Sukereir and El Ramleh, arrived at Selmeh, its appointed destination, some three miles due south of Jaffa, after a march of some forty-five miles. Of this march the Battalion War Diary records that " it had afforded a good test. About thirty or forty men turn out to be unable to march owing to age and infirmities. These men are mostly recent transfers from garrison battalions in Egypt and had not marched in their former units."

On arrival at Selmeh the Battalion appears to have been temporarily posted to the 54th Division. (Map, Palestine, page 351, Volume II.)

The Battalion was inspected on the 8th March by the XXI. Corps Commander, who directed all officers to make themselves thoroughly acquainted with the country to the front, with special reference to the ground about Mulebbis and the Auja River ; and from the 12th to the 14th the Battalion, now in corps reserve, was bivouacked at Bald Hill, some five miles out of Selmeh. It was back again at Selmeh on the 18th, and furnished a guard-of-honour of three officers and one hundred non-commissioned officers and men, under Captain A. F. P. Knapp, on the occasion of the visit to Jaffa of Field-Marshal H.R.H. The Duke of Connaught.

On the 24th March, 1918, the news reached Palestine by wireless that the great German offensive had opened on the Western Front, and that very heavy fighting was in progress.

The 5th April saw the Battalion moved to Mount Synia, south of Mulebbis, and from here on the 11th it marched to El Mire, with orders to take over a portion of the line there held by the 1/5th Suffolk Regiment, coming here under some heavy long-range shelling from the Turks and witnessing a considerable aeroplane activity by the enemy. In the operations which were at the moment in contemplation the Battalion played no part, its services being now urgently called for in another theatre of the World War.

CHAPTER XXXIX

April, 1918–May, 1919

FRANCE AND FLANDERS

THE CLOSING BATTLES OF THE WAR

THE BRITISH ARMY OF OCCUPATION IN GERMANY

THE situation which arose in France consequent upon the German offensive which opened on the 21st March, 1918, necessitated the serious reduction of the force at General Allenby's disposal in Palestine. In his despatch of the 18th September, 1918, he there describes the changes which then took place : " The dispatch of troops to France, and the reorganization of the force, has prevented further operations of any size being undertaken, and has rendered the adoption of a policy of active defence necessary. During the first week in April the 52nd Division embarked for France, its place being taken by the 7th (Meerut) Division which had arrived from Mesopotamia. The departure of the 52nd Division was followed by that of the 74th Division, which left Palestine during the second week in April. The 3rd (Lahore) Division was sent from Mesopotamia to replace the 74th Division, but it was not till the middle of June that the last units disembarked. In addition to the 52nd and 74th Divisions, nine Yeomanry regiments, five and a half siege batteries, ten British battalions, and five machine-gun companies were withdrawn from the line, preparatory to embarkation for France."

In all twenty-three battalions of British infantry were withdrawn from Palestine, all of these, except the 2nd Battalion The Loyal North Lancashire, being Territorial, or Service, Battalions.

On the 15th April the Battalion was "warned for service with another expeditionary force," and was at once relieved in the positions it was then holding by the 1/4th and 1/5th Battalions of the Suffolk Regiment, and moved back to Mulebbis. From here on the 23rd the Battalion marched by way of Surafend to Ludd, where it boarded two trains and proceeded by rail to Gabbari Railway Station, Alexandria, the entraining strength being thirty-three officers and 941 non-commissioned officers and men. A few days were spent in Alexandria in camp, until, on the 18th May, the

Battalion was sent by train to Port Said where it embarked in the hired transport "Huntspill" and sailed immediately for France. The voyage was wholly uneventful, Marseilles being reached on the 26th, when the Battalion was put ashore and spent the next four days in camp at Montfuron.

Entraining again on the 31st the journey was made by Moulins Males-herbes, Abancourt, Noyelles, Etaples, Boulogne and Calais, the Battalion finally arriving at Aire very early on the morning of the 4th June, when it marched six miles to Racquinghem, where it found itself in the 94th Brigade of the 31st Division. The Brigade was commanded by Brigadier-General A. Symons, the Division by Major-General J. Campbell, and the 94th Brigade was composed of the 2nd Battalion The Royal Munster Fusiliers and the 2nd Battalion The Royal Dublin Fusiliers. The 31st Division was in the Second Army.

On the 8th June the Battalion marched, via Wizernes, to the Lumbres area where it went into camp ; and a few days later moved to Racquinghem, where, on the 20th June, notification was received that the Battalion was again to be transferred, this time to the 102nd Brigade of the 34th Division, and from the Second to the First Army.

The 34th Division, when originally raised in June, 1915, was a typical New Army Division, and had seen much hard fighting on the Somme, at the Battles of Arras, at Poelcapelle and in the German Offensive of March, 1918. A considerable difficulty had been experienced of late in the matter of reinforcements, and towards the end of April of this year it had been decided that the infantry of the Division must be reduced to cadres, three battalions only being retained intact and these being sent to other divisions. The reduction to cadre strength was carried out in the middle of May, and the cadres were employed in the training of American troops.

In June Major-General J. Nicholson, C.B., C.M.G., began the task of reconstructing the 34th Division, and " the artillery and field companies returned, and also the machine-gun battalion, but the infantry was all new, and some came from India, others had been employed in Gallipoli, Egypt and Palestine, but had had no experience of war as waged in France." [*]

The Battalion had been initially told off to the 102nd Brigade, but was almost at once transferred to the 101st, which contained also the 2/4th Battalion The Queen's and the 4th Battalion The Royal Sussex Regiments, and was commanded by Brigadier-General W. J. Woodcock, D.S.O.

The latter part of June was passed by the Battalion at Herzeele, from where on the 2nd July it marched to Proven, where training was carried on and organization was completed. But on the 16th orders were received

[*] Shakespear, *The 34th Division*, 1915–1919, p. 253.

to entrain for " an unknown destination " which proved to be the Senlis area, in which the 34th Division was concentrated by the 18th, then marching, via Largny, to the Vivières–Puisieux–Soucy–Longavesnes area, the Battalion arriving at Puisieux on the early morning of the 21st July.

The 34th Division now came under the orders of General Penet, commanding the XXX. Corps of the Tenth French Army, under General Mangin, and was intended to assist our allies in the great counter-offensive which Marshal Foch had been preparing on the front between Chateau Thierry and Soissons.

" On the 21st orders were received to relieve the 38th French Division in the line opposite Hartennes and Taux the next day, and before this was commenced came orders to take part in an attack early on the following day, 23rd July. Under the most favourable circumstances this would have been difficult for any troops, but for a newly-constituted division, composed, as regards infantry, of troops which had not yet been in action in France, and which had just completed a trying movement by rail, bus and route march, it was a very severe test. There was no time for reconnaissance ; the country was entirely new ; there were no organized trench systems on either side. The enemy positions were never actually known till they had been captured. To all these difficulties there were added those inseparable from acting for the first time with foreign troops." *

From Puisieux at 4 a.m. on the 22nd the 101st Brigade moved to Villers Helon, the remaining brigades of the Division following later, and all then taking up positions of readiness in the valleys and woods to the north of that place.

The general plan was that the XX. Corps on the left was to turn the wood on the left of Hartennes and Taux, while the right of the XXX. Corps was to turn the two woods of St. Jean and du Pleissier ; the 34th Division, with two French divisions on its right and left, was to connect the two turning movements and advance due east to the high ground east of the Soissons–Chateau Thierry road ; the 34th Division was not to move, however, till the XX. Corps on the left had crossed this road.

The following is the Battalion account of the very costly operations which now commenced and which endured for some ten days :

On the night of the 22nd–23rd July the 34th Division relieved a French Colonial Corps, the relief being completed by 1 a.m. on the 23rd when the 101st Brigade held the right half sector, the 102nd the left, the 103rd Brigade being in divisional reserve. In the 101st Brigade the Battalion was on the right, the 2/4th Queen's on the left, the two occupying a frontage from a wood 500 yards north of Contremain as far as Parcy Tigny.

* *The 34th Division,* p. 254.

In the Battalion " C " and " D " Companies were on the right and left of the front line respectively, with " A " in support of " C," and " B " of " D."

The direction of the advance was to be due east ; the artillery preparation was to last for ten minutes, the attack commencing on the barrage lifting.

At eight o'clock " C " Company's first wave advanced, but after going forward for some fifty yards it was practically wiped out, the survivors falling back under heavy enemy machine-gun fire and an artillery barrage which came down on the front trench within one minute of the advance commencing. In the meantime " D " Company went forward on the left of the Battalion and covered the right of the Queen's to within 600 yards of the Hartennes–Chateau Thierry road ; the company drove in the enemy's advanced machine-guns, but the Germans, counter-attacking at about 9.30, forced back the Queen's on to " D " Company's left, obliging that company to retire also, having suffered some sixty casualties.

For the rest of the morning the enemy maintained very heavy gun and trench mortar fire on the wood 500 yards north of Contremain, on which the right of the Battalion rested, causing here some seventy casualties. In the afternoon the two front-line companies were ordered back to battalion reserve, when " A " Company occupied the small salient and wooded spur on the right of the Brigade and " B " the small re-entrant on the low ground to its left, so joining up with the Queen's. The night was passed in collecting casualties, burying the dead, and improving the defences.

The 24th was a tolerably quiet day, beyond some intermittent shelling by the enemy ; that night the men were employed in deepening the shallow trenches, and in wiring off the salient at the east end of the wood, while a strong point was completed and wired in at the end of this wood—500 yards north of Contremain.

On the 24th there were three casualties from shell fire, and another on the following day.

On the night of the 26th–27th the German patrols were active, and early on the 27th, after a bombardment of twenty minutes, a patrol of twelve men attacked a post on the extreme right of the Battalion, wounding the sentry and taking three men prisoners ; it was evident that this German patrol had drawn near disguised in French steel helmets, for two of these were found in the trench. On this day the right company of the Battalion, assisted by the Trench Mortar Battery, attacked and silenced an enemy strong point 150 yards south of the salient, which had been giving much trouble. At last on the night of the 27th–28th the 2nd Bn.

The Loyal North Lancashire was relieved in the front line by the 48th French Infantry Regiment and, with the remainder of the 34th Division, fell back under cover of darkness to Bois de Bœuf, and at once set to work to prepare for an attack which it was intended to make next day in the Oulchy le Chateau area, some five miles to the south.

The date of this operation had been more than once changed ; it was at first fixed for the 30th July, but as the French had had some success on the 27th and indications of the enemy being about to retreat increased, it was decided to attack on the 29th ; but as the troops did not reach the Bois de Nadon till the early hours of the 28th, there was little time for reconnaissance of the routes to the " jumping off " line, near and south of the Bois de Baillette.

The 101st Brigade marched off very early on the morning of the 28th to its assembly position some 1,000 yards south-west of the Grand Rozoy Railway Station, the order being that the 34th Division was to attack at 4.30 a.m. on a frontage of 800 yards in a north-easterly direction, the objective being the Grand Rozoy ridge, the XI. French Corps being on the right and the 25th French Division on the left. The 34th Division was disposed with the 103rd Brigade on the right and the 101st on the left, each having a frontage of 400 yards ; the 102nd Brigade was in divisional reserve.

Of the 101st Brigade the 4th Sussex was on the right, the 2/4th Queen's on the left and the 2nd Loyal North Lancashire in brigade reserve ; the front battalions each had two companies in the attacking line, the third and fourth companies each following 150 yards behind, while the Battalion moved 300 yards in rear of the leading battalions, its companies being disposed in depth with 150 yards between each company.

The events of this day are described as under in the Divisional History :—

" The advance started punctually close behind a heavy rolling barrage in dense fog, and the ' Green Line ' was taken without any trouble. The battalions halted there and reorganized before pushing on at 6 a.m. So far everything had gone according to plan, and for some time the progress continued satisfactory. By 7 a.m. the Beugneux–Grand Rozoy road had been cleared of the enemy, but his machine-guns were strongly posted and numerous in the rear of the wood in Beugneux and on Hill 158. The 8th Scottish Rifles,* in spite of heavy losses pushed on as far as the foot of the Hill, and the 5th King's Own Scottish Borderers * passed round the north-west of Beugneux and got well up the slopes of Hill 189. Here they came in touch with ' A ' and part of ' C ' Companies of the 2nd Loyal

* Both of the 103rd Brigade.

North Lancashire, under Captain G. P. Atkinson, who, though in support of the Royal Sussex, had, in the stress of battle, found their way through the woods and seized the crest of Hill 189 by 7.40.   Lieut.-Colonel Jourdain was killed about this time. . . .   At about 10.20 a.m. the situation was roughly as follows : the French had taken Grand Rozoy and pushed to the north-east of it, but not far ; then came some of the Queen's stretching up the slope towards Point 189, but not in touch with Captain Atkinson, and the small party of Loyal North Lancashire and King's Own Scottish Borderers, to the east of which were some of the Royal Sussex, who were also out of touch on their right."

Several attempts were now made to turn Hill 158 and the village from the south, but unsuccessfully, for the fire, chiefly from machine-guns, was too strong, and the 102nd Brigade was ordered up to counter-attack ; but the Germans now launching a heavy attack on the French on the left, the whole line fell back before the intended counter-attack could materialize and took up a new position.   The Battalion retired to the vicinity of Grand Rozoy Railway Station, where it reorganized ; its strength now was no more than six officers and 230 other ranks, but stragglers gradually rejoined.

" As a result of the operations of the 29th July," so the Divisional History states, " the XXX. Corps line now ran from Bois de la Terre d'Or, inclusive, along the road to Grand Rozoy, round the northern end of that village, and thence about one hundred yards south of the road to Beugneux as far as the eastern edge of the wood, and thence to some buildings at the station side of Hill 158, thence parallel to and south of the Beugneux–Cramaille road."

On the 30th July the Battalion was temporarily placed in divisional reserve, but was again called forward to take part in the further operations which were to have been resumed on the 31st, but were later postponed to the 1st August.   The 103rd and 101st Brigades were again to be on the right and left of the divisional front, with the 102nd Brigade in reserve, and in the 101st Brigade the Battalion was at the outset in reserve.

On the 31st Captain R. V. Taylor joined with eighty men from the Divisional Reinforcement Camp at Largny.

At 1 a.m. on the 1st August the Battalion—now only seven officers and 380 other ranks—moved to the assembly position in a sunken road 700 yards south-east of Grand Rozoy, having a trying march through a gas-filled area ; and the attack by the 101st Brigade is described as follows in the Divisional History :—

" The 101st Brigade had been completely successful, overcoming considerable opposition in the woods north of the Grand Rozoy–Beugneux road, where there was fierce fighting with bayonets, and one section 101st

L.T. Battery, under Lieutenant Archibald, did good work silencing machine-guns, of which twelve were captured with five of the enemy, some fifty were killed, and the rest bolted and were chased by the Loyal North Lancashire, who captured forty-one more. By 6 a.m. the Queen's, Royal Sussex and Loyal North Lancashire were on the crest of the ridge near the objective, but were enfiladed by machine-gun fire from Hill 203, which was promptly cleared by Captain Atkinson, commanding the Loyal North Lancashire, sending ' D ' Company of that battalion to form a defensive flank.

" During the rest of the day the line remained stationary, but about 5 a.m. it became evident that the line was not far enough advanced to cover the valleys on either side of Hill 199, and that hostile action in the valley to the east of that hill was causing trouble to the 68th French Division in Servenay. Therefore at 7 p.m. under a creeping barrage the line was pushed forward some 300-400 yards along the whole of the 34th Division and the left of the 68th Division front."

During the night that followed the enemy fell back quietly under cover of a thick fog, and on the 2nd August the 25th French Division passed through the depleted ranks of the 34th and pursued the Germans, now in full retreat. The 34th Division was then withdrawn to the rear, and by the night of the 4th, the Battalion was disposed in billets in Ormoy Villiers, where it was joined by thirteen officers and ninety other ranks from Largny.

The Division had been in the line since the night of the 22nd-23rd July, and had in that time fought three general actions, and had lost 153 officers and 3,617 other ranks killed, wounded and missing. To this total the Battalion had contributed its full share, having lost from the 22nd July to the 3rd August three officers and 76 other ranks, killed or died of wounds, wounded fourteen officers and 318 men, and thirty-two men missing—a total casualty list of 443.

The officers who were killed were Lieut.-Colonel C. E. A. Jourdain, D.S.O., Captain R. V. Taylor and 2nd Lieutenant J. R. T. Jones ; wounded were Captains A. F. P. Knapp, G. P. Atkinson and G. R. Brockbank, Lieutenants C. Crosby, W. E. Martin, H. J. Soppitt, J. B. Martindale, H. B. Leonard and H. Wilkinson, 2nd Lieutenants C. C. Dutton, J. A. Mercer, E. W. W. Brown, and C. G. Nightingale.

On the 34th Division leaving the French Corps area, General Mangin, commanding the Tenth French Army, issued General Order No. 343, of which the following is a translation :—

" Officers, Non-Commissioned Officers and Men of the 15th and 34th British Divisions.

" You entered the battle at its fiercest moment. The enemy, already once vanquished, again brought up against us his best divisions, considerably outnumbering our own. You continued to advance step by step, in spite of his desperate resistance, and you held the ground won in spite of his violent counter-attacks. Then, during the whole day of the 1st August, side by side with your French comrades, you stormed the ridge dominating the whole country between the Aisne and the Ourcq, which the defenders had received orders to hold at all costs.

" Having failed in his attempt to take the ridge with his last reserves, the enemy had to beat a retreat, pursued and harassed for twelve kilometres.

" All of you, English and Scottish, young soldiers and veterans of Flanders and Palestine, you have shown the magnificent qualities of your race, courage and imperturbable tenacity.

" You have won the admiration of your companions in arms. Your Country will be proud of you, for to your Chiefs and to you is due a large share in the victory which we have gained over the barbarous enemies of the free.

" I am happy to have fought at your head, and I thank you.

(Signed) " MANGIN."

The Division now went back for rather over a fortnight to a rest area, after which the units composing it began to return to the front in the Ypres sector ; and on the 30th August the 101st Brigade relieved a brigade of the 41st Division in the Scherpenberg sector. Here the front of the 34th Division extended for some 3,000 yards, facing south-east about midway between Kemmel Hill and Scherpenberg, in the left portion of the XIX. Corps front ; the 30th British Division was on the right and the 27th American Division on the left.

From the 7th to the 13th August the Battalion was at Bissezeele, and while here Lieut.-Colonel T. McG. Bridges arrived and assumed command ; while the following officers joined from the 3rd and 9th Battalions of the Regiment : Lieutenant T. L. Pritchard, 2nd Lieutenants G. R. Sharpe, R. Hay, J. Draper, S. Jellicoe, M. H. Tutt, D. McK. Morison, A. Giddins and H. L. McKay.

It now seemed certain that the enemy must vacate Kemmel Hill, and accordingly on the 30th August Major-General Nicholson gave orders that the battalions in the front line should at once push forward patrols, follow up the enemy should he retire and seize Kemmel Hill. The forward movement began all along the line, and by five o'clock that evening the Battalion had passed through Kemmel village and had occupied the Vierstraat Switch

Line with but small opposition, in the Battalion one man being killed and thirteen wounded.

On the 1st September the Division continued its advance, the 101st Brigade on the left and the Battalion on the left of its brigade ; " C " Company, under 2nd Lieutenant Tutt, was on the right of the Battalion, its right resting on Suicide Road, " A " was on the left with its right on the road running through the map point N. 22 Central, while " B " Company, under Lieutenant Pritchard, and " D," under Lieutenant Sharpe, supported " C " and " A " Companies respectively. The 106th American Regiment was detailed to advance on the left of the Battalion.

By about 11.30 a.m. the two leading companies had reached their first objective and had established protective posts in their front : a halt was now made until 4.30 p.m., at which hour another battalion passed through and advanced on the second objective—the line Peckham–Maedelstede Farm–Petit Bois, but was held up by German machine-guns some 300 yards in the front. This line was held during the night under some heavy though intermittent shelling. In the morning of the 2nd the enemy aeroplanes were tolerably active and many shells fell upon " B " Company in the Alberta dug-outs, and at noon " D " Company suffered to some extent from the fire of the German machine-guns and snipers. At 3.20 the Battalion was relieved by a battalion of the 102nd Brigade and went back to the Scherpenberg area, heavily shelled by the enemy as it marched back by the La Clytte–Kemmel road.

Late on the night of the 3rd the Battalion moved back to the front, reoccupying part of the Vierstraat Switch Line, and here the whole of the 4th was spent under shelling with lachrymatory and mustard gas, in the evening of the 5th moving forward and occupying positions in the vicinity of Spy Farm.

And so matters went on until the 15th when the Battalion was at last relieved and went back to the Frenchbank area where the 101st Brigade was in support, but considered responsible for the defence of the Scherpenberg–Dickebusch system.

During these operations, lasting from the 1st to the 15th September, the casualties in the Battalion had been by no means light, these numbering one officer and nine men killed, five officers and seventy-nine other ranks wounded ; Lieutenant A. F. R. Linaker was killed and the wounded officers were Captain F. L. Morgan, Lieutenants P. R. Thomson and J. Hughes, 2nd Lieutenants M. H. Tutt and A. Giddins.

On the 25th the Battalion returned to the front to take part in further operations, the general scope of which is described as follows in the Divisional History : " These were to commence on the 28th September, and were to extend along the whole Belgian and British front, from Dixmude to the line of the Ypres–Comines Canal. The task of the 34th Division was to establish itself on the Ypres–Comines Canal, south of the bend at Hollebeke. This involved capturing the Wytschaete Ridge. To achieve this by direct assault, with only the support of the divisional artillery, would have been a costly business. It was therefore decided to work up as close as possible to the crest of the ridge in order to seize it, when a turning movement of the 41st Division from the north should have sufficiently loosened the enemy's hold on it. The advance began at 5.30 a.m. on the 28th September, by strong patrols under cover of a smoke barrage."

The advance was almost immediately successful, the Battalion, on the front of the 101st Brigade, early capturing Warsaw Crater and many enemy posts, killing and making prisoners a large number of Germans and also capturing two machine-guns. At 3.30 p.m. good progress had been made on both flanks, and the Division was then ordered to advance beyond the Wytschaete Ridge and clear the ground as far as the Canal before dark. The advance was for a time held up by machine-gun fire from Wytschaete, but the movement was resumed at dark and continued during the night, and very early on the morning of the 29th " B " Company of the Battalion succeeded, by a turning movement, in gaining possession of Wytschaete, the defenders having now made up their minds to retreat.

The advance of the 30th and 41st Divisions had now squeezed the 34th out of the line, and this was accordingly assembled on and west of Wytschaete Ridge, the Battalion withdrawing to Alberta dug-outs.

The fighting strength of the Battalion on going into action was nineteen officers and 377 non-commissioned officers and men, and its losses were eleven killed, five officers and 42 other ranks wounded and eleven men missing ; the wounded officers were, Lieutenants G. R. Sharpe, J. Spencer and W. A. Hopkins, Herefordshire Regiment, attached, 2nd Lieutenants L. S. Smith and E. R. Schofield. The Battalion had captured fifty-two of the enemy, one field-gun and five machine-guns.

The 34th Division moved on the 2nd October to an area east of the Ypres–Comines Canal about Zandvoorde, and that same night took over the Werwicq–Menin line from the 35th and 41st Divisions, the 102nd and 103rd Brigades being in the front and the 101st in reserve in rear about Zandvoorde. This line ran from about 2,500 yards north of Werwicq to Gheluwe, a total front of some 3,500 yards, nearly the whole of which was under direct enemy observation from north and east of the Lys.

On the 8th 2nd Lieutenants H. Mewha and J. Hughes joined from England, and on the 11th Lieutenant J. A. Mercer was wounded.

On the 14th the XIX. Corps again attacked a position, of which the village of Gheluwe was roughly the centre, the 34th Division occupying the Corps centre with the 30th Division on the right and the 41st on the left. The line held this morning by the XIX. Corps ran south-west from a point about 400 yards north-west of the northern end of Gheluwe, through Quack Farm to the Ypres–Gheluwe road, thence due south to the Werwicq–Gheluwe road, and thence again south-west about one hundred yards to the divisional boundary.

On this occasion the 101st Brigade was in divisional reserve and consequently the battalions composing it took no very active part in the operations, which were wholly successful. The casualties were comparatively low and the captures many, 568 of the enemy being taken prisoner, with three field-guns, many trench mortars, machine-guns, and much light railway material and rolling-stock.

Menin was occupied by the 102nd Brigade on the 15th and posts established on the right bank of the Lys, the 103rd carrying on the line along the Wevelghem road to the east of Tent Farm. Then during the night of the 15th–16th the 101st Brigade prolonged the line to the left, its left extending as far as the north-eastern outskirts of Wevelghem. The Battalion was on the right of the Brigade with the Royal Sussex on the left and the Queen's in support. Both front-line battalions sent forward patrols early on the 16th and those from the Battalion cleared Wevelghem, so that by 10 a.m. the north bank of the Lys was effectively held.

At 9.30 on the 17th " B " Company of the Battalion crossed the river near Royal Farm—one man at a time—by means of an improvised raft, and established posts in a semicircle covering the crossing-place. An hour later " D " Company was ordered to cross and advance on Lauwe, supported by Lewis-gun fire by " A "; and by 2 p.m. Lauwe was occupied, and on the arrival of " C " Company a defensive flank was formed facing north-east between the Courtrai and Arbeke roads.

" On the 18th General Woodcock and the headquarters of the 101st Brigade made a triumphant entry into Lauwe, which was the first Belgian town we had entered which was still inhabited. The inhabitants gave the General a demonstrative and enthusiastic welcome. The enemy was evidently in full retreat, and crowds of liberated civilians were met on all sides."

The advance was resumed on the 19th, the Battalion moving in support of the 2/4th Queen's, which provided the advanced guard. By midday some 6,000 yards had been covered and then there was a slight check in front of Belleghem, which was occupied by the enemy, but " B " and " C " Companies of the Battalion moved round the side of the village, encircling it.   This movement took some time and it was midnight before the Courtrai road, east of Belleghem, was reached ; and on the 20th the 101st Brigade was withdrawn to Halbeke, the 34th Division now becoming corps reserve and remaining tolerably quiescent until the 25th—so far as the 101st Brigade was concerned.

On this day the G.O.C. was informed that the 34th Division was to be transferred to the II. Corps, and on the 26th the 101st Brigade moved to a new area south-east of Hartebeke, the Battalion having a trying march during which it crossed the Lys three times.   In the course of the night 26th–27th the Brigade took over the line, from the 36th Division, reaching from Kleineberg to the railway bridge over the Krommebeke.   On the following night, on relief, the 101st Brigade went to the Harlebe–Deerlyck area.   The Battalion suffered some casualties during the relief, 2nd Lieutenants J. Draper (died later of wounds) and S. Hacking and some men being wounded, the total casualties during the month of October being twelve killed or died of wounds, thirty-nine wounded and eleven missing.

There was renewed fighting during the advance on the 31st October and 1st November, but the 103rd Brigade only of the 34th Division appears to have taken any very active part in it ; though, as stated in the Divisional History, the Battalion was ordered up to Sterhoek on the night of the 31st in view of a possible attack in the early hours of the 1st November.

At 1 p.m. on the 1st November, however, the divisions on the right and left of the 34th joined hands across the front of the latter at Elseghem, then advancing to the line of the Scheldt, when the 34th was drawn into reserve, marching on the 3rd to the west of Courtrai, the Battalion going into billets at Wevelghem.

It was here that on the 11th the Battalion received the news that an Armistice had been arranged, and that the war had at long last come to an end.

On the 17th November the Division marched to the Lessines area and was now transferred to the X. Corps, moving again on the 12th December to an area in the angle formed by the Meuse and Somme at Namur, the headquarters of the 101st Brigade being at Malonne, and the Battalion being quartered in a large convent at Ollignies.   Here it remained until the middle of January, 1919, by which time demobilization had begun, and the march to the Rhine commenced.   This was concluded on the 29th, when the 34th Division occupied the right sector of the Cologne bridgehead, the 101st Brigade being at Siegburg.

While here the divisional boxing competition was won by the 2nd Battalion, The Loyal North Lancashire Regiment, which took three out of the six events.

On the 15th March, the 34th Division dropped its old number and became the Western Division, the battalions of which it had been composed being transferred to other divisions or reduced to cadre and their places being for the most part taken by the Young Soldiers' Battalions now coming out to Germany.

To the units which had for so long fought and marched under his command, Major-General Nicholson issued on the 4th March the following farewell order :—

" I cannot allow the infantry battalions, which are now leaving the Division on re-organization, to go without expressing my great appreciation of their conduct and bearing, both in and out of action, since they joined the 34th Division.

" These battalions, coming from different brigades and divisions in the East to new conditions of warfare and to commanders who were unknown to them, were almost immediately put into action with the French army, south of Soissons, in the early days of the French offensive of July, 1918. The conduct of all in the hard fighting and under the strenuous conditions was beyond all praise, and gained much praise from our Allies.

" Subsequently in the months of August, September and October in Flanders and Belgium, they showed the same qualities of endurance, gallantry and discipline in action.

" I am proud to have had such battalions under my command, and part with them with the greatest regret, and wish all ranks the best of fortune in the future."

It was not until the 17th May that the cadre of the Battalion left Siegburg and proceeded by way of Antwerp and Tilbury to the Depot at Preston, the following officers accompanying it : Lieut.-Colonel T. McG. Bridges, Captain C. S. Chambers, Lieutenants H. Wilkinson, E. G. Hooper and E. Molyneux.

CHAPTER XL

THE REGIMENTAL DEPOT.
THE 3RD BATTALION
THE LOYAL NORTH LANCASHIRE REGIMENT.
THE GREAT WAR

1914–1919

THE REGIMENTAL DEPOT.

FULWOOD BARRACKS, PRESTON.

AFTER the completion of the mobilization of the Regular and the Special Reserve Battalions in August, 1914, the Depot was re-formed, the staff being composed of officers from the Reserve of Officers and re-enlisted ex-Warrant and Non-commissioned Officers. Lieut.-Colonel E. G. Costobadie was gazetted to the command on the 9th of September, whilst Major F. H. F. Evans and Major W. Bentley were appointed adjutant and quartermaster respectively.

The Depot became a reception centre, where recruits were received, clothed and equipped and then dispatched in drafts to the 3rd (Special Reserve) Battalion, where they received their training before being sent to one or other of the battalions of the Regiment abroad. Casualties from such units were also dealt with by the Depot ; all the sick and wounded arriving back in England from the Front came automatically on the supernumery strength and so remained until posted to the 3rd Reserve Battalion on expiration of sick furlough, after discharge from hospital.

Prior to March, 1916, it was further the duty of the Officer Commanding Depot to obtain recruits for the Regiment, and recruiting parties, accompanied by a band, were accordingly sent out to the surrounding neighbourhood of Fulwood Barracks, with satisfactory results. After the passing of the Military Service Act, recruits, after having been called up, were conducted from the various recruiting offices to the Depot.

In the autumn of 1914 the Regimental Comforts Fund was inaugurated for the purpose of forwarding articles of warm clothing, tobacco and other additional luxuries to those of the Loyal North Lancashire who were on active service overseas. Subscriptions were readily forthcoming from past and present members of the Regiment and also from their relatives and friends. These gifts were much appreciated and the supply of these comforts was steadily maintained throughout the period of the War.

THE DEPOT, FULWOOD BARRACKS, PRESTON.

Likewise a Regimental Committee was formed to look after the interests of those who had been unfortunate enough to fall into the hands of the enemy and were retained as prisoners-of-war ; some had been wounded before being captured and all suffered the worst privations in the various internment camps.   Parcels of food, and clothing of a special pattern, were dispatched at stated intervals, through the agency of the Red Cross Society ; without the receipt of which many would have died of starvation and cold.   Those interned in the neutral countries were also not forgotten. These activities continued until the signing of the Armistice, on 11th November, 1918, when the prisoners-of-war were generally released.

The 3rd Battalion, The Loyal North Lancashire Regiment

(Special Reserve)

War having been declared by Great Britain against Germany on the 4th of August, 1914, mobilization commenced almost automatically, and the Special Reserve was called up for service.

On the 6th August the first party of Special Reservists of the Battalion was mobilized and proceeded on the same day to Felixstowe to take over barracks ; this party was composed of Lieut.-Colonel P. W. Harrison and twenty-six non-commissioned officers and men.   On the same day Captain H. F. B. Ryley, Lieutenants R. C. Mason and J. G. W. Hyndson were sent to Aldershot, the first-named officer to take over details from the 1st Battalion, and the two subaltern officers to join the Battalion and complete establishment, proceeding overseas with it.

Two days later the 3rd Battalion was mobilized and was dispatched at once to its war station, Felixstowe, where it arrived early on the morning of the 9th, its disentraining strength being twenty officers and 638 non-commissioned officers and men.   There were seventeen absentees on mobilization, but these were all satisfactorily accounted for.

The following officers accompanied the Battalion : Colonel T. Cowper-Essex, Lieut.-Colonel P. W. Harrison, Major A. H. W. Saunders-Knox-Gore, Captains J. G. Fairlie, F. W. Greenhill, G. W. Hay, H. Powell, E. C. Miller, R. E. Crane and G. Loch ; Lieutenants S. T. Lucey, F. G. Wynne, J. H. Miller and V. L. Henderson ; Captain and Adjutant F. H. E. Torbett and Lieutenant and Quartermaster E. C. Mudge.

On arrival in this area the Battalion found itself brigaded with the Third Battalions of the Suffolk, Norfolk and Bedfordshire Regiments under the command of Colonel the Marquis of Salisbury.   The companies of the Battalion were distributed in different posts, all fortified and all forming part of the Harwich fortress defences.

At the end of August the Battalion adopted the double-company system, when the existing eight companies became " A," " B," " C " and " D " ; but in course of time as the recruits, enlisted for the period of the war only, came up in ever-increasing numbers, it became necessary to form five more companies known as " E," " F," " G," " H " and " K," and these were accommodated in newly-erected hutments.

On the 14th November, 1914, Field-Marshal Lord Roberts, Honorary Colonel of the Battalion, died while on a visit to the Army in France ; the funeral took place on the 19th of that month in St. Paul's Cathedral, London, a detachment of the 3rd Battalion being present. On the 1st May, 1915, Colonel L. Bonhote was appointed to succeed him as honorary colonel, and on the 22nd March, 1916, Colonel T. Cowper-Essex was gazetted to the honorary colonelcy of the Battalion.

Between the 4th August, 1914 and the 23rd July, 1918, no fewer than one hundred and five officers, mostly of course second-lieutenants, joined the Battalion, while sixty-seven were transferred to other corps ; of the officers who at one time or another had previously served with the 3rd Battalion, thirty-five were killed or died of wounds, or were wounded, during the course of the War.

The first draft sent out to the Expeditionary Force in France, from the 3rd Battalion, was on the 9th August, 1914, and these succeeded each other with tolerable frequency until the conclusion of hostilities. By the 12th April, 1916, the total number of men sent out during the preceding months was 5,309, for the most part to the Regular and Service Battalions of the Regiment. The functions of the Battalion during the whole of the War were thus of a dual kind—coast defence and draft finding.

The strength of the Battalion was maintained by the steady flow of recruits, and by the casualties from the overseas units of the Regiment, who rejoined through the Depot, after leave following discharge from hospital. Before departing for active service all recruits had to be put through an intensive course of training ; whilst the rejoined casualties from the battalions abroad underwent a special course of hardening so as to enable them once again to take their places in the trenches of France and Flanders, or wherever else they might be called upon to go.

The Battalion remained in and about Felixstowe until the 25th February, 1919, when it was sent to Aldershot, moving to Blackdown on the 24th April ; finally, on the 2nd August, 1919, it was absorbed by the 2nd Battalion ; the cadre of the 3rd Reserve Battalion having returned to Preston on the 28th July.

A representative detachment of the 3rd Battalion took part in the " Victory March " in London, on Saturday the 19th July, 1919.

CHAPTER XLI

THE 4TH (LATER 1/4TH) TERRITORIAL BATTALION
THE LOYAL NORTH LANCASHIRE REGIMENT

1914–1916

THE GREAT WAR

FRANCE AND FLANDERS

FESTUBERT, THE BATTLES OF THE SOMME

IN the summer of 1914 the West Lancashire Division had assembled for its usual annual training under its commander, Major-General W. F. Lindsay, and the 4th Battalion, The Loyal North Lancashire Regiment, was in the North Lancashire Brigade of the Division, with the 4th and 5th Battalions The King's Own Royal Lancaster Regiment and the 5th Battalion of The Loyal North Lancashire ; but the units composing the Division had scarcely settled down in their training area at Kirkby Lonsdale, when they were recalled to their peace stations under Mobilization Order No. 281 of the 4th August. On the 10th Field-Marshal Lord Kitchener, now Secretary of State for War, wrote to the Director-General of the Territorial Force, asking for early information as to what Territorial battalions would volunteer for service abroad, and what others wished to remain with the Home Defence Force only. On the question being put before the units of the West Lancashire Division, the response was immediate and emphatic—every unit in the Division volunteered !

The needs of the military situation abroad made it unfortunately impossible for the Division to go out as a complete unit, as had been intended, since reinforcements for the Regular Army were urgently required ; the result was that many units of the Division were sent singly to France for attachment to the Regular Army, and from October, 1914 to May, 1915 there was a steady flow of such.

On the 14th August the 51st (Highland) Division arrived at Bedford, its war station, and here it was joined by the reconstituted North Lancashire Brigade of the West Lancashire Division. The Brigade now contained the 4th Bn. The King's Own Royal Lancaster, the 8th Bn. The

King's Liverpool, the 5th Bn. Lancashire Fusiliers and the 4th Bn. The Loyal North Lancashire Regiment. The Brigade proceeded abroad with the Highland Division and remained with it until January, 1916, when the West Lancashire Division was re-formed.

On the 13th April, 1915, orders were received for the 51st Division to prepare for embarkation for service overseas, and by the 5th May all the units composing it had been landed in France.

On the 2nd May an advance party, of three officers and one hundred and four other ranks of the Battalion, left Bedford by train, and, on arrival at Southampton, embarked with the whole of the Battalion transport in the S.S. " Rossetti " for Havre. Disembarking here, the party marched to No. 5 Rest Camp where the night was spent.

The rest of the Battalion left Bedford on the evening of the 3rd in two trains, and made for Folkestone, where it went on board the S.S. " Onward," sailing very early on the morning of the 4th for Boulogne where on arrival it was accommodated in Ostrohove Rest Camp. The same evening, however, it was sent on by train to Berguette, being joined en route by the advance party and the transport. At Berguette the train was left and the Battalion marched by way of Lillers to Chalons where it went into billets along the Robecq road.

The total strength of the Battalion on this date was thirty-one officers and 1,003 non-commissioned officers and men; the officers were Lieut.-Colonel R. Hindle, Major F. W. Foley, Captain and Adjutant C. C. Norman, Royal Welsh Fusiliers, Captains H. Nickson, E. H. Booth, C. G. R. Hibbert, J. H. Peak, J. L. Whitfield, J. A. Crump, H. Parker and J. O. Widdows, Lieutenants R. Ord, W. Smith, E. M. Rennard, K. H. Moore, J. L. Brindle, E. M. Gregson and L. Duckworth, 2nd Lieutenants A. T. Houghton, A. L. Harris, W. A. Davis, H. Lindsay, H. Rogerson, P. Parker, H. Bryce-Smith, N. G. Craven and E. Rawsthorn, Lieutenant and Quartermaster F. W. S. Baker, Captain T. H. C. Derham, R.A.M.C., in medical charge, and the Rev. V. P. Powell, Chaplain.

The Division was now concentrated in the area Busnes–Robecq–Lillers, and formed part of the Indian Army Corps in the First Army.

" At this period the general situation on the Western Front was as follows : the Second Battle of Ypres, prepared by the discharge of asphyxiating gases, had begun on the 22nd April, and was to continue with great intensity for over a month. During the early part of this period the French were preparing an attack to be launched on the 9th May between Arras and the right of the British line. The First British Army, having been ordered to support this operation by an attack, had issued instructions directing the IV. Corps against the German position in the neighbourhood of Richebourg—south-west of Fromelles—and the I. and Indian Corps against the German trenches between Givenchy and Neuve Chapelle. These attacks as planned were accordingly delivered on the 8th, 9th, and 10th May, 1915. They, however, met with little success. It was therefore decided that the First Army should concentrate on the southern point of attack, and renew the operations on the 12th May. This attack was subsequently postponed until the 15th owing to low visibility." *

In the meantime the Division had received a number, and became on the 11th May the 51st (Highland) Division, the North Lancashire Brigade being the 154th Brigade of that Division.

During the early portion of the operations known as the Battle of Festubert the 51st Division remained in reserve to the Indian Corps, being held ready to move up to the front at short notice ; but on the 14th May it marched to the area Caestre–Borre–Merris–Meteren and came into G.H.Q. Reserve ; and from this date until the evening of the 18th the 4th Battalion remained in billets on the east and north-east sides of the town of Meteren.

The 51st Division was now to relieve the 2nd on the line of the La Quinque Rue–Bethune road in the area La Gorgue–Vielle Chapelle and the Battalion moved to Locon and remained here until the 25th, while the other two brigades of the Division were taking over the ground from the 2nd Division and Canadians in the Neuve Chapelle and Richebourg sectors. It was consequently not until the 25th May that the Battalion moved out of its billets at Locon and relieved the 7th Black Watch of the 153rd Brigade, taking over a sector about one mile west-north-west of Festubert, the right resting on La Quinque Rue and the left on the road from Rue de l'Epinette to Ferme Cour d'Avoine. " A " and " D " Companies and the machine-gun section occupied the fire trenches, with " C " in support and " B " Company in reserve.

Of the trenches occupied at this stage and in this theatre of the war, the Divisional History states that " in the case of the front taken over by the Division, the normal difficulties were accentuated by the fact that digging in was only possible to a depth of from two to three feet. Everywhere in the Flanders mud, below that level, water was encountered. It was therefore necessary to erect above ground double rows of traversed breastworks, between which the men must live and have their being. The difficulty of consolidation in this mud country requires to have been experienced to be fully appreciated."

Against the trenches taken over by the Battalion the Germans kept up an intermittent fire all day of shrapnel and high-explosive shells ; here the first casualties of the war were experienced, and before relief on the

* Bewsher, *The History of the 51st Highland Division*, pp. 10 and 11.

1st June by an Indian regiment, the Battalion had had one man killed, 2nd Lieutenant H. Bryce-Smith and thirteen men wounded. On relief the Battalion was withdrawn to billets at Cornet Malo, half a mile to the north-west of Locon Church.

By this time the 51st Division had been transferred to the IV. Corps.

" On the 7th June orders were issued from the IV. Corps to attack the enemy's positions about Rue d'Ouvert and Chapelle St. Roch and further south on the morning of the 11th, with the object of gaining ground towards Violaines. Later this attack was postponed until the 15th, but on the 12th the operation order was issued. The objective of the IV. Corps was ' the German positions from the Chapelle St. Roch along the Rue d'Ouvert to L.12. The Canadian Division was to attack on the right and form a defensive flank ; the 7th Division was allotted the Chapelle St. Roch and the southern end of the Rue d'Ouvert as its objective ; and the 51st Division the extreme end.

" ' The actual objective given to the 51st Division were the houses at L.11., L.12., L.13 and K.7. At the last-named they were to join hands with the 7th Division. The 154th Infantry Brigade were detailed for the attack, their right being directed on the south-west corner of the German salient—that is, a point about 150 yards east by south of L.8. The left of this attack was to be directed through L.9.' " *

The Battalion had moved up to the front again on the 13th June—having 2nd Lieutenant A. T. Houghton and one man wounded during the relief—in readiness for the attack to be made on the 15th, of which the following general account, so far as the work of the 154th Brigade is concerned, is abridged from the Divisional History :

At 6 p.m. on the 15th June the attack was launched by the 4th Loyal North Lancashire and the 6th Scottish Rifles, which latter battalion had lately taken the place of the 2/5th Royal Lancaster in the 154th Brigade. The attack was at first successful ; the west end of the German salient was carried, and the attack pushed on to the main German line near the Rue d'Ouvert, and for a time the third German trench line was occupied and held. Three companies of the 4th King's Own Royal Lancaster were accordingly sent forward to reinforce the Scottish Rifles. Unfortunately the attack by the division on the right of the 51st made little or no progress, and when night fell the 154th Brigade had penetrated the German line on a narrow front, but had both its flanks in the air. The attack consequently failed, but as stated in the Divisional History, " great praise is due to the 154th Infantry Brigade for their advance in the face of heavy artillery

* *History of the 51st Division,* pp. 16, 17.

and close-range rifle and machine-gun fire. There is little doubt but that had the operations on their flanks been successful, they would have had every prospect of holding their gains."

The following is from the Battalion account of the day's operations ! The German position had been subjected throughout the earlier part of the day to as heavy a bombardment as our somewhat limited resources in heavy guns and ammunition permitted, and it had been arranged that this would increase in intensity at 5.30 p.m., concentrating at this hour on the enemy wire. At 6 p.m. the guns were to lift on to the German fire trench, then on to their communication trenches, at 6·45 forming a barrage in rear of the road.

At 5.30 " B " and " D " Companies of the Battalion moved up the communication trenches towards the fire trench, while " A " came up from the reserve to the support trench. The German guns now subjected the communication trenches to a murderous fire, and the troops experienced the very greatest difficulty in making their way to the front.

At 6 p.m. " C " Company charged forward from the fire trench, its platoons led by 2nd Lieutenants Parker, Craven and Davis, and within three minutes of starting they were in possession of the German trench, experiencing casualties mainly from rifle and machine-gun from the main trench, since in the advanced trench, which " C " Company captured, the majority of the defenders were found sheltering in dug-outs. These were dealt with in splendid fashion by the bombing parties of the Brigade.

Telephonic communication with Brigade headquarters now broke down and messages had to be sent by runners, and the course of the action now necessarily becomes somewhat obscure. " B " Company suffered severely —all its officers becoming casualties—in crossing the deep and heavily wired ditch in front of the German fire trench, and this company, and also " A " and " D," experienced most of its losses from the German guns, the fire from which had by now redoubled in intensity. " B " Company was, however, able to reinforce " C " on our right, while " D " was used to strengthen the left of the front line.

Meanwhile the attack had swept on past the enemy's fire trench, and would have actually carried the main trench also, but for coming up against a mass of uncut barbed wire, and it was checked, losing many men from enfilade fire.

The Scottish Rifles were attacking on the left of the Battalion, but their advance was also stopped by uncut wire, and they halted and lay down in the open under a very galling fire, also losing heavily ; and the 4th Loyal North Lancashire, not being able to advance, was ordered to dig in in the ditch where it had been checked, the ditch being fringed on the east by rows of pollard willows, while on the other side it was protected by a low bank.

Here the Battalion entrenched itself as well as was possible, and sent out parties to try and establish touch with the troops on the flanks, but without any success.

By this time Lieut.-Colonel Hindle had been wounded, and Major Foley had established battalion headquarters in rear, Major Nickson being in command of the front line.   About 11 p.m. the German gun-fire slackened, and Major Nickson sent back to Major Foley, explaining the situation and asking for orders ; but about midnight, and before any reply was received, the Germans counter-attacked, bombing the trenches, putting one of the Battalion machine-guns out of action and cutting off communication with the Scottish Rifles.

Major Nickson now gave orders for withdrawal, some men lining the shell-craters, holding up the enemy for two hours and allowing of the retirement being carried out, the party finally getting away under cover of the early morning mist on the 16th.

The attacking battalions withdrew to the reserve trenches about 5 a.m., the line being taken over by the 8th Battalion, King's Liverpool (Irish).

On arrival at Le Touret only 243 men answered to their names when the Battalion roll was called, for in this its first general action the total casualties numbered 431 killed, wounded and missing ; actually there were killed, or died of wounds, four officers and nineteen other ranks, six officers and 255 non-commissioned officers and men were wounded, while two officers and 145 men were missing.   Of the officers Captain J. L. Whitfield, Lieutenant W. Smith, 2nd Lieutenants E. Rawsthorn and W. A. Davis were killed or died of wounds ; Lieut.-Colonel R. Hindle, Captain C. C. Norman, adjutant, Lieutenants K. H. Moore and J. L. Brindle, 2nd Lieutenants P. Parker and N. G. Craven were wounded, and Captains C. G. R. Hibbert and J. H. Peak were missing.

The attack was renewed, though with no better success, on the 16th, but the Battalion took no part in it, remaining during the next week or more in brigade reserve.   In the meantime, however, on the 16th the following message was received from the Commander of the IV. Corps :—

" The Corps Commander wishes you to convey to the troops of the 51st Division his appreciation of their gallant conduct yesterday and to-day, particularly to the assaulting battalions—viz. the 6th Scottish Rifles, the 4th Loyal North Lancashire Regiment and the 8th King's Liverpool Regiment."

On the 24th June orders were received for the 51st Division to rejoin the Indian Corps and to relieve the Lahore Division in the sector south of Laventie.   Accordingly on this day the Battalion marched with the 154th Brigade by Lestrem, La Gorgue, Estaires and Laventie to Fauquis-sart, where it took over trenches on a front extending from a point 300 yards north-west of Rue d'Enfer for about 400 yards, the Scottish Rifles being on the left and the Royal Lancaster on the right.   The Laventie defences consisted of little more than a single line of breastworks, with, some 200–400 yards in rear, a series of detached posts at intervals of from 300 to 500 yards.   About one thousand or fifteen hundred yards in rear of the supporting posts was the reserve line, the whole overlooked from Aubers Ridge, occupied by the enemy.   Here the Battalion remained until the 27th July, much being done to improve the existing defences.

The 51st Division was now to be transferred to the X. Corps, under the command of Lieut.-General Morland, of the newly-formed Third Army, and to the Neuilly area east of Amiens ; the X. Corps was one representa-tive of the British Army of this date, containing as it now did the 5th Regular Division, the 51st Territorial Division and the 18th Service Division. The relief of the 51st in the Laventie area by the 8th and Lahore Divisions began on the 26th and was completed by the 29th July.

The Battalion left La Gorgue by train on the 27th and moved by Calais, Abbeville and Amiens, finally detraining at Corbie and marching thence by way of Ribemont to Martinsart, in the neighbourhood of which place the Division relieved a portion of the XI. French Corps, taking over the line from near Becourt on the River Ancre, the 154th Brigade occupying the right sector lately held by the 22nd French Territorial Regiment ; the Battalion, however, remained during the greater part of August in divisional, or brigade, reserve, but the front line was a tolerably quiet one and casualties were few.

On the 21st August the Battalion was joined by a draft 101 strong provided by the 2/4th Battalion ; it was accompanied by four subaltern officers—2nd Lieutenants A. B. Bratton, H. W. Strong, J. S. Walker and M. W. Nolan.   Earlier in this month 2nd Lieutenant G. Norwood had also joined for duty.

In September preparations began for the Battle of Loos, and though the Third Army took no part in the attack, every effort was made by the units composing it to keep the enemy occupied in their front, leading him to be on the outlook for a possible offensive, and so making him disinclined to transfer troops from here to the scene of the actual operations.

On the 7th October Brig.-General G. T. G. Edwards, C.B., assumed command of the 154th Brigade in place of Brig.-General G. L. Hibbert, wounded ; and towards the end of this month an enemy high-explosive shell killed Major H. Nickson and wounded 2nd Lieutenant A. B. Bratton and six men, while a few days later, 2nd Lieutenant M. W. Nolan and two other ranks were also wounded.

There is little of importance to chronicle during the remainder of the time the Division remained in these parts, during which it appears to have been largely employed as an instructional division to New Army Divisions now arriving in France, and which were attached to it for periods of instruction in the line.

The end of the year 1915 found the 4th Battalion, The Loyal North Lancashire Regiment, occupying the trenches about Authuille; but the 51st Division was now under orders for transfer to a new area and a different Corps, and some of its units had already commenced to move away. The Battalion, however, was about to sever its connection with the 51st Division, and was once again to become part of the 55th (West Lancashire) Division.

It was on the 3rd January, 1916, that the 55th Division commenced reconstruction in France; the batteries which had been serving at the front since the previous September with one of the Canadian divisions, had received orders in mid-December to proceed to the neighbourhood of St. Omer; while, later, the other units of the original West Lancashire Division, which had been serving with other divisions, were directed to leave them and proceed to the back areas where all the units of the old Division were to be reconcentrated, and henceforward play their part in the war with the 55th Division. It was therefore a division composed of units possessing no small war experience which began to assemble in and around Hallencourt, near Abbeville, in the first week of January, 1916.

The Battalion was not, however, to leave the 51st Division without a serious loss befalling it, for on the 1st January, while up in the trenches near Authuille, an enemy shell blew in one of the dug-outs, killing 2nd Lieutenant F. R. Best and wounding 2nd Lieutenants H. Rogerson, R. A. Ostrehan and three men.

On the 3rd the Brigade left the 51st Division and marched by Henen-court and St. Gratien to Rainneville, where some thirty-six hours were spent, and here the Battalion became part of the 164th Brigade, of which the other units were the 4th Royal Lancaster, the 8th King's Liverpool and the 2/5th Lancashire Fusiliers; the commander was Brigadier-General G. T. G. Edwards, C.B., and when it first began to concentrate it was in the XIII. Corps. Within a very few days, however, the 55th Division was ordered to join the XIV. Corps commanded by Lieut.-General the Earl of Cavan.

On the 7th January the Battalion moved independently to billets at Airaines, where the remainder of the month was passed: here training of all kinds was put in hand and seventy-two men joined as reinforcements and also the following subaltern officers—2nd Lieutenants F. K. Matthew, H. S. F. Agostini and C. T. Silveira.

On the 3rd February the Battalion left Airaines, for the 55th Division had been detailed to relieve the 88th French Division at the time occupying the sector south of Arras, from Wailly to Bretencourt. February and March were comparatively uneventful months, for the sector was a tolerably quiet one and casualties were happily few; but there was heavy snow followed by a thaw and the trenches became very wet and the discomfort experienced was great. At times the enemy aeroplanes showed a certain amount of activity. During these months, and in April and May also, small reinforcements of officers and men joined, but on the 30th May 2nd Lieutenant W. Eccles was killed in the trenches.

Raids were now the order of the day and these occurred with greater frequency and increasing strength, and in the middle of June a special battalion raiding party was organized and practised continually. This party was composed of Captain E. M. Gregson, 2nd Lieutenants Martin, Roscoe and Walker and sixty other ranks, and " on June 28th a daylight raid on a pretentious scale took place. The preparations were careful and detailed; gas and smoke were to be discharged on a two-mile front, to be followed by raids in no fewer than six different places by parties from the 2/5th Lancashire Fusiliers, 1/4th Loyal North Lancashire, and the 1/5th, 1/6th, 1/7th and 1/9th Liverpool Regiment. Unfortunately at the crucial moment a change of wind took place and the discharge of gas was only partially successful. In addition, the raiding parties were received by heavy rifle and machine-gun fire, with the result that two of the parties were unable to penetrate the enemy trenches. The remainder, however, were successful, and many of the enemy were killed." *

In the battalion raiding party ten were killed, including Captain Gregson; while 2nd Lieutenant A. Martin and 2nd Lieutenant J. S. Walker and seventeen other ranks were wounded. Corporal Thompson did admirable work in maintaining telephone communication between the advanced parties and Brigade headquarters, and he and Private Clarke remained out in a shell-hole until after nightfall observing the enemy's movements:

A private of the raiding party wrote of this affair: " Captain Gregson was there—I never saw him look better, he was always one of the smartest officers in the Battalion, but he seemed to have been got up for the show with greater care than usual. The smoke lifted like a curtain. We were in full view of the Boche trench. We went on till within fifty yards of it, and then he opened out with machine-guns, rifles and trench mortars. It was hell let loose and someone shouted ' On the Kellys,' and on we went

* Coop, *The Story of the 55th Division*, p. 27.

but were cut down like corn. The Jerrys were two deep in their trench and we realized we were done."

The following Special Order of the Day was issued on the 29th June by the Divisional Commander :—

" Yesterday six raids on the enemy's trenches were carried out by the 2/5th Lancashire Fusiliers and 1/4th Loyal North Lancashire Regiment of the 164th Brigade, and by the 1/5th, 1/6th, 1/7th and 1/9th King's Liverpool Regiment of the 165th Brigade, assisted by detachments of the R.E. These raids were carried out in daylight in unaccustomed and very difficult circumstances, and in the face of very determined opposition. In spite of these obstacles the results arrived at were successfully obtained, and great damage and loss inflicted on the enemy. The gallantry, devotion and resolution shown by all ranks were beyond praise, and the Major-General Commanding is proud to be able to congratulate the West Lancashire Division on the discipline and soldierly spirit exhibited—a discipline and spirit which the most seasoned troops could not have surpassed.

" He deeply regrets the loss of those who fell, but the spirit they showed will have its effect on the enemy. When the opportunity comes of avenging their deaths, the Major-General Commanding is confident that the Division will not forget them."

" It was on the 25th July that the Division was relieved by the 11th Division and proceeded south to play its part in the Battle of the Somme. . . . The journey south was accomplished rapidly and without incident, and on July 30th the Division had taken its appointed place in the line opposite the village of Guillemont—already a storm centre—and presently to receive dread notoriety. Guillemont had proved to be a thorn in the British side and had held up more than one attack. Its capture was of supreme importance to the success of the general advance, and a further attack, which was entrusted to the Division, was to take place.

" The Division, therefore, took over the line opposite Guillemont on July 30th and the 164th Brigade occupied the front, having the 39th French Division on its right and the 2nd Division on its left. . . . The attack was timed to take place at 4.20 on the morning of the 8th August. The order of battle was as follows : the 165th Brigade on the right was to capture the line, roughly the Hendecourt–Guillemont road, and to couple up with the French on their right. The 164th Brigade on the left, employing the 1/4th Royal Lancaster and the 1/8th Liverpool Regiment, with two companies of the 4th Loyal North Lancashire, was to take the northern and southern portions of Guillemont village, the two companies of the Loyal North Lancashire following up the attack and occupying the German front line."

Prior to the opening of the attack the Brigade—and also the Battalion —had suffered much from the German guns during the preliminary occupation of the line, the Battalion having three men killed, 2nd Lieutenants Orrell, Crone, Munro and Hunt and thirty-one men wounded.

On the 5th and again on the 6th August " D " Company, under Major Parker, with Lieutenant De Blaby and 2nd Lieutenant Hague, made several attempts to dispossess the enemy of a ridge he was occupying about 150 yards to the front, and in these operations two men were killed and twenty-five were wounded, while 2nd Lieutenant A. E. Hague was missing.

On the night of the 8th the Battalion assembled in trenches east and west of the road which ran south from the east corner of Trones Wood, " C " Company being detailed to consolidate the right of the enemy line. " D " was to consolidate the left of the line on the west side of Guillemont, while " A " and " B " Companies were to act in conjunction with the 4th Royal Lancaster and 8th Liverpool Regiments respectively. The attack was not a success. The right was held up from the start by the switch line and the attackers had to fall back to their starting-point, though the Liverpool Regiment went through the village on the left, and " D " Company of the Battalion had begun consolidation, when the enemy, getting between them and the Liverpool Regiment, obliged " D " Company also to retire.

Considerable confusion was caused by the mist and the employment by the enemy of smoke bombs, and the Battalion reserve platoons, though not called upon to act, suffered very heavily. Of the Battalion three officers—Captains E. M. Rennard and H. Lindsay and Lieutenant R. S. De Blaby—and nine other ranks were killed or died of wounds, Lieutenant A. J. D. Evans, 2nd Lieutenants E. L. Fairclough, T. A. L. Bigger and 97 non-commissioned officers and men were wounded, and 2nd Lieutenants O. H. Ducksbury and J. F. Holden and 107 men were reported missing.

The attack was renewed on the 9th, but the 164th Brigade did not participate, and, though gallantly pressed, it again failed.

The 55th Division was relieved on the night of the 14th–15th August and moved back to the west of Abbeville to rest and refit, having done good work while up in the front : during the period from the 30th July to the 15th August the line had been advanced 500 yards on the right and 300 yards on the left, while 13,000 yards of new trenches had been dug and over 3,000 yards of trench-line deepened and improved.

Having received two strong drafts from the Manchester and East Lancashire Regiments, totalling 219 non-commissioned officers and men, the Battalion spent the rest-period in billets at Saigneville and later at Millencourt. On the 7th the Brigade was recalled to the front, and the Battalion, now reinforced by two officers, Captain S. B. Donald of The Buffs and Captain C. B. Bolingbroke of the Norfolk Regiment, marched from Fricourt for Montauban ; here the sector of the front line taken over extended from the eastern edge of Delville Wood in the direction of Ginchy, the Battalion and the 2/5th Lancashire Fusiliers occupying the trenches. Of the Battalion " B " and " C " Companies were in front with " A " Company in support.

" The situation here," so the Divisional History states, " was a peculiar one. The enemy was still holding on with determination to about twenty yards of the south-east corner of Delville Wood, and Ginchy was still in his hands, having been recaptured from the 7th Division a week after its capture by them. To the south and south-east a line running to the north of Guillemont was held by the 16th and 36th Divisions.

" Orders were received from the XV. Corps that the attack would be renewed at 4.45 in the afternoon of the 9th September. The 16th Division of the XIV. Corps was to attack on the right of the 55th and capture Ginchy, and the 1st Division of the III. Corps was to attack on the left. . . . The task of the 164th Brigade was first to take a line of trenches running roughly from the outskirts of Ginchy to the east corner of Delville Wood, and, secondly, to capture Hop Alley and Ale Alley. . . . The 166th Brigade was to co-operate with the 164th by making a bombing attack on Ale Alley from the north-east corner of Delville Wood."

The following is taken from the Battalion War History : " The British artillery were in action all day and at 4 p.m. the barrage started ; at 4.45 the Division on our left attacked. Our objective was to capture Hop Alley with ' B ' and ' C ' Companies, whilst the Lancashire Fusiliers were to go over with us and take Ale Alley. At 5.25 the Battalion went over, and the first objective, Hop Alley, was gained, but the second wave did not succeed in reaching Ale Alley, and as Hop Alley had become untenable under intense machine-gun barrage and gun-fire, the remnant of ' B ' and ' C ' Companies withdrew and fell back to their original line. Supporting companies from the 1/8th King's Liverpool and 1/4th Loyal North Lancashire Regiments were sent up to strengthen the line, whilst working parties consolidated the position. Sergeant H. Farnworth was awarded the D.C.M. for good work in this attack.

" The casualties were heavy ; amongst the twenty-four killed were 2nd Lieuts. W. E. Pyke and E. F. Falby, whilst, in addition to 125 men, Captains S. B. Donald and C. B. Bolingbroke, Lieut. H. W. Strong and 2nd Lieuts. W. V. Gray, P. Pollard, F. E. Vipond, C. H. Forshaw and W. H. Bury were wounded. Under the heading of missing were seventy-nine of the rank and file. As the result of these heavy losses the Battalion

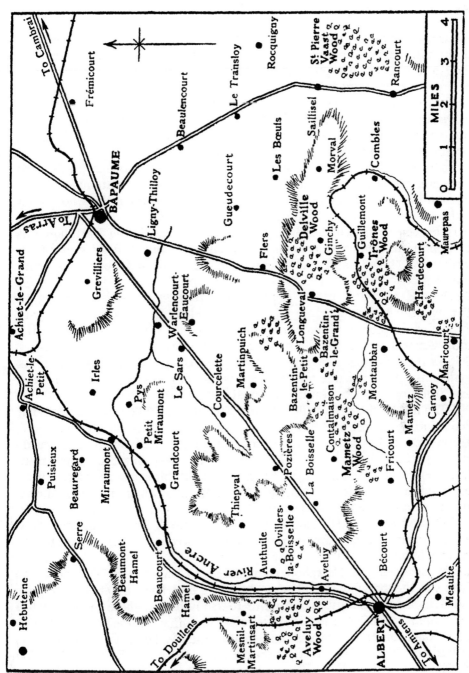

BATTLEFIELDS, NORTH OF THE RIVER SOMME.

1916.

169

was withdrawn from the front to the support line and rested for the day. In the afternoon we stood-to in view of a possib˙ attack by the enemy. Though remaining in support the Battalion was moved 1,000 yards nearer the front for the remainder of its stay, until the 41st Brigade came up as relief on September 12th, when we marched to bivouacs near Fricourt."

On the 18th September Brigadier-General C. I. Stockwell, D.S.O., relieved Brigadier-General Edwards in command of the 164th Brigade, retaining the command until the Armistice.

Following upon some days in billets at Fricourt and Mametz, the Brigade was again brought up to the front in the last week in September, as the Division was now to take part in the general attack along the whole front of the Fourth Army. In the operations which took place about Gueudecourt on the 27th, while the 164th Brigade attacked, the Battalion was in support and suffered comparatively slightly, but 2nd Lieutenant R. Forrest was killed, and 2nd Lieutenant Duerden and four men were wounded.

The end of the month of September witnessed the relief of the 55th Division prior to its departure for the north, where it was to take over part of the Ypres Salient and remain for many months. On leaving the Fourth Army General Sir H. Rawlinson issued the following farewell order :—

" As the Division is now leaving the Fourth Army I desire to express to all ranks my gratitude for the good work that has been done, and my congratulations on the results achieved.

" The hard fighting in which it took part about Guillemont and Delville Wood during August and September was a severe strain on all ranks, and the progress made in these areas reflects great credit on all concerned. When put into the line for the third time to carry out the attack near Gueudecourt on September 27th, the Division exhibited a spirit of gallantry and endurance which was wholly admirable, and which resulted in the capture of all the objectives allotted.

" I regret that the Division is leaving the Fourth Army, and trust that on some future occasion I may have the good fortune to find it again under my command."

On the 30th the Battalion commenced to move from Dernancourt, where for the previous twenty-four hours it had been billeted, and proceeded by train and by march-route to Brandhoek, where an unusually large number of officers joined or rejoined for duty ; these were Captains A. T. Houghton and A. Walsh, 2nd Lieutenants G. Tong, F. C. Jenkinson, V. Mather, A. O. Knight, I. Haworth, F. L. Vernon, E. G. Faber, A. Bardsley, A. Ashton, E. E. Tweedale, H. Holden, H. Swaine, R. V. Reed, B. H. Williams, J. E. Ordish, R. Bissett, J. H. Ogden and H. K. Vipond.

The Division was now in the VIII. Army Corps (General Hunter-Weston) of General Sir H. Gough's Second Army, and the portion of the line taken over by it from the 29th Division ran from Wieltje to the south of Railway Wood.   For the first few months at least of occupation this may be described as a quiet sector, though casualties did not altogether cease, and during the last three months of the year 2nd Lieutenant L. M. Walton was killed and 2nd Lieutenants T. Higson, J. F. Walmesley and J. H. Ogden were wounded.

During these months the Battalion was engaged in no major operations ; but the extent of the general wastage suffered by an infantry unit during this war may be gauged from the following return of the killed, wounded and missing in the 1/4th Battalion, The Loyal North Lancashire Regiment, during the year 1916 :

In the case of the officers these came to a total of thirty-five, while the casualties among the other ranks numbered 593.

The Battalion came out of the trenches on the evening of the 24th December, and Christmas Day was celebrated in comfortable billets in the town of Ypres—the enemy unaccountably refraining from " sending stuff over."

CHAPTER XLII

THE 1/4TH (TERRITORIAL) BATTALION
THE LOYAL NORTH LANCASHIRE REGIMENT

1917–1919

THE BATTLE OF YPRES, THE BATTLE OF CAMBRAI,
THE BATTLE OF THE LYS

THE first five months and more of the year 1917 were spent in the same area and in very much the same kind of operations as those which marked the close of 1916, and the 55th Division as a unit was not actively engaged in the June operations which resulted in the capture of Messines Ridge by the Second Army. The Division did, however, all it could to help the good work which others were carrying out, for as the Battalion History relates : " On the 14th June both sides were active. We were preparing an elaborate programme of smoke and other bombs, to be discharged at the same hour as the Messines battle was timed to start, also putting scaling ladders against the parapet—this work was under Captain Harris. The Huns shelled Ypres pretty heavily in the evening and set two large dumps on fire.

" At 10.30 a.m. on the 7th July the Messines battle started with a literal earthquake—nineteen mines being blown up at once, the barrage starting at the same time on our front among others. The enemy shelled us for about half an hour, by which time he found out we were bluffing him and stopped. Our casualties were five killed, 2nd Lieut. Agostini and ten others wounded."

By this time—the change-over actually took place on the 10th June —the 55th Division had been transferred to the XIX. Corps of the Fifth Army, the Corps and Army Commanders being Generals Watts and Gough.

" The objective of what was called the Third Battle of Ypres was the capture of the enemy's Gheluvelt–Langemarck system. It was also hoped to obtain a footing upon the Gravenstafel Spur, but this was not to be pushed and was contingent upon circumstances. It was, in fact, not intended to attack any position in which strong resistance was offered by the enemy other than the Gheluvelt–Langemarck line.

"The attack was to be made by the Fifth Army in conjunction with the Second Army and the First French Army. The XIX. Corps was to attack with the 15th Division on the right and the 55th on the left. The 16th and 36th Divisions were in reserve. The XVIII. Corps was to attack on the left of the 55th Division, which was to attack with the 165th Brigade on the right, the 166th on the left and the 164th in reserve. All units were to be in their zero positions by 2 a.m. on Zero day." *

The attack was to be made in three stages. The First Objective of the 55th Division was the enemy's front-line system of trenches up to and including the Blue Line, and this was to be captured by the leading battalions of the two front-line brigades. The Second Objective, the enemy's second line, or Stutzpunkt, was to be taken and consolidated by the remaining battalions of these brigades. The Third Objective, the Gheluvelt–Langemarck Line, was to be seized by the 164th Brigade, which was, for this purpose, to pass through the leading brigades of the Division, then halted on the Second Objective.

The weather had been fine throughout June and July, but on the 29th July a very heavy thunder and rain storm broke out, and all the shell-holes were filled with water, while the roads became almost impassable; it was still dull and damp when at 3.30 a.m. on the 31st the barrage opened, and it is said that never before had so intense and so effective a barrage been put down by our artillery.

The 165th and 166th Brigades had very heavy fighting before it was reported that they were in possession of the Second Objective, when the 164th Brigade was to advance through them and go on to the capture of the Third Objective. Part of the German second line was, however, still in the enemy's possession, while other portions had not been finally cleared, so that the work of consolidation and the construction of supporting points, though carried on vigorously, were being fiercely disputed.

The following twenty-two officers went into action this day with the Battalion, and of these four only came through unhurt :—

Lieut.-Colonel Hindle, Captain Ord, second-in-command, Lieutenant Buckmaster, adjutant, 2nd Lieutenant Ashcroft, signalling officer, 2nd Lieutenant Williams, intelligence officer, 2nd Lieutenant Bardsley, transport officer, Captain Shegog, R.A.M.C., medical officer, and the Rev. W. Caley, chaplain.

"A" Company : Captain Harris, 2nd Lieutenants Ordish, Tyldsley and McSweeny.

"B"   ,,   Lieutenant Ogden, 2nd Lieutenants Vincent, Easterby and Rigby.

* The Story of the 55th Division, p. 47.

" C " Company; Captain Hore, 2nd Lieutenants Higson and Mather.
" D "   „   Lieutenant Ostrehan, 2nd Lieutenants Fullerton and Holden.

The following account of the Battalion's share in the action is taken from the War Diary : at zero, plus four hours forty minutes, the 164th Brigade moved off from the assembly trenches in Congreve Walk, the Battalion and the 2/5th Lancashire Fusiliers in front on the right and left respectively, with the 1/4th Royal Lancaster and 1/8th Liverpool Regiment in support. During the actual advance the casualties were few, but 2nd Lieutenant Ashcroft was killed. At 10.10 a.m. the Brigade formed up under the protective barrage some 200 yards on the German side of the Black Line, experiencing some annoyance by the enemy snipers lying out in shell-holes, and then moved forward to attack and consolidate the Green Line, the Battalion, as it advanced, establishing touch with the flank battalion of the 15th Division.

During this advance the casualties became very heavy, especially among the commissioned ranks, these being caused by machine-guns and by shells from guns firing from the high ground beyond the Green Line and by others on the right. Several strong points—known as Keir Farm, Gallipoli and Somme Farm—had to be dealt with while moving forward and from these some sixty prisoners were taken. The Green Line was occupied by 11.40 and consolidation was put in hand ; but the protective barrage now ceased, ammunition was beginning to run short, and about 2.35 p.m. the enemy counter-attacked in strength, obliging the Brigade to fall back to the Black Line. Here shortly after midnight it was relieved by the 165th Brigade, and the Battalion was withdrawn to its original front line between Warwick Farm and Lone Street, near Wieltje.

The Battalion casualties had again this day been heavy, fifty-one of all ranks being killed or dying of wounds, while 192 were wounded and 77 were missing ; the officers killed were Captains A. L. Harris and R. W. Shegog, R.A.M.C., 2nd Lieutenants G. Ashcroft, B. H. Williams, V. Mather, F. Fullerton and J. H. Ogden ; wounded were Captain R. Ord and the Rev. W. L. B. Caley, chaplain, Lieutenant D. H. Ostrehan, 2nd Lieutenants C. Rigby, H. Tyldsley, H. C. Vincent, F. C. Jenkinson, E. M. Easterby, L. Howarth and J. E. Ordish ; 2nd Lieutenants D. H. McSweeny and H. S. Holden were missing.

On the following day a message was received from General Jeudwine, saying : " Well done, One-Six-Four. I am very proud of what you did to-day. It was a fine performance, and no fault of yours you could not stay." This was forwarded by the Brigadier, who added : " I congratulate all units on having earned this praise, which I know to be well deserved."

By 2 p.m. on the 1st August only ninety men of the Battalion had assembled in the old front line ; more eventually straggled in by ones and twos, though some had remained out with battalions of the other two brigades in the Black Line, and did not rejoin until twenty-four hours or more after the Battalion had been relieved. Very heavy losses had, however, been inflicted on the enemy, while over 600 of all ranks had been captured with many guns, trench mortars and machine-guns. The severity of the fighting is evidenced by the Division's casualty list—168 officers and 3,384 other ranks from noon on the 30th July until its final relief at midday on the 4th August.

Many congratulatory messages were received from the Army, the Corps and the Division commanders.

The 55th Division was now relieved by the 36th and was withdrawn to the vicinity of St. Omer for rest and training, the move being completed by the 7th August, and the Battalion found itself in billets in Audrehem, " a small village where there was just sufficient room." Before the month of August was out 174 men had joined in drafts and the following officers had also arrived : Major de W. Fenton, Captain C. M. Denton, Lieutenant W. L. Price, 2nd Lieutenants R. Grisdale, A. P. Smith, J. F. Holden, H. C. Vincent, H. Swaine, F. Shippobottom, A. B. Fergie, J. Hailwood, A. Martin, A. H. Doleman, S. A. H. Pruden, B. Iners, H. W. C. Griffiths, H. Dance and J. Oldham.

While the 55th Division was away in the Recques area, recouping, reorganizing and refitting, at least two unsuccessful attempts had been made by other divisions to advance from the Black Line ; so that when the Division was recalled to the front the line it took over on the 15th September was the same as that which it had handed over six weeks before. It was called upon to do over again the work it had done on the 31st July, as may be seen by the following operation order of the 18th September :—

" The Second and Fifth Armies are to resume the offensive on Z day, the date of which will be notified later.

" The attack of the V. Corps * will be carried out by the 9th Division on the right and the 55th Division on the left. The 38th Division—XVIII. Corps—will be on the left of the 55th Division.

" It is the intention to capture and secure the final objective—the Green Line—and to this end the whole strength of the Division will be devoted. The capture and retention of Hill 37 is of special importance."

" On the night of the 19th–20th September the 164th and 165th Brigades

* When the 55th Division was transferred from the XIX. to the V. Corps is not clear.

closed up to an area east of the Stutzpunkt Line, with the leading waves aligned on a line of posts in shell-holes which were already in our hands." To each brigade a battalion of the 166th Brigade was attached, the other two being in divisional reserve. Zero was 5.40 a.m. on the 20th September, at which hour the barrage opened on the German front line, while the leading waves moved forward to the assault, forming up close under the barrage, which lifted at 5.45 and moved forward fifty yards at a time.

In the 164th Brigade the Battalion advanced in rear of the 1/4th Royal Lancaster, which was to capture the two German front lines, the Battalion then passing through to the capture and consolidation of the Green Line. " The assaulting battalions, immediately upon advancing, came under very severe rifle and machine-gun fire from the front and from both flanks. On the right the hostile barrage caused the 1/4th Loyal North Lancashire to close up with the 1/4th Royal Lancaster, who were in front of them, and they became involved in the fighting earlier than had been anticipated. In fact, they became engaged, and suffered considerable losses, in the neighbourhood of Aisne Farm, which the 1/4th Royal Lancaster had swept past in the assault, but had inadequately mopped up. . . . The 1/4th Loyal North Lancashire had suffered heavily from machine-gun fire from the right flank ; and a portion of the Battalion having become involved in the capture of Gallipoli, only small parties reached the leading lines of the Royal Lancaster who were occupying the Dotted Red Line. . . .

" The situation at 8.15 p.m. was as follows : the left Brigade, 164th, held the Dotted Red Line in strength, with posts in shell holes as far forward as the Green Line. The Capitol was held and also Gallipoli Copse. Hill 37 was in our hands, together with the Snag east of it, and we joined up by a series of short trenches to Waterend House on the right of the divisional front. The assault had been a success. Hill 37 was ours and was firmly held. The Green Line too for the most part was ours and the troublesome Schuler Farm was to fall to us next day." *

Gallipoli Copse and Hill 37 are situated on the outskirts of Fortuin, to the east.

There was some lively shelling by the enemy at dawn on the 21st, but some further captures were made by our troops : in the afternoon, however, very violent counter-attacks were launched by the Germans on Hill 37 and the division on the left of the 55th, which was subjected to an intense bombardment along its whole length of front. The enemy gained a footing here and there in our defences, but was vigorously expelled, and the troops held their ground until the 24th September, when the Division was finally relieved.

* *The Story of the 55th Division,* pp. 57–62.

In the four days' fighting the Battalion had again experienced very severe losses, amounting to thirty-one killed, 176 wounded and eleven missing. Among the officers Captain F. W. S. Baker, 2nd Lieutenants A. B. Fergie, C. B. Holmes and H. Holden were killed or died of wounds, and Captain R. H. Tautz, 2nd Lieutenants E. G. Baker, A. P. Smith, H. Dance, J. Oldham, R. Grisdale, A. Martin and B. Myers were wounded.

The Division now went south to join the Third Army and relieved the 35th Division in the line south of Cambrai, taking over a front of some 8,000 yards, running, roughly, from west of Honnecourt Wood, north-east of Epéhy, to New Post, south-east of the villages of Lempire and Ronssoy.

The Battalion proceeded by road and train and by short stages, via Watou, Hopoutre, Arras, Bapaume, Ytres, Aizecourt-le-Bas and Villers Faucon to Lempire, where it arrived on the 11th October and was in the area of the III. Corps, becoming support battalion to the right brigade.

During these moves 173 non-commissioned officers and men joined or rejoined from the Reinforcement Camp or from the Base, and also the following officers : Major J. A. Crump, 2nd Lieutenants J. O. Firth, J. H. Livesey, H. Ramsbottom, P. Adamson, E. M. Easterby, V. L. Smith, W. H. F. Smith, F. C. Smith, D. Carmichael, J. E. F. Nicholson, R. B. Wilkinson, C. Taylor, L. Frost, F. G. Green and C. Milne. Later in October 2nd Lieutenants W. G. E. Taylor, C. A. Rush and R. Hornby arrived with a small draft, and by the end of October the strength of the Battalion stood at thirty-nine officers and 777 other ranks, so that it had, to some extent at least, recovered from the losses incurred while serving in the Ypres Salient.

On the 17th November the Battalion had relieved another in the Guillemont sector, " C " and " D " Companies, under Lieutenants Lonsdale and Shippobottom, occupying the front line, while " B," Captain Buckmaster, and " A," Captain Houghton, were respectively in support and reserve. At 5.30 on the morning of the 18th the enemy opened a hurricane bombardment of the Guillemont Farm sector ; out of some eighty officers and other ranks occupying the twelve advanced posts only Sergeants Hartley and Hogg and half a dozen men remaining alive, all the rest, including the officer, Lieutenant J. O. Firth, being killed and buried under the débris. Some 200 of the enemy entered the Battalion line and began to work forward, but Lieutenant Lonsdale and the survivors of " C " Company managed to hold them until " A " Company, under Captain Houghton and Lieutenant Adamson, was seen coming up to reinforce, when the Germans began hurriedly to fall back, not however escaping before some twenty or more had been bayoneted. Lieutenant Shippobottom was killed by a bomb from those of the enemy who had entered " D " Company's trenches, and Lieutenant Hornby was wounded, the total casualties in this affair numbering eighty.

During the Cambrai operations, which began on the 20th November and endured until the 3rd December, the task of the 55th Division was merely to contain the Germans in its front and prevent them from moving troops to the assistance of their forces further north ; while its special duty was to attack and, if possible, to capture and hold Guillemont Farm and the Knoll.   That the attack was not to be forced should the enemy offer any really serious resistance, seems clear from the fact that only one brigade, the 164th, with two attached battalions, was employed.   The Battalion took no active part in this attack, it being detailed to hold the brigade front, while it was directed on no account to move forward in support of the assaulting battalions.

The operation was successful, and was a costly one, but it achieved its object, the enemy being prevented from diverting troops elsewhere. The Battalion had twelve casualties, and on the 22nd was withdrawn to the Vaucellette Camp area.

On the 28th November it was noticed that the enemy appeared to be reconnoitring the British position from low-flying aircraft, while there were signs of abnormal activity behind his lines, and it seemed probable that he was contemplating an attack.   All units of the Division were warned to be on the alert, and those in reserve were brought up nearer to the front. "In accordance with these instructions, that same afternoon the 1/4th Loyal North Lancashire from the Reserve Brigade moved up to Vaucellette Farm, leaving one company at St. Emilie, and the 2/5th Lancashire Fusiliers moved from Tincourt to Villers Faucon and occupied the billets vacated by the 1/4th Loyal North Lancashire.   The orders given to Lieut.-Colonel Hindle were to counter-attack at once in case of an attack by the enemy, and to hold Villers Guislain Spur at all costs.   These orders were most loyally carried out.   Movement on the enemy's roads and back areas was again abnormal on the 29th. . . .

"It must be mentioned that on the 29th October the Division had taken over from the 20th Division an area of approximately a battalion front, thereby extending our line northwards to just beyond the Banteau Ravine—a distance of 2,500 yards.   The Division was, therefore, now holding a frontage of 13,000 yards, supported by only two brigades of field artillery.   This wide frontage could not, of course, be continuously held ; it consisted of platoon posts connected by travel trenches, and distributed in depth so far as circumstances allowed." *

At dawn on the 30th heavy firing was heard in the north, and this

* *The Story of the 55th Division*, pp. 73, 74.

gradually increased in violence, so that at 7.30 Colonel Hindle sent his Intelligence Officer, Lieutenant Fazackerley, to find out what was going on, and Lieutenant Johnson to the 166th Brigade for orders—the remaining battalions of the 164th Brigade were at this time resting in rear at Hamel. The report brought back by Lieutenant Fazackerley was to the effect that the enemy was advancing all along the immediate front, and Colonel Hindle then made the following distribution of the companies : "A" to hold the left, "B" the centre in front of Vaucellette Farm, "D" to hold the right at the head of Linnet Valley ; "C" Company, as stated, was still in rear at St. Emilie. All companies were quickly in position, fire was opened and great execution was done, the enemy ceasing to advance and taking up a position on a line running from the Beet Factory to Chapel Crossing.

The Battalion was now completely isolated, no troops being in position on either flank. At 11 a.m. orders came from the G.O.C. 166th Brigade for the Battalion to clear the enemy out of Villers Guislain, and an advance in extended order at once began, the men moving forward, firing as they went, and the Germans commencing to fall back. Ammunition now began to run short, the enemy was reinforced, and the Battalion then slowly fell back on Vaucellette Farm. Here, on the east side, a defensive line was taken up, and all began to dig themselves in. At 12.55 p.m. reinforcements arrived from the 12th Division, and half an hour later "C" Company came up, when a fire trench was dug across the whole front of the farm and wire was put up.

At 1 a.m. on the 1st December the Battalion was relieved and marched back to billets at Hamel.

From the 30th November to the 1st December inclusive the Battalion had lost three officers and eleven other ranks killed, eight officers and eighty-four non-commissioned officers and men wounded and fifteen men missing. The officers who were killed were Lieut.-Colonel R. Hindle, D.S.O., Captain R. N. L. Buckmaster and 2nd Lieutenant J. H. Livesey, while wounded were Captains A. T. Houghton, M.C., and F. K. Matthew, 2nd Lieutenants E. M. Easterby, R. B. Wilkinson, P. Adamson, F. G. Green, J. E. P. Nicholson and R. J. Johnson.

From everybody in high position did the services of the Battalion receive fullest recognition : Major-General Jeudwine wrote to the Brigadier, saying : "I saw the Corps Commander to-day, and he said that they (i.e. the 1/4th Loyal North Lancashire Regiment) had saved the situation. He had seen the Commander-in-Chief and he had agreed."

The History of the 55th Division tells us that "a magnificent counter-attack early in the morning by the 1/4th Loyal North Lancashire, weak in numbers but indomitable in spirit, had not only caused the enemy very heavy losses, but had checked his advance towards Heudicourt. It was here that their gallant commander, Lieut.-Colonel Hindle, D.S.O., fell, shot through the heart at the head of his Battalion. The North Lancashire suffered heavily, but the result of their action was that the enemy never gained a real footing on the Lempire–Epéhy–Chapel Crossing Ridge. In a day of outstanding events, probably this counter-attack and subsequent stand at Vaucellette Farm is the most noteworthy, and was the most decisive in its result."

Then in a letter to Colonel Hindle's father, Major-General Jeudwine wrote :

" He had made his Battalion one of the finest, if not the finest, in the Division. . . . It will, I am sure, be some consolation to you to know that the fine fight he made with his Battalion was the means of definitely checking the German advance in that part of the field, and of preventing their reaching a position which would have endangered large forces."

During the month of December the Battalion made several moves— from Hamel to Tincourt, thence to Flamicourt, where Captains Duggan, M.C., and Hore, M.C., and twenty-two other ranks rejoined : then to Maroeuil, Lattre St. Quentin, Tinques, Bryas, Henchin and finally Delettes, where Christmas was spent and the year was seen out. The Division was now in the I. Corps of the First Army.

The Division had only just arrived in its new area when, under circumstances fully described in an earlier chapter of this History, a reduction in the establishment of divisions and brigades was initiated, and on the 14th January notification was received from the I. Corps that the number of battalions per division was to be reduced to nine ; a week later an order was issued directing three battalions to proceed from the 55th to the 57th Division. Each brigade in the 55th Division lost one of its four battalions, that taken from the 164th Brigade being the 1/8th Bn. The King's Liverpool Regiment.

On the 19th January, 1918, the Brigade was inspected by General Horne, the First Army Commander, and between this date and the end of the first week in February the Battalion had been joined by some thirty officers and 165 other ranks as reinforcements, some from the Reinforcement Camp and some from other regiments, or battalions : the names of the officers are Captains T. D. Collett, B. J. Phillips and R. W. B. Sparkes, M.C., Lieutenant G. B. Wardle, 2nd Lieutenants H. A. Latham, H. Ramsbottom, J. Dawson, W. Hughes, N. Smith, T. Stanley, O. R. Cooper, R. Hodgson, G. H. Frost, E. H. Studdard, L. O. Halliwell, J. S. Hampson, T. H. Scott, W. E. Pasley, J. H. Friar, F. Greaves, A. James, T. McLachlan, M.C.,

J. T. Taylor, R. Smith, G. Kirkly, H. Bailey, P. B. Beresford, R. E. Horsfall, J. H. Symes and G. Haworth.

As a result of these accretions the strength of the Battalion on the 7th February stood at sixty-three officers and 946 non-commissioned officers and men ; the Battalion had not been so strong in numbers since the Battle of Festubert, while the rest and training had proved of the greatest benefit to all ranks.

The Division received its orders to move forward on the 4th February, and at 10 a.m. on the 15th it relieved the 42nd Division in the left sector of the I. Corps front. The portion of the line taken over extended northwards from beyond the La Bassée–Cambrin road to Cailloux road, north-east of Festubert ; but on the 5th March that portion of the divisional area south of the La Bassée Canal was taken over by the 46th Division.

Casualties continued to be suffered, and before the great German offensive opened on the 21st March, the Battalion, in raids and counter-raids and in the more ordinary course of trench warfare, had in the first three months of this year several killed, wounded and missing, including a large percentage of officers, for 2nd Lieutenant P. Adamson, M.C., was killed and 2nd Lieutenants S. B. Westwood and A. James were wounded.

The events connected with the German offensive are described as follows in the Battalion War History : " On March 21st the long-expected attack against the allied front commenced. The Fifth Army, on the right of the Third Army, was driven back and the enemy almost reached Amiens. In order to fill the hole thus made, the First and Second Armies were denuded of reserves, and as a direct result of this the 164th Brigade, which was in divisional reserve, was constantly being rushed up to points of concentration at night in case the Boche attacked. On about April 1st at the Corps Headquarters it was decided that the Division must risk all on the line Givenchy–Festubert, supporting battalions of brigades being close up behind their battle line. The establishment of the main line of defence on the line of Festubert village made the position of Givenchy difficult, as the line of defence of the right brigade holding the position was 800 yards in front of the left brigade."

The position of the Division on the morning of the 9th April is given as under in the Divisional History :—

" The 164th Infantry Brigade on the right was holding the line from the La Bassée Canal to the north of Givenchy. The 1/4th King's Own Royal Lancaster held the right of this line and the 1/4th Loyal North Lancashire held the left. The 2/5th Lancashire Fusiliers were in support at Gorre, with two companies at Windy Corner. The 165th Brigade on the left was holding from the north of Givenchy to the left boundary—including Festubert.   The 166th Brigade was in reserve."

Early on the morning of the 9th April a very heavy bombardment opened on the whole divisional front, but this slackened about 6.30, breaking out again with renewed violence at 8 o'clock, when the Portuguese troops on the left of the 55th Division were driven out of their trenches, thus exposing the whole of the left flank of the Division.   The enemy's infantry attack now commenced, made by a German division specially brought up for the purpose, the energies of its component parts stiffened by the information that "the 55th was a tired division, only fit to hold a quiet sector of the line"!   The general plan was to attack the Givenchy salient on the flanks, striking towards Windy Corner on the north and to Pont Fixe on the south, each attack being carried out by three battalions, supported by storm troops and heavy machine-guns.

Owing to the thick fog and the large amount of wire, the fighting, from the very commencement of the infantry attack until late in the afternoon, consisted of isolated combats carried on all over the area by small parties of officers and men.

The heavy mist—visibility was limited from twenty to thirty yards—enabled the German infantry to get close up to our positions before being exposed to any really effective fire, and consequently they succeeded, on the 164th Brigade front, in penetrating the front line and actually entered the Battalion headquarters.   About 9.30 a.m. Moat Farm was surrounded and the ruins of Givenchy Church occupied by the enemy.   South of Givenchy the attack had reached as far as Gunner Siding on the Cuinchy–Givenchy Road, Death or Glory Sap was cut off; while on the extreme left of the 164th Brigade the enemy had broken through to Le Plantin South, had penetrated beyond the Pont Fixe–Festubert road, had occupied some houses at Windy Corner, while his patrols had reached as far as Lone Farm.

Counter-measures were now taken and the situation was quickly restored, the whole of the ground occupied was recaptured, many prisoners and machine-guns being taken; while before dark all the forward posts and saps were again in our possession, and at the end of the day the Brigade held every inch of its original ground.   "The close of the day's fighting, therefore, found the Division, with the assistance of the 154th Brigade, holding a front of about 11,000 yards—from the La Bassée Canal to the west of the Lawe Canal, 2,000 yards north-east of Locon—whence it was prolonged, though not continuously, by troops of the 51st Division. Practically every rifle in the Division had been put into the line,—the right brigade, the 164th, held the whole of its original line intact; the left brigade, the 165th, held the whole of its line of resistance and had in addition thrown

"SOMEWHERE IN FRANCE."

1918.

The Imperial War Museum—Copyright.

back a flank at right angles for some 2,000 yards. Both brigades had, moreover, a very substantial haul of prisoners."

The casualties in the Battalion were one officer—2nd Lieutenant L. Brooke, M.C.—and forty-three other ranks killed, 2nd Lieutenants R. E. Horsfall, G. C. Horner, G. Haworth and P. B. Beresford and 100 men were wounded; while the Rev. L. N. Forse and Lieutenant W. H. Jenkins, the Medical Officer, and fifty other ranks were missing. Other casualties followed during the next few days, and among these were Captain Collett and 2nd Lieutenant Vincent wounded, while 2nd Lieutenant S. B. Westwood was killed.

The splendid services this day of the 55th Division were everywhere recognized and cordially acknowledged; from Field-Marshal Sir D. Haig came the following telegram : " Please convey to General Jeudwine and to all the Officers and Men of the 55th Division my congratulations on their splendid fighting yesterday, especially at Festubert and Givenchy."

Similar telegrams and messages were received from the Army and Corps Commanders and from the Divisions which had fought alongside the 55th ; while in both the despatches dealing with these operations the Field-Marshal pays repeated and eloquent tribute to the work of the 55th West Lancashire Division.

Between the 14th and the 17th April the Division was relieved by troops of the 1st and 3rd Divisions and went back to the Auchel area—the 164th Brigade being the last to move, the Battalion proceeding to billets at Lozinghem ; the rest period was, however, a comparatively short one, for by the 23rd the Division was back again in the line, relieving the 1st Division in the Givenchy and Festubert sections.

On the 14th May, when up in the line, " A " Company of the Battalion carried out a raid against the enemy's front-line post in a trench known as Willow Drain, penetrating his line at one point and establishing a block which was held until 10.30 p.m., when a strong counter-attack developed and the party was forced to withdraw, having sustained many casualties. While moving across No-Man's-Land—a mass of shell-holes—2nd Lieutenant G. S. Ibbotson was first wounded and then killed by a shell ; 2nd Lieutenant C. Milne was killed by a bomb while passing through the enemy wire ; and 2nd Lieutenant W. R. Cooper was wounded by a bullet in the throat, causing the loss of his voice, but he gallantly continued writing his orders in his pocket-book and " carried on " until killed by a second bullet. Among the other ranks of the raiding party six were killed, forty-seven were wounded and five were missing.

During June, July and the greater part of August events proceeded more or less normally, with intermittent and heavy bombardments by the enemy and occasional small raids, in some of which 2nd Lieutenants Archibald and Dawson distinguished themselves; and towards the close of this period 2nd Lieutenant H. Fazackerley was killed—a great loss to the Battalion. The Brigade was engaged on the 24th August in the successful capture of the enemy line of craters east of Givenchy, which had for long afforded the Germans good observation over a large portion of our defensive system; but during this fighting the Battalion remained quiescent, holding the right and left sub-sectors.

On the 1st September orders were given that all must be prepared to press the enemy, who was showing increased signs of an intention to fall back, and he was to be followed up and all ground made good. On the 14th part of " A " and " C " Companies were detailed as carrying parties for the 2/5th Lancashire Fusiliers who were attacking the enemy, holding what was known as Canteleux Trench. The attack was initially successful, but the enemy counter-attacked, the situation being later restored. Of " A " and " C " Companies 2nd Lieutenant L. B. Smith was killed while assisting the attack of the Lancashire Fusiliers and six men were wounded.

On the 19th September the I. Corps, in which the 55th Division was serving, was transferred from the First to the Fifth Army, and on the night of the 20th–21st the 164th Brigade took over part of the front south and north of the La Bassée Canal.

" The I. Corps issued instructions on September 27th to the effect that the enemy was believed to have made all arrangements for a withdrawal on the Fifth Army front. All divisions in the I. Corps were to push forward posts simultaneously south of the La Bassée Canal on the morning of September 30th. In accordance with these instructions two companies of 1/4th Loyal North Lancashire Regiment attacked south of the Canal at 6.18 a.m. on September 30th. The objectives of the attack were Canal Alley–the junction of Drain and Azimuth Alley–Distillery; the last-named was a strong place and believed to be used as an enemy observation post. The attack was at first successful, and all objectives gained with forty-eight prisoners. The 16th Division on our right was unable to make headway against strong opposition and at noon a powerful enemy counter-attack drove back the posts of the 1/4th Loyal North Lancashire Regiment to their original line, after very severe fighting in which our casualties were heavy.

" On the morning of October 1st the 1/4th Loyal North Lancashire repeated the attack, and gained and held all the objectives, the 16th Division pushing forward posts on our right in touch with us. By the end of September our line had been advanced about 4,000 yards in the left brigade sector and about 2,500 yards in the right brigade sector. The outpost line was 1,000 yards west of La Bassée." *

Two platoons each of "B" and "D" Companies were employed in these operations and they captured fifty-eight prisoners, but themselves suffered considerable loss; 2nd Lieutenant W. Byrne and sixteen other ranks were killed, 2nd Lieutenants J. Cairns, W. C. Griffiths, H. Parkinson, G. Haworth and T. G. Bowles and fifty-two other ranks were wounded, and two men were missing.

On the 8th October the 55th Division was transferred in its existing position from the I. to the III. Corps, and on the same day the Battalion marched to billets at Bethune, where the following officers joined for duty —the Rev. R. J. Cross, chaplain, and 2nd Lieutenants W. E. Crossley, M.C., M.M., G. R. Blount, H. G. Towers, W. H. A. Kennett and R. G. Lathom.

The Battalion was up again in the front by the 13th and all along the line our troops were now pushing forward, the enemy everywhere fighting a delaying action; in some places our troops found the marshy country almost impassable, the water being as much as eight feet deep in parts. At noon on the 16th "D" Company and half of "B" crossed the Haute Deule Canal and advanced to the attack of the strongly held bridge-head at Bac de Wavrin, "A" and "C" Companies supporting. The bridge-head was taken and the patrols pushed on to the Seclin Canal which was bridged, when other troops took up the pursuit.

On the 19th the Battalion moved forward again, assisting in the capture of four villages: thereafter the German resistance again stiffened for a time and counter-attacks were delivered, and on this day the divisional outpost line was east of the Custom House—east of Bois de Moudry—east of Bachy. On the last day of October the Battalion had been withdrawn for rest and was occupying billets at Wannehain; from here it did not again move forward until the 9th November when it marched by Esplechin and Barry to Villers St. Amand, where—on the 11th—the news of the signing of the Armistice reached the troops.

During the operations from the 9th October to the 11th November the casualties had continued, and these amounted to the following: two officers —2nd Lieutenants J. Hailwood and J. T. Taylor—and seventeen other ranks had been killed or died of wounds; three officers—Captain W. L. Price, Lieutenant E. Bury and W. E. Crossley—and seventy-four non-commissioned officers and men were wounded, and three officers—2nd Lieutenants W. G. E. Taylor, G. A. Blount and J. Chambers—and forty-three men were missing.

* *The Story of the 55th Division,* pp. 135, 136.

Since the 1st November the resistance of the German troops had been completely shattered. In spite of his superior numbers the enemy had been in retreat before the whole of our battle-front, his best divisions had been defeated, his lateral communications had been cut and his defensive powers destroyed. The enemy had no alternative than to sign the Armistice on 11th November; for a continuance of hostilities could only have meant utter disaster to the whole of the German Army.

During the three and a half years that the Battalion had served at the seat of war one hundred and fifty-five officers and 3,195 non-commissioned officers and men had been killed or had died of wounds or had been wounded!

The Battalion marched to Leuze on the 14th and to Wattine Chapelle some ten days later, whence, on the 2nd December, an escort, consisting of Captain S. H. Pruden, M.C., Lieutenant A. E. Bulling, Company Sergeant-Major Roberts and two sergeants, was sent to England to bring out the Colours; these arrived on the 10th and were paraded for the first time on the 13th. While the Battalion remained abroad it was quartered at Uccle in the vicinity of Brussels.

Demobilization now set in, and during January and February, 1919, officers and men were leaving the Battalion for England in parties of varying strength; and on the 24th March what remained of the 1/4th The Loyal North Lancashire was formed into a cadre company under the command of Captain R. H. Smith, and by the 12th June it had reached Preston to be received with acclamation by the Mayor and townspeople.

There being only one battle-honours list granted to a regiment, as a whole, for services rendered during the Great War, 1914–1918, the Territorial Battalions received exactly the same honours as those accorded to the Regular and Service Battalions of the Regiment. (See Appendix III.)

A detailed description of the Territorial Force War Medal and the other British medals and decorations awarded to those who served overseas during the period of the Great War will be found in Appendix VI.

CHAPTER XLIII

THE 2/4TH (TERRITORIAL) BATTALION
THE LOYAL NORTH LANCASHIRE REGIMENT

1914–1919

THE BATTLE OF YPRES, THE BATTLE OF THE SCARPE,
THE BATTLE OF CAMBRAI

THOSE battalions of the Territorial Force which had offered themselves for Imperial Service, had scarcely left England, when it became clear that extra reserve units would be needed to take the places of the Imperial Service units, and also to act as feeders for the replacement of war wastage. As a result of this, Army Order No. 399 was published in September, 1914, authorizing the formation of a home unit for each unit of the Territorial Force which had been accepted for Imperial Service.

It was very soon realized that even this expansion of the Territorial Force would not be sufficient for the very large scale upon which the war was to be conducted, and in view of the abnormal wastage which might well be expected ; and on the 24th November an order was issued from the War Office directing that when an Imperial Service Unit proceeded overseas and was replaced at home by its reserve unit, a second reserve unit should at once be raised at the Depot, or peace-time headquarters, of the original unit.

So soon as the units composing the 1st West Lancashire Division—later numbered the 55th—were warned for service abroad, the 2nd West Lancashire Division came into existence, being formed of second-line units of the original division. The 2nd West Lancashire Division then was formed in September, 1914, but it was not until the 10th August, 1915, that it was numbered the 57th (West Lancashire) Division.

In the months immediately preceding the departure of the Division for France, it was engaged in training at Willsborough, Barham Downs and in and about Aldershot. The 2/4th Bn. The Loyal North Lancashire Regiment was in the 170th Brigade.

At 7.30 on the morning of the 7th February, 1917, the 2/4th Battalion,

The Loyal North Lancashire Regiment, marched by wings from Blackdown to Frimley Railway Station and there entrained for Southampton at a strength of thirty-two officers and 926 non-commissioned officers and men ; the following are the names of the officers who accompanied the Battalion : Lieut.-Colonel the Hon. R. Lygon, M.V.O., M.C., Major C. E. C. Bartlett, Captains R. R. Rothwell, W. H. Dawson, J. Eccles, H. A. Whittaker, J. Hunt, G. L. Austin and J. R. Beckett, Lieutenants P. S. Wigney, M. Proctor-Gregg, M. C. Marckx, R. Parker, V. A. Lawrence, W. C. Newton and L. W. Newsholme, 2nd Lieutenants H. N. King, C. A. Atkins, E. W. Edgley, R. de P. Eddison, J. S. Kay, A. Blackhurst, A. McL. Currie, R. J. Wilson, E. L. Fairclough, C. Roscoe, A. B. Douglas, S. L. Partridge, B. Osborne, N. H. Fisher and J. W. Webster, adjutant ; Lieutenant and Quartermaster W. A. Pritchard.

The companies embarked, under Major C. E. C. Bartlett, at 4.30 p.m. the same day in the " Duchess of Argyll," sailing half an hour later, while headquarters, under Lieut.-Colonel the Hon. R. Lygon, left Southampton docks at eleven o'clock at night in the S.S. " Lydia," both parties arriving at Havre early on the morning of the 8th February and marching to the Rest Camp where the day and night were spent.   Two officers and twenty-nine other ranks, with the Battalion transport, were unable to leave England until the 8th, and consequently did not join up with the rest of the Battalion until the 9th.

On this day the Battalion moved off from Havre in the evening in two trains, arriving at Bailleul on the 11th and 12th respectively, and marching thence to billets at Meteren, where it remained until the 13th, on which day it was moved on seven miles to Sailly on the Lys.   Here the 57th Division was in the II. Anzac Corps Area of the Second Army, the 170th Brigade about Sailly, the 171st in the Merris area and the 172nd in the neighbourhood of Borre.   The troops of the newly-arrived Division were, for the first two days, attached to units of the 1st New Zealand Division, which they were under orders to relieve before the end of the month.

On the 14th the 107th Brigade commenced the relief of the battalions of the New Zealand Rifle Brigade ; the Battalion began to take over sectors, company by company, from the 1st Battalion New Zealand Rifle Brigade on the 15th and it was the 17th of the month before the relief was completed.   During the remainder of February the Battalion took it in turns with the 2/5th Battalion of the Regiment to be up in the line or in billets in rear, but from the 26th February to the 3rd March the Battalion was back in brigade reserve.

The sector was a quiet one and during its occupation throughout February only one man was wounded.

In *The New Zealand Division*, Vol. II, p. 151, we are told that the
II. Anzac Corps line "extended from the front of Sailly to St. Yves, a
distance of approximately thirteen miles. The trenches were necessarily
held thinly. On the right, in the Cordonnerie, Boutillerie and Bois Grenier
sub-sectors, was the newly-arrived 57th Division ; the central sub-sectors,
Rue de Bois, l'Epinette and Houplines, were held by the 3rd Australian
Division ; and now the New Zealanders were extending their knowledge
of the Lys flats in the sub-sectors of Le Touquet and Ploegsteert, on the
left bank of the river. The trenches were of the poorest description, accommodation was hopelessly inadequate and drainage had been neglected.
The thaw made conditions doubly uncomfortable. Not merely unoccupied
gaps, but portions of the fire trenches also were under water. The communication trenches were narrow, deep in mud, and all but impassable.
The parapet was low, and in bad repair, and the enemy enjoyed marked
superiority in sniping."

It will be seen from the above extract that the conditions governing
the initiation of the troops of the 57th Division in trench warfare were by
no means ideal, and the inferiority of the British position soon led the
enemy to an increased activity on this part of the allied front.

Twice during the month of March—on the 9th and again on the 19th
—did the enemy attempt small isolated attacks upon portions of the trench
line held by the Battalion, on both occasions hoping to enter the trenches
under cover of a bomb attack. Each time the raiders were driven off,
not, however, without loss being incurred, and during this month the
casualties were two killed, eleven wounded and one missing.

During the same period, however, five officers and forty-five other ranks
joined from the Base, and at the beginning of April the Battalion numbered
thirty-seven officers and 904 non-commissioned officers and men.

Early in April 2nd Lieutenant N. H. Fisher was killed in the trenches,
but on the night of the 19th–20th the Battalion made an effort to "get
some of its own back." A small patrol, officered by Lieutenants Fairclough
and Jump, went out from the trenches as a special reconnoitring party,
but was unfortunately overtaken by daylight before it had proceeded far,
and experienced great difficulty in regaining the lines. The enemy brought
a very heavy fire to bear upon the patrol and two men fell. Believing
that they were only wounded, a rescue party, composed of Lieutenant
Kay and three men, was at once organized and went out to bring the men
in, but one of this party was at once killed by the enemy fire, and Lieutenant
Kay and one of those with him managed to reach the two men only to
find that they were dead. Lieutenant Kay was now wounded in the foot,
and was helped back to safety by Lance-Corporal Atherton.

There had been a good deal of sickness in the Battalion due to the unhealthy condition of the trenches, and early in May it was found necessary to reorganize the companies, temporarily, on a three-platoon basis. On the last day of May the Battalion was relieved by the 1/5th Battalion The West Riding Regiment and marched to Armentières, where it formed part of a detached force from the 57th Division under command of Lieut.-Colonel G. W. Geddes, D.S.O.

In the *New Zealand History*, the following appreciation is given of the general situation on this particular part of the British front during the time that the Battle of Messines was in prospect : " Under General Godley, the Corps Commander, at the beginning of May were the 57th, the 3rd Australian, the New Zealand and the 25th Divisions. The Corps was reinforced in the middle of the month by the 4th Australian Division from the I. Anzac Corps, then forming part of the Fifth Army. The divisions earmarked for the attack lay approximately in their assembly areas. On the right, from St. Yves to the Douve, the 3rd Australian Division held a frontage of some 2,000 yards. The New Zealanders, in the centre, from the Douve to just north of the Wulverghem–Messines road, occupied some 1,500 yards. On the left, where the II. Anzac was divided from the IX. Corps at the Wulverghem–Wytschaete road, the frontage allotted to the 25th Division was still narrower, in view of the greater distance that lay between them and the crest. On the Corps front south of the Lys the 57th Division had extended its positions to the north to include the sub-sectors of l'Epinette and Houplines just south of the river, and now held a frontage of 18,000 yards, formerly garrisoned by three divisions, each with two strong brigades in the line.

" Towards the end of May, to relieve the Second Army and II. Anzac Corps of responsibilities outside the active area, the 57th Division sector right up to the Lys was transferred to the XI. Corps of the First Army. The defensive front of the Corps, as contrasted with the offensive front on which the three divisions were preparing their spring on Messines, was thus restricted to the short sector from the Lys to St. Yves, held by the 3rd Australian Division. To relieve its garrison a separate force of two battalions of the already extended 57th Division was brought up on the 3rd June north of the Lys and attached for tactical purposes to the 3rd Australians."

The two battalions here mentioned, as detached from the 57th Division, were the 2/4th and 2/5th Battalions of The Loyal North Lancashire Regiment, and in the War Diary of the Battalion it is stated that the task of this two-battalion detachment was " to hold the front from the River Lys to St. Yves as a defensive front on which other operations will pivot."

With this small detached force the Battalion remained for some ten days, taking its share of duty with Australian battalions, and during almost the whole period of its absence from the Division being subjected to an especially heavy bombardment by all descriptions of "heavy stuff." The casualties suffered were naturally very many—probably in proportion almost as heavy as those incurred by battalions actually engaged in the Messines battle ; these amounted to one officer—2nd Lieutenant W. H. Dickson—and fourteen other ranks killed, Lieutenant and Adjutant J. S. Kay and one hundred non-commissioned officers and men wounded.

On the 11th June the Battalion was recalled from this special duty and marched to billets at Estaires. Before, however, the two battalions of The Loyal North Lancashire Regiment left the Second Army under which they had temporarily been serving, they received a very appreciative message from Major-General Monash, commanding the 3rd Australian Division, expressing his entire satisfaction with the part played by the detached force. Further, on arrival at Estaires the Battalion was inspected by Lieut.-General R. G. Broadwood, commanding the 57th Division, who congratulated the Battalion on the good work it had performed ; only a very few days later this general officer died from wounds received in Armentières.

On the night of the 28th–29th July "D" Company of the Battalion carried out a very successful raid on the enemy. The raiding party consisted of four officers—Captain Dawson, 2nd Lieutenants Jump, Driver and King—and 135 other ranks, divided into three platoons, of which two platoons composed the raiders and one platoon the covering party. The raiders left the first-line trench at 10.30 p.m. on the 28th, and everything was proceeding "according to plan," when the left platoon under 2nd Lieutenant Jump came in contact with an enemy sentry group, when there was an immediate exchange of bombs, the platoon then charging with the bayonet. Of the German sentry group one man was killed and the others fled. Hearing now that an attack had been opened on his bombing section, 2nd Lieutenant Jump took his men back to its help, and en route encountered a party of the enemy twenty-five strong. This he at once engaged, killing six and wounding several others, while the remainder effected their escape.

The platoon under 2nd Lieutenant King, fifty-one in number, came upon a smaller party of Germans who opened upon our men with bombs and rifle fire. After some hand-to-hand fighting this lot of the enemy was dispersed, but almost immediately afterwards another party of some forty Germans appeared on the right and were at once attacked with the bayonet and fled precipitately.

2nd Lieutenant Driver, with the thirty-five men under his command, arrived at the position told off to him, and straightway saw an enemy body approaching and this at once charged. A sanguinary struggle ensued, but the enemy had soon had enough and fell back, leaving one prisoner behind them.

There seems no doubt that this raid by " D " Company of the Battalion coincided with one arranged by our opponents, thus leading to an unusual situation.

Our raiding party was not to have withdrawn until 2 a.m. on the 29th, but, as the fighting had been heavy, the losses not inconsiderable and the enemy had wholly disappeared, Captain Dawson decided upon a withdrawal, taking his prisoners with him, and from some of these much useful information was obtained.

In the Brigade report on this raid it is stated that " the enemy showed a far inferior fighting spirit and were lacking considerably in morale compared to our troops, in spite of the fact that they belonged to a Sturmtruppen Company. All ranks of the raiding party behaved magnificently throughout the operation and showed determination and eagerness to get at the enemy."

The Divisional Commander's remarks were as follows : " The Divisional Commander congratulates the Battalion on the success of last night's raid. The fighting spirit shown by the men on meeting the enemy at close quarters was excellent."

In the course of the raid one officer and thirty-seven other ranks of the Battalion were wounded and five men were missing.

Two nights later—on the 31st—another raiding party went out under 2nd Lieutenant Ball, and again some loss was caused to the enemy.

On the 2nd August the Battalion went back into brigade reserve at l'Epinette, but immediately on return to the trench line some ten days later, it came under heavy shelling and 2nd Lieutenant R. de P. Eddison and four men were killed and nine were wounded.

In the middle of September a move was made from the neighbourhood of Armentières to Ligny-les-Aires, where the Division remained in training for the best part of a month, then marching to Proven and thence to Boesinghe, where on the 24th October the Battalion took over trenches. The line occupied was from Besace Farm to the Watervliet Stream, one company being in the front line, with two in support and one in reserve. This sector was tolerably quiet, except for some intermittent shelling.

The 57th Division was now in the XIV. Corps with the 50th and 58th Divisions, and was to take part in the Second Battle of Passchendaele on the 26th October, the Division attacking with the 58th Division on its right and the 50th on the left.   In the 170th Brigade the 2/5th Loyal North Lancashire was on the right, the 2/4th was in the centre, and the 4/5th Battalion of the Regiment on the left, the 2/5th Battalion King's Own Royal Lancaster Regiment being in support.   The Battalion was to assault with three companies in front line and one in support.

By 3.40 a.m. on the 26th October the Battalion was formed up in its assembly position, and moved off to attack at 5.40 : within a very few minutes the Mendling and Rubens Farms had been captured, and, although the losses had been comparatively light during the advance, all four company commanders early became casualties.   The centre of the attack was now held up by the fire from the enemy pill-boxes, but, supported by The King's Own Royal Lancaster, the attack was resumed, when the pill-boxes were captured and a position taken up on some dominating ground.   From here any fresh advance was found to be impossible by reason of the very heavy German machine-gun fire from all sides ; but the Battalion was able to hold its ground until relieved on the night of the 26th–27th by the 2/8th King's Liverpool Regiment, and moved back to Proven.

The Battalion on this occasion captured eighteen Germans and destroyed several enemy machine-guns.   The ground advanced over was very bad, swampy and covered with shell-holes.

In this day's battle the 57th Division encountered very severe losses, in which the Battalion bore its full share : three officers—Lieutenant P. H. F. Wiseman, 2nd Lieutenants J. B. Horn, A. Bellingham—and fifty-eight other ranks were killed or died of wounds, eight officers and 251 non-commissioned officers and men were wounded and thirty-eight men were missing—a total of 358 killed, wounded and missing !   The wounded officers were Captains R. Herbert and P. S. Wigney, 2nd Lieutenants D. Evans, J. H. Driver, L. E. G. Judge, J. Hopwood, W. Demaine and J. F. Downes.

From Proven the Battalion went for some weeks' training to Bonningues, then back to Proven, and from there to Boesinghe, where Christmas Day was spent ; and the end of the year found the Battalion in the Proosdy area, from where on the 3rd January, 1918, it was transferred to Erquinghem, where it provided many working parties when out of the line, and carried out some very useful patrol work when up at the front.   The Battalion was now, however, much weakened in numbers, counting twenty-five officers and no more than 480 other ranks ; during February, however, reinforcements of twelve officers and 250 other ranks joined, and these, with other accretions, brought up the strength, by the end of the month—when the Battalion was at Merville—to thirty-seven officers and 815 non-commissioned officers and men.

The first three weeks of March were spent at Pont de Nieppe—a rest area, the amenities of which were, however, occasionally disturbed by fire from long-range, high-velocity enemy guns ; and on the 21st March the Brigade marched to Fleurbaix, towards the end of the month relieving a brigade of the 38th Division in the Wez Macquart sector, the Battalion taking the place of the 17th Royal Welsh Fusiliers in the left sub-sector—pronounced on first arrival to be a fairly quiet part of the line. Hereabouts the Division remained until early in May, engaged in no events of outstanding importance ; and then on the 7th of this month the 57th Division began to move to the Bucquoy area, south of Arras, there to relieve the 42nd Division, which had suffered considerable losses in the fighting connected with the German offensive of this spring.

In this area what was known as the Purple Line was the main line of resistance, and this, so the 42nd Division History states, " rejoiced in the possession of Beer, Stout and Rum Trenches, but whether the names had been given with the idea of raising false hopes in the breasts of thirsty Teutons and luring them on to destruction is not known " ! By this date —the 7th May—the Battalion had relieved the 8th Manchester Regiment of the 127th Brigade, 42nd Division. The Battalion was now in brigade reserve at Coigneux, and on the day after taking over, it sent working parties to Beer Trench—the old British front line, east of Fonquevillers and Hébuterne ; but when it later moved up to the front line, Stout Trench was the one the Battalion mainly occupied, and here much heavy shelling was experienced, while enemy aircraft became daily more active.

In this area the Division remained until the last week in August, when a move took place, and the Battalion marched to Bailleulmont, where it arrived on the 25th of the month. It rested here during that day, late in the afternoon going up to the Hindenburg Line and taking up its position in Shaft Avenue in support to the 172nd Brigade.

The Division was now in the XVII. Corps, which contained also the 52nd, 56th and, later, the 63rd Divisions, and these were now to take part in the Battle of the Scarpe. The 52nd and 56th Divisions had attacked on the 25th August, the former taking Henin-sur-Cojeul and gaining a footing in St. Martin-sur-Cojeul, while the 56th had heavy fighting about Croisilles and on the high ground to the north-west known as Henin Hill. In regard to the fighting which then followed, the despatch of the 21st December, 1918, tells us that " yielding before the persistent pressure of our attacks, in the early morning of the 29th August the enemy evacuated Bapaume, which was occupied by the New Zealand Division. On the same day the 18th Division entered Combles, while to the north of Bapaume a gallant thrust by the 56th and 57th Divisions penetrated the enemy's positions as far as Riencourt-les-Cagnicourt. Though our troops were unable at this time to maintain themselves in this village our line was established on the western and northern outskirts of Bullecourt and Hendecourt. By the night of the 30th August the line of the Fourth and Third Armies north of the Somme ran from Clery-sur-Somme past the western edge of Marnière Wood to Combles, Lesboeufs, Bancourt, Fremicourt and Vraucourt, and thence to the western outskirts of Ecoust, Bullecourt and Hendecourt. Any further advance would threaten the enemy's line south of Peronne along the east bank of the Somme, to which our progress north of the river had already forced him to retreat."

The following is the Battalion account of the operations of the 29th August in which, with the 57th Division, it played a prominent part :—

" Moved up to the front line, taking over from the 2/4th South Lancashire. Zero hour was 1 p.m. and our first objective was the Hendecourt–Bullecourt road, the second being Greyhound Trench. The first objective was to be taken without a barrage ; and our left flank was unprotected owing to the Canadians being 1,000 yards away. We succeeded in gaining our objective, and the battalion on our right, the 2/5th King's Own Royal Lancaster, captured Riencourt. Our objective was taken by 2 p.m.

" The Battalion held on to its objective during the night of the 29th–30th, although the enemy attacked about 12.35 p.m. on the 30th in large numbers, he was beaten off three times, suffering heavy casualties. Owing to the battalion on our right having to retire from Riencourt, we were ordered about 1.30 p.m. to withdraw to Cemetery Avenue, and this line the Battalion held until relieved about 4 p.m. by the 171st Brigade, when we moved back to the support area, and the following night was passed in Tunnel Trench."

From here on the 2nd September the Battalion moved back to the Hendecourt area, where for the next three days it was employed in salvage and burying work, and does not appear to have been employed in what is known as " the storming of the Drocourt–Quéant Line," which was carried out in the opening days of this month.

On the 11th, however, orders were received directing that " the 170th Brigade, in conjunction with the 171st on the left, will attack and capture the line of the Canal du Nord and will exploit success to the east of the Canal. The 1/5th Loyal North Lancashire Regiment, with two companies of the 2/4th Loyal North Lancashire Regiment attached (for mopping-up purposes), will carry out the attack ; objectives the Canal du Nord from E.15.C.1.0. to E.20.D.7.0. Posts to be pushed forward and established " (at certain map reference numbers). " Defensive flank from Leopard Avenue to be formed. On completion of mopping-up the two attached companies to occupy defensive positions east and south-east of Moeuvres. . . . Zero hour 6.15 p.m."

In the continuous fighting which now followed during the next four days, the companies of the Battalion each appear to have fought separate and individual actions; nominally to be employed only for mopping-up and carrying duties, they appear to have over and over again been called upon by any unit, in whose immediate neighbourhood they happened to be in any moment of stress, to fill a gap, to assist in stemming a counter-attack, or to hold on to and consolidate any ground won. It was late on the night of the 15th before the Battalion could be reunited and relieved, by which time it had suffered close upon seventy casualties, two officers and thirteen other ranks having been killed, while 2nd Lieutenant Harrop and forty-five men were wounded and six were missing; the two officers who died were 2nd Lieutenants H. W. Marsden and P. Hutchinson.

The Battalion was now to take part in the Battle of Cambrai which opened on the 27th September and culminated on the 5th October in the capture of the last remaining sectors of the Hindenburg Line. To quote from the despatch of the 21st December of this year: " Between the neighbourhood of St. Quentin and the Scheldt, the Fourth, Third and First Armies in the order named occupied on the evening of the 26th September a line running from the village of Selency (west of St. Quentin) to Gricourt and Pontruet and thence east of Villeret and Lempire to Villers Guislain and Gouzeaucourt, both inclusive. Thereafter the line continued north-wards to Havrincourt and Moeuvres, and thence along the west side of the Canal du Nord to the floods of the Sensée at Ecourt St. Quentin." Then, after describing the difficulties facing each of the armies to be engaged, the despatch goes on to say that a very heavy bombardment along the front of the three armies, on the night of the 26th–27th September, was to be followed on the following morning by an attack by the corps com-posing the First and Third Armies on a front of thirteen miles from Gouzeau-court to the neighbourhood of Souchy Lestrée. " The northern portion of the Canal was too formidable an obstacle to be crossed in the face of an enemy. It was therefore necessary for the attacking divisions to force a passage on a comparatively narrow front about Moeuvres, and thereafter turn the line of the Canal further north by a divergent attack developed fanwise from the point of crossing. This difficult manœuvre was carried out successfully, and on the whole front of attack our infantry, assisted by some sixty-five tanks, broke deeply into the enemy's position."

Of these events the Battalion recounts its personal experience as follows :

" 25th September. The Battalion moved by rail and road and by way of Saulty to bivouacs at Noreuil.

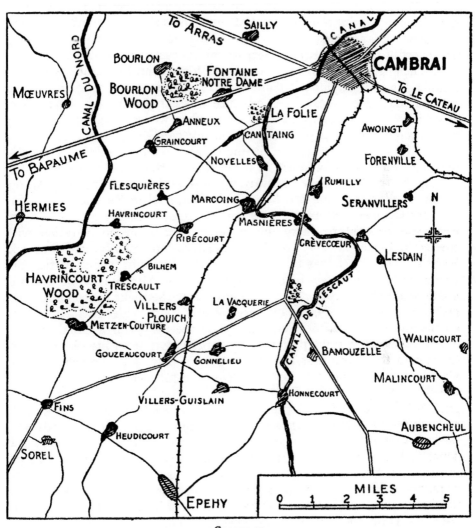

To Arras
Sailly
CANAL
CAMBRAI
Mœuvres
CANAL DU NORD
Bourlon
Bourlon Wood
Fontaine Notre Dame
To Le Cateau
Anneux
La Folie
Graincourt
Cantaing
Awoingt
To Bapaume
Noyelles
Forenville
Flesquières
Marcoing
Rumilly
Hermies
Havrincourt
Seranvillers
Ribécourt
Masnières
Bilhem
Crèvecœur
Lesdain
Havrincourt Wood
Trescault
N
Villers Plouich
La Vacquerie
Metz-en-Couture
CANAL DE L'ESCAUT
Gouzeaucourt
Gonnelieu
Walincourt
Bamouzelle
Villers-Guislain
Honnecourt
Malincourt
Fins
Heudicourt
Aubencheul
Sorel
MILES
0   1   2   3   4   5
Epehy

CAMBRAI.

1917, 1918.

197

" 27th. 4.30 a.m. moved forward through Pronville to Tadpole Copse and crossed the Canal du Nord at noon, then halting for three hours to allow the artillery to cross and take up positions. By 9 p.m. we were in position in the Sunken Road near Graincourt where the night was spent.

" 28th. 6 a.m. Moved forward under harassing fire from the enemy in support of the 2/5th King's Own Royal Lancaster. On reaching Marcoing Trench ' A,' ' B ' and ' C ' Companies formed up for attack with ' D ' Company in reserve, our left flank on the Bapaume–Cambrai road and our right on La Folie Wood. The advance was carried out by short rushes under heavy machine-gun fire until 11.30 when we were held up by a very severe bombardment in front of the enemy wire.

" 29th. 8 a.m. Battalion, having suffered many casualties, was withdrawn to refit and reorganize in a position to the south of Anneux.

" 30th. 5 a.m. Moved forward again to a position at La Folie Wood, in the evening relieving the 8th King's Liverpool in the line.

" 1st October. Spent morning consolidating and at 3 p.m. ' A ' Company was ordered to carry out a minor attack in co-operation with the 2/5th Battalion The Loyal North Lancashire, its objective being Z. Trench. The trench was taken by ' A ' Company with few casualties, but owing to the non-success of the right attack a gap of some 1,000 yards in depth was left exposed. ' A ' Company spent the night consolidating the position, but the other companies were out of touch with ' A.' At 10 p.m. on the 2nd a man of ' A ' Company swam the St. Quentin Canal, landing at ' C ' Company's right post with a verbal report from his platoon commander to the effect that the enemy was in rear of Z. Trench. During the night every effort was made to re-establish touch with ' A,' but they failed.

" 3rd October. The Battalion scouts were sent forward at 5 a.m. to try and get in communication with ' A ' Company, but all the roads were covered by the fire of machine-guns and snipers and one of the scouts was killed. At 7 a.m. aeroplane report stated that ' A ' was still holding on. At 3 p.m. a counter-attack on Z. Trench was organized and attempted by platoons of ' B ' and ' D ' Companies, assisted by the Trench Mortars of the 170th Brigade, but the platoons were unable to get further forward than 300 yards and suffered very considerable loss.

" 4th October. What remained of ' A ' Company fell back, and that company and the others occupied a line in touch with the Canadians on the left. At midnight the Battalion was relieved and went back for a brief rest."

It was brought up to the front again on the 7th and remained for rather over twenty-four hours, being then again withdrawn and spending the best part of a week moving from one—so-called—rest area to another.   It was about this time that the 57th Division was taken out of the XVII. Corps and transferred to the XI. Corps of the Fifth Army.

From the 21st October the Division was in the Templeuve area, where some very active patrolling was carried out and the Battalion had three men killed, three officers and twenty-four other ranks wounded.

The 1st November found the Battalion—having fought its last fight—in tolerably comfortable billets in Hellèmes, and here on the 11th the news of the signing of the Armistice was received, and all then settled down to training, inspections, courses of all kinds, and—finally—to demobilization.

By the beginning of 1919 the Battalion had moved to Marne Camp at Agnez les Duisans, and here it remained during the first six months of this year.

On the 1st April—very many officers, non-commissioned officers and men having by this time left for home—the Battalion was reduced to cadre strength of five officers and forty-four other ranks ; on the 31st May it was announced that the whole of the 170th Brigade would make a move homewards on the 2nd June, and on this day all the battalions left Agnez les Duisans for Dunkirk, whence on the 6th they sailed in several transports for Southampton—and home.

A King's Colour was presented, in 1919, to each Second Line Battalion of the Territorial Force which had served abroad during the Great War, 1914–1918.   (See Appendix II.)

CHAPTER XLIV

THE 3/4TH (RESERVE) BATTALION
THE LOYAL NORTH LANCASHIRE REGIMENT

1915–1918

ON the 1st June, 1915, the 3/4th Battalion of The Loyal North Lancashire Regiment was raised, the nucleus being formed by the transfer of certain officers and non-commissioned officers from the 2/4th Battalion which was then undergoing training at Oxted in Surrey. The unit itself was formed at Weeton Camp, near Kirkham in Lancashire, and its original officers were Major G. D. Hale, Captains T. G. Sandeman and W. K. Kershaw—who was appointed adjutant early in June, 1916— Lieutenants T. S. Wilding and E. S. Healey, with Major and Quartermaster H. J. Whitehead.

Recruits were sent to the new Battalion from the Territorial Headquarters at Avenham Lane, Preston, for the necessary training, and the first draft dispatched to France to join the active service battalions, left in September, 1915. From these battalions were received in exchange all officers and men sent home from overseas or discharged from hospitals in England, after sick furlough.

Towards the end of the year the Battalion was moved for the winter into billets in the neighbourhood of Blackpool, from where further large drafts were sent abroad.

In the spring of 1916 the unit was again moved, this time to a hutment camp at Park Hall Camp, Oswestry, which contained the Third Line units of all the battalions of the West Lancashire Division. In August of this year Army Order No. 259 was issued, and in this it was announced that His Majesty The King had been graciously pleased to approve the formation of a new corps of Infantry to be designated " The Training Reserve," and that instructions regarding its formation and establishment would shortly be issued. These appear in Army Council Instruction No. 1528 of the same month and year, and in paras. 2 and 3 we read as follows :—" With the object of preserving the territorial connection as far as possible there will, however, be retained as regimental reserves in each regiment the Special

Reserve Battalion, the Extra Special Reserve Battalion, if any, and the Territorial Force Reserve Battalions shown in Schedule A attached.

" The remainder of the Infantry Reserve Battalions, at present known as 2nd Reserve and Local Reserve Battalions, will become the ' Training Reserve.' They will discard their present regimental designations and be given consecutive numbers as battalions of the Training Reserve. The constitution of the Training Reserve, showing the old and new designations and establishments of each battalion, is shown in Schedule B attached."

In Schedule A, or Appendix No. 135, of this Army Council Instruction it is officially notified that " the 4th, 5th and 12th Reserve Battalions of The Loyal North Lancashire Regiment are henceforth to be known as the 4th Reserve Battalion of the Regiment with a total establishment, all ranks, of 2,085."

Of the 4th Reserve Battalion, The Loyal North Lancashire Regiment, Major, now Lieut.-Colonel, Hale assumed command, with Captain Healey as adjutant. By this time the unit had increased in strength from a beginning of six officers and some 200 non-commissioned officers and men to about 120 officers and 2,000 other ranks.

In January, 1918, Lieut.-Colonel A. S. Bates, D.S.O., relieved Colonel G. D. Hale in command, and very shortly afterwards the Battalion was sent to Ireland, where it was at first under canvas in Phœnix Park, then moving into Wellington Barracks, Dublin, where it remained until finally disbanded.

CHAPTER XLV

THE 5TH (LATER 1/5TH) TERRITORIAL BATTALION
THE LOYAL NORTH LANCASHIRE REGIMENT

1914–1919

THE GREAT WAR

THE BATTLE OF THE SOMME, THIRD BATTLE OF YPRES, THE BATTLE OF CAMBRAI, THE BATTLE OF ARRAS

O N the 1st August, 1914, the Battalion—994 strong of all ranks— had proceeded to camp at Kirkby Lonsdale, when at 5 p.m. the same day a telegram was handed to the Commanding Officer containing the brief command—"Return at once." Camp was left at five o'clock next morning, and on reaching Bolton three hours later the Battalion was dismissed, but ordered to hold itself in readiness to re-assemble. On the 4th came the order to mobilize and by 8.30 a.m. the Battalion had re-assembled over 1,200 strong, many men falling in with it who had completed their time. On the 10th August the 5th Battalion, 1,030 strong, entrained for Chipping Sodbury in Gloucestershire and for some days was employed in guarding the railway line from Wootton Basset to Avonmouth.

The 5th Battalion formed part of the North Lancashire Brigade of the West Lancashire Division, and the Brigade contained also on mobilization the 4th and 5th Bns. The King's Own Royal Lancaster Regiment and the 4th Bn. The Loyal North Lancashire Regiment.

At this time the Commander of the Division was Major-General W. Lindsay, but he left almost at once to join the Headquarter Staff of the British Expeditionary Force, Major-General Hammersley then taking his place ; but this officer also proceeded overseas after a very brief period of command, and the West Lancashire Division was then ordered down to train in Kent under Major-General J. B. Forster.

It had been hoped and indeed intended that the Division should go out to the seat of war as a complete unit, but the exigencies of the military situation in France and the urgent need for reinforcements did not permit this arrangement to be adhered to ; and nearly all the infantry battalions proceeded abroad, some individually, while the North Lancashire Brigade was reconstituted, the 5th Battalion, The Loyal North Lancashire Regiment, being taken out of it, and, as elsewhere stated, that Brigade went to France with the 51st Division.

It was from Sevenoaks that the 1/5th Battalion left on the 12th February, 1915, for the port of embarkation, proceeding in three trains at 7.30, 9.35 and 11 a.m., and on arrival at Southampton sailing at seven o'clock the same evening in the S.S. " Tintoretto," escorted by three destroyers.

The embarking strength of the Battalion was twenty-six officers and 1,058 non-commissioned officers and men, the following being the names of the officers who accompanied it : Majors G. Hesketh and A. H. C. Haslam ; Captains C. K. Potter, C. R. Shaw, P. A. O. Read, C. F. Bouchier, G. J. Bouchier, P. C. Pilling, T. Entwisle and A. V. Makant ; Lieutenants W. A. Grierson, T. O. Smith, T. Entwisle, A. E. B. Dixon, H. A. Richardson, A. R. B. Chapman, R. W. B. Sparkes, J. D. Thompson, F. K. Mallet, W. C. Whalley, F. W. Musson, H. Chronnell and R. K. Makant, Captain and Adjutant W. R. H. Dann, Captain and Quartermaster T. R. Griffiths and Lieutenant T. R. W. Atkins, R.A.M.C.

Disembarkation was effected at Havre on the morning of the 13th, when the Battalion prepared to join the division to which it had now been transferred. In the *Short History of the 6th Division*, compiled by its commander, Major-General T. O. Marden, in dealing with the events of the opening of the year 1915, when the 6th Division was about Armentières, he writes that each of his brigades received at that time a fifth—a Territorial—battalion, and that " the 5th Bn. The Loyal North Lancashire Regiment joined the 16th Infantry Brigade of the 6th Division on the 15th February."

In the Battalion War Diary this arrangement is very briefly referred to, for under date of the 13th February we read : " Battalion in 16th Brigade, 6th Division, III. Army Corps. 14th. Left by train and arrived Armentières ; in Brigade, 8th Buffs, Leicester, Shropshire and York and Lancaster Regiments. Brigade Commander, Major-General Ingouville-Williams, Divisional Commander, Lieut.-General Sir W. Pulteney, Army Commander, General Sir H. L. Smith-Dorrien."

On the 22nd February parties of the Battalion went up to the front line for instruction in trench duties by more experienced battalions, and on the 27th the first casualties of the war occurred, two men of the Battalion being wounded. On the same day news was received of the promotion to commissioned rank of four men of the Battalion, viz. Lance-Sergeant Kenyon, Lance-Corporals Marshall, Ward and Glaister ; these were all gazetted to the rank of 2nd Lieutenant.

On the 13th March the Battalion suffered its first fatal casualties, one man being killed, while Captain A. V. Makant died of wounds.

In the middle of March the 6th Division began to move north to the Ypres sector, the 16th Brigade moving off first, but the Battalion was then attached as a temporary measure to the 17th Brigade of the Division, and on the 8th April took over part of the centre sector of the front line, and had the supreme satisfaction, on its first appearance in the front line trenches " on its own," of capturing a German flag. During the night of the 22nd–23rd the enemy, in a moment of vainglory, had placed a German flag midway between their trenches and those held by the Battalion ; and the very same night two men of the 5th Loyal North Lancashire— Privates Holt and Parkinson—went out and brought it in.

At the beginning of June the Battalion moved with the remaining units of the Division, and occupied hutments one and a half miles north-west of Ypres, and on the 6th when up in trenches near St. Jean many casualties were sustained and Lieutenant A. E. B. Dixon died of wounds received.

The time was now at hand when the Battalion was to join another Division, and on the 10th June it paraded before the G.O.C. 16th Brigade, Major-General Ingouville-Williams, who addressed the officers and men in the following flattering terms :—

" I come here to say good-bye. I am very sorry to lose the Battalion from the Brigade. When I first saw the Battalion I made up my mind it was a good Battalion and well trained, and I may say that my opinion was well justified. I can safely say that your work has been thoroughly satisfactory and I shall have great pleasure in telling your Brigadier my opinion of you. I am very sorry you are going away, and I am confident that so long as the 5th Loyal North Lancashire are here they will always keep their good name and do their work loyally and thoroughly.

" I wish you every success in your new sphere and shall follow your career with great interest."

On the 11th June the Battalion moved to the neighbourhood of Vlamertinghe, where it was attached to the 151st Brigade of the 50th Division and held in general reserve for the attack by the 3rd Division on the enemy's trenches ; this attack was initially successful, but in the end the 3rd Division was obliged to fall back, and on the 17th June the Battalion, then in reserve at Hooge, was ordered up to reinforce the Border Regiment of the 149th Brigade. Accordingly at 1.30 a.m. it moved forward to Sanctuary Wood, to the south of Hooge and east of Zillebeke. The Battalion was not, however, very seriously engaged, and by the 20th was back again in bivouacs some two miles to the south-west of Vlamertinghe, having during the preceding days suffered rather under twenty casualties.

At the end of June the Battalion was occupying trenches about a mile and a half to the west of Kemmel, when out of the line being at Locre. On the 16th July the Battalion marched with the 151st Brigade—one wholly composed of battalions of the Durham Light Infantry and now under the command of Brigadier-General J. S. M. Shea—to Armentières, where several weeks were now to be passed, and while here—in September —Lieutenant E. Blackburn was wounded.

During the latter part of this month the 50th Division was occupying the Houplines sector of the line, with the 7th Division on the right and the 23rd on the left, the troops when out of the line being in billets at Tissage.

For purposes of training the Division went back on the 10th November to the neighbourhood of Steenwercke, but here the weather was deplorable, all the roads were flooded and the level ground was everywhere eighteen inches under water, so that any idea of outdoor training had, at least temporarily, to be abandoned. The Battalion can hardly, therefore, have felt any keen regret when in December information was received that the 55th (West Lancashire) Division was very shortly expected to arrive in France, when the Battalion was to be re-transferred back to it. On the 21st December it left the 151st Brigade, 50th Division, being for the time being attached to the 26th Brigade of the 9th Division ; but at last, on the 9th January, 1916, the Battalion marched to Bailleul, then going on by rail and road to Vergies-sur-Somme, where it rejoined its original Division then just arrived in France, and to the command of which Major-General H. S. Jeudwine, C.B., had been appointed. The Battalion was posted to the 166th Infantry Brigade, which also contained the 1/5th King's Own Royal Lancaster, the 1/10th (Scottish) King's Liverpool, and the 1/5th South Lancashire Regiments, the commander being Brigadier-General L. F. Green-Wilkinson, D.S.O.

At Vergies-sur-Somme 2nd Lieutenants E. H. Taylor, F. Alker, R. E. Ford and 208 non-commissioned officers and men joined.

" On January 29th, 1916, the Division paraded as a complete unit, for the first time since the outbreak of the war, for inspection by Lieut.-General the Earl of Cavan, commanding XIV. Corps, and a few days later " —on the 4th February—" proceeded to relieve the 88th French Division —at that time occupying the sector south of Arras from Wailly to Bretencourt. The relief was completed by the 16th February and the Division immediately began to make its presence felt. To harass the enemy as much as possible ; to keep him ever upon the alert ; to lose no opportunity of inflicting casualties upon him—these were from the first the methods drilled into the Division, and the enemy was not slow in learning to appreciate them." *

The Battalion reached Bellacourt, its destination, on the 11th, and while waiting in the village street on the following day to take over the trenches from the French, a German shell burst in the ranks, killing five men and wounding eleven.

The trenches when taken over were found to be in bad condition, very muddy and difficult to move about in and from, but none the less on the 22nd February two men of " C " Company captured and brought in three prisoners ; these men, though of good physique, surrendered comparatively weakly and complained with some bitterness of being "fed up" with the war!

On the 30th May the following officers joined from England : Captain G. M. Hesketh, 2nd Lieutenants J. J. Crabtree, C. Carr, W. J. Curtis, B. Kearney, J. C. Frankland and J. Faulkner.

The months of May and June were passed in the Gouy area, and here on the 5th June Lieutenant A. R. B. Chapman was killed in the trenches ; on the 26th 2nd Lieutenants C. E. Haslam and E. Harling joined.

The time had now come for the Division to move south and play its part in the Battle of the Somme. Some of the units, the Battalion among them, began to move on the 9th July and after many long marches it arrived at Meaulte on the 30th, proceeding next day to the front-line trenches. Here it came under very heavy enemy shelling, and on the 6th August there were twenty-one casualties among all ranks, five officers—Captains P. C. Pilling, T. Entwisle and H. Whitehead, Lieutenant and Adjutant W. Tong and 2nd Lieutenant R. Crompton—being wounded, the first-named dying of his wounds.

In the chapters dealing with the services of the 1/4th Battalion of the Regiment, something has been said of the preliminaries of the great battle of this month and of the part taken in it by the 55th Division, and this need not here be repeated. In the operations of the 8th August the two other brigades of the Division were in the front line, but very early on this day the Battalion moved forward into Dublin and Casement Trenches as reserve to the 164th Brigade, which was attacking on the left of the Division. From here " B " and " C " Companies were sent on to occupy trenches running north between the Trônes–Guillemont road and Railway Support Trench, " C " going still further forward and joining the 8th King's Liverpool in the front line : " A " and " D " Companies were soon after ordered to trenches at the time held by the 2/5th Lancashire Fusiliers, 164th Brigade, and moved up accordingly.

* The Story of the 55th Division, p. 25.

The Battalion now joined in the attack then launched, advancing in four waves, with the Liverpool Scottish on the right and the 2nd Division on the left, the first objective being the enemy front line and, that captured, the village of Guillemont. The opening of the attack was somewhat delayed and hampered by the extreme congestion of the assembly trenches, but it was finally launched at 5.25 a.m. On the left things went well, but on the right the companies were held up by an intense machine-gun fire and every officer of these companies, with one exception, became a casualty. Further advance was deemed to be out of the question and the 164th Brigade, and the Battalion with it, was withdrawn to the original line.

On the 10th August the Battalion was moved still further back ; on the 15th it withdrew to Meaulte and on the 19th it proceeded by train and march route to Acheux.

The casualties in the battle were four officers and twenty-nine other ranks killed, two officers and eighty-three other ranks wounded, while twenty men were missing. Of the officers, Lieutenant Edward Blackburn, 2nd Lieutenants Ernest Blackburn, E. W. Rice and J. Farnworth were killed, and Captain T. Entwisle and Lieutenant E. H. Ward were wounded.

Of the attack by the Battalion the Divisional History gives the following brief but eulogistic account : " On the left the 1/5th Loyal North Lancashire, owing to the lateness of the hour at which orders were received ; to the narrowness and crowded condition of the trenches, due to reliefs ; and to the heavy casualties to officers, were unable to get into position until after 5 a.m. In spite of this, and in spite of the fact that the artillery barrage had lifted at 4.23 a.m. as arranged, they made a most gallant assault. They were, however, unable to reach the German trenches, and were compelled to fall back to their starting point."

During the month of August three drafts numbering 127 non-commissioned officers and men joined, and also the following officers : 2nd Lieutenants G. Glaister, W. A. Arthur, C. B. Wray, W. Ingham, T. S. Morris and G. E. Riding ; so that when on the 30th the Battalion left for Meri-court the strength was twenty-eight officers and 820 other ranks.

On the 5th September " the Division came back into the line, and the 165th and 166th Brigades with two companies of the 1/4th South Lancashire (Pioneers), relieved the brigades of the 24th Division from a point midway between High Wood and Delville Wood, across the Longueval–Flers road, round the front of Delville Wood to Ale Alley, east of Delville Wood." Here the 55th Division had the 7th on its right and the 1st on the left, and the Battalion had two of its companies in the front line and two in support.

" Here the situation," so runs the Divisional History, " was a peculiar one. The enemy was still holding on with determination to about twenty yards of the north-east corner of Delville Wood and Ginchy was still in his hands " ; and it was during an unsuccessful attempt made on the 6th September by the 7th Division to capture Ginchy, that the Battalion had some losses, four men being killed, and 2nd Lieutenants T. S. Morris, E. Rigby and thirty-eight other ranks being wounded.

The 166th Brigade took no active part in the fighting of the 9th September, nor in that of the 27th of the month, during the latter operation being apparently in occupation of some reserve trenches 800 yards north-east of Delville Wood ; but the Battalion had Lieutenant H. A. Richardson wounded.

At the end of September the relief of the 55th Division by the 41st commenced, and during the first days of October the Battalion followed to Ypres, where it occupied a reserve line on the Yser Canal, coming under frequent and heavy shelling, casualties being many and the parapets being constantly damaged and needing daily repair.

Here, on the 22nd, eleven officers joined the Battalion—four from the 8th Manchester, one from the 9th Manchester and six from the 4th Royal Welsh Fusiliers.

The Division was now in the Second Army, and except for two periods of rest—in January and in August—it remained in the Ypres Salient until the end of September, 1917. The portion of the line which on arrival it had taken over from the 29th Division, ran from Wieltje to the south of Railway Wood, and during the first few months at least of occupation the sector might reasonably be described as " quiet." There is consequently no outstanding event to record for this period ; but in January, 1917, four officers and 140 other ranks of the Battalion carried out a raid on the German trenches, which was, however, only partially successful, since the opposing enemy were numerous, strongly posted and evidently aware of what was in view ; and the casualties in the raiding party were heavy in proportion to the number engaged. 2nd Lieutenant J. C. Frankland and seven men were killed, 2nd Lieutenants F. F. Wood, C. W. Whitaker, A. Jones and forty-eight other ranks were wounded and two men were missing.

During January, 2nd Lieutenants D. S. Hamilton and R. B. Knowles joined.

There is nothing to be recorded during the months of February to May inclusive ; but more pressing matters were now to engage the attention of the 55th Division. On the 13th June the XIX. Corps, to which it belonged, was transferred to the Fifth Army, and, though not engaged in the June operations resulting in the capture of Messines Ridge, the Division was employed in the period immediately preceding the battle of the 31st July in providing carrying parties for the forward area, in patrolling, and in raids upon the enemy's trenches. All this good work could not be performed without the usual accompanying casualties, and between the 22nd and 30th July 2nd Lieutenants D. S. Hamilton, P. O. Davies, F. F. Wood and J. Kennedy were wounded.

The Fifth Army was detailed, in conjunction with the Second British and the First French Armies, to attempt on the 31st July the capture of the enemy's Gheluvelt–Langemarck system. The XIX. Corps was to attack with the 15th Division on the right, the 55th on the left, and with the 16th and 36th in reserve ; on the left of the XIX. Corps was the XVIII. The 55th Division was to advance with the 165th Brigade on the right, the 166th on the left and the 164th in reserve, and of the 166th Brigade the 1/5th Royal Lancaster and the 1/5th Loyal North Lancashire were in the front line.

At 5.30 a.m. on the 31st July the Battalion advanced to and attacked the German trench on a front of some 350 yards and penetrated for 400 yards into the German position ; the first and second objectives were captured, many prisoners taken, and the divisional objective, the Green Line, was reached. In the afternoon the Germans counter-attacked and the Brigade fell back to the Black Line, where a position was strongly established and held throughout the 1st August ; and shortly after midday on the 2nd the 36th Division relieved the 55th which went back to the Recques area, near St. Omer, for rest and training.

During the five days, from noon of the 30th July to noon on the 4th August, the casualties in the Division numbered 168 officers and 3,384 other ranks, to which the contribution of the Battalion was eight officers and 150 other ranks killed, wounded and missing. Of the officers, Acting Captain H. Chronnell, Lieutenants G. Glaister and J. S. Carr were killed, and Lieut.-Colonel T. O. Smith, Acting Captain S. L. Redfern, 2nd Lieutenants W. H. Tutt, R. T. Thornley, and J. M. Woods were wounded.

By the 14th September the Division was back again in its old area, and the Battalion supplied many working parties on the Canal Bank ; two days after return Captain R. K. Makant and 2nd Lieutenant J. H. Jones were wounded while so engaged.

While the 55th Division had been out of the line many attempts to advance from the Black Line—associated with the earlier fighting of this year—had been made by other divisions, but all these had failed, and the Division was now to be called upon to attempt the capture of its former objective. The Second and Fifth Armies were to attack on the 20th September, and in the V. Corps the 9th Division was to be on the right and the 55th on the left, while on the left of the 55th Division was the 38th of the XVIII. Corps.

The 164th and 165th Brigades of the Division were in the front line, and to each of these a battalion of the 166th Brigade was attached—the 1/5th Loyal North Lancashire to the 165th Brigade ; the two remaining battalions formed the divisional reserve. The two attached battalions assembled in rear of the leading brigades in the old German front-line system.

Zero hour was 5.40 a.m. on the 20th September and at that hour the barrage opened on the enemy's front line. Directly the leading battalions of the 165th Brigade went forward they were met with particularly heavy rifle and machine-gun fire from several strong points, and severe fighting followed in which the supporting battalions became involved. Four of the strong points were captured soon after 8 a.m., but several about Hill 35 were still holding out, and at 9.45 the 1/5th Loyal North Lancashire was ordered to reinforce the 1/6th King's Liverpool and attack Hill 37. By eleven o'clock two of the Battalion companies had captured this hill, but twenty minutes later they were counter-attacked and driven back, the enemy then occupying Hill 37 in great strength.

No further movement was made until reinforcements had come up, when another attack was launched, and soon after five o'clock that afternoon it was reported that Hill 37 had been captured and that the position was being consolidated.

The part taken in this day's operations by the 164th Brigade, on the left of the divisional front, has been described in the chapter dealing with the 1/4th Battalion of the Regiment, so that it will now be sufficient to say that the assault had, generally speaking, been a success. Hill 37 was ours and so was also the greater part of the Green Line. Telegrams of hearty congratulation were received that night from the Army and Corps Commanders, thanking all ranks for their " splendid efforts."

The position gained was held all through the 21st under a very heavy enemy barrage, and several attacks were made but were repulsed with loss ; and on the night of the 22nd–23rd the Division was relieved, having suffered casualties amounting to 127 officers and 2,603 other ranks. Those in the Battalion totalled 167, for twenty men were killed, 2nd Lieutenants S. J. Curtis, F. Howard, F. R. Pritchard and 140 other ranks were wounded, while 2nd Lieutenant G. H. Mewha and three men were missing.

The 23rd and 24th September the Battalion spent at Watou, and here Brigadier-General F. G. Lewis, C.B., D.S.O., who was now in command of the 166th Brigade, complimented the Battalion on its " splendid achievements " during the operations of the 20th–23rd, and also read out a congratulatory message he had received from the G.O.C. 165th Brigade.

On the 25th September the Division proceeded south to join the Third Army and relieved the 35th Division in the line south of Cambrai, the Battalion on the 26th taking over trenches in the Longavesne area. Here eleven subaltern officers—all from the 3rd Battalion—reported for duty— 2nd Lieutenants H. N. Hobson, A. Fraser, E. L. Hall, E. N. O. Weighill, J. Rankin, C. B. Cowan, J. S. Smith, T. A. Barter, A. B. Robson, W. B. Leigh and C. A. Bryan.

The line now occupied by the Division ran, roughly, from west of Honnecourt Wood, north-east of Epéhy, to New Post, south-east of the villages of Lempire and Ronssoy, a total frontage already of some 8,000 yards and shortly to be even further extended; moreover, it was not a continuous trench system, but a number of fortified posts with connecting trenches.

In the part of the Cambrai battle fought on the 20th November, only one brigade, the 164th, was engaged, but in the fighting on the 30th, the remaining units, and especially the 1/5th Loyal North Lancashire, took their full share.

On the 29th the divisional front had been nearly doubled, now extending to 13,000 yards, and the artillery support was limited to two field artillery brigades only. On the morning of the 30th " the portion of the line, extending from Banteau Ravine to Wood Road, was held by the 1/5th South Lancashire Regiment. South of them, in the Honnecourt sector, were the 1/5th Loyal North Lancashire, and in the Ossus sector the 1/10th Liverpool Scottish. The 1/5th King's Own Royal Lancaster Regiment was in support." The 165th Brigade was on the right and the 164th was in divisional reserve.

At seven on the morning of the 30th, in thick fog, a very heavy bombardment opened on the whole front of the Division, and all roads and tracks were under fire; communication with the South Lancashire was completely broken off, and it appeared that large bodies of Germans had got through on the left of that battalion and were advancing rapidly on Villers Guislain, the situation of which soon became precarious.

" Meantime, as late as 7.57 a.m.," so the Divisional History, " the 1/5th Loyal North Lancashire had reported—' no infantry action,'—but at 8.15 a.m. a message was received from the Liverpool Scottish on their right, stating that the enemy was advancing from its trenches at Ossus II. A quarter of an hour later an indistinct message from the 1/5th Loyal North Lancashire was received at the Headquarters of the 166th Brigade, to the effect that the enemy was through on the left—the line was then cut. By 8.30 a.m. the enemy was reported to have penetrated our line at Holt's Bank, and a few moments after large bodies of the enemy were seen in Pigeon Quarry—north of the Liverpool Scottish and between them and the 1/5th Loyal North Lancashire. . . . The advance had been rapid and almost bewildering. Our troops, reduced in numbers, and holding, nevertheless, a front of nearly seven miles, had not merely been attacked by overwhelming numbers, but had suddenly found themselves seriously outflanked. The situation at 10.45 a.m. was undoubtedly precarious and, unless restored, might have had grave consequences. It was restored !

" It is needless to say that the battalions, though sadly at a disadvantage, resisted splendidly. . . . The 1/5th Loyal North Lancashire, placed in a very hazardous position owing to what had happened on their left, made a gallant stand and, with the Liverpool Scottish, held on at Adelphi and Gloucester Road, causing very severe casualties to the enemy, and very considerably delaying his advance. These troops, however, became sadly reduced in numbers, and eventually, when in danger of being entirely surrounded, were compelled to withdraw, though Meath Post did not fall till 4.30 in the afternoon, and Limerick Post, garrisoned by a composite party of the 1/10th Liverpool (Scottish) and 1/5th Loyal North Lancashire, though cut off and surrounded, resisted until 5 a.m. next day, when they succeeded in reaching their own lines. . . .

" During the night of the 1st–2nd December the 164th and 166th Brigades were relieved by the 21st Division," when the scanty remains of the Battalion were withdrawn to Buire.

The losses in this fighting had been appalling, two men had been killed, three officers and twenty-seven other ranks wounded, two officers were wounded and missing, while sixteen officers and 384 non-commissioned officers and men were missing—a total casualty roll of 434 !

On the 9th December the Battalion moved to Noyelles and then passed the rest of the month training at Erny St. Julien, where towards the end of January, 1918, three officers and seventy other ranks were cross-posted to the 2/4th Battalion of the Regiment and fourteen officers and 271 other ranks to the 1/4th Battalion. The Battalion now severed its connection with the 55th Division, consequent on the decision recently come to in regard to the reduction in the number of battalions per division.

Three battalions—the 1/8th King's Liverpool from the 164th Brigade, the 1/9th King's Liverpool from the 165th Brigade, and the 1/5th Loyal North Lancashire from the 166th Brigade were ordered to join the 57th Division and they accordingly marched away on the 31st January, the last-named battalion moving to Erquinghem at a strength of no more than fourteen officers and 301 other ranks, exclusive of fifty men of the transport and other details remaining behind to follow on later. On arrival in the 57th divisional area the Battalion was posted to the 170th Brigade.

On the 14th February the Battalion was at Cottes in the St. Hilaire area, where it was in reserve of the XV. Corps, on the 1st March moving to Pont de Nieppe, where some days were spent in training : and then on the 20th taking over trenches in the Fleurbaix area, a tolerably quiet part of the front compared with more lively spots in which the Battalion had before served. During March considerable reinforcements must have joined, for at the end of the month the strength of the Battalion stood at 40 officers and 994 other ranks.

For the months of April and May, spent, for the most part, in Couin and Coigneux respectively, there is nothing of interest to record, and it was in fact not until well past the middle of August that any of the units of the 57th Division were called upon to take part in any major operations.

In the *History of the 51st (Highland) Division*, it is recorded that on the 14th August this division came under the orders of the XVII. Corps and began to take over trenches in the Bailleul–Fampoux area, and that " at the same time the 170th Brigade, 57th Division, south of the Scarpe, came under the orders of the G.O.C. 51st Division," which was then hold-ing a front of some 7,600 yards extending from Tilloy-les-Moufflaines on the south to Bailleul on the north. From this front the British forces were to attack the German front-line system on a front extending from the south of the Scarpe down to the right of the British line. The 170th Brigade occupied the right of the 51st Division front, and on the 17th and 18th patrols were sent forward, and a subsequent advance found the enemy's line unoccupied, though in other places it was held in strength. " From the information obtained in these encounters, it was decided that the 170th Brigade should continue its advance, while north of the Scarpe a series of operations were planned in order to gain the enemy's outpost zone from the Scarpe as far north as the Arras–Gavrelle road.

" It was hoped by this means to gain a good jumping-off line for an advance which the Division had now been ordered to carry out on the left of the Canadian Corps on the 26th August." [*]

On the night of the 18th–19th the Battalion moved up into the forward trenches, and at 1 a.m. on the 19th " B " and " D " Companies attacked the enemy trenches, just south of the River Scarpe, on a frontage of 600 yards. Ireland and Ionian Trenches were captured and consolidated, and Moray Trench was also secured by 2.30 a.m. Numerous counter-attacks were made by the enemy and successfully repulsed during the day, and at 10.30 on the night of the 19th the Battalion occupied and garrisoned Indian Trench. Very early on the morning of the 20th the Germans strongly attacked this trench and at the third attempt secured a footing

[*] Bewsher, *The History of the 51st (Highland) Division*, p. 359.

in it, the garrison being then forced to withdraw to Moray Trench. The enemy shelled the trenches held by the Battalion until dark, and at nine o'clock the troops withdrew to the original line.

During these operations the casualties in the Battalion amounted to five men killed, two officers—2nd Lieutenants F. A. Wyles and W. W. Long—and twenty-four other ranks wounded.

On the 21st the Battalion moved to Arras and next day to rest billets at Anzin, where congratulations on the good work done were received from the Corps Commander.

The 170th Brigade now returned to its own Division, having been relieved in the 51st area by the Canadians ; and the 55th Division now, as part of the XVII. Corps of the Third Army, re-entered the battle area on the 27th August, experiencing very severe fighting between that date and the 2nd September.

On the night of the 27th the Battalion slept in the open in Delville Wood, moving up into the line on the following day and acting as " moppers-up " to the 172nd Brigade, which attacked in front of Hendecourt and Riencourt, the Battalion thereafter taking up a position ready to attack Riencourt on the following day. Moving forward on the 29th it was in close support of the 2/5th King's Own Royal Lancaster, which attacked and captured Riencourt, and during the 30th it guarded the western out-skirts of that town against any possible German attack, on relief on the 31st going back into support. It came forward again, however, on the following day, first occupying Copse and Crux Trenches and then advancing in support of the 171st Brigade, by which Riencourt was captured that evening : this day 2nd Lieutenant Dean was rather badly gassed. On the 2nd September there was hard fighting by the XVII. and Canadian Corps, whereby the enemy was pushed back to the Canal du Nord, when one of the companies of the Battalion followed on clearing the trenches forward of the Drocourt–Quéant line, and liaison posts were established with the 2/4th South Lancashire. On the 3rd the Battalion moved back to the Hindenburg Support Line, to the south-west of Fontaine-les-Croisilles. On this day 2nd Lieutenant Lees was shell-shocked.

It was the 9th of the month before the Battalion came up to the front again, on which day it relieved the Irish Guards in Moeuvres, remaining here throughout this day and the following one under enemy bombing ; it attacked again on the evening of the 11th and established a line just west of the Canal du Nord. The enemy was still offering a stout resistance, and late on the 12th he succeeded in passing some of his infantry into Moeuvres on the left of the Battalion, enveloping the company on that flank. After two hours' hard fighting this company succeeded in making its way through the village and took up a defensive position to the west. At dawn on the 13th the company attacked, cleared the enemy out of the village and established itself in the new line.

That night the Battalion was relieved by the 2/5th King's Own Royal Lancaster and withdrew into reserve in the Hindenburg Line : here it remained until the 16th, when it marched and travelled by rail to billets at Saulty.   The Division was now in the XI. Corps of the Fifth Army.

In the latter part of September and throughout practically the whole of the month of October the Division was constantly engaged, the enemy, though nearly everywhere falling back, putting up a stiff resistance and causing no small loss to their opponents.   " Though troops could still be found to offer resistance to our initial assault, the German infantry and machine-gunners were no longer reliable, and cases were being reported of their retiring—without fighting in front of our artillery barrage."

By the end of October, when the Battalion was in the Templeuve area, the losses suffered during the preceding days had risen to the following very high totals : three officers and forty-four other ranks had been killed in action or had died of wounds received ; six officers and 156 non-commissioned officers and men had been wounded ; while one officer and twenty men were missing, at least half of whom were known to have been wounded.   The officers who were killed were Lieutenants G. B. Cook (R.E., attached) and R. T. Thornley and 2nd Lieutenant A. Wallis.

On the 1st November the 170th Brigade was withdrawn to Hellèmes, and it was quartered here when, on the 11th, the signing of the Armistice with Germany was made known.   Early in December the Brigade made a further move, to Agny-les-Duisans, and here on the 17th the Colours which had been sent for to England were handed over to the Battalion with all due formality.   At the end of the year the Battalion stood at a strength of forty-three officers and 811 other ranks, Major F. W. Seward being then in command.

In January, 1919, this establishment began very rapidly to be reduced as demobilization set in, and on the 27th February the numbers had fallen so low, that those non-commissioned officers and men who remained were formed into one company.

It was not, however, until the 2nd June that any homeward movement was made, and on this date the cadres of all the battalions of the 170th Brigade left Agny-les-Duisans by train for Dunkirk, remaining here in camp until the morning of the 8th when the cadre of the 1/5th Bn. The Loyal North Lancashire Regiment marched down to the docks, and, embarking there in the S.S. " Mogileff," sailed at seven in the morning for Southampton.

CHAPTER XLVI

THE 2/5TH (TERRITORIAL) BATTALION
THE LOYAL NORTH LANCASHIRE REGIMENT

1914–1919

THE BATTLE OF YPRES, THE BATTLE OF THE SCARPE, THE BATTLE OF CAMBRAI

IN the chapter dealing with the 2/4th Battalion of the Regiment mention has been made of the raising of the Second-Line units of the Territorial Battalions. The 2/5th was raised in 1914, very much about the same time as the others, and was also posted to the 170th Brigade of the 57th Division.

Immediately after the order was received for the raising of the Second Line Battalions of the Regiments of the Territorial Force, in September, 1914, there was, throughout the Country, a rush of recruits of the very best type as regards physique, education and intelligence, and in the course of a week, or so, the full establishment was obtained. The rate of enlistments was only regulated by the number of men who were able to be examined, and passed, by the medical officers from day to day. At first the military authorities were unable to supply anything in the way of uniform, arms, and equipment, as all the available stocks were required for the use of the British Expeditionary Force overseas ; neither was accommodation even available and all ranks were therefore billeted for a time in their own homes—but these difficulties were speedily overcome and training began in earnest, in spite of the shortage of qualified instructors.

The 2/5th Battalion embarked for France with the other units of the Division, leaving Blackdown early on the morning of the 8th February, 1917, and being established in billets in the outskirts of Outtersteene before midday on the 12th.

The strength of the Battalion on leaving England was thirty-seven officers and 983 non-commissioned officers and men, and of the officers : Lieut.-Colonel C. F. Hitchins was in command, with Major W. Ainsworth as second-in-command.

On the 18th the Battalion moved up nearer to the front and took the place in divisional reserve of a battalion of the 3rd New Zealand Brigade, and two days later began relieving one of the battalions of the 55th Division in the trenches, when casualties almost immediately occurred, before the end of the month five men being killed, while 2nd Lieutenant H. L. Bangham and four men were wounded. On the 14th April another officer —2nd Lieutenant E. W. Meadows—was wounded, and on the following day the Battalion had its first fatal officer casualty, Major W. Ainsworth, the second-in-command, being killed.

By this time the Battalion had " found its feet," and in May two silent raids were carried out on the enemy trenches. At eleven o'clock on the night of the 19th a raiding party—three officers and thirty-four other ranks —left our lines, but the German trenches were found to be deserted, the occupants having apparently cleared away preparatory to one of the enemy's favourite " trench-mortar shoots," which opened on the raiding party leaving our lines. No prisoners were, therefore, taken and the party had happily no casualties.

Another raid, but on a smaller scale, took place on the 24th, when two officers—Lieutenants Crampton and Marshall—and fifteen men started off. These had just reached the enemy's support line when a German patrol was heard approaching, and the raiders divided into two parties ; one charged the enemy with the bayonet and a sharp fight ensued, two Germans being killed and four captured ; two of these last were wearers of the Iron Cross ribbons and all looked very fit and in good condition. Of the raiding party only one—Lieutenant P. Crampton—was wounded.

On the 1st June the Battalion marched to Armentières, and on the following day relieved an Australian Infantry battalion in Ploegsteert Wood, the left sub-sector of the Le Touquet sector ; and from this date the Battalion, together with the 2/4th Battalion of the Regiment, was detached from the 170th Brigade, and became part of the force under Colonel Geddes, serving under the orders of the 3rd Australian Division, the operations of which have elsewhere been described. It was, as stated, to form the right flank of the attack on Messines Ridge by the Second Army.

The frontage, which the Battalion now took over under tolerably heavy enemy shell fire, but fortunately without any loss, extended from the Warnave Stream to Westminster Avenue, both inclusive.

The Second Army attack opened on the 7th June, and during the four days that the Battalion remained up in the trenches it was under a heavy and an almost continuous shell fire, while the German infantry in the immediate front was very active and enterprising and their machine-guns were continuously in action ; the whole front was also shelled by the enemy with " whizz-bangs."

When the Battalion was finally relieved by the 3rd Canterbury Battalion, of the Australian Corps, and went back into billets in Armentières, it had suffered the following casualties, viz. two men killed, four officers and fifty-seven other ranks wounded and one man missing : the wounded officers were Lieutenants W. Canty, G. Murray and E. H. Farmer and 2nd Lieutenant R. Malpass.

On the 11th the Battalion marched from Armentières to Bac St. Maur, where it was paraded before the G.O.C. 57th Division, who complimented officers and men on their excellent work and devotion to duty during the intense bombardment to which they had day and night been subjected during the eight days that the Battalion held the right flank of the Second Army attack under command of the 3rd Australian Division.

July, August and the greater part of September the Division remained in the Armentières sector of the line, during which time casualties regularly occurred among all ranks, and three subaltern officers were at various times wounded—2nd Lieutenants S. Eastwood, E. K. Edge and H. Kilner. Then on the 15th September the Battalion marched to the neighbourhood of La Gorgue and thence to Cantraine, and from there to Westrehem, where billets were taken over and intensive training commenced. During the last few days of September a draft of 127 other ranks joined and also four officers—2nd Lieutenants W. Boyle, W. Walton, L. F. Guy and J. Middlehurst.

The time had now come when the 57th Division was to play its part in its first great battle of the war, and for this purpose it left the neighbourhood of Westrehem about the middle of October. The Battalion moved by road, by train and by bus, and by way of Renescure, Proven, Boesinghe and Marsouin, and on the afternoon of the 24th moved up to the line about Poelcappelle, completely equipped and rationed for four days' operations.

The Division was still in Lord Cavan's XIV. Corps, and in the front line of this now were the 50th Division, next to the French, the 35th and the 57th ; and in the chapter dealing with the services in this action of the 2/4th Battalion of The Loyal North Lancashire, something has been said of the fighting which took place and of the terrible state of the ground over which the attack was made on this October day.

In the War Diary of the 2/5th we are told that " the leading waves had scarcely gone more than fifty yards before they came under an intense machine-gun barrage which caused a great number of casualties, and it seemed that our barrage had missed locating the positions of the enemy machine-guns. All the company officers of the Battalion became casualties during the early stages of the attack and the sergeants and junior non-commissioned officers then carried on the advance in a most determined manner. Small groups of men reached and held some shell-craters about 500 yards in advance of our original line ; and it was only by reason of the particularly heavy losses and the very thin line that was being held that it was decided to withdraw to our original position and there consolidate.

" The enemy seemed to have anticipated the attack and had pushed forward small groups of men very close to our line under cover of the darkness. These groups were untouched by our barrage and surprised the leading waves, thus causing the heavy casualties in the initial stages of the attack. The enemy's snipers were especially efficient.

" The ground which had to be advanced over was dreadful, and it speaks well for the men that they got along at all as it was almost impassable. The German machine-guns were mostly emplaced in shell-holes, bringing a cross-fire to bear on the Battalion frontage ; though covers were used for the rifles it was found almost impossible to fire them owing to the mud which collected on the rifles as the men fell in and out of shell-holes waist deep in water."

Throughout the 25th the Battalion held the line under the very worst possible conditions of rain and mud, the enemy keeping up a heavy if intermittent shelling, which caused fifty-three casualties ; and about five o'clock on the morning of the 26th the companies formed up to attack an objective which was distant about 1,000 yards from the original line.

At 5.40 the Battalion moved off in attack formation, three companies being in the front line and one being held in readiness as a counter-attack company, each platoon having a frontage of about 160 yards. The " going " was almost impossible, but the men pushed on steadily if slowly. Owing to the state of their weapons it was practically impossible to use either rifle or Lewis gun, and the men had to trust to the bayonet, in the wielding of which the men of the 2/5th excelled themselves, and it is estimated that the non-commissioned officers and men accounted for some five hundred of the enemy and captured eight machine-guns. One sergeant attacked and killed the detachments of two German machine-guns single-handed, and was still advancing when he himself became a casualty.

On the evening of the 26th the 2/8th King's Liverpool Regiment came up in relief, when the Battalion moved back to Huddleston Camp, and from there by way of Boesinghe to Peddington Camp near Proven, where it rested and reorganized. The strength on the last day of October was no more than twenty-three officers and 615 non-commissioned officers and men, since in the Passchendaele Battle the losses had been serious, amounting to 288 all ranks killed, wounded and missing. Six officers—Captains A. B. Hoare and H. Morris, Lieutenant N. Grey, 2nd Lieutenants J. E. Hartley, J. Middlehurst and W. Boyle—and forty-two other ranks were killed or died of wounds, nine officers and 144 non-commissioned officers and men were wounded, and eighty-seven men were missing. The wounded officers were Captain A. C. Eames, Lieutenants J. Bryans and H. W. Lawrence, 2nd Lieutenants G. M. W. Knott, W. Paton, W. Walton, A. J. Marshall, I. W. E. L. Bigger and H. Drysdale.

The Battalion remained in the Proven area until the 8th November, when it was sent to Audenfort near Audruicq, but at the end of the year 1917 it was back again in the Proven area, about Proosdy.

On the 2nd January, 1918, the Battalion was again on the move, this time to the Steenwerck area, where immediately on arrival it went into the line, there relieving the 44th Australian Battalion of the 3rd Australian Division, and here it was in close support of the Wezmacquart sector, three of the companies being in the Subsidiary Line and one company in what was known as Fleurie Switch. This company was mainly occupied in improving the local defences. The periods out of the line were usually spent in billets in Erquinghem.

It was while quartered in this village early in February that a very great change was made, somewhat unexpectedly as would appear, in the organization, training and future employment of the 2/5th Battalion, The Loyal North Lancashire Regiment. Mention has elsewhere been made of the reorganization of divisions which took place early in 1918, and the reasons for and nature of which are set forth in the Field-Marshal's despatch of the 20th July of this year. So far as this reorganization affected other battalions of the Regiment with which this History has up to the present treated, the result had usually been that some battalions were transferred to other divisions than those with which they had hitherto served, while in one or two cases battalions were broken up and their personnel distributed among others whose existence was not threatened.

The effect of the new order of things was wholly different in the case of the 2/5th Battalion, for in the War Diary under date of the 5th February, 1918, we read that " the Battalion was selected to be the Pioneer Battalion to the Division as from 6 p.m." on this day. It was at once placed at the disposal of the C.R.E. 57th Division, and set to work under his orders on the reinforcement of the defences of the Divisional Sector.

The Divisional Commander, General R. Barnes, had always found the Battalion in every way so satisfactory that he was very averse to its being broken up or disbanded, and being aware that it contained an unusually large number of miners, the following was directed to be put to the men :

A. That the unit should be kept together as the Pioneer Battalion of the Division, when its fighting days would not be brought to a close :

B. That the Battalion should be disbanded.

All ranks unanimously agreed to remaining on as a Pioneer Battalion, and in its new sphere all served on right well to the end of the war.

On the 11th two large drafts arrived and were taken on the strength of the Battalion—nine officers and 230 other ranks from the 8th and 150 other ranks from the 9th Service Battalion.

A move was made on the 14th to the Estaires area, where the Battalion took over a " job of work " from a Pioneer Battalion of the Welsh Regiment, the companies being employed separately, but generally in the improvement of the defences from Fleurbaix to Laventie. The Battalion now stood at a very high strength—fifty-one officers and 968 non-commissioned officers and men, and it was at this time enacted that it should be reorganized on a three-company basis, the change not to be immediately and drastically made, but to be carried out by a process of natural attrition and not by any large or immediate transfers of personnel.

On the 20th March the Battalion relieved a Northamptonshire Pioneer Battalion in the Sailly area, and carried out work under the C.R.E. of its own Division—the 57th ; but that this had to be executed under the usual attentions from the enemy is proved by the reports of casualties which were constantly occurring, most of them from shell fire.

During April the Battalion was much moved about, being sent wherever important defence work had to be done and never remaining more than a very few days in any one place : at the end of April it was in Coigneux, and the " attrition " above referred to seems indeed to have been of a gradual nature, for there were still fifty-one officers and 850 other ranks serving with the Battalion.

In and about Coigneux the Battalion remained until the beginning of July when it moved to St. Leger-les-Authies, and at the end of the month the 57th Division was transferred to the VI. Corps Reserve, and the Battalion marched with the 170th Infantry Brigade Group to Wanquetin, and from there on the 1st August to billets in Arras. The Division was now in the XVII. Corps of the Third Army, this corps containing also the 52nd and 56th Divisions. Here the companies were at once set to work on the defences in the forward system.

On the 19th of the month the Battalion was on the move again, marching from Arras to Marquay, thence by Noyelles, Beaudricourt and Bavincourt to Blaireville, and here taking over the work of the repair of all roads in the forward area from Heninel to Croisilles.

During the September fighting of this year the Battalion was distributed by companies among other units of the Division, following up closely in rear of the advance and improving the roads as progress was made. At the end of the month it was temporarily in trenches to the west of Bourlon

Wood, and from here on the 1st October the Battalion moved to billets in the sunken road south-west of Fontaine-Notre Dame, and was then again dispersed among other units and was employed in carrying out road repairs and in the construction of strong posts on the Marcoing Line.

In the Field-Marshal's despatch of the 21st December, 1918, he writes as follows of the operations of the 8th–12th October, known as the Battle of Cambrai : " during the night of the 9th October the Canadian Corps captured Ramillies and crossed the Scheldt Canal at Pont d'Aire. Canadian patrols entered Cambrai from the north and joined hands with patrols of the 57th Division working through the southern portion of the town." It was no doubt on this occasion that the 2/5th Battalion, The Loyal North Lancashire, was among the very first of our troops to enter Cambrai, where they came upon a very large clothing-store completely equipped with clothing and equipment of all kinds for the German troops, much of it full-dress, intended to be worn on the ceremonial entry into Paris. From here on the 10th it was sent to Moeuvres, and from there by road and rail and by Noeux-les-Mines to Formelles, where it took the place of a battalion of the 47th Division near Redinghem.

There was now to be a brief relief from pioneer work, for the 2/5th Battalion was to take part in something of an almost spectacular character, since on the 19th it was at Cantelieu and there provided a guard-of-honour for M. Clémenceau, the President of the French Republic, on the occasion of his visit to Lille on the release of that city from four long years of German domination—a city which the Battalion was among the very first of the British troops to enter.

From the 21st to the 31st October the Battalion was working on the roads about Cornet, then moving to Ronchin and from there to Tournai, where news of the signing of the Armistice was received ; a return was then made to Ronchin, where all the many educational and other courses were inaugurated and where demobilization now very shortly commenced.

At the end of the year, when the Battalion was at Arras as part of the 171st Brigade, the strength stood at thirty-seven officers and 660 non-commissioned officers and men ; but these numbers now began very rapidly to diminish until the time arrived, in the early summer of 1919, for the Battalion to return home with what remained of the Division with which it had embarked for the war just over two years previously.

THE 2ND/5TH BATTALION ENTERING CAMBRAI.

10th October, 1918.

The Imperial War Museum—Copyright.

CHAPTER XLVII

THE 3/5TH (RESERVE) BATTALION
THE LOYAL NORTH LANCASHIRE REGIMENT

1915–1918

THIS Battalion was formed in April, 1915, at Fletcher Street Barracks, Bolton, when the 2/5th Battalion had been completed ; and in June it proceeded to Weeton near Kirkham, where it was placed under canvas in company with the other units of the North Lancashire Brigade of the Third Line Battalions. The 3/5th Bn. The Loyal North Lancashire Regiment contained at this time 1,250 non-commissioned officers and men, but no more than five officers, the Commanding Officer being Captain C. F. Bouchier, while Captain J. W. Hough was the adjutant. The difficulty of handling, instructing and training so large a number of men, with so wholly inadequate a number of commissioned officers, was of course very great.

In October Lieut.-Colonel F. W. Foley took over command from Captain Bouchier, and in the same month the Battalion was sent to Blackpool and was there accommodated in billets in the South Shore District, remaining there until the spring of 1916. It was then moved to Oswestry and went under canvas in a large camp south of the hutments at Park Hall.

The Battalion was wholly a training unit and was used for preparing drafts for the battalions overseas, these being replaced by men who returned home wounded or sick from the 1/5th or 2/5th Battalions.

At this time Lord Derby, the Honorary Colonel of the 5th Battalion, was Under-Secretary of State for War, and on the 18th April, 1916, he sent the following telegram to the O.C. 3/5th Battalion :—

" Could and would you get two hundred of your men to volunteer to-day for the 2/4th Royal Lancaster Regiment, which is badly in want of men. It would be most patriotic of them if they would go and if you could spare them."

To this Colonel Foley was able to reply as follows on the 19th :—

"Two hundred and twelve volunteers 2/4th Royal Lancaster. Await instructions to transfer."

Lord Derby's appreciation of this prompt and patriotic action is contained in the following letter, dated Derby House, Stratford Place, London, 19th April, 1916 :—

"DEAR COLONEL FOLEY,—

"I got your telegram and took it at once to the Adjutant-General and he has asked me to write to you specially to thank you and your men for your action. His expression was—'Splendid. I wish there were more like them.'

"I cannot sufficiently thank you for what I know must be rather a severe wrench parting with such men, but you have done a most patriotic action and so too have the men who have volunteered. Will you convey to them my most sincere thanks. They are going to an even older Regiment than the Loyal North Lancashire in the Royal Lancaster, and I believe it is a first-rate battalion. Please wish the men good luck from me.

"Yours sincerely,

(sd.) "DERBY."

The Battalion continued training at Oswestry until September of this year when the 3/4th and 3/5th Battalions were amalgamated in one unit under the command of Lieut.-Colonel G. D. Hale, Lieut.-Colonel Foley having been transferred to a battalion serving in France.

Under Army Order No. 259 of the 1st August, 1916, it was announced that "His Majesty has been graciously pleased to approve the formation of a new Corps of Infantry to be designated 'The Training Reserve'"; and in Army Council Instruction No. 1528 of the 6th of the same month special orders were issued on this matter, while in Appendix No. 135, accompanying this Instruction, it was announced that the 4th, 5th and 12th Reserve Battalions, The Loyal North Lancashire Regiment, were thenceforth to be designated "the 4th Reserve Battalion, The Loyal North Lancashire Regiment", with an establishment, all ranks, of 2,085 ; and under this title the newly-constructed unit continued to exist until final disbandment took place.

CHAPTER XLVIII

THE 4/5TH (TERRITORIAL) BATTALION
THE LOYAL NORTH LANCASHIRE REGIMENT

1916–1918

THE BATTLE OF YPRES, BATTLE OF PASSCHENDAELE

THE 4/5th Territorial Battalion appears to have come into being in June, 1916, and was posted to the 170th Brigade of the 57th West Lancashire Division, a brigade almost wholly composed of battalions from North Lancashire. The latter part of the training of the Division was carried out in the neighbourhood of Aldershot, and it was not until the beginning of 1917 that the 57th Division received orders to proceed to France.

At 11.30 p.m. on the 11th February the Battalion left Blackdown and marched to Farnborough where it entrained for Folkestone, and, leaving here early on the afternoon of the 12th, it reached Boulogne the same evening and spent that night and the whole of the next day in Ostrohove Camp. Leaving this camp early on the 14th for the concentration area, the whole Brigade was settled by the 19th in billets at Rouge de Bout, and the Battalion, having now been joined by the transport section which had landed at Havre, the total strength was twenty-seven officers and 908 non-commissioned officers and men.

The Battalion was almost immediately on arrival in this area sent up to the trenches, and on the 26th experienced its first casualties, one man being killed and three wounded. On the 1st March a patrol went out from the Battalion examining the enemy's wire in the left sector, and on return reported that the German trenches appeared to be in bad condition and the line but weakly held. The enemy on this part of the front does not seem to have been especially enterprising, for on the 2nd a patrol of five non-commissioned officers and men went out under 2nd Lieutenant G. Green, entered the German front line immediately opposite the Battalion right sub-sector, and patrolled the trenches for some 150 yards, meeting neither sentries nor patrols and bringing back a number of stick-bombs found lying on the parapet.

About the end of the first week in March the Division was moved to the Fleurbaix sector, Fleurbaix being described by an officer of the Division as a "ruined village, though some of the neighbouring farms were intact and flourishing. The church was a mere skeleton and whole sides of some of the streets were in a state of collapse." On taking over this area the new-comers had been told that the enemy bombarded it heavily at regular intervals, and this was found to be the case, the Germans also using gas and smoke bombs freely.

On the 13th the Battalion suffered its first officer casualties, Captain G. B. Hill being this day wounded in the trenches and also four men of his company.

Throughout the remainder of the stay here, extending to some months and during which the front held by the Division was increased to a distance of some 16,000 yards, the raiding by small parties of the Battalion went actively on whenever its companies were up in the line, prisoners were now and then brought in, and, considering the activity displayed, the casualties cannot be regarded as especially heavy. On the 7th June, however, 2nd Lieutenant H. Gittins was hit by a sniper when up in the Boutillerie sub-sector and died of his wounds.

On the 2nd August the Battalion marched from Fleurbaix to Armentières, which was found to be under heavy enemy shell fire, but the cellar billets afforded tolerably satisfactory cover. On the 18th September, the Battalion set off for a rest area about Rély and marching by Neuf Berquin, Robecq, Busnes, La Perrière, Lillers, Faucquenhem and Lières, reached Rély on the 21st, the next four weeks being spent in training hard for the attack. On the 19th October the Brigade left for Proven.

The time was now at hand when the brigades and battalions of the 57th Division were to profit by the training they had undergone at home and in Flanders, and to take part in the closing operations of this year's Battle of Ypres. The operations which had now for some time endured, had been seriously hampered by continuous bad weather : but as Sir Douglas Haig writes in his despatch of the 25th December, 1917, he was in hopes that "by limited attacks made during intervals of better weather, however, it would still be possible to progress as far as Passchendaele, and in view of other projects which I had in view it was desirable to maintain the pressure on the Flanders front for a few weeks longer."

The 23rd and 24th October were still very wet and unsettled, but the 25th was fine with a drying wind, and it was resolved to attack on the 26th on a front extending from the Ypres–Roulers railway to Poelcappelle.

The 57th Division was now in the XIV. Corps with the 35th and 50th

Divisions, and a historian * of the War quotes the description of the ground to be passed over as given by an officer of the 170th Brigade : " I have never seen such a sight as that country was in the valley of the Broombeek and Watervlietbeek just south of the Houthulst Forest. Nothing on earth but the wonderful courage of the Lancashire lads enabled them to get so far as they did. We went over with our rifles and Lewis guns bound up with flannel so as to keep the mud out, and with special cleaning apparatus in our pockets, but you can't clean a rifle when your own hands are covered an inch thick ! We killed a great number—one of the sergeants in the Loyals laid out thirteen with his bayonet ; altogether we actually killed over six hundred with the bayonet ; but, as I say, the ground was too heavy to allow us to out-manœuvre the pill-boxes, and though we took three or four the rest did us in. In one box we got thirty-eight Germans and killed them all with a Lewis gun through the porthole."

The following is the Battalion account of the events of the 26th October :—

" At 4.30 a.m. on the 26th the Battalion was drawn up on the forming-up line ready to move forward. At 5.40, Zero hour, our barrage fell and the Battalion moved forward with the leading waves from 25–50 yards behind the barrage. At 5.45 a light enemy barrage dropped just behind our original front line, and the company in reserve had to pass through this barrage, suffering a few casualties in so doing. The enemy barrage continued on this line until about 7.45 a.m. Despite the mud and water-logged shell-craters the line advanced steadily behind our own barrage, and under slight enemy machine-gun fire until about 6 a.m., and at about 6.20 the troops were finally held up on the Green Line, a barrier of machine-gun fire being opened up by the machine-guns in the pill-boxes immediately in front and on the flanks of our troops.

" A party of men succeeded in working round a pill-box in the ruins of a farm building. This strong point held thirty men, who were killed or wounded by Lewis gun and rifle fire and bombs.

" Enemy aircraft to the number of forty machines repeatedly flew over our troops at a low altitude and inflicted several casualties, and enemy artillery—apparently resultant upon aeroplane reconnaissance—opened fire on our new line, but fortunately their shells fell about 100 yards beyond our men, and this fire was kept up most of the day. From 6.30 a.m. the troops, with the exception of Lewis gunners and snipers, were compelled to lie low in water-logged shell-holes owing to the sweeping machine-gun fire and constant sniping from men posted in trees, shell-craters and pill-boxes.

" About 7.30 a.m. about one hundred men appeared from the vicinity

* Conan Doyle, *The British Campaign in France and Flanders*, Vol. IV, p. 226.

of Devoust Farm with the apparent object of delivering a counter-attack. The men were, however, totally disorganized and in no formation for attack when they advanced towards Vandyck Farm ; some wore steel helmets, some soft caps, all wore greatcoats, none wore equipment and many had no rifles. They were easily dispersed by Lewis gun and rifle fire and their casualties were estimated at about forty.

" The battalion on our left apparently experienced serious difficulties and it was not possible to secure touch with it. The battalion on the right continued to advance after our line was held up at 6.20 a.m., and apparently gained the first objective, but being unable to hold the position, withdrew to its original front line ; unfortunately in the withdrawal many casualties were inflicted by enemy machine-gun fire. Communication with Battalion headquarters was almost impossible by runners owing to enemy sniping, and many runners were shot down in attempting to get back with reports. Communication by Lucas lamps was not secured, owing either to destruction of the apparatus by shell fire, or to casualties among the signallers. Of the pigeons taken forward, two were killed and two were utilized. Telephone communication was maintained only with the battalions on the left.

" The ground over which the troops advanced was badly cut up by shell fire, and all shell-holes were full of water ; the going was very difficult, and before the day was far advanced, Lewis guns and rifles were rapidly becoming useless. Heavy rain began to fall about midday. The right and left flanks were in the air, with the exception of a small flank party on the left ; most of the Lewis guns and rifles were out of action, and the men reduced in numbers and much exhausted through exposure and through being in water-logged shell-craters for two days and two nights. For the above reason it was considered necessary to withdraw to the original line and this was effected by 9 p.m. During the withdrawal most of the wounded were brought back into our lines."

By the 29th of the month the Battalion was back again in camp at Proven, for a well-earned rest.

The casualties, in this the Battalion's first battle of the war, had been very heavy ; killed, were three officers and 63 other ranks, five officers and 165 non-commissioned officers and men were wounded, twenty-six men were missing and twenty-seven wounded and missing, a total in all of 289 casualties ! The three officers who were killed were Lieutenants J. Bryans and F. G. Carrie and 2nd Lieutenant W. Rimmer.

At Proven the Battalion remained until the 9th November when it went by rail and road to Licques, where one officer and seventy-five other ranks joined as reinforcements ; it was sent back on the 10th December to Proven and in a camp near this town Christmas Day was spent.

At the beginning of 1918—on the 2nd January—the Division left Proven by train and proceeded to Steenwerck, whence the 170th Brigade marched to Erquinghem, where the Battalion relieved the 41st Australian Infantry and became support battalion in the Chapelle sector. The Germans were here found to be more than usually aggressive, attempting several raids upon our front line ; and at midnight on the 12th they made a raid, the point of attack being what was known as Agnes Post in the first support line. The first sign of anything was the dropping by the enemy of a smoke bomb into the Post, the corporal in charge of which took the smoke for gas and ordered his men to put on their respirators. While this was being done, the enemy suddenly attacked, stunned one of the garrison of the Post and dragged him out of the trench.

The corporal was also tackled, but he was able to make use of his bayonet, whereupon the attackers hurriedly withdrew. The corporal then put up a Véry light, when the adjoining Lewis gun post opened fire, the retreating enemy releasing their captive and bolting. Two dead Germans were found on the ground and one of the men of our post was slightly wounded.

In the chapters of this History dealing with the services of the 1/5th Battalion of the Regiment, it has already been recorded that in January, 1918, the 1/5th Battalion left the Brigade and Division in which it had so long served, and was transferred to the 57th Division where it was amalgamated with the 4/5th Battalion, which latter battalion thereupon ceased to exist, from this month, as a corporate unit.

CHAPTER XLIX

THE 6TH (SERVICE) BATTALION
THE LOYAL NORTH LANCASHIRE REGIMENT

1914–1916

GALLIPOLI, EGYPT AND MESOPOTAMIA

WHEN on the 6th August, 1914, Field-Marshal Lord Kitchener became Secretary of State for War, he at once realized that the Army required to be rapidly and largely augmented, but he was at the same time faced by the fact that there was little or no Regular Army foundation upon which to build. Under these circumstances three courses presented themselves to him :—

(1) To expand the Special Reserve ; (2) to use the organization of the Territorial Force, which at least provided a framework of fourteen mounted brigades and fourteen infantry divisions ; or (3) to create entirely new formations. The objections to (1) were that it would disorganize the Special Reserve of the Regular Army, while the number of the Special Reserve units was small and they were almost wholly composed of infantry. The chief objection to (2) was the inadequacy of the framework upon which to raise the hundred divisions upon which Lord Kitchener was already counting ; duplication and reduplication of these small nuclei would eventually entail new formations ; such measures—the duplication and reduplication for dilution by the untrained manhood of the country —would render these formations immobile and, temporarily at least, disorganize them ; while home defence would be paralysed, and the possibility of using any units already existing and organized for reinforcements would be neutralized.

Lord Kitchener therefore decided upon the immediate creation of wholly new divisions, retaining the Special Reserve for its maintenance functions, and at the same time encouraging the recruiting, training and duplication of the Territorial Force, so as to relieve the Regular Army units in distant garrisons, and to supply immediate unit reinforcements to the field army ; further, as soon as the Territorial Divisions, not broken up for the two above-mentioned purposes, were sufficiently trained, to put them into the field as complete divisions.

While, therefore, the existing Territorial units were training for war, and in some cases were relieving Regular troops in overseas garrisons, the creation of the New Armies proceeded with extraordinary rapidity and smoothness. On the 8th August, 1914, Lord Kitchener asked for 100,000 men, and within a week that number was in camp; on one single day the enlistments numbered over 30,000—indeed the men came in more quickly than they could be clothed or equipped.

The 6th (Service) Battalion, The Loyal North Lancashire Regiment, appears to have come into existence on the 8th August, 1914, the first officers to be appointed to it on that day being Captain G. S. Rowley-Conwy and Lieutenant F. G. Wynne; while the first official intimation of the existence of the new unit appears in Army Order No. 324 published on the 21st August of this year, in which it is stated that His Majesty The King had approved of the addition to the Army of six divisions, these being numbered from 8 to 13 inclusive. In an appendix to this Army Order the composition of these divisions is given, and the 6th (Service) Battalion, The Loyal North Lancashire Regiment, is found to be included in the 38th Brigade of the 13th (Western) Division, a division wholly composed of battalions of the New Armies.

The 13th Division was commanded by Major-General R. G. Kekewich, C.B., and was in the First New Army under General Sir A. Hunter, G.C.B., G.C.V.O., D.S.O.; the 38th Brigade contained the 6th (Service) Bn. The King's Own (Royal Lancaster Regiment), the 6th (Service) Bn. The East Lancashire Regiment, the 6th (Service) Bn. The Prince of Wales's Volunteers (South Lancashire Regiment) and the 6th (Service) Bn. The Loyal North Lancashire Regiment; its commander was Brigadier-General A. H. Baldwin.

In the Army List for October, 1914—none was published for September—the following officers appear as on the strength of the 6th Battalion: Major (Temporary Lieut.-Colonel) R. R. Bowlby, Captains J. G. Fairlie, G. R. Trefusis and G. S. Rowley-Conwy, Lieutenants N. S. Mann, F. G. Wynne, P. A. Edwards and M. A. Cross, 2nd Lieutenants J. D. Crichton, M. Thomas, C. N. Hathorn, R. M. Wilson, J. T. Kewley, H. F. A. Turner, G. H. Grimshaw, J. C. Marson, G. B. Lockhart, L. C. Rice, N. L. Wells, H. Wright and C. Cammack, and Lieutenant and Quartermaster J. W. Atherley.

The training of the 13th Division was for the most part carried out on Salisbury Plain, but towards the end of its time in England the Battalion was at Blackdown, near Aldershot.

In the spring of 1915 it was decided to send reinforcements to General Hamilton's force in the Gallipoli Peninsula, and the 10th, 11th and 13th

Divisions were ordered to prepare for embarkation. Accordingly, on the 14th June the Battalion transport, with Lieutenants Broadwood and Mann, left Farnborough Station for Avonmouth, there to embark in the "Japanese Prince"; later in the same day the headquarters entrained at Frimley for the same port, followed a couple of hours later by the remainder of the Battalion, the total strength being thirty-one officers and 946 other ranks.

The following officers embarked with the Battalion: Lieut.-Colonel H. G. Levinge; Majors J. G. Fairlie and G. S. Rowley-Conwy; Captains B. W. O. Thompson, J. W. Mather, A. S. Walter, G. G. Wilson, H. Wright, N. S. Mann (adjutant), H. G. Mann and C. C. de Fallot; Lieutenants J. B. Pennefather, G. E. Cash, G. M. Smyth, R. M. Wilson, J. D. Crichton, H. F. A. Turner, G. B. Lockhart, N. L. Wells and W. A. Broadwood; 2nd Lieutenants C. N. Hathorn, J. T. Kewley, G. H. Grimshaw, L. C. Rice, G. P. Guilleband, T. D. Penrice, H. W. Mann and C. W. Creasey; Lieutenant and Quartermaster J. W. Atherley and Captain Binks, R.A.M.C.

On arrival at Avonmouth the Battalion went on board the "Braemar Castle," but did not sail until 11 a.m. on the 17th and then, steaming on by Malta, Alexandria and Mudros, the Battalion was landed at Cape Helles on the night of the 6th July and went into bivouac at Seghir Dere in Gully Ravine. The 13th Division was now under Major-General F. C. Shaw.

The force originally sent to the Dardanelles under General Sir Ian Hamilton had landed at Cape Helles on the 25th April, but had not been able to penetrate inland, remaining since that date in possession of little more than the coast-line and suffering heavy casualties from the fire of the Turks. The troops which had originally landed had now been reinforced, and counting the fresh arrivals and those now on their way out to join, Sir Ian Hamilton should actually have had available for any fresh operations a total force of thirteen divisions and five brigades; all these units were, however, greatly under strength and it is doubtful if the force exceeded 110,000 men. With the help of the new-comers General Hamilton proposed to reinforce the Australians and New Zealanders at Anzac, to effect a landing at Suvla Bay, and from there to attempt the capture of the main peak of Sari Bair and so grip the narrows of the Peninsula.

Almost immediately on arrival the Battalion was sent forward into the front line, relieving, for the most part, troops of the 29th Division, which had suffered much in the landing operations; but on the last day of July the 13th Division was sent temporarily to Mudros, where four days were spent. While up in the line during July, however, the Battalion had already suffered its first casualties of the war—Captain C. C. de Fallot and six other ranks being killed or dying of wounds, while Captain H.

Wright, Lieutenants G. M. Smyth, J. D. Crichton and twenty-four non-commissioned officers and men were wounded, and one man was missing.

In General Hamilton's despatch of the 11th December, 1915, in which he describes the fighting which had taken place on the Gallipoli Peninsula in June and July, he states that after the action of the 31st July had been fought a large proportion of his reinforcements had arrived, and that he had relieved the war-worn 29th Division at Helles by the 13th under Major-General Shaw. " The experiences here gained," he continues, " in looking after themselves, in forgetting the thousand and one details of peace-soldiering and in grasping the two or three elementary rules of conduct in war-soldiering, were, it turned out, to be of priceless advantage to the 13th Division throughout the heavy fighting of the following month."

The Battalion returned from Mudros to Anzac on the 4th August and occupied bivouacs in Victoria Gully, where on the 6th, as the result of enemy shelling, two men were killed and 2nd Lieutenant L. C. Rice and thirty-one other ranks were wounded.

On this date the army under General Hamilton's command was distributed as under :—

At Anzac : the 13th Division, the Australian and New Zealand Corps, an Indian Brigade and a Brigade of the 10th Division.

At Helles : the 29th, 42nd, 52nd and Royal Naval Division and two French Divisions.

At Mitylene : the 31st Brigade and part of the 30th of the 10th Division.

At Lemnos : the remaining battalions of the 30th Brigade.

At Imbros : the 11th Division.

The following was the general plan of attack in the offensive now proposed to be launched : (1) A feint was to be made at the head of the Gulf of Saros, as though it was the intention to take the Bulair Lines in flank and rear. (2) A strong offensive was to be made in the Helles area against Achi Baba with the hope of attracting the Turkish reserves to Krithia. (3) The Anzac Corps was to endeavour to gain the heights of Koja Chemen Tepe and the seaward ridges. (4) A simultaneous and new landing was to be effected in Suvla Bay.

If then the Anafarta Hills could be seized, and the right of the Suvla Bay force be linked up with the left of the Australians, the British would hold the central crest of the uplands running through the western end of the Peninsula, cutting the Turkish communications and leading to the capture of the Achi Baba and the Pasha Dagh tableland.

In General Hamilton's despatch of the 11th December, 1915, he states that the troops at the disposal of General Birdwood in the Anzac area amounted, at the opening of the above operations, to 37,000 men and seventy-two guns.   These were to be divided into two portions, one remaining to hold the existing Anzac position and make frontal assaults therefrom ; while the other was to assault the Chunuk Bair ridge.   This portion consisted of the infantry of the New Zealand and Australian Divisions, the 13th Division (less five battalions), the 29th Indian Infantry Brigade and the Indian Mountain Artillery Brigade.   The 29th Brigade of the 10th Division and the 38th Brigade of the 13th Division were held in reserve.

When on the night of the 6th August the advance from Anzac commenced, two battalions only of the 13th Divisions were employed, the remainder being kept in hand as a reserve.

On the morning of the 7th August the 6th Battalion, The Loyal North Lancashire Regiment, was marched to the foot of the Chailuk Dera, and on the night of the following day it was detached from its brigade and was sent forward to a point on the Chailuk Dera, known as the Apex, as a reinforcement to Brigadier-General Johnston's New Zealand Brigade.

On the 9th three columns were sent forward to complete the conquest of Chunuk Bair, where the fighting had already been very severe, and in one of these columns were included the remaining battalions of the 38th Brigade.   These trenches were sited about 150 yards short of the crest of the hill, then allowing the Turks to mass for attack not only at close quarters but in dead ground.   " A," " B " and " C " Companies of the Battalion were in the firing-line with " D " Company in support.

The summit of the ridge was held with desperate valour throughout a day of terrible heat and under repeated attacks by the Turks, covered by heavy shelling, and the attack ended in failure, by the evening of the 9th only small parties of exhausted troops clinging to the summit of Chunuk Bair.

During the night the worn-out troops on the ridge were relieved and were replaced in the so-called trenches by the 6th Loyal North Lancashire and the 5th Wiltshire Regiments, while the 10th Hampshire were in support. The first-named battalion arrived on the ground first and its commanding officer, Lieut.-Colonel Levinge, hastily tried to improve the trenches.   The Turks, realizing full well that if the summit of Chunuk Bair were held, the Narrows would be endangered, shelled the ridge vigorously at dawn on the 10th and then hurled against the position a whole division and three extra battalions.   The Wiltshire Regiment was caught in an exposed trench, was literally almost annihilated, while the 6th Loyal North Lancashire was simply overwhelmed by sheer weight of numbers.   The Battalion made a gallant resistance, doing all men could do, Captain Mather's company doing especially well and charging three times with the bayonet.

The official despatch states : " The two battalions of the New Army chosen to hold Chunuk Bair were the 6th Loyal North Lancashire Regiment and the 5th Wiltshire Regiment. The first of these arrived in good time and occupied the trenches. Even in the darkness their commanding officer, Lieut.-Colonel H. G. Levinge, recognized how dangerously these trenches were sited, and he began at once to dig observation posts on the actual crest and to strengthen the defences where he could ; but he had not time given him to do much. The second battalion, the Wiltshires, were delayed by the intricate country ; they did not reach the edge of the entrenchment until 4 a.m., and were then told to lie down in what was believed, erroneously, to be a covered position. At daybreak on Tuesday, 10th August, the Turks delivered a grand attack from the Chunuk Bair Hill-Q against these two battalions, already weakened in numbers, though not in spirit, by previous fighting. First our men were shelled by every enemy gun, and then, at 5.30 a.m., were assaulted by a huge column, consisting of no less than a full division, plus a regiment of three battalions. The North Lancashire men were simply overwhelmed in their shallow trenches by sheer weight of numbers, whilst the Wiltshire, who were caught in the open, were literally almost annihilated. The ponderous mass of the enemy swept over the crest, turned the right flank of our line below, swarmed round the Hampshires and General Baldwin's column, which had to give ground and were only extricated with great difficulty and very heavy losses. . . . Towards this supreme struggle the absolute last two battalions from our general reserve were now hurried, but by 10 a.m., the effort of the enemy was spent. Soon their shattered remnants began to trickle back, leaving a track of corpses behind them, and by nightfall, except prisoners or wounded, no live Turk was left upon our side of the slope.''

In General Hamilton's despatch, he wrote : '' Generals fought in the ranks and men dropped their scientific weapons and caught one another by the throat. So desperate a fight cannot be described. The Turks came on again and again, fighting magnificently, calling upon the name of God. Our men stood to it and maintained, by many a deed of daring, the old traditions of their race. There was no flinching. They died in the ranks where they stood.''

Here Brigadier-General Baldwin, the commander of the 38th Brigade, was killed, as was also of the Battalion, Lieut.-Colonel H. G. Levinge. The casualties in the Battalion were very heavy, ten other officers and eight men being killed, while thirty other ranks were wounded and 445 were reported missing, the majority of these, of course, '' presumed killed.'' The officers who died were Lieut.-Colonel H. G. Levinge, Major G. S. Rowley-Conwy, Captains J. W. Mather, H. G. Mann, and B. W. B. Osborne,

Lieutenants G. P. Guilleband, G. B. Lockhart, N. L. Wells and R. M. Wilson, 2nd Lieutenants C. N. Hathorn and H. W. Mann.

After five hours' fighting, the Turkish attack was spent ; but the enemy held the top of Chunuk Bair, and our great attack had been admittedly a failure.

The Battalion withdrew and was temporarily attached to the 40th Brigade, rejoining the 38th on the 18th in Aghyl Dere. Here for several days all were engaged on working parties, certain reinforcements arrived, with Lieutenants Hebblewhite and Horsfall, and on the 28th the Battalion was formed into a composite battalion with the 6th Battalion, The South Lancashire Regiment, under the command of Major J. G. Fairlie, of the Loyal North Lancashire.

On the 29th this Composite Battalion relieved a similar unit of the Dorsetshire and Manchester Regiments in the support trenches at Kazlar Bair ; but during the first week in September substantial and much-needed reinforcements reached the Battalion, these amounting to four officers and 265 other ranks.

There was now to be a readjustment of divisions and on the 31st August the 13th Division was sent to Suvla Bay, the 54th Division being transferred to Anzac in exchange. At Suvla the Battalion was in reserve trenches in No. 3 Sector ; a week later, however, it was moved to the 31st Brigade headquarters just west of Chocolate Hill, and took over trenches near Green Hill.

By this time Major-General Shaw had been invalided to England and his place as commander of the 13th Division had been taken by Major-General Maude.

During November more reinforcements arrived, both in officers and other ranks, and by the end of the month the strength of the Battalion was fifteen officers and 619 non-commissioned officers and men.

On the evening of the 26th November a terrific rainstorm came on and in a few minutes every dug-out and trench was flooded out. The Division occupying the flat ground to the right of Chocolate Hill was washed out of its trenches and there were several casualties from drowning, while the Salt Lake came right up to the foot of Chocolate Hill. " Then, on a sudden," so writes a historian, " the wind swung round to the north and fell upon the wrecked and inundated scene with icy blast. For nearly two days and nights snow descended in whirling blizzards, and two days and nights of bitter frost succeeded the snow. The surface of the pools and trenches froze thick. The sentries and outposts in the advanced trenches could not pull the trigger of their rifles for cold. Few can realize the suffering of those days."

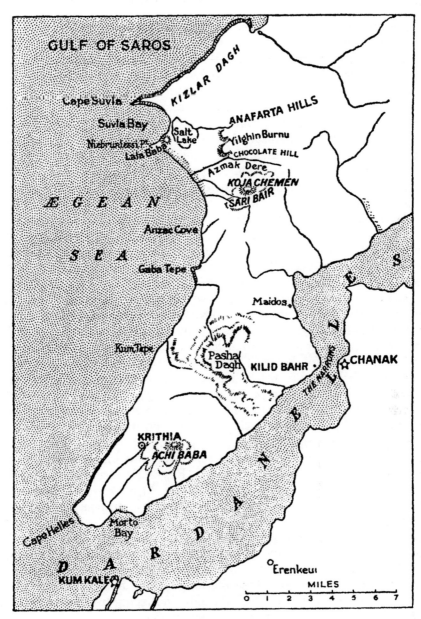

THE GALLIPOLI PENINSULA.

—

1915.

237

On the 30th October General Sir Charles Monro had arrived on the Peninsula in relief of General Sir Ian Hamilton, who had been recalled to England to discuss with the heads of the Government the proposed evacuation of Gallipoli ; the new commander had very strongly urged the discontinuance of the struggle and the complete withdrawal of the troops, and orders for the evacuation had been issued in the early part of November. There was, of course, much to be done before this could be carried out, since at Suvla and Anzac alone there were over eighty thousand men with an abundance of stores of all kinds, all of which would have to be embarked from an open beach in the presence of an active and enterprising enemy, whose trenches in some places were no more than twenty paces distant from those of the British.

At the time when the decision to evacuate the Peninsula was arrived at, there were at Suvla the 11th, 13th, 29th and 53rd Divisions, also the Mounted Division ; but the 29th and 53rd were almost at once sent round to Helles, so that when the evacuation actually commenced on the 10th December, only three divisions remained to be moved. In General Monro's despatch of the 9th March, 1916, he writes that " in the rear of the front-line trenches at Suvla the G.O.C. IX. Corps broke up his area into two sections, divided roughly by the Salt Lake. In the southern area a defensive line had been prepared from the Salt Lake to the sea, and Lala Baba had been prepared for defence ; on the left the second line ran from Karakol Dagh through Hill 10 to the Salt Lake. These lines were only to be held in case of emergency—the principle governing withdrawal being that the troops should proceed direct from the trenches to the distributing centres near the beach, and that no intermediate positions should be occupied except in case of necessity."

The Turkish shelling continued to be heavy and on the 11th December, three officers—Lieutenant E. C. Grey, Royal Fusiliers, 2nd Lieutenants E. C. Tydeman, Middlesex Regiment, and J. C. Stokoe, Manchester Regiment—all attached to the Battalion, were hit by shrapnel, the last-named being killed.

From the 10th to the 18th December the withdrawal proceeded gradually and smoothly, until by the latter date the garrisons of all posts had been reduced to the numbers decided upon as the absolute minimum ; from the 13th to the 16th three officers and one hundred other ranks of the Battalion were employed at Lala Baba in digging trenches which might require to be held during the final evacuation.

On the 15th December Captain Le Feuvre left the Peninsula for Mudros to make the necessary arrangements for a camp for the 38th Brigade, and on the 18th Captain Cragg, six other officers and 343 other ranks sailed

SUVLA BAY, GALLIPOLI.

1915.

The Imperial War Museum—Copyright.

for the same destination, the last party of the Battalion finally embarking from the South Pier, Lala Baba, on the 20th. At Lemnos the whole Battalion was reunited, re-embarked on the 21st and sailed in the S.S. " Huntsgreen " for Mudros, on arrival here marching to a camp at Portianos.

Just a month was spent here, for on the 20th January, 1916, the Battalion was put on board the " Ascanius " and proceeded to Alexandria, thence moving to a camp at Port Said, where the companies were greatly dispersed employed on the Canal defences.

Already before the evacuation of the Gallipoli Peninsula was finally completed, the situation in Mesopotamia had assumed a somewhat serious aspect. In November General Townshend had advanced upon Baghdad, and gaining a victory some thirty miles short of that city, had fallen back in face of greatly superior forces and was now besieged in Kut. An attempt had been made to effect his relief, but this had been repulsed, the two Indian divisions which earlier had reached Mesopotamia from France had suffered heavy losses, and the Home Government now decided to move a British division from Egypt to the scene of action. On the 30th January, 1916, General Maude was informed that his division had been selected for the new undertaking.

The Battalion returned to Port Said on the 8th February and at once. began to equip for the new theatre of war to which it had now been ordered to proceed. The 38th Brigade began embarkation at Port Said and Suez on the 12th and at 3.45 p.m. on the 13th went on board the hired transport " Corsican," the strength of the Battalion now being twenty-nine officers and 1,015 non-commissioned officers and men.

Leaving Port Said early on the morning of the 14th the " Corsican " entered Koweit Bay on the 27th, and, after spending a few days here at anchor, the Battalion was transhipped on the 3rd March to the hired transport " Thongwa " and proceeded up the Shatt-al-Arab. Basra was reached on the afternoon of the 5th and here all embarked in river boats and commenced the journey up the river. Passing Qurna, Ezra's Tomb, Amara and Ali Gharbi, the boats arrived on the 11th at Sheik Saad, where camp was pitched in rain, and Battalion training was at once put in hand with the special object of hardening the men for long marches.

In Callwell's *Life of Sir Stanley Maude* we are told that " two days before Maude quitted Basra "—he actually began moving up the river on the 10th March—" General Aylmer had after six weeks' pause undertaken an offensive against the Turkish position about the Dujaila Redoubt, which, had all gone well, might have achieved a success of immense importance. . . . Whether success ought not to have been achieved has been the subject of a good deal of controversy ; but what actually occurred was that an attack was not delivered at once with the troops which had arrived, that the operation proved unsuccessful when the attack was delivered, and that the relieving army suffered a somewhat serious reverse."

By the 23rd March the 39th and 40th Brigades, the artillery and practically the whole of the 13th Division was assembled at Sheikh Saad; some ten days previously General Gorringe had succeeded General Aylmer in command of the Tigris Corps, and he now had at his disposal an effective combatant strength of some 30,000 rifles and 127 guns.

On the 1st April General Gorringe issued his orders for the attack on the 5th on the Turkish position in the Hannah defile ; this position " consisted of five entrenched lines one behind the other, covering a depth of about one and a half miles, with a number of gun positions behind the third line and a wire entanglement in front of their advanced line. On the right bank their forward position, just east of the Abu Roman Mounds, ran roughly southward from the Tigris for about two miles." *

The 13th Division was detailed for the assault, and its orders were that after capturing the enemy's second line of defence, this was to be consolidated prior to attacking the third line ; the 7th Division was to support the 13th. The 3rd Division on the right bank was to contain the enemy in its front, and prevent any enemy movement on the left bank between the Falahiyeh Bend and the Suwaikieh Marsh. Two brigades were to be left to hold the camp, while the Cavalry Brigade guarded the left and rear.

"At 4.55 a.m. on the 5th April "—the strength of the 6th Battalion was now thirty-two officers and 949 other ranks—" the 13th Division moved forward to the assault, and, meeting with only slight opposition, carried the enemy's first and second lines in quick succession. A further immediate advance was only rendered impossible by the fire of the British artillery, who, not knowing that there was no enemy opposition and being unable in the dim light to distinguish the infantry signals, did not lift their fire until about 5.35 a.m. A few minutes later, the Turkish third line was occupied and found empty ; and, continuing to advance, the 13th Division had occupied the enemy's fourth and fifth lines by 7 a.m." In these attacks the Battalion moved at the outset in the support line, the 38th and 39th Brigades having been in front with the 40th in reserve.

While the two brigades which had attacked were re-forming, the 40th was sent forward to secure a line some 2,000 yards eastward of the Falahiyeh position, but went slightly further than had been intended and suffered rather heavy casualties, and the 38th was then advanced in support, the 39th remaining in reserve. Later, General Maude sent both these brigades

* *Mesopotamia Campaign*, Vol. II, p. 373.

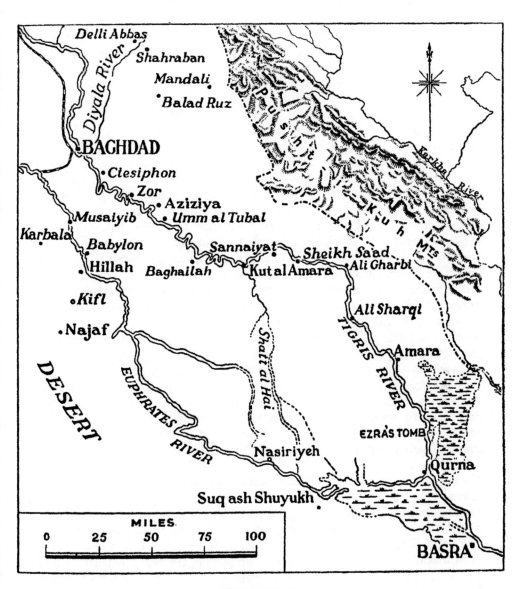

MESOPOTAMIA.

———

1916–1918.

to take up positions on the flank of the 40th, but they were checked by very heavy hostile fire and had to dig in on the line they had reached. It was now arranged to postpone any resumption of the attack on the Falahiyeh position until nightfall, the brigades in the meantime retaining their positions.

"About 7 p.m. the 38th and 39th Brigades, which, passing through the 40th, were to deliver the assault, began forming up in four lines, and at 7.15 the artillery bombardment commenced. The four lines of the 38th Brigade consisted each of one battalion on a frontage of one thousand yards, the 6th Loyal North Lancashire being in front, with the 6th King's Own, 6th East Lancashire and the 6th South Lancashire behind them in that order. . . . At 7.35 p.m. the 38th and 39th Brigades began their advance ; and in spite of strong resistance by the enemy, the 38th Brigade had, by a fine advance, captured their objective by 8.15 p.m. Not long afterwards the 39th Brigade, whose advance had been delayed by the broken ground over which their forward movement lay, also captured their portion of the position. . . . The captured trenches were consolidated and were taken over from the 13th Division by the 21st Brigade of the 7th Division. This relief took some time and was not completed till after midnight, when the 13th Division withdrew to bivouacs in rear." *

In General Sir P. Lake's despatch of the 12th August, 1916, he writes that "the 38th Infantry Brigade and the Warwicks and Worcesters of the 39th Brigade did particularly well in this assault," but the losses in the 13th Division were not far short of 2,000, while in the Battalion they totalled ninety-seven, two officers—Lieutenant Bird and 2nd Lieutenant J. Leggatt—and ten other ranks were killed or died of wounds, four officers and seventy men were wounded and eleven were missing. The four wounded officers were Major N. S. Mann (died of wounds), Captain G. M. Smyth, Lieutenant L. C. Rice and 2nd Lieutenant R. S. Perry (died of wounds).

There was renewed, but unsuccessful, fighting on the 6th, 7th and 8th during which an assault had been attempted on the Sannaiyat position, and it was now arranged that the 13th Division should be brought up and renew the attack on the morning of the 9th. In this attempt the 38th and 40th Brigades were to be in front on the right and left respectively, each brigade having all its battalions up in line, the 6th Loyal North Lancashire being on the right of the Brigade and Division ; the 39th Brigade was in support.

The following is General Maude's story of the action as recorded in his diary : "Line deployed quite successfully, no noise, and everything with

* *Mesopotamia Campaign*, Vol. II, pp. 378, 379.

utmost regularity. . . .   At 4.30 a.m. line moved forward to assault, orders being to rush the first three lines. . . .   Line advanced steadily and noiselessly till 4.28, when leading line was within 100 yards of position.   The Turks then sent up a flare from their left which made our left lose direction slightly.   About half a minute later another flare went up from the enemy's right, followed by heavy outburst of machine-gun and rifle fire.   Second line lay down while first line pushed on.   Consequently first line, which did splendidly, got into Turks' trenches in a good many places—North Lancs, King's Own, Welsh Fusiliers and Wilts especially.   But being unsupported by second line had to give way. . . .   We held on tenaciously where we were all day, the troops scratching holes in the ground and digging themselves in as best they could, and at night we withdrew into the trenches we started from in the morning."

In this action the Battalion had seven men killed, six officers and seventy-nine other ranks wounded, while four officers and 165 non-commissioned officers and men were missing.   The four missing officers were Captain R. de Chazal, Lieutenant Armstrong, R. L. Manderson and E. L. Tottenham.

Captain and Adjutant Pennefather writes of this action : " It was after the attack had failed and while the troops were trying to dig in under intense machine-gun fire, that the Rev. W. R. F. Addison, the C. of E. Chaplain attached to the Battalion, gained the Victoria Cross for his unceasing attention to the wounded throughout the whole morning under incessant fire on perfectly flat ground within 400 yards of the Turks.   I saw him myself, having been wounded early in the morning."

" In this attack," the *Official History* records, " the 13th Division sustained 1,807 casualties, to which the 6th King's Own, 6th Loyal North Lancashire, 5th Wiltshire and 8th Royal Welsh Fusiliers each contributed over 26 per cent. of their respective strengths."

The British commanders now discussed the situation and decided that another assault on the Sannaiyat position could only be successfully attempted by sapping up to it ; this meant delay and time was getting short if Kut were to be relieved before starvation forced surrender ; it was now arranged to make an attack upon the enemy's right, on the right bank of the Tigris.

On the morning of the 17th the Beit Aiessa position, which covered and controlled the river bunds, was captured by the troops of the 3rd Division, and orders were then issued for the 13th, which had been held back in reserve near the Falahiyeh bridge, to move up and relieve the 3rd Division after dusk.   Before, however, the relief had actually commenced, the 3rd Division was very violently attacked, and General Maude hurried up and flung in five of his battalions, which played an important part in restoring the situation at some points where the 3rd Division had been compelled to give way. Of the assistance then given the G.O.C. 3rd Division wrote to Brigadier-General O'Dowda, who was now in command of the 38th Brigade : " It is hardly possible that my worn-out troops could have held on without the assistance so loyally accorded by your troops."

On the 18th the 13th Division relieved the 3rd in the Beit Aiessa position, and a fresh attack was made on the Sannaiyat position by the 7th Division and other troops, the 3rd and 13th Divisions doing what they could during the days that followed to keep up pressure on the enemy on the right bank.

" Casualties especially heavy in officers and we are having bad luck in this respect," wrote General Maude in his diary on the 21st ; " some of the battalions have only five or six, including the colonel and adjutant, left." In this respect the Battalion was on the 20th and 21st particularly unfortunate, having one officer wounded, while Lieut.-Colonel J. G. Fairlie and Captain H. F. C. Horsfall were killed, and by the end of April the strength of the Battalion had dropped to ten officers and 508 other ranks.

On the 28th April Kut had surrendered after a defence lasting for five months, and after 24,000 men had been killed, wounded or taken prisoner in trying to bring it aid ; of these 24,000 casualties, 10,000 may be said to have occurred since the 13th Division was first engaged.

On the 2nd May the Commander of the Tigris Corps received the following very gratifying message from His Majesty The King-Emperor :—

" Although your brave troops have not had the satisfaction of relieving their beleaguered comrades in Kut, they have under the able leadership of yourself and subordinate commanders fought with great gallantry and determination under most trying conditions. The achievement of relief was denied you by floods and bad weather, and not by the enemy whom you have persistently pressed back. I have watched your efforts with admiration, and am satisfied that you have done all that was humanly possible and will continue to do so in future encounters with the enemy."

In the early part of May the Turkish force confronting the Tigris Corps had been considerably reduced, owing to the necessity for sending a cavalry brigade and two infantry divisions to oppose the body of Russian troops which, under General Baratoff, was advancing on Baghdad ; and this left only three Turkish divisions to oppose the force under General Gorringe. His troops were, however, greatly in need of rest, drafts and reorganization, while it was also urgently necessary that a regular and abundant supply of stores of all kinds should be assured. From April to September there was much sickness in the Tigris Corps, causing extraordinarily heavy casualties ; as early as the 28th April General Maude records in his diary

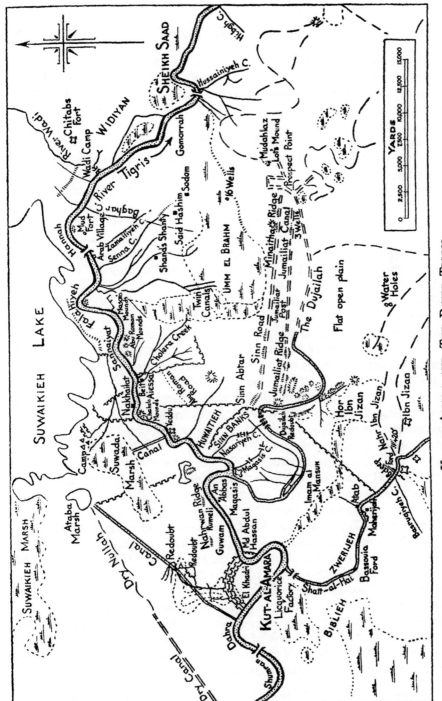

KUT-AL-AMARA AND THE RIVER TIGRIS.

1916.

245

that in his division there were from twenty to thirty cases of cholera daily and from five to eight deaths.* As a result of the above, and for the seven or eight months following the fall of Kut, the British and Turkish forces on the Tigris settled down into a condition of comparative inactivity which endured until the end of 1916.

During May and part of June the Battalion remained about Beit Aiessa, during July and the greater part of August it was at Sheikh Saad, where it became for a time part of the Sheikh Saad Mobile Column. The heat was now very great, the temperature being on some days as high as 124 degrees F. in the shade.

With the view of easing the supply situation and of allowing of the building up of a sufficient reserve of supplies at Sheikh Saad, the 13th Division was now ordered to withdraw to Amara. The Battalion accordingly left Sheikh Saad on the 25th August and marching by Dawwayah, Ali Gharbi, Sufait, Mukarramat, Ali-es-Sharqi, Tannaz, Dar-al-Faratisha and Mikala, arrived at Amara on the 3rd September.

During this period several changes had been made in the higher commands of the Mesopotamia Force ; on the 11th July General Maude had relieved General Gorringe in the command of the Tigris Corps, and on the 28th August he had taken the place of General Sir Percy Lake as commander of the forces in Mesopotamia ; Major-General Cayley had been promoted from the command of the 39th Brigade to that of the 13th Division, while Lieutenant-General W. R. Marshall had been selected for the command of the Corps vacated by General Maude.

Many small reinforcements had reached the Battalion, both in officers and men, but these scarcely made up for the casualties caused by sickness, the strength at the end of October being no more than ten officers and 689 non-commissioned officers and men.

"At the beginning of December the enemy still occupied the same positions on the Tigris front which he had occupied during the summer. On the left bank of the Tigris he held the Sannaiyat position, flanked on one side by the Suwaikieh Marsh and on the other by the river. In this position he had withstood our attacks on three occasions during the previous April. Since then he had strengthened and elaborated this trench system, and a series of successive positions extended back as far as Kut, fifteen miles in the rear. The river-bank from Sannaiyat to Kut was also entrenched. On the right bank of the Tigris the enemy held the line to which he had withdrawn in May when he evacuated the Es Sinn position. This line extended from a point on the Tigris three miles N.E. of Kut in

* According to the *Official History* of the Campaign, there were 800 cases of cholera in the Tigris Corps during April and May.

a S.W. direction across the Khadiari Bend to the River Hai, two miles below its exit from the Tigris, and thence across the Hai to the N.W. . . . The enemy occupied the line of the Hai for several miles below the bridge-head position with posts and Arab auxiliaries. On the left bank of the Tigris our trenches were within 120 yards of the Turkish front line at Sannaiyat. On the right bank our troops were established some eleven miles from those of the Turks opposite the Khadiari Bend, and some five miles from his position on the Hai." *

The operations now to be undertaken were in order as follows :—

1. To secure possession of the Hai.
2. To clear the Turkish trench systems on the right bank of the Tigris.
3. To sap the enemy's strength by constant attacks.
4. To compel him to give up the Sannaiyat position.
5. To cross the Tigris and cut his communications.

The army had by this been reorganized, the Tigris Corps having been divided into two Army Corps, the I. Indian Army Corps (3rd and 7th Divisions) under General Cobbe, and the III. Indian Army Corps (13th and 14th Divisions) under General Marshall. "As regards the general distribution, the I. Corps was to be on the right on both sides of the river, with the III. Corps on its left, the latter taking over some of the ground previously held by troops of the I. Corps as soon as the 13th Division came up to the front from Amara." †

The III. Corps was concentrated before Es Sinn on the night of the 13th December, crossed the Hai at six the following morning, and, moving north, drove in the enemy's advanced posts. By the 18th December General Marshall had extended his grip on the Turkish defences and had cut in opposite Kut between the outer Turkish defences east of the Hai and those to the west of it. In the meantime General Cobbe had been engaged in heavily bombing the Sannaiyat position, in bridging the waterway and in making new roads.

* General Maude's despatch of the 10th April, 1917.
† Callwell, *Life of Sir Stanley Maude*, p. 250.

CHAPTER L

THE 6TH (SERVICE) BATTALION
THE LOYAL NORTH LANCASHIRE REGIMENT

1916–1919

MESOPOTAMIA

WHEN on the 14th December, 1916, the British offensive commenced, the 13th Division was concentrated at Imam-al-Mansur, whither it had marched or travelled by river from Amara.

In General Maude's despatch on the operations now to begin, he gives his plan as follows: "first, to secure possession of the Hai; secondly, to clear the Turkish trench systems still remaining on the right bank of the Tigris; thirdly, to sap the enemy's strength by constant attacks and give him no rest; fourthly, to compel him to give up the Sannaiyat position, or in default of that to extend his attenuated force more and more to counter our strokes against his communications; and lastly, to cross the Tigris at the weakest part of his line as far west as possible, and to sever his communications."

The I. Corps on the left bank was to open a heavy bombardment of the Sannaiyat position with the object of making the Turks believe that the attack was to be delivered upon this part of their defences, while the III. Corps—the 13th and 14th Divisions, with the Cavalry Division attached—was to secure and entrench a position on the Hai.

The advance commenced about 3 a.m. on the 14th and Basrugiya was reached by the cavalry at 6 a.m. and Atab by the 13th Division about 5.45. The Turks were surprised and the force, pivoting on its right, moved up the eastern bank of the Hai, driving the enemy's advanced troops back on to the Hai bridge-head position which was strongly held. During the early part of the 15th the 13th Division remained halted and consolidated the line gained, the right of the 6th Battalion, Loyal North Lancashire, resting about 250 yards to the south-west of the Ruins. About 4 p.m. the advance was resumed and the 38th and 39th Brigades pushed on to within 600 yards of the Turkish position on the Hai bridge-head and there dug in.

During this day the Battalion losses were Major E. W. Maples, the commanding officer, and five other ranks killed, Lieutenant R. B. Rathbone, 2nd Lieutenants A. L. Goff and R. L. A. Underwood and forty-eight men wounded. By this time six officers—Lieutenants J. G. Burt, O. B. White and P. Wade, 2nd Lieutenants K. Kinna, J. H. M. Meredith and E. T. Covington—had joined for duty.

From the 16th to the 19th there was little or no change in the position of the Battalion, which was occupied in consolidating and digging new trenches ; but on the 22nd more line was taken over and held by twelve posts each containing a garrison of twenty men and each 200 yards apart. Casualties continued and before the year closed seven men had been killed and nine—including three officers—had been wounded ; the officers were 2nd Lieutenants J. H. W. Collins, F. H. Gibson and W. Hopkins. On the last day of December Lieutenant H. C. Beaumont, 2nd Lieutenants W. H. Kingsberry and R. C. Henderson—all of other battalions of the Regiment—joined with a draft sixty-five strong.

The reason for the comparative inaction of the 13th Division at this time may perhaps be found in the fact that on the 26th December General Maude was informed of the possibility of the Division being withdrawn from Mesopotamia ; the question remained for some weeks in abeyance, and it was not until well into March, 1917, that General Maude learnt that the 13th Division was to remain under his command.

From the 20th January to the 5th February the III. Corps under General Marshall was engaged in operations for the reduction of the Hai Salient, the extensive trench system which the Turks held astride the Hai River near its junction with the Tigris, and ground was slowly gained until, on the 24th January, our trenches were within 400 yards of the enemy's front line. At 2 a.m. on the 28th " C " and " D " Companies of the Battalion attacked the Turkish front line and gained their objective without serious opposition. The line held was, however, found to be of but small value since the field of fire therefrom was very limited. The line was consolidated and further small advances made until the 2nd February, when the Battalion withdrew with its Brigade into corps reserve.

On the 3rd the Brigade crossed the river by the Bassouia Bridge, remaining in divisional reserve until 6.15 p.m. when it moved to a position of reserve to the 14th Division which was then operating against the enemy positions on the right bank of the Hai. There was no further movement until the evening of the 4th when the Brigade occupied the trench system on the right bank of the Shatt-al-Hai, there relieving the 35th Brigade of the 14th Division ; two battalions were here in the front line and two—one of these being the 6th Loyal North Lancashire—in reserve. There was no further movement for some days, though trench fighting continued, and 2nd Lieutenant Strong was wounded on the 9th.

The operations which now commenced are described in General Maude's despatch as those of the Dahra Bend, wherein the Turks had been enclosed so that they were now fighting with their backs to the Tigris. Here the centre of the enemy position was the main objective, and it was decided that the 40th Brigade, with the 6th Battalion, The Loyal North Lancashire, attached—was to carry out the assault, while the 14th Division on the right and the 39th Brigade on the left were to give support with rifle and machine-gun fire directed against the left bank of the Tigris, from which the enemy might enfilade our advance. The Battalion was on the left of this attack, and of it General Maude writes in his despatch of the 10th April, 1917, that "early on the 15th the Loyal North Lancashires captured a strong point opposite our left, which enfiladed the approaches to the enemy's right and centre, the retiring Turks losing heavily from our machine-gun fire."

The Battalion War Diary contains the following more personal account :—

"15th February. 'D' Company under Captain C. B. O'Connor attacked and secured the nullah in front of the Ruins, few casualties, but during the occupation of the trench, which was very shallow, casualties became heavier. Two platoons went out later under 2nd Lieuts. Hampson and Wade and were largely instrumental in capturing two officers and ninety men. Casualties, 2nd Lieut. N. Hampson and thirty-seven killed, Lieut. F. C. Burt, 2nd Lieut. G. O. Preston and forty-five men wounded.

"16th. By night the whole of the Dahra Bend was cleared of Turks."

The despatch above quoted from continues as follows : " Thus terminated a phase of severe fighting, brilliantly carried out. To eject the enemy from his horse-shoe bend, bristling with trenches and commanded from across the river on three sides by hostile batteries and machine-guns, called for offensive qualities of a high standard on the part of the troops. That such good results were achieved was due to the heroism and determination of the infantry, and to the close and ever present support of the artillery, whose accurate fire was assisted by efficient aeroplane observation."

On the 19th the Brigade was withdrawn to Bassouia, but came forward again on the 24th.

" Although the right bank was practically clear of the enemy, the Tigris still covered and afforded protection to the main Turkish force in its entrenched positions extending from Sannaiyat to Shumran and to its communications along the left bank. Further attacks would, there-

---

* *Mesopotamia Campaign*, Vol. III, p. 149.

fore, have to be carried out on the left bank, either against Sannaiyat or by crossing the Tigris above Sannaiyat ; or by a combination of both. . . . General Maude finally came to the conclusion that his best plan was to attack both the enemy flanks, i.e. at Sannaiyat and Shumran simultaneously." *

On the 16th February General Maude directed that when the present heavy rain, which had now set in, should cease, the III. Corps was to continue to operate vigorously against the enemy's troops on the right bank of the Tigris in the river bend west of Shumran ; the I. Corps was to attack Sannaiyat next day. The III. Corps was at this time occupying, with two brigades, a line of picquets along the river-bank up to the Canal and thence along that canal, while the rest of the Corps was more or less concentrated in rear.

The final attack on the Sannaiyat position was made by the I. Corps on the 22nd, while by the morning of the 24th, the troops of the III. Corps were on the left bank of the Tigris in considerable strength, and, by keeping up a constant pressure on the enemy within and beyond the Shumran Bend, gradually overcame all opposition, the enemy retiring up the river in disorder.

"When darkness closed in on the 24th, what was left of the Ottoman forces was in full flight from the scene of their triumphs of a few months before, and that night the British gunboats, pushing up from Falahiyeh, moved off Kut." *

The Battalion War Diary gives the following account of the moves of the remaining days of this month :—

"25th February, 5.40 a.m. The Battalion advanced as advanced guard to the Division up the left bank of the river and came under shell fire. Advance continued under heavy shell fire over very flat country ; had to halt till dark about 400 yards from enemy position : dug in.

"26th. 6 a.m. Advance continued. Battalion in support—2nd Lieut. T. H. Ellis wounded. Enemy found to have withdrawn during night. Brigade on advanced guard to Division until Imam Mahdi was reached about 11 a.m. 27th. At 1 p.m. the Brigade moved to Baghailah, which was reached about 5.30 p.m.

"28th. No move."

This brief account makes hardly sufficient mention of the fighting in which the Battalion was engaged on the 25th of this month, and which may be epitomized as follows from the *Official History of the Mesopotamia Campaign* :—

At 6 a.m. on the 25th the advanced guard of the 13th Division—containing the 38th Brigade—started from the Shumran peninsula and

* *Sir Stanley Maude*, p. 263.

advanced up the left bank of the Tigris, the Cavalry Division moving off three-quarters of an hour later well to the north of the 13th Division. The mounted troops at the head of the advanced guard drove the enemy out of some posts in front of the Turkish left, and occupied them, and at 11 a.m. the head of the 38th Brigade reached the north-east corner of the Husaini Bend, coming under fairly heavy Turkish shell fire. Covered by the fire of our guns with the vanguard, the leading battalions of the Brigade continued their advance and drove in the enemy's advanced posts, the naval flotilla on the river also co-operating with their guns in the 38th Brigade attack. By 12.30 p.m., however, the 38th Brigade advanced line —6th King's Own, 6th East Lancashire and 6th Loyal North Lancashire, in this order from the right—had been definitely checked by heavy rifle and machine-gun fire some 700 yards from the enemy's trenches and was beginning to dig itself in. The fourth battalion of the Brigade, the 6th South Lancashire, was sent to the right to try and turn the enemy's left, and held on till dark in the position arrived at.

It being now evident that the 38th Brigade could make no further progress unsupported, the 39th was brought up at 2 p.m. to attack the Turkish left, captured the position and took many prisoners, holding on against more than one counter-attack. The Turks finally withdrew at 2 a.m. on the 26th.

On the 28th February the British cavalry reached Aziziya, which was found clear of the enemy, and during this day the I. Corps closed up to Shaikh Jaad, while the III. Corps stood fast.

The 13th Division began to move forward again on the 1st March, when the Battalion marched to Umm-al-Tubal, and then, going on by Zor and Ctesiphon, was at Bustan on the night of the 6th. Here the Turks had prepared a rearguard position, but had later decided not to hold it and they were found to be entrenched on the further bank of the Diyala River, the attempt to cross which was now to be made.

On the morning of the 7th the Battalion was sent forward to support some cavalry and guns which were to make a reconnaissance towards the river. At 2.30, the two batteries had taken up a position, while, of the Battalion, " A " Company was occupying a mound 500 yards in front of the guns, " D " was 400 yards to the left of " A " and the remaining two were 1,000 yards in rear in reserve ; all dug in as Turkish shells were coming over. Later " D " was sent forward to a mound in front and " C " then took its place, the whole Battalion, when darkness set in, moving off to take up a position on the river-bank, in order to prevent any enfilade fire being directed at the spot where it was intended to bridge the stream by pontoons. Bridging operations here had, however, to be for the time

abandoned owing to machine-gun fire and some of the pontoons being sunk
by the Turkish shells.   A second attack also failed, and the two battalions
of the 38th Brigade which had been engaged in these attempts now dug
in on the river-bank, and the Battalion was withdrawn to the Brigade
area early on the 7th, having suffered no casualties.

"The following dispositions had been arranged by the 38th Brigade
for crossing the Diyala during the night of the 8th–9th March.   The 6th
King's Own and 6th East Lancashire would remain along the river bank in
the vicinity of the village ; the 6th Loyal North Lancashire, two companies
8th Welsh Pioneers and the 72nd Company R.E. would carry out the
crossing on the right of the East Lancashire ; the 6th South Lancashire
would prolong the line to the right of the North Lancashire ; the Brigade
machine-gun company would support the crossing from several positions ;
and the artillery would open an intense bombardment at midnight." *

What follows is taken from the Battalion War Diary :—

"Four columns were formed, composed of one company each with the
addition of rowers and carriers from the R.E. and Pioneers, and they proceeded in this formation towards the river where each column was led
to a position of readiness, opposite the place where each crossing was to
be made.   One pontoon only was available for each column.   On arrival
at the bund on the river each column prepared positions from which they
could cover the launching of the pontoons.

"At midnight, under cover of an intense artillery barrage, pontoons
were launched ; 'A' Company's pontoon reached the opposite shore with
2nd Lieut. J. H. W. Collins and nine men, but as it was being ferried back
again it was sunk by machine-gun fire, 2nd Lieut. E. J. Covington and
Lieut. Mason, R.E., were killed, and the operations for the time being of
this column were delayed.   'B' Column's first pontoon reached the opposite
shore with Lieut. H. C. Beaumont and twelve men, but after the second
journey all the rowers were hit and the pontoon was lost.   Subsequently,
by the aid of two pontoons from up-stream, 'B' Column was able to pass
over four more boat-loads, but during the operations 2nd Lieut. J. J. W.
Lassetter was killed.

"'C' Column's pontoon was able to make six trips carrying ten men
at each trip.   'D' Column's pontoon, owing to the steepness of the bank,
was not launched.   Heavy shell, machine-gun and rifle fire by the Turks
at this juncture sunk the two remaining pontoons, and the situation now
was that four officers and one hundred men had reached the opposite bank
and were endeavouring to consolidate the further edge.   An urgent request
had already been made for more pontoons and we were told that six more

* *Mesopotamia Campaign,* Vol. III, pp. 225, 226.

were on their way; but an hour and a half went by before these were seen approaching. Star shells were then sent up by the Turks and the pontoons came under a very severe shrapnel fire, two being riddled by bullets and rendered unfit for use.

"Dawn was now breaking and further attempts to cross had to be abandoned; but during the 9th successive attempts were made by means of rifle grenades, rockets and lines procured from the Navy to throw a line to the further bank in order to replenish the supply of bombs and ammunition of the party there isolated. This party had established itself in a small depression on the bank. All attempts to help met with no success.

"From reports rendered it appears that those of 'A' Column who reached the opposite bank had hung on where they landed; 'B' Column had done the same; while the party from 'C' Column under Captain O. A. Reid, reduced by casualties from fifty to fifteen effectives, had moved down the bank, joined up with 'B,' and, sending for the remnant of 'A,' had collected in the depression where they were all consolidating. During the rest of the night, and especially at dawn, the Turks continuously attacked from the adjacent wood and tried to bomb them out of their defences. All these attacks were repulsed with heavy loss to the enemy, and during daylight our guns materially assisted the defence by shell fire.

"During the morning the C.O., Lieut.-Colonel Harrison, reconnoitred the bank higher up, to try and find suitable places where further attempts to cross the river might be made, and also to relieve Captain Reid's party; and at a Brigade conference held during the afternoon the following arrangements were made: two battalions of the 40th Brigade were to be sent up the Tigris past the mouth of the Diyala in motor lighters, landing in rear of Diyala village on the north bank, then work up the bank and attack the rear of the Turks who were facing that part of the river held by the Battalion; another battalion of the 40th Brigade was to cross at a bend in the river above the 6th South Lancashire who were lining the bank on the flank of the 6th North Lancashire; the 6th East Lancashire was to cross at another point.

"This movement was timed for 4 a.m. on the 10th; but at 9 p.m. on the 9th the Turks opened an especially heavy bombardment, just at the very moment when Private C. Miller of 'D' Company, who had volunteered to try and open communication with Captain Reid's party, had entered the river for this purpose with a line tied round his shoulders. Having got half-way across, Private Miller was unable to get further owing to the strength of the current and got back in an exhausted condition. Lieut. L. A. Soman, who was paying out the line to the swimmer, noticing that the line had become caught on a bush, ran forward to disengage it.

thereby being silhouetted against the bank by the light of the moon, was seen by a Turkish sniper and shot dead.

" At 4 a.m. on the 10th the battalions of the 40th Brigade effected a crossing, the Turks fell back, followed by the 38th Brigade, a bridge was thrown across the Diyala and the 13th Division passed over the river, encamping about Dadawiya."

All the accounts of these operations—the crossing of the Diyala— whether official or unofficial, unite in speaking in the very highest terms of the services of the 6th Bn. The Loyal North Lancashire Regiment on this occasion, and especially of the stand made by the small and isolated party under Captain O. A. Reid.

In the *Official History* we read * : " The Turkish account of their attempts to drive out this British detachment affords a fine testimony to the gallant tenacity of these men of Lancashire. The Turkish 2/44th Regiment, in a series of determined efforts, suffered very heavy casualties, including their commander and most of their other officers. The regimental commander, arriving at the front about 2 a.m., led the 3rd Battalion and the remnants of the 2nd forward in person to the attack no less than five times. This regiment, which had played a distinguished part at Ctesiphon, Dujaila and Sannaiyat, did its utmost to add to its fine record and lost many officers and hundreds of men. But as Muhammad Amin says : ' the small result of these bloody assaults was to confine to the palm grove near the crossing place an enemy force estimated at fifty to sixty men and two machine-guns.' "

In the *Life of General Maude* it is recorded † : " Some of the Loyal North Lancashire did manage to gain a footing on the further bank, and they not only gained a footing but they maintained their grip upon a small loop in the river embankment, unsupported except by fire from the other side, for nearly twenty-four hours, in spite of every effort of the enemy to dislodge them."

The III. Corps Commander, Lieut.-General Marshall wrote ‡ : " One ferry managed to get some seventy men of the Loyal North Lancashire Regiment across the river, but was then shot to pieces. The party established itself in a loop of the river bank, and there they held out for twenty-two hours, though they were being shot at from three sides. The party held its position and remained confident and cheery during the following day : they even exchanged badinage with their comrades on the opposite bank ! "

" Eyewitness " described this incident at greater length and even more

* Vol. III, p. 227.   † pp. 272, 273.
‡ *Memories of Four Fronts*, p. 225.

enthusiastically * : " Some sixty men had got over. These joined up and started bombing along the bank. They were soon heavily pressed by the Turks on both flanks, and found themselves between two woods. Here they discovered a providential natural position. A break in the river bund had been repaired by a new bund, built in the shape of a half-moon on the landward side. This formed a perfect lunette. The Lancashire men, surrounded on all sides save towards the river, held it through the night and all the next day against repeated and determined attacks. These assaults were delivered in the dark or at dawn. . . . At midnight of the 9th–10th, the Turks were on the top of the parapet, but were driven back. One more determined rush would have carried the lunette, but the little garrison, now reduced to forty, kept their heads and maintained a cool control of fire. A corporal was seen searching for loose rounds and emptying the bandoliers of the dead. In the end they were reduced almost to their last clip and last bomb ; but we found over a hundred Turkish dead outside the redoubt when they were relieved at daylight on the morning of the 10th."

The total losses in the Battalion during these operations amounted, in addition to the officers already mentioned, to thirty-one killed, two died of wounds, sixty-five wounded and two men missing.

By 10 a.m. on the 10th March the whole of the 38th Brigade had crossed the river to the right bank, and was holding a bridge-head to the depth of one mile from the stream, with patrols pushed out well beyond. By the 12th the Division was encamped at Es Salekh, near Baghdad, and here it remained until the 26th of the month.

The following wire was received from General Maude : " Please convey my best congratulations to my old Division and especially to the die-hards of the Loyal North Lancs. who stuck to their post so grimly and manfully."

The London Gazette of the 8th June, 1917, announced the award of the Victoria Cross to Captain O. A. Reid, 4th Bn. The King's Liverpool Regiment, attached 6th Bn. The Loyal North Lancashire Regiment, " for conspicuous bravery in the face of desperate circumstances " during the operations on the Diyala River.

On the 11th March Baghdad had been occupied by our troops.

On the 26th March the 13th Division was moved forward ; on the 28th the 39th and 40th Brigades attacked the enemy, who retired to the line of the Adhaim River. The 38th Brigade was not engaged in this action, during which it was in support to the 39th, and on the 30th it was withdrawn and occupied an outpost line from Abu Tamar to the railway bridge in front of Jadida.

* *The Long Road to Baghdad*, Vol. II, pp. 90, 91.

THE KOTAH BRIDGE AND RIVER TIGRIS, BAGHDAD.

1917.

The Imperial War Museum—Copyright.

On the evening of the 8th April the Battalion moved forward again and took over an outpost line along the Shatt-al-Adhaim front near the junction with the Tigris to about two and a half miles up-stream, and here it remained for several days. " The position on the 10th April on the left bank of the Tigris was that the bulk of the XVIII. Turkish Corps was holding the line of the Shatt-al-Adhaim near the junction of that stream with the main river, while the XIII. Turkish Corps was for the most part disposed in the stretch of the Jabal Hamrin which extends between the Diyala and the Shatt-al-Adhaim, threatening any Anglo-Indian forces in flank that might advance with the idea of forcing a passage across the latter stream and of defeating the XVIII. Turkish Corps. It had been intended that General Marshall should attack the line of the Shatt-al-Adhaim on the night of the 10th–11th with his III. Corps ; but the enemy XIII. Corps suddenly came down on the 10th from the Jabal Hamrin on Marshall's flank. This Turkish move gave rise to some lively encounters which lasted over two days, but which by the 14th had terminated in a notable triumph for the III. Corps, the enemy drawing off northwards through the defiles of the Jabal Hamrin." *

In those " lively encounters " the Battalion played no part, continuing to hold the outpost line ; but on the night of the 17th the companies moved into a position of readiness on the river-bank with a view to forcing the passage at dawn on the 18th at the mouth of the Nahrwan Canal. The South and East Lancashire Battalions—the left of the former on the Tigris —were to ferry across at 2.20 a.m. on the 18th and assault the cliff edge some 1,000 yards from the river-bank ; while in order to take off the attention of the Turks from this crossing, and, further, to force him to dangerously extend his defensive line, the Battalion was to cross the stream by wading and attacking about two miles higher up and near where the road crosses by a bridge which had been destroyed. This attack was so timed as to take place simultaneously with that by the South and East Lancashire.

" B " and " D " Companies waded through the river under command of Major Thorne, and formed up on the further bank, then moving forward again at the schedule time. Their advance was undiscovered until they arrived within a hundred yards of the edge of the cliff, when a sharp, but wild and inaccurate fire was opened upon them from machine-guns and rifles. By a quick rush the leading lines stormed the cliff and established a footing on the top, extending their position by bombing down the side nullahs. At this moment a stray shot unhappily killed Major Thorne as he was directing the operations.

Dawn was now breaking, and the fire from the covering parties and

* *Sir Stanley Maude*, p. 283.

from two British batteries kept down the enemy's fire and enabled the assaulting columns to establish themselves and to consolidate the position, the Turks gradually falling back to positions in rear, while the Battalion extended its line northward to the upper ford and also to the south-west-ward. By 2 p.m. the other two battalions, whose advance had been checked, had come into line on the left, our guns opened a heavy barrage and the infantry advanced. The Turks fled, being pursued along the Nahrwan Canal by the 35th Brigade and by a Cavalry Brigade and Horse Artillery guns, which had crossed by a bridge which had been thrown across, and the result was a complete success.

During these operations the casualties in the Battalion may be said to have been light, one officer—Major Thorne—and one man killed and five men wounded.

The Battalion remained in bivouac on the left bank opposite Al Habbab until very early on the morning of the 24th, when it moved out with the 38th Brigade as part of a force which was to assist in an attack upon the enemy who was preparing a position north-west of Dahuba, and from which it was desirable to eject him before he should be reinforced. As dawn broke about 5 a.m. on the 24th the enemy was seen occupying a line of mounds in front of the 38th Brigade, when the 6th King's Own and 6th Loyal North Lancashire at once moved forward, supported by three batteries. Our infantry soon came under sharp rifle and machine-gun fire, most of which fell on the Battalion, which was on the left and whose line was somewhat in advance of that of the King's Own. The force attacked without waiting for a supporting column which had been delayed in its advance, the King's Own and 6th Loyal North Lancashire moving forward, the last-named being still somewhat in front. " Under a heavy, though inaccurate, rifle and machine-gun fire, the King's Own and South Lancashire gradually got level with the North Lancashire, when all three battalions advanced together, gaining ground by short rushes. It soon became evident that the Turks were retiring, and by 9.30 a.m. the Lancashire Brigade had rushed the enemy's line, capturing about seventy prisoners."

The column, of which the 38th Brigade and Battalion formed part, now occupied a defensive line running east and west and resting on the Adhaim, the Battalion being on the right flank.

In General Maude's last despatch, that dated the 15th October, 1917, he writes :—

" As a result of the fighting during the month of April the enemy's XIII. and XVIII. Corps had been driven back on divergent lines, the former into the Jabal Hamrin and the latter to Tekrit. . . . The objectives which we had set out to reach had been secured, and the spirit of the enemy's troops was broken. . . . The increasing heat now rendered it necessary that the troops should be redistributed for the hot weather, and that every provision possible under existing conditions should be made with a view of guarding against the trying period which was rapidly approaching."

The Battalion spent the months May to September occupying different camps in the neighbourhood of Sindiya, enduring very great heat and losing some men from heatstroke ; but reinforcements joined, both in men and officers, and by the end of September, when the resumption of active operations was to be expected, the strength of the Battalion stood at nineteen officers and 796 other ranks. The 38th Brigade had no part in the one action which occurred during the summer—that of Ramadi— and all that any of the Battalion saw of the enemy was some Arab horsemen in the far distance.

At the beginning of October, " on the extreme British right, British detachments occupied Mandali and Balad Ruz, while the 14th Division held a line which extended from the neighbourhood of Shahraban to and along the left bank of the Diyala as far south as Windiya, westward of which the 13th Division held a line to a point on the Tigris just north of Sindiya. Opposite the British III. Corps was the Turkish XIII. Corps holding a very extended line in no great strength, with its advanced troops along the western slopes of the Jabal Hamrin." For some time past General Maude had been anxious to occupy the Jabal Hamrin, both to make his right flank more secure and to deny to the Turks this screen for movements against his flank and into Persia. Many reasons had hitherto prevented its occupation, but with the coming of the cooler weather, the extension of the railways and the improvement in the military situation, General Maude felt in a position to carry out his project.

It was arranged that the III. Corps was to occupy the Jabal Hamrin on the Diyala left bank, and General Marshall's plan was to drive the enemy out of his advanced position about Delli Abbas, holding him in front while a main attack developed against the Turkish left. To this end the force to be employed was divided into three groups, and in the left group were included the 38th and 40th Brigade of the 13th Division.

The forward concentration commenced on the 16th, and on the 18th the left group, meeting with little opposition, occupied an east and west line to the north of Delli Abbas, connecting on the right with the centre group ; by 11 a.m. on the 19th, to the west of the Diyala, the 38th Brigade had occupied Mansuriya village and a line to the north-west of it. The Brigade had come under enemy shell fire and the Turks were still occupying trenches in the foothills, to attack which flat and exposed ground would have to be advanced over. Consequently, the attack was for a time postponed. Early on the 20th the troops of the left group advanced on the Turkish trenches, but the enemy had retired during the night, and by midday the 38th Brigade had occupied an east and west line astride the Jabal Hamrin with the right on the Diyala, about one and a half miles northward of Mansuriya, and its left about Mujariyin. On the night of the 20th the Battalion camped just east of Mansuriya.

In the *Official History* it is stated that " General Marshall had gained his objective with the loss of only thirty-seven casualties "; but in the War Diary of the 6th Bn., The Loyal North Lancashire, it is recorded that " Total casualties were 137 wounded, one of whom died in the ambulance. No officer casualties."

On the 18th November General Maude died of cholera in Baghdad after two days' illness ; Lieut.-General Sir W. R. Marshall was appointed to succeed him in chief command in Mesopotamia, and Major-General Egerton now took command of the III. Corps.

In General Marshall's despatch of the 15th April, 1918, he states as follows :—

" Towards the end of November I determined to attack that part of the XIII. Turkish Army Corps which was holding the Diyala River above Mansuriya, the passes over the Jabal Hamrin and Kara Tepe. The Turkish forces were well placed for defence, and the task set to our troops included the forcing of the passages of the Diyala and Narin Rivers, as well as the Sakaltutan and Abu Zenabil passes through the Jabal Hamrin." The III. Corps was detailed for these operations and by dark on the 2nd December the troops were in their appointed places, the 38th Brigade being to the west of the Diyala and two and a half miles north of Mansuriya. This Brigade, having established itself during the night of the 2nd–3rd on a three-mile east and west line with its right on the Diyala about one mile south of Abu Zenabil, was to advance early on the morning of the 3rd towards Suhaniya and the Sakaltutan Pass.

The following is the Battalion account of the operations that now followed :—

" On the night of the 2nd–3rd, the Battalion moved to position of readiness, and at 5.30 a.m. on the 3rd advanced against the Turkish picquet line, with the left on Howitzer Hill and right on the Diyala River, supported by the 6th King's Own, echeloned on the left and keeping touch with the 6th East Lancashire, two miles to their left and on the right of Longride Hill. The 6th East Lancashire were in reserve at Longride Hill.

" The Battalion attack was supported by an 18-pounder battery on the left bank of the Diyala, other guns also supported, and a section of the 26th Mountain Battery advanced with the Battalion. ' A ' and ' B ' Companies were in front, ' C ' was in reserve and ' D ' protected the right. ' A ' and ' B ' met with but little opposition, and by 7 a.m. had established themselves on Howitzer Hill and to the north-east of it, the Turks withdrawing to the main ridge of the Jabal Hamrin and up the right bank of the Narin River. When the 6th East Lancashire had broken through the picquet line and were ready to move forward, the advance was continued smoothly, until by 4 p.m. the line was halted and the Battalion threw out outposts and bivouacked for the night. The casualties this day were two men wounded, one of whom died later.

" At 4.45 a.m. on the 4th the advance was continued towards the Sakaltutan Pass along the main ridge of the Jabal Hamrin, and this was reached about noon, no opposition being met with, the Turks having retired during the night towards Narin Kopri. That night the Battalion spent in brigade reserve near the Suhaniya Post. It had been a long and trying day, but the weather was fortunately cool. All battalions were now engaged in making and improving a defence line."

At the end of the year 1917 the 13th Division, west of the Diyala, held the line of the Jabal Hamrin from Abu Zenabil to the Sakaltutan Pass with a brigade group, and the remainder of the Division was between Delli Abbas and Sindiya.

The Battalion spent the months of January, February and March, 1918, tolerably quietly in camp, engaged in training and in assimilating one or two drafts which joined during that period. At the beginning of April, however, there were signs of trouble on the Persian border, where certain tribes had been affected by German propaganda, and it became necessary to take action against them in the interests of others of that nation who were friendlily inclined towards the British. The effect of our successful action was to increase the impression in favour of the British, and our line of communication into Persia was safeguarded from any really serious raiding.

In General Marshall's despatch of the 1st October, 1918, he states that " With the object of making the Persian line of communications more secure, I considered it advisable to drive the Turks out of the Qara Tepe–Kifri–Tuz Khurmatli area and to hold both Kifri and Tuz for the future. The general plan of operations decided upon was to simulate a converging attack upon Qara Tepe and Kifri, but in reality to strike first at the more distant objectives of Abu Gharaib and Tuz Khurmatli, with the intention of cutting off and dealing subsequently with any hostile forces southeast and east of these places."

The conduct of the proposed operations was entrusted to the G.O.C. III. Corps, and the force to be employed was divided into five columns, the 38th Brigade being told off to what was known as B.1. Column, the mission of which—in co-operation with Column D.—was to surprise and destroy Abu Gharaib by an advance against that place from Umr Maidan.

" By the morning of the 26th April, Egerton had deployed his forces and that night the various columns moved on their objectives. Despite torrential rain, inky darkness and flooded streams, all columns reached their destinations at daybreak on the 27th. The Turks, however, had at last taken alarm, and, too late, attempted to retreat via Tuz Khurmatli and Kirkuk to the Lesser Zab. . . . Kifri was taken with no opposition, and then Cayley " (commanding 13th Division), "with O'Dowda's and Lewin's brigades ". (38th and 40th), " attacked and captured the strongly defended Turkish position at Tuz Khurmatli, the brunt of the fighting falling on O'Dowda's brigade." *

The Battalion account of these operations is as follows :—

" 25th. The remainder of the Column arrived at Ain Lailah under Brig.-General O'Dowda, and in co-operation with other columns advanced on the 26th to Umr Maidan with a view to clearing up the Kifri area. On the night of the 26th–27th the Column marched to attack the Turks at Abu Gharaib, co-operating with a cavalry column moving up the Adhaim River.

" On the morning of the 27th the Turks were found to have evacuated the Abu Gharaib positions, and the Battalion marched in the evening to Sarah and went into bivouac. On the 28th the march was continued to within four miles north of Tuz Khurmatli, and, leaving its bivouac again at 1 a.m. on the 29th, the Battalion marched by way of Khasradala ford to a position of readiness, from which at 4.45 a.m., with the 6th King's Own Royal Lancaster on the right, it attacked the Turkish position—' A ' Company on the right, ' B ' on the left, ' C ' echeloned to the left rear and ' D ' Company in reserve. During the initial stage of the action the machine-guns were kept on the left flank in support. The Cavalry Brigade was holding picquets covering the roads leading from Tuz Khurmatli, north and north-west, and throughout was working on the left of the Battalion, hemming in the enemy against the foothills north of Tuz.

" The attack progressed rapidly, and near Buyuk village two field and two machine-guns were captured by ' A ' Company. On the left ' B ' Company, assisted by ' D,' and supported by two Maxims and the 55th Field Battery, took three guns, the Turkish battery commander, his men and teams. A little further on another field-gun was found abandoned, while the fire from our Lewis guns compelled the enemy to abandon another.

* Marshall, *Memories of Four Fronts*, pp. 301, 302.

The 6th King's Own took four more guns and ten machine-guns, and the Turks now became completely demoralized, surrendering on all sides, while others were discovered hiding in Tuz Khurmatli, and the Battalion was now able to get some rest, while the cavalry completed the victory, pursuing as far as the left bank of the Tauq Chai."

The dash and rapidity of the attack were irresistible and the Battalion received the hearty congratulations of the Brigade, Division and Corps Commanders.

In the *Official History of the Mesopotamia Campaign*, the losses in the 6th Loyal North Lancashire are given as twenty; in the War Diary of the Battalion, however, they are stated to be four killed, or died of wounds, and twelve wounded. Of the Turks we buried over 200 of their dead, and captured 1,300 prisoners, twelve field-guns, twenty machine-guns and large quantities of ammunition ; among the Battalion captures there is mention of " one pointer dog, Judy " !

During the next two or three days the Brigade remained on the bank of the Aq Su River, to the south of Tuz Khurmatli, engaged in clearing the field of the late action.

It had not been General Marshall's intention to advance any further to the north beyond Tuz Khurmatli ; but on the 29th April the War Office telegraphed directing him to strike at Kirkuk and Sulaimaniya, in order to divert the troops which it was believed that the Turks proposed sending to Persian Azerbaiyan to support a general rising of the Persians. Kirkuk, the new objective, being, as General Marshall points out in his book, " 130 miles distant from railhead, due preparation was required to deal with the supply situation," since it seemed certain that the III. Corps would have, while so employed, to be placed on reduced rations, when, too, the hot weather was approaching.

General Egerton's force was organized in two commands, a striking force of two columns under General Cayley and a force to hold the line of communications under Brigadier-General Lewin. General Cayley's command was subdivided into two columns and the 38th Brigade was detailed to form part of Column B. The advance of General Cayley's force from Tuz Khurmatli towards Kirkuk was to start on the 4th May.

The Battalion left its camp with the 38th Brigade on the 4th May, crossing the Tauq Chai next day by a masonry bridge of fourteen arches which the Turks had failed to destroy ; and on the 7th Kirkuk was occupied, the Turks having withdrawn during the night, leaving behind over five hundred sick and wounded. On the 9th the Battalion moved out to Daraman in support of the cavalry which was to attack the enemy's position at Altun Kopri, but the Turks fell back and our troops then withdrew to Daraman and thence back to Kirkuk.   The almost insuperable difficulties attending upon the supply and maintenance of troops here during the summer months was now fully realized, and by the end of May all the units of the III. Corps were back again on the line of Tuz Khurmatli–Kifri.

The 13th Division took no part, as a complete unit, in any of the remaining operations of this the last year of the Mesopotamia Campaign, but in July the 39th Brigade was detached for service in Persia and took part in the defence of Baku.

During June, July and August the Battalion was in camp at Khalis ; in October it moved to Abu Saida on the right bank of the Diyala River, and here on the 1st November news was received that on the previous day an armistice had been concluded with Turkey.

On the 28th November Captain Turner, Lieutenants Stock, Wade and Hughes and 183 other ranks left the Battalion en route for Salonika, and now demobilization appears to have set in, and farewell messages and orders of the day were issued by the Corps, Divisional and Brigade Commanders, and by Lieut.-Colonel Harrison, commanding the Battalion ; and in this last Colonel Harrison wrote as follows on the 22nd January, 1919 : " Now that the dispersal of the Battalion has commenced in earnest, I wish all ranks to know before leaving how proud I am of having been for the last two years your commanding officer ; how I feel that I have had every officer, warrant officer, non-commissioned officer and man at my back, ready and eager to undertake any duty that the Battalion was called upon to perform.   No man could have had a more loyal body of men serving under him, or upon whom he could rely with such absolute confidence, however difficult, or dangerous, the task might be.   You have indeed not only maintained, but added to, the glorious traditions of the Loyal North Lancashire Regiment and proved to the hilt the unconquerable spirit of the men of Lancashire. . . .

" I wish each one of you a safe return to those who are now so eagerly awaiting you in the Old Country, and may the joy of your home-coming be an augury of happy and prosperous days to come."

The following are the names of the officers present with the Battalion on the 31st January, 1919 : Lieut.-Colonel J. S. N. Harrison, D.S.O. ; Captains J. Thomas, adjutant, P. B. White, F. S. Hebblewhite, M.C., J. M. O'Donohue and H. O. K. Pope ; Lieutenants T. Duncan and R. Hamilton-Smith, Lieutenant T. Black, in medical charge, the Rev. T. H. W. Barker and Lieutenant W. J. Adams, M.C., Devonshire Regiment, attached.

In February the Battalion was sent by train to Kut-al-Amara, marching from there to a camp at Tabar, seven miles to the south ; and while here it was announced that the 6th Loyal North Lancashire had been detailed to form part of the Army of Occupation and was to be posted to the 53rd Infantry Brigade, while temporarily attached to the 34th. Men were now beginning to leave fast as demobilization progressed, and orders were issued that the Royal Welsh Fusiliers, South Wales Borderers and South Lancashire Regiments were each to provide a company to complete the Battalion to war establishment. In March the Battalion joined the 34th Brigade under Brigadier-General A. Wauchope, C.M.G., D.S.O., and remained during the next three months in camp.

On the 3rd June orders were received to join the advanced troops of the 18th Division at Kirkuk ; and starting off on the following day by river and road, Kirkuk was reached on the 15th, and here the companies were accommodated in the Turkish barracks ; later three companies were detached to Kara Anjir, where they were chiefly employed in finding escorts for convoys.

At the end of September the Battalion was in camp at Baiji and was now very weak in numbers, containing no more than nine officers and 222 other ranks, and all must have been greatly pleased to hear on the 31st October of the arrival at Baghdad of the 1st Battalion, Rifle Brigade, which was coming up in relief ; and the War Diary of the Battalion for this month closes with the words—" Undemobilizable details will then proceed to the combined depot on the right bank at Baghdad, and by the first week in November the 6th (Service) Battalion The Loyal North Lancashire Regiment, forming part of the Army of Occupation in Mesopotamia, will have ceased to exist, as such."

Great disappointment was felt by all that the Battalion should be sent home to England in small parties and not as a complete unit.

The following list of the officers who were serving with the Battalion at the end of September, shows how very small was then the percentage of those actually belonging to the North Lancashire Regiment :—

Lieut.-Colonel J. S. N. Harrison, D.S.O.	Somerset Light Infantry.
Captain (acting Major) F. S. Hebblewhite, M.C.	Loyal North Lancashire.
Captain H. C. Wancke . . .	Royal Welsh Fusiliers.
Lieutenant (acting Captain) J. M. O'Donohue	Loyal North Lancashire.
Lieutenant (acting Captain) J. Thomas	Somerset Light Infantry.
Lieutenant C. J. Newman . .	Royal Welsh Fusiliers.

Lieutenant V. J. Matthews .   . South Lancashire.
Lieutenant A. Bouchier.   .   . Royal Welsh Fusiliers.
Lieutenant H. R. Searby   .   . Oxford and Bucks Light Infantry.
Lieutenant R. Paterson.   .   . King's Own Scottish Borderers.
Lieutenant R. Hamilton-Smith   . Royal Highlanders.
2nd Lieutenant R. B. Jones .   . South Wales Borderers.
Captain B. L. Blampied   .   . Royal Army Medical Corps.

There being only one battle-honours list granted to a regiment, as a whole, for services rendered during the Great War, 1914–1918, the Service Battalions received exactly the same honours as those accorded to the Regular and Territorial Battalions of the Regiment. (See Appendix III.)

In recognition of the services of the 6th (Service) Battalion, the Loyal North Lancashire Regiment was awarded the following battle-honours : " Suvla," " Sari Bair," " Gallipoli, 1915," " Egypt, 1916," " Tigris, 1916," " Kut-al-Amara, 1917," " Baghdad," " Mesopotamia, 1916–18 "—the honours " Suvla " and " Baghdad " having the distinction of being now borne on the Colours.

A King's Colour was subsequently presented to each Service Battalion which had served overseas during the Great War. (See Appendix II.)

CHAPTER LI

THE 7TH (SERVICE) BATTALION
THE LOYAL NORTH LANCASHIRE REGIMENT

1914–1918

THE BATTLES OF YPRES AND THE BATTLES OF THE SOMME

IN Army Order No. 382, published on the 11th September, 1914, it was announced that His Majesty The King had been graciously pleased to approve of a further addition to the Army of six divisions and Army Troops, the new divisions to be numbered from 15 to 20. In the 56th Brigade of the 19th Division were the following Service Battalions : the 7th Bn. The King's Own Royal Lancaster Regiment, the 7th Bn. The Loyal North Lancashire Regiment, the 7th Bn. The East Lancashire Regiment and the 7th Bn. The Prince of Wales's Volunteers (South Lancashire Regiment).

The stations allotted to the 19th Division were Tidworth, Bulford and Swindon ; it formed part of the Second New Army,—the 19th Division was commanded by Major-General C. G. M. Fasken, and the 56th Brigade by Brigadier-General B. G. Lewis, D.S.O. The actual date of the raising of the Battalion appears to have been the 6th September, 1914, since that is the date on which its first officer—Temporary Lieut.-Colonel T. H. O'Brien—was posted to it.

The Battalion remained at home busily training, until, on the 6th July, 1915, the commanding officer was verbally informed by the Brigadier that mobilization had been decided upon ; the 7th was the first day of mobilization, when all underwent medical inspection, and the greater part of the officers and other ranks were allowed to go on a few days' leave pending embarkation. Early on the morning of the 16th three officers and 110 non-commissioned officers and men left for Southampton with the transport, embarking at that port for Havre. The rest of the Battalion did not leave Tidworth until the afternoon of the 17th, when it proceeded in two trains to Folkestone and crossed over to Boulogne.

The strength of the 7th Loyal North Lancashire was now 30 officers and 900 other ranks.

The Battalion made no prolonged halt at the Boulogne Rest Camp, but left again on the afternoon of the 18th and took the train to Watten, whence it set off by march route to join the Indian Corps, to which the 19th Division had been assigned. On the 30th July the Battalion was settled in billets, taken over from the 2nd Battalion South Wales Borderers, in the village of Paradis, two and a half miles south of Merville.

The Indian Corps had lately been withdrawn to rest, having suffered severely in the recent fighting of April, May and June. In his book, *With the Indians in France*, General Willcocks, the Commander of the Corps, writes that "from the finish of the Battle of Festubert until the Indian Corps took part in the subsidiary attack in front of Mauquissart on the opening day of the Battle of Loos in September, 1915, was for us what was called in France a quiet time. No big attack was undertaken and no special features marked this period. The troops, however, had plenty of hard work."

So far as the Battalion was concerned, the "hard work" during the weeks immediately following its arrival at the front, took the form of intensive training in all forms of trench warfare ; to this end it was sent into the trenches with other regiments of British and Indian brigades ; officers and men attended lectures on the employment of trench weapons ; and practical instruction was given in the use of trench mortars and gas helmets. The latter part of August was passed at Le Sart, and on the 31st the Battalion marched to billets at Les Lobes, just to the north of Locon, where the Brigade formed part of the Army reserve, but the remaining two brigades had taken over a sector between Festubert and Richebourg l'Avoué.

At Les Lobes the Battalion remained until the 13th September, when it marched to the neighbourhood of Locon, taking over reserve billets at the Rue de Chavattes from the 10th Battalion The Worcestershire Regiment. From here, however, a large party was sent forward to occupy various defence posts, and on the 16th two men were killed and two wounded in what was known as the Orchard Salient.

On the 19th September Lieut.-Colonel T. H. O'Brien gave up command of the Battalion and returned to England, his place being taken two or three days later by Lieut.-Colonel C. S. Shephard, D.S.O.

The 19th Division was now busy preparing to take some part in the operations of the Battle of Loos, which had already been for some days in progress, and on the 25th September, as stated in the *Official History*,* "the 19th Division of the Indian Corps on the left of the I. Corps had been ordered to co-operate with the 2nd Division by attacking the Rue d'Ouvert as soon as the attack of the 5th Brigade had developed. The

* *France and Belgium,* 1915, Vol. II, p. 258.

57th Brigade being in Army reserve, and the 58th and 56th in the line, the 56th was ordered to take over part of the 58th Brigade line so that the latter could attack on a front suitable to its strength." The 56th Brigade in general and the Battalion in particular did not, however, take any prominent part in this day's action, the 58th Brigade only being employed, as appears from the account in the Battalion War Diary of this date.

"Stood to arms at 4.30 a.m.," so we read ; "messages re impending gas and smoke attacks received at 5.7 a.m. At 5.30 an intense bombardment began and between 5.50 and 6 a.m. the whole front of the Brigade was covered with white smoke. The bombardment continued violently till 6.30 a.m. The Battalion was in divisional reserve, but could in case of urgent necessity be called on by the Brigadier, but was not required for any action. From 1 to 5 p.m. dug-outs were improved and fresh ones made. It rained very heavily from 4 p.m. till about midnight, but all the Battalion had some kind of shelter. A large number of enemy shells fell close to Battalion headquarters, but only three of them exploded."

On the 28th the Battalion took over a portion of the front and at once began to be very active, improving the trenches and frequently sending out officers' patrols.

The Indian Corps was now commanded by Lieut.-General Sir C. A. Anderson, who had relieved General Willcocks early in September.

To the northward of the Loos battle area the Battalion spent the month of October, either up in the forward positions between Richebourg l'Avoué and Festubert or in rear in billets ; and though this period may be described as comparatively peaceful, casualties were by no means few in number, 2nd Lieutenant J. E. Lord being among the wounded. During November the German artillery was very active, while the weather became particularly trying, constant rain being followed by intense cold, the trenches were full of mud, men had sometimes to be hauled out and there were many cases of "trench feet." On the 21st November orders were received for the relief of the 19th Division by the 7th, the former to move back into general reserve. Two days later the relief was completed and the Battalion moved back to billets to the north of Merville, settling down there to platoon and company training in very cold weather.

This period of training did not last much more than ten days, for on the 3rd December the 19th Division was ordered back to the front to relieve the 46th Division in the line between Richebourg l'Avoué and Neuve Chapelle. Here trenches were held and billets occupied during this month.

Towards the end of the month a new divisional commander arrived in the person of Major-General G. T. M. Bridges, and on the 30th Captain

M. Thomas, of the Battalion, was wounded by a German sniper, dying within a few hours.

Early in November the Indian Army Corps had been broken up and its units had left France, and the 19th Division was then transferred to the XI. Corps.

On the 11th January, 1916, orders were received directing that the 56th Brigade was shortly to move from Merville, near which it was then stationed, and take over billets then occupied by the 1st Guards Brigade at Robecq, and by the evening of the 12th the Battalion had relieved the 2nd Bn. Grenadier Guards at Calonne. Here training of all kinds set in with renewed severity, but the War Diary strikes a note of regret when it remarks that "no battalion drill could be held owing to the difficulty of getting on to the only field large enough, the field being surrounded by a wide ditch full of water!"

In the middle of February a further move was made, the Brigade taking over the trenches about Neuve Chapelle, the billeting area, when out of the line, being at Croix Barbée, and this, too, appears to have been a tolerably quiet sector, no incident of importance taking place. In the middle of April it was announced that the Division was now to be withdrawn into general reserve for training; the move began about the 24th, when the Battalion marched to Estrée Blanche and settled down to company and battalion training which went on until early in May.

A Fourth Army had been formed on the 1st March and to the command of this General Rawlinson had been transferred from that of the First Army; and in the *Official History* * it is stated that "on the 24th March the headquarters of the III. Corps (Lieut.-General Sir W. P. Pulteney) had arrived in the Fourth Army, and shortly after, although only its 8th Division was available, took over the front near Ovillers la Boisselle, between the XIII. and X. Corps. The 19th and 34th Divisions, assigned to the corps, did not arrive until early in May." It is clear, therefore, that about the time mentioned the 19th Division had been transferred from the XI. to the III. Corps.

Estrée Blanche was left on the 7th May and, moving by Lillers, Longeau and Amiens, the Battalion arrived at Tremont in the new corps area on the afternoon of the following day. Here it remained, engaged in hard training, until the 16th June, when it marched to Rainneville and, after spending a few days at this place, moved on again to Henencourt Wood, where on the last day of the month it took over trenches to the north-east of Albert.

On the 1st July, so the *Official History* records,† "the position of the III. Corps between Bécourt and Authuille, lay on the forward slopes of

* *France and Flanders*, 1916, Vol. I, p. 249.   † *Ibid.*, p. 371.

a long low ridge between Albert and La Boisselle, marked by Tara and Usna Hills, a continuation of the spurs of the main Ginchy–Pozières ridge on which the village of Ovillers stands. . . . The enemy first position, with its front line higher than the British, lay across the upper slopes of the three spurs which reach out south-westwards from the main ridge towards Albert. The distance between the opposing lines varied from 800 to 50 yards, the trench nearest to the enemy, opposite La Boisselle, being known as ' Glory Hole.'

" The right of the Corps faced the western slope of the long Fricourt spur ; its centre, the La Boisselle spur, with the village of that name almost in the German front line ; whilst in front of its left was the upper part of Ovillers spur, with the village within the German front defences. . . . The great Thiepval spur—actually opposite the X. Corps, next on the left —overlooked practically all the first belt of ground over which the divisions of the III. Corps had necessarily to advance."

The two assaulting divisions of the III. Corps were the 8th and 34th, and these were to effect the capture of two fortified villages and six lines of trenches, then advancing into the enemy position to a depth of some two miles on a front of 4,000 yards.

" The 19th Division, in corps reserve, but with its guns in action under the other divisions, was to be in a position of readiness in an intermediate position north of Albert, and as the 34th and 8th Divisions moved forward to the assault, the two leading brigades of the 19th Division were to take their places in the Tara–Usna line, ready to move forward to relieve them when they had secured their objectives."

The 34th Division attacked the La Boisselle Salient with all its battalions on the morning of the 1st July, while the whole weight of the infantry of the 8th Division was employed in the assault on the Ovillers spur, and it had been intended that two brigades of the 19th Division should carry out an attack on La Boisselle after dark. The operations were conducted with conspicuous gallantry, but Ovillers and La Boisselle remained in the enemy's hands, while the casualties in the two attacking divisions amounted to over 11,000 ; consequently " at 4.15 p.m., in view of the poor prospect of success, the difficulty in getting the troops up owing to congestion in the trenches, and the fact that it appeared doubtful if any British troops were still alive and uncaptured in the German positions, the order for the 5 p.m. assault was cancelled."

On the 7th Battalion's share in the events of this day the following account appears in the War Diary :—

" 1st July, 8 a.m. Left intermediate line for the Usna–Tara Line in reserve to the 8th Division. Captain Leverson wounded.

" 3 p.m. Battalion moved to old British front line preparatory to attack on Ovillers from north-west ; attack to take place at 5 p.m.

"4.45 p.m. Message received, attack cancelled. C.O. summoned to 25th Brigade, 8th Division headquarters at once. Battalion then placed in reserve trenches as reserve for 25th Brigade till dawn. About twenty-five casualties."

On the 2nd July the Battalion was relieved and went back to the railway cutting near Albert, where, in a field, the day, and part of the following night, was passed ; but at 3 on the morning of the 3rd all were again on the move, going up again to the Usna–Tara line on the right of the main Albert–Pozières road. Here the Battalion remained until night, being in support to the 7th Royal Lancaster Regiment which was then in the old German front-line trench. At 1 a.m. on the 4th the Battalion was sent to the trench line about La Boisselle—" very much knocked about and full of dead "—and it was here when at eight o'clock fighting was renewed.

On the 3rd the 57th and 58th Brigades had attacked the village of La Boisselle, and by the evening of the 6th the whole village was solidly consolidated by the 19th Division, which had broken up a strong counter-attack from the direction of Pozières, and had extended its gains so as to include an enemy redoubt known as Heligoland.

For the activities of the Battalion during these epoch-making days we must consult the War Diary again :—

" *4th July*, 8.30 a.m. Three companies sent up at intervals during the morning to help. Heavy bombing in village of La Boisselle. Lieut. Hughes did very well with Lewis guns. Lieut. L. Milbourne and the bombing sergeant were both killed. Towards dusk it became quieter.

" 10 p.m. our line heavily shelled ; about 40–50 prisoners came through our line.

" *5th July*, 12.30 a.m. Aid post found very overcrowded. Quiet morning.

" 2 p.m. 7th East Lancashire made bombing attack, ' D ' Company and the Battalion bombers went up to help. ' C ' Company was up in reserve, when at 3 p.m., owing to some misunderstanding on the left, the East Lancashire withdrew back to the old German front line and old British front line. ' C ' Company was at once ordered to charge to regain the lost ground, went over the open in very good order and retook the line vacated by the East Lancashire. This was a very fine performance. Lieut. Wilkinson on the left held up some Germans with a machine-gun as they were advancing down a trench, and by his prompt action stopped a determined rush by the enemy. For this he was recommended for the Victoria Cross by the O.C. Sherwood Foresters.   Soon after this Lieut. T. O. L. Wilkinson was unfortunately killed in trying to rescue a wounded man forty yards in front of our parapet.   Captain Maule rendered great assistance in getting the trench re-occupied by the East Lancashire.

"Intermittent shelling during the whole night."

The Battalion remained up in the trench line near La Boisselle until 11 p.m. on the 7th, when it was relieved by the 13th Bn. The Rifle Brigade, and went back to bivouac in heavy rain in rear of the Usna–Tara line.

The taking by the 19th Division of La Boisselle completed the capture of the German first line of defence in the centre section of the wide battlefield ; further to the right Fricourt, Mametz and Montauban had also fallen to our assaults ; and plans were now in preparation for attacking the German second-line system.   This ran from Guillemont through Longueval and along Bazentin Ridge to Pozières.   Certain intermediate positions had, however, first to be captured, and one of the strongest of these, the fortified village of Contalmaison, lay in front of the III. Corps.

Reinforcements to the number of 109 reached the Battalion on the 11th, but these scarcely made good the losses during the past ten days' fighting which totalled seven officers and 164 other ranks.

A good many days in the middle of the month of July were spent by the Battalion in camp in Henencourt Wood near Albert, but on the 19th the 56th Brigade received orders to be ready to move to bivouacs near Fricourt ; that evening the Brigade marched off and before dawn on the 20th the Battalion had relieved a unit of the 98th Brigade at Bazentin-le-Petit, later in the day taking over an advanced and very extended line —one of a thousand yards in length—for the holding of which no more than four hundred and eighty rifles were available.

"7 p.m. our Lewis guns," so the War Diary tells us, "brought down a German aeroplane just in front of our front line.   It burst into flames and both men were burnt to death."

At this time the central British position was not by any means a favourable one, since it formed a long salient bending from High Wood through Delville Wood to Guillemont, and it was everywhere exposed to direct observation from the German position.   Since the 15th July several attempts had been made to drive the enemy from High Wood, mainly by the 33rd Division, and in one of these a brigade of the 19th Division, the 56th, had taken part : the Battalion was not, however, engaged.   None of these attempts had met with the wished-for success, and now, on the morning of the 23rd July, the 19th Division was to attack the Switch Line in company with the 1st Division in the centre and the Australians on the left of the line.

"B" and "C" Companies of the Battalion moved forward to the attack at 12.20 on the morning of the 23rd and reached their objective, having suffered very heavy casualties, and "C"—now only forty-five strong—then advanced up a road on the left, but was held up by machine-gun fire on passing over the crest of the hill. "A" Company was then ordered to prepare to renew the attack, but at this moment, Lieutenant Porter, the commander of "C" Company, came back and reported that his company had incurred heavy losses, that his men had advanced to within two yards of the German trench and could get no further by reason of the opposing machine-gun fire. "A" Company's attack orders were now cancelled and its commander was directed to consolidate the front line and endeavour to hold it against any counter-attack.

A report now came in from 2nd Lieutenant Tovani that Captain Thompson and 2nd Lieutenant H. Hoyle of his company had been killed, and that the company had been held up by German machine-gun fire only a few yards short of the enemy front line ; and 2nd Lieutenant Tovani then withdrew the small remnant of the company—some fifty men only—to our front line. Companies of the East Lancashire and Cameron Highlanders now came up to strengthen the position. A Field Company R.E. was also sent up and helped to consolidate the captured first objective, to wire the front and help to dig communication trenches back from the right towards Crucifix Corner.

At 8.50 p.m. the Battalion was relieved and went back to dug-outs in Mametz Wood, having during the last four days had eleven officers and 290 other ranks killed, wounded and missing. Of these eleven officers the following were killed : Lieutenant W. A. Dawson, 2nd Lieutenants H. J. R. Hosking, H. Hoyle, R. W. Jardine and McK. F. Turpie.

The Battalion remained in Mametz Wood until the end of the month, the artillery on both sides being very active and some fifteen men being wounded by enemy shells ; and there were frequent reports that the Germans were making, or intended to make, attacks on the divisional or corps front.

On the 31st the Battalion was relieved and marched by Albert and Fricourt to Franvillers, where it occupied fairly comfortable billets.

The Battalion was now to be temporarily shifted to the Flanders front, where for the time a more peaceful atmosphere reigned ; but just before, during and just after the move considerable reinforcements arrived, and in many cases these belonged to regiments other than that to which they were dispatched and even in some cases the men composing them belonged to regiments, battalions of which were actually in the same brigade as the 7th Loyal North Lancashire Regiment ! Thus on the 2nd August a draft of 141 other ranks arrived to join the Battalion, and of these eighty-six belonged to the Royal Lancaster and over fifty to the East Lancashire Regiments, both of which corps had battalions in the 56th Brigade !

Later on a second draft of thirty men joined.

On the 3rd August the Battalion marched to Frechencourt Railway Station and there entrained for Longpré, whence it moved by Villers-sur-Ailly and Bailleul to Kemmel where it was accommodated in huts by the 7th of the month. Here the 19th Division took over the line facing Messines Ridge ; but on the 3rd September the Battalion was relieved by the 38th Battalion Canadian Infantry, the 19th Division being under orders to move again to the south to take the place of the 23rd Division in the Ploegsteert area. Marching by way of Dranoutre, Neuve Eglise, Ramarin and Papot, the Battalion took over on the 5th a somewhat long front line from the 11th Bn. West Yorkshire Regiment, the length of the line requiring that all the companies should occupy the front trenches. At first all were employed on working parties ; but when about the middle of the month fighting recommenced with increased vigour on the Somme front, the troops occupying the front line in Flanders were directed to make demonstrations so as to keep the enemy facing them from detaching troops to other points, and to this end many raids were carried out during the rest of the time that the Division remained here. On the 19th the 7th Division began to relieve the 19th which moved back for training, and by the 22nd the Battalion was accommodated in billets at Outtersteene, where training of all kinds was entered upon.

The London Gazette of the 26th September, 1916, announced the award of the Victoria Cross to Lieut. T. O. L. Wilkinson, 7th Battalion, for his " magnificent example of courage and self-sacrifice " at La Boisselle on 5th July, 1916.

On the 2nd October it was intimated that the 19th Division was very shortly to move back again to the Somme area, and on the 5th the Battalion marched to and entrained at Bailleul for Doullens, from where it marched via Serton, Authie, and St. Leger to Coigneux. Some few days were spent here, during which training was continued, special attention being paid to the practice of the attack, to bayonet fighting and bombing.

Later in the month the Division marched to the neighbourhood of its old fighting ground of the previous July—about Albert and La Boisselle, and in these regions it had been intended to employ the newly-arrived troops in an attack up the valley of the Ancre, but there was incessant rain, the ground was no better than a morass and the proposed attack had to be postponed.

At the beginning of November the 56th Brigade was holding the front line of the sector about Aveluy, the weather had improved, and the 19th Division was now to take part in the Battle of the Ancre, the closing effort of the year.

" On Sunday, 12th November, Sir Hubert Gough's Fifth Army held the area from Gommecourt in the north to the Albert–Bapaume road. Opposite Serre and extending south to a point just north of Beaumont Hamel lay the 31st, 3rd and 2nd Divisions. In front of Beaumont Hamel was the 51st Division. On their right, from a point just south of the famous Y Ravine to the Ancre, lay the 63rd Naval Division. Across the river lay the 39th and the 19th Divisions. The boundary of the attack on the right was roughly defined by the Thiepval–Grandcourt road." *

The objectives of the proposed attack were Miraumont, Beauregard, Dovecot, Serre, Pys, Irles and Achiet-le-Petit, and the 19th Division was to pass over Grandcourt Trench to a final line on the Miraumont–Beaucourt road. In the 19th Division the 56th and 58th Brigades took part in the attack on the 13th November, the 57th Brigade, which had been having a very hard time in the trenches, being kept back in reserve.

On the night of the 12th–13th the Battalion moved forward to its position of assembly in front of Stuff Trench, and at zero hour on the 12th —5.45 a.m.—" B," " C " and " D " Companies advanced in two waves, " A " remaining behind to hold Stuff Trench. The whole attack went well and the objective was gained in ten minutes, thanks to the fine leading of Captain H. C. Bennett, while the very thick mist materially assisted the advance. The Germans appear to have been completely taken by surprise and nearly two hundred prisoners, of some five different battalions, were captured by the 7th Loyal North Lancashire, the casualties in which numbered five officers and eighty-one other ranks. Owing to the mist the companies had become very much mixed up and in some cases the objective had been overrun ; but the new line was consolidated during the day, the 7th East Lancashire and the 1st Hertfordshire Regiments being on the right and left of the Battalion respectively.

On the night of the 13th–14th the Battalion was ordered to make a raid along Battery Valley, and this was successfully carried out at 1.40 a.m. on the 14th by " A " Company under 2nd Lieutenant Nightingale, five prisoners being taken, while our line was slightly advanced, but the Company had one officer and sixteen men hit.

The Battalion was withdrawn on the evening of the 17th to Wolseley Huts near Aveluy after some seven especially trying days and nights up at the front, and consequently took no part in the renewed attack made

* Buchan, *History of the Great War*, Vol. III, pp. 210, 211.

by the Division on the 18th and of which a historian * gives the following account :—

"The movement of the 19th Division was difficult and complex, with Grandcourt as a possible objective. It meant an attack upon a maze of trenches under the worst possible terrestrial conditions, while the advance had really to be in three different directions—due north, north-east and almost due east. At 6 a.m. upon November 18th, in a sharp snow-storm, the advance began. It was the last concerted operation of the year, but it was not unfortunately destined for success. The garrison of the trenches appear to have been as numerous as the stormers and far more advantageously placed, while the ground was such that an advance over it without opposition would have been no easy task. . . . It is difficult to exaggerate the extreme hardships which had been suffered by the whole of General Jacob's corps during these operations amid the viscid mud slopes of the Ancre. Napoleon in Poland had never better cause to curse the fourth element. The front trenches were mere gutters, and every attempt to deepen them only deepened the stagnant pool within. The communications were little better. The mud was on the men's bodies, in their food, and for ever clogging both their feet and their weapons. The hostile shelling was continuous. It was a nightmare chapter of the campaign."

The 19th Division was now due for relief by the 11th, and on the evening of the 21st the move began, and the Battalion proceeded by Aveluy, Warloy, Vadencourt and Beauval to Berneuil, where it arrived in pouring rain on the morning of the 25th and took over what the War Diary describes as "filthy billets." Here the glad tidings were received that the Battalion would probably remain in Berneuil for the whole period of six weeks' training.

During the month of November of the officers who became casualties, Captain F. E. G. Porter and 2nd Lieutenant H. Fletcher had been killed.

The Battalion remained at Berneuil during the whole of the month of December, chiefly engaged in training and in the absorbing of drafts ; of these the following arrived :—

On the	3rd December	.	44 non-commissioned officers and men,			
,,	,, 4th	,,	.	26	,,	,, ,, ,,
,,	,, 5th	,,	.	55	,,	,, ,, ,,
,,	,, 8th	,,	.	15	,,	,, ,, ,,
,,	,, 9th	,,	.	22	,,	,, ,, ,,
,,	,, 11th	,,	.	14	,,	,, ,, ,,
,,	,, 17th	,,	.	151	,,	,, ,, ··

* Conan Doyle, *The British Campaign in France and Flanders*, Vol. III, pp. 324–6.

the last, under charge of Lieutenant Bryan, making a substantial addition to the strength of the Battalion of 327 ; but from the remarks made in the War Diary some deterioration in the physique of the reinforcements now coming in seems to have already become noticeable.

On the 9th January, 1917, the Battalion marched from Berneuil and proceeded by Beauquesnes to Authie and St. Leger, two companies being billeted at each of these places, the weather being still very trying, wet and cold with occasional snow. After some ten days here, a fresh move was made, the Battalion going up into brigade support and being again split up, with two companies in Hébuterne Keep and two in Sailly-au-Bois. From here the Battalion took its share of duty in the front line which from time to time was heavily shelled ; and on the 28th the Brigadier, who had only comparatively recently assumed command of the 56th Brigade—Brigadier-General W. Long—was killed by a shell, and at the same time the Brigade Major, and Captain Bryan and 2nd Lieutenant Cooper of the Battalion were wounded.

At the end of February the Battalion was sent to Juniper Huts at Courcelles, where no more than two or three days were spent, and in March many moves were made ; on the 3rd from Courcelles via Louvencourt to Vauchelles, thence on the 9th to Gezaincourt and so on by way of Rebreuve, Gauchin-Verloingt, Cauchy-à-la-Tour, Estrée Blanche, Wittes, Sereus, and St. Omer to Mentque, which was reached on the 21st and where the rest of the month was quietly spent. In April again was the Battalion much shifted about until on the 18th it found itself in the Diependaal Sector in the Dranoutre area of the Flanders front. May was spent in the same quarters ; and the 19th Division had now for some six months past taken no part in any major operations, when early in June it was required to engage in the Flanders offensive of this year, known as the Battle of Messines, which endured from the 7th to the 14th June.

The Battalion was now in the IX. Corps of the Second Army, the Corps being under the command of General Hamilton-Gordon, while the Second Army was under General Plumer ; the 19th Division had lately come under a new commander in Major-General Shute.

" The British front of assault was held by three of the six corps of the Second Army. From opposite Mount Sorrel, astride the Ypres–Comines Canal to the Grand Bois just north of Wytschaete, lay the X. Corps with the 23rd Division on its left, the 47th Division in the centre, the 41st Division on the right and the 24th Division in support. Opposite Wytschaete was the IX. Corps, with the 19th, 16th and 36th Divisions in line from left to right, and the 11th Division in support. South lay the II. Australian Corps, with the 25th Division on its left, the New Zealand Division as its centre, the 3rd Australian Division on its right astride the Douve, and the 4th Australian Division in support. The two southern corps had the task of the direct assault on the ridge, while the X. Corps, with a much longer front, had to clear the hillocks towards the Ypres Salient, and advance upon the ridge and the Oosttaverne line from its northern flank." *

On the night of the 6th June the Battalion moved up to its assembly position in a violent thunderstorm, which happily cleared away before the hour fixed for the attack on the morning of the 7th.

For the assault by the 19th Division upon its objective, the Oosttaverne line, the 56th and 58th Brigades were in the front, the 57th in reserve, and the ground to be moved over presented many difficulties, being mainly through a region of shattered woods.

At 3.10 a.m. on the 7th June nineteen huge mines were simultaneously exploded under the German defences, and at the same moment our guns opened and the infantry everywhere advanced to the attack. " C " and " D " Companies led the Battalion, all objectives were captured and the Red Line was reached by 3.45, when consolidation at once commenced, while communication was established with the battalions on the flanks and by runners with the Battalion headquarters in the rear. Some forty Germans were taken prisoner and as many were killed; in the Battalion Captain W. H. F. Maule, D.S.O., was wounded, while there were some sixty casualties among the other ranks.

The Battalion now took over the whole frontage of the Green Line, the headquarters being established in some old German dug-outs in Onraet Wood.

In the despatch of the 25th December, 1917, it is stated that " by 3.45 p.m. the village of Oosttaverne had been captured. At 4 p.m. troops from the northern and western counties of England entered the Oosttaverne Line east of the village and captured two batteries of German field guns. Half an hour later other English battalions broke through the enemy's position further north. Parties of the enemy were surrendering freely, and his casualties were reported to be very heavy. By the evening the Oosttaverne Line had been taken and our objectives had been gained."

The 57th Brigade had now moved forward and taken the place of the troops in the front, the 56th Brigade remaining to consolidate the Green Line, and the Battalion providing large carrying parties for the brigade in front. The enemy still, however, displayed considerable activity, and on the 10th, when the Battalion was up in the front line, an enemy raiding party, about fifty strong, suddenly made its appearance near one of the Lewis-gun posts. The post at once opened fire, while a platoon charged

* Buchan, A History of the Great War, Vol. III, pp. 574, 575.

out on the flank, cutting off one German officer and three men who were brought in.   The German gun-fire continued to be very heavy, and before the Battalion was relieved on the 12th and moved back into support, the casualties during the last week had risen to five officers and 165 other ranks, killed and wounded.

In the latter part of June the Brigade was withdrawn to a camp near Kemmel, where a brief period of greatly-needed rest was entered upon.

Nearly the whole of July was spent in various training camps—Moore Park Camp, Butterfly Camp, Weston Camp and finally Rossignol Camp ; and on the 3rd all ranks were greatly cheered by the sight of their King, His Majesty, accompanied by H.R.H. The Prince of Wales and General Plumer, the Army Commander, visiting the 19th Division area.

As the month drew to its close the time had arrived when the 19th Division was to play its part in the operations known as the Third Battle of Ypres, which had commenced on the 1st June and which was to endure until nearly the middle of November. As stated in the official despatch of the 25th December, 1917, "the front of the Allied attack," arranged for the 31st July, "extended from the Lys River opposite Deulemont northwards to beyond Steenstraat, a distance of over fifteen miles, but the main blow was to be delivered by the Fifth Army on a front of about seven and a half miles, from the Zillebeke–Zandvoorde road to Boesinghe, inclusive." The First French Army was on the left of our Fifth Army, and on its right was General Plumer's Second Army. The task of the Second Army was to cover the right of the Fifth and advance only a short distance, it being intended that it should increase the area threatened by the attack and so prevent the enemy from concentrating the whole weight of the fire of his guns on any special portion of the front.

The general arrangements for the attack, so far as these affected the Second Army in general and the 19th Division in particular, are given as under in the *History of the 19th Division.** "The X. (41st Division) and IX. Corps (19th and 37th Divisions) were to capture the Blue Line, which, in the area of the 41st Division, included Hollebeke, and along the 19th Divisional front ran from Bee Farm on the south to just east of Forret Farm on the north. The 56th Brigade had received orders to carry out the attack along the front of the 19th Division on a three-battalion frontage. The 7th Royal Lancaster on the right, 7th East Lancashire in the centre, and 7th North Lancashire on the left, were the assaulting battalions ; the 7th South Lancashire was in support."

On the 29th July the Battalion moved up to the trenches from Rossignol Camp, and by 9.45 p.m. on the 30th the companies had taken up their

* The 37th Division was on the right, the 19th in the centre, the 41st on the left.

positions in the front line in the following order from right to left—" A," " C," " D " and " B." Zero hour was at 3.50 a.m. on the 31st, when the attack started on a line from north of Pilckem to south of Green Wood, the 56th Brigade being thus at the extreme south point of the attack, and the Battalion at the north of the Brigade front. The attack was to be launched on a front of approximately 700 yards against no definite trench system, but against a line marked on the map as " the Blue Line," which was some 500 yards short of the actual objective.

Of the progress of the attack the Battalion War Diary tells us that " no reports were received until 4.30 a.m. when it was heard that ' A ' Company had reached its objective, but was not in touch with ' C ' Company on the left. It appeared later that ' C ' Company had been held up by machine-gun fire and was 100 yards in rear of ' A,' while ' B ' and ' D ' Companies were in front of ' C ' but were not on their objectives. Report received that the 122nd Brigade, 41st Division, on the left, had gained its objective, including Forret Farm and part of Hollebeke, with slight casualties. Further report from ' C ' Company that it was held up by machine-gun fire from the road in front and that its present strength was now only forty all ranks. ' D ' Company now reported that Forret Farm was in the hands of the enemy who were using machine-guns against our troops ; these were trying to dig in, but were suffering casualties. Our machine-guns got into position 200 yards to the west of the Twins. Communication was very difficult across the open ground, but runners managed to reach battalion headquarters with information, and the general position was said to be as follows : ' A,' ' B ' and ' D ' Companies were held up 100 yards short of their objective, while ' C ' was echeloned 150 yards to the left rear of ' A.'

" The enemy had started a counter-barrage to our artillery and machine-gun barrage about fifteen minutes after the attack opened, and the Ravine was heavily shelled with 4·2's and 5·9's up to midnight on the 31st. No movement was possible during daylight, and all were employed in digging in on the line arrived at, and in the endeavour to establish communication with troops on the flanks. Three enemy aeroplanes flew low over the new British lines and directed artillery registration upon them, the enemy thereafter keeping up a shell fire on these lines, this increasing in intensity towards night.

" At 11.30 p.m. a message was received saying that the enemy was preparing for a counter-attack, but this did not materialize. It was now learnt that the 122nd Brigade had not captured Forret Farm, and the enemy holding this had caused our two left companies many casualties ; by nightfall the Battalion had Captain Justice died of wounds, 2nd Lieut.

Priestland wounded, and ninety killed and wounded among the non-commissioned officers and men.

" 1st August. Forret Farm continues to be held by the enemy and a good deal of enfilade fire comes from the right and causes many casualties. Battalion H.Q. in the Ravine heavily shelled from 3–7 a.m. and the evacuation of the wounded is only effected with the utmost difficulty, as the stretcher bearers are sniped, but the work of clearing the area of the advance is proceeding slowly. The conditions on the front-line trenches are now very bad owing to the heavy rain which has made the ground water-logged and swampy ; the men cannot leave their improvised trenches, which are now ankle-deep, and in some places knee-deep, in water.

" The divisional front was reorganized on a two-brigade frontage, the 58th Brigade coming up to take over the southern portion of the 56th Brigade front, one company of the South Lancashire relieving the right company of the Battalion, thus reducing our frontage from 700 yards to 333. Rain continues to be heavy and conditions are severely taxing the men's physical endurance. ' Trench Foot ' is making itself evident and men have to be evacuated owing to exhaustion."

Consolidation was now the order of the day, further captures were made and by the 3rd August the 19th Division was in possession of all the objectives allotted to it in the original operation orders ; the casualties in the Division had, however, been heavy, amounting to forty-one officers and 829 other ranks killed, wounded and missing.

On the night of the 3rd–4th August the 57th Brigade relieved the 56th in the front line, the Battalion marching to Vierstraat and being conveyed thence by lorries to Locre, where it was put up in Doncaster Huts. On the 5th the Brigadier—Brig.-General E. Craig-Brown—ordered a special parade of the Battalion, when he thanked all ranks for their behaviour in the trenches.

On the 5th the enemy, by a sudden attack, recaptured part of the front line, but was driven out again by the troops of the 19th Division.

Then on the night of the 7th–8th August the 19th Division was relieved and moved back to the Lumbres area for training, the 56th Brigade being located about Colembert, the Battalion in billets to the north of Mt. Kokereele.

The Division remained out of the line, engaged in training, until the night of the 11th–12th September, when it took over part of the Klein Zillebeke sector, one bounded on the right by the Ypres–Comines Canal, the front line running in a north-easterly direction through Opaque Wood along the eastern outskirts of Imperfect Farm and thence to about 150 yards west of Greenburg Farm, the ruins of which lay half-way between the British and German trenches.   Klein Zillebeke itself was on the left rear of the divisional front.   The 57th and 58th Brigades were, shortly after, withdrawn from the line for the purpose of training and making final preparations for the operations known as the Battle of the Menin Road Ridge, which took place on the 20th 25th September.

"The front selected was just over eight miles in extent, running from the Ypres–Comines Canal, north of Hollebeke, to the Ypres–Staden Railway, north of Langemarck. . . .   The 19th Division was one of the twelve divisions to be employed, and was on the extreme right.   The main object of the attack of the IX. Corps, to which the 19th Division belonged, was to secure the right flank of the X. Corps (attacking on the left of the 19th Division)." *

The 57th and 58th Brigades were in the front line and the 56th in reserve, and none of the units of the latter seems to have been called upon to take any part until the close of the action, when one of its battalions came up to hold some of the ground gained.

On the night of the 19th the Battalion moved up to Bois Carré, and from the opening of the battle early on the following morning reports of its successful progress came through, verified by the arrival throughout the day of batches of German prisoners passed down from the front to the IX. Corps cage.

The 56th Brigade relieved the other two of the Division on the night of the 21st, the Battalion being in reserve ; and by this date the Division had again captured all its objectives, despite the very determined resistance put up by the enemy.   In this action the Divisional Commander, Major-General Bridges, was very severely wounded, and was replaced by Major-General G. D. Jeffreys.   The Battalion does not, however, appear to have incurred any loss until the 27th September, when an enemy shell exploded in a dug-out of "A" Company, occupied by two officers and twelve non-commissioned officers and men, and of these 2nd Lieutenant F. H. Dyke and four men were killed, Captain W. H. F. Maule, D.S.O., and eight other ranks were wounded.

At the end of the month the Battalion was back again in Bois Carré, and here on the 3rd October it was joined by a draft of 207 men from England.

The Battle of Broodseinde opened on the 4th October, but the infantry of the 19th Division was not called upon to attack, though the battalions up in the front line had a hard time of it, for mud was everywhere and some of the posts were quite uninhabitable.

"On the 4th November orders were received at Divisional Headquarters

* Wyrrall, *The History of the 19th Division*, p. 107.

stating that the 19th Division was to be relieved by the 37th by 10 a.m. on the 10th; on relief the Division was to proceed to the Blaringhem area for training. The 56th Brigade, having been relieved by the 57th on the 5th, came out of the line and moved from the support area on the 8th to the Locre area. By the 12th all moves were completed, the 19th Divisional Headquarters being at Blaringhem, and the three infantry brigades in the neighbourhood, i.e. the 56th at Blaringhem, the 57th at Mont d'Hiver and the 58th at Ebblinghem " * ; the Battalion being in tolerably comfortable billets at the village of La Belle Hôtesse.

Since the 5th September the 56th Brigade had been under the command of Brigadier-General F. G. Willan.

" The Division was out of the line for not quite a week," thus the *History*, † " for on the 4th December a wire arrived at Headquarters ordering the Division, less the artillery, to be prepared to leave the Second Army and proceed by rail, on or after the 6th, to join the Third Army on the Somme. . . . Operation orders for the move were issued on the 5th and the following day the Division entrained for the Third Army area. On the 10th the 57th Brigade relieved the left brigade of the 6th Division in the Ribecourt sector ; on the 12th the 58th Brigade took over the right subsector, the 56th Brigade being in divisional reserve. . . . The divisional front ran from the most westerly of four sunken roads south of Marcoing in a north-westerly direction to east of Flesquières ; Ribecourt was included in this sector. The old Hindenburg Support Line was the divisional support and reserve line : a line of posts formed the outpost line ; the whole front was 4,500 yards in extent."

The following extracts from the Battalion's War Diary for December give some idea of the conditions prevailing in this particular sector : " This sector appears very quiet, but great keenness and alertness are necessary owing to the probability of the enemy attempting to regain his lost position " ; and again : " Great importance is laid on patrolling, since the dispositions and intentions of the enemy have not been ascertained and even identifications are lacking."

The Battalion had moved up to the front line on the 15th, and next day came in for some shelling, an enemy shell falling just outside Battalion headquarters, killing one man and wounding six others, among the latter being Lieutenant Baxter and 2nd Lieutenant Brickell.

The month of January, 1918, was one of many rumours and counter-rumours ; it was often reported that the enemy appeared to be massing for attack, and later reasons for these operations were even stated ; it was known that many German divisions were in process of transfer from

---

* *History of the 19th Division*, p. 120.   † *Ibid.*, pp. 123, 124.

A TYPICAL SCENE IN FLANDERS.

1918.

The Imperial War Museum—Copyright.

the eastern to the western theatre of the war; and early in December orders were issued having for their object immediate preparations to meet a strong enemy offensive.

Several battalions of the 19th Division, and the 7th Battalion, The Loyal North Lancashire Regiment, amongst them, were not, however, destined to see the ultimate result of all these measures. For reasons which have been given in an earlier chapter dealing with the latter part of the Great War, it had early in 1918 been found necessary to disband some units in order that others might be brought up to strength. On the 24th January orders to this effect were received at the headquarters of the 19th Division; all four battalions of the 56th Brigade were to be disbanded, the Brigade being re-constituted with surplus battalions from the two other brigades of the Division and with one taken from the 63rd Division.

In a letter to the Commander of the Third Army, Sir Douglas Haig wrote: "I know how deeply officers and men will feel the severance of the ties binding them to the units in which they have served and fought with such splendid gallantry and success, and with which they had hoped eventually to return home after the great struggle had been won and their task achieved. But I know also that since this reorganization has to be, it will be accepted with the loyalty and devotion with which every trial has been met by British officers and men throughout the War."

In promulgating to all concerned the contents of this letter, Major-General Jeffreys added: "I know that all ranks of the 19th Division join with me in deeply regretting the loss of old comrades and in wishing them good-bye and the best of luck wherever they may go."

On the 6th February, then, the 7th (Service) Battalion, The Loyal North Lancashire Regiment, was disbanded, and so ceased to exist as a unit of the Regiment, the good name of which all ranks had striven so manfully —and successfully—to uphold.

CHAPTER LII

THE 8TH (SERVICE) BATTALION
THE LOYAL NORTH LANCASHIRE REGIMENT

1914–1918

FRANCE AND FLANDERS

THE SOMME, YPRES, MENIN ROAD

THE 8th and 9th Service Battalions of the Loyal North Lancashire Regiment both came into existence very shortly after the opening of the Great War, the commission of the first officer gazetted to the 8th Battalion—2nd Lieutenant P. R. Shields—being dated the 31st August, 1914. On the 13th September Army Order No. 388 was published, announcing that the Army was to be further increased by the addition of six divisions numbered from 21 to 26. The 25th Division contained three brigades—74th, 75th and 76th—and in the first of these were the 8th (Service) Bn. The Royal Lancaster Regiment, the 8th (Service) Bn. The East Lancashire Regiment and the 8th and 9th Service Bns. The Loyal North Lancashire Regiment. The 25th Division was to form part of the Third New Army under Lieut.-General Sir E. T. H. Hutton, K.C.B., K.C.M.G., while the Division and Brigade commanders were Major-General F. Ventris and Brigadier-General A. J. W. Allen, C.B.

In the Army List for October, 1914—none was published for September—the following officers appear as belonging to the 8th (Service) Battalion, The Loyal North Lancashire Regiment : Major (Temporary Lieut.-Colonel) G. A. Faulder, Lieutenant W. Milne, 2nd Lieutenants P. R. Shields, A. Harrison, G. P. Guilleband, J. B. Pennefather, G. M. Smyth, G. D. Keeble, F. Gregory, J. M. Ford, H. Hamer, E. S. Underhill, H. Dipple and S. G. Millar, and Lieutenant and Quartermaster B. Bartholomew.

The Battalion remained in England for a full year after the date it came into existence, training and growing in strength, until at the beginning of September, 1915, it was announced that the Division was very shortly to sail for " an unknown destination."

The Transport and Machine-Gun Section of the Battalion left Aldershot on Saturday the 24th September, under the command of Major A. F. S.

Caldwell, and proceeded by train to Southampton, embarking there and reaching Havre that night. At 10 a.m. on the 25th Major Caldwell's party went on by train to Lillers, where it arrived on the 27th.

The rest of the Battalion left Aldershot for Folkestone, under the command of Lieut.-Colonel W. H. Biddulph, and crossed from there to Boulogne ; on arrival here the commanding officer was at first told that he was to proceed by train with his battalion to Berguette, and had this order held good the Battalion might have been involved in the very hard fighting then in progress at La Bassée. The destination was, however, later changed, and the 8th Battalion went by train to Caestre and spent the night of the 27th–28th in billets at Rouge Croix, a small village between Caestre and Strazeele. Next day the march was continued to Bailleul, and on the 30th the Battalion joined up with the rest of its brigade which was now concentrated at Armentières ; here the party under Major Caldwell came in.

For about a week now the Battalion was attached to a unit of the 50th Division for instruction in trench duties, and it was during this time that the first casualty occurred, Private Flanagan, of " B " Company, being shot through the head while undergoing instruction in the front line.

On the 6th October the Battalion moved into brigade reserve at Le Bizet, remaining here for a week at the disposal of the R.E., busied in improving the communication trenches and the reserve line. From the 13th to the 20th the Battalion was up in the front line and the guns were busy on both sides, and even when in reserve again at Le Bizet the companies were under heavy shelling.

On the 26th October there was some re-shuffling of the component parts of brigades and divisions. Sir John French had from the first been very averse to the employment in the field of " inexperienced divisions," such as those of the New Army which were now arriving in France ; and after the Battle of Loos several of the new divisions were stiffened by some of their battalions being exchanged for battalions of the Regular Army. " Thus the 17th Brigade of the 6th Division took the place of the 71st Brigade in the 24th Division and then exchanged one battalion with each of the 72nd and 73rd Brigades. In the 62nd, 63rd and 64th Brigades of the 21st Division, one battalion each was exchanged, the 1st Lincolnshire and 4th Middlesex from the 3rd Division, and 1st East Yorkshire from the 6th Division, being received in their places. Similarly the 2nd, 3rd, 5th, 7th and 8th Divisions made exchanges with the 33rd, 25th, 32nd, 30th and 23rd Divisions." *

As a result of the above the 76th Brigade was removed from the 25th

* *Military Operations, France and Flanders,* 1915, Vol. II, p. 274.

Division, in which the 7th Brigade from the 3rd took its place ; the composition of the 7th Brigade now appears to have been as follows : the
10th Bn. The Cheshire Regiment, 3rd Bn. The Worcestershire Regiment,
1st Bn. The Wiltshire Regiment, and the 8th Bn. The Loyal North
Lancashire Regiment.

On the transfer of the Battalion from the 74th to the 7th Brigade the
following complimentary farewell order was issued by the Brigadier :—

" On the departure of the 8th Bn. The Loyal North Lancashire Regiment
to join the 7th Infantry Brigade, the G.O.C. 74th Brigade desires to place
on record his appreciation of the good work all ranks have performed since
the raising of the Battalion. He is sure that the Battalion will under all
circumstances uphold the traditions and reputation of the noble Regiment
to which they belong, and in saying farewell he wishes the officers, non-
commissioned officers and men all good fortune in the future."

During the latter part of November some very useful reconnaissance
work was carried out by 2nd Lieutenants Ramsay and Howard and on
one occasion when a patrol returned and one of the party was found to
be missing, every man of the patrol volunteered to go back and search for
him, in spite of the fact that it was now bright moonlight and the German
trenches were only a hundred yards distant : fortunately the missing man
turned up just as the search party was moving out. 2nd Lieutenant
Ramsay was wounded about this time.

The weather had now turned bitterly cold and the length of the tour
of duty in the trenches was reduced to five days. Very wet weather was
experienced at the beginning of December and the parapets and many ·
of the dug-outs fell in.

On the 11th a message was received from the G.O.C. 74th Brigade
reporting a gallant act by No. 13431 Corporal McCullough, of the Battalion,
who was employed with a Salvage Section in Armentières. A house
in the town was set on fire by a shell and a woman was said to be inside
the building, when the Corporal dashed in through the flames and rescued
her.

Lieutenant Jones was slightly wounded on the 12th December, and
2nd Lieutenant Howard on the 20th.

At Christmas time the Battalion was in divisional reserve at Papot,
and all were greatly cheered by the receipt of presents of all kinds from
friends in England ; and so the first Christmas to be spent by the Battalion ·
at the front came to an end, and the New Year was inaugurated by
a tolerably heavy bombardment being opened from both sides.

The month of January, 1916, was spent by the Battalion in the same
area, subject to considerable shelling by the enemy, and during this period

Captain G. E. C. Clark and four other ranks were killed, while Captain W. Furness and four men were wounded. In the last week in January the 25th Division was relieved by the 9th and withdrew into corps reserve, the Battalion marching by La Crèche to Outtersteene, where intensive training of all kinds commenced, special instruction being given in the handling and use of grenades and of the Lewis gun.

On the 14th February Lieut.-Colonel W. H. Biddulph left the Battalion and went home, Major A. F. S. Caldwell taking over the command from him.

About this time a return was published in the Division giving the number of men per battalion who had been admitted to hospital from the 15th October to the 31st January ; the 8th Battalion, The Loyal North Lancashire Regiment, came out well at the head of this list, having had no more than sixty-seven admissions, the 9th Battalion coming next with 104, while the admissions among the other battalions of the Division were considerably higher, one battalion having no fewer than 255 !

Two subaltern officers joined on the 13th, 2nd Lieutenants A. Sumner, from the 3rd, and W. V. Brunger, from the 11th Battalion of the Regiment, and on the 27th Major G. B. Marriott, Royal Warwickshire Regiment, took over the command of the Battalion.

During the latter part of February there had been several rumours that the Division was to move to another area, but these had come to nothing : on the 9th March, however, definite orders for a move were received, for the 25th Division was to be transferred from the II. to the XVII. Corps area, and on the following day the Brigade left Outtersteene and marching through Vieux Berquin, Merville, Calonne, Robecque, Busnes, La Perrière, Lillers, Berbure, Pernes and Hestrus, the Battalion reached billets in Maizières on the 14th, where the 25th Division was for a time in corps reserve.

The following farewell order was published by the II. Corps Commander :—

" On the departure of the Division from the II. Corps, I would like to express my great regret at the severance of our connection, and my sincere congratulations and thanks for all the good work that the Division has done during the last six months. Commanders of all grades, staff and units, have worked most loyally and whole-heartedly, and I know that they will keep up the reputation which the Division has already made for itself.

" I wish the Division the best of luck and success in the future."

After the arrival of the 7th Brigade at Maizières, the Brigadier issued the following, which was published in Battalion Orders of the 16th March :—

" The Brigadier wishes it to be known by the Battalion that he is very pleased at the way in which they have performed the marches.

"The Battalion has marched better than any other in the Brigade. He is particularly pleased with those men who, though they had bad feet, stayed the marches without falling out. This, he considers, shows a proper spirit."

At the end of March two companies were sent to Maroeuil, under the command of Major Caldwell, to provide carrying parties for the 51st Division; here the remaining companies of the Battalion joined up on the 11th April, and a few days later the whole went up to the trenches in front of Mont St. Eloi, relieving there a battalion of the 46th Division. Opposite this part of the line the enemy now began to show considerable activity, his bombardment being at times exceptionally heavy, and during the month the Battalion had five men killed, 2nd Lieutenant A. Marshall and thirty other ranks wounded.

On the night of the 18th–19th May the Germans, by a sudden attack, succeeded in capturing certain of our posts about what was known as "Broadmarsh Crater," and the Battalion was thereupon ordered to provide, on the evening of the 19th, a party one hundred strong to counter-attack and endeavour to recover the lost ground. Our guns bombarded the Crater until 9.15 p.m., when the barrage lifted and the Battalion's parties went "over the top."

No. 1. Party, twenty strong, under 2nd Lieutenant Howard, was to crawl forward in two lines, each of ten men, to within twenty yards of the enemy position, and was then to charge home with the bayonet, rifle fire and the bombs which each man carried, being only used if absolutely necessary.

No. 2. Party, of the same strength, under 2nd Lieutenant Tatam, was to leave the front trench when No. 1. Party commenced to charge, carrying a good supply of bombs, and also sandbags for consolidating the position when recaptured. To this party ten more men were attached whose duty it was to see that a good supply of bombs was kept up, passing these along to the men in front by a small trench running to the right of the Crater.

No. 3. Party. Fifty men, under 2nd Lieutenant Walsh. These were to be held in reserve and to be employed to follow up and complete the work of consolidation. A Lewis gun was to provide covering fire from a block half-way up the small communication trench running up to the right of the Crater; this block was between the British and German trenches.

On the attack opening, No. 1. Party left the trench and 2nd Lieutenant Howard very skilfully led his men unobserved to within twenty yards of the enemy position, then charging with a cheer. The officer was almost at once wounded by a bomb, when Sergeant Powell took charge of the party which gained the lip of the Crater, holding it under heavy fire. 2nd

Lieutenant Walsh now came up from the rear and took charge of the further operations which he conducted with much skill and judgment.   The Germans had now decamped in great haste, leaving behind much ammunition and some rifles.   The enemy guns now, however, opened a terrific bombardment of our trenches, keeping it up for some three-quarters of an hour, but the casualties therefrom were not heavy.

On the position being taken consolidation at once began, while a constant stream of bombs was hurled into the enemy trenches ; and then in the early morning of the 20th the original party was relieved by a fresh one under 2nd Lieutenant Kewley, and the work of consolidation was continued.

In these operations the Battalion's casualties were, killed or died of wounds, 2nd Lieutenants L. C. Tatam and C. C. Howard and seven other ranks, wounded were Captain A. T. Marsden, 2nd Lieutenant G. R. Kewley and eighteen non-commissioned officers and men, while four men were missing.

During the 21st the German guns fired very heavily, communication with our front line was cut off, and about 7.30 p.m. the Germans exploded a mine a few yards to the south of Broadmarsh Crater and then attacked in successive lines of infantry.   The fire of the Battalion did great execution and fighting was heavy and prolonged with rifle, bomb and bayonet.   The ammunition and bomb supply at last began to run out, but the men of the 8th Battalion, The Loyal North Lancashire Regiment, held their ground admirably led by Lieutenant Jones, Sergeant Grayson and Corporal Coates, and the men were at last reduced to " bombing " the Germans with lumps of chalk, flint and even empty bomb boxes !

The men now began to fall back, halting whenever possible to stay the German advance, and the advanced position was finally evacuated about 10 p.m.

The German attack on Broadmarsh Crater was part of an assault on the whole front of the brigade on the left, and the enemy succeeded in occupying both the line of resistance and the support line.   About 10 p.m. the Battalion was ordered to counter-attack, but the only information to hand was that the battalion on the left was holding a support trench running from the main communication trench on the left of the 7th Brigade, while the enemy was believed to be in possession of nearly all the other front lines.   The Battalion was to deploy in front of a small trench connecting Central and Lassalle communicating trenches and attack with the bayonet alone at 2 p.m. on the 22nd, the Division on the left attacking at the same hour.

The Battalion had deployed for attack by 1.45 a.m. under command of Major F. G. Wynne, and began to crawl forward under shell and machine-gun fire, when the Germans commenced to fall back to the line in rear. The Battalion losses had by this been heavy, part of the line was checked by uncut wire, and there being as yet no sign of any attack by our troops on the left, Major Wynne decided to advance no further.   Parties were, however, pushed out to make blocks, no Germans being encountered, and the whole line was strengthened and made as defensible as possible, and the position was held until 8.45 p.m. when the Battalion was relieved by the 3rd Bn. Worcestershire Regiment and withdrew to dug-outs in rear.

The casualties on the night of the 21st–22nd had been by no means light, especially in officers, Lieutenants R. B. B. Jones and E. J. Nicholls being killed; while Captain T. M. Foote, Lieutenants L. T. Taylor (later died of wounds) and F. Gregory, 2nd Lieutenants W. V. Brunger, R. D. Muir and W. J. Whitehead being wounded; of the other ranks twenty-seven were killed, 103 were wounded and fifteen were missing.

By the end of the month the whole Division was withdrawn to a rest area at Monchy Breton.

On the 27th May the following Special Order of the Day was published by the Commander of the Second Army :—

" The Army Commander has read with interest and pleasure the account of the successful attack on the Broadmarsh Crater carried out by a party of the 8th Loyal North Lancashire Regiment on the night of the 19th–20th May.   Please convey the Army Commander's congratulations to all the troops who took part in the operations."

The 25th Division spent the greater part of June training to the west of St. Pol, but in the last week of that month it moved south to join the Fourth Army ; and when the Battle of the Somme opened on the 1st July the Division lay about Warloy, some four miles behind the front line, being, with the 13th Division, in the Fourth Army Reserve.   The Battalion was on the 1st July at Lealvillers, when orders were received to move to Force-ville, to make room for the 38th Division.

On the night of the 2nd the 7th Brigade was transferred to the X. Corps and proceeded to Aveluy Wood where it was held in corps reserve ; but on the night of the 3rd the whole Brigade moved up to the front and relieved the 14th Brigade in the trenches, the Battalion, however, forming the brigade reserve in dug-outs at Crucifix Corner.   Here it remained until the 7th subjected, periodically, to rather heavy shelling ; and on the afternoon of the 5th all ranks experienced a great personal loss, the Rev. Father D. O'Sullivan, attached to the Battalion, being killed by a shell outside the advanced dressing station of the 75th Field Hospital.

At about 2 p.m. on the 7th orders were received for the Battalion to move from Crucifix Corner up to the front line, " A " and " B " Companies going up first, while " D " moved into trenches near Campbell Post in the support line in front of Aveluy village, and " C " was placed at the disposal of the O.C. 3rd Worcestershire Regiment. " A," " B " and " C " were later moved into the trenches of the Leipzic Salient, which had that morning been captured by the Wiltshire Regiment. At 8.30 p.m. " D " Company was also sent into the Salient, and the defence of this position was taken over from the Worcestershire Regiment. This position was no easy one to hold, particularly as the Battalion had taken it over in the dark ; no attack, however, transpired, and the night passed quietly except for some desultory shelling and sniping, and the Battalion was relieved in the early morning of the 8th, having had two officers and five men killed or died of wounds, thirty-four men wounded and two missing. The officers were 2nd Lieutenants T. White and P. Walsh.

During the 8th, and part of the 9th, the 7th Brigade was near Albert in support of the two other brigades of its division, which were then hold-ing the newly-won German line about Ovillers and La Boisselle ; but on the afternoon of the 9th the Battalion was sent up to take over an advanced position of the trench system immediately south of Ovillers, relieving there part of the 74th Brigade, which had been working under another division ; and the 25th Division now occupied the front previously held by the 12th Division, with the 19th and 32nd Divisions on the right and left respectively.

On the 10th July attacks were made northwards towards Ovillers by the 7th and 74th Brigades, that by the latter being the more successful of the two.

" About 1 p.m.," so the Battalion War Diary records, " orders were received to occupy several points in the enemy line running across our front and joining our trenches on the right. At 2.30 p.m. an advance was made from our block and a heavy hostile barrage was opened on the trench, but in spite of very large casualties we reached Point 25, where we were held up by enemy bombing parties, and heavy shelling and bombing continued for about two hours without any gain on either side.

" The enemy then tried to outflank us, both on right and left, moving across the open, but was driven off and the night passed quietly, a block being established just short of Point 25. A detached post under Sergeant Holmes of ' C ' Company on the left of our line held its ground all day, although it experienced many casualties and no supports could reach it. The post was relieved during the night of the 10th–11th. The enemy had shown signs of massing for a counter-attack at various points, notably at Pozières Wood, and, our artillery being informed of this, opened a heavy bombardment, causing serious loss to the enemy.

" It is believed that at one time the Battalion was opposed by no fewer than three Prussian battalions.

" Desultory shell fire was continued until the Battalion was relieved in the front line on the evening of the 11th, moving back into dug-outs in La Boisselle."

The casualties in the Battalion had been heavy : 2nd Lieutenants H. Day, C. E. Pringle, H. T. Emerson, G. H. Grimshaw and thirty-three other ranks were killed ; Major F. G. Wynne, Captains O. H. Hadley and H. C. Bennett, Lieutenants H. Haworth and A. Sumner and 156 men were wounded, while forty-nine other ranks were missing, " believed killed."

The Battalion was brought forward again after a very brief interval, in order to provide a carrying party for an attack which the 10th Cheshire Regiment was to make on the 14th, in conjunction with the 75th Brigade, with a view of capturing a line of trenches to the south of Ovillers. The attack duly took place at eleven o'clock at night on this date, and the line of German trenches was reached, but had to be vacated as it was swept by enemy machine-gun fire from above ; none the less a few casualties were incurred, Captain A. N. Falkner, Lieutenant P. R. Shields and eleven men being wounded, while three were killed and four were missing.

The 7th Brigade was relieved on the 15th by the 74th, which the same day effected the capture of Ovillers, and the Division was then withdrawn for a few days to rest and refit in the neighbourhood of Authie, the 7th Brigade being in huts in the Bois de Warnimont. Here two drafts joined the Battalion, the one of sixty, the other of ninety men, mostly of other regiments. At the end of July the Battalion was at Engelbelmer, where two more drafts arrived of 138 and 214 other ranks respectively.

The London Gazette of the 5th August, 1916, announced the award of the Victoria Cross to Lieutenant R. B. B. Jones, 8th Battalion, " for most conspicuous bravery " on the night of the 21st–22nd May.

The 25th Division during the early days of August was holding a sector of the line from the River Ancre northwards, and took no part in any offensive operations, moving back again on the 10th for rest and training to the Bois-les-Artois. On the 24th two companies of the Battalion took part with two battalions of the Brigade in an attack on the main Hindenburg trench ; but when on the 26th the 7th Brigade was relieved, the Battalion remained up in the line, having been " placed at the disposal of the 75th Brigade in order to attack a small pocket of Germans who were still holding on to a small portion of the Hindenburg trench on our left. The belief that the remnants of the enemy's garrison was demoralized through want of food and water and therefore likely to surrender was unfounded. An attack by ' D ' Company, 8th Loyal North Lancashire, under Captain Cash with Lieut. May and Lieut. Copeman, was made at 6 p.m. The information as to the condition of the garrison of this strong post, called the Wunderwerk, turned out to be incorrect, and the enemy was very much more numerous and better prepared for resistance than had been expected. The first wave succeeded in entering the enemy's position, but though reinforced by a second and third wave the North Lancashire were unable to maintain themselves and were finally forced to retire to their original line, Captain G. E. Cash and Lieut. S. H. May being killed.

" The 26th August the 74th Brigade was relieved by troops of the 49th Division." *

The Battalion's losses in this engagement were, killed, or missing and believed killed, four officers and eighty-five other ranks, while wounded were three officers and 181 other ranks.

The following was received on the 30th from the Corps Commander, Lieut.-General Jacob : " The Corps Commander has read the report of the minor operations carried out on the afternoon of the 26th inst. by the 8th Battalion, The Loyal North Lancashire Regiment. The attack, although unsuccessful, was carried out most gallantly ; the arrangements made by the Battalion commander were good, and it was due to no fault of his or his men that the operations failed. While regretting the heavy casualties, the Corps Commander congratulates Lieut.-Colonel Marriott and all ranks of the 8th Bn. The Loyal North Lancashire Regiment, on the spirit and gallantry with which the attack was made. The men fought splendidly and their work was worthy of high praise."

" The Divisional Commander thoroughly agrees with the remarks of the Corps Commander. Please communicate to O.C. 8th Bn. The Loyal North Lancashire Regiment."

During the first three weeks of September the 25th Division remained in a rest camp near Abbeville, commencing to move back to the forward area about the 25th. During the previous fortnight Thiepval had been captured and our troops held a line approximately east and west along the Thiepval Spur ; from the right of the divisional front we had observation over the Grandcourt valley, but on the left, from Stuff Redoubt west-wards, the Germans held the crest of the ridge. Several minor operations were now undertaken with a view to the capture of the high ground north of Stuff Redoubt and to push forward posts to obtain fuller observation over the Grandcourt valley. One such attack was made on the 9th October by the 10th Cheshire Regiment of the 7th Brigade ; on the following day this unit was relieved by the Battalion, when preparations were made for

* Kincaid-Smith, *The 25th Division in France and Flanders*, p. 17.

a further attack on the high ground known as "The Mounds" immediately north of the Stuff Redoubt.

Before, however, this attack was launched, the Germans made a very determined attempt to recapture Stuff Redoubt, coming forward with great resolution on the evening of the 12th October; and by the use of special "Storm Troops" he gained a footing at one point of the line, but was finally ejected, having suffered many casualties. In the Battalion, however, Captain E. S. Underhill was killed, 2nd Lieutenant J. F. Holden died of wounds, Captain H. D. Copeman, M.C., and Lieutenant L. B. Panchard were wounded, and eighty-eight other ranks were killed or wounded.

"The attack was finally carried out by 'A' and 'B' Companies of the 8th Loyal North Lancashire at 2.46 p.m. on the 14th, although at 2.40 p.m., just before our attack was timed to begin, the Germans put down a heavy barrage on our position. This was carried out by 'A' and 'B' Companies under Captain Shields, with Lieut. Bolton and Lieut. Turner. The distance to be covered was roughly 200 yards, but the left party, under Lieut. Alford, had further to go before reaching their objective. The artillery was most effective and the men kept well up to the barrage. It was afterwards learnt from prisoners that the enemy had observed our troops preparing to advance, but the German officer in command, however, appears to have thought that no attack was contemplated and to have ordered the enemy's artillery to stop firing by 2.40 p.m.

"When our barrage was put down at 2.46 p.m. the enemy's barrage had died down, and our troops gained their objective with but slight casualties. This fine piece of work resulted in the capture of one officer and one hundred German prisoners, as well as several machine-guns, and also gave us the required observation all along the ridge." *

On this day eight men of the Battalion were killed, while Lieutenant P. L. Bolton and twenty other ranks were wounded.

During the last week of October the 25th Division was relieved and moved back to the neighbourhood of Doullens, being thus transferred from the Fifth to the Second Army, and moved on the 29th October to the Bailleul area, the Battalion being quartered in billets about Nieppe. But before leaving the Fifth Army, in which it had been fighting on and off for four months, the following message was received from the Army Commander :—

"It is with great regret that the Commander of the Reserve Army bids farewell to Major-General Bainbridge and the 25th Division. This Division has the proud distinction of having served longer in the Somme Battle than any other in the Army. During the last four months it has been

* *The 25th Division in France and Flanders*, pp. 19, 20.

successful in many engagements, has taken many prisoners and has inflicted very heavy losses upon the enemy.   These successes are due to good leadership and sound organization in the higher ranks, and to a spirit of cheerfulness, courage and resolution in the junior ranks, officers and men. It has every reason to be proud of these achievements and this spirit.''

On the 31st October the 25th Division took over the Ploegsteert sector, which had a frontage of some 6,000 yards, the line extending from the River Lys on the right to Hill 63 on the left ; this last was later taken over by the Ulster Division, when St. Yves became the normal boundary of the divisional front.   The line was held by two brigades of the Division in front and one in reserve about Bailleul.

The sector now for some months to be held by the 25th Division was a comparatively quiet one ; when first taken over the trenches were in a very bad state, drainage being practically non-existent, but very much was done to improve them, both from a defensive and hygienic point of view, while the Division remained in occupation.

During November and December the casualties remained low, 2nd Lieutenant A. P. Hill and six men only being wounded during the last month of the year ; while four drafts, amounting in all to 250 non-commissioned officers and men, joined the Battalion, but the majority of these are noted as '' untrained,'' and were consequently not fitted for employment in the front-line trenches.

In January, 1917, four more small drafts arrived, these amounting to one officer and 147 other ranks.   Then, on the 24th February, the Division was withdrawn from the line and moved back to the training area in the neighbourhood of St. Omer, the Battalion being in billets in farms in the Berthen area, where every advantage was taken for training in musketry and especially in field firing.   Before, however, the Battalion moved back a few casualties had been incurred, Acting Captain Smith and Lieutenant J. S. Hill, M.C., being wounded among others.

On the 21st March the Division was transferred to the II. Anzac Corps, at once moving up into corps reserve in the Merris and Caestre area ; and a week later it relieved the New Zealand Division in the Wulverghem sector, where it was called upon to supply large working parties for road-making, cable-burying and constructing shelters and bomb-proof dug-outs, in view of the offensive which was expected to be shortly opened.   At the end of March the Battalion was quartered in Kortepyp Camp.

During April there were many changes of quarters ; from Kortepyp Camp to Neuve Eglise, thence to La Crèche, from there to Le Bizet, then for a brief period holding a portion of the front line from the River Lys to Le Gheer, back again to Le Bizet, and then to St. Marie Cappel and

Noote Boom ; and finally at the end of the month moving into the Strazeele area, where the Division was once more in corps reserve.   Here it remained until the 11th May, when it again relieved the New Zealand Division in the Wulverghem sector, all ranks making ready to play their part in the approaching battle for the Messines–Wytschaete Ridge.

At the beginning of June the Battalion was up in the line, when orders were received to carry out a raid on the enemy position known as Nutmeg Trench and Nutmeg Reserve, and " D " Company, one hundred strong, with Captain S. Ramsay and 2nd Lieutenant E. S. Williams, was told off to carry out the enterprise in collaboration with a party of equal strength provided by the 3rd Worcestershire Regiment.   The object of the raid was to examine the enemy defences and obtain identifications.   The raid made by the Battalion failed of its purpose, owing to the party coming under our own barrage and having to retire, Captain Ramsay, who was in command of the first wave, being killed.   Lieutenant Williams again went forward with a strong patrol for the object of recovering Captain Ramsay's body, but the Germans were by this time well on the alert, the party could not get far out and Lieutenant Williams was killed on the way back to the lines.

" On the 7th June, 1917, the Second Army attacked with three Army Corps the German defences along the line of hills from Messines to Wytschaete.   The capture of this line by the British troops was necessary before any attack could be developed further north and to the east of Ypres. . . .   The front of attack allotted to the 25th Division extended from the Wulverghem–Messines road to the Wulverghem–Wytschaete road. The New Zealand Division attacked on the right and the 36th Division on the left of the 25th Division respectively.   The objective of the 25th Division lay in front of the village of Wulverghem and comprised the strip of ground with a front of about 1,200 yards on the German front line to a depth of about 3,000 yards, but narrowing towards the top of Messines ridge to about 700 yards.   A short forward slope followed by a descent into the Steenebeek valley.

" From this point the ground rises steeply, flanked on either side by Hell Farm and Sloping Roof Farm, with Four Huns Farm, Chest Farm, Middle Farm on the crest of the ridge, and Lumms Farm a little further on to our left front.   These farms, both naturally and tactically strong points, had been converted by military science into positions of immense strength and importance. . . .   Along this line of advance, which was considerably deeper than the ground to be covered by the New Zealand Division on the right, there lay nine distinct lines of enemy trenches to be stormed and captured." *

* *The 25th Division in France and Flanders*, pp. 50, 51.

The 25th Division was to attack with two brigades in line, the 74th on the right, the 7th on the left and the 75th in reserve, and each brigade had two battalions in the front line, in the 7th the 8th Loyal North Lancashire was on the left and the 3rd Worcestershire on the right.

By midnight on the 6th the Battalion was in its assembly position in Onslow and Fusilier Trenches, and at 3.10 a.m. on the 7th, following the explosion of several mines and under cover of an intensive bombardment, the attack was launched. The objectives of the two leading battalions of the 7th Brigade—Nutmeg Trench and Nutmeg Reserve Trench—were captured with small loss seven and a half minutes after the start, and the whole Division then swept irresistibly forward, capturing the Ridge and penetrating about 6,000 yards into the enemy's position.

In this advance the Battalion companies were commanded as under :—

" A," Lieutenant Andrews, " B," Captain Hadley, " C," Lieutenant G. W. Tollett, and " D " by Captain C. P. Tindall-Atkinson.

The battalions of the 75th Brigade now passed through those of the 7th, which remained consolidating the position arrived at, and the 75th Brigade, moving on, captured the furthest objective. The Battalion remained in its position all through the 7th and 8th, and on the evening of this day it was ordered forward and took over from the 75th Brigade what was known as " the dotted line." Just at the hour appointed for the advance the enemy opened a very heavy shell fire, but on this slackening about 10 p.m. the Battalion moved up and then relieved the 11th Bn. Cheshire Regiment, the relief, however, owing to inexperienced guides and want of preliminary reconnaissance, not being completed until 3.15 a.m. on the 9th. Here the Battalion remained, subject to considerable enemy shelling, until the night of the 11th–12th, when on relief it marched back to camp near Wulverghem.

During the period from the 6th to the 12th the Battalion had lost thirty-six non-commissioned officers and men killed, four officers and ninety-eight other ranks wounded and seven men missing. The wounded officers were Captain O. H. Hadley, Lieutenant A. H. Chaworth-Musters, 2nd Lieutenants E. V. Everard and J. A. Grant.

The Division was again brought up to the front to carry out a further attack on the 14th and advance the line about 800 yards beyond the line then held by the II. Anzac Corps, the front of attack allotted to the Division being one of 1,500 yards between the Blauwepostbeek and the La Douve River. This attack was made by the 75th Brigade, the 7th being in support, and the battalions of the latter being employed in the digging of communication trenches in the forward zone. There was continuous enemy shelling, but casualties in the Battalion were happily but few.

During the night of the 22nd–23rd the 25th Division was finally with-drawn from this sector of the line, and on the 24th moved back for a pro-longed and well-earned rest to the Bomy area, south of St. Omer.

Of the capture of Messines Ridge, General Haig wrote in his despatch of the 25th December, 1917 : " The position assaulted was one of very great natural strength, on the defence of which the enemy had laboured incessantly for nearly three years. Its position, overlooking the Ypres Salient, was of the greatest tactical and strategical value to the enemy. The excellent observation he had from this position added enormously to the difficulty of our preparation for the attack and ensured to him ample warning of our intentions."

" As soon as the attack and capture of the Messines and Wytschaete Ridge had been successfully accomplished on the 7th June and the follow-ing days, preparations were made for the main offensive east and north of Ypres. On the 10th June the Fifth Army took over command from Boesinghe to the north with the II., XIX., XIV. and XVIII. Corps. The 25th Division, which had been resting round Bomy, fifteen miles south of St. Omer, since the 24th June, moved up on the 7th and 8th July by route march and omnibus to Ypres and the II. Corps' forward area, with the ex-ception of the 74th Brigade, which remained. in the training area for another fortnight." *

The Battalion commenced its move on the 6th July and on the evening of the 9th took up its quarters in Ypres, where the 1st Wiltshire Regiment was also accommodated, the other two battalions going up into the line in the Hooge sector. During the final march to Ypres, the road followed by the Battalion was very heavily shelled, and one shell fell close to the headquarter party, killing Regimental Sergeant-Major Proctor and causing eight other casualties ; another enemy shell exploded almost immediately afterwards and killed Major T. M. Foote, who was moving along the road.

Four days were spent in Ypres, where all roads and approaches and gun positions were constantly and heavily shelled, while a number of casual-ties were caused by gas shells, and the Battalion had here its first experience of the new " mustard gas " employed by the Germans.

On the night of the 14th–15th the Battalion went up to the right sub-sector of the Brigade front, and on the 18th a raid was carried out by one hundred men of " C " Company under 2nd Lieutenants H. Brown and S. D. Appleby, the objectives being the enemy's front line and support trenches known as " Ignorance " and " Support " Trenches, and the idea being to capture Germans, destroy trenches and secure identifications.

The raid started at 10.30 p.m. and reached the German trenches, which

_____
* *The 25th Division in France and Flanders*, p. 87.

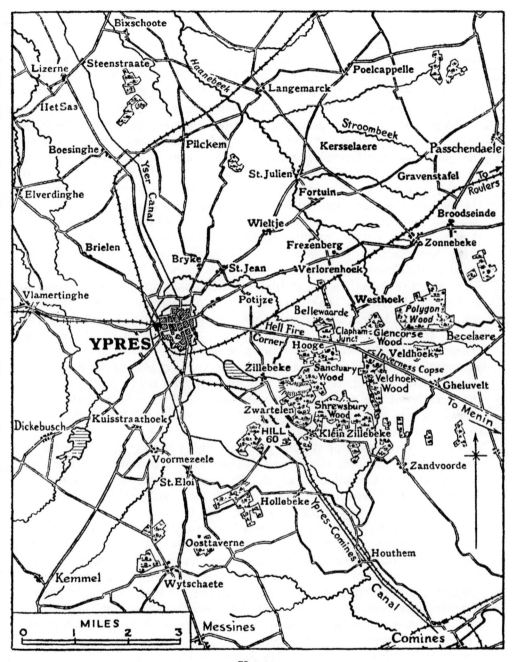

YPRES.

———

1914–1918.

were, however, found to be unoccupied. The dug-outs were bombed and
the enemy then put down a heavy barrage on his own front and support
lines, causing many casualties among the raiding party, 2nd Lieutenant
Appleby and two men being killed, while 2nd Lieutenant Brown and nineteen other ranks were wounded and eleven men were missing.

Preparations for the proposed offensive were completed by the 26th
July, but the attack was postponed for a few days, and it was not until
the 30th that the Battalion moved forward from the Reninghelst area,
where for a day or two it had been resting and refitting, and marched to
Belgian Chateau, near Ypres, the concentration area of the 7th Brigade.
On the 31st the Fifth Army delivered its assault on the German main line
defences, the Second Army making a subsidiary attack on the right and
the First French Army moving forward on the left. " The front of the
Fifth Army attack extended from the Zillebeeke–Zandvoorde road to
Boesinghe inclusive, a distance of about seven and a half miles. The II.
Corps attacked with the 24th, 30th and 8th Divisions in the line, supported
by the 18th Division in the centre and the 25th Division on the left in corps
reserve " ; the last-named Division also acted in support of the 8th, which
was to attack the German front-line system, and the 25th was to push on
should the 8th Division gain its furthest objective. " The 7th and 75th
Brigades were held in readiness about 2,000 yards in rear of the assaulting
troops. As, however, the attack was unexpectedly held up on the right,
the brigades of the 25th Division were not called upon to undertake the
rôle previously assigned to them and to pass through the 8th Division and
to carry on the advance."

On the early morning of the 31st July the 7th Brigade moved up to
Halifax House dug-outs and remained there all the remainder of this day
and the whole of the following night. In broad daylight on the 1st August
the Battalion relieved a unit of the 8th Division on Westhoek Ridge, the
relief being carried out under some difficulties owing to the exact position
of the battalion to be relieved not being accurately known, while the whole
operation was executed in full view of the enemy, who was still holding
Glencorse Wood. Here the Battalion remained until the night of the
5th when it withdrew to Winnipeg Camp, having during this tour suffered
considerable hardship from the very inclement weather and the difficulty
of getting up supplies of all kinds, and also many casualties from the enemy ;
these amounted to seven officers and 147 other ranks, killed, wounded and
missing ; the seven wounded officers were Lieut.-Colonel A. F. S. Caldwell
(accidentally), Captain C. P. Tindall-Atkinson, Lieutenant A. Sumner, 2nd
Lieutenants P. J. Knight, A. M. Fairweather, R. V. Gilliatt and H. Hield.

" Owing to the incessant rain and bad weather conditions, the troops

HELL FIRE CORNER, MENIN ROAD.

1917.

Australian Official Photograph—Copyright.

in the front line were, during the next few days, relieved every forty-eight hours, and at the same time preparations were energetically pushed forward for another attack on the German line of defences along Inverness Copse, Glencorse Wood and the Westhoek Ridge. The capture of these positions was most important in order to give observation to the east and south-east."

During the next few days the 25th Division was not employed as a complete unit, its brigades, and even battalions, being made use of with other formations ; and the Battalion was not called forward again until the 29th August when the 7th Brigade was placed at the disposal of the G.O.C. 23rd Division, the Battalion and the 1st Wiltshire being directed to take over the line in the Clapham Junction area. On the 30th the Battalion moved up to the front-line neighbourhood in buses, and relieved a battalion of the 23rd Division in front of Glencorse Wood. Here the Battalion remained until the afternoon of the 5th when it was relieved, and the Division moved to the First Army area in the neighbourhood of Bethune, the Battalion being in billets at Burbure, near Steenbecque. During this last tour at the front one officer—2nd Lieutenant R. O. Weber—and eight other ranks had been killed or had died of wounds, while 2nd Lieutenant F. M. Taylor and fourteen men had been wounded.

On the 4th October the 25th Division " took over the Givenchy sector from the 2nd Division in the XI. Corps area, the divisional headquarters being at Locon, two and a half miles north of Bethune. All three brigades were in the line, with two battalions in front, one in support and one in reserve respectively ; the 7th Brigade on the right, the 75th in the centre and 74th on the left. The line held was approximately 8,000 yards, with the La Bassée Canal running almost through the centre of the 75th Brigade sector. Givenchy was the dominating position of the whole line, with the Aubers Ridge on the left front.

" During the seven weeks in which the Division was holding this front, nothing of importance occurred to put on record. No operations of any magnitude were undertaken and the work of the units in the line consisted in denying No-Man's-Land to the enemy by means of active patrolling every night. A few prisoners were taken, and the battalions likewise had slight losses whilst carrying out these tactics ; the enemy was also kept on the alert by constant heavy concentration of medium and heavy trench-mortar fire, assisted on one occasion by a Portuguese medium trench-mortar battery. The Portuguese Division was now holding the sector on our left, and all through November fresh Portuguese battalions were serving under our brigades for training purposes and to gain experience."

On the 1st December orders were received for the 7th Brigade to move with its Division to join the IV. Corps of the Third Army in the Somme area ; and on the 3rd the Battalion entrained at Wavrans and on the 9th relieved the 1st Northumberland Fusiliers of the 3rd Division in the left sub-sector of the trenches near Barastre, the Division being now in the Quéant area, due south of Bullecourt.

" The line, about 6,000 yards, was held with two brigades in front and one brigade in reserve. On the right the right sector of the IV. Corps was held by the 51st Division, and on our left we were in touch with the 59th Division of the VI. Corps. The front line in the sector consisted of a series of disconnected posts, with very few communication trenches. The Division now spent all its energies in digging a continuous front system, with several strong belts of wire, communication trenches and reserve lines. Owing to the very cold and frosty weather digging was extremely difficult, but in spite of this good results were obtained. Unfortunately when the frost broke, the trenches collapsed and for several days were quite impass-able. During these days all movements by troops on both sides was more or less above ground and in full view of one another." *

In these various activities the Battalion played its part, and when Christmas Day came round again—the last that the 8th Battalion, The Loyal North Lancashire Regiment, was to spend in France—the Brigade was in divisional reserve at Favreuil.

It had gone up into the line again at the end of January, 1918, and had just been relieved on the 1st February and withdrawn into brigade support, when intimation was received that the Battalion was to be disbanded. Within the next few days drafts of officers and men were sent away to other units of the Regiment—nine officers and 200 other ranks to the 9th (Service) Battalion in the 74th Brigade, 300 to the 2/4th and 230 to the 2/5th Battalions, and then on the 10th February what was left of the 8th Battalion marched to a camp at Courcelles where on the 16th it was absorbed into No. 5 Entrenching Battalion, ceasing on that date to exist as a separate and individual unit.

The heavy fighting of 1917 had resulted in an enormous casualty list ; divisions were now weak in numbers and the difficulty of supplying adequate reinforcements was daily increasing. The policy of disbanding certain battalions was inevitable, being the only means whereby other battalions in the field could be maintained at full strength ; all divisions were so affected.

---

* *The 25th Division in France and Flanders,* pp. 127, 128.

CHAPTER LIII

THE 9TH (SERVICE) BATTALION
THE LOYAL NORTH LANCASHIRE REGIMENT

1914–1918

THE BATTLES OF THE SOMME, PLOEGSTEERT, MESSINES, BAPAUME, LYS, SECOND BATTLE OF THE AISNE, KEMMEL

THE 9th (Service) Battalion of the Regiment was raised in September, 1914, and, as stated in the last chapter, was, under Army Order No. 388 of 1914, posted to the 74th Brigade of the 25th Division, the Brigade containing the 8th Bn. The King's Own (Royal Lancaster Regiment), and the 8th Bn. The East Lancashire Regiment, as well as the 8th and 9th Battalions of The Loyal North Lancashire Regiment. The Divisional Commander was Major-General F. Ventris and Brigadier-General A. J. W. Allen, C.B., was the Commander of the 74th Brigade.

The Army List for October, 1914, shows the following officers then serving in the 9th Battalion, with the dates of their appointments, and from this it would seem that the Battalion came into existence on the 19th September of this year.

Major (Temporary Lieut.-Colonel) C. E. M. Pyne	.	1st Oct., 1914.
2nd Lieutenant G. W. Anson	.	19th Sept., 1914.
,, ,, F. W. Simmons . . .	.	,, ,, ,,
,, ,, M. C. Perks . . .	.	,, ,, ,,
,, ,, J. H. P. Lindesay . . .	.	,, ,, ,,
,, ,, C. Dalziel	.	22nd Sept., ,,
,, ,, W. Furness	.	,, ,, ,,
,, ,, E. W. Hardman . . .	.	,, ,, ,,
,, ,, G. E. Cash	.	5th Oct., ,,
Lieutenant and Quartermaster R. M. Calvert .	.	22nd Sept., ,,

The Battalion remained training in various camps in England until the autumn of 1915, at which time the 74th Brigade was quartered at Aldershot, where the Battalion was occupying Blenheim Barracks.

On the 24th September the advance party and the Transport left under the command of Major W. A. Jupp, at a strength of three officers and 109 other ranks, and on arrival at Southampton crossed over from there to Havre. The remainder of the Battalion marched to Farnborough Station on the 25th under Lieut.-Colonel C. E. M. Pyne and left the same evening for Folkestone, and, embarking in the S.S. "St. Seiriol," crossed the Channel to Boulogne, and on arrival, very early on the 26th, marched to a rest camp two miles out of the town where some twenty-four hours were spent.

The strength of the 9th Battalion on arrival in France was twenty-seven officers and 889 non-commissioned officers and men.

The units composing the 25th Division were now hurriedly pushed up to the more forward area, and the Battalion, moving by rail and road and by way of Calais, St. Omer, Hazebrouck, Caestre, Strazelle and Bailleul, finally arrived in billets at Armentières on the 29th. Here the Transport and the advance party rejoined, and all ranks were attached by batches to various battalions of the 150th Brigade for instruction in trench duties. This instructional period lasted no more than a week, for on the 6th October the Battalion marched to Le Bizet, where it was held in reserve to the 11th Lancashire Fusiliers and 13th Cheshire Regiment, which were holding the front line of trenches. The Battalion itself moved up to the front on the 12th, remaining in occupation until the 20th, and during this time the first casualties of the war were incurred, four men being killed, or dying of wounds, while five were wounded.

In this sector the remaining weeks of the year were spent, and when Christmas Day came round the Battalion had just been relieved in the advanced trenches, and was back in reserve billets at Le Bizet.

Some time before the year 1916 opened, the reshuffling of battalions and brigades, mentioned in the previous chapter, as resulting from Sir John French's decision to " stiffen " some of the New Army Divisions, had taken place, and the 74th Brigade was now composed of the 2nd Bn. Royal Irish Rifles, the 11th Bn. Lancashire Fusiliers, the 13th Bn. Cheshire Regiment and the 9th Bn. The Loyal North Lancashire Regiment. The 76th Brigade had left the Division and its place had been taken by the 7th, to which the 8th Bn. Loyal North Lancashire had been transferred from the 74th Brigade. The 9th Battalion was now under the command of Lieut.-Colonel C. B. Messiter.

On the 19th January the Battalion took part in its first offensive operation of the war, being detailed to support an attack made by the 2nd Royal Irish Rifles on Le Touquet Salient, causing a diversion by means of a feint attack. The operation was entirely successful, but the Battalion had sixteen killed and wounded, including two officers—Lieutenant J. H.

Pullin and 2nd Lieutenant R. D. Robinson—the former dying of his wounds two days later.

Throughout the whole of February the Division remained in corps reserve, the Battalion being at Steenewerck, and while here five officers and forty-three other ranks joined for duty from the 25th Base Depot; the officers were Lieutenant C. C. Yates, 2nd Lieutenants B. J. Edwards, M. C. Perks, H. J. Priestland and J. Moser.

During the next three months the Battalion was a good deal moved about, periods in the front-line trenches alternating with stays in billets at Neuf Berquin, Ostreville, Tinques, Maizière and Camblain l'Abbé, and several officers joined and also some very small parties of men, either from England, or recovered sick and wounded from hospital. Among the officers who arrived were Major S. J. Jervis, Captains A. S. Walter and W. H. M. Wienholt, Lieutenant J. D. Crichton and 2nd Lieutenants R. W. K. Reid and T. H. S. Bullough. The casualties were, however, very numerous during the months of March, April and May, especially among the commissioned ranks, for Lieutenants C. C. Yates and R. Willis were killed in action; Captain A. C. Hay, Lieutenants C. P. Gillies, L. F. Jenkin, J. D. Crichton and F. G. Laurie, 2nd Lieutenants F. C. Happold, H. J. Priestland, C. W. Sayers, and E. U. Green were wounded.

The Battalion remained at Ostreville during the first half of June, and then, reinforced by the arrival of six officers—Captain O. S. Darby-Griffith, Lieutenant Robinson, 2nd Lieutenants Cooper, Stevens, Lanham and Tiley—the Battalion marched south with its Division to join the Fourth Army, and at the end of June it was at Warloy, about four miles behind the front line, where the 12th and 25th Divisions constituted the reserve for the Fourth Army.

Very shortly after arrival in this area the other two brigades of the 25th Division were placed at the disposal of other corps or divisions to assist in the operations of the Somme battle then in progress; but the 74th Brigade remained at Warloy until the night of the 3rd–4th July when it was moved to Bouzincourt in support of the 7th and 75th Brigades then up in the front line, where the 25th Division had just relieved the 32nd. "On the 5th July the 74th Brigade was detached and joined the 12th Division, taking over a sector of the line in the village of La Boisselle, which had been captured the previous day by the 19th Division. On the morning of the 7th it participated in an attack by the 12th Division on Ovillers and the trenches to the right across the Pozières road. The attack was carried out by the 9th North Lancashire and 13th Cheshire, with the 2nd Royal Irish Rifles and 11th Lancashire Fusiliers in support. The attacking battalions, after an intense bombardment from massed artillery of all calibres, moved forward at 8.5 a.m. and successfully reached their first objectives after heavy fighting. Mainly owing to the heavy losses, great difficulty was experienced in reaching the second objectives the same day, but, during the night of the 7th–8th and the following morning, bombing parties eventually established themselves in the enemy's line just south of the Pozières road." *

Up to this two at least of the brigades of the 25th Division had been working under other divisions, but from the 9th July on the Division worked as a whole, and it now took over the front lately held by the 12th Division, with the 19th and 32nd on its right and left. It went back to Beauval and neighbourhood for a rest on the 17th July and then from the 23rd July to the 10th August it occupied a sector of the line from the River Ancre northwards. During this time the brigades had no part in any actual offensive operations, but the Battalion experienced fresh losses early in August, 2nd Lieutenant J. Moser and seven men being killed, and 2nd Lieutenants Rodwell and Williams and ten other ranks being wounded. Later in the month 2nd Lieutenant S. R. F. Empey was killed by a bomb, and before the month came to an end Major R. M. Everett and 2nd Lieutenant E. Sonnenthal were wounded.

On the 11th September the Division was relieved by the 11th Division and marched back some twenty miles to a camp near Abbeville for rest and training, remaining here until the 25th when it began to move forward again to the front. The 74th Brigade remained in corps reserve during the attack on Thiepval, thereafter taking over a section of the line immediately south of the Ancre. At the beginning of October the Battalion was in reserve billets and dug-outs about Aveluy, but on the 5th moved up to the front and took over a line of front trenches, and at this time several subaltern officers were temporarily attached from other battalions. During the early attacks upon Stuff Redoubt the 74th Brigade was not actively employed, although there were several casualties from the enemy shells ; but preparations were during this time being pushed on for an attack upon Stuff and Redoubt Trenches.

It had originally been intended that this attack should be launched on the 19th, but by reason of bad weather it was postponed until the 21st, when at 12.6 p.m. the troops of the 74th and 75th Brigades moved out under cover of the barrage.

" Owing," so the Divisional History relates, " to the weakness of the battalions of the 74th Brigade, the assault was carried out by three battalions in the front line, going forward in three waves. The Lancashire Fusiliers on the right, 9th Loyal North Lancashire in the centre and the 13th Cheshire Regiment on the left, with the 2nd Royal Irish Rifles and

* *The 25th Division in France and Flanders*, pp. 12, 13.

1st Wiltshire in support. The four companies of the 9th Loyal North Lancashire were commanded by Lieut. Motherwell, 2nd Lieuts. Tiley, Wardle and Dobbyn. All the battalions kept well up to the rolling barrage and reached their objectives without much difficulty, but some stiff fighting took place in Regina Trench."

In the 9th Battalion War Diary it is stated that " at 12.6 p.m. the Battalion got out of Hessian Trench in three lines and crossed No-Man's-Land immediately behind the barrage, very few casualties occurring until we reached the enemy's wire, when a considerable amount of trouble was caused by an enemy machine-gun and snipers. This machine-gun was outside a dug-out in the Sunken Road and was put out of action by 2nd Lieut. G. M. Jones and three bombers, the gun being captured. Many prisoners were taken, chiefly from the Sunken-Road dug-outs, not many of the enemy being in the front line. About two hundred prisoners were taken, including one officer who said that he was a battalion commander. As soon as they had taken the trench the men did remarkably good work consolidating, and an outpost line was immediately organized and put out by 2nd Lieut. G. M. Jones. On the 22nd the Battalion was relieved and proceeded to the Rest Camp."

During the whole time the Battalion had been up in the trenches—fourteen days—the casualties numbered four officers and forty-eight other ranks killed, eight officers and 148 other ranks wounded and eighteen men missing. The officers who died were 2nd Lieutenants C. F. S. Brown, S. A. Talbot, G. C. Tiley and J. E. Motherwell; the wounded officers were Captains E. U. Green and O. S. Darby-Griffith, Lieutenant E. W. Taylor, 2nd Lieutenants F. Mitchell, G. M. Jones, H. Dobbyn, W. L. Kirkham and J. P. Oliver.

From the rest camp at Bouzincourt the Battalion moved by motor-bus to huts at Toutencourt, thence by march to billets at Beauval, from there to Candas and on by train to Caestre in the Second Army area ; here the following officers joined for duty : 2nd Lieutenants R. V. Read, W. S. Hartley, H. M. Coke, D. I. Lewis, R. C. Newth, T. E. Church and H. Everett.

On the 31st October the 25th Division took over the Ploegsteert sector, a frontage of some 6,000 yards, extending from the River Lys on the right to Hill 63 on the left, and here the Division remained until the middle of February, 1917, the sector being a comparatively quiet one.

Lieut.-Colonel C. B. Messiter, D.S.O., left the Battalion for duty in England on the 1st December, Lieut.-Colonel H. M. Craigie-Halkett from the 2nd South Lancashire Regiment assuming command in his place. Three drafts, totalling 244 men, arrived, and Christmas Day, 1916, was spent in the trenches about Ploegsteert Wood.

During the months of January and February, 1917, several subaltern officers joined the Battalion, but drafts appear to have been few ; among the officers were 2nd Lieutenants E. Leggatt, T. F. McCarthy, R. J. Court-hope-Wilson, G. C. Davis, R. C. S. Stark, F. Nuttall, T. G. Skingley, F. G. Edge, T. Sefton, W. A. Dundas, R. Hay, A. Cross and T. H. Elkington, while during the same period 2nd Lieutenant T. Davenport was wounded.

During the first half of the year 1917 the Division was considerably moved about ; on the 24th February to the training area about St. Omer ; on the 21st March it was transferred to the II. Anzac Corps and went into corps reserve in the Merris and Caestre areas ; a week later the Division took the place of the New Zealand Division in the Wulverghem sector ; on the 30th April it was once more withdrawn into corps reserve and remained there till the 11th May when it returned to the Wulverghem sector, having the good fortune to remain here holding the portion of the line allotted to it in the coming Messines battle.

During this latter period there was much activity along the whole front, many raids were organized and casualties were not few : on the 26th April Lieutenant M. C. Perks was killed in the trenches about Neuve Eglise.

The preliminaries of the Battle of Messines, and the objectives generally allotted to the 25th Division, have been stated in the preceding chapter dealing with the 8th Battalion, and it may be enough here to open the account of the part played by the 9th Battalion in the action, by recording that at 1.30 a.m. on the 6th June, when the 25th Division was assembled in order of battle, the 74th Brigade was on the right, with the 7th on its left and the 75th in reserve. The 2nd Royal Irish Rifles and the 13th Cheshire Regiment were on the right and left front of the 74th Brigade respectively, the 9th Loyal North Lancashire and the 11th Lancashire Fusiliers being on the right and left in support of them. The plan was that the two leading battalions of each of the front-line brigades were to capture all enemy trenches up to the Steenbeek, the two rear battalions following and passing through to the capture of the further objectives.

" Away on the right the 9th Bn. Loyal North Lancashire Regiment and the 11th Bn. Lancashire Fusiliers had left the assembly positions in artillery formation immediately behind the rear waves of the two leading battalions of their brigade. The four companies—' A,' ' B,' ' C ' and ' D ' of the 9th Bn. Loyal North Lancashire were commanded by Captain Laurie, Lieut. Pollitt, Captain Godfrey and Lieut. Lanham respectively. Unfortunately, the enemy's barrage caught the carrying parties of the leading companies, causing some casualties : however, passing through the leading battalions, the two battalions advanced across the Steenbeek, which was found to be dry and to present no serious obstacle.

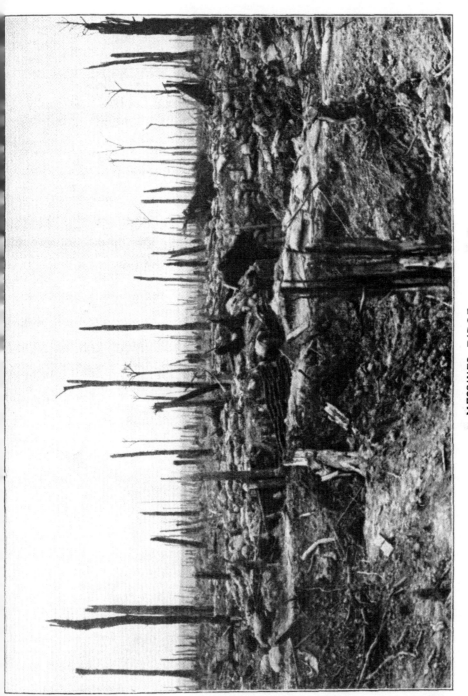

MESSINES RIDGE.

1917.

The Imperial War Museum—Copyright.

" The 11th Lancashire Fusiliers got two machine-guns, but little resistance was met with until the German support line was reached, when the 9th Bn. Loyal North Lancashire Regiment and 11th Bn. Lancashire Fusiliers each took two more machine-guns. . . . On the capture of their final objective the 9th Bn. Loyal North Lancashire and 11th Bn. Lancashire Fusiliers pushed forward outposts and consolidated a line of shell-holes in advance of their new position.

" Messines and the Ridge had been captured in one hour and forty minutes " * ; but not without very serious loss to the Battalion, in which Captain R. D. Robinson and seventy-seven other ranks were killed, twelve officers and 272 non-commissioned officers and men were wounded and six other ranks were missing. The wounded officers were Captain F. G. Laurie, Lieutenants G. R. Sharpe, H. J. Shipp, L. H. Lanham and M. W. Nolan, 2nd Lieutenants T. Sefton, T. Pollitt, R. Hay, A. Cross, W. A. Dundas, T. H. Elkington and R. L. Brock.

The Battalion was relieved on the 9th and went back to some trenches close in rear, returning, however, more than once to the front before, on the 25th, it marched to Radinghem in the Bomy area, south of St. Omer, for rest and training ; here 2nd Lieutenant L. A. Kemp joined the Battalion and also five drafts, totalling 255 non-commissioned officers and men.

Two of the brigades of the 25th Division moved in the first week of July to the forward area of the II. Corps about Ypres, but the 74th Brigade remained on in the training area for another fortnight and it was the 26th before the Battalion reached Abeele. Three of the battalions of the Brigade, including the 9th Loyal North Lancashire, were now placed at the disposal of the C.R.E., II. Corps, for work on the roads and in connection with the water supply, and did much very useful work during the days that followed, opening up communication with the forward line, digging communication trenches, and consolidating the new front line.

It was consequently not until the 4th August that the 74th Brigade rejoined its division, which was now holding the Westhoek and Bellewaarde Ridges, the 74th being in the front line, the 75th in support at Ypres, and the 7th Brigade in reserve west of Ypres.

" To complete the capture of the Westhoek Ridge was now "—10th August—" the task allotted to the 74th Brigade. On the right the 55th and 54th Brigades of the 18th Division had as their objectives the capture of Inverness Copse and Glencorse Wood. The 74th Brigade attacked with all four battalions in the front line, along a front of about 2,000 yards, with its left flank on the Ypres–Roulers railway.

" The assembly of the assaulting troops was complete by 3.25 a.m. on

* *The 25th Division in France and Flanders*, pp. 57, 58.

the 10th August. At 4.25 a.m. the whole line moved forward to the attack and was well clear of our line when the enemy's barrage came down a few minutes later." From right to left were the 13th Cheshire, 2nd Royal Irish Rifles, 9th Loyal North Lancashire and 11th Lancashire Fusiliers. "The four companies of the 9th Loyal North Lancashire, commanded by Captain W. F. Loudon, Captain E. U. Green, M.C., killed and succeeded by 2nd Lieut. L. A. Kemp, Lieut. H. J. Priestland, wounded and succeeded by 2nd Lieut. T. F. McCarthy, and Captain H. Everett respectively. The supporting artillery of five brigades R.F.A. opened simultaneously, and throughout the day replied with great promptitude to all signals for assistance against numerous attempted counter-attacks.

" The attack was a complete success in every way, and notwithstanding some severe fighting, particularly on the right, the whole Brigade was firmly established on its objectives by 5.30 a.m. Several strong points, pill-boxes and fortified houses garrisoned with machine-guns, offered considerable opposition, but were quickly rushed and captured by assaulting troops. . . . The Irish Rifles rushed Westhoek, together with the two strong points, and took the garrison before the enemy realized they were being attacked. The 9th Loyal North Lancashire advanced in three waves. The first company was held up by a strong point which they quickly surrounded, capturing a machine-gun and its detachment. The Battalion had many casualties from snipers, especially on the right flank. German aeroplanes flew low and fired on any bodies of troops moving in the open. . . .

" From first to last the plans and their execution reflected the greatest credit on all concerned. The progress of the troops was in exact accordance with the time-table previously laid down. . . .

" Private Seal, 9th Loyal North Lancashire Regiment, whilst carrying a message from brigade headquarters, was badly wounded by a shell in both legs and head. In spite of his wounds, this runner crawled on through the heavy bombardment and succeeded in delivering his message. He afterwards received the D.C.M." *

The officer casualties on this occasion were Captain E. U. Green, 2nd Lieutenants C. Lunt and H. H. Swift killed, and Lieutenant H. J. Priestland and 2nd Lieutenant H. C. W. Ferguson wounded.

The Battalion remained in the newly-won front line, with the other units of the 74th Brigade, subjected to several very determined counter-attacks by the enemy, until the night of the 11th–12th August, when they were relieved by the 75th Brigade, and about the 17th the 25th Division was withdrawn to the Steenwoorde and Eecke area. Here it remained until the beginning of September, when it moved to the front again and

* *The 25th Division in France and Flanders*, pp. 90–2.

relieved other divisions on the Westhoek Ridge and in the trenches in front of Glencorse Wood and Stirling Castle ; but on the 9th September the Division was moved once again, this time to the First Army area south of Bethune, where it remained for some three weeks or more engaged in reorganizing and training.

No events of any outstanding importance occurred during the last three months of the year, and January, 1918, was for the most part spent by the Battalion in a reserve camp in the Pronville sector.   Early in February the 8th Battalion of the Regiment was disbanded and its personnel was distributed among other units, on the 16th February ten officers from the 8th joining the 9th Battalion.   Two days later a draft, eighty-three strong, joined, so that the Battalion was now as strong as it had ever been.

At the end of the month the 25th Division was withdrawn to the Achiet-le-Petit area, some four miles to the north-west of Bapaume, the Battalion settling down for ten days or so in Buchanan Camp.   On the 12th March it moved to Fremicourt, and was still here when, later on in the month, the many rumours as to a probable German offensive were confirmed, and on the 21st the Battalion was sent forward to support the 51st Division, being detailed to assist the 153rd Brigade near the Beetroot Factory, north of the Cambrai–Bapaume road.

It had been expected that the 25th Division would be employed in counter-attack and certain objectives had been pointed out, but " events moved too rapidly for this plan to materialize, and, owing to the exigencies of the military situation, brigades and battalions of the Division were used piecemeal to reinforce the 51st and 6th Divisions.   In fact, from the opening phases of the battle up to a time six days later when the Division was finally withdrawn, it was fighting continuously under strange commanders and a strange staff."

The 74th Brigade had barely reached its position of support when it became clear that the advancing enemy had not only forced his way through our front defensive system, but in places was actually in the second line ; and the G.O.C. 51st Division now ordered the 74th Brigade to move forward and place itself outside the Cambrai–Bapaume road.   The 11th Lancashire Fusiliers were south of the road, " the 9th Loyal North Lancashire Regiment to the north of the road, ' A,' ' B,' ' C ' and ' D ' Companies being commanded by 2nd Lieut. E. M. Scott, Captain J. D. Crichton, Captain R. L. C. Keays and Captain H. Everett, with the 3rd Worcestershire in support about 1,000 yards behind.   The portion of the Corps line held by the 51st Division to their immediate front was, however, still intact.

" The position up to the evening of the 21st March was very favourable. The Corps line of defence was intact except in places at Vaulx Wood and

Maricourt Wood, where the enemy had effected a lodgment, and the casualties throughout all units of the Division had been comparatively slight. The night of the 21st–22nd March was mainly spent in reorganizing along the Corps line and getting ready for the battle next day.

"Enemy shelling began early, soon after dawn on the 22nd, and by 7.30 the first attack was well on its way all along the line. . . . From midday onwards, owing to reports received of the enemy massing astride the Bapaume–Cambrai road, the 9th Loyal North Lancashire were moved gradually up to reinforce the 6th Black Watch and 7th Gordons in that part of the Corps line immediately north of the road. The Germans were continually pressing on in large numbers, and very heavy casualties were inflicted on them by the 9th Loyal North Lancashire Regiment and other troops in this portion of the line. About 4 p.m. a small party of the enemy with machine-guns broke through on the left of the Battalion, and, with their numbers steadily increasing, the line north of the Bapaume–Cambrai road became intolerable ; Major F. M. King " (King's Royal Rifles, attached to the Battalion) " had been killed and many other officers and other ranks had become casualties, when the O.C. 9th Loyal North Lancashire decided to withdraw to the right and line the south side of the Bapaume–Cambrai road, with a view to a counter-attack on those of the enemy behind his line ; but before this could be organized and carried out, it was found that the Germans had also broken through south of the road. This increased their difficulties so much that by 5.30 p.m. most of the men were casualties and the remainder were successfully withdrawn in small parties to the new position.

" The 9th Loyal North Lancashire then moved south of the road, throwing back a defensive flank to face northwards in touch with the 6th Seaforths, 51st Division, in the Corps line south of the road. This battalion sent a company to reinforce the 9th Loyal North Lancashire, and the position was held till midnight, when orders were received to withdraw from this portion of the line. The remainder of the Battalion then took up a position on the south side of Beaumetz, facing north, until the following morning, when orders were received to withdraw to Fremicourt.

" ' D ' Company, during the first withdrawal, became detached from the Battalion and joined the 11th Lancashire Fusiliers, with whom it remained throughout the fighting of that day. Lieut. Brown and 2nd Lieut. Short led their men with great ability, and 2nd Lieut. Swift, for his excellent work in charge of the Battalion signallers, received the Military Cross. Sergeants Schofield, Cowap and Phillips received the D.C.M. for their exceptional coolness and courage when leading their platoons to reinforce the Corps line east of Morchies. Lance-Sergeant Jones and Private Llewellyn did fine work with their Lewis guns.   Private Crew as a Battalion runner and Privates Barnes, Livesay, Lowe and Glease and Lance-Corporal Goodwin were all conspicuous for their bravery and disregard of danger in attending to and bringing in wounded.   Corporal Atherton was responsible for rations reaching the men in the front line." *

The 74th Brigade had concentrated at Bihucourt, near Achiet, on the afternoon of the 23rd, and later dug in along the front just west of Bienvillers, crossing the Bapaume–Achiet road and prolonging south as far as Grevillers—this line to be in support to the 75th Brigade covering Sapignies and Behagnies; but on the morning of the 25th the enemy occupied Bienvillers in some force and the battalions of the 74th Brigade began a gradual withdrawal to a position east of Bihucourt, and twenty-four hours later had taken up a line from the north-east corner of Gommecourt Wood, through Pigeon Wood facing south-east, the Battalion being on the right and the 11th Lancashire Fusiliers on the left.   Late that night orders reached all three brigades of the 25th Division to withdraw from their positions and assemble west of Fonquevillers on the Souastre road and from there to concentrate at Couin ; from here on the 27th the Division marched to the area south of Doullens, the Battalion being then quartered at Candas.

During the months of February and March the casualties in the Battalion were as follows : killed, six officers and seventeen other ranks ; wounded, eleven officers and 113 non-commissioned officers and men ; missing, one officer and 215 other ranks ; the officers who were killed or died of wounds were Major F. M. King, Captain J. D. Crichton, Lieutenant R. V. Reid, 2nd Lieutenants W. D. James, R. A. Tait and L. A. Kemp; wounded were, Captains H. Everett, M.C., and R. L. C. Keays, Lieutenant T. B. Harker-Thomas, 2nd Lieutenants F. Brown, H. Short, F. N. Scott, J. F. Hepburn, A. Hughes, H. S. A. Brien, J. Ridyard and W. Swift ; 2nd Lieutenant G. Holt was wounded and missing.

At the end of March the 25th Division entrained at Doullens and Canaples for Caestre in the Second Army area, here joining first the Australian and then the IX. Corps, and the Division taking over the Ploegsteert sector, a line some 7,000 yards in length.   On arrival at Caestre, the 74th Brigade found itself in divisional reserve, the other two brigades being up in the line ; the command of the Brigade was now assumed by Colonel H. M, Craigie-Halkett vice the Brigadier, promoted to the command of a division, and Major W. H. M. Wienholt took over charge of the Battalion.

During the early days of April the Battalion received no fewer than six drafts, amounting in all to 477 other ranks ; but as pointed out in the Divisional History, these drafts now arriving from England were nearly

* *The 25th Division in France and Flanders*, pp. 139–50.

all of the " 19-Year Old Class, who had been training for the last nine months in England, and were of most excellent material, but the absence of older men suitable for promotion to N.C.O.'s rank, was, in some units, a serious disadvantage." The Division could not at the time be given the training necessary for assimilating these reinforcements, and it had consequently been placed in what was hoped would be a comparatively quiet sector for at least an appreciable time.

" At 11 a.m. on the 9th April, however, news was received at Divisional Headquarters that the Germans had made a vigorous attack soon after daybreak on the British line south of Armentières as far as Givenchy, the sector held by the Portuguese and the troops of the XV. Corps. At the same time the 34th Division in front of Armentières was heavily shelled with mustard gas. The enemy appeared to have quickly gained possession of Fleurbaix, Laventie and the whole British line of defence nearly as far south as Givenchy. They at once pushed on west and north-west through Estaires and Bac St. Maur towards Merville and Steenwerck. To meet this menace on our right flank the 74th Brigade was ordered about midday to move to Steenwerck to be at the disposal of the 34th Division, XV. Corps.

" At 1 p.m. the Brigade started and by 4 p.m. was in touch with the enemy south of Steenwerck. At this moment the Germans had already penetrated as far as Croix du Bac. Here the 9th Bn. Loyal North Lancashire was held up by machine-gun fire, and at about 6.30 p.m. Lieut.-Colonel Wienholt, in command, had his horse shot under him in the village and he, himself, was wounded ; Major E. P. Nares then took over command of the Battalion. . . . Owing to the importance of driving the enemy south of the Lys before daylight, a counter-attack was organized at 2 a.m. on the 10th.

" The counter-attack was launched at 3 a.m. with the 9th Loyal North Lancashire on the right, 11th Lancashire Fusiliers in the centre and the 3rd Worcestershire on the left. The 9th Loyal North Lancashire attacked with ' A,' ' B ' and ' C ' Companies in front and ' D ' Company in support, commanded by Captain Loudon, Lieut. Edwards, 2nd Lieut. Barrett, succeeded by Captain Hartley, and Captain F. Smith (wounded), succeeded by 2nd Lieut. Ridyard. . . . The first attack at 3 a.m. failed to dislodge the enemy, who was in some force with numerous machine-guns in and around the village of Croix du Bac. Captain Hartley won a Military Cross for the gallant way in which he reorganized and led his company in the counter-attack, and also Lieuts. Wilson and Brittorous ; Lance-Corporals Diggle, Dodd and Lake received the Military Medal for their fine work in command of their men. Lieut. Edwards, of the Battalion, with his company beat off two attacks, but was badly wounded and missing during the counter-attack in the early morning of the 10th. A further attack was organized for 4.30 a.m., and this time the 9th Loyal North Lancashire went straight through the village, and established themselves on the north bank of the River Lys.

"Further to the left, the Brigade was less successful, with the result that the 9th Loyal North Lancashire found themselves under enfilade machine-gun fire and suffered heavy casualties, and about 7 a.m. the Battalion was forced to withdraw from the river-bank. At 9 a.m. the Brigade was ordered to make a further attempt to drive the enemy across the river ; but by this time the Germans were firmly established on the northern bank with large reinforcements of infantry and machine-guns. About 10.30 a.m. the enemy began to get round the left flank of the 11th Lancashire Fusiliers, and by 3.30 p.m. they had succeeded in working round both sides of Steenwerck, more especially on the east of the village. For the moment the position was somewhat critical, but a new line was successfully formed from Pont de Pierre through Steenwerck Station, in touch with the 88th Brigade on the left and the 40th Division to the right, under whose orders the Brigade was now placed." *

The following momentous Special Order of the Day, issued by Field-Marshal Sir Douglas Haig on 11th April, 1918, best summarises the critical situation of the Allied forces then on the Western Front :—

"Three weeks ago to-day the enemy began his terrific attacks against us on a fifty-mile front. His objects are to separate us from the French, to take the Channel Ports, and destroy the British Army.

"In spite of throwing already one hundred and six divisions into the battle, and enduring the most reckless sacrifice of human life, he has, as yet, made little progress towards his goals. We owe this to the determined fighting and self-sacrifice of our troops.

"Many amongst us now are tired. To those I would say that victory will belong to the side which holds out the longest.

"The French Army is moving rapidly, and in great force to our support.

"There is no other course open to us but to fight it out. Every position must be held to the last man : there must be no retirement. With our backs to the wall, and believing in the justice of our cause, each one of us must fight on to the end.

"The safety of our homes, and the freedom of mankind depend alike upon the conduct of each one of us at this critical moment."

* *The 25th Division in France and Flanders,* p. 195 *et seq.*

Early on the morning of the 12th April the enemy attacked heavily all along the front, as well as to the right and left of the divisional sector, and a retirement became necessary after continuous hard fighting. By the night of the 13th the 74th Brigade, retiring in touch with the 101st and 88th Brigades on right and left respectively, was established on the high ground east of Bailleul. The Germans again followed up and the outpost line on the Bailleul–Armentières road was driven in : late in the afternoon of the 13th, parties of the enemy succeeded in reaching the high ground, but they were immediately counter-attacked by some of the Battalion, led by 2nd Lieutenant A. E. Downing, together with a few men of other corps, and many Germans were killed, the rest put to flight and several machine-guns were captured.

On this day Company Sergeant-Major Crote, Privates Bromley, Kay, Prescott, Cobbold, Parker and Hayward, of the Battalion, all did good service.

During the early hours of the 15th the 74th Brigade was relieved and the Battalion moved back to Mt. Noir. In the meantime the line had been reinforced by other troops, both British and French, which had been hurried up, and by the 17th April, when the 74th was holding a portion of the line south of St. Jean Cappel, the situation was relieved from all anxiety. About the 20th the 25th Division was withdrawn and marched to the Poperinghe–Proven area, coming there into the Second Army Reserve ; the Battalion was accommodated in Dirty Bucket Camp, where fourteen officers joined from the Base.

On the 23rd and 24th the Germans bombarded and attacked the allied positions on and about Kemmel Hill, and at 11.30 a.m. on the 25th the Division was ordered to the support of the XXII. Corps, the enemy having established himself in Kemmel Village and on Kemmel Hill.

By 9.20 p.m. on the 25th the Battalion—strength eighteen officers and 402 other ranks—was in an assembly position 300 yards north of La Clytte cross-roads.

" The 25th Division now came under the orders of the II. French Cavalry Corps, and a counter-attack was organized for the following morning in conjunction with French troops. At 3 a.m. on the 26th the counter-attack started, the 74th Brigade on the right, the 7th on the left, with the 75th in support. On the right was the 3rd Worcestershire, and on the left the 9th Loyal North Lancashire, with four companies commanded by Captain A. Sumner, Captain L. C. Rice (wounded), succeeded by Lieut. L. Bolton, Lieut. A. E. Bulling, and Captain B. A. D. Leverson (wounded), succeeded by 2nd Lieut. J. Draper, and the 11th Lancashire Fusiliers in support."

The Brigade advanced at the appointed hour, but the flooded state of the Kemmel Beek made it difficult for the troops to keep up with the barrage, but by 4.55, the leading battalions had gained their first objective with comparatively few casualties, capturing several machine-guns and some fifty prisoners. Some of the Battalion entered Kemmel Village and pushed on further, but the other troops on the right of the Division had not been equally successful, and by 9 a.m. the 7th and 74th Brigades withdrew to the line of the Kemmel Beek.

Of the Battalion, Sergeant Stourbridge and Private Murphy had pushed on in front of the main attack and captured or killed some twenty Germans ; also Sergeant Rowe, Corporal Newnham and Lance-Corporal Watson showed great ability in reorganizing their men for the attack.

During the remainder of the month fighting continued and the losses mounted up, but the relief of the brigades of the 25th Division began on the 1st May, and by the 5th it was concentrated in an area about ten miles to the west of Poperinghe.

In the fighting of April, 1918, the 9th Loyal North Lancashire had suffered cruel losses, six officers and thirty-nine other ranks being killed or died of wounds, while seventeen officers and 474 non-commissioned officers and men were wounded and 285 were missing—a total casualty list for the month of April of 821 ! The six officers who died were Lieutenants A. A. Baldwin, W. K. Tyldesley and B. J. Edwards, 2nd Lieutenants T. F. McCarthy, J. G. Barrett and J. C. Lancaster ; wounded were Lieut.-Colonel W. H. M. Wienholt, Captains F. Smith, P. R. Shields, L. B. Rice, B. A. D. Leverson, W. H. Cullen and W. S. Hartley, Lieutenants W. H. Mohr and R. L. Bolton, 2nd Lieutenants H. W. Summerson, R. Wilson, J. H. Sloane, W. Ashworth, E. S. Morris, R. L. Isherwood, G. Wolstenholme and J. H. McKercher.

On the 9th May the 25th Division entrained at various small stations to the north-west of Poperinghe, and started on a journey of some thirty hours' duration to the district near Fismes, twenty miles south-east of Soissons in Champagne, where the Division came again under the commander of the IX. Corps.

In Sir Douglas Haig's despatch of the 21st December, 1918, he gives the following reasons for the transfer of this and other British divisions to the Sixth French Army : " At the end of April and early in May, the 8th, 21st, 25th and 50th Divisions, subsequently reinforced by the 19th Division and constituting the IX. British Corps, under command of Lieut.-General Sir A. Hamilton Gordon, had been placed at Marshal Foch's disposal. These divisions had been dispatched by him to the Sixth French Army to take the place of certain French divisions concentrated behind

Amiens.   Of these divisions, the 19th, 21st, 25th and 50th had taken part in both the Somme Battle and the Battle of the Lys.   The 8th Division had been involved south of the Somme in some of the heaviest fighting of the year, and had behaved with distinguished gallantry.   All these divisions had but lately been filled up with young drafts, and despite their high spirit and gallant record, were in no condition to take part in major operations until they had had several days' rest."

Marshal Foch had himself described the sector to which these divisions were now sent as " a quiet place on the Aisne " ;   his local commanders had assured him that the position here was impregnable ;   while he seems himself to have made up his mind that if the enemy made here any attack at all, it would be between Arras and Montdidier.   In any case the position taken up along the so-called Chemin-des-Dames was not a good one from any point of view, since it was too narrow.

The 25th was the last of the British divisions to reach the Champagne area, arriving at a time when the 8th, 21st and 50th Divisions were gradually relieving the French troops on both banks of the Aisne ;   and on arrival the 25th Division was placed in reserve to the other three about midway between the Aisne and the Marne, the headquarters being at Arcis-le-Ponsart, with the 7th, 74th and 75th Brigades respectively at Arcis, Coulanges and Vendeuil.

The Division had lost some two-thirds of its strength during the April fighting, in addition to close upon 3,500 men during the latter part of March ; many reinforcements of young soldiers had reached the different battalions within the last few days ;   and all were hoping to be able to settle quietly down to reorganizing and training.

About the middle of May, however, from various reports which came to hand, it seemed that the enemy was elaborating preparations for an attack ; on the 22nd May the 25th Division was moved up nearer to the line, the 74th Brigade marching to Vendeuil ;   and on the 26th definite information was received that the Germans intended on the following morning to attack along the whole allied front.   That night the brigades of the 25th Division were brought up in close support of the three front-line divisions, the 74th Brigade being at Muscourt, two or three miles south of the Aisne, in support of the 8th Division.

At 1 a.m. on the 27th the Germans opened a very heavy and sustained bombardment of the front-line and back areas as far as Fismes with gas shells of every kind and high explosive ;   and at 4 a.m. the infantry attack followed, eight German divisions in all taking part in the assault on the IX. Corps front, while twenty-one were employed against the French front of about thirty miles.   The initial attack was entirely successful, the French being forced back from the Chemin-des-Dames, while very many British guns were captured and our battalions holding the front line were swept away.

The 25th Division now received orders to hold the second line of defence south of the Aisne, and by 10 a.m. was in position from Cormicy on the right to Maizy on the left; each brigade was now placed at the disposal and under the command of other divisions, the 74th Brigade on the left, in the line from Concevreux to Maizy, coming under the 50th Division. The Battalion, on the left, occupied the front line with the 11th Lancashire Fusiliers on its right, and its companies at the outset were commanded as follows: " A," by Captain Loudon and then by Lieutenant Sanderson, " B," by Captain Sumner, later by Lieutenant Readman, " C," by Captain Shields and later by 2nd Lieutenant Morrison, and " D " Company by Captain Marshall.

By midday the Germans were across the river, while the retreat of the French south of the stream had caused an undefended gap of some two miles on the flank of the 74th Brigade; and strong enemy attacks developed against its battalions, necessitating a withdrawal to the high ground south of the village of Concevreux. " During their retirement the 3rd Worcestershire suffered heavily, and early in the battle Major Darby-Griffith, commanding the 9th Loyal North Lancashire, was killed. Major Lloyd, 105th Field Company, R.E., at once took over the command of the Battalion. 2nd Lieut. Baines handled his men with great skill and held on until nearly surrounded, ably assisted by Lance-Corporal Blodwell, when all other non-commissioned officers had become casualties. Private Still did excellent work with his Lewis gun. Corporal Farnworth and Corporal Wood were conspicuous for their courage in attending wounded under heavy fire, also Privates Cartwright and Lane as stretcher-bearers; Private Lever, in spite of his knee being smashed by a bullet, successfully delivered a message entrusted to him, and Sergeant Carr, with complete disregard of danger, repaired telephone wires under heavy machine-gun fire."

Before dark the line gradually retired to new positions in rear, and by the morning of the 28th the 7th Brigade was along the high ground east of Prouilly, the 74th held the high ground north-west of Montigny and the 75th was south of the river. All the battalions of the 25th Division were by this time greatly reduced in numbers, the average strength being about one hundred men per battalion.

On the evening of the 28th the 74th Brigade came under the orders of the G.O.C. 8th Division, and that night was fairly quiet; on the morning of the 29th, however, a bombardment started and was followed by an attack. By this time French reinforcements were coming up, and on the morning of the

30th the 8th Division was relieved and the 74th Brigade retired to Ville-en-Tardenois. " About 9 a.m. German infantry were reported advancing on Romigny in large numbers, and to meet them a composite battalion of the 50th Division which had just been formed and sent up to reinforce the 74th Brigade, was ordered up to the high ground north and east of Romigny. These were unable to push back the German infantry, and by midday the Brigade was falling back on the line Sarcy–Ville-en-Tardenois, with the 3rd Worcesters on the right and the 9th Loyal North Lancashire on the left, in touch with troops of the 19th Division on their right. . . . By noon the enemy had obtained possession of the village of Romigny and the neighbouring high ground, and the left flank was now forced back to the high ground south-west of Ville-en-Tardenois.

" 2nd Lieut. Morrison, 9th Loyal North Lancashire, commanded his company with great skill. During the attack he reorganized his men and formed at a critical moment a defensive flank. Lance-Corporal Wass, with his Lewis-gun team, and Private Bailey as a runner, were conspicuous for their courage."

There was renewed fighting during the 30th and 31st, but on the 1st June what remained of the 74th Brigade was withdrawn to reorganize and to be in reserve to the 19th Division : the Brigade had fought without a break for five days. The Battalion, its strength now only eight officers and thirty-nine other ranks, was ordered to concentrate at the south-west edge of the Bois de l'Eglise, where the remnants of the Division were formed into what was called " the 1/25th Composite Battalion " under Lieut.-Colonel Traill, 3rd Worcestershire, the Battalion forming part of No. 1 Company of this Composite Battalion. It remained in or near the front until the middle of the month, when it was relieved and the North Lancashire Company was sent by Gaye and Germaine to Fère-en-Champenoise.

The retreat of the Allied forces was actually stayed on the 6th June, following upon two final desperate attacks made by the enemy on the Montagne-de-Bligny, which were repulsed ; and the situation was relieved by the arrival of large reinforcements, mainly American and Italian.

In an Order of the Day issued by the Commander of the Sixth French Army he wrote as follows :—

" With a tenacity, permit me to say, wholly British, you have re-formed in the remnants of your divisions, submerged in the hostile flood, the new reinforcements which you have thrown into the fight, and which have finally allowed us to build a dam against which the German flood has beaten itself in vain. All this, no French witness can ever forget."

In this the Second Battle of the Aisne, which endured from the 26th May to the 14th June, 1918, the Battalion had two officers and six other ranks killed, six officers and 220 other ranks wounded, and six officers and 139 other ranks missing; so that during the last two months of its existence as part of the Loyal North Lancashire Regiment the 9th Battalion had suffered no fewer than 1,200 casualties killed, wounded and missing; while if one may accept the figures given in the Divisional History, the total loss suffered by the Battalion in the whole course of the war was 3,499!

In the Second Battle of the Aisne Major O. S. Darby-Griffith, M.C., and 2nd Lieutenant H. W. Summerson were killed; Lieut.-Colonel A. M. Tringham, D.S.O., Captain A. Sumner, 2nd Lieutenants J. B. M. Lightbody, W. Readman and A. McGregor were wounded, and Captains P. R. Shields, R. J. P. Hewetson and 2nd Lieutenant A. E. Downing were missing, the last-named also wounded.

To the great regret of all ranks it was now learnt that the infantry battalions of the 25th Division were to be broken up, and the Service Battalions used as reinforcements for other battalions. On the 17th and 18th June the three Divisional Composite Battalions were withdrawn from the line; the Regular Battalions of the 25th Division were distributed among the 19th, 21st and 30th Divisions; while a Composite Brigade was made up from the remaining infantry battalions for employment with the 50th Division till finally disbanded a few weeks later. The 8th Border Regiment and the 9th Loyal North Lancashire Regiment formed No. 2 Battalion of the 50th Divisional Composite Brigade.

CHAPTER LIV

THE 10TH (SERVICE) BATTALION
THE LOYAL NORTH LANCASHIRE REGIMENT

1914–1918

THE BATTLES OF THE SOMME AND THE ANCRE, YPRES

THE first official intimation of the existence of the 10th (Service) Battalion, The Loyal North Lancashire Regiment, seems to be contained in Army Order No. 388 of 1914, wherein it appears as forming one of the battalions detailed as divisional troops for the 22nd Division of the Third New Army. The 22nd Division contained the 65th, 66th and 67th Infantry Brigades, and was commanded by Major-General R. A. Montgomery, C.B., C.V.O., and the Army List for October, 1914, gives the name of one officer only as forming the Officer Corps of the 10th Battalion of The Regiment: this was Brevet Colonel W. A. B. Dennys, Indian Army, the date of whose appointment to command the Battalion is given as the 1st October, 1914.

The Battalion's experience of service with the 22nd Division lasted a bare six months, for early in April, 1915, it was transferred to the 112th Brigade of the 37th Division, which assembled at Ludgershall, Wiltshire, the Brigade going under canvas on Windmill Hill.

The 37th Division was commanded by Major-General Count Gleichen, and the 112th Brigade by Brigadier-General J. Marriott, the Brigade containing the 11th (Service) Bn. The Royal Warwickshire, the 6th (Service) Bn. The Bedfordshire, the 8th (Service) Bn. The East Lancashire and the 10th (Service) Bn. The Loyal North Lancashire Reigment.

While the Division was engaged in training on Salisbury Plain it was inspected by His Majesty King George, and also by Field-Marshal Lord Kitchener.

In view of the heavy losses which the original Expeditionary Force had suffered since the commencement of the Great War, there was every desire on the part of the military authorities to push the New Army divisions out to France as soon as their training could be regarded as being in any way completed, and about half-way through the year 1915 the 37th Division received orders to prepare for embarkation for France.

On the 30th July the 10th Battalion transport entrained at Ludgershall under the command of Major R. H. Milvain—strength three officers and 103 other ranks—very early in the morning, while the rest of the Battalion—thirty officers and 846 non-commissioned officers and men—did not leave until the evening of the 31st; the whole arrived at Boulogne at 2 a.m. on the 1st August and marched off at once to the Ostrohove Rest Camp, where the following twenty-four hours were spent.

The Army List for August, 1915, shows the following officers as being at that time on the strength of the Battalion : Brevet Colonel W. A. B. Dennys ; Majors A. McC. Webster and R. H. Milvain ; Captains J. B. D. Dryden, C. R. Maude, F. D. T. Coke, adjutant, R. M. Dennys, H. F. King, A. Caldicott, R. E. Besant and G. W. Ainsworth ; Lieutenants N. Nicholson, C. G. Steel, H. F. L. Williams, C. P. Tindall-Atkinson, W. H. Proctor, J. A. Gravett, H. St. H. Peskett and J. C. Brown ; 2nd Lieutenants L. G. Jude, E. Howell, K. C. Watson, J. R. Couper, H. J. G. Duggan, G. L. Brown, B. C. Macnamara, H. S. Boxer, R. A. Preeston, R. F. Andrews, D. R. C. Lloyd, P. Bee, R. L. Stahlschmidt, N. S. Willis, R. W. K. Reid, C. T. Rostron, J. S. Hill and C. A. S. Bidwell ; Lieutenant and Quartermaster J. Dempster.

Leaving Boulogne on the 2nd August the Battalion proceeded by rail and march route to Hazebrouck, where the headquarters remained for some days, a large fatigue party being detached to Locre under Major Webster for work on the second-line defences.

While in these parts the 37th Division formed part of the Second Army, but about the middle of August the Division was transferred to the Third Army which had recently been formed under the command of Lieut.-General C. Monro ; and on the 26th the Battalion left by train for the neighbourhood of Doullens where the Division came into the area of the VII. Corps, which was commanded by Lieut.-General Sir T. Snow. On the day following arrival in this area the Battalion was sent to Engelbelmer, where it was billeted and where also it was attached to the 11th Infantry Brigade for instruction in trench duties. While thus engaged the first casualties occurred, two men of the Battalion being wounded while up in the trenches. This period of instruction closed on the 5th September, when the Battalion marched to St. Amand to rejoin the Brigade, and on the 15th took over trenches " on its own," all four companies being in the firing-line.

On first occupation it appeared that this was a comparatively quiet portion of the line, the enemy trenches were quite 1,000 yards distant and apparently only lightly held. Patrols from the Battalion found, however, that the Germans were on the alert and some casualties were incurred on the 20th and 21st, 2nd Lieutenant C. A. S. Bidwell and two men dying of wounds received, while Lieutenant H. P. Williams, the machine-gun officer, and two other men were wounded.

In November the condition of the trenches about Hennescamps, whither the companies usually went when their turn came to relieve other troops in the line, had become very bad, due to the heavy rain which had lately fallen. The sector was a very low-lying one and it was practically impossible adequately to drain the trenches, some of them were two feet deep in water, some of the parapets collapsed and dug-outs fell in, in one case completely burying a man of the Battalion, who was only extricated after thirty minutes' hard work.   The reliefs took a very long time to carry out.

In spite of the weather much useful work was done by the patrols and sniping parties.

During November Lieutenant J. A. Gravett, grenade officer, was wounded while instructing a squad, and 2nd Lieutenant N. H. H. Chamberlain joined from the 11th Battalion of the Regiment.

The Battalion spent its first Christmas Day in France up in the same trenches about Hennescamps, but on relief next day went back to Bienvillers in brigade reserve.

Early in May, 1916, the enemy suddenly showed signs of increased activity, bombarding the whole front of the Division and concentrating his fire on the Le Monchy salient, while he also raided the trenches held by the Battalion and the losses were somewhat heavy, during this month 2nd Lieutenant J. R. O'Keefe and four men being killed and thirty-two wounded.

During the months that the 37th Division had spent in this area, it had taken no part in any of the large-scale operations of this period, and though its units had been doing very useful work and had gained much experience, their casualties had been low—and indeed almost negligible— compared with those of some of the other divisions engaged in other areas. In the 34th Division, for instance, the total casualties suffered in its three brigades during the July fighting of this year came to a total of 6,591— that is, in the infantry of the Division alone.   These casualties " rendered it impossible for the Division to remain in the line, unless it were speedily reconstituted, and therefore the 102nd and 103rd Brigades, whose effectiveness would take longer to restore owing to the severe losses they had sustained in their higher ranks, were transferred to the 37th Division, their places being taken by the 111th and 112th Brigades of that Division. . . . The exchange of troops took place without delay by buses and lorries on the 6th and 7th July " * ; the 110th Brigade of the 37th Division was at the same time transferred to the 21st Division.   The 34th Division was

* Shakespear, *The Thirty-fourth Division*, 1915–1919, p. 54.

commanded by Major-General E. C. Ingouville-Williams, C.B., D.S.O., and the 112th Brigade commander was now Brigadier-General P. M. Robinson, C.M.G., while at the time this transfer took place Lieut.-Colonel R. P. Cobbold was the C.O. of the 10th Battalion, The Loyal North Lancashire Regiment.

The 34th Division was in the III. Corps of the Third Army.

On the 6th July the Battalion moved by buses to Albert via Millencourt, and on the 11th took over trenches on Usna-Tara Hill. On this day the two brigades just arrived from the 37th Division " were ordered to push forward strong patrols, and try to occupy a line of trench running from the north-west corner of Contalmaison, westward to the fork formed by the junction of two tracks from Pozières and Ovillers, and prolonged northwards to the Pozières–Albert road, which it crossed about 1,000 yards west of the former village. This meant an advance of about 500 yards, and though the patrols pushed forward vigorously they did not make much progress. All the afternoon and evening the front line was heavily shelled. . . . Later an attack by both brigades was ordered, and had begun before the orders cancelling it reached the battalions concerned. This sad contretemps caused severe losses."

On the 13th the Battalion was relieved in the front line and went back into close support, but on the 16th was ordered up again in support of the 111th Brigade and moved to the Chalk Pit, carrying spare ammunition and bombs to form a dump there. The 111th Brigade attack on Pozières was made at 9 a.m. on the 16th but failed, the Brigade sustaining very heavy losses. The attack was renewed in the afternoon, the Battalion forming the fourth wave of the assaulting line. " Again, however," so the Battalion War Diary relates, " our objective was not realized as the whole village of Pozières bristled with machine-guns." The Divisional History takes up the story, saying that " before being relieved," on the 18th, " the 10th Loyal North Lancashire had established itself firmly in the most westerly of the two orchards at the south-east end of Pozières, so that the sad losses of the 15th had not been quite in vain, for our line had been advanced about 1,000 yards and a foothold obtained in the defences of Pozières."

The Division was relieved on the 19th and 20th by the 1st Australian Division, which captured Pozières on the 25th July after most severe fighting. The 112th Brigade now went to billets at La Houssaye, the Battalion moving into Albert, where it remained until the 31st when the 112th Brigade marched by way of Bresle to Bécourt Wood.

During this month's fighting the Battalion suffered losses as under :—
Killed or died of wounds, Captain R. M. Dennys and twenty-three

other ranks ; wounded were Captain J. B. D. Dryden, Lieutenants H. St. H. Peskett, C. P. Tindall-Atkinson, 2nd Lieutenants J. R. Couper, P. Bee, R. F. Squibb, T. T. Wren, E. C. Wooley and F. Hayes.

On the 22nd July the Divisional Commander, Major-General Ingouville-Williams, was killed by shell fire while visiting the front line : he was succeeded by Major-General C. L. Nicholson.

On the 31st the Division went back into the line, this time more to the east than before, only one brigade was up in the front and the 112th Brigade was in reserve in Bécourt Wood ; but the enemy guns were at this time very active and their shells far-reaching, for on the 1st August the battalion bivouacked on the left of the 10th Loyal North Lancashire had nearly fifty casualties from their fire. On the 6th the Brigade took over the front line, the Battalion occupying trenches east of Bazentin-le-Petit, and at 2 a.m. on the morning of the 11th, so the Divisional History tells us, " the turn of the 10th Loyal North Lancashire came. Immediately on the tail of a heavy bombardment, ' C ' Company, under Lieut. J. A. Garratt," (should be Gravett) " sprang out of our trench on the right of the barrier, and dashed along the top of the Boche trench, hurling down bombs on its occupants. ' A ' Company, under Lieut. W. H. Proctor, followed, and, passing ' C,' pushed on, sprang down into the trench and bayoneted the defenders, clearing the trench up to the Martinpuich road. Lieut. Duggan, with a building party, then put up a barricade fifty yards from the road, which was completed by 2.50 a.m. Both the company commanders and their seconds-in-command, 2nd Lieuts. E. Y. Wadeson and A. F. Gordon, having been wounded (the latter died later), Duggan took command and beat off three determined counter-attacks with heavy loss to his assailants. At 7 a.m. ' B ' Company took over the three hundred yards of trench won by ' C ' and ' A,' and later a company of the 9th North Staffordshire came up and consolidated the gain. The casualties were : killed, one officer and twenty other ranks ; wounded, three officers and seventy-seven other ranks ; of the wounded men, three died later."

On the evening of the 15th August the 34th Division was relieved by the 1st, and the Battalion went back by Bresle, La Houssaye and Allonville to Longpré, where it arrived on the afternoon of the 18th and found itself in excellent billets. The Brigade was now to have another change of Division, for on the 20th all proceeded by rail and road, and by way of Bailleul and Neuf Berquin, to La Gorgue, where they arrived on the evening of the 22nd and there rejoined the 37th Division. Though now actually belonging again to the 37th Division, the Brigade was temporarily lent, first at Bruay to the 16th Division in the IV. Corps of the First Army, and twenty-four hours later it was placed at the disposal of the G.O.C.

40th Division then at Mazingarbe and forming part of the I. Corps of the First Army. Here the Battalion was at the outset in brigade reserve.

On the 2nd September the Battalion marched to Beugin and joined the 37th Division again. At Beugin four officers—2nd Lieutenants Bennett, Band, Travers and Beastall—joined for duty from the 14th Battalion The Sherwood Foresters.

The 37th Division remained in these parts until the last week in October when it was moved to the Doullens area, the Battalion marching over very bad roads to Beausart. On arrival here it was announced that an attack was impending and that the 112th Brigade was to be attached to the 2nd Division and was in support of the 99th Brigade. Nothing seems, however, to have come to pass in connection with this order, and by the 31st October the Battalion was back again in the Doullens area and was quartered in good billets in that town. Here four officers joined—Captain Chew of the 1st Battalion North Staffordshire Regiment, and 2nd Lieutenants Vipond, Vernon and Tonge from the 1/4th Battalion Loyal North Lancashire Regiment, and the Battalion settled down to the usual training.

In the course of this a terrible bombing accident happened on the 8th, caused by the premature explosion of a Mills bomb, and unhappily 2nd Lieutenants Travers and Vernon were killed, and 2nd Lieutenant Stacey, a sergeant and two privates were seriously injured.

The Battalion was now to take part with its Brigade in the Battle of the Ancre, lasting from the 13th to the 18th November ; and on the 12th it left Doullens and moved via Vauchelles to Bertrancourt, which was reached on the evening of the 13th and here it found itself in reserve to the V. Corps and at the disposal of the G.O.C. 3rd Division. The accounts received on reaching Bertrancourt of the progress of this day's action seemed satisfactory, the attack having been successful all along the line except at Serre, where the 3rd Division had been held up. Next day the Brigade marched from Bertrancourt to Mailly Maillet, where it came under the orders of another Division—the 2nd—and that evening the Battalion and the 8th East Lancashire were detached and held in readiness to reinforce the 5th Infantry Brigade of the 2nd Division, and, alternatively, to relieve the other two battalions of the 112th Brigade, which, earlier in the day, had been detailed to carry out an attack.

In the Battalion War Diary under date of the 15th November, we read : " This morning at 2 a.m. the Battalion was formed up in artillery formation, and, with the 51st Division on the right and the 8th East Lancashire on the left, we advanced towards a German line known as the Munich Trench. Our own bararge was intense, but very inaccurate, causing a great many casualties. At 1 p.m. reports came in that we had failed to gain a footing in Munich Trench ; among the killed were Captain Chew, Lieuts. Couper and Jude, 2nd Lieuts. Bennett, Stainer and Andrews, while the officers wounded were 2nd Lieuts. Howarth, Beastall, Woodbury —died of wounds—Band and Macnamara."

The Battalion was relieved in its advanced position on the afternoon of the 16th and retired to the original German second line, falling back still further on the following day to Englebelmer, where all arrived greatly exhausted. Little rest was, however, possible, for by midday on the 19th the Battalion had again gone forward and was occupying a sunken road running in a valley from Beaucourt to Beaumont Hamel, being here in support to another battalion of its brigade. On the following night an enemy shell burst in the middle of a group of officers, and Major Milvain, Captain Donovan, R.A.M.C., 2nd Lieutenants Woodward, Rendal, Dunn, Allen and Watson, and four other ranks were wounded, or otherwise injured.

On the night of the 22nd–23rd the Battalion was up in the front again, and was detailed to attack an enemy trench on the afternoon of the 23rd, establishing posts at its junction with another trench known as Leave Alley. The attack was carried out by two companies under Captain C. G. Steel and 2nd Lieutenant A. C. Smith. The operation was only partially successful and 2nd Lieutenant Smith and nine men were killed, twenty-five being wounded.

On the last day of November the Battalion was at Rubempré, where five officers joined, or rejoined, and early in December the strength was appreciably increased by the arrival of nine officers and 244 other ranks.

Practically the whole of December was spent in the neighbourhood of Le Touret, the 112th Brigade headquarters being at Bethune. There was no change until the end of January, 1917, when the Division was withdrawn from the line to G.H.Q. Reserve ; and finally on the 6th February orders were received intimating that the 37th Division was shortly to move down to the Loos Salient and there relieve the 24th Division in the I. Corps, the 112th Brigade to be in the Les Brebis area.

On the 10th the four battalions of the Brigade marched off at half an hour's interval, and moving by Zelobes, Locon, Bethune and Noeux-les-Mines, Les Brebis was reached on the same evening, and the Battalion moved up next day to the trenches in the Loos Salient, holding the line from the Loos Crassier to Boyeau 31, the 8th East Lancashire being on the right and a battalion of another brigade on the left : two companies were in front and two in support in the cellars in an enclosure just outside Loos.

At the beginning of March the 6th Division took the place of the 37th which moved back into a training area beyond Arras. It moved forward

A RATION PARTY.

1917.

The Imperial War Museum—Copyright.

again on the 5th April to take part in the great Arras offensive of this
year, the hard fighting in connection with which began on the 9th April
and was not over before the 4th May ; in these operations three cavalry
and twenty-six infantry divisions of the British Expeditionary Force,
contained in six Corps and two Armies, the First and Third, took part.

When the operations began, the 37th Division was in the VI. Corps
under General Haldane, of the Third Army under General Allenby ; the
Third Army contained four Corps, of which the VII., VI. and XVII. were
in line in that order from right to left ; the VI. Corps was composed of
four divisions, the 3rd on the right, the 12th in the centre and the 15th
on the left, and the 37th was in support ; the reserve of the Third Army
was the XVIII. Corps of four divisions. The First Army was on the left
of the Third, and the Fifth was on the right.

On the 9th the Battalion was kept busy drawing iron rations, tools,
bombs, Véry lights and rifle grenades from the equipment dump to the
west of Arras. But during the night it moved forward to a trench line
known as Iceland where it was in support to the Bedfordshire and East
Lancashire battalions of the Brigade ; and, continuing to advance, the
37th Division found itself by the middle of the afternoon in the German
second-line system. As evening fell the Division pressed on in the hope
of capturing Monchy, but the advance was directed rather too much to
the south, and the line came up to a field of barbed wire where it was for
a time held up. During the 10th the battalions of the brigade dug themselves in, the Battalion being still in support ; but during the night it
received orders to go through the leading battalions in the early morning
and attack objectives known as the Green Line and the Wood in O.8. Central.

Of the resulting operations the War Diary tells the following story :—

" 11th. 5 a.m. The Battalion having got into position for such an
advance, immediately came into full view of the enemy and met with very
heavy machine-gun and shell fire, and we received orders not to advance
until our barrage opened, but by this time we had carried by assault the
enemy trench east of the Sunken Road, and were establishing ourselves
in shell-holes 100 yards further east. It was at this time that Captain
H. St. H. Peskett and 2nd Lieut. E. Ibbotson were killed, 2nd Lieut. R. E.
Quesnel having been wounded the day before.

" During the assault we suffered very heavy casualties and were enfiladed
from Monchy le Preux.

" The right flank, perceiving that they were in the air and appreciating
the fact that if the flank remained thus there was a likelihood of their
being outflanked, boldly determined to risk all and assault a small trench
running south from the Cambrai road in the direction of Guémappe and

about thirty yards east of the Sunken Road above mentioned. A tank now came up to their aid. On obtaining possession of the trench Corporal Leonard, Lance-Corporal Dinwoodie and six men were all that were left, but these eight men boldly bombed along the trench to the southward, killing more than a dozen Germans, taking three prisoners and then found themselves in complete possession. To their surprise seven German officers now appeared, apparently from nowhere, and were at once shot down.

" Two machine-guns were also taken in this gallant assault, and were put out of action. These men retained possession of this trench, while Captain Gravett, ably assisted by 2nd Lieut. Deacon—now the only two officers left—and Company Sergeant-Major Webster, with sixty men, made themselves masters of the corresponding trench running northwards from the Cambrai road. Here they remained throughout the day, and during that time 2nd Lieut. Deacon received two wounds, but refused to leave his captain or his men. Some of the dismounted men of the 3rd Dragoon Guards came up on the left and relieved the situation, while men of other battalions of the Brigade were collected from shell-holes and helped to hold the line, until Captain Gravett was completely master of the situation. No further advance was at present permitted as this party of the Battalion was already forward of the troops on either flank.

" At 1 a.m. on the 12th the Battalion was relieved and marched back, all greatly exhausted, to Tilloy Wood, and from there next day to billets in cellars at Arras, the losses in this fighting totalling thirteen officers and 286 other ranks killed, wounded and missing."

A week was passed at Ambures, resting and reorganizing, until on the 19th April the Division moved up to the forward area again about St. Nicholas, south of Arras, the Division having now been transferred to the XVII. Corps, commanded by General Ferguson.

In the afternoon of the 23rd April the Battalion again attacked and the following is taken from the War Diary :—

" At 4.50 p.m. we received orders to move to Chili Trench and to be in readiness to advance and attack the Brown Hill by 5.45 p.m. During the move the Battalion met with a very heavy barrage of artillery and suffered casualties. At 6 p.m. our guns opened a shrapnel barrage for twenty-five minutes followed by H.E. for five minutes, during which we halted in a trench in rear of Chili Trench, the East Lancashire being on our left. At 6.30 we moved into Chili Trench, and during this advance we suffered tremendously from the enemy's guns, and Captain W. H. Proctor was killed and only three officers remained unwounded.

" The Battalion failed to reach the Blue Line, so remained in shell-holes till dark, when the C.O. collected all the men he could and held on

in Clyde Trench for the protection of the right flank, at the same time
deepening and consolidating Clyde Trench. At this time only 140 non-
commissioned officers and men were left, but at 8 p.m. a section of machine-
guns came up and got into position on the flank.

" We held on all that night and until the night of the 24th, subjected
to heavy shelling, then relieving the 63rd Brigade in the Blue Line.

" The attack on the 23rd undoubtedly failed, but this cannot be
wondered at considering the nature of the ground over which we had to
advance, also the heavy enemy barrage of artillery and machine-guns;
but the officers and other ranks of the Battalion were magnificent in their
endeavours, but in spite of all we were checked before reaching the Blue
Line, so naturally failed to take Greenland Hill, our real objective. During
the 25th and 26th we held Clasp Trench as our forward line and a trench
in the Sunken Road as our support line.

" 27th. Received orders to attack Greenland Hill at dawn next day.
Made all necessary arrangements and decided that the Battalion should
' go over ' in two waves.

" 28th. 4.25 p.m. Barrage opened, Battalion already in position for
the attack. Battalion advanced and reached a point where the enemy
had commenced to dig a trench, and during this movement the losses had
been heavy and only one officer—2nd Lieut. Jones—was left. We at once
began to improve the newly-begun trench under enfilade fire from the
direction of the Chemical Works on the right, and in this trench and adjacent
shell-holes what remained of the Battalion hung on until the early hours
of the 29th when the 112th Brigade was relieved and withdrawn to St.
Nicholas, from where the Battalion was sent on in lorries to Ambures."

During these operations of April, 1917, the Battalion had twenty-one
officers and 478 non-commissioned officers and men killed, wounded and
missing.

The Division now, after its very heavy losses in the Arras battle, was
given some time to reorganize its units and was put into what was generally
spoken of as " quiet sectors " of the line ; and until well on into September
the 112th Brigade spent most of its time in the Kemmel sector, but towards the end of that month the 37th Division took over the line south
of the Menin Road on the right of the 5th Division.

Even in the so-called " quiet sectors " casualties were met with, and, on
the 28th May, Captain Macnamara and 2nd Lieutenant Way were wounded.

When on the 23rd September the Division relieved the 39th Division
in the Menin area, the Battalion took over the line from a unit of the 118th
Brigade just on the right of Tower Hamlets in Shrewsbury Forest, where
it was in support to the 6th Bedfordshire of its brigade ; and in carrying

out the relief 2nd Lieutenants H. N. King, G. Brydon and twenty men were wounded, and casualties now began quickly to mount up, and on relief, after only four days in the line, ninety-four men in all had been killed and wounded.

On the 8th October Lieutenant J. H. Simpson was wounded, and on the following day in an attempt to capture a German post fresh casualties were incurred, 2nd Lieutenant A. C. Baker being badly wounded with some of his party. The shelling was always very heavy and very rough weather was experienced ; and though the 37th Division was not actually engaged in the front line in any of the battles of October and November of this year, it probably had as unenviable an experience of the Ypres Salient as any other division which had served there.

On the 15th October the Battalion, with the 8th East Lancashire, moved into Ypres for work on the roads, and here these battalions were temporarily attached to the III. Australian Corps, and while here a large draft of one hundred and thirty men joined. The first half of December was spent in the front and support trenches about La Clytte, and on the early morning of the 9th the garrison of one of the posts held by the Battalion did very fine work.

" At 3.30 a.m. the enemy raided our No. 7 Post and received a good reception. The post was approached by two parties on the north and south, a barrage being put down just behind the post, and under cover of this the wire was cut and the raiders attacked. The garrison of the post consisted of Corporal Grindrod, in command, Privates White, Linton, Compton and Gregson. As soon as the bombs began to fall and the raiders were seen, the garrison rushed forward to meet them. Private White engaged single-handed two of the enemy, and though severely wounded by the butts of rifles and with his head cut open, he fought on and eventually killed one and took the other—a sergeant-major—prisoner. One cannot speak too highly of this man's determination and gallantry, and his action was undoubtedly responsible for the success. Corporal Grindrod displayed coolness and judgment, working his Lewis gun with deadly effect, and he was most ably supported by the rest of the garrison who beat off the attack, causing very heavy losses—three being killed and two captured. The strength of the raiding party was from twenty to twenty-five, and as they fell back, they were followed up by the fire of the Lewis gun, causing further casualties."

The 112th Brigade appears to have been the last of the units of the 37th Division to move to the Hollebeke area, for it was not until the 9th January, 1918, that the Battalion left Ridge Wood, where for some days it had been encamped, and proceeded by rail and road to Wallon Cappel, where very comfortable billets were taken over. The weather was now exceptionally rainy and all were no doubt thankful not to be, for the present, up in the trench line. On the 22nd the Battalion was sent to Vierstraat and was engaged in work on the line.

It was while here that, under date of the 27th January, the War Diary strikes the following very mournful note : " Our Death Knell has rung ! The order has been received to-day that we are to be disbanded. For the moment no one can realize it. The Battalion that has been our home for so long, that we have fought and worked for, is to be broken up ; the Battalion which we have all prided ourselves in being members of, and whose good name has been unsullied since the outbreak of hostilities, is to fade away and be a thing of the past. It is indeed hard ! Both officers and men, in spite of the blow, have decided to carry out to the best of their ability the splendid traditions of the Battalion to the last."

On the 1st February the Battalion went back by train to Ebblinghem and thence by road to Racquinghem ; but before moving off there was a very special and somewhat mournful parade, when the Battalion buried, with all honours, the Flag which it had carried during so many years of war and through so many very trying times. The ceremony ended with the Commanding Officer, Lieut.-Colonel E. A. Cameron, D.S.O., delivering a speech of farewell to all ranks.

Leaving Racquinghem on the 15th the Battalion proceeded by train to Ebblinghem, where the Divisional Commander, Major-General H. Bruce-Williams, C.B., D.S.O., was waiting to bid the Battalion good-bye, and the companies then went on to Wippenhoek. Here the Battalion came under the XXII. Corps of the Fourth Army."

On the 19th February it was made known that " the 10th (Service) Bn. The Loyal North Lancashire Regiment will become surplus on the 21st February," being then made up to an establishment of 1,100 and becoming No. 15 Entrenching Battalion of the Fifth Army.

On the 21st February, then, the 10th (Service) Battalion, The Loyal North Lancashire Regiment, ceased, as such, to exist, but the spirit of the Battalion lived on as may be read in the words inscribed on the last page of the War Diary : " In spite of the heavy blow that has fallen on them, officers, non-commissioned officers and men have voiced with one accord their determination to uphold the good traditions of the Battalion in whatever Regiment, or Corps, they may be called upon to serve."

In the Army List for February, 1918, the month in which the 10th Battalion was disbanded, the following appear as the names of the Officers then serving with it : Lieut.-Colonel E. A. Cameron, D.S.O. ; Majors H. R. Dewar and J. A. Gravett, M.C. ; Captains C. G. Steel, B. C. Macnamara,

E. Howell, M.C., J. C. Brown, P. Bee, H. Crank and W. J. Plant ; Lieu-
tenants A. A. Pepper, C. T. Rostron, C. F. Allen, H. L. Jones, E. H. B.
Nobbs, adjutant, H. Booth, F. Hayes, M.C., G. A. Goodman, F. H. A.
Woodward, F. H. Beastall and J. J. Sweetenham ; 2nd Lieutenants W. L.
Howarth, E. C. Wooley, A. C. Baker, M.C., J. B. Blakeway, S. B. Smith,
M.C., A. L. Howard, H. N. Roberts, C. A. Tasker, W. B. Weatherell, L. B.
Smith, R. E. Quesnel, W. E. Crossley, M.C., H. N. King, J. Kay, H. J.
Lancaster, C. L. Kelly, P. S. Maingot, N. J. Carline, J. F. Mills, J. Buchan,
P. Catterell, H. D. Crane, H. Dillon, J. A. Jackson, G. H. Coldbeck, H. F.
Lea, C. H. Law, C. S. Irons, B. W. Peachey, E. Wrigley, and Lieutenant
and Quartermaster G. E. Welch.

Field-Marshal Sir Douglas Haig wrote in one of his despatches : " The
feature of the war which to the historian may well appear the most noteworthy is the creation of our New Armies. To have built up successfully,
in the very midst of war, a great New Army is an achievement of which
the whole Empire may be proud. . . . At the outset the lack of deep-
seated and instinctive discipline placed our new troops at a disadvantage
compared with the methodically trained enemy ; this disadvantage, however, was overcome, and during the last two years the discipline of all ranks
of our New Armies, from whatever part of the Empire they had come, was
excellent. . . . Drawn from every sphere of life, from every profession,
department and industry of the British Empire, and thrust suddenly into
a totally new situation full of unknown difficulties, all ranks have devoted
their lives and energies to the service of their Country in the whole-hearted
manner which the magnitude of the issues warranted. Young officers,
whatever their previous education may have been, have learnt their duties
with enthusiasm and speed, and have accepted their responsibilities unflinch-
ingly. Promotion has been entirely by merit, and the highest appointments have been open to the humblest, provided he had the necessary
qualifications of character, skill and knowledge. . . . As a body, generally, new officers have understood that the care of their men must be their
first consideration, that their men's comfort and well-being should at all
times come before their own, that without this they cannot expect to win
the affection, confidence, loyalty and obedience of those they are privileged
to command, or to draw the best from them ; moreover they have known
how to profit by the experience of others, and in common with their men
they have turned willingly to the members of the old Regular Army for
instruction and guidance in all branches of their new way of life. . . .
The general absence of jealousy and the readiness to learn, which in the
field has markedly characterized all ranks of our New Armies, is proof both
of the quality of our Old Army and of the soundness of our pre-war training."

CHAPTER LV

THE 11TH (RESERVE) BATTALION
THE LOYAL NORTH LANCASHIRE REGIMENT

1914–1917

THE 11th Reserve Battalion of the Regiment was raised at Felixstowe in November, 1914, and the first officers to join were Lieut.-Colonel F. C. L. Logan, in command, Major J. L. Burbey, Captain R. E. Crane, adjutant, and Lieutenant and Quartermaster J. Gee.

From Felixstowe the Battalion was moved early in 1915 to Chichester and Brighton, went from there in June to Billericay in Essex, and from thence in October to Seaford, remaining here until September of the following year, when it became merged in, and in fact provided the major portion of the nucleus of, the 17th Training Reserve Battalion.

This Battalion was formed at Seaford on the 1st September, 1916, under Army Council Instruction No. 1528 of 1916, under which Second Reserve Battalions ceased to exist.

Prior to the above date the 4th Reserve Infantry Brigade was quartered at Seaford and was composed of the following seven Second Reserve Infantry Battalions—the 11th Gloucestershire, 10th Border, 11th Loyal North Lancashire Regiments, the 14th and 15th Battalions The King's Royal Rifle Corps and the 14th and 15th Battalions The Rifle Brigade.

In the reorganization under the above-quoted Army Council Instruction, the 11th Battalion, The Loyal North Lancashire Regiment, formed the basis of the 17th Training Reserve Battalion, in which the 10th Battalion, The Border Regiment, was included, and to which some seven hundred men of the disbanded 14th Battalion, The King's Royal Rifles, were transferred. As a result the 17th Battalion commenced its existence under the command of Lieut.-Colonel F. C. L. Logan at a strength of 2,264 non-commissioned officers and men, made up as under :—

412 Other Ranks of the 11th Bn. Loyal North Lancashire Regiment,
327   ,,   ,,   ,,   ,,   10th Bn. Border Regiment,
708   ,,   ,,   ,,   ,,   14th Bn. King's Royal Rifle Corps,

while, attached, were 367 of the Border Regiment and 450 of the Loyal North Lancashire Regiment.

The difficulties of the situation were increased by the fact that immediately prior to the commencement of this reorganization, it was decided by the War Office that a large number of partially trained men of the Border and Loyal North Lancashire Regiments, who had been transferred to their respective Special Reserve Battalions and were on the point of proceeding to them, were to remain and complete their training with the 17th Training Reserve Battalion, before joining their new units.

As a result of the formation of one new battalion from three old ones, a very large number of officers and other ranks came on the strength of the new battalion, and the following are the names of the officers, by regiments :—

Border Regiment : Captains H. Johnson and M. J. D. Cockle and 2nd Lieutenant P. Reader.

Loyal North Lancashire Regiment : Lieut.-Colonel F. C. L. Logan, Major J. L. Burbey, Captains L. F. Crane, G. W. Ainsworth and A. M. Hollins, 2nd Lieutenants H. D. Anthony, G. L. Brown and W. Allsup and Lieutenant and Quartermaster J. Dempster.

King's Royal Rifle Corps : Majors C. H. N. Seymour, D.S.O., and G. N. Prendergast, Captain J. Marshall and 2nd Lieutenant G. E. Ingram.

In addition to the above-named officers, two majors, two captains and over fifty subaltern officers were brought in on the strength of the 17th Battalion on the 1st September, 1916, or were attached pending the receipt of orders for them to embark or to proceed to join their various Special Reserve Battalions ; but of these the majors and captains and all but seventeen of the subaltern officers had left by the 1st February, 1917.

The surplus warrant and non-commissioned officers were gradually absorbed, until by the 1st February, 1917, all had been taken on with the exception of certain company sergeant-majors and company quartermaster-sergeants.

On the 28th September, 1916, the Battalion sent away its first draft, this, consisting of thirty other ranks, going to the Rifle Brigade in France.

In the following month it was proposed to send the Battalion to Northampton, but on its being found that sufficient accommodation was not there available for so strong a unit, Luton, in Bedfordshire, was selected as the future station of the Battalion, and on the 1st November it proceeded there by train and was accommodated in billets.

Before this latter date, however, four more drafts had been dispatched overseas, one twenty strong for the Rifle Brigade, another of the same strength for the Loyal North Lancashire, and two, respectively 105 and 162 in numbers, to the Border Regiment. Before the end of the year seven more drafts, containing in all 240 other ranks, had been sent to various regiments in different theatres of the war.

On the 5th April, 1917, orders were received that the Battalion had been selected to receive " A. IV." recruits, and arrangements were accordingly made for the transfer of all men, other than boys under the age of 18 years and 8 months and a few other details, to the 16th Training Reserve Battalion at Northampton. These " A.IV." Recruits commenced to arrive on the 10th April and within ten days 1,223 of them had joined the Battalion. These came for the most part from country districts and from Depots at Norwich, Bury St. Edmunds, Northampton, Warley, Bedford, Mill Hill, Hounslow, Kingston, Maidstone, Chichester and Guildford.

On the 25th April, 1917, Field-Marshal Lord French, Commanding the Home Forces, accompanied by the G.O.C. Eastern Command, inspected the Battalion in Stockwell Park, which had recently been taken over as the site for a summer camp. The Field-Marshal expressed himself as highly pleased with all he saw.

On the 12th May, under instructions from the G.O.C. Eastern Command, tables were drawn up and sent in showing the ages of all category " A. IV." men of the Battalion in ten distinctive groups ; and as a result thirty men were now transferred to the Machine-Gun Corps, and 208 others to the 18th and 19th Training Reserve Battalions at Northampton. A few weeks later, however, a draft 283 strong was received from the 19th Training Reserve Battalion, and on arrival at Luton this was formed into a special company.

The Battalion was moved to Harwich on the 4th July, thus leaving the 4th Training Reserve Brigade, its departure drawing the following very complimentary farewell order from Brigadier-General G. H. Colomb, commanding the Brigade :—

" In bidding good-bye to the Battalion on leaving the 4th Training Reserve Brigade, the G.O.C. wishes to place on record his sincere and grateful thanks to Lieut.-Colonel Logan, Major Burbey and all the officers, non-commissioned officers and men who have so freely given their whole hearts, their time, and their energy to the one object of making that Battalion, sometimes under the most trying circumstances, what it is now, viz. a unit which any G.O.C. might be proud to have under his command.

" The loyalty and spirit of the Battalion, as fostered by Lieut.-Colonel Logan, reflects the greatest credit upon all who have had the making of it, and it is with profound regret that the Brigadier-General finds himself compelled to say good-bye, but he wishes the Battalion the best of luck in the future that lies before it."

The Battalion was now in the 6th Training Reserve Brigade, commanded by Brigadier-General C. V. Humphreys, in the Harwich Garrison under Major-General Stanton, and took over part of the defensive position in the Harwich section ; and on the morning of the 22nd July it was ordered into the trenches owing to the presence of enemy aircraft. Several bombs were dropped near the camp, but happily no casualties were sustained by the Battalion.

On the 31st July it was intimated that the Battalion was to be re-organized from a Junior Training Reserve Battalion into a Graduated Training Reserve Battalion, and as a result of this change the following transfers of personnel were carried out :—

To the 3rd Bn. Suffolk Regiment, Felixstowe . . .	50 Men.
„ „ „ „ Essex „ „ . . .	50 Men.
„ „ „ „ Bedfordshire „ „ . . .	34 „
„ „ 22nd Training Reserve Bn., Dovercourt . . .	155 „
„ „ 25th „ „ „ Luton	540 „

While there were transferred to the Battalion :—

From the 22nd Training Reserve Bn., Dovercourt . .	225 „
„ „ 25th „ „ „ Luton . .	109 „
„ „ 16th „ „ „ Bedford . .	169 „
„ „ 24th „ „ „ Sittingbourne . .	21 „

On the completion of the reorganization, attention was now given to the training of the various specialists to be included in a Graduated Training Reserve Battalion, and men were trained as Lewis gunners, bombers and signallers. At this time the Battalion had sixteen Lewis guns on charge, as well as four German converted machine-guns.

On the 24th September the Battalion moved into camp at Broome Park, near Canterbury, and was now in the 202nd Infantry Brigade, of the 67th Division, Southern Army. Here it took over the lines, mobilization stores, transport, etc., of the 2/4th Bn. The Buffs, and also assumed a new title, being now, under War Office letter 27/Gen. No. 6273 (A.G.2.) of the 1st September, designated the 284th Infantry Battalion.

During 1917 the Battalion sent 252 men to regiments overseas in drafts of varying size.

CHAPTER LVI

THE 1/12th (TERRITORIAL) BATTALION (PIONEERS)
THE LOYAL NORTH LANCASHIRE REGIMENT

1915–1919

FRANCE, MACEDONIA, PALESTINE, FRANCE AND FLANDERS
THE BRITISH ARMY OF OCCUPATION IN GERMANY

BEFORE the campaign on the Western Front had settled down to a condition of siege or trench warfare, it had been decided to proceed with the creation of Pioneer Battalions, and to add one to each of the New Army Divisions. The 12th Territorial Battalion, The Loyal North Lancashire Regiment was, in accordance with the above decision, raised in August, 1915, and it appears for the first time in the Army List for October of that year, when the following officers are shown as belonging to it : Colonel W. T. C. Beckett, Captain B. Musgrave, 2nd Lieutenants G. W. Parkinson, T. Watters and A. Walsh. The date of Colonel Beckett's appointment was the 20th August, 1915, that is presumably the date when the Battalion came into being. On 1st September the Battalion, strength eight hundred, entrained at Bolton for Lytham, where billets were provided and training commenced. At first there was a general shortage of rifles, clothing and equipment. In March, 1916, the Battalion was reported upon as being ready to go overseas, and was ordered to Norfolk for the completion of its practical training both in infantry and engineering duties, in conformity with the intended rôle.

It was not, however, until the end of April, 1916, that the Battalion joined, at Warminster on Salisbury Plain, the 60th Division with which it was to see service in so many different theatres of the World War. This Division had been originally formed as the 2nd London (Reserve) Division, from the very large number of recruits for the 2nd London Territorial Division, who had come forward in response to Lord Kitchener's appeal of the 10th August, 1914 ; but it was not until January, 1916, that the Division officially received an independent denomination and number of its own and became the 60th (London) Division, its brigades being numbered 179th, 180th and 181st.

The commander of the Division was Major-General E. S. Bulfin, C.B.

The Battalion, as above stated, joined the 60th Division in April, and of the new arrivals their G.O.C. eventually gave the following impression :—

" We were fortunate also in getting during April the 1/12th Battalion The Loyal North Lancashire Regiment, which came to us as our Pioneer Battalion, under a most capable officer, Lieut.-Colonel Beckett. They were a hard-bitten, thirsty lot of Lancashire miners, but what they could do with a spade was a perfect revelation. The Division owed a great deal to this fine Battalion for the splendid work they did on the Vimy Ridge, and I attribute our comparatively low casualty returns to the rapidity with which these pioneers, assisted by the various battalions, managed to lower the depth of the trenches eighteen inches in record time."

In the middle of May the Division was officially informed that it would probably embark for France in a month's time ; and on the 14th June it was notified that the Division was to commence embarkation on the 21st.

The Battalion left Sutton Veny, Warminster, early on the morning of the 21st and proceeded by train to Southampton where it embarked, the Headquarters and companies in the S.S. " Cesarea " and the Transport in the " City of Dundalk," crossing over by night to Havre ; on landing it marched to No. 1 Rest Camp, Point St. Addresse, and remained here until the evening of the 23rd June.

The disembarkation strength was over one thousand with twenty-one officers ; the officers who landed in France with the Battalion were Lieut.-Colonel W. T. C. Beckett, Major, A. Buckley, second-in-command ; Captains W. Longbottom, adjutant, G. W. Parkinson, T. Watters, J. P. Bayley, A. Walsh, H. Wilkinson and M. Montgomery, Lieutenants J. M. Marshall, C. D. M. Keyworth, A. Gillespie, R. T. Powell, S. H. D. Faulkner, F. Barton-Smith, T. C. L. Farrar and J. White ; 2nd Lieutenants C. T. Jackson, G. Wood, G. Bryers, P. H. Pettiford, L. A. Cooke, R. Hodgkinson, J. E. S. Bodger, J. G. L. Piveteau, A. M. Pawsey, H. E. Ward and S. C. H. Webster, and Lieutenant and Quartermaster G. D. Chambers and Captain N. P. Laing, R.A.M.C.

Leaving Havre at 9 p.m. on the 23rd the Battalion proceeded by train to St. Pol and marched from there by Ternas to Haute Avesnes, " C " and " D " Companies then going on to Acq and Headquarters with " A " and " B " Companies to Louez, billets being arrived at about midnight on the 26th. The Battalion was now much split up on pioneer duties of all kinds, repairing front-line and communication trenches and also in carrying out work in connection with the light railway under the C.R.E. XVII. Corps.

As intended, the 60th Division took over this sector, facing Vimy Ridge, from the 51st Division, which was under orders to move, in connection with the forthcoming operations on the Somme. The opening artillery bombardment of the Somme battle was soon to commence.

The Battalion remained much separated, " A " Company and the greater part of " B " Company going to the centre sector at La Maison Blanche, " D " Company to the right sector about Ecurie and Anzin, while " C " worked in the left sector at Neuville St. Vaast ; the work allotted to the companies being to put the whole of the front-line trenches in a thorough state of repair, while lowering all to a depth of seven feet.

When engaged in this work the 1/12th Bn. The Loyal North Lancashire suffered its first casualties of the war, seven men being wounded during the month of July.

" The divisional area included the district between Suchez and Arras, extending westwards to the town of Aubigny, where railhead was established, and south to Hermaville, in the ancient chateau of which Divisional Headquarters were established. The line of front extended from the ruined village of Roclincourt on the right to beyond Neuville St. Vaast, similarly in ruins, on the left, running, roughly, about a thousand yards east of those places. In rear were the partially ruined villages of Ecurie, Anzin, Maroeuil, Bray, Ecoivres and Mont St. Eloi." *

On the 8th August ten officers reported for duty on arrival from the Reserve Battalion of the 12th which had been established at Oswestry when the 60th Division embarked for France ; these officers were Captain J. M. Turnbull, 2nd Lieutenants R. W. Williams, S. N. Bradbury, G. M. McCorquodale, W. F. Hedges, C. A. Young, J. J. Tinker, H. N. C. Chase, E. H. Treacy and E. J. Hart. During this month the Battalion suffered its first fatal casualties, one man being killed and another dying of wounds.

The War Diaries for these months give details of the vast amount of work done by the Battalion in strengthening and improving the trenches occupied by the Division, and fully bear out what General Bulfin has put on record as to the services of the Battalion on Vimy Ridge.

In September two more subaltern officers joined from the Reserve Battalion—2nd Lieutenants H. S. Lewis and H. P. Muckleston.

Orders for the 60th Division to be relieved by the 3rd Canadian Division were received on October 19th. The Division was to go into General Headquarters reserve sector, preparatory to proceeding to the Somme area. All the companies of the Battalion were withdrawn from the trenches on the 24th October, and next day the Battalion marched from Louez and arrived about midday on the 29th at Boisbergues in the Fourth Army area. This place was left again on the 3rd November when the Battalion proceeded

* Dalbiac, *History of the 60th Division*, p. 44.

to Ailly le Haut Clocher, where on the 5th the connection of the 12th Battalion with the 60th Division came, happily only temporarily, to a close.

There seems to have almost from the first been some doubt as to whether the destination of the Division was really, as notified, to be the Somme area. Throughout the month of October rumours had been current that it was to move to a different theatre of war altogether ; and finally, on the 1st November, Sir Douglas Haig personally informed General Bulfin, that as the 60th was one of the strongest divisions on the Western Front, it had been selected to proceed to Salonika. The Division accordingly began entraining at Longpré on the 14th November, arrived at Marseilles on the 28th and following days, and by the 12th December the units of the Division were at sea and on their way to Salonika.

In the meantime the Battalion had received orders for attachment to the 32nd Division, and it joined its new command at Englebelmer on the 18th November, and during the remainder of the month it was employed in the usual trench duties in front of Beaumont Hamel. On the 25th, however, the 32nd Division was relieved by the 7th, but the Battalion remained behind in the Beaumont Hamel sector, and was for a time attached to the 7th Division, rejoining the 32nd again on the 22nd December at Puchevillers. During the month of November reinforcements joined to the number of 180 non-commissioned officers and men. Christmas Day, 1916, was spent in billets at Puchevillers.

On leaving the 7th Division the commander—Major-General H. V. Watt—forwarded the following letter to the G.O.C. 32nd Division :—

" I wish to bring to your notice the excellent work performed by the 12th Battalion The Loyal North Lancashire Regiment (Pioneers) during the time they have been attached to the Division under my command.

" They have done most useful work, under great difficulties and under conditions of considerable discomfort, and have shown a willingness and energy which merit the highest praise."

During December 2nd Lieutenant E. H. Treacy was wounded by shell-fire, dying within an hour of his wounds.

On the 5th January, 1917, the Battalion left Puchevillers by rail and road for Abbeville, and on arrival here found orders awaiting it to leave the 32nd Division and rejoin the 60th at Salonika. From Abbeville the companies marched, Headquarters and " B " and " C " Companies to Maroeuil and " A " and " D " to Caubert, and at these places the Battalion had only the very shortest possible time to make ready for service in an entirely new theatre of war. On the 10th all entrained for Marseilles, which was reached in the afternoon of the 12th, when the Battalion marched

DOIRAN AND THE LAKE.

1917.

The Imperial War Museum—Copyright.

off at once to the docks and embarked in the S.S. " Menominée," finally sailing for Salonika at 4.15 p.m. on the 14th.

The embarking strength was thirty-five officers and 964 other ranks.

Touching en route at Messina, the transport reached Salonika on the morning of the 23rd, when all disembarked and marched to a camp on the Seres road, the rest of the month being taken up with drawing stores and mules.

What was known as " the Allied Army of the Orient " serving in Greece and Macedonia was composed of British, French, Italian, Russian and Serbian contingents, all under the command of the French General Sarrail, the British portion of the Army being under Lieut.-General Sir G. F. Milne. The arrival of the 60th Division in December, 1916, had brought the strength of the British force up to six divisions, of which the 10th, 27th and 28th formed the XVI. Corps, while the 22nd, 26th and 60th Divisions composed the XII. Corps, under the command of Lieut.-General Sir H. Wilson.

" The front occupied by the Allies extended from the Struma River, on the east, to Monastir and the Albanian frontier on the left. The British held the right sector of the line, from the mouth of the Struma up the river to Lake Tahinos, and then in a westerly direction by Lakes Butkovo and Doiran to the River Vardar. The XII. Corps was responsible for the line from Butkovo to the Vardar; the front ran along the mountains known as the Krusha Balkans, as far as about two miles east of Doiran, when it turned southwards, and lay on the lower grounds bordering on Lake Ardjan. The Bulgarian Second Army which faced the XII. Corps from Butkovo to Doiran, was formidably entrenched along the Belashitza Range in a series of almost inaccessible positions from 1,500 to 2,000 feet higher than the Krusha Balkans; while from Doiran to the Vardar their positions completely dominated the British lines, especially at the point about Doiran, known as the Grand Couronné, rising to a height of nearly 2,000 feet.

" The French and other allied contingents extended the general line west of the Vardar, across the Cerna bend to Monastir and into Albania. At the time that the 60th Division arrived active hostilities were at a standstill. . . . Ever since then the setting in of exceptionally severe and inclement weather, continuous heavy rains and storms of snow, had rendered operations, except on a very minor scale, impossible." *

Marching out of Salonika on the 6th February the Battalion, after some delay, due to the inclement weather, arrived at Snevce camp in the 60th Division area on the 13th, when the companies were at once set to work on the Snevce–Karamudli road, the material for repair of the same being obtained from the quarries at Karamudli. The companies also worked separately and independently under various units of the Division.

* *History of the 60th Division, pp. 67, 68.*

It had been given out that the spring offensive on the Doiran front
was to open during the first week in April, and at the end of February
the 6oth Division was ordered to take over the section of the front line
between the Vardar and Lake Doiran ; and by the end of March the
divisional headquarters was established at Karasuli, the brigades occupying a general line southwards along the east side of Lake Ardjan, through
Mihalova and Cavalanci to Avret Hissar.

From the 11th to the 18th March the Battalion was engaged in work
under the C.R.A. of the Division, from whom the following letter was
received :—

" I feel I must send you a few lines to thank you very much indeed
for the work your men did for my Divisional Artillery Headquarters from
the 11th to the 18th March.   They worked most splendidly, and were as
good in pitching the camp, etc., as they are at every job they seem to
take on.

" I cannot thank you sufficiently for the help they gave us."

By this time the Battalion was on the march to join the Headquarters
of the 6oth Division, and much of the journey had to be carried out by
night as the road was under enemy observation.   The difficulty inseparable
from marching on unknown roads in the dark, and for three miles through
a swamp, was increased by the driving snow, while a stream which was
in flood and some thirty yards wide had to be forded.

On arrival in camp at Sal de l'Abri all set to work digging " Shell Slits,"
making communication trenches and dug-outs and preparing horse lines.

2nd Lieutenant L. A. Cooke reported for duty from England on the
31st March.

The attack on the Doiran front, originally fixed by General Sarrail for
the first week in April, was deferred for various reasons until the last week
of the month, and in the meantime the enemy became slightly aggressive,
and, as stated in the Battalion War Diary, " during the early hours of the
morning of the 1st April, 2nd Lieut. W. F. Hedges' platoon was working
on the trench at Bowl's Barrow.   The Bulgars, after a stout bombardment,
raided this trench and carried away with them four of our men, two of
whom escaped before reaching the enemy lines.   One of these men was
shot at and bayonetted by his captors.   The captor of the other man was
shot by his comrades who apparently thought he and his prisoner were
part of a raiding party from our lines.   One of the two remaining men is
believed to have been killed by the enemy.   The platoon sergeant was
wounded during the enemy bombardment."

An enemy squadron of German aeroplanes and heavy bombing machines
had now reached this front and began to be very aggressive.   On the 5th

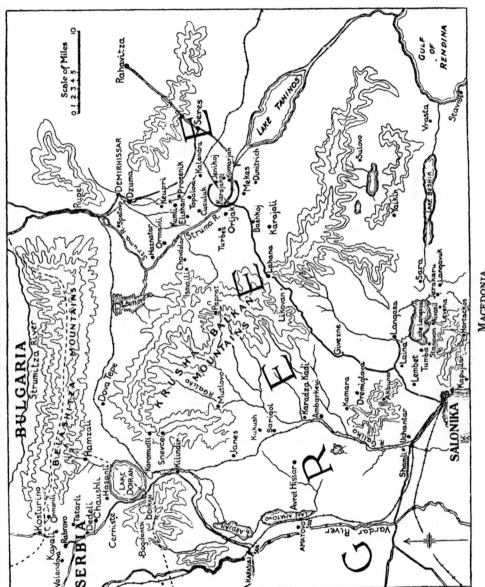

MACEDONIA.

1917.

April an air raid on Karasuli Station was carried out by twelve enemy planes, which dropped a number of bombs in the vicinity of divisional headquarters. Two salvage parties, each fifty strong, were sent to Karasuli Station from the Battalion, but were unable to be of any assistance owing to the continuous explosion of ammunition dumps caused by the bombs.

The long-projected attack on the Doiran front opened on the 20th April, and the 60th Division gained its objectives, the Battalion being busily employed during the days that immediately followed in consolidating the positions captured ; the same procedure was followed when the attack east and west of the Vardar was renewed on the 8th and 9th May.

Further fighting continued without any very outstanding success, and on the 24th May, General Sarrail gave orders for offensive operations to be for the present discontinued, and the 60th Division was now relieved by the 26th, being ordered to occupy the sector near Lake Doiran ; the Battalion was relieved by the 8th Bn. The Oxfordshire and Buckinghamshire L.I. (Pioneers) and moved back to Hill 231, Vladaja Ravine.

About this time the news seems to have got about that the Division was likely to be moved to yet another theatre of the war, and on the 2nd June the Battalion started off on its march down-country, the Division being now under orders to embark for Egypt. On the 6th the Battalion arrived at Uchantar Camp, near Salonika, where all the units of the Division were concentrating, preparatory to embarkation. On the 18th the camp was quitted, and on arrival at the quay the Battalion at once embarked in the transport " Huntspell," and, escorted by two destroyers, the ship sailed for Alexandria, which was reached late on the morning of the 22nd. From here the Battalion—now twenty-five officers and 1,029 other ranks —proceeded in two trains to the base camp of the Egyptian Expeditionary Force at Moascar, near Ismailia on the Suez Canal, where from a fortnight to three weeks was spent, during which time the Division was re-equipped on the Egyptian scale.

Prior to the transfer of the 60th Division from Salonika to Egypt, the advance of the Egyptian Expeditionary Force across Sinai and into Palestine had been brought to a halt before Gaza, and this phase of the campaign had ended with a rebuff. On the 11th June, General Sir A. Murray, the commander who had confronted the early difficulties with forces which he had judged and reported to be inadequate, and who had made all the preparations for the invasion of Palestine, was informed that a change in the command was considered desirable and that General Sir E. H. H. Allenby had been appointed to succeed him.

" When General Sir E. Allenby arrived in Cairo on the 27th June, 1917, the British Government had already decided upon their policy with regard to the campaign in Palestine. . . . But the defeat of the enemy and the eventual destruction of his forces, the capture of Jerusalem, and the expulsion of the Turks from Palestine were fixed as the final goals to endeavour." *

Early in July the 60th Division began moving across the Sinai Desert into Palestine, and on the 19th the Battalion had arrived at Deir-el-Belah, where, by the 23rd, the whole Division was concentrated in readiness to proceed to its allotted section of the line. Massey, in his book *How Jerusalem was Won*, writing of the arrival of the 60th Division, says :—

" The 60th Division came over from Salonika, and we were delighted to have them, for they not only gave us General Bulfin as the XXI. Corps Commander, but set us all an example of dash and doggedness, which earned them a record worthy of the best in the history of the Great War —no one had any misgivings about that cheery crowd."

On the 26th July the Division was ordered to relieve the 53rd Division on the Wadi Ghuzze in the Shellal Gamli section of the line, and the relief was carried out on the 28th and two following days ; the Battalion did not, however, move until the 31st when it marched to and camped about three-quarters of a mile north-east of El Gamli, part of the men being employed in the construction of a Decauville railway line at Gamli East, while the rest of the Battalion was engaged in training.

General Allenby had been promised that another division—the 10th— was to be sent him from Salonika, but this did not arrive until the end of August ; early in that month, however, the Egyptian Expeditionary Force was reorganized and formed into three Corps—a Desert Mounted Corps, a XX. and a XXI. Corps, and the second of this was to contain the 10th, 53rd, 60th and 74th Divisions, with four brigades of Heavy Artillery. General Bulfin was promoted from the command of the 60th Division to that of the XXI. Corps, and Major-General J. S. M. Shea, C.B., D.S.O., succeeded to the command of the 60th Division in his place. The Commander of the XX. Corps was Lieut.-General Sir P. W. Chetwode.

General Allenby announced his intention of taking the offensive as soon as he had seven divisions ready for action, the main attack to be made on the Turkish left, operations being at the same time undertaken against the right and right centre, the main attack being carried out by the XX. and Desert Mounted Corps. " After the initial operations of the XXI. Corps an advance on Beersheba would be made by the XX., and a portion of the Desert Mounted Corps, to capture the place, and, if possible, annihilate its garrison. The XX. Corps, with sufficient mounted forces to protect its right, would then advance north and north-west against the left flank of

* *Military Operations, Egypt and Palestine*, Vol. II, Part I, p. 1.

the enemy and drive him from his positions at Tell-esh-Sheria and Hareira. While these operations were in progress a portion of the Desert Mounted Corps would be retained at Shellal, in the gap between the XX. and XXI. Corps, in case enemy forces should move against the left flank of the former." *

On the 7th September the Battalion Commander was notified by the C.R.E. XX. Corps that the Battalion was now to be considered as G.H.Q. troops temporarily lent to the XX. Corps, remaining under the 60th Division for administrative purposes only ; and for some little time all ranks were employed in making new roads across the Wadi Ghuzze—a wide water-course with steep banks, 150–200 yards wide, flowing into the Mediterranean at Tel-el-Ajjul—to facilitate the passage of troops, and in deepening the reservoirs in the wadi, training being carried on whenever possible.

On the 22nd September a draft of 173 non-commissioned officers and men joined the Battalion, and by the end of the month the total strength was forty-one officers and 1,124 other ranks.

During October the men of the Battalion were kept hard at work laying the Decauville railway of which 5,000 yards were completed—no small effort when it is remembered that in addition the working parties had to march eight miles daily to and from their work. Such spare time as remained was spent in company and battalion training, and after the war was over Field-Marshal Lord Allenby, as he had then become, paid a special tribute to the zeal and energy which all ranks of the 60th Division put into their training, saying that " before it attacked Beersheba it was training so hard to keep fit that the General Officer Commanding had to order his men to eat and drink more, and not work so hard."

On the 18th October the C.O., the Second-in-Command and three other officers made a reconnaissance towards Beersheba for the purpose of selecting a route for future railway construction.

The XX. Corps began to move forward on the night of the 20th–21st October ; ten days later the 60th Division was in its position of assembly south of Beersheba, and by the evening of the 31st the town was in our hands. The Battalion had, however, been ordered not to commence its forward movement until information came through that Beersheba had been taken, and it was consequently not until the afternoon of the 1st November that the Battalion marched through the town, crossing the Wadi Saba and bivouacking on the south side. Fatigue parties were at once furnished for clearing the many wells in and about the town which the enemy had done his best effectually to damage before he fell back.

On the 2nd the Division began to move forward again, and when on

* *Egypt and Palestine*, Vol. II, Part I, p. 17.

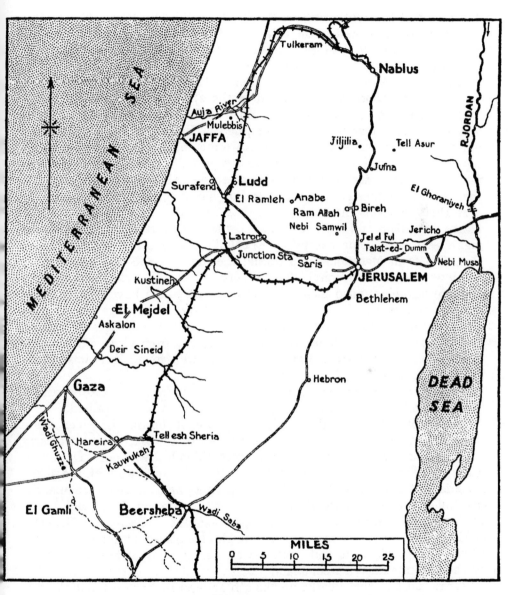

PALESTINE.

—

1917–1918.

the next day the 179th Brigade followed, " A " Company of the Battalion was attached to it, and in the attack made on Sheria on the 6th it formed part of the brigade reserve ; thereafter this company was for some time attached to the 2/14th Battalion London Scottish.

In the attack on Sheria, 2nd Lieutenant R. M. Ashton, of the Battalion, was killed in action, when attached to the 2/19th London Regiment.

The Battalion headquarters remained in Beersheba until the 11th, by which time the town was almost emptied of British troops, and marched out to Kauwukah, and the companies were employed in road making and repairing, gradually moving on to Gaza where all arrived on the 19th, the remaining companies now being also attached to the 179th Brigade. By the 24th the greater part of the Battalion had reached Saris, and here the War Diary contains the information that " we have now got into the hills before Jerusalem and a great change in the temperature is noticeable, the nights especially being exceptionally cold." Sickness had come with the Battalion from Macedonia and during the month there had been a good many admissions to hospital—four officers and 156 other ranks—only three of these being wounded men. The sickness may also have been in some measure due to the large quantities of fruit available, since the History of one battalion of the Division records that " so many oranges were eaten on the march that, later on, drafts marching up from Gaza were known to have followed the trail of orange-peel, and thus found their way across Palestine to Jerusalem " !

During the month the pursuit of the Turks had been relentlessly carried on and Ramleh, Ludd, Enab and Nebi Samwil had been captured.

In the operations resulting in the capture of Jerusalem, which commenced on the 4th December, two companies of the Battalion took part, " C " Company being attached to the 179th Brigade ; while of " D " Company, two platoons served with the 180th Brigade, and two with the 301st Brigade, Royal Field Artillery, the headquarters and remaining companies continuing their railway work at Saris, Junction Station, Ludd and Jaffa. This went on until the 20th December when the G.O.C. 52nd Division specially asked that these companies might be placed at his disposal to assist in preparing rafts and pontoons for the crossing of the Auja River by the troops under his command.

Jerusalem had surrendered on the 9th December, but on the 26th and 27th the Turks made very desperate attempts at its recapture, some of the heaviest of the fighting which resulted being on the front of the 60th Division ; all attacks were heavily repulsed, and by means of counter-attacks by our troops, we gained an advance of 4,000 yards on a six-mile front. On the 28th the XX. Corps was ordered to make a general advance

JERUSALEM, FROM THE MOUNT OF OLIVES.

1918.

The Imperial War Museum.—Copyright.

northwards, and, after four days' fighting, it had advanced on a front of twelve miles to a depth varying from six miles on the right to three on the left. " All that remained of the III. Turkish Corps, that set out to recapture the Holy City, was a mob of demoralized men streaming north."

At the beginning of the New Year, 1918, the 53rd and 60th Divisions changed places, the latter moving to the extreme right of the line and the immediate neighbourhood of Jerusalem, its task being to cover Jerusalem and the Jerusalem–Nablus road, and also to protect the Bethlehem–Hebron road as far as Hebron. The Division was now, to some extent, at rest, leave was opened to Egypt and elsewhere, but work and training of all kinds was carried on, and the Battalion companies found plenty to do in digging trenches, making roads and improving communications.

Early in February preparations were taken in hand for an advance on Jericho, distant some sixteen miles from Jerusalem by a good road. The enemy was known to be holding a position across the Jerusalem–Jericho road at Talat-ed-Dumm, eight miles east of Jerusalem. An attack was to be made upon this position in the middle of February, and this was to be carried out by the 60th Division and two mounted brigades; for these operations two companies of the Battalion were attached to the 181st Brigade and did much useful work while so employed.

The rest of the Battalion remained at work in rear, plate-laying and converting the Turkish line.

That the extent and quality of the work done by the Battalion was appreciated by those in authority is revealed in a letter received by the commander of the 60th Division from the G.O.C. XX. Corps :—

" MY DEAR SHEA,—

" Will you thank your troops for the splendid work they have put in on the laborious and uncongenial task of road-making in your area, which has not only rendered possible further offensive operations, but in the event of the enemy ever being in a position to attack Jerusalem has quadrupled our powers of defence by permitting the free movement of troops in the mountains.

" Yours sincerely,
(sd.) " PHILIP W. CHETWODE."

During March and April the 60th Division was engaged in various raids which were carried out across the Jordan, the Battalion continuing to be very much broken up and working by separate companies and under different commands; but finally, on the 10th April, all the companies came together at Surafend, when the Battalion was re-united for the first time since early in November, 1917.

Early in 1918 the War Office had decided considerably to reinforce
General Allenby's army in Palestine by dispatching thither large numbers
of Indian troops.   The launching on the 21st March of the German offensive
in France, however, not only caused many of the proposed reinforcements
to be wholly withheld or their arrival delayed, but, as stated in an earlier
chapter of this History, dealing with the services of the 2nd Battalion,
General Allenby was called upon to transfer large bodies of his troops
from Egypt to France.

On the 3rd April the G.O.C. 74th Division was informed that his division
would very shortly embark for France ; on the 14th it was concentrated
at Ludd, on the 16th it was at Kantara and two days later embarkation
commenced at Alexandria for Marseilles.   Owing no doubt to the fact that
the 60th Division was to be wholly re-organized, for seven of its battalions
were taken from it and sent to France, while two others were disbanded,
it was decided to transfer the 1/12th Battalion, The Loyal North Lancashire
Regiment, to the 74th Division, and on the 10th April orders to this effect
reached the Battalion.   Three days later it marched from Surafend to
Ludd, there entraining in four trains for Kantara, where all had arrived
by the 14th.   There was no further movement until the 29th, when the
Battalion was sent by train to Alexandria, embarking there in the " Kaiser-
i-Hind," at a strength of thirty-six officers and 980 other ranks and sailing
for Marseilles on the afternoon of the 1st May.

The voyage was somewhat delayed by reports of the presence in these
waters of enemy submarines, and Marseilles was not reached until the
morning of the 7th, and on the following day the journey was commenced
to the front, the Battalion arriving at Noyelles—where the remaining units
of the 74th Division were by this time concentrated—on the 11th May.
Here the Battalion was billeted in the area Hautvillers–Ouville, and on
the 16th it was re-organized on a three-company basis in conformity with
the orders regarding the establishment of a Pioneer Battalion.

By the 25th May a fresh move had been made, the Headquarters of the
74th Division being then at Le Couroy in the Doullens area, the Battalion
being in billets at Fosseux, where it was inspected on the 29th by Major-
General E. S. Girdwood, the commander of the Division.   In these parts
the Battalion remained until the 25th June, when " the 74th Division
moved to Norent Fontes, where it was at four hours' notice for the purpose
of reinforcing either the XI. or XIII. Corps, and at twenty-four hours'
notice for G.H.Q. reserve.   Work on rear defences was carried out for both
Corps, and training continued until the 10th July, when, in accordance
with the XI. Corps orders, the Division started to relieve the 61st Division
in the line.   The line occupied by the Division was between the La Bassée

Canal and the River Lys, with the left resting on the small village of Corbie. The town of Merville, in enemy hands, was some 3,000 yards away." *

During July the companies carried on as usual, and some work of a more or less novel character was also started, parties working with a Tunnelling Company, R.E. : there were some casualties during the month, 2nd Lieutenants Chappell and Carruthers being wounded by shell fire while engaged on work in connection with a Decauville railway near St. Venant. Early in the month the Battalion experienced a great loss, Lieut.-Colonel W. T. C. Beckett, D.S.O., who had served with it uninterruptedly since it was raised and commanded it throughout the war, relinquishing the command on the 9th July; he was succeeded by Major W. Longbottom.

The line remained quiet until the 4th August, and there were now signs that the enemy was falling back, consequently orders were issued for an advance, when the Division moved forward some 3,000 yards, meeting with comparatively trifling opposition and that mostly from machine-gun fire. Marshal Foch, who in March had assumed the command of the Allied Armies, now issued the following order for the August offensive :—

" The British Fourth Army and the French First Army will advance on the 8th, under the command of Field-Marshal Sir D. Haig, the former north and the latter south of the Amiens–Roye road. The offensive, covered by the Somme, will be pushed as far as possible towards Roye. The French Third Army will attack the left flank of the Montdidier Salient on the 10th inst. The French Tenth Army in the Oise Valley, on the left bank, will continue to advance eastwards."

The Battalion remained at work about St. Venant during the early part of August, occasionally having to change billets owing to the very accurate fire from the enemy's guns, which on the 1st occasioned the death of a young officer, 2nd Lieutenant C. W. Fryer; but when on the 8th the advance began, " A " and " C " Companies were pushed up to the front to make good the roads in the forward area, repair bridges and fill in shell holes ; later in the month the remainder of the Battalion was sent forward to do the same work, under, however, heavy shelling.

The Division was relieved on the 26th by the 59th Division and began to leave for the Somme area, the Battalion entraining at Aire, and proceeding by St. Pol, Doullens and Amiens to Méricourt l'Abbé, where it was billeted for a few days.

In the action of the 2nd September the III. Corps attacked the spurs west and south-west of Nurlu, the 74th Division being on the right, the 47th in the centre and the 18th on the left. Only one company, however, of the Battalion—" B "—moved forward with the advance, this being attached

* Dudley-Ward, *The 74th (Yeomanry) Division in Syria and France*, p. 208.

to the 229th Brigade and held in readiness to form crossings for the guns
over the Canal du Nord ; the infantry of the Brigade was, however, unable
to get sufficiently far forward, and the company withdrew to the Battalion ;
the other companies worked on the roads, moving forward as the troops
advanced, also repairing the light railway and the pipe line.

When on the 21st September, during the Battle of Epéhy, the situation
at one time became somewhat critical, the whole of the Battalion was
ordered forward to take up battle stations in the reserve line, remaining up
here until the 24th when they went back to camp. At the end of the
month the whole Battalion was quartered in billets near Chocques.

The advance continued, the Battalion following up closely, repairing
the main and side roads and filling in shell holes and mine craters, in fact
making good all the damage which the enemy attempted to do in his retreat.
On the 16th October the crossings of the Canal on the divisional front
having been secured, the companies worked with the R.E. in throwing
pontoon and other bridges across at Habourdin and at La Planchée des
Saintes, later on helping in the laying of a heavy trestle bridge. During
the whole of this month the companies were much separated and worked
more or less independently.

Early in the morning of 7th November, 1918, Marshal Foch, then at his
head-quarters at Senlis, received a wireless message from the Germans to
the effect that an immediate suspension of hostilities was desired and that
their emissaries were waiting to know how and where they could enter the
Allied lines to sue for an armistice. The deputation was duly ordered to
present itself before the French outposts at La Capelle, by 5 p.m., the same
day, where it would be received and conducted to the place fixed for interview. In the meantime Foch took up his quarters in his own special train
which moved to a railway siding near Rethnodes Station, in the Forest of
Laigle. At 9 a.m., two hours after their arrival there, on the following day,
the 8th, the German plenipotentiaries were ushered into the presence of
the Marshal and the other Allied commanders, who after having examined
their credentials read out the conditions imposed by their Governments ;
a period of seventy-two hours being granted for consideration of the terms.
At 12.30 a.m. on 11th November, authority having been received from
the German head-quarters at Spa, the envoys requested a further interview
in order to sign the Armistice. By 5.15 a.m., all outstanding questions
had been decided upon and the various signatures appended whereby the
Armistice was to come into force six hours later, namely at 11 o'clock that
morning.

When on the 11th November information was received of the signing
of an Armistice the Battalion was concentrated in billets at Frasnes, having

been at work during the previous days in the neighbourhood of Tournai. The cessation of hostilities did not put an end to the work of a Pioneer Battalion, for there was very much to be done in the improvement of communications of all kinds.

On the 6th December the Battalion marched to Mansart, where the 74th Division was inspected by His Majesty The King.

On the 10th, demobilization having commenced, the first batch of men left for home.

The 1st January, 1919, found the whole Battalion billeted in Lessines, and during the month officers and other ranks left for England in parties of varying size, some on short periods of leave and some on demobilization, those remaining being employed in clearing the area and engaging in educational and other forms of training.

On the 24th February the Battalion—now containing only eleven officers and 131 other ranks—left Lessines and went by train to Bonn, on arrival there being billeted at Dottendorf and in Kessinech.   Here, during February, the Battalion began to be made up to strength again :—

On the 8th Lieutenants G. S. Harris, J. E. Orrell, 2nd Lieutenants J. B. Gore, C. J. Sollitt, W. Wilcock, C. G. Helliwell, K. R. Harvey and 272 other ranks reported for duty from the 1st Battalion of the Regiment.

On the 10th, Lieutenants A. Dawson, R. P. Hargreaves, G. H. Tasker and fifty men joined from the 2/4th and twelve more from the 1st Battalion.

On the 12th Lieutenants C. A. Atkins, G. W. Slack and fifty-four other ranks arrived from the 2/5th, and Lieutenants G. W. Rushton, T. L. Pritchard, W. Strong, 2nd Lieutenants J. Bonnington, H. V. Carwin, H. J. Gibbs, J. E. Higgins, E. R. Schofield, W. E. Ulyatt, C. W. Donnellan, T. R. Smith, W. E. Knowles, and 166 other ranks joined from the 2nd Battalion, and other very small parties followed.   Officers and men were, however, leaving the Battalion almost daily on demobilization or for transfer to other units of the Army of Occupation, but on the 31st March the Battalion stood at the remarkable strength of sixty-eight officers and 1,265 non-commissioned officers and men.

On the 5th July the Battalion paraded for the presentation of the King's Colour by Lieut.-General Morland, commanding X. Corps, and early in September a move was made to the infantry barracks in Bonn.   Here the strength of the Battalion began appreciably and rapidly to decline, and it was accordingly re-organized on a two-company basis under Captains C. A. Atkins and W. R. Harness.   The end was now very near ; the last official record of the 12th (Pioneer) Battalion, The Loyal North Lancashire Regiment, shows it still at Bonn on the 31st October, 1919; the following month it returned to England for final disbandment.

CHAPTER LVII

THE 2/12TH (TERRITORIAL) BATTALION (PIONEERS)
THE 13TH (HOME SERVICE) BATTALION
THE 14TH (TERRITORIAL) BATTALION
THE LOYAL NORTH LANCASHIRE REGIMENT

1916–1918

THE 2/12TH (TERRITORIAL) BATTALION (PIONEERS)

A SECOND Battalion for the 12th Pioneers was raised early in 1916, and it made its first appearance in the Army List for April of that year, when the following officers appear as posted to it : Captains J. M. Turnbull and W. E. James (adjutant) ; Lieutenants S. J. Hughes and A. Walsh ; 2nd Lieutenants R. W. Williams, G. Tong, H. E. Ward, B. Moore, S. N. Bradbury, S. H. Bailey, P. P. Butters, A. M. Pawsey, C. A. Young, W. F. Hedges, G. M. McCorquodale, D. Harrop, J. J. Tinker, H. N. C. Chase, E. H. Treacy and H. C. Palmer, with Lieutenant and Quartermaster J. Lalor.

In August 1916 the Battalion was amalgamated with the 3/4th and 3/5th Battalions of the Regiment, under the title 4th Reserve Battalion.

Over three thousand men were recruited, many being drafted to the 1/12th Battalion overseas. The Battalion remained on home service.

THE 13TH (HOME SERVICE) BATTALION

This would appear to have been raised during the winter of 1916, since it is first shown in the Army List for January, 1917, with the following two officers only : Lieut.-Colonel G. C. Ashworth and Major and Quartermaster B. Goacher. It had but a comparatively brief existence since it does not appear in the Army List after that for August, 1918, when only eight second-lieutenants remained. A number of officers from the London Regiment were attached for duty.

THE 14TH (TERRITORIAL) BATTALION

The 14th Battalion of the Loyal North Lancashire Regiment was raised in the early spring of 1917, and made its initial appearance in the April Army List of that year ; the following are the officers shown as having been appointed to it : Captains G. V. Williams and J. B. Morrison ; Lieutenants J. H. Lee, A. E. Sholl, T. A. Ridshaw, A. P. Smith, H. Maxwell, A. M. Tomlinson, L. R. B. Grainger and F. H. B. Hodgson. It ceased to appear in the Army List after the issue of January, 1918, in which month only the adjutant, Captain G. H. Dickson, was shown. Headquarters were at Bolton.

CHAPTER LVIII

THE 15TH (SERVICE) BATTALION
THE LOYAL NORTH LANCASHIRE REGIMENT

1918–1919

THE BATTLES OF YPRES AND COURTRAI

THE genesis of the 15th (Service) Battalion, The Loyal North Lancashire Regiment, may be traced in a statement contained in Sir Douglas Haig's despatch of the 21st December, 1918, wherein he describes the operations which took place between May and November of that year; in this he writes that by the end of April " it had become impossible to maintain at an effective strength the full number of our divisions. At the beginning of May no less than eight divisions had been reduced to cadres and were temporarily written off altogether as fighting units."

The 14th Division was one of them, the date of its reduction to cadre being the 27th May, 1918, and on the 17th June it returned to England, and proceeded to Bullswater Camp, near Pirbright, where it at once began to recruit and reorganize. From the cadre of one of the units of the Division —the strength of which unit can hardly have exceeded ten officers and forty other ranks—a new battalion very speedily began to rise. Between the 18th and the 20th June drafts amounting to thirty-three officers and something like 900 non-commissioned officers and men joined, and before the end of the month the strength of the new Battalion stood at forty-three officers and 937 other ranks. Within a few days, however, 254 of the new arrivals were found to be medically unfit for active service and were sent back to Oswestry, while officers surplus to establishment were ordered to Cromer.

Under date of the 19th June it is stated in the War Diary—" Battalion definitely named 15th Bn. The Loyal North Lancashire Regiment (Pioneers) "; but this title would seem to have been later changed, though no mention of such occurs in the Diary, for in the Army Lists for the period during which the Battalion endured, it is always shown as the " 15th (Service) Bn., The Loyal North Lancashire Regiment."

Its initial appearance in the Army List is in that for October, 1918; here the names of the following officers occur with dates of appointment :—

Lieut.-Colonel S. Bingham, D.S.O. . .	18th June, 1918
Major H. Johnson, M.C. . . .	18th ,, ,,
,, G. J. Harris, M.C. . . .	18th ,, ,,
Captain R. G. Chadwick . . .	18th ,, ,,
,, H. Paget, adjutant. . .	18th ,, ,,
,, H. Hallam	18th ,, ,,
Lieutenant R. Attwood . . .	19th ,, ,,
,, J. S. Flood . . .	27th ,, ,,
,, J. Wright	19th ,, ,,
2nd Lieutenant J. H. Dodds . .	18th ,, ,,
,, A. Manning, M.M. . .	18th ,, ,,
,, V. Jones . . .	27th ,, ,,
,, H. Short, M.C. . .	27th ,, ,,
,, A. B. Robson . .	27th ,, ,,
,, F. T. Stevens . .	19th ,, ,,
,, W. S. Taylor . .	27th ,, ,,
,, D. S. Wilson . .	27th ,, ,,
,, H. H. Pollock . .	27th ,, ,,
,, J. R. Case . . .	27th ,, ,,

The 14th Division was now once again complete, and was to return to France, the Battalion forming part of the divisional troops. Leaving Brookwood by train—the transport under 2nd Lieutenant Howell on the 3rd and the headquarters on the 4th July—the Battalion crossed over from Folkestone to Boulogne, and moving on thence with the Divisional Head-quarter Group, it was settled by the 13th July in billets at Mentque. Here a draft of 152 men joined from Étaples, bringing the strength of the Battalion up to 33 officers and 798 non-commissioned officers and men.

The 14th Division was now in the X. Corps of the Second Army.

The Battalion remained at Mentque until the 18th August, when it was moved to the neighbourhood of Poperinghe, and was here for some time employed under the orders of the II. Corps in work on a light rail-way and the improvement of the Vlamertinghe defence line.

On the 1st September, when the companies were up in the front line working separately under other brigades of the Division, one of them was badly shelled and 2nd Lieutenant A. C. Ramsdale was killed and one man was wounded. The Battalion continued doing useful work, training in such spare time as was available, until the 28th September, when the 14th Division was to take part in the Battle of Ypres of this year.

In Sir Douglas Haig's despatch of the 21st December, 1918, he states that " at 5.30 a.m. on the 28th September the XIX. and II. Corps of the

Second Army attacked without preliminary bombardment on a front of some four and a half miles south of the Ypres–Zonnebeke road. The 14th Division (Major-General P. C. B. Skinner), 35th Division, 29th, and 9th Divisions delivered the initial assault, being supported in the later stages of the battle by the 41st and the 36th Divisions. On the left of the II. Corps the Belgian Army continued the line of attack as far as Dixmude." (The 14th Division was now in the XIX. Corps.)

" On both the British and Belgian fronts the attack was a brilliant success. The enemy, who was attempting to hold his positions with less than five divisions, was driven rapidly from the whole of the high ground east of Ypres, so fiercely contested during the battles of 1917. By the end of the day the British divisions had passed far beyond the furthest limits of the 1917 battles, and had reached and captured Kortewilde, Zandvoorde, Kruiseecke and Becelaere. On their left Belgian troops had taken Zonnebeke and Poelcappelle, and cleared the enemy from Houlthulst Forest."

When on the above date the 14th Division attacked astride the Ypres–Comines Canal to St. Eloi Crater and the Bluff, the Battalion companies stood by at Melon Copse with the 1st Field Company, R.E., ready to go forward in two shifts to carry out repair work on the Voormezeele-Hollebeke road as far forward as possible. When the night came on and work had to cease, the Battalion bivouacked north-east of Dickebusch, carrying on again early the following morning and working on the road from St. Eloi via Hollebeke as far as the banks of the Comines Canal. During the first week of October the companies worked on the roads east of Messines, Wulverghem, Ploegsteert and near other towns.

At this time the German Chancellor was addressing appeals to President Wilson suggesting the conclusion of an armistice between the warring nations. This produced something of the nature of a special warning from Army Headquarters in the field, which was issued to " all concerned " on the morning of the 7th October : " There are indications that the attention of officers and men is in danger of being diverted, by insidious rumours, from their single task of defeating the enemy, and the Field-Marshal Commanding-in-Chief warns all ranks against the disturbing influence of such unfounded peace talk. He wishes it to be clearly understood that at no time has there been a greater need of relentless effort or a fairer promise of great results, and the Army will concentrate its entire energy in bringing the operations in the field to a successful and decisive issue."

When on the 14th the Second Army continued the attack, the 14th Division stood by awaiting results, crossing the Lys River in the afternoon. The attack, as the despatch informs us, was on the whole front between the Lys River and Comines and Dixmude, the British sector extending for a distance of between nine and ten miles from Comines to the hamlet of St. Pieter on the Menin–Roulers road, and was launched by the X., XIX. and II. Corps of the Second Army. The attack was attended by complete success, and on the afternoon of the 16th the troops of the Second Army held the north bank of the Lys from Frelinghien to opposite Harlebeke. The enemy now was rapidly retreating.

Following up our advancing troops, the companies of the Battalion worked hard at improving the roads to the bridge approaches, and towards the close of the month were busy about the divisional area east of Dottignies.

During October six additional subalterns joined the Battalion.

The Battalion was about Estaimpuis when on the 11th November the news came in that the Armistice had been signed with Germany; but there was no rest for the companies and work went on as usual, until the 16th, when the Battalion moved to Tourcoing, and here a Divisional Agricultural Company was formed from farm labourers of different units and lent to the country people to assist them with work on their long-neglected farms. Then on the 20th demobilization commenced, miners and railway employés being the first to leave the Army and the Battalion.

Inspections were now the order of the day; educational courses of all kinds were arranged; and men continued to leave for England and civil life in small but almost daily parties. On Christmas Day, 1918, the War Diary contains the curt but expressive remark—" No parades."

On the 25th January, 1919, there was a divisional parade when the Commander of the XV. Corps, Lieut.-General Sir H. B. de Lisle, presented the King's Colour to the Service Battalions of the 14th Division, the ceremony taking place in the Grande Place at Roubaix; each battalion sent a representative party, that of the 15th Battalion being under the command of Captain J. S. Flood.

The Battalion had now become so weak in numbers that on the 7th February it was re-organized into one company of three platoons under the command of Major G. J. Harris, M.C. Five weeks later—on the 15th March—the following officers were transferred to the 12th Battalion of the Regiment, they having volunteered to remain in Germany with the Army of Occupation—Captains Manning, Flood and Harkess, Lieutenant Johnson, 2nd Lieutenants Case, Hogg and Pendlebury.

On the last day of March the Battalion was reduced to cadre strength, this being, including attached, fifteen officers and fifty-five other ranks.

At last, on the 3rd June, orders were received for the cadre to return to England, and on the 14th a start was made for Boulogne by way of Lille, the Colour being in charge of 2nd Lieutenant Jones and the cadre itself under the command of Major H. Paget. Disbandment then followed.

APPENDICES

I–VIII

By

K. R. WILSON

APPENDIX I

THE COLONELS OF THE REGIMENT

THE 47TH REGIMENT

NAME.	DATE OF APPOINTMENT.	
Colonel J. Mordaunt	15th January	1741
General P. Lascelles	13th March	1743
Lieut.-General Lord Guy Dorchester, K.B.	2nd April	1772
Major-General A. Williamson	16th July	1790
General W. Dalrymple	19th March	1794
General Hon. R. Fitzpatrick	25th February	1807
General Hon. Sir Alexander Hope, G.C.B.	26th April	1813
General Sir William Anson, Bart., K.C.B.	25th March	1835
Major-General Sir Henry G. W. Smith, Bart., G.C.B.	18th January	1847
Lieut.-General T. Dalmer, C.B.	16th April	1847
General Sir James Shaw Kennedy, K.C.B.	27th August	1854
Major-General Sir Charles T. Van Straubenzee, K.C.B.	31st May	1865
Lieut.-General J. Patton	8th December	1867
General Sir William O'Grady Haly, K.C.B.	2nd November	1875
General Sir William S. R. Norcott, K.C.B.	20th March	1878

THE 81ST REGIMENT

Major-General Albemarle Bertie	19th September	1793
Major-General W. Blathwayte	31st December	1794
Major-General Hon. C. Norton	25th March	1795
Major-General G. Forbes	24th January	1797
Major-General Sir Hew Dalrymple	8th August	1797
Major-General J. G. Simcoe	18th January	1798
General Sir Henry Johnson, Bart.	18th June	1798
Lieut.-General Sir James Kempt, G.C.B., G.C.H.	12th July	1819

GENERAL SIR JAMES WILLCOCKS, G.C.B., G.C.M.G., K.C.S.I., D.S.O.

Colonel
The Loyal North Lancashire Regiment
1916-1926.

NAME.	DATE OF APPOINTMENT.
Lieut.-General Sir Richard D. Jackson, K.C.B. . .	8th January 1829
Major-General Sir John Waters, K.C.B. . . .	15th June 1840
Lieut.-General Sir Maurice C. O'Connell, K.C.H. . .	6th December 1842
Major-General Sir George H. F. Berkeley, K.C.B. . .	15th January 1844
Lieut.-General Sir Neil Douglas, K.C.B., K.C.H. . .	11th July 1845
General T. Evans, C.B.	12th July 1847
General Sir William F. Forster, K.H.	12th February 1863
General H. Renny, C.S.I.	9th June 1879

THE LOYAL NORTH LANCASHIRE REGIMENT

General Sir William S. R. Norcott, K.C.B. . . .	20th March 1878
General H. Renny, C.S.I.	9th June 1879
General Sir Richard T. Farren, G.C.B.	14th September 1885
Major-General H. T. Jones-Vaughan, C.B. . . .	31st December 1909
General Sir James Willcocks, G.C.B., G.C.M.G., K.C.S.I., D.S.O.	12th April 1916
Lieut.-General Sir Gerald F. Ellison, K.C.B., K.C.M.G. .	19th December 1926
Brigadier-General J. B. Wells, C.M.G., D.S.O. . .	18th August 1931

APPENDIX II

THE COLOURS

The Colours may be said to be the concrete embodiment of the soul of the regiment ; so long as the Colours remain and there is even one man left to carry them, a regiment can never die and can recruit again around that one man and so continue on its path to future glory with the same old traditions behind it, together with the same atmosphere surrounding it.

When the 47th was raised in 1741 the practice of carrying one Colour per company throughout a battalion had ceased, and the establishment allowed for one pair, or " stand," of Colours per battalion ; these consisted of a " King's," or Union, and a " Regimental " Colour, as at present, save that they were larger than those of to-day, measuring six and a half feet by six feet, on a nine-foot pole. Although the records of the Colours of some regiments have survived from these days, particular mention of those of the 47th Regiment cannot be traced ; it may be assumed, therefore, that they conformed more or less to the standard pattern laid down for the Infantry of the Line. At this time, and for more than a century afterwards, the Colours were provided by the Colonel of the Regiment and slight variations of pattern were liable to occur.

Prior to 1743 the patterns of regimental Colours had been optional with colonels of regiments ; on the 14th September of that year instructions were issued that no colonel was to be permitted to put his arms, crest, device, or livery, on any part of the appointments of his regiment. The regulations were as follows : " The First Colour of every marching Regiment of Foot is to be the Great Union. The Second Colour to be the colour of the facing of the regiment, with the Union in the upper canton, except those regiments which are faced with white or red, whose Second Colour is to be the Red Cross of St. George in a white field, with the Union in the upper canton. In the centre of each Colour is to be painted, in gold Roman figures, the number of the rank of the regiment, within a wreath, except those regiments which have royal devices or ancient badges ; the numbers of their rank are to be painted towards the upper canton."

From records, changes of pattern and other reliable data, it may be safely concluded that the 47th and 2/47th (The Tarifa Battalion), between them, have had eleven different stands of Colours, but only three can be found to-day.

The first set possessed by Mordaunt's may have been carried at Prestonpans, 21st September, 1745, but as to what became of it there is now no knowledge ; it is just possible that, the conflict being a civil war, the Colours were left behind at Edinburgh. In 1750 the Regiment was, for the first time, officially numbered

" 47th " ; this would involve a new set of Colours in the ordinary course of events, but as the 47th was by this time in Nova Scotia, the change was much delayed.

The Regulations of 1751 styled the First and Second Colours respectively the " King's " and " Regimental," and they have been so termed ever since.

The first official notice of new Colours is contained in an Inspection Return of 1767, which states that new Colours had been given in 1760 ; from this may be drawn two inferences—either the original set was replaced then, or else the second set had been so shot to pieces in the two hot actions of Quebec and St. Foy that it was no longer fit to be seen ; the latter is the more probable.

The designs on the Colours were originally hand painted, but in 1768 instructions were given that they could be either painted or embroidered ; about 1820 painted Colours ceased to be made and only embroidered were henceforth brought into use.

The next record is again gleaned from an Inspection Return of 1771, which tells us that the Regiment had new Colours in 1770 ; this was an ill-fated set, for it went through the Siege of Boston, the Battle of Bunker's Hill, and was carried at last through the New England forests to the fatal lines of Saratoga. What happened to it on the surrender of Burgoyne's army is unknown ; certainly it cannot be traced now among the captured British Colours still in America. When the 47th was re-constituted in 1782 and became the " Lancashire Regiment " it received another new set of Colours—so much is gathered from an Inspection Report dated 9th of November of that year—and that set lasted till 1803, when the 47th came back from Bermuda to find that the incorporation of the Cross of St. Patrick in the Union Jack, consequent on the Union with Ireland, had rendered another change of pattern necessary. This is the first set of which there is any pictorial record still extant. In the archives of the Inspector of Regimental Colours (which Office came into existence about the end of the eighteenth century) there is a sketch showing the Regimental Colour in 1807. No county title, however, appeared on the Colours of any regiment of the Infantry of the Line before the year 1816 at the earliest. In the same archives there is a hand-painted book showing the Colours of every regiment in the Army of 1820, collected by order of H.M. King George IV ; in this series the contemporary records of the Colours of both battalions of the 47th and 81st Regiments appear.

Until 1825 Colours were not formally presented, being received and accounted for as ordinary stores.

The next record comes again from the files of the Inspector of Regimental Colours, where there is a letter from Mr. Horne—a well-known Colour maker of the period—dated 1st of March, 1831, asking for working drawings for a new set of Colours for the 47th Foot ; and incidentally, it may be mentioned that the 1/47th had been abroad for twenty-four years without a break, that the old Colours had been subject to the stress of war and weather in places as far apart as the Rio de la Plata, the Persian Gulf and the Burmese jungle ; this set is the earliest one of the 47th Regiment which has yet been traced, and is referred to in some old regimental accounts which show an entry dated 9th August, 1831 : " Paid Mr. Horne for a pair of Colours, £40." Again on 4th September, 1832, there is a further payment of £4 to the same individual for " two pairs of tassels for the Colours."

Although the Digest of Services does not give the exact date when it was taken into use, it is clear that this set was carried by the 47th from 1832 to 1858 ; consequently it went through the Crimean campaign with the Regiment, so that it was the last set of Colours carried by the 47th Foot in action.   On the 20th of September, 1854, the Regiment, forming part of the Second Division, crossed the Alma just above the blazing village of Bourliouk and advanced up the hill against the Russian centre ; the Queen's Colour was badly torn by a plunging shot, which killed two N.C.O.s of the Colour party, and the Regimental was also injured ; both the ensigns escaped unwounded.   When the 47th returned from the Crimea, the Colours being considered too dilapidated to be emblazoned with the new honours, a fresh set was requisitioned and the old ones were laid up in the Parish Church of Lancaster, late in 1858.   It must be remembered that at this time the 47th was the only regular Lancashire regiment.   (See Illustration facing page 136, Volume I.)

The dimensions of the Colours of the Infantry had remained practically unchanged ; in 1855 it was prescribed that the size was to be in future six feet in the fly and five feet six inches on the pike, namely, six inches less both ways. In 1858 a Royal Warrant authorized a further reduction in the size of the Colours, namely, four feet flying and three feet six inches deep ; it was also ordered that the Queen's Colour was to be edged with a gold fringe mixed with crimson silk, whilst that on the Regimental was to be the hue of the regimental facings. The poles were surmounted by the Lion and Crown instead of the ornamental spear-head ; the cords and tassels of crimson silk and gold were attached as heretofore.   A subsequent alteration in size was made in 1868, reducing flag dimensions to three feet nine inches flying and three feet on the staff, which measurements are still those of the present day.   In 1904 the length of the pike was reduced from nine feet ten inches, including the four-inch Crown and Lion on top, to that of eight feet seven and a half inches.

The next set of Colours was presented to the 47th Regiment by Major-General Sir James Yorke Scarlett at Aldershot on 19th of November, 1858, and was carried on parade until 1912—a remarkable achievement that two sets of Colours should have spanned eighty years between them !   All that is left of this last set now reposes in Preston Parish Church ; the Regimental is still quite recognizable, but the King's is almost beyond identification.   It is rather interesting to note that as far back as 1896 the 1st Battalion of the Loyal North Lancashire Regiment put in a requisition for new Colours to replace those issued in 1858, but by the time the new set followed the 1st Battalion to Ceylon, it had left for South Africa ; this was early in 1899.   The incidence of the South African War, and various other reasons, delayed the presentation, so that it was not until May, 1912, that the 1st Battalion received the new Colours from the hands of H.M. King George V at Aldershot.   This accounts for the fact that the present 1st Battalion Colours bear the pattern of Crown characteristic of Queen Victoria's reign.

Immediately after the signing of the Armistice and the consequent cessation of hostilities in France and Flanders, on the 11th November, 1918, the Colours of the 1st and 2nd Battalions, Loyal North Lancashire Regiment, were brought out from England and were carried by these battalions on the march to the Rhine. During the early part of 1919, the 1st Battalion was quartered at Bornheim and the 2nd Battalion at Siegburg, being units of the British Army of Occupation in Germany, and were for the first time in the history of the Regiment stationed in the vicinity of each other. The illustration facing page 74, Volume II, shows the Colours of the 1st and 2nd Battalions, together, on the banks of the Rhine, in March, 1919.

It may be mentioned that the Crimean Colours at Lancaster were found in 1925 to be in a very bad state of dilapidation; they had been roughly netted, and the frayed and perished silk was fast tearing away from the support; they were consequently entirely re-netted and re-mounted, and are now restored to their old positions in Lancaster Parish Church.

The 81st Regiment appears to have been more fortunate in the matter of the preservation of their old Colours; out of nine stands of Colours traceable to the 1st and 2nd Battalions of the Loyal Lincoln Volunteers, seven can actually be seen.

It has been mentioned previously that in the eighteenth century, and until 1855 in the nineteenth, Colours were provided by the Colonel of the Regiment out of his " off reckonings," or deductions, from the grant per man enlisted, which were allowed to the Colonel to clothe and equip his men. It was a natural thing, then, that as the old sets of Colours passed into retirement they should be returned to the source from which they originally came. Following this line of argument, a set was traced home to the family of General Albemarle Bertie, who raised the Loyal Lincoln Volunteers. The family records showed that a set of Colours belonging to the 81st Foot had hung for years in Uffington Church, until they had decayed and were deemed too disreputable to be kept there any longer; so they were turned out, to be found long afterwards in a coach-house by Lord Lindsey, who then gave them a place of honour in Uffington Hall. One night, in the spring of 1904, Lord Lindsey and his household were awakened by an alarm of fire; and in a very short time the old mansion was a mass of smouldering ruins. When morning came, only one of the Colours could be found, the King's, and the fact that there was no crimson where the Cross of St. Patrick should have shown, put the date before 1801—it was the original King's Colour of the 81st, having waved at St. Domingo and the Cape, and was probably retired when the 81st Regiment came home from South Africa in 1802, as a new pattern would be required on account of the Union with Ireland.

The next record occurs in the correspondence of the Inspector of Regimental Colours, and brings us to the year 1807. In the meantime the Regiment had taken part in its first battle and the name of Maida was fresh on everyone's lips. The Inspector of Colours seems to have been charged with the somewhat thankless task of ascertaining that the Colours of all Regiments conformed to standard pattern, and to this end he issued a circular letter calling for a return of the pattern of Colour in use and for " reasons in writing " for any divergence from that laid

B B

down.   The sketch returned by the O.C. 1/81st has preserved for us the pattern of the Colours carried at Maida, and it is particularly interesting in that it shows the honour " MAIDA " embroidered on both the Colours in a quite unique fashion : that is, on a diamond-shaped label, within a wreath.   " MAIDA " was one of the earliest honours authorized to be borne on the Colours and possibly the way in which the name was affixed thereto was determined by the individual ideas of commanding officers.   It is said that this particular set of Colours was laid up in a church in Lincolnshire, but it has not been possible, so far, to trace them.

King George IV's Book in the archives of the Inspector of Regimental Colours (1820) gives the contemporary record of the sets carried by the 1/81st, and the 2/81st, disbanded four years previously, bearing the honours " MAIDA," " CORUNNA," and " PENINSULA."

In 1826 the 81st was in Canada ; by a happy coincidence Lieut.-General Sir James Kempt, G.C.B., who had been Colonel of the Regiment since 1819, was at the time Lieutenant-Governor of Halifax, and he presented the Battalion with a new set of Colours at Halifax on the 14th of June of that year.   The Digest of Services gives a detailed account of the ceremony, including the speeches, in one of which there is a remark from which it may be inferred that the set retired on this occasion was the one carried at Maida ; if so, the embroidery must have been altered when the Peninsular honours were put on, as it is entirely different in the 1820 book from the design shown in the 1807 return.   This point cannot be cleared up until the Maida Colours are located, if ever.

About the year 1839 the use of Arabic numerals on new Colours practically ceased ; the space in the centre of the girdle bearing the County title being occupied solely by the number in Roman characters, the abbreviation " Regt." being dispensed with.

At St. Ann's, Barbados, on the 8th of December, 1840, the 81st received its next set from the hands of " The Lady of Lieut.-General John Maister," as the Digest quaintly puts it ; this last-mentioned set, with the 1826 set of the 81st, together with that of the 2/81st, are now honoured in the Soldiers' Chapel in Lincoln Cathedral, where a tablet on the wall serves to remind the inhabitants of that ancient City of the last visible link which exists between themselves and the Regiment which still bears their City arms on its badge.   The manner in which they came there is not without interest, and may be briefly retold.   In 1912, Colonel Churchward, after finishing his period of command of the 2nd Battalion, Loyal North Lancashire, was serving in the Eastern District, where he came across some records which led him to think that there were some 81st Colours at Lincoln Cathedral.   He went there to investigate, and found that nearly half a century before some sets had been sent there for safe custody ; but at that time a distinctly anti-military feeling existed among the ecclesiastical authorities, wherefore the unwelcome charge had been passed on to the City Corporation. The latter body had taken them over and the Colours had reposed ever since in the vaults of the " Stone Bow " (one of the old City gates), being taken out from time to time to decorate the Guildhall on festive occasions.   After some negotiations, the City Council was induced to agree to the return of the Colours to their proper resting-place within the Cathedral walls ; for by this time the Dean and Canons were more than anxious to recover them and were prepared to accord them every possible honour. At length the matter was arranged satisfactorily, and on the 24th of September, 1913, a party of the 2nd Battalion, led by Colonel Jackson and Colonel Churchward, took over the Colours and carried them to the Cathedral, where they were handed over to the Dean for " safe and honourable custody." In handing them over Colonel Jackson, himself a Mutiny veteran, reminded his hearers that one of the sets was that carried by the 2/81st at Corunna, and that under it fourteen officers and over one hundred other ranks had fallen, dead or wounded, in the course of the Battle.

Battle-honours, to be borne on both Colours, were first introduced into the Army about the year 1784, but in 1844 these were forbidden on the Queen's Colour of the regiments of the Infantry of the Line ; being borne on the Regimental only. The practice was now discontinued of placing any regimental device upon the Royal Colour, more than the number of the regiment, surmounted by the Crown.

In 1854, at Meerut, the 81st Regiment received new Colours from their Colonel, Lieut.-General T. Evans, C.B. ; this was the last set of large Colours carried by the Regiment, and it was not until 1903 that the great six-foot silken squares—the Regimental having for its ground the familiar buff of the old 81st facings—disappeared from parade, to be replaced by a set of the regulation type (small) Colours, which were quietly taken into use without ceremony. Concerning this latter set, it is worth noting that they were made and passed for service by the Inspector of Regimental Colours in 1878, so that they still bore in the centre the old number " LXXXI " ; having been kept in store for twenty-five years ! The 1854 set went through the Indian Mutiny, but it cannot be said with certainty that they were flown in action, for Sir Colin Campbell issued an order that Colours were not to be uncased in face of the mutineers ; it is quite certain however that they were the last Colours of The Loyal Regiment to be exposed to the fire of an enemy, for they were on the hillside at Ali Masjid in November, 1878, where one of them was carried by Colonel Churchward—then an ensign. These are now laid up in the Parish Church of Preston.

The Illustration facing page 256, Volume I, depicts the Colours of the 81st Regiment, as presented in 1854.

On the re-organization of the Army on the 1st July, 1881, General Order No. 41 of that year stated : " All distinctions appearing hitherto on the Colours, as borne by either of the Line Battalions of a Territorial Regiment, will in future be borne by both those battalions." With the introduction of the Territorial system there disappeared from the Regimental Colour the small Union in the dexter canton, when it was directed that : " in regiments which are faced with white the Second Colour is to be the Red Cross of St. George, in a white field, with the Territorial designation and the title displayed within the Union wreath of Roses, Thistles, and Shamrocks, ensigned with the Imperial Crown." This order only applied to the design of new Colours and was not intended to alter those already in use.

A Circular Letter was addressed to all commanding officers in 1882, pointing out that, in consequence of the altered form of attack and the extended range of firing, the Colours would not necessarily in future be taken with a battalion on active service ; but should be left at the base of operations, unless otherwise deemed expedient.

Under the Royal Warrant of June, 1885, all arrangements for the issue of Colours, clothing and accoutrements were to be made by the newly constituted Army Clothing Department.

The disposal of retired Colours on replacement was left to the discretion of commanding officers of units down to 1909, in which year the following instruction was issued : " When Standards, Guidons, or Colours, are replaced, they remain the property of the State and should be deposited in some church or other public building. Officers Commanding will forward proposals for their disposal to the General Officer Commanding for submission to the War Office. No one is entitled to sell old Standards, Guidons, or Colours, or to deal with them in any way. In no circumstances may Standards, Guidons, or Colours, be allowed to pass into the possession of any individual."

Shortly before Colonel Churchward's completion of his command in 1909 it was decided that with the disappearance of the last " 81st " officer from the 2nd Battalion, it was appropriate that the " LXXXI " Colours, 1903, should be retired ; and that the new " Loyal North Lancashire " Colours, which had been requisitioned shortly before, should come into use. Effect was given to this decision on 19th August, 1909, at Mauritius, when the Governor of the Island, Sir Cavendish Boyle, presented new Colours to the 2nd Battalion.

The accompanying illustration shows the present-day Colours of the 2nd Battalion, bearing on the King's, the ten battle-honours awarded to the Regiment for services rendered during the Great War, 1914–1918.

Regarding the Colours of the 3rd Battalion, the old 3rd Royal Lancashire Militia, there is now very little information available. There are records in the archives of the Inspector of Regimental Colours of a set having been issued in 1816 and 1853, and there must have been a set, or sets, prior to these dates, but their details and present whereabouts are unknown. Presumably the King's and Regimental Colours were in accordance with the standard pattern of the time ; if so, at the close of the eighteenth century, the universal practice was, according to the Ordnance Department books at the Public Record Office, London, for the Regimental Colour of Militia units to bear simply the heraldic coat-of-arms of the Lord-Lieutenant of the County, the King's bearing that of the Union. From 1801 to 1871, when the Militia was transferred from the Home Office and the Lord-Lieutenants of Counties to the War Office, the King's, or Queen's, Colour was the Union having usually within the centre a circular disc, or roundel, bearing the Royal Cypher, surrounded by a wreath of Roses, Thistles and Shamrocks. The Regimental, or " County," Colour, as it was frequently termed, was of the same colour as the regimental facings and bore in addition to the universal Union in the upper left-hand corner, as in Line Regiments, variously the arms of the Lord-Lieutenant, or the County emblem, or the arms of the County town ; in all probability the design of the Red Rose was adopted.

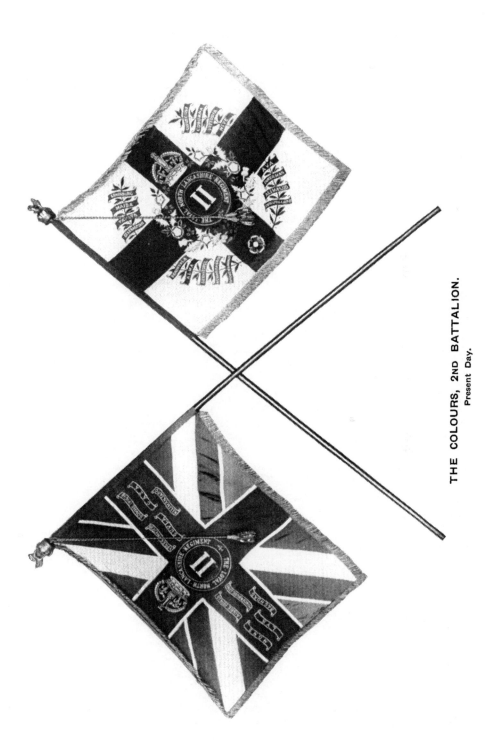

THE COLOURS, 2ND BATTALION.
Present Day.

In July, 1879, the Regiment was subdivided into two battalions, and in 1881 a new set of Colours was presented to both the 3rd and 4th Battalions ; this latter set remained in use until 1896, in which year the 4th Battalion ceased to be a separate unit, being amalgamated with the 3rd Battalion.

From 1881 onwards Militia Battalions bore Colours similar to those of their Regular Battalions, but without the battle-honours awarded for war services. There is a set of Colours at the Depôt, Preston, which was issued in 1891 ; the Regimental bears the Militia honours " MEDITERRANEAN," " MEDITERRANEAN, 1900–01,"and " SOUTH AFRICA, 1901–02," the two latter being subsequently added. It may be noted that the first honour was awarded in 1856 to the 3rd Royal Lancashire Militia for service abroad during the period of the Crimean War.

By Army Order No. 251 of the 1st October, 1910, it was decreed that the battle-honours borne on the Colours of the Regular Battalions were in future to be borne also on the Colours of their Special Reserve Battalions, and the honours received when the latter were Militia were in consequence to lapse.

Although the various Volunteer Companies of the early part of the nineteenth century carried their own Colours, the Volunteer units formed on the revival of the movement in 1859, after a few years, were not allowed to do so ; but when these battalions came under the Territorial Act of 1907 the privilege was restored and new Colours were presented. Under these conditions, Colours were carried by the 4th and 5th Territorial Battalions from 1909. The Regimental of both battalions bore the battle-honour " SOUTH AFRICA, 1900–02," which was awarded to the 1st and 2nd Volunteer Battalions at the conclusion of that campaign ; and they are now emblazoned also with those battle-honours of the Great War, granted to the Regiment, which they helped so gallantly to earn. When the 1/4th Battalion was mobilised in August, 1914, their Colours were handed to the Mayor of Preston for safe custody and in his care they remained for nearly five years ; similarly the Colours of the 1/5th Battalion were retained at Bolton.

In Preston Parish Church there hang two King's Colours, those of the 6th and 10th Service Battalions of the Regiment. Both Battalions rendered devoted service to their Country and brought honour to the name of the " Loyals," particularly the 6th, to which the Regiment owes the honours of " SUVLA " and " BAGHDAD " ; both suffered heavily, both are disbanded. So there these Colours rest, the last visible evidence of the existence of these Service Battalions which rallied so nobly to their Country's call in the hour of need. Their disposition and permanent resting-place are in accordance with Army Council Instruction No. 444 of the 21st July, 1919, which is as follows :—

" His Majesty the King has been graciously pleased to approve of the presentation of a silk Union Flag to each Service, Graduated and Garrison Battalion of the Regular Army, and to each Second and Third Line Territorial Force Battalion, which has served abroad during the Great War.

" His Majesty has been further pleased to command that these Flags, which will represent the King's Colour, are to be consecrated and to be granted all the salutes and compliments authorized to be paid to Colours.

" In the case of Battalions which have been disbanded or otherwise ceased to exist, the final disposal of the Flags rests with the Commanding Officer and Officers of the Battalion at the time of disbandment, subject to the proviso that they are to be deposited in some sacred or public building in the locality, where the unit was raised. It is to be distinctly understood that the Flags remain the property of the State, and are not to pass into the possession of, or be handed over for custody to, any private individual.

" The Flags as issued are plain Union Flags, and no additions (except titles and numerals) can be sanctioned."

The design for a King's Colour is as follows :

" The King's Colour of every Battalion is to be the Great Union, the Imperial Colour of the United Kingdom of Great Britain and Ireland, in which the Cross of St. George is conjoined with the Crosses of St. Andrew and St. Patrick on a blue field, as modified by Her late Majesty Queen Victoria in 1900. The Colour is to bear in the centre the Territorial designation on a crimson circle, with the Royal or other title within, the whole surmounted by the Imperial Crown. The number of each Battalion is to be placed in the dexter canton.

" When Regiments have not a combination of Territorial and Royal or other special designations, the number of the Battalion will be placed within the circle bearing the name of the Regiment, instead of in the dexter canton."

The award of Battle-Honours to the Regiment for services rendered during the Great War of 1914–1918 and the bearing of same on the Colours is detailed in Appendix III.

APPENDIX III

THE BATTLE-HONOURS

The following are the Battle-Honours awarded to the Regiment prior to the outbreak of the Great War, in 1914 :—

BATTLE-HONOUR.	BATTALION.
" LOUISBURG "	47th
" QUEBEC, 1759 "	47th
" MAIDA "	81st
" CORUNNA "	2/81st
" TARIFA "	2/47th
" VITTORIA "	2/47th
" ST. SEBASTIAN "	2/47th
" NIVE "	2/47th
" PENINSULA "	2/47th, 1/81st, 2/81st
" AVA "	47th
" ALMA "	47th
" INKERMAN "	47th
" SEVASTOPOL "	47th
" ALI MASJID "	81st
" AFGHANISTAN, 1878–79 "	81st
" DEFENCE OF KIMBERLEY " . . .	1st
" SOUTH AFRICA, 1899–1902 " . . .	1st

THE GREAT WAR

The conditions under which Battle-Honours were awarded to regiments in recognition of their services during the Great War were announced in Army Orders Nos. 338 and 470 of 1922.

There was to be only one list for a regiment ; an Infantry Regiment was to include the Regular, Special Reserve, Territorial and Service Battalions of the Regiment concerned.

The guiding principle in the selection and allotment of Battle-Honours was that headquarters and a minimum of fifty per cent. of the effective strength of the unit, exclusive of drafts which although in the area had not actually joined, must have been present in the specified theatre of war to qualify for the particular Honour ; the Report of the Battles Nomenclature Committee giving the official tabulated lists of engagements, etc., having been already published.

Following the Honours previously earned, and at the head of the list of Honours granted for the Great War, the words " THE GREAT WAR," together with the total number of the battalions of the regiment which participated, were directed to be recorded in the Army List.

Regimental Committees were set up, and from the Honours sanctioned a maximum number of ten was to be taken and borne on the Colours and Appointments, these Honours being identical for all battalions comprising the regiment, and are shown in the Army List in thicker type.

The announcement that Battle-Honours had been awarded to The Loyal Regiment (North Lancashire) was first made in Army Order No. 163 of May, 1924—" List No. 4."

Army Order No. 55 of 1925 notified the cancellation of the above and substituted a revised and complete list in accordance with that compiled from the war diaries and rolls furnished by the Regimental Battle-Honours Committee ; this list will be found on page xx, Volume II ; the ten, printed in CAPITALS, being those chosen to be borne on the Colours and Appointments, were as follows :—

" MONS "	" HINDENBURG LINE "
" AISNE, 1914, '18 "	" SUVLA "
" YPRES, 1914, '17, '18 "	" GAZA "
" SOMME, 1916, '18 "	" BAGHDAD "
" LYS "	" KILIMANJARO "

During the years 1914–1918 the number of battalions of the Regiment was increased to twenty-one ; active service was seen in France and Flanders, Macedonia, Gallipoli, Egypt, Palestine, Mesopotamia and East Africa, for which no less than sixty-eight separate Battle-Honours were awarded. Of the twenty-one battalions, fourteen went overseas ; all, except the 6th Battalion, saw service in France and Flanders at one time or other.

The Battle-Honours " DEFENCE OF KIMBERLEY " and " KILIMANJARO " are borne by no other Regular Infantry Regiment of the British Army.

The following appeared in *The Lancashire Lad* of December, 1924, and shows the complete list of Battle-Honours awarded to the Regiment, together with the numbers of the separate Battalions which gained them :—

BATTLE-HONOUR.	BATTALION.
" MONS "	1st
" Retreat from Mons "	1st
" Marne, 1914, '18 "	1st, 2nd
" AISNE, 1914, '18 "	1st, 9th
" YPRES, 1914, '17, '18 "	1st, 2nd, 1/4th, 2/4th, 1/5th, 2/5th, 7th, 8th, 9th, 10th, 15th
" Langemarck, 1914 "	1st
" Gheluvelt "	1st

BATTLE-HONOUR.	BATTALION.
" Nonne Bosschen "	1st
" Givenchy, 1914 "	1st
" Aubers "	1st
" Festubert, 1915 "	1/4th
" Loos "	1st, 7th, 8th, 9th
" SOMME, 1916, '18 "	1st, 1/4th, 1/5th, 7th, 8th, 9th, 10th, 12th
" Albert, 1916 ".	1st, 7th, 8th, 9th
" Bazentin "	1st, 7th, 8th, 9th
" Pozières "	1st, 8th, 9th
" Guillemont "	1/4th, 1/5th
" Ginchy "	1/4th, 1/5th
" Flers-Courcelette "	1st, 1/4th, 1/5th
" Morval "	1st, 1/4th, 1/5th
" Ancre Heights "	7th, 8th, 9th
" Ancre, 1916 "	7th, 10th, 12th
" Arras, 1917, '18 "	1st, 1/5th, 10th
" Scarpe, 1917 "	10th
" Arleux "	10th
" Messines, 1917 "	1st, 7th, 8th, 9th
" Pilckem "	1/4th, 1/5th, 8th, 9th
" Menin Road ".	1/4th, 1/5th, 7th, 8th, 10th
" Polygon Wood "	7th, 10th
" Poelcappelle "	7th, 10th
" Passchendaele "	1st, 2/4th, 2/5th, 4/5th, 7th, 10th
" Cambrai, 1917, '18 "	1/4th, 2/4th, 1/5th, 2/5th
" St. Quentin ".	9th
" Bapaume, 1918 "	9th
" Lys "	1st, 1/4th, 9th
" Estaires "	1/4th, 9th
" Bailleul "	9th
" Kemmel "	9th
" Bethune "	1st
" Scherpenberg "	9th
" Soissonnais-Ourcq "	2nd
" Drocourt-Quéant "	1st, 2/4th
" HINDENBURG LINE "	1st, 2/4th, 12th
" Epéhy "	1st, 12th
" Canal du Nord "	2/4th, 1/5th
" St. Quentin Canal "	1st
" Courtrai "	2nd, 15th
" Selle "	1st
" Sambre "	1st

BATTLE-HONOUR.	BATTALION.
" France and Flanders, 1914–'18 " . . .	1st, 2nd, 1/4th, 2/4th, 1/5th, 2/5th, 4/5th, 7th, 8th, 9th, 10th, 12th, 15th
" Doiran, 1917 "	12th
" Macedonia, 1917 "	12th
" Suvla "	6th
" Sari Bair "	6th
" Gallipoli, 1915 "	6th
" Egypt, 1916 ".	6th
" Gaza "	12th
" Nebi Samwil "	12th
" Jerusalem "	12th
" Jaffa "	12th
" Tell 'Asur "	2nd
" Palestine, 1917, '18 "	2nd, 12th
" Tigris, 1916 ".	6th
" Kut-al-Amara, 1917 "	6th
" Baghdad "	6th
" Mesopotamia, 1916–18 "	6th
" Kilimanjaro "	2nd
" E. Africa, 1914–16 "	2nd

Theatres of War

1914–1918

	Battalions.
France and Flanders . . .	1st, 2nd, 1/4th, 2/4th, 1/5th, 2/5th, 4/5th, 7th, 8th, 9th, 10th, 12th, 15th
Macedonia	12th
Gallipoli	6th
Egypt.	6th
Palestine	2nd, 12th
Mesopotamia.	6th
East Africa	2nd

APPENDIX IV

THE VICTORIA CROSS

No. 2040 Pte. J. McDermond

The 47th Regiment

" For saving the life of Colonel Haly, on the 5th November, 1854, by his intrepid conduct in rushing up to his rescue when lying on the ground disabled, and surrounded by a party of Russians, and killing the man who had disabled him." (*The London Gazette, 24th February, 1857.*)

No. 8655 Pte. H. Kenny

1st Bn. The Loyal North Lancashire Regiment

" For most conspicuous bravery. Pte. Kenny went out on six different occasions on one day under a very heavy shell, rifle and machine-gun fire, and each time succeeded in carrying to a place of safety a wounded man who had been lying in the open.

" He was himself wounded in the neck whilst handing the last man over the parapet." (*The London Gazette, 30th March,* 1916.)

Lieut. R. B. B. Jones

8th Bn. The Loyal North Lancashire Regiment

" For most conspicuous bravery. He was holding, with his platoon, a crater recently captured from the enemy. About 7.30 p.m. the enemy exploded a mine forty yards to his right, and at the same time put a heavy barrage of fire on our trenches, thus isolating the platoon.

" They then attacked in overwhelming numbers. Lieut. Jones kept his men together, steadying them by his fine example, and shot no less than fifteen of the enemy as they advanced, counting them aloud as he did so to cheer his men. When

379

his ammunition was expended he took a bomb, but was shot through the head while getting up to throw it.

" His splendid courage had so encouraged his men that when they had no more ammunition, or bombs, they threw stones and ammunition boxes at the enemy till only nine of the platoon were left.   Finally, they were compelled to retire." (*The London Gazette, 5th August,* 1916.)

Lieut. T. O. L. Wilkinson
7th Bn. The Loyal North Lancashire Regiment

" For most conspicuous bravery.   During an attack, when a party of another unit was retiring without their machine-gun, Lieut. Wilkinson rushed forward and with two of his men, got the gun into action, and held up the enemy till they were relieved.

" Later, when the advance was checked during a bombing attack, he forced his way forward and found four or five men of different units stopped by a solid block of earth, over which the enemy was throwing bombs.

" With great pluck and promptness he mounted a machine-gun on the top of the parapet and dispersed the enemy bombers.   Subsequently he made two most gallant attempts to bring in a wounded man, but in the second attempt he was shot through the heart, just before reaching the man.

" Throughout the day he set a magnificent example of courage and self-sacrifice." (*The London Gazette, 26th September,* 1916.)

"FOR VALOUR"

APPENDIX V

UNIFORM, ARMS AND EQUIPMENT

It has not been proposed to attempt anything approaching a complete account of the dress, etc., of the British Infantry, even so far as the 47th, 81st and Loyal North Lancashire Regiments were concerned; want of space itself would preclude. All that has been done is to try and give a general impression of the uniform, arms and equipment of these regiments, with a brief outline of some of the more important changes, or differences, during the period of their existence, now of nearly two hundred years.

THE 47TH AND 81ST REGIMENTS

The 47th Regiment was raised in 1741 and in the following year a work was produced, entitled *A Representation of the Clothing of His Majesty's Household, and of All the Forces, etc., giving a coloured plate of a private soldier of every Regiment in the Service.*

The 47th (Mordaunt's Foot) will be found under the number " 48 "; the private of the battalion companies, here depicted, wears the three-cornered felt hat of the period, trimmed with white lace; the usual black cockade of the Royal House of Hanover on the left side; the frock-coat, of red cloth, is most voluminous, without any collar, but with chest lapels and huge cuffs of white cloth; the extension skirts are doubled back, showing a white lining round the neck and lapels; round all buttonholes, pockets, and the outside seams and edges of the coat, appears the peculiar lace worn by the Regiment, about three-quarters of an inch in width, of white worsted, ornamented with a light blue line down the outer edge and small blue star-like devices down the centre. The various patterns of lace worn by regiments had a most marked effect, distinguishing one corps from another; it may have been put on with the idea of strengthening the buttonholes, but one thing is certain, viz. that the particular pattern varied from time to time, possibly according to the whim, or fancy, of the colonel of the Regiment, who provided the clothing. Our Infantry wore coloured striped lace until 1836, when it gave way to plain white tape. The waistcoat of red cloth reaching half-way down to the thigh with sleeves and trimmed on the front with lace, red breeches, and long white gaiters completed the costume. The equipment consisted of a broad leather shoulder-belt, supporting the huge black pouch, brass buckle in front, therefrom depending the little brush and picker, used in the days of flint and steel, a broad waist-belt carried the small sword and the bayonet in a frog, on the left side.

Notes on the Uniform of The 47th Regiment, 1742–1848, by S. M. Milne, are incorporated in this Appendix.

The next evidence is to be found in a series of oil pictures at Windsor Castle, representing a grenadier of every foot regiment, the work of David Morier ; there is no date attached, but for all practical purposes it may be fixed about 1751. The coat presents much the same appearance and cut as in 1742, but the regimental lace has undergone a change, the pattern now being two black zigzags on the outer edges and one yellow zigzag down the centre of the white lace. The grenadier is especially notable for his high mitre-shaped cap, the front of white cloth (the regimental facing), the Royal cypher " G.R. " in black worsted embroidery in the centre, surmounted by the Crown in yellow and red ; just above the man's brow appears a flap, or turn-up, of red cloth bearing the White Horse of Hanover with the motto " Nec aspera terrent," this badge and motto being common to the grenadiers of every regiment. The equipment remains much as in 1742, with the exception that the brass match case appears to be fastened to the centre of the shoulder-belt ; this article was intended to hold the lighted slow match, or fuse used for igniting the hand grenades. This grenadier at Windsor is in full marching order, his knapsack of goatskin is over his right shoulder, the haversack being slung over the other shoulder ; a light tin canteen, or water carrier, is also shown over the right shoulder. No greatcoats were used in those days ; the sleeved waistcoat and the voluminous coat, of stout cloth, were evidently considered enough.

Cloth grenadier caps were abolished by the Warrant of July, 1768, which stated that " black bearskin caps be supplied to the fusilier regiments, companies of grenadiers and drummers, as often as shall be necessary."

The next general clothing warrant was issued in December, 1768, but in the meantime a great change had taken place in the fashion and cut of the uniform ; the turn-down collar, or cape as it was called, met across the chest, the waist being quite exposed, the lapels becoming simply ornaments ; the skirts turned well back, lined as before with white, coat pockets much smaller, and the length of the waistcoat shortened ; the large cuffs entirely disappeared, smaller ones, without any slit, taking their place ; the sword was dispensed with excepting for sergeants and grenadiers, the latter picked men were probably considered strong enough to carry a sword as well as a musket and bayonet.

In the Prince Consort's Library, Aldershot, there is a manuscript book giving a coloured drawing of a grenadier of every regiment according to the new regulation of 1768 ; from which may be gathered that the new cap was of black bearskin, having in front a black metal plate, the King's crest in white metal ; this plate, however, was common to the grenadiers of all regiments. The coat of red cloth had wings on the shoulders of the same material, ornamented with six loops of regimental lace and a border of the same round the buttons ; white turned-down collar ; the pattern of the lace had changed again, now it was white with two stripes, a black one on the outer edge and a red one in the centre. A considerable amount of regularity had been introduced, the pattern of lace for each regiment was described in the Army List and it was not permitted to be changed without special authority ; every regiment had its own distinct pattern, but the loops on the buttonholes were of different forms, some being square-headed, some pointed,

1742—Private.

1751—Grenadier.

1768—Grenadier.

1798—Officer.

THE 47TH REGIMENT.

others flowered, some set at equal distances, some by twos, so that at any period between 1768 and 1836, anyone conversant with the various facings and patterns of lace, could tell to what regiment a man belonged without the necessity of closely examining the small pewter buttons for the regimental number.

The different patterns of lace appear for the first time in Millan's Army List for 1769 ; that for the 47th being described as white, with two black stripes down the outer edges and a red in the centre ; it will be noticed that the lace in 1768 had only one black stripe ; however, as it was first described in Millan's list so it continued till 1836 ; it remained still on the drummers' coats a little broader but the identical pattern, until all regimental drummers' laces were abolished in 1871 and the universal pattern adopted.

The waistcoat in 1768 was white, the breeches were the same colour, with long black gaiters. The accoutrements still continued ; a pouch shoulder-belt, and frog waist-belt, but of lighter make and pipeclayed, the brass match case occupying its old position as an ornament only. It is now time to inquire what uniform was worn by the officers at this early period of the Regiment's existence. Not very much light can be thrown on this question in the absence of such information as may be gathered from portraits and miniatures ; the earliest entry in the Inspection Returns bearing on this point is as follows : Athlone, 23rd May, 1768. Report of Lieut.-General R. Armiger. " Officers' uniform scarlet coat, lapelled to the waist with white cloth, slash sleeve with white round cuffs, white waistcoats, lining and breeches, buttons unnumbered, plain hats with silver buttons and loops, no shoulder knots or epaulettes ; grenadier officers with red leather sword-belts, with silver buckles and tips worn across the shoulders ; all the officers in boots. Men with black gaiters, hats laced with white linen, four rank and file clothed as fifers. Grenadiers appeared without swords, a new set ordered not having arrived. Accoutrements white and clean, but they wear their pouches quite behind their hip, which occasions many of the men to take out their cartridges and tuck them between waist-belts and clothes, that they may more readily load."

With regard to the buttons it may be mentioned that a Royal Warrant was issued 21st September, 1767, requiring that the number of the regiment should appear on the buttons, which hitherto had been quite plain. Next year the Inspecting Officer remarked that the officers had hats edged with silver scalloped lace.

The Clothing Warrant of 1768 did not probably come into full operation for a year or two ; but when it did the uniform of the officers and men would be as follows :—

Officers' scarlet coats lapelled with white cloth to the waist, lapels 3 inches wide, fastened back by silver buttons, bearing the regimental number and placed at equal distances, the buttonholes being perfectly plain. The cape, or collar, of white cloth turned down and fastened by a button at each end, in fact buttoned to the top button of the lapel ; small round white cloth cuffs, 3½ inches wide, thereon four buttons, cross pockets in line with the waist with four buttons, one button on each side of the slit behind. Skirts lined and turned back, white. Officers of the grenadier company had an epaulette of silver lace and fringe on each shoulder ;

battalion officers one on the right shoulder only ; waistcoat and breeches white cloth, black linen gaiters with black buttons and small stiff tops coming above the knee, and black gaiters, the crimson sash tied round the waist, silver gorget with the Royal Arms engraved thereon, and fastened to the neck with rosettes and ribbons ; gilt sword hilt, with a crimson and gold striped sword knot ; hats, black beaver, cocked in front-laced with silver, a black cockade on the left side fastened down with a loop and button. Officers of the grenadier company wore black bearskin caps, the King's crest on the front in gilt metal on a black japanned ground ; they carried fusils, and had white shoulder-belts and pouches.

Other officers carried espontoons, a light steel-headed spike with a small ornamental cross-bar just below the blade, some seven feet in length. A silver breastplate would be worn on the sword shoulder-belt, but of what pattern cannot now be determined. Sergeants' coats were similar to those worn by the officers, the buttons of white metal and buttonholes bound round with white worsted lace, perfectly plain ; hats laced with silver, black cockade, crimson worsted sashes with a stripe of white, swords and halberds were carried, the latter a light orna- mental kind of battle-axe with a long handle or shaft. Corporals' and private soldiers' coats, laced with regimental lace, as before described, white metal buttons with number ; breadth of shoulder-belt 2¾ inches, that of the waist-belt, support- ing bayonet, 2 inches ; the corporals were distinguished by a silk epaulette on the right shoulder. Towards the end of the century the gaiters became shorter, only reaching to the knee ; the collar, probably following the French fashion of the day, began to be worn turned up ; the lace loop and button which had been used to fasten it down was attached to the new front, becoming simply an ornamental appendage, and so remained for half a century. The coat became still more scanty across the chest and in the skirts ; the waistcoat shrinking quite up to the waist. About this period, the date cannot be exactly determined, the buttons were set on the coat two and two, a fashion which continued till 1855. There are indications taken from two different metal workers' order books, 1783, that the silver breast- plate worn by the officers was a heart-shaped shield, surmounted by a Crown, having thereon the number and County title " Lancashire " engraved. All other regiments had a square, or an oval, plate ; so this shape would be most peculiar and distinct. The buttons now had the design of the Lion and Crown above the regimental number, " 47." It is interesting to note that some old buttons of the 47th Regiment have been dug up recently on the various camping-grounds of the British troops, who were engaged in the War of American Independence ; these buttons prove that the Regiment wore the Royal Crest in those days.

Hitherto the white shoulder-belt of the infantry officer, from which the sword was suspended, had been worn under the coat and over the waistcoat, but by 1776 it had become the custom to wear this belt outside the coat.

An Inspection Report on the 47th Regiment of the 20th June, 1788, stated : " Sergeants of Flank Companies have pouches with shoulder-belts and slings. Light Infantry in half gaiters."

The 81st Regiment was raised in 1793 ; and whereas the regimental facings of the 47th were white those of the 81st were buff, which colours were retained until the amalgamation of the two units in 1881. It must be borne in mind that the various changes in uniform, arms and equipment, which took place applied to every Regiment of the Infantry of the Line ; of course each regiment always retained with pride their individual distinctions, such as facings, badges, etc. In the event of a regiment being on foreign service there was frequently a considerable lapse of time before the approved changes were effected.

When the 81st Regiment was raised, the British Army had been armed, for more than a century, with the long, heavy and cumbersome musket. The " Brown Bess " was a flint-lock, fitted with a pan, and weighed about ten pounds ; the calibre was ·753 inch ; the round leaden bullet was more than one ounce in weight. The maximum range was some three hundred yards, but no satisfactory result could be relied upon further than that of one hundred yards, beyond which distance the firing line depended on the collective effect of the volley, rather than on the shooting of the individual men. In order to obtain certain ignition by the snapping of the flint, the butt end of the cartridge had to be torn open by the teeth before being inserted in the musket barrel and a splash of powder was thrown into the pan to catch the spark and so communicate it to the cartridge ; the latter was driven down the barrel by an iron ramrod. The bayonet was long and triangular, and its weight, when fixed, did not tend to make the marksmanship more accurate. Such was the weapon used at the Battle of Maida, the Retreat to Corunna, throughout the Peninsular War, and in Burma.

The breastplate worn by the officers of the 81st Regiment in 1793 was of polished silver, oval shaped, somewhat convex ; having the numerals " 81 " within a circle in the centre, otherwise perfectly plain ; the approximate size was $3\frac{1}{4}$ by $2\frac{1}{2}$ inches.

The Warrant of 1796 authorized a very considerable change in the fashion and cut of the coat ; the lapels were continued down to the waist, and so made either to button over occasionally, or to fasten closely with hooks and eyes ; the white, or buff, lapels being buttoned back ; the stand-up collar for the officers very high and roomy so as to admit the large neck cloth then coming into vogue.

A light infantry jacket was introduced, very short in the skirt, the pocket flaps placed thereon in a slanting direction, and not level with the waist as in the long-tailed coat, the latter being the parade and full-dress coat of the battalion officers.

The men's coat, or jacket, was single-breasted without lapels, ten loops of regimental lace with buttons by twos down the front ; the white, or buff, collar laced all round, four loops and buttons on the white, or buff, cuffs ; faced linings to the cut-away skirts, edged with lace, slash pockets with four loops and buttons on the skirt, and a triangle of lace between the two waist buttons at the back.

As regards the 47th no doubt these changes were gradual, the Regiment being stationed at Bermuda. When inspected on 8th March, 1798, the Inspecting Officer remarked : " The men wear round hats which are necessary here, of good shape and worn in a military manner, trousers also are worn."

An Inspection Report on the 81st Regiment, when quartered in Guernsey, dated 2nd August, 1798, stated : " No grenadier caps or pioneers' appointments ; officers' coats of scarlet cloth faced with light buff cloth, round cuffs, cross pockets, white buttons with the number of the Regiment ; buff cloth waistcoats and breeches ; lace epaulettes with silver fringe, uniform, hats, swords and sword knots, according to the King's Regulations. The bayonet belts two inches wide only, and the pouch belts two and a quarter inches wide, throughout the Regiment.''

By now, powdering the hair, except for officers, had gone out of fashion. Horse Guards Warrant dated 22nd April, 1799, directed officers and men of infantry, excepting the flank companies, to wear their hair queued, to be tied below the upper part of the collar of the coat and to be 10 inches in length, including one inch of hair to appear below the binding.

The cockaded hat worn by the men was discontinued by a General Order dated 24th February, 1800, and a cylindrical shako, with straight leather peak introduced ; this head-dress was made of lacquered leather ornamented with a large brass plate in front about 6 inches high, thereon engraved the regimental number with the King's cypher surrounded by a trophy of arms, which, with the exception of the number, was universal for the infantry ; a worsted tuft was fixed in front, rising from a black leather cockade ; there was no chin strap. The colour of the tufts worn by the battalion companies was red and white, whilst the grenadier company had a white and the light infantry a green. The approximate height of this shako was 7 inches and the measurement across the top 6½ inches.

The warrant stated that the grenadiers might wear their shakos when not using their fur caps. Officers retained their cocked hats, indeed many used them through the earlier stages of the Peninsular War, sometimes worn across, and sometimes fore and aft ; in 1811 infantry officers were ordered to discontinue wearing cocked hats and to wear a head-dress similar to that of the men.

The following order, dated 9th of April, 1800, is significant : '' Commanding Officers who shall direct, or knowingly permit, any alteration whatsoever to be made in any part of the cloathing or appointments, so that the same shall differ in the smallest degree from the patterns of the several articles sealed by Our Cloathing Board, and sent to the respective regiments, or shall allow any deviation from our existing Regulations for the cloathing and appointments of our Forces, shall be considered as guilty of disobedience of orders, and be liable to such punishment for the same, as by a general court-martial shall be awarded.''

The same order enumerated the list of necessaries to be provided by stoppage from the pay of soldiers of Regiments of Infantry of the Line, when on home service : Two pairs of black cloth gaiters, a second pair of brushes, one hair leather, one pair of shoes including mending and shoe soles, three pairs of socks, three shirts, one forage cap, one knapsack—once in six years, pipeclay and whiting, one clothes brush—once in two years, three shoe brushes, black-ball, worsted mitts, black stock, hair ribbon, two combs, washing at four pence per week ; total amount per annum £3 16s. 1½d. In addition a man was also liable to stoppage for straps to carry his greatcoat and for the extra price of his shoes in lieu of half-mounting, beyond the sum of five shillings and six pence.

At the beginning of the century greatcoats for the rank and file were coming into use, and in April, 1801, a warrant was issued granting each man of the Infantry of the Line who was not then possessed of a serviceable greatcoat to be

1798—Officer.

1805—Private.

1815—Sergeant.

1822—Officer, Grenadier Company.

THE 81ST REGIMENT.

provided with one.   Prior to this order only a limited number of greatcoats was maintained regimentally for the use of men on sentry at night and other similar duties.

An Inspection Report of the 2/81st, when stationed at Plymouth in 1804, stated the " accoutrements were of black leather."

A black canvas knapsack, with the regimental number in white, was authorized in 1805.   Orders were also issued that greatcoats were only to be worn when on duty and never on fatigue.

In October, 1806, a new pattern of shako was approved, and was first introduced about the year 1809, whereupon the lacquered leather shako fell into disuse. This was made of black felt and was fitted with cap lines—gold and crimson for officers, white for the rank and file, except the light company, which were green. The size of the brass plate in front was reduced.   No alteration was made in the colour of the plumes.   The peak was rounded and gave some shade to the eyes. The height in front was just 7 inches, the back being 1 inch less.

By General Order dated 20th July, 1808, the queues were abolished and the ˋhair ordered to be cut short in the neck, a small sponge was ordered to be added to the soldier's list of necessaries " for the purpose of frequently washing his head."

During the year 1813 the 81st Regiment adopted a new breastplate ; oval shaped, size $3\frac{1}{2}$ by $2\frac{3}{4}$ inches ; the foundation was silver, bearing the numerals " 81 " in centre, within a garter inscribed with the battle-honours " Maida," " Corunna," all in gilt ; on either side a wreath of laurel, in silver, tied with a ribbon at the base.   This was worn until the year 1830, when the silver lace on the officers' uniforms was changed to that of gold, in accordance with the General Order.

In 1814 the officer's costume was as follows : Long-tailed coat for parade, levées, etc., white, or buff, chest lapels buttoned back with ten silver buttons set in pairs with corresponding twist buttonholes of silk the colour of the cloth they were sewn on ; these twist buttonholes were dummies, 7 inches long, and took the place of the gold, or silver, lace buttonholes of more gorgeously attired regiments. In those days and until 1829 more than one half of the infantry regiments had these dummy buttonholes instead of lace ; the buttons were silver, slightly convex, with the number thereon ; faced collar edged all round scarlet with one loop and button at each side ; plain, round, cuffs of cloth, with four buttons and loops by twos ; cross pocket flaps with the same loops and buttons and edged ; skirts of the coat tails white, or buff, and turned back, fastened at the bottom with skirt ornaments ; breeches and black legging boots for home, and grey trousers for active service.   Instead of the long-tailed coat, a short jacket, very similar to that worn by the men, was adopted by officers for the field, being double-breasted and buttoning over, without any chest lapels.

The long straight sword, black leather scabbard, gilt mounting, with crimson and gold sword knot, was worn according to regulations, suspended in a frog from a white buffalo shoulder-belt, the latter ornamented with the regimental breast-plate of silver.

Officers of the light infantry company carried the curved light infantry sabre suspended by slings from the shoulder-belt ; on service this weapon was carried generally by all officers.

A crimson silk sash was worn round the waist.   Officers' rank was distinguished by the silver epaulettes ; according to the General Order of February, 1810, field officers wearing two, a colonel having a silver star and crown embroidered on the strap ; lieutenant-colonel, a crown ; major, a star ; whilst captains and subalterns wore a single epaulette on the right shoulder ; officers of the flank companies, two wings with gilt grenades, or " bugles," thereon respectively.   The adjutant wore in addition to his epaulette an epaulette strap on the left shoulder.   The epaulettes of field officers and captains, together with the wings of captains of the flank companies were edged with silver bullion ; those of subalterns with silver fringe. Paymasters and surgeons wore the regimental coat single-breasted but without epaulettes or sash, the sword being suspended by a plain waist-belt under the coat. Private soldiers wore short single-breasted red cloth jackets, laced across the breast with loops of regimental lace, 4 inches long, and set on in pairs ; white pewter buttons ; lace round the high collar of white, or buff, cloth showing frill in front ; red shoulder-straps edged with lace and terminated by a small worsted tuft ; in the flank companies by a wing of red cloth, trimmed with diagonal stripes of lace, edged with an overhanging worsted fringe ; gaiters, breeches and trousers as officers.   Sergeants were dressed as the privates but in finer cloth ; chevrons of rank on their arms, these latter were introduced by a General Order of July, 1802, the lace being plain white tape ; their sash of crimson worsted with a stripe of the same colour as the regimental facings, they carried a straight sword suspended from a shoulder-belt ; their other weapon being the halberd, a plain steel spear-head with cross-bar, very similar to the espontoon formerly carried by officers, the battle-axe headed halberd having fallen into disuse in 1792.   It may be mentioned that the sergeant-major and staff-sergeants wore silver lace ; this was the usual custom in all infantry regiments, quite regardless whether their officers wore gold or silver lace, and was so maintained until 1855.

After the Waterloo campaign in 1815, the British troops forming part of the army of occupation in the French capital were encamped side by side with the picked battalions of the other Allied Powers, and although practical, the " Wellington " shako was not nearly so imposing as the shakos worn by most of our Allies. Since the early days of the nineteenth century the armies of Europe, especially the Prussian, had been increasing the size of their head-dresses in order to obtain decorative effect.   Such inferiority on our part could not be tolerated, and on the 22nd August, 1815, the Prince Regent decided on a new pattern of head-dress, modelled on that of the Prussian.   The material was black felt ; height $7\frac{1}{2}$ inches, measurement across the top 11 inches ; feathered red and white plume, 12 inches high for officers ; the wide drooping peak was of black leather ; the chin scales were allowed to be fastened up in front below the black cockade ; the silver-gilt plate in front was of a star pattern, size about 4 by $3\frac{1}{2}$ inches ; 2 inches of lace round the top and $\frac{1}{2}$ inch round the bottom.   Grenadiers retained their bearskins with embroidered tassels for their officers and white for their men, and the light company had a green feather and a " bugle " badge.   On service in the field the plume was generally removed and in wet weather it was customary to protect the shako with a waterproof cover. The design of the shako plate subsequently brought into wear by the battalion companies of the 47th Regiment was as follows : an eight-pointed silver star having " XLVII " in centre, within a garter ribbon, inscribed " Lancashire," surrounded by the battle-honours, on scrolls, " Vittoria," " St. Sebastian " and " Peninsula " within a wreath, the whole thereon surmounted by the Crown and Lion ; it will be observed that the honour " Tarifa " was omitted, this being later placed on the buttons, above the Crown and Lion, which latter custom has been so retained.

For the next fifteen to twenty years the uniform of the British infantry was at its highest splendour.

In the year 1816 the 47th Regiment having received permission to adopt the battle-honours " Tarifa " and " Peninsula," a new breastplate was consequently introduced ; it was of silver, square in shape, bearing the number " XLVII " in the centre, surrounded by a girdle thereon " Lancashire " ; over the girdle the Crown and Lion, on each side of the girdle a laurel wreath ; above, a scroll with the word " Peninsula," and below one with " Tarifa." A new skirt ornament for the officers was also worn, embodying these two battle-honours.

Short-tailed coats, or jackets, for all ranks were done away with in 1820 and the breeches and gaiters in 1822, blue-grey trousers and half-boots being substituted. One day in 1824 the clothing department suddenly discovered that " it frequently happens that tall men have short necks and short men have long necks " ; so after serious deliberation and much correspondence it was decided that, for the future, coat collars were to be sent out to regiments separately in the piece and no longer issued on the coats ; in spite of the best intentions this arrangement proved thoroughly unworkable and it was not long before these instructions were countermanded. In 1826 the coat of the private soldier was altered in shape, the lace loops across the chest being made broader at the top and tapering down narrower to the waist, the lace was taken off the skirts.

In 1826 the officer's sword had a half basket hilt, with G.R. IV inserted in the outward bars, and lined with black patent leather, the grip of black fish skin bound with three gilt wires, the blade of 32½ inches long, 1⅜ inches wide at the shoulder, with round back, terminating off to a shampre within 9 inches of the point and very little curved.

The horse furniture for mounted officers of infantry, now in use, comprised a saddle cloth of the same colour as the regimental facing with silver lace and scarlet edging ; the bridle was of black leather, bent branch bit with bosses, having the Rose, Shamrock and Thistle in centre, encircled with the words " Infantry Mounted Officers " and the Crown above, the front and roses corresponded in colour to the facing of the regiment ; the collar was white, or buff, and the holsters covered with black bearskin, except in tropical climates where they were to be covered with black patent leather.

In 1827, on the officer's shako of the 47th Regiment, a very handsome star ornament of cut silver was introduced, in the centre of this star was a girdle with buckle of gilt metal with the words " Tarifa," " Vittoria," " St. Sebastian,"

" Peninsula," the centre all blue enamel, thereon the number " 47," above it the Lion and Crown in silver metal, underneath two small laurel branches in gilt metal.

The scarlet coats with long tails or skirts were much as described for 1814 ; the epaulettes, wings, etc., being larger, and more important. From an old laceman's books we are enabled to give a description of the epaulettes of the 47th ; as will be seen a good deal of black is mixed with the silver, how long this had been so, in the absence of reliable evidence, is not known. Epaulette strap 2¼ inches wide, silver vellum pattern, with six black stripes, corded round, with alternate black and silver button, the crescent on end of the shoulder, filled up with black and silver cord with a silver rose at each end, the hanging button fringe of silver, the wings, for the light, and grenadier companies' officers were also corded with black. Trousers of light blueish grey, of very full shape, were worn ; down the dress trousers broad silver lace, same pattern as on the shako.—At this period a new regulation cut-and-thrust sword came into use and was worn in the frog of the shoulder-belt. Light company officers wore whistles and chains, and a blue great-coat, otherwise frock-coat, was authorized for undress, the crimson sash was worn with it, and the sword suspended in a frog from a black leather waist-belt. The paymaster, quartermaster, surgeon, and assistant-surgeon wore single-breasted scarlet coats ; silver buttons and notched holes, the imitation buttonholes, across the chest by pairs ; regimental collar and cuffs as other officers ; black leather sword-belt under the coat, no epaulette or sash ; all these wore cocked hats, the pay and quartermaster with gold loop and tassel, the former without a feather, surgeons plain, black silk loop and button, without feather. Sergeants still carried the halberd, for which, however, fusils, short muskets, were substituted by Warrant dated 31st July, 1830.

In December, 1828, another change took place in the shako, the height was now reduced to 6 inches and the plume to 8 inches, all the silver lace was removed and replaced by bands of black leather, also the time-honoured Hanoverian cockade disappeared. The only ornament for the front was the universal star plate with Crown attached on the top some 6 inches by 6½ broad. Regiments were per-mitted to put what devices they liked in the centre ; the gilt scales to fasten under the chin remained and cap lines were introduced, the latter to be worn on parade occasions only wound round the shako across the front in a heavy braided festoon, and then hung down terminating in two tassels which were looped up to one of the coat buttons ; of gold lace for the officers, white worsted for battalion companies, and green worsted for the light infantry.

The greatest variety of appearance was now presented by infantry officers, some regiments wore a profusion of gold and silver lace, and others wore none at all on the coats saving the epaulette ; the 47th came under the latter category ; as a consequence the authorities ordered that one single pattern coat with exactly the same quantity of lace should be worn by all regiments.

In February, 1829, a warrant was promulgated authorizing the well-known double-breasted coatee which remained, with scarcely any alteration, the dress of officers until after the Crimean War.

The coatee authorized for the 47th had two rows of silver buttons down the

1800—Officer, Light Company.

1812—Corporal, Light Company.

1835—Officer.

1854—Corporal, Grenadier Company.

THE 47TH REGIMENT.

front by pairs, a collar of white cloth edged scarlet of the so-called Prussian shape fastening up the front, on each side two loops of the new regimental lace (silver vellum pattern with a narrow black stripe down the centre), white round cuffs with a scarlet slashed flap with four buttons and small loops of lace in pairs ; scarlet slashed pockets in the coat tails, edged white with four buttons and loops by pairs, white turnbacks to the skirt and a new skirt ornament larger and more pretentious than the old one, which consisted of a large silver eight-pointed star embroidered on black velvet in the centre of the star, a red and white " Old English Rose," above it the " Lion and Crown " in mixed silver and gold, two silver laurels round the Rose. Large silver epaulettes were worn on each shoulder for the first time, in the case of captains and subalterns of Infantry, excepting the grenadiers and light infantry, who still adhered to the silver wings, the epaulettes' fringe button varying a little in length according to rank. The new " Oxford mixture " was now substituted as a colour for the old blue-grey trousers and a blue forage cap with a large stiff top with white band was for the first time authorized. A plain scarlet shell jacket was ordered to be worn by officers at some stations but with the exception of certain tropical climates they sat down to mess in the full-dress coatee.

The subject of the regimental lace of the 47th on the promulgation of the 1829 Warrant must now be considered. Regiments without lace were ordered to choose their own pattern. It is easy to gather that the officers of the 47th adopted the black striped silver vellum pattern exactly the same, indeed, in every respect as was then, and had been for many years worn by the 13th and 63rd Regiments (laced regiments). The authorities at once objected not only to the black stripe, but also to the black striped epaulettes, the regulation being that the epaulette strap should be striped with silk the colour of the facings ; the epaulettes were allowed, however, but the black stripe in the lace was rigidly forbidden. There is evidence to prove that at least one or two coats were made ornamented with the silver black striped lace, so the objections of the ruling powers must have been overcome in the early part of the year 1830.

The origin of the black stripe in the lace is obscure ; it is a long-cherished tradition that it was worn as an emblem of mourning for General Wolfe ; but whether this is correct or not, in spite of most diligent search, has been so far impossible to either prove or disprove. If the date, 1751, assigned to the pictures by David Morier, previously mentioned, be correct, it would appear that some black was introduced into the regimental lace of the 47th Foot at least eight years before the death of General Wolfe, at Quebec. In 1768, however, it was officially laid down that the pattern of the regimental lace was white, with a black stripe on the outer edge and a red in the centre (see pages 382 and 383).

In 1830 a red fatigue jacket was substituted for the white one hitherto worn by the rank and file, which had originally sprung from the old white waistcoat with sleeves.

At this period white trousers were worn during the summer months.

The accession of H.M. King William IV was marked by considerable changes. By the General Order dated 2nd August, 1830, gold lace was substituted for silver on the officer's coatee, the gorget abolished, the feathered plume of the officer's shako was to be all white ; the light company to wear a green tuft, instead of feather, and the band was ordered to be dressed in white.

The black stripe in the lace of the 47th Regiment must have firmly settled, for it at once appeared on the gold lace and a certain amount of black cord was retained round the gold epaulettes and wings. As regards the skirt ornament the star was altered to gold embroidery and the Rose in the centre made entirely of red silk, no white. Of course this alteration to gold lace necessitated a change in the officer's silver breastplate, worn since 1816 ; a very handsome gilt one was now introduced, and worn probably without any alteration until these ornaments were dispensed with in 1855, size 4½ inches by 3½ inches of bright gilt, thereon an eight-pointed silver cut star nearly covering the plate ; in the centre of the star " XLVII " within a garter, thereon " Lancashire " ; immediately under the garter a Rose ; on scrolls at the top and sides " Peninsula," " Vittoria," " St. Sebastian " ; above the upper scroll the Lion and Crown ; the whole surrounded by two laurel branches ; at the bottom on the branches two scrolls with " Ava," " Tarifa."

The gorget, abolished 1830, which first came into use during the early years of the fifteenth century, remained the last survival of ancient armour. In the days when complete armour was worn, each portion of the body had its proper protection ; that for the neck and collar-bone being termed the " gorget," which was fitted over the cuirass, or corselet. After the Restoration in 1660 when armour gradually fell into disuse, the gorget was worn alone in place of the cuirass. In the nineteenth century the size was about 5 inches deep ; made of brass and engraved with the Royal Arms. This relic of the past was worn by officers when on duty, either suspended from a riband round the neck, or attached from the top button of the lapels of the coat ; naturally at the latter period it was more ornamental than useful. (Illustration, page 135, Volume I.) In one of the modern standard dictionaries, the definition of the word " gorget " is given as " a piece of armour for defending the throat, or neck ; a kind of hollowed breast-plate like a half-moon ; a metallic ornament formerly worn by officers on the breast "—an adequate explanation of its description and various usages.

The Clothing Warrant of 1830 stated that each man was to be issued with the following, as specified : cap, complete with scales, plate and feather or tuft, biennially ; a coat, pair of cloth trousers and short boots annually. The bearskin caps of the grenadier companies were the established head-dress of these companies and considered as articles of clothing to be supplied by the colonel to the men once in every six years, but on stations where the bearskin caps were not worn by the grenadiers, the men be furnished biennially with the common regulation caps.

For some time mounted officers had worn their swords suspended by slings from a white shoulder-belt bearing the regimental breastplate, but in 1832 field officers were ordered to wear them suspended by slings from a white waist-belt ; the scabbard to be brass, instead of leather ; the adjutant to wear a steel scabbard and to retain the old method of wearing the sword ; this necessitated that a sword-belt clasp be used, and one was designed having the regimental crest and number, with the battle-honours thereon.   In 1834 a new forage cap was ordered to be worn by officers ; of blue cloth with a black silk band-oak leaf pattern, the numerals in gold embroidery in front.   The officer's undress uniform now presented a very handsome appearance, for the blue frock-coat was ornamented with shoulder-straps laced with regimental gold lace and terminated with gilt metal crescents ; the sword carried in the black leather waist-belt over the crimson sash.

About this time the narrow welt of red cloth down the outer seam of the trousers was first brought into use.

By now it was beginning to be realized that the size of the shako was somewhat unwieldy ; on the 27th August, 1835, a new pattern was approved which was made of black beaver ; 6 inches in height (raised to $6\frac{3}{4}$ inches in 1842), 11 inches across the top ; the plumes were replaced by ball tufts, red and white for the battalion companies and green for the light company ; other details remained practically unchanged.   The shako plate as worn by the 81st Regiment was a gilt star surmounted by the Crown ; " LXXXI " in centre of garter inscribed " Loyal Lincoln Volunteers " ; the battle-honours " Maida," " Corunna " and " Peninsula " on silver scrolls, a wreath in silver on either side.

By General Order dated 10th October, 1836, the striped regimental lace so long worn by the rank and file was abolished, and plain white tape took its place, but the peculiar mode of wearing it was retained, namely square-headed loops, by pairs across the chest.

Sergeants were directed to wear double-breasted coats without any lace on the chest, epaulettes or wings.   Coloured lace was still worn by the drummers, of the regimental pattern ; until 1857 the drummers wore a coat, generally cut like that of the men, but laced across the chest, collar, skirts, and back seams ; they also wore large wings like the grenadiers.

About the year 1841, the bearskin caps of the grenadiers were ordered to be discontinued ; this of course necessitated an alteration in the shako ball tufts, the grenadiers took their original white tufts ; the battalion companies retained their red and white, and the light company the green ; this change, however, was not completed until 1846.

In 1842 a new model musket on the percussion principle was adopted, with a back sight for one hundred and fifty yards, calibre ·753 inch ; hitherto regiments had been armed with the old muzzle-loading flint-lock, which, in spite of several attempts for improvement, had remained the standard weapon.

The " Albert " shako, copied from the contemporary French and Austrian models, was authorized on the 4th December, 1843 ; it was made of black beaver, height $6\frac{3}{4}$ inches, $6\frac{1}{4}$ inches across the top, and had a chain chin-strap for officers, other ranks one of leather.   No alteration was made in the size and colour of the ball tufts ; a drooping peak, both back and front, afforded some protection to the neck as well as to the eyes.   The men had a small round brass plate in front, thereon the Crown over the numerals.   Officers of the 47th Regiment had a new shako plate, of universal pattern, and size $4\frac{1}{2}$ inches in diameter, and an eight-pointed gilt star with Crown over ; in the centre " 47 " within a garter, thereon " Lancashire," surmounted by the Lion and Crown.   On one side a palm branch, and on the other the laurel, " Peninsula " on a scroll under the girdle ; below that again a " Rose," whilst the four other battle-honours appeared on the gilt star rays.

The red and white, and red and buff, waist sashes of the sergeants were abolished by General Order, 6th August, 1845, and a plain crimson one 2½ inches wide substituted.

A General Order, 30th June, 1848, abolished the frock-coat with shoulder scales, and a plain shell jacket of scarlet cloth with collar and pointed cuffs was introduced ; it had shoulder knots of gold twisted cord ; a black patent-leather sling sword-belt was worn with it ; a grey greatcoat in lieu of the blue cloak was also adopted for officers.

The ornament on the buff facing on the skirt of the coatee as now worn by the officers of the 81st Regiment had " 81 " in the centre within a garter inscribed " Lincoln Volunteers " on blue silk ; Crown, above, with silver bullion beading ; decorative wreaths on either side ; all in gold embroidery. That on the forage cap was of similar pattern but without the Crown ; and the garter was plain, bearing no words thereon. In 1850 a plain shoulder-belt, with breastplate, to carry the men's pouches was authorized, the bayonet being hung in a frog from the waist-belt. The following is a description of the breastplate worn by the rank and file of the 47th Regiment ; size 3½ inches by 2½, a solid heavy ornament in the form of a six-pointed star and crown ; girdle thereon " Lancashire " ; within the girdle " XLVII " with two roses, one above and one below the number ; four battle-honours on the star rays and one on a label below.

The Minié rifle was introduced in 1851, the diameter of the bore being ·702 inch, and sighted up to one thousand yards ; it was never generally issued, although used by some of our troops during the earlier stages of the Crimean War. It is interesting to note the dimension of the diameter of the bore of each successive rifle, showing the gradual diminution in size, which has since so continued.

The Enfield rifle was issued in 1855 and was used during the closing actions of the Crimean War, having there replaced the Minié rifle, 1851 pattern, and the percussion musket of 1842 ; it was also used by the British troops during the Indian Mutiny. The diameter of the bore was ·577 inch, and the range twelve hundred yards. This rifle remained the weapon of the infantry until the general introduction of the breech-loader in 1867.

The experiences of the Crimean War hastened the end of the old coatee ; for in 1855 the double-breasted tunic was first introduced, the gilt buttons being all placed at equal distances ; no lace was worn except a little on the cuff slashes and tail pockets, the coat and collar edges being piped. Officers lost the handsome epaulettes and wings with the coatee, the only gold lace being round the cuffs, skirts and collar, the latter carrying the following distinctions of rank : ensign, silver embroidered star ; lieutenant, silver embroidered crown ; captain, silver embroidered crown and star ; major, gold embroidered star ; lieutenant-colonel, gold embroidered crown ; colonel, gold embroidered crown and star. The crimson sash was now worn across the left shoulder. A double-breasted blue frock-coat was adopted by officers for undress, having a plain stand-up collar and gilt regimental buttons ; the sword being carried in the white sling belt.

1831—Sergeant, Light Company.

1854—Officer.

1856—Officer.

1865—Private.

THE 81ST REGIMENT.

Prior to this date the buttons on the men's tunics had always been made of pewter.

The " Albert " shako was remodelled, being now of black felt ; height in front 5¼ inches, rising to 7⅛ inches at the back.   The diameter on the top was one inch less than that of the bottom ; ball tufts as before.   Black patent-leather chin strap.

Sergeants now wore their crimson worsted sashes over their right shoulders.

Between the years 1830 and 1855 the shoulder-belt plate of the 81st Regiment was of a somewhat unusual and distinctive character ; made of gilt brass, burnished, having only the numerals " LXXXI " mounted thereon, otherwise perfectly plain, the size was 3¾ by 3⅛ inches.   On the introduction of the tunic in 1855, the shoulder-belt, or breast, plate, disappeared throughout the Army.

By 1856 clothing was no longer supplied by commanding officers, but had become an issue chargeable to the public funds.

Patterns for the drummer's lace and fringe were approved, by authority, on the 2nd May, 1857 ; the fringe was to be 1¾ inches long and arranged in a width of ½ inch of each colour ; that of the 47th Regiment being alternately black, white, red ; and that of the 81st Regiment blue, red and buff.   These were worn until 1871 when they were replaced by a new universal pattern of lace, white with red Crowns, and a red and white fringe of a smaller size.

With the new issue of clothing in 1858 the double-breasted tunic became obsolete, and the single-breasted was introduced ; that for the officers had eight buttons in front at equal distances, collar rounded off in front, slashed sleeves, scarlet flaps at the plaits behind, buttons on flap and waist, collar and cuffs of the regimental facings ; on the left shoulder, there being no shoulder-straps, a crimson silk cord with button retained the sash, gold lace on collar, cuffs and skirts ; rank badges on collar.   Between the 15th October and 30th April trousers of Oxford mixture with a scarlet welt down the outer seam were worn, and from the 1st May to 14th October those of dark blue with the same scarlet welt, ¼ inch broad.   Officers continued to wear the white gloves, two-buttoned, of regulation pattern.

In this year, the abolition of the flank companies, i.e. the grenadier and light, came into force ; and all companies were henceforth to be clothed alike.

Until the year 1859, the coatee, succeeded by the tunic, had been the recognized mess dress for officers ; but in many regiments it had been customary to wear the shell jacket open with a waistcoat, the pattern of which was decided solely by commanding officers.   The wearing of the shell jacket at mess was officially sanctioned by a Circular Memorandum, dated 9th June of that year.

In 1860, all the parts of the rifle and lock were made to interchange, an incalculable advantage for a military arm, particularly in the field, and it was directed that the Army should only be so equipped in the future.

Yet another alteration took place in the shako in 1861 ; the material was now of blue ribbed cloth, having a peak, now straight, only in the front.   The height was 4½ inches rising to 7¾ inches at the back.   Dimensions on top 6 × 5¾ inches. Ball tufts red and white, now, for all companies.   The plate was a gilt star of eight points, having the number of the regiment within a garter, the whole surmounted by a Crown. No alterations were made in the patent-leather chin-strap.

The black leather leggings, as now worn, were 9 inches high for a man of 5 feet 8 inches, with a variation not exceeding 1 inch for a man above 5 feet 10 inches, or under 5 feet 6 inches.

In 1866 officers' black leather scabbards were replaced by those of steel ; whilst field officers retained theirs of brass. In 1867 the officer's patrol jacket was sanctioned which took the place of the blue frock-coat ; and in the following year the slashed cuff on the tunic was replaced by the pointed, having gold lace, the amount of which varied according to rank. For levées, etc., the officer's sash was ordered to be of gold and crimson, and gold lace was to be worn on the trousers and sword belt. A similar alteration was also made to the cuffs on the tunics of the men, which so remained until 1882.

During the year 1867, the Snider rifle was approved as a temporary expedient, and there was no difficulty in fitting this breech action to the existing Enfield rifle.

On 1st June, 1869, a new blue cloth shako was officially approved, the height of which was 4 inches, the back 6½ inches. Dimensions on top 6 × 5½. Gold braid ornamented those of the officers, the other ranks being plain. The straight black leather peak and the red and white ball tuft were retained. The plate was gilt and consisted of a cut-out regimental number on a frosted background within the garter ribbon, supported by laurels, tied at the base, supporting the Crown above. A gilt chained chin-strap for officers.

After the issue of the Snider-Enfield rifle in 1867, the principle of breech-loading arms was in a transition state, and as the result of many exhaustive and prolonged experiments, the Martini-Henry rifle was recommended in 1871 for adoption ; a period of some three or four years necessarily elapsed before all units, at home and abroad, were completely supplied. The diameter of the bore was ·45 inch. This rifle, as before, had a long triangular bayonet, tapering towards the point, and was used by the British regiments in Afghanistan, 1878–1879.

In 1871, the Wallace valise equipment was adopted and in due course was taken into wear by all infantry regiments. About the same year the colour of the men's tunics was changed from brick red to scarlet and the Glengarry cap became generally worn by the Line Regiments for undress and walking out purposes ; the cap badges of which were for the 47th Regiment the figures " 47 " within a garter inscribed " Lancashire Regiment," the whole surmounted by a Crown ; that of the 81st Regiment being of a similar design and shape bearing " Loyal Lincoln Volunteers " ; and the numerals " 81 " in the centre. Owing to the great variety of the officers' mess uniforms in vogue, a universal pattern was introduced in 1872 ; this was made to fasten at the neck and both the jacket and vest were edged with stud buttons. In 1874 the men's shell jacket was discarded in favour of a loose scarlet frock, for undress. The buttons of regimental pattern worn by the men were ordered to be replaced, throughout the Army, in 1871, by a general service type bearing the Royal Arms. The following Regimental Order of the 81st Regiment, dated 2nd March, 1874, announced : " The distinctive button hitherto worn by the Regiment bearing the words ' Maida,' ' Corunna,' having been abolished in consequence of the adoption of a universal pattern button for all Line Regiments, H.R.H. the Field-Marshal Commanding-in-Chief approves of a distinctive collar badge being worn by the Regiment ; the design being the Lincoln Shield, surmounting a scroll with the words ' Maida,' ' Corunna.' "

This change of buttons did not generally apply to officers, who continued to wear those of regimental pattern, introduced in 1855 ; that of the 47th Regiment being of gilt brass, circular and convex, the numerals " 47 " below the Lion and Crown ; above the word " Tarifa " ; bay and laurel wreath around, tied with ribbon at base. The button of the 81st Regiment was similar in make, having the numerals " 81 " in centre, with the words " Maida " above, and " Corunna " below, within a circle.

The Lincoln Shield of the 81st Regiment was the heraldic shield of its birthplace, the City of Lincoln, and bore the Red Cross of St. George with the fleur-de-lis thereon.

The year 1878 saw the shako displaced by the blue cloth helmet, with fittings of gilt brass ; at the top a gilt spike was mounted on a cross-piece base ; curb chain chin-strap with rose fastenings at sides ; the chin-strap when not required to be worn under the chin could be fastened up to a hook at the back ; the plate in front consisted of an eight-pointed star, regimental number in centre within a garter ribbon, on either side a laurel branch tied at base, the whole surmounted by the Crown.

In 1880, in conformity with the general order, the officers' embroidered badges of rank were removed from the collar and placed on the shoulder-straps of the tunic, etc. ; at the same time an alteration and re-arrangement of the " crown " and " star " signifying the respective ranks was effected. The collar was thus free to acquire the regimental badge. The tunic was now to be fitted with shoulder-straps of twisted round gold cord, lined with scarlet ; gold lace ornamented the collar and pointed cuffs, the amount of which still varied according to rank ; the collar was no longer rounded in front but cut square.

Prior to 1881, the Lion on the regimental badge, as worn by the 47th Foot, was uncrowned.

THE LOYAL NORTH LANCASHIRE REGIMENT

On the re-organization of the Army on the 1st July, 1881, consequent upon the introduction of the Territorial system, the regimental numbers were abolished. The 47th and 81st Regiments were amalgamated and became respectively the 1st and 2nd Battalions, The Loyal North Lancashire Regiment. All battle-honours, distinctions, mottoes, badges, which appeared hitherto in the Army List, or on the Colours, as borne by either of the Line Battalions were in future to be borne by both battalions of a Territorial Regiment. The facings of all English regiments, except those entitled " Royal," were to be white ; and a special instruction was issued to the effect that the black line was to be retained in the lace of Territorial Regiments, any of whose battalions were authorized to wear it ; thus the 47th continued to wear their white regimental facings, whilst the 81st lost their facings of buff and adopted those of white. On the amalgamation, the badge of the 47th, the Red Rose surmounted by the Lion and Crown, was utilized for that of the head-dresses, and the Lincoln Shield of the 81st became the collar badge. The new regimental button, a combination of the two, was as follows : gilt brass, convex ; centre, the Shield of the City of Lincoln surmounted by the Lion and Crown, the whole within a garter inscribed " Loyal North Lancashire Regiment." The design of the helmet plate was an eight-pointed star, gilt, surmounted by a Crown ; in centre, the Red Rose surmounted by the Lion and Crown in silver-gilt within the Garter ribbon, inscribed " Honi Soit Qui Mal Y Pense " ; on either side a laurel branch of gilt brass ; at foot, a silver scroll having the words " Loyal North Lancashire Regiment " thereon. The numerical shoulder titles were replaced by those bearing the designation of the County, " N. Lancashire," and in a similar manner, amongst other changes, the design of the officer's sword-belt plate was altered to the following : the Red Rose, surmounted by a silver Lion and Crown, on frosted gilt background ; within a circle inscribed " Loyal North Lancashire Regiment." The gold lace on the tunic of the officers was replaced by that of the rose pattern, universally worn by all English regiments ; the black stripe being retained.

The plain round cuff, the colour of the regimental facing, replaced the pointed one on the men's tunics in 1882 ; which latter was restored in 1903.

During the year 1884, the new pattern, 1882, valise equipment was issued to the various battalions serving at home ; brown gloves were first worn by officers in 1887, for drill order and undress. In 1888 the new Slade-Wallace equipment was approved and in due course was generally adopted by the infantry.

The Lee-Metford magazine rifle was finally approved in 1889, when its manufacture immediately commenced ; calibre ·303 inch ; originally the magazine was made to contain eight cartridges only, but in the later marks it was enlarged to hold ten. An aperture sight was also introduced for the purpose of the longer ranges. Cordite cartridges were first issued in 1892. In 1895 a safety catch on the rear end of the bolt was added, which, when turned up, locked the striker, and prevented the bolt being opened. The bayonet was sword-shaped.

In 1890 the scarlet serge patrol jacket was taken into use by officers ; the collar, shoulder-straps and pointed cuffs were of white ; a patch pocket with pointed flap and small button on each breast ; five small regimental buttons down front ; there was no collar badge. The officer's forage cap, at this period, was made of blue cloth, straight up, 3 inches high, with black patent-leather drooping peak, and chin-strap ; the peak ornamented with half-inch full gold embroidery ; band 1¾ inches wide of black oak-leaf lace ; badge, in front, the Rose of Lancaster, surmounted by the Lion and Crown ; below the Rose a scroll inscribed " Loyal North Lancashire."

The Glengarry cap was abolished in 1893 on the introduction of the new field service cap ; this latter was made of blue cloth with folding peak in front ; flaps at the sides to let down ; lower flaps to fasten under the chin when unfolded ; when folded these were fastened in front by two small buttons ; regimental badge in brass on the left-hand side.

The charger loading Lee-Enfield was officially sanctioned in 1895—this rifle with a slight alteration in the sighting and form of rifling was similar in all other respects to the Lee-Metford. This was the rifle used throughout the War in South Africa, 1899–1902.

White headropes were ordered in 1896 to be substituted for the steel chain reins.

In 1897 the mess jacket with white roll collar, cuffs and waistcoat was introduced, with the addition of rank badges on the shoulder-straps ; in some regiments these were in miniature.

During the war in South Africa, 1899–1902, either khaki helmets, or slouch hats, were worn with the service dress.

The Sam-Browne belt was introduced for officers in 1900.

Sabretaches, worn by mounted officers only, were abolished throughout the Service in 1901, and the officers' gold and crimson sash for levées, together with the gold lace on the trousers, were discarded.

In May, 1902, in conformity with the general order, the rank badges for a captain, lieutenant and second-lieutenant were changed to : captain, three stars ; lieutenant, two stars ; second-lieutenant, one star—prior to which (since 1880) a captain wore only two stars ; lieutenant, one star ; whilst a second-lieutenant had no distinguishing mark. The rank badges of the field ranks remained unchanged, namely, major, crown ; lieutenant-colonel, crown and star ; colonel, crown and two stars.

About this time, the design of the Royal Crown having been officially changed from that of the Stuart to that of the Tudor, the regimental badge underwent a corresponding alteration.

After the conclusion of the war in South Africa, in 1902, certain changes in uniform took place. The infantry officer's tunic was shorn of the varied braiding according to rank, all were henceforth to wear the same amount of decoration on the sleeves and collar as had formerly been used for subalterns, and the skirts were altered ; the officer's sash was now to be worn round the waist instead of over the left shoulder ; a double-breasted blue frock-coat, with gilt buttons, was reintroduced for officer's undress, taking the place of the red serge and mohair braided patrol jackets ; the gold lace sword slings being worn under the tunic and over the frock-coat ; the brass spurs and sword scabbards of field officers were replaced by those of steel. Khaki became the recognized dress for undress parades and work in the field. A new cap, of a somewhat nautical appearance, of dark-blue cloth, with the regimental badge in front, was served out to the non-commissioned officers and men, which pattern was sometimes termed the " Brodrick " ; their tunics had now a pointed cuff and slashed flaps and buttons on the skirts. The blue forage cap of the officers had a sloping black patent-leather peak and chin-strap ; the peak embroidered for field officers and plain for others ; gilt regimental badge in front, and a narrow red welt round the top seam. The short black leather leggings were withdrawn. During the year 1905, a new round walking-out cap, with drooping black patent-leather peak, for the other ranks, was taken into use ; and by then the khaki greatcoat had become general for all purposes, both dress and undress. In the meantime a further alteration in the design of the regimental button had taken place, which was now as follows : gilt brass, convex ; centre, the Shield of Lincoln surmounted by the Lion and Crown ; a laurel branch on either side ; above the word " Tarifa " ; inscribed " Loyal North Lancashire " around.   The sizes of these buttons had remained unchanged and were approximately three-quarters of an inch in diameter for the larger and five-eighths of an inch for the smaller ; for the khaki service dress the buttons bore a similar device, but were of bronze, sizes and shape as before mentioned.   Swords were now carried on the saddle by mounted officers, in all mounted orders of dress, other than review order.

The short Lee-Enfield rifle (1907 pattern) was introduced in 1910, the barrel which screwed into the body being a trifle thinner and 5 inches shorter than that of the former Lee-Enfield, whilst the sword bayonet was 5 inches longer.   The diameter of the bore was ·303 inch, and the number of cartridges in the magazine was also ten.   This was the rifle used by the British troops, of all arms, on the several fronts throughout the Great War.

By 1910 the whole of the Regular Army had been equipped with the new web equipment, 1908 pattern.

During the year 1913, an alteration was made in the officer's blue serge frock ; the step collar taking the place of the stand-up, which necessitated only four buttons in front instead of five ; a white linen collar and black tie, tied in a sailor's knot, were now worn ; no alterations were made in the blue pointed patch pockets and cuffs ; the shoulder-straps still remained of the same material as the jacket, fastened with a small regimental button, having the badges of rank in metal thereon.

On the outbreak of the Great War in August, 1914, the wearing of full-dress uniform immediately ceased, and service dress clothing and equipment only were henceforth worn, both at home and overseas.

During the summer of 1916 the round steel helmets, commonly termed " tin hats," were first issued to the troops serving in France and Flanders, prior to which the regulation khaki, peaked, cloth field-service caps were worn throughout all engagements.

After the cessation of hostilities in 1918, in the interests of economy, it was decreed that the regulation khaki service dress should be maintained for all pur- poses, both dress and undress ; and the issue of full dress clothing continued to be temporarily in abeyance, which order has so far not been rescinded.   Of late years, however, a little colour has been added for ceremonial and walking out purposes ; for sergeants have been permitted to wear their crimson sashes over their right shoulders, when in khaki ; and the non-commissioned officers and men their white pipeclayed waist-belts.

THE LOYAL REGIMENT (NORTH LANCASHIRE)

The title of the Regiment was changed on the 1st January, 1921, to " The Loyal Regiment (North Lancashire)," but it was specially laid down that in order to avoid undue expense, the necessary changes in the uniform, and on the appoint- ments, should only be made gradually and not before the existing stocks were

1887—Officer.

1897—Lance-Corporal.

1907—Officer.

1914—Private.

THE LOYAL NORTH LANCASHIRE REGIMENT.

exhausted ; the new metal shoulder titles on the men's tunics were to bear the designation " Loyals " only.

For the first time since khaki became the service dress of the Army, the other ranks of the Loyal Regiment started, in 1924, to wear the Lincoln Shield, in brass, as a collar badge ; the pattern was the same as worn by the officers on their jackets, except that the scroll was omitted.

In 1925 the ten selected battle-honours awarded to the Regiment for their services during 1914–1918 were ordered to be added to those already on the appointments.

THE MILITIA AND SPECIAL RESERVE

The Militia were the descendants of the ancient Constitutional Force of Great Britain and date back to the earliest period of the nation's military history. Previous to 1881 the Militia regiments existed as separate units and had their own titles, regimental numbers and badges, the latter being derived generally from the insignia of the County to which they belonged ; the regiments of Lancashire all wore the Red Rose as their badge. In 1881 the Militia regiments lost their individuality, on the re-organization of the Army, and became additional battalions to the Regular Line Regiments of their respective Counties. In many cases their old badges were adopted and are still displayed by the Regular Battalions, for strangely enough, although most Regular Infantry Regiments bore County titles, few had previously to 1881 worn any badge, or device, denoting their County connection. Prior to 1830, quite a number of Militia regiments wore gold lace and buttons with their scarlet uniforms, but the same order that decreed the Regulars to wear gold, ordered the Militia to wear silver. The patterns of lace and of the buttons differed according to the period, as in the Regular Army.

Before the introduction of the Territorial system in 1881, the two battalions of the 3rd Royal Lancashire Militia (" The Duke of Lancaster's Own ") were clothed in scarlet and being a Royal Regiment their facings were blue ; having silver lace and buttons in accordance with the Army Order of the 2nd August, 1830. In some units the pewter buttons on the men's serge frocks were maintained until 1881. In recognition of their services during the period of the Crimean War the honour " Mediterranean " was borne on the appointments.

On the 1st July, 1881, the 1st and 2nd Battalions of the 3rd Royal Lancashire Militia became respectively the 3rd and 4th (Militia) Battalions, The Loyal North Lancashire Regiment ; their blue facings were discarded in favour of the white worn by the 1st and 2nd Battalions of the Regiment, the badges and buttons were made to conform to those of the Regular Battalions, the silver lace and buttons were substituted for gold ; whilst the distinction " Mediterranean " was retained on the appointments. Officers wore the letter " M " below the rank badges on the shoulder-straps, the other ranks also wore the uniform of the corresponding ranks of the Line, with the letter " M " and the number of the battalion over the County title " N. Lancashire " on their shoulder-straps. Full-dress uniform was worn by the officers, but dress tunics and helmets were, as a rule, not issued to the rank and file, and all parades were attended by them in the scarlet frock, and the Glengarry until the latter was superseded by the field service cap.

The various changes in the uniform, including the khaki service dress, arms and equipment of the Militia were in accordance with those of the Regular Army ; although some little time frequently elapsed before the requisite alterations became effective.

During the year 1896, the 3rd and 4th Battalions were amalgamated, under the title 3rd Battalion.

The honours " Mediterranean, 1900–01 " and " South Africa, 1901–02 " were granted to the 3rd Battalion after the conclusion of hostilities in South Africa, 1902, and were borne on the appointments until 1910.

When the Battalion was converted into one of the Special Reserve, in 1908, the wearing of the letter " M " on the shoulder-straps of the officers and men became obsolete ; otherwise no other alteration in the uniform was made at the time.

By an Army Order of 1910 it was laid down that the battle-honours borne by the Regular Battalions of a regiment were in future to be borne also by their Special Reserve Battalion, and those honours awarded when the latter were Militia units were in consequence to lapse ; thus the 3rd Battalion was authorized to bear the full list of battle-honours as shown in the Army List ; whilst the two " Mediterranean " honours were not only lost to the 3rd Battalion, but to the Regiment generally.

After the outbreak of war in August, 1914, the regulation khaki service dress and equipment only were issued, in accordance with the general instructions.

THE VOLUNTEER AND TERRITORIAL BATTALIONS

The establishment of the Volunteer force was sanctioned on the 12th May, 1859. As regards particulars of the uniform, arms and equipment, the War Office Circular of that date announced that the details were to be settled by the members themselves. In view of the fact that the various companies, or corps, were to be trained as riflemen, the colour of the clothing usually selected was either one of green or grey, and not red as in the Regular Army. In the early days of the movement the uniform, which was as simple in character as possible, consisted of a shako or peaked cap ; tunic, single-breasted, braided and cut long in the skirts ; trousers or knickerbockers of the same material and leather leggings. Greatcoats of a military pattern were rarely issued ; haversacks, water-bottles and knapsacks were practically unknown. The pouch belt, worn over the left shoulder, and the waist-belt with bayonet frog were of black, or brown, leather. The rifle with which these rifle corps generally equipped themselves was the Enfield.

In 1863 it was ordained that all companies of an administrative battalion were to be dressed alike and that the cloth for uniforms, cut out and basted, was to be supplied from the Army Clothing Depôt at cost price.

About the year 1863 the red tunic first made its appearance in the dress of the Volunteers, on the plea that in the event of an invasion of our shores an enemy would know immediately whether he were opposed by Regular troops or by Volunteers, by the very colour of their uniform.

In 1872 the Snider rifle had superseded the Enfield. By now the 11th Lancashire Rifle Volunteers had changed from their riflemen's uniform into red, with blue facings ; as had also the 27th Lancashire, but with green facings.

According to the Regulations of 1878, infantry battalions were to wear an Austrian knot on the sleeve, the colour of the regimental facings ; the initials of the County and the number of the Corps were to be placed on the shoulder-straps ; silver lace, badges, and buttons ; with white belts and black pouches. Officers were to wear the cross-belt ; but the crimson sash, worn over the left and right shoulders respectively, by the officers and sergeants of the Regular forces, was not permitted.

In 1880 the facings of the 11th Lancashire were altered from blue to white, whilst the 27th, which was re-numbered the 14th, in the latter part of this year, retained their green.

On the re-organization of the Army and the introduction of the Territorial system on the 1st July, 1881, the 11th and 14th Lancashire Rifle Volunteer Corps became respectively the 1st and 2nd Volunteer Battalions, The Loyal North Lancashire Regiment. White now being the colour of the regimental facings, the 2nd Battalion consequently lost their former green. The badges of rank previously worn on the officer's collar were now placed on the shoulder-straps ; non-commissioned officers were to wear their chevrons on the right sleeve only, instead of both arms. The men's shoulder-straps were to bear the letter " V," in addition to the number of the battalion and the title. Belts and pouches, buff. The lace and buttons of silver were retained. The old individual badges were eventually abolished in favour of the regimental, in silver.

By 1885 the Martini-Henry rifle had been generally adopted and henceforth the various changes in the uniform, arms and equipment were in accordance with the regulations.

As a reward for their services during the war in South Africa, both the 1st and 2nd Volunteer Battalions were duly authorized to bear the battle-honour " SOUTH AFRICA, 1900–02 " on their appointments.

. On the 1st April, 1908, the 1st and 2nd Volunteer Battalions became the 4th and 5th Territorial Battalions of the Regiment, which necessitated certain alterations in the uniform ; the silver lace, buttons, helmet plate, etc., were replaced by those of gold, or gilt brass ; the letter " T " was substituted for that of " V," and when in scarlet, officers were now allowed to wear the crimson sash round the waist and sergeants over the right shoulder.

On the outbreak of the Great War in 1914, the issue of all clothing, except the khaki service dress and equipment, was withdrawn ; which order has so far not been countermanded.

The battle-honours awarded for services rendered during 1914–1918 were announced in 1925. There being only one list for a regiment, the Territorial

Battalions received exactly the same as those also granted to the Regular and Service Battalions ; and the ten selected were ordered to be borne on the appointments of both the 4th and 5th Battalions.

THE SERVICE BATTALIONS

The regulation khaki service dress and equipment, together with the usual necessaries, were alone issued during the period of their existence, 1914–1919.

When the Service Battalions were raised in the autumn of 1914, owing to the pressing needs of the British Expeditionary Force, then overseas, there was a general shortage of uniforms, arms and equipment, available for those serving at home ; so much so that recruits were obliged to wear their own civilian clothing and only a few rifles were obtainable for drill and instructional purposes. In some units a blue serge uniform was issued as a temporary measure. These difficulties, however, which at the time appeared to be almost insuperable, were speedily overcome by the military authorities and it was not so very long before the various battalions were fully clothed, armed and equipped.

As stated above, the battle-honours awarded were the same as those granted to the Regular and Territorial Battalions of the Regiment, but before these honours were published and could be borne on the appointments, the Service Battalions had all been disbanded and the officers and men had returned to civil life.

APPENDIX VI

MEDALS

The following is a detailed description of the war medals, and decorations, awarded for the various campaigns, in which the Regiment has participated.

THE MILITARY GENERAL SERVICE, 1793–1814.

By General Order, 1st June, 1847, H.M. Queen Victoria commanded that a Medal should be struck to record the services of the Army during the wars 1793–1814. Issued 1848 ; to survivors only.

Obverse : Head of Queen Victoria, diademed, *l.*, 1848 below. Legend " VICTORIA REGINA."

Reverse : Queen Victoria standing on a dais, robed, *r.*, placing a laurel wreath upon the head of the Duke of Wellington, kneeling on his left knee, with his field-marshal's bâton in his right hand. At the side of the dais, a British lion, dormant, *r.* Legend " TO THE BRITISH ARMY." Exergue 1793–1814.

Silver. Circular. 1·4 inches in diameter.

Riband, 1¼ inches wide, crimson with blue borders.

Mounting, straight silver bar and clip.

The name, rank, and regiment of the recipient are indented on the edge.

Twenty-nine clasps in all were issued, including " MAIDA," " CORUNNA," " VITTORIA," " ST. SEBASTIAN," and " NIVE " ; the majority of which were for the Peninsular War.

Although this Medal bore the dates 1793–1814, the period of the various actions for which the various clasps were given was only 1801–1814.

"INDIA, 1799–1826."

It was announced by General Order, Horse Guards, dated 21st March, 1851, that " H.M. the Queen had been pleased to signify her assent to a measure which had been proposed by the Court of Directors of the East India Company for granting a Medal, at their expense, to the surviving Officers and Soldiers of the Crown who were engaged in the services in India from 1799–1826 "—this was known as the India General Service Medal.

Obverse : Head of Queen Victoria, diademed, *l.* Legend " VICTORIA REGINA."

Reverse : Figure of Victory, seated, holding in her right hand a laurel branch, in her left a wreath. In the left background a palm-tree and a trophy of weapons. Above " TO THE ARMY OF INDIA." Exergue 1799–1826.

Silver. Circular. 1·4 inches in diameter.

Riband, light blue, 1¼ inches wide.

Mounting, silver scroll bar, attached by a claw clip.
Name and regiment of the recipient are engraved round the edge.
Twenty-one clasps, including " AVA," in all were issued.

THE INDIA GENERAL SERVICE, 1852–1895.

Notified to the Army of India by a General Order of the Governor-General, dated 22nd December, 1853 ; as a reward of the services of Her Majesty's, as well as the East India Company's, land and sea forces, who were engaged in the Burmese War of 1852 and 1853. This Medal has since been issued to commemorate the numerous campaigns that have taken place on the Indian Frontier, including the expedition to the Malay Peninsula.

Obverse : Head of Queen Victoria, diademed, *l.* Legend " VICTORIA REGINA."

Reverse : A figure of Victory, crowning a warrior with a wreath of laurel. In the exergue, a lotus flower, with leaves.

Twenty-three clasps, in all, were authorized, indicative of the service for which awarded, including " NORTH WEST FRONTIER."

Silver. Circular. 1·4 inches in diameter.

Riband, 1¼ inches wide, red with two blue stripes, forming five ¼-inch stripes.

Mounting, silver scroll bar and claw clip.

The name and regiment were either indented, or engraved, round the edge.

Artists : obverse, W. Wyon, R.A. ; reverse, L. C. Wyon.

THE DISTINGUISHED CONDUCT MEDAL.

Granted by Royal Warrant, 4th December, 1854, and awarded for distinguished service and gallant conduct in the field. A gratuity of £15 to a sergeant, £10 to a corporal and £5 to a private was originally given ; but by Royal Warrant, dated 30th September, 1862, these gratuities were withdrawn. A further Royal Warrant of 7th February, 1881, provided for the issue of a Bar, for each subsequent award. Artist, Pistrucci.

Obverse : A military trophy, having an oval shield in centre bearing the arms of the United Kingdom.

Reverse : Plain, inscribed " FOR DISTINGUISHED CONDUCT IN THE FIELD." Below, a spear-head.

Silver. Circular. 1·4 inches in diameter.

Riband, 1¼ inches wide, ribbed, red with a dark blue stripe down centre ; in three equal widths.

Mounting, scroll bar and ornamental claw clip.

The name, etc., of the recipient is engraved round the edge.

On the accession of H.M. King Edward VII, the obverse was changed, as follows :

Obverse : Bust of King Edward VII, *l.*, in Field-Marshal's uniform and the Star and ribbon of the Garter ; greatcoat. Legend " EDWARDUS VII REX IMPERATOR."

In like manner, a further change was effected after the accession of H.M. King George V :

Obverse : Bust of King George V, *l.*, in Field-Marshal's uniform, and the Star and ribbon of the Garter. Legend " GEORGIUS V. BRITT: OMN: REX ET IND: IMP:"

No alterations were made on the reverse and the colour of the riband has remained unchanged throughout.

In undress uniform, when the riband only is worn, the award of the Bar is denoted by a silver rose in centre of same.

THE CRIMEA (BRITISH).

General Order No. 638, 15th December, 1854, stated that H.M. The Queen had been pleased to command that a Medal bearing the word " CRIMEA," with an appropriate device, be conferred upon all those engaged in the campaign in the Crimea, and that clasps with the words " ALMA " and " INKERMANN " thereon be also awarded to those who participated in those battles.   On the 23rd February, 1855, the clasp " BALAKLAVA " was granted, and on the 31st October the clasp " SEBASTOPOL " was added. The Order, dated 2nd May, 1856, authorized the " AZOFF " clasp to the officers and crews of such ships who had served in the Sea of Azoff between the 25th May, 1855 and the 9th September, 1855, which latter date was afterwards extended to the 22nd November, 1855.

Obverse : Head of Queen Victoria, diademed, *l*. Legend " VICTORIA REGINA, 1854."

Reverse : A flying figure of Victory crowning a Roman soldier with a laurel wreath, who bears a sword in his right hand and a shield on his left arm, with a lion in the centre.   The word " CRIMEA " is on the left.

Silver.   Circular.   1·4 inches in diameter.

Riband, 1⅜ inches wide ; light watered blue with narrow yellow borders.

Mounting, foliated bar.   Clasps oak-leaf and acorns.

The name and regiment of the recipient were either indented, or engraved, on the edge.

Artists : obverse, W. Wyon, R.A. ; reverse, B. Wyon.

THE CRIMEA (TURKISH).

H.I.M. the Sultan of Turkey granted a Medal to the British, French and Sardinian troops engaged.

Obverse : Within two laurel branches, tied with a ribbon at the base, the Cypher of Sultan Abdil Mageed Khan II (The Slave of the Good).   Below, in Turkish characters, " CRIMEA," and the date of the Hegira " 1271 " (A.D. 1855).

Reverse : The map of the Crimea, spread over a field-gun, to the right is a mortar and anchor, and to the left three cannon balls, a ramrod, etc.   The flags of Turkey and Great Britain in front, and France and Sardinia behind.   In the exergue " CRIMEA 1855."

Silver.   Circular.   1⅞ inches in diameter with a plain raised border, suspended from a pink watered riband with green edges.

The Medals were issued without names.

The position of the national flags varied according to the nation for which the medal was intended.

A certain number of French and Sardinian Medals were also awarded to the British troops, in recognition of their services during the war in the Crimea of 1854–1855.

THE VICTORIA CROSS.

Established by Royal Warrant on the 29th January, 1856, and revised 23rd April, 1881, " for acts of valour in the presence of the enemy."

A bronze Maltese Cross. 1½ inches in diameter.

Obverse: The British Lion and Crown ; below a scroll with the words " FOR VALOUR."

Reverse : A raised circle in centre, containing the date of the act of bravery.

A pierced lug is attached to the top limb for suspension. Bronze Clasp, laureated, 1½ inches wide, on the reverse side of which are engraved the name and regiment of the recipient.

For each additional award a Bar is given.

On 8th August, 1902, posthumous awards were sanctioned.

Riband 1½ inches wide. Red for Army. Blue for Navy.

In August, 1918, the colour of the riband was officially ordered to be changed to that of the red for all Services.

Army Order No. 290 of 1916, on the award of a Bar, authorized a miniature replica of the Cross in bronze to be worn on the riband, when in undress or service uniform ; one or more according to the exact number of Bars awarded.

Army Order No. 114 of 1917, amended the above Order and directed that when in undress or service uniform, a miniature replica of the Cross in bronze was to be worn on the riband, on the first award. The award of a Bar to the original decoration was marked by a second miniature Cross on the riband, an additional Cross being added for each further Bar.

INDIAN MUTINY, 1857–1858.

Granted by General Order, dated 18th August, 1858, to those troops of Her Majesty and of the East India Company, and those of the Naval Brigade, who were employed in suppression of the Mutiny in India, which broke out on 10th May, 1857.

Obverse: Head of Queen Victoria, diademed, *l.* Legend " VICTORIA REGINA." On truncation, W. Wyon, R.A.

Reverse : A helmeted figure of Britannia standing in front of a lion. Holding out a laurel wreath in her right hand, and on her left arm the Union shield. Above the word " INDIA." Exergue 1857–1858. L. C. Wyon.

Silver. Circular. 1·4 inches in diameter.

Riband, 1½ inches wide. White with two red stripes, forming five ½-inch stripes. Mounting, an ornamental cuspid bar with claw clip attachment.

Five clasps in all were subsequently issued, these clasps were 1½ inches long by ⅜ inch wide at the ends, and reduced to ¼ inch in the centre. The ends are fish-tailed, and the lettering in raised capitals. The clasps are inscribed " DELHI,"" DEFENCE OF LUCKNOW," " RELIEF OF LUCKNOW," "LUCKNOW " and " CENTRAL INDIA."

The name and regiment of the recipient were indented on the edge of the Medal.

AFGHANISTAN, 1878–1880.

Sanctioned by General Order No. 30, dated 19th March, 1881.

Obverse : Bust of Queen Victoria, *l.*, crowned and with veil hanging behind wearing the Star and ribbon of the Order of the Garter. Legend " VICTORIA REGINA ET IMPERATRIX."

Reverse : Anglo-Indian troops on the march in a mountainous country ; a prominent feature being an elephant carrying a mountain gun. The word " AFGHANISTAN " above. Exergue " 1878–79–80."
Silver. Circular. 1·4 inches in diameter.
Riband green, with red edges.
Mounting, plain straight silver bar, with claw clip attachment, fixed by a rivet.
Six clasps in all were issued, including the one for the Capture of " ALI MASJID " on the 21st November, 1878.

THE DISTINGUISHED SERVICE ORDER.

Established by Royal Warrant, dated 6th September, 1886, " in recognition of special service of commissioned officers of the Imperial Forces."
A gold cross patée, convexed, enamelled white, edged with gold.
Obverse : In the centre, within laurel wreath, enamelled green, an Imperial Crown in gold, upon a red enamelled background.
Reverse : Imperial Cypher, within two branches of laurel, also upon a red-enamelled background.
Suspended from a red riband, edged with blue, 1 inch wide, from a gold laureated bar 1¼ inches wide, fastened by two gold loops, and having a similar gold laureated bar with brooch attachment above.
For each subsequent award a Bar is issued ; and when ribands only are worn each additional award is denoted by a silver rose in centre of same.

CANADA, GENERAL SERVICE MEDAL.

Army Order No. 7 of January, 1899, announced that H.M. Queen Victoria had been graciously pleased to approve of a Medal being granted to those who were employed in repelling the Fenian Raids on the Canadian Frontier in 1866 and 1870 ; or engaged in the Red River Expedition of 1870.
Issued to survivors only.
Obverse : Bust of Queen Victoria, l., with diadem and veil ; wearing the Star and ribbon of the Garter. Legend " VICTORIA REGINA ET IMPERATRIX."
Reverse : The Canadian Flag between two branches of maple leaves. Above, the word " CANADA."
Silver. Circular. 1⅞ inches in diameter.
Riband, 1¼ inches wide, scarlet with white stripe down centre, in three equal widths.
Mounting, a straight bar with claw attachment, fixed by a rivet.
Three clasps in all were issued, including that inscribed " FENIAN RAID, 1866." The name of the recipient was either indented or engraved round the edge.

SOUTH AFRICA, 1899–1902 (QUEEN'S).

Army Order No. 94 of April, 1901. H.M. King Edward VII confirmed the order given by Her late Majesty Queen Victoria, in June, 1900, that a Medal be struck to commemorate the operations in South Africa. It was granted to all those who had served, at any time, between 11th October, 1899, and 31st May, 1902.
Obverse : Bust of Queen Victoria, l., crowned and veiled ; wearing the Star and ribbon of the Order of the Garter. Legend " VICTORIA REGINA ET IMPERATRIX."

Reverse : Britannia, *r.*, standing, wearing helmet, holding a standard in her left hand, and in her right a laurel wreath towards troops advancing. A shield, trident and palm branch at her feet. On the left are shown the sea and a man-of-war. Above is the legend " SOUTH AFRICA."

Silver. Circular. $1\frac{3}{8}$ inches in diameter.

Riband, $1\frac{1}{4}$ inches wide, centre orange $\frac{1}{2}$ inch wide, between two narrow stripes of dark blue and red on the borders.

Mounting, straight bar and swivel for suspension.

Twenty-six clasps in all were authorized, including " MODDER RIVER " and " DEFENCE OF KIMBERLEY."

The name, etc., of the recipient is indented on the edge, in capital letters.

Army Order No. 32 of February, 1902, awarded this Medal to those of the Militia who served on garrison duty at Gibraltar, Malta, or in Egypt, during the period of the war. The riband and medal were of the same pattern, but the legend " MEDITERRANEAN " took the place of " SOUTH AFRICA " on the reverse. Those who received the Queen's Medal for South Africa were not entitled to that for the Mediterranean also.

SOUTH AFRICA, 1901–1902 (KING'S).

Army Order, No. 232, October, 1902, stated that H.M. King Edward VII had been pleased to approve that a second War Medal be granted to those of the Imperial forces who were actually serving in South Africa on or after 1st January, 1902, and on that date had completed eighteen months' war service, or subsequently completed such service before 1st June, 1902.

Obverse : Bust of King Edward VII, *l.*, in full dress uniform of a Field-Marshal (with greatcoat), with Star and ribbon of the Garter. Legend " EDWARDUS VII, REX IMPERATOR."

Reverse : Same as the Queen's Medal.

Silver. Circular. 1·4 inches in diameter.

Riband, $1\frac{1}{4}$ inches wide, having three stripes of equal width, of orange, white and green.

Two clasps were granted, inscribed " SOUTH AFRICA, 1901 " to all those who served during the whole of the year 1901, and " SOUTH AFRICA, 1902 " to those who served in South Africa between 1st January, 1902, and 31st May, 1902, both dates inclusive.

Mounting, straight silver bar, with ornamental clip, fixed by a rivet.

The name, etc., of the recipient is indented round the edge in capital letters.

THE MILITARY CROSS.

Instituted 28th December, 1914, and confined to officers below field rank and warrant officers only.

A Silver Cross, ornamented, with four arms, on each of which is an Imperial Crown. In the centre is the Imperial Cypher " G.R.I.," and the Cross is suspended by the top arm, from the plain silver clasp, through which the riband passes. Bars are also awarded for further awards, and in service dress when the riband only is worn, each Bar is denoted by the wearing of a silver rose in the centre.

Riband, white watered, with equal blue line down centre.

The name and rank of the recipient are engraved on the reverse, which is otherwise plain.

THE MILITARY MEDAL.

Sanctioned by H.M. King George V, by Royal Warrant, 5th April, 1916. Available for non-commissioned officers and men who perform individual, or associated, acts of bravery in the field.

For each subsequent award a Bar is given.

Obverse : Bust of King George V, *l.*, wearing the full dress uniform of a Field-Marshal, with Star and ribbon of the Garter. Legend " GEORGIUS V. BRITT: OMN: REX ET IND: IMP: "

Reverse : Inscribed " FOR BRAVERY IN THE FIELD," within a laurel wreath, and surmounted by the Royal Cypher and Crown.

Silver. Circular. 1·4 inches in diameter.

Riband, 1¼ inches wide, dark blue, having in the centre three white and two crimson stripes, alternating.

Mounting, silver scroll bar with claw clip.

The name, etc., of the recipient is engraved round the edge.

In undress uniform, when the riband only is worn, the award of the Bar is denoted by a silver rose in centre of same.

THE GREAT WAR—THE 1914 STAR.

In November, 1917 (Army Order No. 350), a Star in bronze was granted to all those who had served in France and Flanders between 5th August, 1914, and midnight 22nd–23rd November, 1914. No clasp was originally issued.

A four-pointed Star, 1¾ inches in diameter, surmounted by a Crown.

Obverse : Two crossed swords with a ribbon intertwined, bearing the inscription on three scrolls, " AUG.–1914–Nov." within oak wreath, bearing Royal Cypher at base.

Reverse : Plain, name and unit of recipient engraved thereon.

In October, 1919 (Army Order No. 361), the issue of a clasp was sanctioned, to those who had served under fire between 5th August, 1914, and midnight 22nd–23rd November, 1914. This clasp is made of the same metal as the Star, and is inscribed " 5TH AUG.–22nd Nov. 1914," on a frosted ground.

In undress and service uniform, when ribands only are worn, the grant of the clasp is denoted by a small silver rose in the centre of the riband.

The Star is suspended from the riband by a bronze ring. The riband is red, white and blue in colour, shaded and watered.

THE GREAT WAR—THE 1914–15 STAR.

In December, 1918 (Army Order No. 20, 1919), a Star in bronze was awarded to all those who had served in the various theatres of war between 5th August, 1914, and 31st December, 1915, both dates inclusive ; but those who were eligible for the " 1914 Star " were not to receive the " 1914–15 Star."

The decoration is identical, except for the date, to the " 1914 Star " (but no clasp). On the obverse " 1914–15 " appears on the centre scroll, whilst the two smaller scrolls are omitted ; the reverse is plain, bearing the name, etc., thereon.

The riband is also the same as that of the " 1914 Star."

THE GREAT WAR—THE WAR MEDAL.

In July, 1919 (Army Order No. 266), the war having been successfully concluded, it was announced that this Medal be issued to all those of H.M. Forces who left their native shores, whether they eventually entered a theatre of war, or not.

Obverse : Head of King George V, *l.* Legend " GEORGIUS V. BRITT: OMN: REX ET IND: IMP:"

Reverse : Equestrian figure of St. George, facing right, trampling underfoot the eagle shield of the Central Powers, and a skull and cross-bones, the emblems of death. Above the rising sun, the symbol of victory. Legend " 1914–1918."

Silver. Circular. 1·4 inches in diameter.

Suspended from riband by a straight clasp, without swivel.

The riband is orange in the centre, watered, with stripes of white and black on each side, with borders of Royal blue.

The name, etc., of the recipient is engraved round the edge of the Medal.

THE GREAT WAR—THE VICTORY MEDAL.

In August, 1919 (Army Order No. 301), this second Medal was granted to those who had been engaged on active service between 5th August, 1914, and 11th November, 1918.

Obverse : A winged full-length figure of Victory, with outstretched arms. The borders and the background plain, without date or inscription.

Reverse : Inscription " THE GREAT WAR FOR CIVILISATION, 1914–1919," within laurel wreath.

Bronze. Circular. 36 millimetres in diameter.

Suspended by a circular ring from the riband, the colour of which is red in the centre, with green and violet on each side, shaded to form the colours of two rainbows. This Medal is identical in design with that issued by the other Allied Powers. Rim plain.

The name, etc., of the recipient is engraved round the edge.

An emblem of an oak leaf in bronze was authorized in January, 1920 (Army Order No. 3) to be worn on the riband of this Medal, by those who had been " mentioned in despatches."

THE GREAT WAR—THE TERRITORIAL FORCE WAR MEDAL

In April, 1920 (Army Order No 143), this Medal was approved for those members of the Territorial Force who had volunteered for service overseas on, or before, the 30th September, 1914, and who had rendered such service during the years 1916–1919, providing they were serving as Territorials on 4th August, 1914, or had completed a period of not less than four years' service before the outbreak of war and re-joined not later than 30th September, 1914.

Obverse : Head of King George V, *l.* Legend " GEORGIUS V. BRITT: OMN: REX ET IND: IMP:"

Reverse : Inscription " FOR VOLUNTARY SERVICE OVERSEAS, 1914–1919," within a laurel wreath.

Bronze. Circular. 1·4 inches in diameter.

Riband, yellow, with two green stripes.

Mounting, straight bar with claw clip attachment.

The name, etc., of the recipient is engraved round the edge of the Medal.

Those who qualified for either the " 1914 Star," or " 1914–15 Star," were ineligible.

THE BAND, 1ST BATTALION.

1912.

APPENDIX VII

MILITARY MUSIC AND BANDS

Military bands may be said to have been originally copied from the Saracens, whilst the drums were probably introduced into Europe from the East by the Crusaders, or by the Moors into Spain.

The early employment of drums was near the standard, where the lusty beating assured the troops, in the heat of battle, that their flag was still being kept flying.

About the middle of the sixteenth century the fife made its first appearance and speedily attained popularity, being in a great degree responsible for supplanting the bag-pipes from popular favour. Towards the end of this century drums and fifes appear to have become a recognized part of the military establishment. In the infantry, drums at this period were all side-drums, or tambours—" snares " were then unknown.

In addition to their musical duties, drummers were utilized as messengers between opposing armies and had therefore to be men of superior intelligence and sobriety.

A drum-major is mentioned in 1668 as being borne on the establishment of every regiment, and although graded as a staff-sergeant he was not paid by the Government, but by the Regiment ; and whilst his pay was that of a sergeant, his allowances for clothing, etc., were only those of a drummer. It was not until 1810 that marching regiments were permitted by regulations to bear a drum-major on the establishment, with full pay and allowances. His primary duty was to train the drummers and boys in the beating of the drum and instruct them in the bugle calls ; in later years he was also responsible for the carrying out of all corporal punishments awarded, and the carrying of letters. A certain order, dated August, 1800, read as follows : " The drum-major will procure his cat-o'-nine-tails from the quartermaster-serjeant, for which he will pay the sum of one shilling, and which sum he will charge against the punished soldier's account of the muster. The cats are always to be returned to the quartermaster-serjeant after use, each time of punishment ; the quartermaster-serjeant will be answerable that they are made of cord of a thickness never less than what is usually called penny cord. He will also be the carrier of all letters, for which he will receive such price per letter, or parcel, as by a board of officers shall from time to time be agreed upon."

Being considered profane, drums and fifes were laid aside during the period of the Commonwealth in England, and almost ceased to exist as an integral part of military music ; but owing to the efforts of the Duke of Cumberland they were revived in 1748, after the campaign in Flanders, and have continued ever since.

In the earlier days, many of the drums of the infantry had the heraldic arms of the colonel commanding painted on them ; it was subsequently decreed that " the front be painted with the colour of the regimental facing, with the King's Cypher and Crown, and the number of the regiment, under it." In 1789 the wooden drums were replaced by those of brass.

A Circular Memorandum, dated 30th September, 1858, stated : " the allowance in lieu of drums, fifes and bugles, hitherto optional with commanding officers, will henceforth cease, and these articles will, for the future, be issued in kind and of one universal pattern."

General Order No. 104 of 1872 directed that, as considerable want of uniformity existed in the mode of accounting certain non-commissioned officers in the monthly returns, the drum-major should in future be accounted for in the column of drummers, and not in that for sergeants ; this order was counter-manded by General Order No. 107 of 1881.

During the year 1881 the designation of drum-major was changed to sergeant-drummer ; the former title was restored in July, 1928 (Army Order No. 139).

The fife has seldom more than one key ; the compass is about two octaves and as the scale is diatonic, only airs of simple melodic structure can be played upon it.

In the present-day bugle, a valveless instrument, only five of its eight notes are brought into play for the purpose of the various calls, namely C below the stave, and G, C, E, G, in ascending order.

The military band appears to have originated during the reign of King Charles II, about 1678, who introduced the oboe into the British Army from the French ; hence the regimental band was frequently designated in orders as " the hautbois," and the name remained on officially in Army Estimates until 1834. The bands, as a whole, were generally styled " the musick."

The oboe was a non-chromatic instrument, having a reed not unlike that of the modern bassoon.

The number of musicians was usually from four to six, and this strength was maintained until the middle of the eighteenth century, when the clarinet together with the horn and bassoon first began to make their appearance ; the latter being found not sufficiently strong to maintain the bass part, the serpent and trombone were next introduced in support. The serpent was the natural bass of the cornet family and the bassoon became the tenor instrument.

By the Clothing Warrant of 1751 and some subsequent regulations, drummers were ordered to be clothed in garments, the entire colour of which was that of the regimental facings worn by the officers and men of the battalion, but the details do not appear to have been very concise and were possibly misinterpreted—many irregularities were therefore seemingly approved. In some regiments the dress of the bandsmen, with certain modifications, was similar to that of the drummers, whilst others evolved, or even invented, their own particular designs in pattern, colour and embellishment, with the consequential result that the sartorial appear-ance when on parade may be better imagined than described. Many bandsmen had worn the aiguillette for years past ; in some regiments on the right shoulder, in others on the left, but whether a regiment did, or did not, wear these aiguillettes before or after the Warrant of 1751 probably depended on the whim of the commanding officer ; at any rate they were not entirely obliterated, for many units continued to adorn their bandsmen accordingly right up to the outbreak of the Great War, in 1914, after which full dress was temporarily discarded.   Aiguillettes, sometimes termed shoulder-knots, are not legislated for in the dress and equipment regulations and, if used, have always been supplied from other sources.   That the origin is French is obvious from the very name, but as in the case of so many other portions of military dress no exact date of introduction can be absolutely assigned.

The following special instructions regarding the bandmaster and musicians, published in 1777, are not without interest.   " The most skilful of the band ought to be appointed bandmaster.   He should find out and practise the best adjudged pieces and to his care and inspection the others should be subjected ; a man whose regularity, sobriety, good conduct and honesty can most strictly be depended upon ; most remarkably clean and neat in dress, have an approved ear and taste for music and a good method of teaching ; without speaking harshly to the youths, or hurrying them on too fast.   Musicians must attend roll calling at all times when the regiment is on the march or under arms, and when in action are to stay with their respective companies and assist the wounded."

In 1781 the strength of the band was increased to eight ; two oboes, two clarinets, two horns and two bassoons ; sometimes a flute, or trumpet, or bugle was included, but at the expense of one or other of the former instruments.

By a General Order of 5th August, 1803, it was directed that the number of musicians should not be more than one private soldier to each company, and one non-commissioned officer be allowed to act as master of the band ; " the men to be drilled and fall in with their companies completely armed and accoutred, in case of actual service."

The bass-drum and cymbals, as they were introduced into the Army, were eagerly embraced by infantry regiments, together with the tambourine and triangle.   These instruments were frequently played by negroes, who were fancifully garbed, and it was their habit to perform all sorts of gymnastic antics and contortions whilst playing.   These men of colour began to disappear from the regimental establishments about the year 1835, but the present-day leopard, or tiger, skin worn by the big-drummer and the flourishing of the drum sticks, when playing, are survivals of the times when these instruments were played by the black drummers.

Another importation adopted, by some battalions, early in the nineteenth century was the " chapeau chinois," more commonly known as the " Jingling Johnny," which measured about seven feet over all and consisted of a staff surmounted by several brass crescents, to which was attached a number of small silver bells, each of a different tone.   At the end of the crescents, coloured horsehair plumes were suspended.   This spectacular combination was, as a rule, carried in front of the band by the tallest man available in the battalion, who was not necessarily a bandsman, but selected purely on account of his height.   In order to save his coatee, or tunic, from undue wear a white leather apron was generally provided for the bearer.   It is believed the idea was originally taken from the

Moors who had long used it, not only as a musical instrument, but also as a rallying standard for their warriors when in battle.

The key-bugle was invented in 1810, and from this was evolved the ophicleide, a bass key-bugle and an octave lower. Prior to this, valves in brass instruments were unknown, and it was therefore quite impossible for a complete scale to be produced.

The Regulations of the Army of 1811 directed general officers to report half-yearly as to whether the bands played in correct time or not ; and the drum-major was enjoined to use the plummet to practise his men by, and when on the march, at the head of the column, to ensure a regular step " he was to use his staff and plant same every fourth pace, so as to keep time."

It is interesting to note that in 1820, the innovation was made by a certain conductor, who ceasing to play his instrument stood in front of his musicians and wielded his baton ; before which date bands, and orchestras, were directed and given their tempo by their leader, who was invariably one of the players.

In 1822 the number of instrumentalists was officially raised to ten, exclusive of boys or negroes, and in 1823 an increase was sanctioned to fifteen, including the band-sergeant. These numbers, however, were frequently exceeded, in spite of the regulations, by impressing men from the ranks, who were termed " acting bandsmen."

A Circular Memorandum, dated 16th February, 1829, addressed to commanding officers with a view of limiting officers' expenses, read as follows : " Twenty days' pay to be paid by each officer to the band fund on appointment, and an annual subscription, under the discretion of the commanding officer, but not exceeding twelve days' pay, to be paid in support of the band expenses. In all cases of promotion, the same rule to apply to the band, as that laid down for the mess subscription." There was nothing in the Regulations to prevent officers contributing individually what they pleased to the support of the band, but they could not be required to exceed the amount prescribed. Any further donation was entirely optional and the express object of the memorandum was to protect the officer of small means, while it left to the individual whose income might admit of it, the power of an increased contribution, which was to be considered private and not regimental.

By an Army Order of 2nd August, 1830, bands of infantry regiments were " to be dressed in white clothing with the regimental coloured facings ; the trousers and caps were to be conformable in every respect to the pattern of the regiment at large." This order seems to have been the first real attempt on the part of the military authorities to co-ordinate the dress of bandsmen throughout the Service ; before which, as previously narrated, no concise regulations for their clothing and equipment appear to have been laid down, and accordingly all sorts of fancy garments and head-dresses crept in, probably due to the caprices of the individual regimental officers who were also responsible for their supply and payment.

The formation of bands at regimental depôts did not find favour with the higher authorities. A Circular of 18th February, 1835, drew attention to the fact that many musicians were retained in excess of establishment. In some cases bands had been formed and maintained by subscriptions from the officers ; expense was also incurred by the addition of lace and other alterations in the clothing ; non-commissioned officers were employed in charge of the band and thus withdrawn from their other duties. The regulations only allowed four drummers on a depôt establishment, and the proportion of acting drummers was not to exceed six ; these acting drummers were to be clothed as privates, without any addition of lace or ornament. Again, a further memorandum on this subject was issued on 12th February, 1845. There was to be but one band in a regiment, which must as a matter of course accompany the service companies. Any officer in command of a depôt who permitted a band to exist was deemed to have taken upon himself a departure from Her Majesty's Regulations. The plea of training men, or boys, for the regimental band at a depôt was altogether inadmissible, and those specially enlisted for the band should have been sent to the service companies with the first draft after their enlistment, and not retained on the pretence of maintaining a band for the depôt companies. The establishment had been increased by now to six drummers and four boys as fifers or buglers, and these boys only so long as they were of an age or stature not to bear arms ; no man was on any account to be withdrawn from the ranks and employed in an occupation which was intended to be confined to the boys specially authorized to be enlisted for that purpose.

The cornopean, or cornet, was introduced in 1836, and the saxhorn, or euphonium, in 1845 ; the latter took the place of the ophicleide. The saxophone appeared about 1846.

On the march, music had been played mostly from memory, for until now there was little printed music in existence, much less available ; bandmasters were therefore obliged to arrange their own settings in manuscript form for the different instruments ; the repertoire being consequently somewhat limited. Printed music, with the various band parts, was first published and sold about the year 1846. It was not, however, until 1st April, 1883, that General Order No. 54 announced : " With a view to bands of infantry being enabled to perform together, when brigaded or massed, the regimental quicksteps to be used on such occasions have been approved and printed. Commanding officers are recommended to cause these marches to be practised. The music has been prepared and can be procured on payment."

The strength of the band was in 1846 increased to twenty-one, one sergeant and twenty bandsmen.

Hitherto, no school of music for the training of bandsmen existed in any shape or form, and regiments were frequently perforce obliged to engage civilians as their musicians, with the result that not being subject to military discipline, they were a continual source of trouble to their commanding officers and the military authorities generally ; especially as a certain proportion was obtained from the Continent and had little or no knowledge of the English language. No monetary grants, or allowances, were available, still less forthcoming, for the upkeep of the bands and all expenses had to be defrayed personally by the officers of the battalion ; the Government only recognizing the drums and fifes as being on the establishment.

Further, there was no recognized musical pitch and it was courting disaster to attempt to mass bands together.

Before the year 1855, regimental music and musical matters were regulated solely by a branch of the Board of Ordnance.

H.R.H. the Duke of Cambridge, shortly after being appointed commander-in-chief, issued a circular, on the 26th September, 1856, addressed to all commanding officers, inviting their attention to the unnecessary expense caused by the employment of professional civilian musicians as masters of bands, and recommended the formation of a musical class of instruction for the training of those candidates selected from regiments to qualify for the post of bandmaster. The scheme was duly approved on the following 4th December, and a " Military Music Class " was inaugurated at Twickenham on the 3rd March, 1857. This was the foundation of the Military School of Music, Kneller Hall, which was established in the following year. In order that the School should be self-supporting, commanding officers were expected to subscribe from their own regimental funds the initial sum of £5 for the purchase of instruments and an annual subscription of £8 towards the maintenance and training. The premises were Government property. It was not until about the year 1875 that the War Office assumed complete control of military music and matters pertaining thereto.

In 1858, within a year of the foundation of Kneller Hall, the Military School of Music laid down its musical pitch as that used by the Ancient Philharmonic Society, a difference of nearly a semi-tone between music elsewhere, both at home and abroad. This pitch was adhered to in the Army until December, 1928, although the Philharmonic adopted the lower " International " or " Continental " in 1885, with the intention of helping to standardize it throughout the civilised world. Shortly after this decision in 1885, a serious effort was made by Kneller Hall to bring the Army into line ; no objection to the proposed change in itself was raised by the authorities, but owing to the heavy expenditure involved, the project fell through.

The importance of music when recruiting was again emphasized in a Circular Memorandum of 2nd May, 1859 : " Commanding officers, whose regiments are below establishment, will send their bands and drums to one of the nearest towns on all market days, or on such other occasions as may lead to a concourse of people, for the purpose of raising recruits."

In 1862, it was ordered that the key to be used in playing the National Anthem should invariably be that of B flat.

By 1863, the many difficulties which besetted military bands had been practically surmounted and henceforth the bands of all branches of the Service made rapid strides in advancement and improvement.

On the 2nd August, 1871, sanction was given to abolish the white tunics worn by the band, since 1830, in favour of the scarlet worn by all ranks ; at the same time the wearing of a worsted badge of crossed trumpets on the right sleeve was also authorized. The two main reasons advanced for the abolition of the white tunic were, firstly, the medical officers recommended " as the white cloth must be cleaned with pipeclay, which if put on dry causes the soldier to inhale a quantity of dust, and if applied wet renders the tunic damp and unhealthy "; secondly, " it has also been found that the enemy at a distance can easily distinguish the number of battalions in the opposing force, by merely counting the bands."

In the interests of economy, it was also decided, in 1871, to introduce a universal pattern of lace for the drummers, for until now there were still about two hundred various patterns being worn throughout the Army. The drummer's fringe, the pattern of which was sealed in 1857, was also abolished at the same time ; this fringe was $1\frac{3}{4}$ inches long, and arranged in a width of $\frac{1}{2}$ inch of each colour ; that of the 47th Regiment being alternately black, white, red ; and the 81st Regiment blue, red, buff. This new pattern of lace was white with red Crowns, and the fringe of red and white was to be smaller and shorter for the future.

Bandmasters were appointed and recognized as such in 1863, but warrant-rank was not granted until 1881. General Order No. 59, August, 1874, stated : " The salary allowed to military bandmasters from the band fund, in addition to their pay as first-class staff-sergeants, is fixed at £100 a year." This was amended by General Order No. 84 of 1881 : " In consideration of the advantages as to pay, position, etc., to be conferred on bandmasters from 1st July, 1881, the salary allowed to them from the band fund will be reduced to £70 a year, from that date. This rate is, under no circumstances, to be exceeded." The first occasion upon which a bandmaster was gazetted and commissioned an honorary second-lieutenant was in the year 1887.

Army Order No. 46, March, 1904, cancelled the continuance of contributions and subscriptions from officers to the band fund : " After 1st April, 1904, the contributions and subscriptions paid by officers under paragraph 982 of the King's Regulations (1901), will cease to be payable by officers of infantry of the line, when serving at home, or in the colonies. Band property (exclusive of presentation instruments, etc.) will remain in regimental custody and will be replaced when necessary out of the increased allowance provided under paragraph 685 Allowance Regulations, but all such property will be regarded as vested in the Army Council and will not be alienated without the consent of the Council." At the time, this order did not apply to those officers who were serving on the Indian establishment, for paragraph 983 King's Regulations, 1904, laid down the sums to be paid on promotion and by annual subscription, which paragraph was subsequently cancelled by Army Order No. 96, April, 1906. Thus the order became operative throughout the infantry battalions of the Army in 1906.

Army Order No. 175 of June, 1914, announced the conditions under which a bandmaster, of special meritorious service, might be granted a commission as director-of-music, with the honorary rank of lieutenant, who on being promoted was to receive the same rates of regimental pay and allowances as a quartermaster ; a reduction at the rate of £70 per annum was made in the allowance for regimental bands, in the case of a regiment to which a director-of-music was appointed.

The old custom of appointing a regimental bandmaster direct from civil life had long since died out, and bandmasters, many of whom enlisted as boys, must now have all passed through the various ranks and stages and qualified at Kneller Hall, before appointment.

So that uniformity throughout the bands of the Service might be maintained, King's Regulations laid down that all instruments were to be of the pitch known as the " Kneller Hall " pitch, which was 479·3 vibrations per second, at 60° Fahrenheit, for B flat, corresponding to 452·4 for A, and 538 for C, at the same temperature.

During the summer of 1918 an entirely new brass band was formed ; the strength was thirty and consisted of boys, all under sixteen years of age. This band was sent out later to join the 2nd Battalion in Germany, at the time when the British Army was in occupation. The Germans were much astonished to see a body of such youthful musicians, for there was nothing similar in the whole of the German Army. In addition to the usual regimental duties this band gave many public performances in the district around Cologne and gained the merited approval of all. With the assistance of some half a dozen additional bandsmen who rejoined in due course, a high musical standard was ultimately attained, with the result that the band was amongst those selected to play at the British Empire Exhibition, Wembley, in 1924 and 1925.

A set of eleven Silver Drums was purchased by subscription from all ranks of the 1st Battalion in 1922 and now forms a permanent memorial to those of that Battalion who fell in the Great War, 1914–1918 ; a constant reminder of sacrifice and of duty well performed.

In 1928 the question of the proposed alteration of the military band pitch from the old Philharmonic to the new, commonly referred to respectively as " sharp " and " flat " pitch, was renewed, and it was found that a large proportion of the units at home was in favour. Army Council Instruction No. 544 of December, 1928, duly authorized the change and paragraph 1376 King's Regulations, 1928, was amended accordingly ; the approximate number of vibrations per second, at 60° Fahrenheit, now being 465 for B flat, corresponding to 439 for A, and 522 for C, the third space of the treble stave, at the same temperature. The decision was based on the consideration that the change did not necessitate more than the substitution of the low-pitch wood wind for the former high-pitch and the provision of slides to tone down the brass instruments. No high-pitch instruments were henceforth to be purchased and the change was ordered to be proceeded with as quickly as possible, the expense incurred being defrayed by the individual regiment itself, not by the public.

The chief advantage of the standardization of wind instruments was that Army bandsmen are now able to join in performances with organs in places of worship and public buildings, and also with string orchestras ; from which they had previously been obliged to stand aloof. It was also hoped that the makers might be able to reduce the cost of the various instruments, as in the future they would have to manufacture only one type, instead of two.

According to the latest establishment, the strength of the band of an infantry battalion is one bandmaster, one sergeant, one corporal and thirty-six bandsmen (sixteen acting). These, in addition to their musical training and duties, act as regimental stretcher-bearers in the field, when required, and have to qualify accordingly. The number of drummers is sixteen, of which six at least have to be trained in anti-aircraft duties.

Besides being musicians, all bandsmen must nowadays be prepared, literally, to play the part of the soldier too, for paragraph 1359, King's Regulations, 1928, states : " The N.C.O.s and men included as bandsmen, or acting bandsmen, in the establishments of regiments, will be effective soldiers, perfectly drilled, and liable to serve in the ranks."

No regular instrumentation has ever been recommended by official authority, and possibly there are no two bands exactly alike in composition and detail.

Nearly every battalion in the Territorial Army possesses a well-trained brass band under the direction of a capable bandmaster, who wears the prescribed uniform as such ; but nevertheless the rank of bandmaster is not provided for in the present establishment, neither does it carry the pay and allowances for same. The rank of drum-major, however, is allowed for the non-commissioned officer in charge of the drums and fifes.

Throughout the ages, in peace and in war, martial music has ever been a source of inspiration and invigoration to all.

The regimental marches of the several battalions of The Loyal Regiment (North Lancashire) are as follows :—

1st Battalion	" The Mountain Rose."
2nd Battalion	{ " The Red, Red Rose," and " The Lincolnshire Poacher."
3rd Battalion	" The Red, Red Rose."
4th and 5th (T.) Battalions . . .	" The Red, Red Rose."

THE REGIMENTAL CALL.

APPENDIX VIII

CASUALTIES, THE GREAT WAR

1914–1918

The total number of those of The Loyal North Lancashire Regiment who gave their lives for their King and Empire, 1914–1918, is as follows :—

Officers	357
Other Ranks	7,232
Total, All Ranks	**7,589**

The complete nominal rolls of both the Officers and Other Ranks of The Loyal North Lancashire Regiment who were Killed in Action and Died of Wounds or Disease during the Great War, have been published recently, under the authority of H.M. Stationery Office.

INDEX

A

Acton, Capt. J. R., 33
Adamson, 2nd Lieut. P., 177–181
Adcock, Capt. St. J., 24, 28
Ainsworth, Major W., 216–217, 325, 338
Allason, Capt. L. T., 1, 10
Alldred, 2nd Lieut. R. A., 41, 42
Allen, Capt. J. F., 2, 10, 15, 17
Allsup, 2nd Lieut. W., 48, 52, 338
Almond, 2nd Lieut. O. E., 97, 102, 109, 110
Anderson, Lieut. W. H., 77, 88, 96
Andrews, Lieut. C. N., 24–25
Anson, Lieut. C. J. de V. I', 77, 96
Appleby, 2nd Lieut. S. D., 300–302
Ashcroft, 2nd Lieut. G., 173–174
Ashworth, Lieut.-Col. G. C., 358
Atkinson, Capt. G. P., 100, 120–125, 146–147

B

Bands, and music, 413–421
Bare, Capt. A. R., 58
Barker, 2nd Lieut. R. A., 22–29
Bartlett, Major C. E. C., 188
1st Battalion, 1–74, 379
   France and Flanders (1914–1918), 2–70
     Advance, Final, the, 63–68
     Aisne, Battle, 7–8, 11
     Albert, in billets, 43, 46
     Aldershot, departure from, 1
     Armistice, the, 68–69
     Arras, Battles, 48, 58
     Aubers Ridge, attack on, 27–29
     Bazentin, Battle, 38
     Bethune, Battle, 57
     Brigade, re-organization of, 54
     Cuinchy, trenches, 22–24
     Drocourt–Quéant, line, 58
     Epéhy, Battle, 60–61
     Esquehéries, in billets, 2–3
     Festubert, sector, 25
     Flers–Courcelette, line, 42
     Fresnoy-le-Grand, at, 69
     Gheluvelt, Battle, 15–16

1st Battalion—*continued*
     Givenchy, action at, 19
     Havre, disembarked at, 2
     Hindenburg Line, 59–63
     Houthulst Forest, 53
     Langemarck, Battle, 11–12
     Loos, Battle, 30–33, 35
     Lys, the, Battle, 57
     Mametz Wood, 39, 43–44
     Marne, River, passage of, 7
     Memorial, erection of, 20
     Messines, Battle, 49–50
     Mobilization, 1
     Mons, Retreat from, 4–6
     Morval, Battle, 42
     Neuve Chapelle, Battle, 24–25
     Nieuport, attack on, 49–50
     Nonne Bosschen, counter-attack, 18
     Passchendaele, offensive, 51
     Philosophe, trenches, 33
     Pozières Ridge, 39–40
     St. Quentin Canal, 61–62
     Sambre, the, Battle, 66–68
     Selle, the, Battle, 63–65
     Somme, the, Battles, 37–44
     Trench warfare, beginning of, 9
     Troyon, attack at, 8–9, 11
     Victoria Cross awarded to Pte. H. Kenny, 35, 379
     Ypres, 11–19, 51–53
   Germany (1918–1919), 71–74
     Army, British, of Occupation, 71–74
     Bornheim, in billets, 72–74
     Colours, the, 71, 73
     Demobilization, 72–73
     Educational scheme, inaugurated, 73
     England, cadre returns to, 74
     Rhine, the, march to, 71–72
2nd Battalion, 75–153
   Africa, East (1914–1917), 76–136
     Bagamoyo, arrival at, 117
     Battle-honours, awarded, 119
     Bukoba, attack on, 106–108, 121
     Capetown, move to, 115–117, 125
     Company, double, adopted, 97

423

Printed in Great Britain by Butler & Tanner Ltd., Frome and London

Lightning Source UK Ltd.
Milton Keynes UK
17 November 2009

146368UK00001B/16/A